Collins
COBUILD

KEY WORDS
FOR THE
TOEIC® TEST

HarperCollins Publishers
Westerhill Road
Bishopbriggs
Glasgow
G64 2QT

First Edition 2012

Reprint 10 9 8 7 6 5 4 3 2 1 0

ISBN 978-0-00-745883-7

Collins® and COBUILD® are
registered trademarks of
HarperCollins Publishers Limited

www.collinslanguage.com

A catalogue record for this book is
available from the British Library

Typeset by Davidson Publishing
Solutions, Glasgow

Printed in Great Britain by Clays Ltd,
St Ives plc

Acknowledgements
We would like to thank those authors
and publishers who kindly gave
permission for copyright material
to be used in the Collins Corpus.
We would also like to thank Times
Newspapers Ltd for providing
valuable data.

contents

EDITORIAL STAFF

Editorial consultant
Roberta Steinberg

Senior editor
Ian Brookes

Project manager
Lisa Sutherland

Contributors
Daniel Barron
Carol Braham
Jennifer Craig
Julie Moore
Enid Pearsons

For the publishers
Lucy Cooper
Kerry Ferguson
Elaine Higgleton
Susanne Reichert

Computing support
Thomas Callan

Collins COBUILD KeyWords for the TOEIC Test covers the words and phrases that will help you to raise your English to the level required to succeed in the Test of English for International Communication (TOEIC). Mastering the vocabulary in this book will give you the skills you need to operate confidently in an English-medium work environment.

The first section of the book contains alphabetically ordered dictionary-style entries for **key words** and **phrases**. The vocabulary items have been chosen to prepare you fully for the kind of language found in the TOEIC test. This includes some of the more formal vocabulary that occurs mainly in written English, as well as technical terms that you are likely to encounter in commercial correspondence and conversations.

Each word is illustrated with **examples** of natural English taken from the Collins Corpus and reflecting the style of language used in a typical work environment. As well as definitions and examples, entries include useful information about **collocations** and **usage notes** to help you put the vocabulary you have learnt into practice.

Words from the same root (for example, *calculate*, *calculation*, and *calculator*) are shown together to help you to make the vital **links** between words. By understanding how these words relate to each other, you will be able to vary the way you express your ideas, which will help improve your writing and speaking skills.

There are also **synonyms** at each entry to help you widen your range of vocabulary and create more variety and flexibility in your writing style. The **Extend your vocabulary** boxes help you understand the differences between sets of similar words, so you can be sure that your English is accurate and natural, while the **Business correspondence** boxes give tips on expressions that are widely used in specific work situations.

The second section of the book consists of **word lists** organized by subject and topic area. You can use these lists to help **revise** sets of vocabulary or when preparing for writing tasks. The words are grouped into different **business areas** (such as Personnel and Sales & Marketing), **common topics** (such as education and the natural world), as well as according to **functions** (such as talking about problems and solutions or describing location).

We hope you enjoy preparing for the TOEIC using *Collins COBUILD KeyWords for the TOEIC Test*. The vocabulary in this book will not only help you to succeed in the test, but will also equip you for success in your future studies and career.

We have used the International Phonetic Alphabet (IPA) to show how the words are pronounced.

IPA Symbols

Vowel Sounds

ɑ	calm, ah
æ	act, mass
aɪ	dive, cry
aʊ	out, down
ɛ	met, lend, pen
eɪ	say, weight
ɪ	fit, win
i	feed, me
ɒ	lot, spot
oʊ	note, coat
ɔ	claw, more
ɔɪ	boy, joint
ʊ	could, stood
u	you, use
ʌ	fund, must
ɜ	turn, third
ə	the first vowel in about

Consonant Sounds

b	bed, rub
d	done, red
f	fit, if
g	good, dog
h	hat, horse
k	king, pick
l	lip, bill
ᵊl	handle, panel
m	mat, ram
n	not, tin
ᵊn	hidden, written
p	pay, lip
r	run, read
s	soon, bus
t	talk, bet
v	van, love
w	win, wool
x	loch
y	yellow, you
z	zoo, buzz
ʃ	ship, wish
ʒ	measure, leisure
ŋ	sing, working
tʃ	cheap, witch
θ	thin, myth
ð	then, bathe
dʒ	joy, bridge

Notes
Stress is shown by a line below the stressed syllable. For example, in the word *abandon*, /əbændən/, the second syllable is stressed.

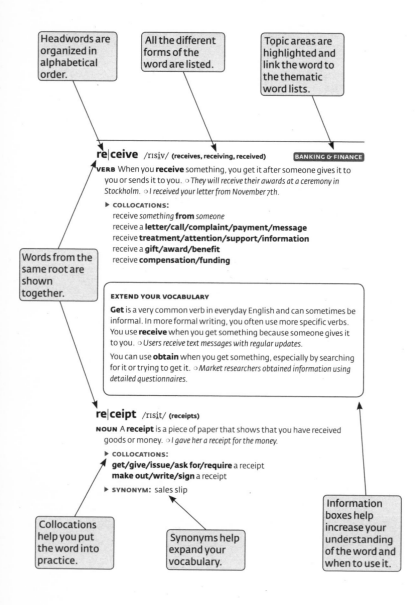

Headwords are organized in alphabetical order.

All the different forms of the word are listed.

Topic areas are highlighted and link the word to the thematic word lists.

re|ceive /rɪsiːv/ (receives, receiving, received)   BANKING & FINANCE

VERB When you **receive** something, you get it after someone gives it to you or sends it to you. ○ *They will receive their awards at a ceremony in Stockholm.* ○ *I received your letter from November 7th.*

▶ **COLLOCATIONS:**
   receive *something* **from** *someone*
   receive a **letter/call/complaint/payment/message**
   receive **treatment/attention/support/information**
   receive a **gift/award/benefit**
   receive **compensation/funding**

Words from the same root are shown together.

EXTEND YOUR VOCABULARY

Get is a very common verb in everyday English and can sometimes be informal. In more formal writing, you often use more specific verbs. You use **receive** when you get something because someone gives it to you. ○ *Users receive text messages with regular updates.*

You can use **obtain** when you get something, especially by searching for it or trying to get it. ○ *Market researchers obtained information using detailed questionnaires.*

re|ceipt /rɪsiːt/ (receipts)

NOUN A **receipt** is a piece of paper that shows that you have received goods or money. ○ *I gave her a receipt for the money.*

▶ **COLLOCATIONS:**
   get/give/issue/ask for/require a receipt
   make out/write/sign a receipt

▶ **SYNONYM:** sales slip

Collocations help you put the word into practice.

Synonyms help expand your vocabulary.

Information boxes help increase your understanding of the word and when to use it.

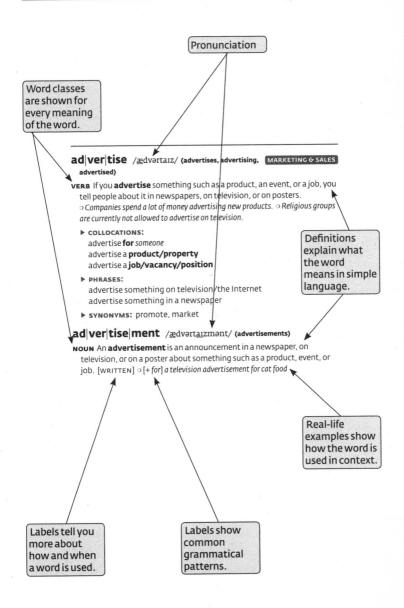

Pronunciation

Word classes are shown for every meaning of the word.

ad|ver|tise /ˈædvərtaɪz/ (advertises, advertising, advertised) [MARKETING & SALES]

VERB If you **advertise** something such as a product, an event, or a job, you tell people about it in newspapers, on television, or on posters. ○ *Companies spend a lot of money advertising new products.* ○ *Religious groups are currently not allowed to advertise on television.*

▶ **COLLOCATIONS:**
advertise **for** *someone*
advertise a **product/property**
advertise a **job/vacancy/position**

▶ **PHRASES:**
advertise something on television/the Internet
advertise something in a newspaper

▶ **SYNONYMS:** promote, market

ad|ver|tise|ment /ədˈvɜːtaɪzmənt/ (advertisements)

NOUN An **advertisement** is an announcement in a newspaper, on television, or on a poster about something such as a product, event, or job. [WRITTEN] ○ [+ *for*] *a television advertisement for cat food*

Definitions explain what the word means in simple language.

Real-life examples show how the word is used in context.

Labels tell you more about how and when a word is used.

Labels show common grammatical patterns.

Grammatical labels

All the words in the dictionary section have grammar information given about them. For each word, its word class is shown after the headword. The sections below show more information about each word class.

ADJECTIVE	An adjective is a word that is used for telling you more about a person or thing. You would use an adjective to talk about appearance, color, size, or other qualities, e.g. *The price of corn and other <u>agricultural</u> products has increased.*
ADVERB	An adverb is a word that gives more information about when, how, or where something happens, e.g. *Children vary <u>considerably</u> in the rate at which they learn.*
CONJUNCTION	A conjunction is a word such as *and*, *but*, *if*, and *since*. Conjunctions are used for linking two words or two parts of a sentence together, e.g. *I have to decide <u>whether</u> or not to take the job.*
NONCOUNT NOUN	A noncount noun is a noun that is used for talking about things that are not normally counted, or that we do not think of as single items. Noncount nouns do not have a plural form, and they are used with a singular verb, e.g. *<u>Debt</u> is a main reason for stress.*
NOUN	A noun is a word that refers to a person, a thing, or a quality. In this book, the label *noun* is given to all count nouns. A count noun is used for talking about things that can be counted, and that have both singular and plural forms, e.g. *America's trade <u>gap</u> widened.*
NUMBER	A number is a word used for telling you how many of a thing there are, e.g. *<u>Forty</u> planes have been grounded.*
PHRASE	Phrases are groups of words which are used together and which have a meaning of their own, e.g. *He was to remain in jail <u>in the interim</u>.*
PLURAL NOUN	A plural noun is always plural, and it is used with plural verbs, e.g. *Some tried to sell <u>assets</u> to pay the debts back.*
PREPOSITION	A preposition is a word such as *by*, *with*, or *from*, which is always followed by a noun group or the *-ing* form of a verb, e.g. *No illness <u>except</u> malaria, has caused as much death as small pox.*
PRONOUN	A pronoun is a word that you use instead of a noun when you do not need or want to name someone or something

directly, e.g. *At school, <u>he</u> enjoyed football and boxing; <u>the latter</u> remained a lifelong hobby.*

QUANTIFIER   A quantifier comes before *of* and a noun group, e.g. *The <u>bulk</u> of the text is essentially a review of these original documents.*

VERB   A verb is a word that is used for saying what someone or something does, or what happens to them, or to give information about them, e.g. *We <u>cancelled</u> our trip to Washington.*

Subject labels

Some words in the dictionary have subject labels to help you identify which words are relevant to you.

BANKING & FINANCE   Covering accounting, general finance, banking, economics, currency, insurance and vocabulary associated with investments and the stock market.

COMMUNICATIONS   Covering the language of business correspondence, discussions, information and different means of communication.

HEALTH & FITNESS   Covering health problems and health care.

JOBS   Covering different job titles, professions and management positions.

LEGAL   Covering legal terms and issues.

LOGISTICS & DISTRIBUTION   Covering the internal structure and operations of an organization, including orders and distribution, import and export, and supplies.

MARKETING & SALES   Covering markets and marketing, sales and pricing.

OFFICE   Covering the practical day-to-day work environment, office buildings, office supplies, IT, and business meetings and conferences.

ORGANIZATION   Covering types of business organization, business sectors and the overall structure of organizations.

PERSONNEL   Covering the tasks and people involved in personnel and HR, recruitment, training, remuneration, terms and conditions of employment, and career development.

R&D   (Research & Development) Covering research and innovation, business planning and business development.

TRAVEL   Covering vocabulary associated with business travel.

Aa

---

aban|don /əbændən/ (abandons, abandoning, abandoned)

1 VERB If you **abandon** a place, thing, or person, you leave the place, thing, or person permanently or for a long time, especially when you should not do so. ○ *He claimed that his parents had abandoned him.* ○ *The road is strewn with abandoned vehicles.*

▶ **COLLOCATIONS:**
abandon a **child/baby**
an abandoned **building/warehouse/mine/quarry/vehicle/car**
hastily/abruptly/temporarily abandon *someone/something*

▶ **SYNONYMS:** desert, leave

2 VERB If you **abandon** an activity or piece of work, you stop doing it before it is finished. ○ *The authorities have abandoned any attempt to distribute food.* ○ *The scheme's investors, fearful of bankruptcy, decided to abandon the project.*

▶ **COLLOCATIONS:**
abandon an **attempt/effort**
abandon a **project/plan/idea**

---

ab|bre|vi|ate /əbriːvieɪt/ (abbreviates, abbreviating, abbreviated)　　**COMMUNICATIONS**

VERB If you **abbreviate** something, especially a word or a piece of writing, you make it shorter. ○ [+ *to*] *The generic name is usually abbreviated to the initial letter.* ○ *Charles' letter was published in an abbreviated form.*

▶ **COLLOCATIONS:**
abbreviate *something* **to** *something*
an abbreviated **version/form**

▶ **SYNONYM:** shorten

a

ab|bre|via|tion /əbriːvieɪʃᵊn/ (abbreviations)

NOUN An **abbreviation** is a short form of a word or phrase, made by leaving out some of the letters or by using only the first letter of each word. ○ [+ for] *The abbreviation for Kansas is KS.*

▶ COLLOCATIONS:
an abbreviation **for** something
an abbreviation **of** something

▶ PHRASE: abbreviations and acronyms

able /eɪbᵊl/ (abler, ablest)

PHRASE If you **are able to** do something, you can do it. ○ *Only larger companies will be able to afford the increasing costs.*

▶ PHRASE: willing and able

abil|ity /əbɪlɪti/ (abilities)

NOUN Your **ability to** do something is the fact that you can do it. ○ *The public never had faith in his ability to do the job.* ○ *He has the ability to bring out the best in others.* ○ [+ of] *the ability of an individual to work on a team*

▶ COLLOCATIONS:
the ability **of** someone
have/possess/demonstrate/show/develop an ability
lack/lose an ability

▶ PHRASES:
skill and ability
willingness and ability

▶ SYNONYM: capability

abroad /əbrɔːd/ `TRAVEL`

ADVERB If you go **abroad**, you go to a foreign country. ○ *I would love to go abroad this year.* ○ *About 65 percent of the company's sales come from abroad.*

▶ COLLOCATIONS:
go/travel/work/love/move abroad
a **trip/vacation** abroad

▶ SYNONYM: overseas

ab|rupt /əbrʌpt/

ADJECTIVE An **abrupt** change or action is very sudden, often in a way that is unpleasant. ○ *an abrupt shift in policy* ○ *the abrupt departure of the company's former chief executive*

▶ **COLLOCATIONS:**
an abrupt **halt/end/departure**
an abrupt **shift/turnaround/transition**

▶ **SYNONYM:** sudden

ab|rupt|ly

ADVERB ○ *He stopped abruptly and looked my way.* ○ *a summit that was abruptly canceled because of differences over proposed political reforms*

▶ **COLLOCATIONS:**
stop/end/cease abruptly
resign/quit abruptly

▶ **SYNONYM:** suddenly

ab|sent /æbsⁿnt/ `PERSONNEL`

ADJECTIVE If someone or something is **absent from** a place or situation where they should be or where they usually are, they are not there.
○ [+ *from*] *Women are conspicuously absent from higher management.*
○ *Employees who are absent without a genuine reason should be disciplined.*
○ *Any soldier failing to report would be considered absent without leave.*

▶ **COLLOCATIONS:**
absent **from** *somewhere/something*
absent from a **list/agenda**
absent from **work/school**
conspicuously/noticeably/notably absent

▶ **PHRASE:** absent without leave

ab|sence /æbsⁿns/ (absences)

1 **NOUN** Someone's **absence** from a place is the fact that they are not there. ○ *a bundle of letters which had arrived for me in my absence* ○ *the problem of high employee absence in the public sector*

▶ **COLLOCATIONS:**
in *someone's* absence
a **lengthy/continued/four-year** absence
an **unexplained/unauthorized** absence

2 NOUN The **absence** of something from a place is the fact that it is not there or does not exist. ○ [+ of] *The presence or absence of clouds can have an important impact on heat transfer.* ○ [+ of] *In the absence of a will the courts decide who the guardian is.*

▶ **COLLOCATIONS:**
the absence **of** *something*
in the absence of *something*
the absence of **evidence/proof/information**
the absence of a **will/explanation/alternative**

▶ **SYNONYM:** lack

ab|so|lute|ly /ˈæbsəlutli/

1 ADVERB If you say something is **absolutely** necessary, you mean it is totally and completely necessary. ○ *You're absolutely right.*

2 ADVERB You say **absolutely** in response to a question if you are saying yes or agreeing with someone strongly. ○ *"Do you think I should call him?"* —*"Absolutely."*

▶ **COLLOCATIONS:** absolutely **right/necessary/essential/certain**

▶ **SYNONYMS:** definitely, certainly

ab|sorb /əbˈsɔrb, -ˈzɔrb/ (absorbs, absorbing, absorbed)

1 VERB To **absorb** something, such as a liquid or gas, is to take it in. ○ *Dust dries air because it absorbs moisture.*

2 VERB To **absorb** changes, effects, or costs is to deal with them without being badly affected. ○ *Manufacturers are absorbing higher production costs rather than passing them on to consumers.*

▶ **COLLOCATIONS:**
absorb **energy/heat/moisture**
absorb a **shock/lesson**
absorb *something* **through/into/by/from** *something*

▶ **SYNONYM:** soak up

aca|dem|ic /ˌækəˈdɛmɪk/

1 ADJECTIVE Academic is used to describe things that relate to the work done in schools, colleges, and universities, especially work which involves studying and reasoning rather than practical or technical skills. ○ *Their academic standards are high.* ○ *the start of the last academic year* ○ *The author has settled for a more academic approach.*

2 ADJECTIVE Someone who is **academic** is good at studying. ○ *The system is failing most disastrously among less academic children.*

▶ **COLLOCATIONS:**
academic **standards/excellence/ability/freedom**
academic **research/work/staff/life**
an academic **qualification/achievement/career**
an academic **journal/institution/study/subject**
the academic **year**

▶ **PHRASES:**
academic and vocational
academic and professional

▶ **SYNONYM:** scholarly

---

ac|cel|er|ate /æksɛləreɪt/ **(accelerates, accelerating, accelerated)**

1 VERB If the process or rate of something **accelerates** or if something **accelerates** it, it gets faster and faster. ○ [+ to] *Growth will accelerate to 2.9 percent next year.* ○ *The government is to accelerate its school construction program.*

2 VERB When a moving vehicle **accelerates**, it goes faster and faster. ○ *Drivers accelerated and braked around traffic islands.* ○ [+ to] *A video showed the police car accelerating to 115 mph.*

▶ **COLLOCATIONS:**
accelerate **to** x
accelerate **pace/growth**
accelerate a **process/trend/timetable**
accelerate **smoothly/gradually/rapidly/sharply**
a **car/driver** accelerates
inflation/growth/decline accelerates

▶ **SYNONYM:** hasten

---

ac|cent /æksɛnt/ **(accents)** COMMUNICATIONS

NOUN Someone who speaks with a particular **accent** says words in a way that shows which country or part of a country they come from, or which social class they belong to. ○ *He had a slight American accent.*

▶ **COLLOCATIONS:**
a **British/American/Southern** accent
a **thick/heavy/slight** accent

a

ac|cen|tu|ate /æksɛntʃueɪt/ (accentuates, accentuating, accentuated)

VERB To **accentuate** something means to emphasize it or make it more noticeable. ○ *His shaven head accentuates his large round face.*

▶ **COLLOCATIONS:**
accentuate *someone's/something's* **size/features**
accentuate **differences/similarities**
accentuate the **problems**
accentuate the **positives**

---

ac|cept /æksɛpt/ (accepts, accepting, accepted)

1 VERB If you **accept** something that you have been offered, you say yes to it or agree to take it. ○ *students who have accepted an offer of admission from the university* ○ *All those invited to next week's peace conference have accepted.*

▶ **COLLOCATIONS:**
accept a **gift/donation/offer/invitation**
gratefully/gladly/reluctantly accept *something*

▶ **SYNONYMS:** take, welcome

2 VERB If you **accept** an idea, statement, or fact, you believe that it is true or valid. ○ [+ *as*] *It is now accepted as fact that the brain and the immune system communicate.* ○ *a workforce generally accepted to have the best conditions in Europe*

▶ **COLLOCATIONS:**
accept *something* **as** *something*
accept *something* as **proof/evidence/fact**
generally/widely/internationally/commonly accepted
readily/reluctantly accept *something*

▶ **SYNONYMS:** acknowledge, recognize

USAGE: *accept* or *except*?

These words sound very similar and are easily confused, so be careful with their spelling.

Accept is a verb meaning to agree to or to believe something.
○ *the generally accepted meaning of the term*

Except is a conjunction used to introduce the only person or thing that something does not apply to. ○ *He remained in America, except for military duty, for the rest of his life.*

ac|cept|able /æksɛptəbᵊl/

1 ADJECTIVE Acceptable activities and situations are those that most people approve of or consider to be normal. ○ [+ *for*] *It is becoming more acceptable for women to drink alcohol.* ○ *The air pollution exceeds most acceptable levels by 10 times or more.*

2 ADJECTIVE If something is **acceptable to** someone, they agree to consider it, use it, or allow it to happen. ○ [+ *to*] *They have thrashed out a compromise formula acceptable to Moscow.* ○ *They recently failed to negotiate a mutually acceptable new contract.*

▶ **COLLOCATIONS:**
acceptable **for/to** *someone*
socially/politically/morally acceptable
an acceptable **level/standard**
an acceptable **compromise/alternative/solution**
acceptable **behavior**
find/consider/deem *something* acceptable

▶ **SYNONYM:** satisfactory

ac|cept|ance /æksɛptəns/ (acceptances)

1 NOUN Acceptance of an offer or a proposal is the act of saying yes to it or agreeing to it. ○ [+ *of*] *The Party is being degraded by its acceptance of secret donations.* ○ *a letter of acceptance* ○ *his acceptance speech for the Nobel Peace Prize*

▶ **COLLOCATIONS:**
acceptance **of** *something*
acceptance of a **proposal/plan/offer/invitation**
an acceptance **speech/letter**

2 NONCOUNT NOUN If there is **acceptance** of an idea, most people believe or agree that it is true. ○ *a theory that is steadily gaining acceptance* ○ [+ *that*] *There was a general acceptance that the defense budget would shrink.*

▶ **COLLOCATIONS:**
gain/win acceptance
general/wide/widespread/growing acceptance
grudging/tacit/resigned acceptance

▶ **SYNONYM:** agreement

---

ac|cess /æksɛs/ (accesses, accessing, accessed) `COMMUNICATIONS`

1 NONCOUNT NOUN If you have **access to** a building or other place, you are able or allowed to go into it. ○ *Does the school have wheelchair access?*

○ [+ to] *Scientists have only recently been able to gain access to the area.*

2 **NONCOUNT NOUN** If you have **access to** something such as information or equipment, you have the opportunity or right to see it or use it.
○ [+ to] *a plan that would give patients right of access to their medical records*
○ *households with Internet access*

▶ **COLLOCATIONS:**
access **to** *something/somewhere*
access to **information/funds**
gain/give/grant/allow/provide access
deny/restrict/block access
fast/high-speed/instant/easy/direct/free access
public/wheelchair access
Internet/broadband/wireless access

▶ **SYNONYMS:** entry, entrance

3 **VERB** If you **access** something, especially information held on a computer, you succeed in finding or obtaining it. ○ *You've illegally accessed and misused confidential security files.* ○ *a service that allows users to access the Internet on their phones*

▶ **COLLOCATIONS:**
access **data/information**
access the **Internet**
access a **file/site/network/service**
instantly/easily/remotely/illegally access *something*

ac|ces|sible /ækˈsɛsɪbəl/

1 **ADJECTIVE** If a place or building is **accessible to** people, it is easy for them to reach it or get into it. If an object is **accessible**, it is easy to reach. ○ [+ to] *The Center is easily accessible to the general public.* ○ *The premises are wheelchair accessible.*

2 **ADJECTIVE** If something is **accessible to** people, they can easily use it or obtain it. ○ [+ to] *The legal aid system should be accessible to more people.*
○ *This device helps make virtual reality a more usable and accessible technology.*

▶ **COLLOCATIONS:**
accessible **to/for** *someone*
easily/readily/publicly accessible
wheelchair accessible
an accessible **area/location**
make *something* accessible

ac|ci|den|tal /æksɪdɛntˀl/

ADJECTIVE Something that is **accidental** happens by chance. ○ *accidental death*

▶ **COLLOCATIONS:** an accidental **collision/injury/death/discovery**

▶ **SYNONYM:** unintentional

ac|com|mo|date /əkɒmədeɪt/ (accommodates, accommodating, accommodated)

TRAVEL

VERB If a building or space can **accommodate** someone or something, it has enough space for them. ○ *Ports are to get longer piers to accommodate all the containers.*

▶ **COLLOCATIONS:** accommodate **guests/visitors/passengers**

▶ **PHRASE:** accommodate up to *x*

▶ **SYNONYM:** hold

ac|com|mo|da|tions /əkɒmədeɪʃˀnz/

PLURAL NOUN Accommodations are the buildings or rooms where people stay or live temporarily. [in BRIT, use **accommodation**] ○ *The price includes flights and hotel accommodations.* ○ *Rates are higher for deluxe accommodations.* ○ *The building provides accommodations for 80 students.*

▶ **COLLOCATIONS:**
provide/offer/book/find accommodations
vacation/overnight accommodations
hotel/B&B/hostel accommodations
student/guest accommodations

ac|com|pa|ny /əkʌmpəni/ (accompanies, accompanying, accompanied)

1 VERB If you **accompany** someone, you go somewhere with them. [FORMAL] ○ *Ken agreed to accompany me on a trip to Africa.* ○ *The Prime Minister, accompanied by the governor, led the President up to the house.*

▶ **COLLOCATIONS:**
accompanied **by** *someone*
accompanied by a **bodyguard/adult/escort**

▶ **SYNONYM:** escort

2 VERB If one thing **accompanies** another, it happens or exists at the same time, or as a result of it. [FORMAL] ○ *This volume of essays was* *designed to accompany an exhibition in Cologne.* ○ *Wakefield's paper was accompanied by a critical commentary.*

▶ COLLOCATIONS:
accompanied **by** something
accompanied by a **photograph/caption/commentary**
accompany a **text/illustration/article**

---

ac|com|plish /əkɒmplɪʃ/ (accomplishes, accomplishing, accomplished)

VERB If you **accomplish** something, you succeed in doing it. ○ *We accomplished our goal.*

▶ COLLOCATIONS: accomplish a **goal/task/objective**

▶ PHRASE: mission accomplished

▶ SYNONYMS: realize, achieve

ac|com|plish|ment /əkɒmplɪʃmənt/ (accomplishments)

NOUN ○ *appreciation for each person's special efforts and accomplishments*

▶ SYNONYMS: achievement, talent

---

ac|cord|ing to

> Pronounced /əkɔrdɪŋ tə/ before a consonant and /əkɔrdɪŋ tu/ before a vowel.

1 PHRASE If someone says that something is true **according to** a particular person, book, or other source of information, they are indicating where they got their information. ○ *Philip stayed at the hotel, according to Mr. Hemming.* ○ *According to current theory, novae are close double stars.*

2 PHRASE If something is done **according to** a particular set of principles, these principles are used as a basis for the way it is done. ○ *Coal is usually classified according to a scale of hardness and purity.* ○ *They must make their own decision according to their own legal advice.*

▶ SYNONYM: based on

3 PHRASE If something varies **according to** a changing factor, it varies in a way that is determined by this factor. ○ *Prices vary according to the quantity ordered.* ○ *The route that the boatmen choose varies according to the water level.*

▶ SYNONYM: depending on

ac|count /əkaʊnt/ (accounts)

BANKING & FINANCE

NOUN An **account** is a written or spoken report of something that has happened. ○ [+ of] *He gave a detailed account of what happened.* ○ *According to police accounts, Mr. and Mrs. Hunt were found dead in their kitchen.*

▶ **COLLOCATIONS:**
an account **of** something
give/write/publish an account
a **full/detailed/brief** account
a **first-hand/eye-witness/personal** account

▶ **PHRASE:** according to accounts

▶ **SYNONYMS:** report, description

ac|count|ing /əkaʊntɪŋ/

NONCOUNT NOUN **Accounting** is the activity of keeping detailed records of the amounts of money a business or person receives and spends. ○ *the accounting firm of Leventhal & Horwath*

▶ **COLLOCATIONS:**
accounting **rules/standards/principles/practices/methods**
an accounting **firm**

ac|cu|mu|late /əkyumyəleɪt/ (accumulates, accumulating, accumulated)

VERB When you **accumulate** things or when they **accumulate**, they collect or are gathered over a period of time. ○ *Households accumulate wealth across a broad spectrum of assets.* ○ [+ in] *Lead can accumulate in the body until toxic levels are reached.*

▶ **COLLOCATIONS:**
accumulate **in** something
accumulate in the **body/lungs/brain/atmosphere**
accumulate **wealth/debt/wisdom/knowledge**
accumulated **losses**
an accumulated **deficit**
evidence/fluids/toxins accumulate

▶ **SYNONYMS:** gather, amass

ac|cu|mu|la|tion /əkyumyəleɪʃən/ (accumulations)

NOUN ○ [+ of] *technological advance and the accumulation of scientific knowledge* ○ [+ of] *an accumulation of fluid in the lungs* ○ *No economy can sustain such a colossal rate of capital accumulation.*

▶ **COLLOCATIONS:**
the accumulation **of** *something*
the accumulation of **wealth/capital/fluid/knowledge**
cause/prevent/increase/reduce accumulation

▶ **SYNONYM:** increase

---

ac|cu|rate /ˈækyərɪt/

ADJECTIVE Accurate information, measurements, and statistics are correct to a very detailed level. An **accurate** instrument is able to give you information of this kind. ○ *Accurate diagnosis is needed to guide appropriate treatment strategies.* ○ *a quick and accurate way of monitoring the amount of carbon dioxide in the air*

▶ **COLLOCATIONS:**
reasonably/historically/scientifically/factually accurate
accurate **information/figures**
an accurate **description/measurement/diagnosis/prediction**

▶ **SYNONYMS:** precise, exact, correct

ac|cu|ra|cy /ˈækyərəsi/

NONCOUNT NOUN ○ [+ *of*] *We cannot guarantee the accuracy of these figures.* ○ *weapons that could fire with accuracy at targets 3,000 yards away*

▶ **COLLOCATIONS:**
the accuracy **of** *something*
the accuracy of a **measurement/diagnosis/test**
the accuracy of **information/figures**
guarantee/ensure/measure accuracy
historical/mathematical/unerring/pinpoint accuracy
an accuracy **rate/level**

▶ **PHRASE:** speed and accuracy

▶ **SYNONYMS:** exactness, precision, correctness

ac|cu|rate|ly

ADVERB ○ *The test can accurately predict what a bigger explosion would do.* ○ *The costs of each part of the process can be measured fairly accurately.*

▶ **COLLOCATIONS:**
accurately **describe/measure/perceive** *something*
determine/predict *something* accurately

▶ **SYNONYMS:** precisely, exactly, correctly

achieve|ment /ətʃivmənt/ (achievements)

NOUN An **achievement** is something that you succeed in doing or causing to happen, usually after a lot of effort. ○ *Reaching this agreement so quickly was a great achievement.* ○ [+ *of*] *Only the achievement of these goals will bring lasting peace.*

▶ **COLLOCATIONS:**
achievement **of** *something*
achievement of a **goal/objective**
a **great/lifetime/crowning** achievement
an **academic/educational/artistic** achievement
celebrate/recognize an achievement

▶ **SYNONYMS:** accomplishment, success

ac|quaint|ance /əkweɪntəns/ (acquaintances)

NOUN An **acquaintance** is someone you know slightly but not well.
○ *He's an old acquaintance of mine.*

▶ **COLLOCATIONS:** a **new/old/casual** acquaintance

▶ **PHRASE:** friends and acquaintances

ac|quire /əkwaɪər/ (acquires, acquiring, acquired)

1 VERB If you **acquire** something, you buy or obtain it for yourself, or someone gives it to you. [FORMAL] ○ *General Motors acquired a 50% stake in Saab for about $400 million.* ○ *efforts to acquire nuclear weapons*

2 VERB If you **acquire** something such as a skill or a habit, you learn it, or develop it through your daily life or experience. ○ *Their sleeping brains were continuing to process the newly acquired information.* ○ *Piaget was convinced that children acquire knowledge and abilities in stages.*

▶ **COLLOCATIONS:**
a **company/purchaser/shareholder** acquires *something*
acquire a **stake/share**
acquire **land/property/assets/wealth**
acquire a **skill/habit/reputation**
acquire **knowledge**
newly/recently acquired

▶ **PHRASE:** an acquired taste

a

EXTEND YOUR VOCABULARY

Get is a very common verb in everyday spoken English. In more formal writing, more specific verbs are often used.

If you get something by paying for it, you can use **buy**, **purchase**, or **acquire**. **Acquire** is especially used to talk about businesses rather than individuals. ○ *The company acquired/purchased properties throughout Australia.*

You can use **acquire** or **obtain** when you get something in other ways, for example, by being given it.

▶ acquire **assets/wealth/ownership/shares**

▶ obtain **information/documents/copies**

You can use **acquire**, **gain**, or **develop** when you get a skill, a reputation, knowledge, etc., gradually over time.

▶ acquire a **skill/reputation**

▶ gain **confidence/acceptance/reputation/experience**

▶ develop a **skill/strategy/relationship/reputation**

---

ac|qui|si|tion /ækwɪzɪʃ°n/ (acquisitions)

1 **NOUN** If a company or businessperson makes an **acquisition**, they buy another company or part of a company. ○ [+ *of*] *the acquisition of a profitable paper recycling company* ○ *the number of mergers and acquisitions made by Europe's 1,000 leading companies*

2 **NONCOUNT NOUN** The **acquisition** of a skill or a particular type of knowledge is the process of learning it or developing it. ○ *the process of language acquisition* ○ [+ *of*] *the acquisition of basic skills*

▶ **COLLOCATIONS:**
the acquisition **of** *something*
the acquisition of **assets/land/property/skills**
land/language acquisition
a **recent/planned/compulsory/further** acquisition
acquisition **costs/activity**
make/finance/fund/propose/complete an acquisition

▶ **PHRASE:** mergers and acquisitions

▶ **SYNONYMS:** purchase, procurement, achievement, attainment

ac|tu|al|ly /ˈæktʃuəli/

ADVERB **Actually** is used for saying that something surprising really is true.
○ *The judge actually fell asleep during the trial.*

▶ **COLLOCATIONS:** actually **see/get/go/do/look**

▶ **PHRASES:**
what I actually meant
what actually happened

▶ **SYNONYM:** really

a|dapt /əˈdæpt/ (adapts, adapting, adapted)

1 VERB If you **adapt to** a new situation or **adapt yourself to** it, you change your ideas or behavior in order to deal with it successfully.
○ [+ *to*] *We will have to be prepared to adapt to the change.* ○ [+ *to*] *They have had to adapt themselves to a war economy.*

▶ **COLLOCATIONS:**
adapt **to** *something*
adapt to **change**
adapt **readily/quickly**
difficulty/problems adapting to *something*

▶ **SYNONYMS:** adjust, acclimate, become accustomed

2 VERB If you **adapt** something, you change it to make it suitable for a new purpose or situation. ○ [+ *for*] *Shelves were built to adapt the library for use as an office.* ○ [+ *for*] *a specially adapted toilet for people with disabilities*

▶ **COLLOCATIONS:**
adapt *something* **for** *a purpose/someone*
specially/skillfully adapted
adapt a **technology/technique/method**

EXTEND YOUR VOCABULARY

Change is a very common verb in English. In more formal writing, more specific verbs are often used.

Adapt and **customize** mean to change something to make it suitable for a particular purpose or situation. ○ *The software can be adapted/ customized to suit the user's needs.*

Modify and **alter** mean to change something slightly. **Modify** is often used to talk about making improvements. **Alter** often refers to changes that just happen naturally or over time. ○ *a slightly modified version of the design* ○ *New technologies are slowly altering the structure of the business world.*

adapt|abil|ity /ədæptəbɪlɪti/

NONCOUNT NOUN Adaptability is the ability to change your ideas or behavior in order to deal with new situations. ○ [+ of] *The adaptability of wool is one of its great attractions.*

▸ **COLLOCATION:** the adaptability **of** something

▸ **SYNONYM:** flexibility

ad|ap|ta|tion /ædæpteɪʃ°n/

NONCOUNT NOUN Adaptation is the act of changing something or changing your behavior to make it suitable for a new purpose or situation. ○ *Most living creatures are capable of adaptation when compelled to do so.*

▸ **SYNONYMS:** adjustment, modification

ad|di|tion|al /ədɪʃən°l/

ADJECTIVE Additional things are extra things apart from the ones already present. ○ *Table 2 gives additional information about participants.* ○ *The insurer will also have to pay the additional costs of the trial.*

▸ **COLLOCATIONS:**
additional **costs/shares/information**
an additional **payment/contribution/expense**

▸ **SYNONYMS:** supplementary, extra

ad|equate /ædɪkwɪt/

ADJECTIVE If something is **adequate**, there is enough of it or it is good enough to be used or accepted. ○ *One in four people worldwide are without adequate homes.* ○ [+ to-inf] *The old methods weren't adequate to meet current needs.*

▸ **COLLOCATIONS:**
adequate **for** something
adequate for a **purpose/task/need**
adequate **protection/provision/compensation/resources**
perfectly/quite/barely/hardly adequate

▸ **SYNONYM:** sufficient

ad|equate|ly /ædɪkwɪtli/

ADVERB ○ *Many students are not adequately prepared for higher education.* ○ *Traditional analysis methods cannot deal adequately with these highly complex systems.*

▶ **COLLOCATIONS:**
respond/function adequately
adequately **deal with** something
adequately **trained/compensated/funded/protected/prepared**

▶ **SYNONYM:** sufficiently

---

ad|ja|cent /ədʒeɪsᵊnt/

ADJECTIVE If one thing is **adjacent to** another, the two things are next
to each other. ○ plans to redevelop the train station and adjacent land
○ [+ to] surveys to monitor toxin levels in the areas adjacent to the canal

▶ **COLLOCATIONS:**
adjacent **to** something
a **site/area** adjacent to something
an adjacent **building/neighborhood**
adjacent **land**

▶ **SYNONYMS:** neighboring, near

---

ad|just /ədʒʌst/ (adjusts, adjusting, adjusted)

1 VERB When you **adjust to** a new situation, you get used to it by
changing your behavior or your ideas. ○ [+ to] We are preparing our fighters
to adjust themselves to civil society. ○ [+ to] I felt I had adjusted to the idea of
being a mother very well.

2 VERB If you **adjust** something, you change it so that it is more effective or
appropriate. ○ To attract investors, Panama has adjusted its tax and labor laws.
○ The clamp can be adjusted to fit any tire size. ○ seasonally adjusted figures

▶ **COLLOCATIONS:**
adjust **to** something
adjusted **for** something
adjusted for **inflation/height/age**
adjust **figures/rates**
adjust something to **reflect/fit** something
seasonally/periodically/automatically/manually adjusted
adjusted **accordingly**

▶ **SYNONYMS:** adapt, change, shift

ad|just|ment /ədʒʌstmənt/ (adjustments)

NOUN ○ [+ to] Compensation could be made by adjustments to taxation. ○ [+ for]
Investment is up by 5.7% after adjustment for inflation. ○ [+ to] A technician
made an adjustment to a smoke machine at the back of the auditorium.

a

▶ **COLLOCATIONS:**
an adjustment **to/in/for** *something*
adjustment for **inflation/age/height**
a **structural/seasonal/slight/minor** adjustment
make/require/need an adjustment

▶ **SYNONYMS:** adaptation, change

---

ad|min|is|tra|tive /ædmɪnɪstreɪtɪv/   `JOBS`

ADJECTIVE Administrative matters relate to organizing and supervising
the way that an organization or institution functions. ○ *Other industries*
have had to fire managers to reduce administrative costs. ○ *The project will have*
an administrative staff of 12.

▶ **COLLOCATIONS:**
administrative **costs/expenses/staff/management**
an administrative **system/structure/procedure**
an administrative **task/duty/error**

▶ **SYNONYMS:** bureaucratic, organizational, secretarial, clerical

ad|min|is|tra|tive as|sist|ant /ædmɪnɪstreɪtɪv əsɪstənt/
(administrative assistants)

NOUN An **administrative assistant** is a person who helps to supervise the
way that an organization functions. ○ *appointments updated by their*
administrative assistants

▶ **SYNONYM:** secretary

---

adopt /ədɒpt/ **(adopts, adopting, adopted)**

VERB If you **adopt** a new attitude, plan, or way of behaving, you begin to
have it. ○ *The Russian Parliament adopted a resolution calling for the complete*
withdrawal of troops. ○ *Students should be helped to adopt a positive approach*
to the environment.

▶ **COLLOCATIONS:**
adopt *something* **as** *something*
adopt *something* as a **policy/standard**
adopt a **stance/approach/attitude/strategy/tactic/policy**
unanimously/formally/widely adopted

▶ **SYNONYMS:** embrace, endorse, support, accept

adop|tion /ədɒpʃⁿn/

NONCOUNT NOUN ○ [+ of] the adoption of Japanese management practices by British manufacturing ○ [+ of] the widespread adoption of renewable energy

▶ **COLLOCATIONS:**
the adoption **of** something
the adoption of a **practice**
the adoption of **technology**
widespread/rapid/mass adoption

▶ **SYNONYMS:** acceptance, endorsement

---

ad|vance /ædvæns/ (advances, advancing, advanced) `R&D`

1 VERB To **advance** means to make progress, especially in your knowledge of something. ○ Medical technology has advanced considerably.

▶ **COLLOCATIONS:**
advance **rapidly/greatly/significantly**
advance **technologically**

▶ **SYNONYMS:** progress, improve

2 NOUN An **advance** in a particular subject or activity is progress in your knowledge of it. ○ Scientific advances have transformed our understanding of DNA. ○ [+ in] Major advances in microsurgery have been made.

▶ **COLLOCATIONS:**
an advance **in** something
technological/medical/scientific advances
a **major/significant/great** advance
make/represent an advance

▶ **SYNONYM:** development

ad|vanced /ædvænst/

ADJECTIVE An **advanced** system, method, or design is modern and has been developed from an earlier version of the same thing. ○ The lamp uses advanced technology to produce a very efficient source of light. ○ the most advanced optical telescope in the world

▶ **COLLOCATIONS:**
advanced **technology/equipment/techniques**
technologically/technically advanced

▶ **SYNONYMS:** up-to-date, modern, cutting edge

ad|van|tage /ædvæntɪdʒ/ (advantages)

1 **NOUN** An **advantage** is a way in which one thing is better than another. ○ [+ of] *The great advantage of this technique is the cost.* ○ [+ over] *These weapons have many advantages over existing ones.*

▸ **COLLOCATIONS:**
the advantage **of** *something*
an advantage **over** *something*
a **big/great/major/huge** advantage
a **distinct/obvious/added** advantage

▸ **SYNONYMS:** benefit, strength, merit, positive

2 **NOUN** An **advantage** is something that puts you in a better position than other people. ○ [+ over] *They are deliberately flouting the law in order to obtain an advantage over their competitors.* ○ [+ to] *A good crowd will be a definite advantage to me and the rest of the team.*

▸ **COLLOCATIONS:**
an advantage **over/to/for** *someone*
an advantage over **competitors/rivals/opponents**
an advantage to/for **employers/consumers/patients**
a **competitive/unfair/distinct/huge** advantage
enjoy/hold/have/obtain/secure/derive an advantage
confer/offer/provide an advantage

▸ **SYNONYMS:** aid, edge

3 **NONCOUNT NOUN** **Advantage** is the state of being in a better position than others who are competing against you. ○ [+ over] *Men have created a social and economic position of advantage for themselves over women.*

▸ **COLLOCATION:** advantage **over** *someone*

▸ **SYNONYMS:** dominance, superiority, privilege

ad|van|ta|geous /ædvənteɪdʒəs/

ADJECTIVE If something is **advantageous to** you, it is likely to benefit you. ○ [+ to] *Free exchange of goods was advantageous to all.* ○ *Coca-Cola enjoyed an extraordinarily advantageous market position during the early twentieth century.*

▸ **COLLOCATIONS:**
advantageous **to** *someone/something*
an advantageous **position/rate/condition**
mutually/economically/politically advantageous

▸ **SYNONYM:** favorable

ad|ver|tise /ˈædvərtaɪz/ (advertises, advertising, advertised) **MARKETING & SALES**

VERB If you **advertise** something such as a product, an event, or a job, you tell people about it in newspapers, on television, or on posters.
○ *Companies spend a lot of money advertising new products.* ○ *Religious groups are currently not allowed to advertise on television.*

▶ **COLLOCATIONS:**
advertise **for** *someone*
advertise a **product/property**
advertise a **job/vacancy/position**

▶ **PHRASES:**
advertise something on television/the Internet
advertise something in a newspaper

▶ **SYNONYMS:** promote, market

ad|ver|tise|ment /ˈædvərtaɪzmənt/ (advertisements)

NOUN An **advertisement** is an announcement in a newspaper, on television, or on a poster about something such as a product, event, or job. [WRITTEN] ○ [+ *for*] *a television advertisement for cat food*

▶ **COLLOCATIONS:**
an advertisement **for** *something*
place an advertisement
an advertisement **appears** *somewhere*
a **television/newspaper** advertisement
a **full-page** advertisement

▶ **SYNONYM:** commercial

ad|ver|tis|ing agen|cy /ˈædvərtaɪzɪŋ ˈeɪdʒənsi/ (advertising agencies)

NOUN An **advertising agency** is a company whose business is to create advertisements for other companies or organizations. ○ *Several big advertising agencies report that ad spending this year is lower than expectations.*

> **USAGE:** *advertising* or *advertisement*?
>
> The noncount noun **advertising** can refer generally to the process or business of telling people about a product or service. ○ *The company has increased its spending on online advertising.*
>
> An **advertisement** (a count noun) is a specific example of something that advertises a product or service, in a newspaper, on television, etc. ○ *a television advertisement for cat food*

a

ad|vice /ædvaɪs/

NONCOUNT NOUN If you give someone **advice**, you tell them what you think they should do. ○ *She has given me some good advice.* ○ [+ *about*] *Don't be afraid to ask for advice about the course.* ○ [+ *on*] *Your doctor can offer advice on health and fitness.*

▸ **COLLOCATIONS:**
advice **on/about** *something*
advice **from** *someone*
give/offer (*someone*) advice
provide/ask for/seek/get/receive advice
take/follow *someone's* advice
good/sound/bad advice
legal/financial/medical/career advice
professional/independent/expert/practical advice

▸ **SYNONYM:** guidance

af|fect /əfɛkt/ (affects, affecting, affected)

VERB If something **affects** a person or thing, it influences them or causes them to change in some way. ○ *Nicotine from cigarettes can adversely affect the heart.* ○ *More than seven million people have been affected by drought.* ○ *The new law will directly affect thousands of people.*

▸ **COLLOCATIONS:**
badly/adversely/directly affect
seriously/severely/greatly affect
affect the **outcome/quality/performance of** *something*
affect **people/everyone**

▸ **SYNONYMS:** influence, impact

USAGE: *affect* or *effect*?

Affect is a verb. The noun that comes from **affect** is **effect**. You can say that something **affects** you, or that it has an **effect** on you. ○ *Noise in factories can seriously affect workers' health.* ○ *Noise in factories can have a serious effect on workers' health.*

---

af|flu|ent /æfluənt/

ADJECTIVE If you are **affluent**, you have a lot of money. ○ *Cigarette smoking used to be more common among affluent people.*

▶ COLLOCATIONS:
affluent **people/families**
an affluent **area/neighborhood/suburb/society/country**
an affluent **lifestyle**

▶ SYNONYMS: prosperous, wealthy

• **The affluent** are people who are affluent. ○ *The diet of the affluent has not changed much over the decades.*

---

af|ford|able /əfɔːdəbəl/   MARKETING & SALES

ADJECTIVE If something is **affordable**, most people have enough money to buy it. ○ *the availability of affordable housing*

▶ COLLOCATIONS:
affordable **housing/childcare/insurance**
an affordable **lifestyle/home/car/price**
make/keep *something* affordable

---

agen|da /ədʒɛndə/ (agendas)

NOUN You can refer to the issues that are important at a particular time as an **agenda**. ○ *Does television set the agenda on foreign policy?* ○ *This is sure to be an item on the agenda next week.*

▶ COLLOCATIONS:
on the agenda
the **domestic/national/legislative/political/social** agenda
pursue/push/outline an agenda
set the agenda
dominate/top the agenda

---

agent /eɪdʒ³nt/ (agents)   LOGISTICS & DISTRIBUTION

NOUN A chemical that has a particular effect or is used for a particular purpose can be referred to as a particular kind of **agent**. ○ *the bleaching agent in white flour* ○ *a chemical agent that can produce birth defects*

▶ COLLOCATIONS:
a **chemical/biological** agent
a **bleaching/clotting/bonding** agent

---

ag|gres|sive /əgrɛsɪv/

ADJECTIVE An **aggressive** person or animal behaves in an angry or violent way toward others. ○ *The man became aggressive when the flight attendant asked him to sit down.*

a

▶ **COLLOCATIONS:**
increasingly/overly/extremely aggressive
an aggressive **campaign/strategy**
aggressive **behavior**
be/get/become aggressive

▶ **SYNONYMS:** hostile, forceful

agree|ment /əgriːmənt/

NONCOUNT NOUN If there is **agreement** between two accounts of an event or two sets of figures, they are the same or are consistent with each other. ○ [+ with] *Many other surveys have produced results essentially in agreement with these figures.* ○ [+ between] *There is a measure of agreement between these accounts.*

▶ **COLLOCATIONS:**
in agreement
agreement **between** *things*
in agreement **with** *something*

▶ **SYNONYMS:** concurrence, correspondence

ag|ri|cul|tur|al /ægrɪkʌltʃərəl/   `ORGANIZATION`

ADJECTIVE If something is **agricultural**, it is concerend with the business or activity of farming. ○ *agricultural land* ○ *The price of corn and other agricultural products has increased.*

▶ **COLLOCATIONS:**
agricultural **land**
an agricultural **product/subsidy/worker**
the agricultural **industry**

air|port /ɛərpɔrt/ (airports)   `TRAVEL`

NOUN An **airport** is a place where airplanes come and go, with buildings and services for passengers. ○ *Newark Airport*

▶ **COLLOCATIONS:** a **major/international** airport

al|low /əlaʊ/ (allows, allowing, allowed)

1 VERB If someone **is allowed to** do something, it is all right for them to do it. ○ [+ to-inf] *The children are not allowed to watch violent TV programs.* ○ [+ to-inf] *The Government will allow them to advertise on radio and television.* ○ *Smoking will not be allowed.*

> SYNONYMS: permit, let

2 VERB If you **are allowed** something, you are given permission to have it or are given it. ○ *Gifts like chocolates or flowers are allowed.* ○ *He should be allowed the occasional treat.*

> SYNONYM: permit

3 VERB If you **allow** something **to** happen, you do not prevent it. ○ [+ to-inf] *He won't allow himself to fail.* ○ [+ to-inf] *If the soil is allowed to dry out the tree could die.*

> SYNONYMS: permit, let

al|low|able /əlaʊəbəl/

ADJECTIVE ○ *Capital punishment is allowable only under exceptional circumstances.* ○ *Her expenses were allowable deductions.*

> SYNONYM: acceptable

al|low|ance /əlaʊəns/ (allowances)

NOUN A particular type of **allowance** is an amount of something that you are allowed in particular circumstances. ○ *Most of our flights have a baggage allowance of 44 pounds per passenger.*

> COLLOCATIONS:
> an allowance **of** x
> a **baggage/mileage/vacation** allowance

al|ter /ɔltər/ (alters, altering, altered)

VERB If something **alters** or if you **alter** it, it changes. ○ *Little had altered in the village.* ○ *attempts to genetically alter the caffeine content of coffee plants*

→ see note at **adapt**

> COLLOCATIONS:
> alter the **course/outcome** of something
> alter the **composition/balance/structure** of something
> alter the **facts/perceptions/wording**
> **radically/fundamentally/structurally/genetically** alter something

> SYNONYMS: change, adapt

al|tera|tion /ɔltəreɪʃən/ (alterations)

NOUN An **alteration** is a change in or to something. ○ [+ to] *Making some simple alterations to your diet will make you feel fitter.* ○ [+ in] *an alteration in hormone balance which causes blood sugar levels to fall*

▶ **COLLOCATIONS:**
an alteration **in/of/to** *something*
make/propose an alteration
require/undergo alteration
a **structural/genetic** alteration
a **minor/major/necessary/significant** alteration

▶ **SYNONYM:** change

amaze|ment /əmeɪzmənt/

NONCOUNT NOUN Amazement is the feeling you have when something surprises you very much. ○ *I looked at her in amazement.*

▶ **COLLOCATIONS:**
express amazement
utter/sheer amazement

▶ **SYNONYM:** surprise

am|bigu|ous /æmbɪgyuəs/

ADJECTIVE If you describe something as **ambiguous**, you mean that it is unclear or confusing because it can be understood in more than one way.
○ *This agreement is very ambiguous and open to various interpretations.*
○ *The Secretary of State's remarks clarify an ambiguous statement issued earlier this week.*

▶ **COLLOCATIONS:**
deliberately/somewhat/highly ambiguous
remain/seem ambiguous
an ambiguous **relationship/position/result/phrase/statement**
ambiguous **language/wording**

▶ **SYNONYMS:** vague, unclear, obscure

am|biva|lent /æmbɪvələnt/

ADJECTIVE If you say that someone is **ambivalent about** something, they seem to be uncertain whether they really want it, or whether they really approve of it. ○ [+ *about*] *She remained ambivalent about her marriage.*

▶ **COLLOCATIONS:**
ambivalent **about** *something*
feel/remain ambivalent

▶ **SYNONYM:** unsure

am|biva|lence /æmbɪvələns/

NONCOUNT NOUN ○ [+ toward] *a profound ambivalence toward households and family policy*

▶ **COLLOCATIONS:**
ambivalence **about/toward** something
express/display/show/reflect ambivalence

am|ple /æmpᵊl/ (ampler, amplest)

ADJECTIVE If there is an **ample** amount of something, there is enough of it and usually some extra. ○ *The navy had ample opportunity to intercept them at sea.*

▶ **COLLOCATIONS:**
ample **opportunity/time**
ample **evidence**
ample **money/space/room/parking**
an ample **supply**

ana|lyze /ænəlaɪz/ (analyzes, analyzing, analyzed)

1 VERB If you **analyze** something, you consider it carefully or use statistical methods in order to fully understand it. ○ *McCarthy was asked to analyze the data from the first phase of trials of the vaccine.* ○ [+ what] *This book teaches you how to analyze what is causing the stress in your life.*

2 VERB If you **analyze** something, you examine it using scientific methods in order to find out what it consists of. ○ *Thompson and her colleagues analyzed the samples using the antibody test.* ○ *They had their tablets analyzed to find out whether they were getting the real drug or not.*

▶ **COLLOCATIONS:**
analyze **data/statistics/results/trends**
analyze a **sample**
analyze something **critically/carefully/scientifically**

▶ **SYNONYMS:** examine, study, inspect, investigate

analy|sis /ənælɪsɪs/ (analyses)

NOUN ○ *The main results of the analysis are summarized below.* ○ [+ of] *This involves mathematical analysis of data from astronomy.* ○ [+ of] *an analysis of President Bush's domestic policy*

▶ **COLLOCATIONS:**
analysis **of** something
analysis of **data/samples**

undertake/conduct/perform an analysis
a **statistical/technical/chemical/forensic/scientific** analysis
a **detailed/thorough/comparative/objective** analysis
analyses **indicate/show/suggest** *something*

▶ SYNONYMS: examination, study, investigation, inspection

---

an|nounce|ment /ənaʊnsmənt/   COMMUNICATIONS
(announcements)

NOUN An **announcement** is something that is told to a lot of people to give them official information. ○ *He made his announcement after talks with the president.* ○ *There has been no formal announcement by either government.*

▶ COLLOCATIONS:
make an announcement
a **formal/official/public** announcement
a **surprise** announcement

▶ SYNONYMS: declaration, statement

---

an|nual /ænyuəl/

1 ADJECTIVE **Annual** events happen once every year. ○ *the society's annual conference* ○ *In its annual report, UNICEF says at least 40,000 children die every day.*

2 ADJECTIVE **Annual** quantities or rates relate to a period of one year. ○ *The electronic and printing unit has annual sales of about $80 million.*

▶ COLLOCATIONS:
an annual **conference/event**
an annual **vacation/celebration**
annual **fees/costs/sales/profits**
an annual **income/salary/budget**

▶ SYNONYM: yearly

---

anony|mous /ənɒnɪməs/

ADJECTIVE If you remain **anonymous** when you do something, you do not let people know that you were the person who did it. ○ *You can remain anonymous if you wish.* ○ *anonymous phone calls*

▶ COLLOCATIONS:
remain anonymous
an anonymous **phone call/caller/letter/donor**

▶ SYNONYMS: unknown, unidentified, unnamed

an|tici|pate /æntɪsɪpeɪt/ (anticipates, anticipating, anticipated)

VERB If you **anticipate** an event, you realize in advance that it may happen and you are prepared for it. ○ *Surveyors anticipate further price declines over coming months.* ○ [+ that] *It is anticipated that the equivalent of 192 full-time jobs will be lost.* ○ [+ that] *Officials anticipate that rivalry between leaders of the various drug factions could erupt into full-scale war.*

▶ **COLLOCATIONS:**
anticipate a **decline/slowdown/surge/advance/reaction**
widely anticipated

▶ **SYNONYM:** expect

anx|ious /æŋkʃəs/

ADJECTIVE If someone is **anxious**, they are feeling nervous or worried about something. ○ *He appeared anxious to end the conversation.*

▶ **COLLOCATIONS:**
an anxious **wait/moment/parent**
be/feel/become anxious

▶ **SYNONYMS:** eager, uneasy

apolo|gize /əpɒlədʒaɪz/ (apologizes, apologizing, apologized)   COMMUNICATIONS

VERB When you **apologize**, you say that you are sorry. [in BRIT, also use **apologise**] ○ [+ for] *He apologized for being late.* ○ *I spelled your name wrong — I do apologize!*

▶ **COLLOCATIONS:**
apologize **publicly**
apologize **for** *something*

▶ **PHRASE:** apologize for the inconvenience

▶ **SYNONYM:** ask forgiveness

BUSINESS CORRESPONDENCE: Apologizing

There are several common expressions used to apologize for problems, delays, etc., in business correspondence. Be careful not to confuse the verb form **apologize** and the noun **apology** (plural **apologies**). ○ *I would like to apologize for* the error with your order. ○ *Please accept our apologies for* the delays in dealing with your request. ○ *We regret* any inconvenience this has caused.

ap|par|ent /əpærənt/

1 **ADJECTIVE** An **apparent** situation, quality, or feeling seems to exist, although you cannot be certain that it does exist. ○ *the apparent government lack of concern for the advancement of science* ○ *There are two reasons for this apparent contradiction.*

▸ **COLLOCATIONS:**
an apparent **contradiction/lack**
an apparent **failure/inability**
an apparent **reason/attempt**

▸ **SYNONYMS:** seeming, supposed

2 **ADJECTIVE** If something is **apparent** to you, it is clear and obvious to you. ○ *It has been apparent that in other areas standards have held up well.* ○ *[+ that] It will be readily apparent from Fig. 108a that there is a link between the monetary side of the economy and the real economy.* ○ *[+ from] The shrinkage of the tissue is not immediately apparent.*

▸ **COLLOCATIONS:**
apparent **to** *someone*
apparent **from** *something*
readily/immediately/increasingly apparent

▸ **SYNONYMS:** clear, obvious

ap|par|ent|ly /əpærəntli/

ADVERB You use **apparently** to refer to something that seems to be true, although you are not sure whether it is or not. ○ *The recent deterioration has been caused by an apparently endless recession.*

▸ **COLLOCATIONS:** apparently **random/unrelated/healthy/unaware**

▸ **SYNONYMS:** seemingly, ostensibly

ap|peal|ing /əpiːlɪŋ/

ADJECTIVE Someone or something that is **appealing** is pleasing and attractive. ○ *There was a sense of humor to what he did that I found very appealing.*

▸ **COLLOCATIONS:**
appealing **to** *someone*
look/seem appealing
find *something* appealing
an appealing **feature/option/aspect/prospect/idea**

▸ **SYNONYM:** attractive

ap|pear|ance /əpɪ̯ərəns/ (appearances)

NOUN Someone's or something's **appearance** is the way that they look.
  ○ She used to be so fussy about her appearance. ○ [+ of] He had the appearance of a college student. ○ [+ of] A flat-roofed extension will add nothing to the value or appearance of the house.

▶ **COLLOCATIONS:**
  the appearance **of** someone/something
  something's **physical/external** appearance
  improve/enhance someone's/something's appearance

▶ **SYNONYM:** look

ap|pli|ance /əplaɪ̯əns/ (appliances)

NOUN An **appliance** is a machine that you use to do a job in your home.
  [FORMAL] ○ domestic appliances

▶ **COLLOCATIONS:** a **household/kitchen/electrical/stainless steel** appliance

▶ **SYNONYM:** device

ap|ply /əplaɪ/ (applies, applying, applied)   PERSONNEL

1 VERB If you **apply for** something such as a job or membership in an organization, you write a letter or fill in a form in order to ask formally for it. ○ [+ for] I am continuing to apply for jobs. ○ [+ to-inf] They may apply to join the organization.

▶ **COLLOCATIONS:**
  apply **for** something
  apply for a **job**
  apply for a **license/visa/permit/passport**
  apply for a **grant/loan**
  apply for **membership**

2 VERB If something such as a rule or a remark **applies to** a person or in a situation, it is relevant to the person or the situation. ○ [+ to] The convention does not apply to us. ○ The rule applies where a person owns stock in a corporation.

3 VERB If you **apply** something such as a rule, system, or skill, you use it in a situation or activity. ○ These psychologists are applying psychological principles in order to improve the effectiveness of industrial organizations. ○ [+ to] His project is concerned with applying the technology to practical business problems.

▶ COLLOCATIONS:
apply **to** *someone/something*
a **rule/principle/condition** applies
apply a **principle/technique/rule/criterion**

▶ SYNONYMS: pertain, be relevant, use

ap|pli|cant /ˈæplɪkənt/ (applicants)

NOUN An **applicant** is someone who formally asks to be considered for a job
or course. ○ *job applicants* ○ *The firm recently had fifty applicants for one job.*

▶ COLLOCATIONS:
screen/interview/reject an applicant
a **job/successful** applicant

ap|pli|ca|tion /ˌæplɪˈkeɪʃən/ (applications)

1 NOUN An **application for** something is a formal written request for it.
○ [+ *for*] *His application for a student loan was rejected.* ○ [+ *to-inf*] *Turkey's
application to join the European Community* ○ *Applications should be submitted
as early as possible.* ○ *Tickets are available on application.*

▶ COLLOCATIONS:
an application **for** *something*
file/submit an application
receive/accept/reject an application
a **job/visa/passport/loan/grant** application
an application **form**

2 NOUN The **application of** a rule or piece of knowledge is the use of it in a
particular situation. ○ [+ *of*] *Students learned the practical application of the
theory they had learned in the classroom.* ○ [+ *to*] *The book provides a succinct
outline of artificial intelligence and its application to robotics.*

▶ COLLOCATIONS:
the application **of** *something*
something's application **to** *something*
the application of a **principle/theory/rule**
the application of **technology**
a **practical/commercial/clinical/specific** application

▶ SYNONYMS: use, relevance

ap|pli|ca|tion form /ˌæplɪˈkeɪʃən fɔːrm/ (application forms)

NOUN An **application form** is a written list of questions that you have to
answer when you apply for a job. ○ *I enclose my completed application form
for the position of Administrative Assistant.*

▶ SYNONYM: résumé

a

ap|pre|ci|ate /əpriːʃieɪt/ (appreciates, appreciating, appreciated)

VERB If you **appreciate** a situation or problem, you understand it and know what it involves. ○ *Those arguing the case often do not appreciate the difference between an island nation and a continental one.* ○ [+ that] *It is essential to appreciate that addictive behavior can compromise energy levels.*

▶ **COLLOCATIONS:**
   appreciate the **importance/significance** of something
   appreciate the **seriousness/extent** of something
   appreciate a **fact**
   fully appreciate

▶ **SYNONYMS:** acknowledge, recognize

BUSINESS CORRESPONDENCE: Polite requests

There are several common expressions used to make polite requests in business correspondence. Longer expressions are often used in more formal contexts: ○ *I would appreciate it if you could return two signed copies to me.* ○ *I would be grateful if you could forward me the complete list of candidates.*

Simpler, less formal polite expressions include: ○ *I wonder if you could give me a call to confirm the dates.* ○ *Could you please let us know how many people you expect to attend?*

---

2 VERB If you **appreciate** something that someone has done for you or is going to do for you, you are grateful for it. ○ *Friends appreciated his effort in joining the crew for the race.* ○ *We appreciate your help in the market research survey.*

▶ **COLLOCATIONS:**
   appreciate a **gesture/sacrifice/donation**
   appreciate someone's **kindness/generosity/help**

▶ **PHRASE:** I really appreciate it

ap|pre|cia|tion /əpriːʃieɪʃᵊn/ (appreciations)

NOUN An **appreciation of** a situation or problem is an understanding of what it involves. ○ [+ of] *They have a stronger appreciation of the importance of economic incentives.* ○ [+ of] *The WTO showed a deeper appreciation of the need for environmental exemptions.*

▶ **COLLOCATIONS:**
   appreciation **of** something
   appreciation of the **importance/significance** of something

appreciation of the **need** for *something*
show appreciation

▶ **SYNONYMS:** grasp, understanding

ap|pre|ci|able /əprɪ̠ʃiəbəl, -ʃəbəl/

ADJECTIVE An **appreciable** amount or effect is large enough to be important or clearly noticed. [FORMAL] ○ *It contains less than 1 percent fat, an appreciable amount of protein, and a high content of minerals.* ○ *This has not had an appreciable effect on production.* ○ *There was no appreciable difference in test results.*

▶ **COLLOCATIONS:**
  an appreciable **amount/proportion**
  an appreciable **effect/difference**

EXTEND YOUR VOCABULARY

If an effect or a difference is **appreciable**, **noticeable**, or **discernible**, it is large enough to be clearly noticed. ○ *This distinction makes no appreciable difference in our analysis.*

You can talk about a **visible** effect or change if you can physically see it. ○ *There may be no visible signs of infection.*

A **significant** change or difference is large enough to be important. ○ *Numerous studies appear to show a statistically significant increase in risk.*

---

ap|pren|tice|ship /əprɛ̠ntɪsʃɪp/ (apprenticeships) `PERSONNEL`

NOUN An **apprenticeship** is an arrangement for someone to learn a skill by working for someone who has that skill. ○ *After serving his apprenticeship as a toolmaker, he became a manager.*

▶ **COLLOCATIONS:**
  serve an apprenticeship
  an apprenticeship **program**

▶ **SYNONYMS:** training, internship

---

ap|proach /əpro̠ʊtʃ/ (approaches, approaching, approached)

1 VERB When you **approach** a task, problem, or situation in a particular way, you deal with it or think about it in that way. ○ *The Bank has approached the issue in a practical way.* ○ *Employers are interested in how you approach problems.*

▶ **COLLOCATIONS:** approach a **task/issue/problem**

▶ **SYNONYMS:** tackle, address

2 NOUN Your **approach to** a task, problem, or situation is the way you deal with it or think about it. ○ [+ to] *We will be exploring different approaches to gathering information.* ○ *The program adopts a multidisciplinary approach.*

▶ **COLLOCATIONS:**
an approach **to** *something*
adopt/take/prefer an approach
a **pragmatic/cautious/different/innovative** approach

▶ **SYNONYMS:** methodology, procedure, technique

---

ap|pro|pri|ate /əprouʹpriːt/

ADJECTIVE Something that is **appropriate** is suitable or acceptable for a particular situation. ○ [+ to] *Dress neatly and attractively in an outfit appropriate to the job.* ○ *The teacher can then take appropriate action.*

▶ **COLLOCATIONS:**
appropriate **to/for** *something*
appropriate to/for a **purpose/occasion/task**
appropriate **action/treatment/punishment**
an appropriate **measure/response**
deem/consider *something* appropriate
wholly/entirely/perfectly/highly appropriate

▶ **SYNONYMS:** suitable, acceptable

ap|pro|pri|ate|ly

ADVERB ○ *Dress appropriately and ask intelligent questions.* ○ *It's entitled, appropriately enough, "Art for the Nation."*

▶ **COLLOCATIONS:**
respond/act/dress/behave appropriately
appropriately **named/titled**

▶ **SYNONYMS:** suitably, acceptably

---

ap|prove /əpruʹv/ (approves, approving, approved)

VERB If someone in a position of authority **approves** a plan or idea, they formally agree to it and say that it can happen. ○ *The Russian Parliament has approved a program of radical economic reforms.* ○ *The Senate approved the bill on Thursday.*

▶ **COLLOCATIONS:**
approve a **plan/bill/measure/proposal/request**
approved by **Congress/voters**
approved by a **committee/board/majority**
unanimously/formally/officially approved

▶ **SYNONYMS:** sanction, authorize, allow

ap|prov|al /əpruːvəl/

NONCOUNT NOUN **Approval** is a formal or official statement that
something is acceptable. ○ [+ *of*] *The testing and approval of new drugs will
be speeded up.* ○ [+ *of*] *The initiative is awaiting the approval of the medical
research ethics committee.*

▶ **COLLOCATIONS:**
the approval **of** *something*
the approval **of/from** *someone*
seek/obtain/await/gain/grant approval
subject to/pending approval
formal/final/regulatory approval

▶ **SYNONYM:** authorization

ap|proxi|mate (approximates, approximating, approximated)

> The adjective is pronounced /əprɒksɪmɪt/. The verb is pronounced
> /əprɒksɪmeɪt/.

1 **ADJECTIVE** An **approximate** number, time, or position is close to the
correct number, time, or position, but is not exact. ○ *The approximate cost
varies from around $150 to $250.* ○ *The times are approximate only.*

▶ **COLLOCATIONS:**
an approximate **cost/value/price/age/height/size**
an approximate **guide/definition/location**

▶ **SYNONYM:** rough

2 **VERB** If something **approximates** something else, it is similar to it but is
not exactly the same. ○ *By about 6 weeks of age, most babies begin to show
something approximating a day/night sleeping pattern.*

▶ **COLLOCATIONS:** **closely/roughly** approximate

ap|proxi|mate|ly /əprɒksɪmɪtli/

ADVERB ○ *Approximately $150 million is to be spent on improvements.* ○ *Each
session lasted approximately 30 to 40 minutes.*

▶ **SYNONYMS:** roughly, about, around

ar|bi|trary /ɑrbɪtrɛri/

ADJECTIVE If you describe an action, rule, or decision as **arbitrary**, you think that it is not based on any principle, plan, or system. It often seems unfair because of this. ○ *Arbitrary arrests and detention without trial were common.* ○ *a seemingly arbitrary deadline*

▶ **COLLOCATIONS:**
an arbitrary **arrest/imprisonment/execution**
an arbitrary **limit/deadline/distinction/code**
seemingly/purely arbitrary

▶ **SYNONYMS:** random, unfounded

archi|tect /ɑrkɪtɛkt/ (architects) `JOBS`

NOUN An **architect** is a person who designs buildings.

▶ **COLLOCATIONS:**
an architect **designs/builds** *things*
a **renowned/modernist/chief** architect

ar|gu|ment /ɑrgyəmənt/ (arguments)

NOUN An **argument** is a statement or set of statements that you use in order to try to convince people that your opinion about something is correct. ○ [+ *for*] *There's a strong argument for lowering the price.* ○ [+ *against*] *The doctors have set out their arguments against the proposals.*

▶ **COLLOCATIONS:**
an argument **for/against** *something*
an argument **in favor of** *something*
someone's **main/basic/general** argument
put forward/advance/present an argument
a **strong/powerful/persuasive/compelling** argument

▶ **PHRASES:**
a line of argument
both sides of an argument

▶ **SYNONYMS:** statement, case, reasoning

ar|range|ment /əreɪndʒmənt/ (arrangements) `OFFICE`

1 NOUN Arrangements are plans and preparations which you make so that something will happen or be possible. ○ [+ *for*] *The staff is working on final arrangements for the conference.* ○ [+ to-inf] *She telephoned Ellen, but made no arrangements to see her.* ○ *I prefer to make my own travel arrangements.*

▶ **COLLOCATIONS:**
arrangements **for** *something*
make/discuss/negotiate arrangements
travel/security arrangements

▶ **SYNONYM:** plans

2 NOUN An **arrangement** is an agreement that you make with someone to do something. ○ *The caves can be visited only by prior arrangement.*
○ [+ to-inf] *Her teacher made a special arrangement to discuss her progress once a month.* ○ *Our policy is to try and come to an arrangement with the owner.*

▶ **COLLOCATIONS:**
an arrangement **with** *someone*
come to/make an arrangement

▶ **PHRASE:** by prior arrangement

▶ **SYNONYM:** agreement

ar|ti|fi|cial /ɑrtɪfɪʃəl/

ADJECTIVE Artificial objects, materials, or processes do not occur naturally and are created by human beings, for example, using science or technology. ○ *a diet free from artificial additives, colors, and flavors* ○ *The city is dotted with small lakes, natural and artificial.*

▶ **COLLOCATIONS:**
an artificial **limb/leg/heart**
an artificial **sweetener/additive/flavoring/fertilizer**
an artificial **lake/surface**
somewhat/wholly/highly/totally artificial

▶ **PHRASE:** artificial intelligence

▶ **SYNONYMS:** synthetic, manmade

as|sem|bly /əsɛmbli/ (assemblies)   `OFFICE`

1 NOUN An **assembly** is a large group of people who meet regularly to make decisions or laws for a particular region or country. ○ *the campaign for the first free election to the National Assembly*

▶ **COLLOCATIONS:**
elect/convene/dissolve an assembly
a **regional/national/legislative** assembly

2 NONCOUNT NOUN The **assembly** of a machine, device, or object is the process of fitting its different parts together. ○ [+ of] *For the rest of the day, he worked on the assembly of an explosive device.* ○ *car assembly plants*

▶ **COLLOCATIONS:**
the assembly **of** something
an assembly **plant/line**
assembly **instructions**

▶ **SYNONYMS:** construction, manufacture

---

as|sess /əsɛ́s/ (assesses, assessing, assessed)

VERB When you **assess** a person, thing, or situation, you consider them in order to make a judgment about them. ○ *Our correspondent has been assessing the impact of the sanctions.* ○ *The test was to assess aptitude rather than academic achievement.* ○ *[+ whether] It would be a matter of assessing whether she was well enough to travel.*

▶ **COLLOCATIONS:**
assess the **damage/impact/risk/progress**
assess a **situation**
assess **objectively/independently/accurately/properly**

▶ **SYNONYMS:** evaluate, judge, test

as|sess|ment /əsɛ́smənt/ (assessments)

NOUN ○ *[+ of] There is little assessment of the damage to the natural environment.* ○ *Everything from course learning materials to final assessment is completed via the Web.* ○ *[+ by] He was remanded to a mental hospital for assessment by doctors.*

▶ **COLLOCATIONS:**
assessment **of** something
assessment **by** someone
assessment of a **situation**
risk/damage assessment
undergo/conduct/complete an assessment
a **frank/objective/accurate/detailed** assessment
a **blunt/gloomy/initial/preliminary** assessment
a **psychiatric/psychological/environmental** assessment

▶ **SYNONYMS:** evaluation, test, appraisal

---

as|set /ǽsɛt/ (assets)   BANKING & FINANCE

1 NOUN Something or someone that is an **asset** is considered useful or helps a person or organization to be successful. ○ *[+ of] Her leadership qualities were her greatest asset.* ○ *His Republican credentials made him an asset.*

▶ **COLLOCATIONS:**
an asset **of** something
a **valuable/great** asset

▶ **SYNONYMS:** distinction, advantage

2 PLURAL NOUN The **assets** of a company or a person are all the things that they own. ○ [+ of] By the end of 1989 the group had assets of 3.5 billion francs. ○ Some tried to sell assets to pay the debts back.

▶ **COLLOCATIONS:**
assets **of** $x
the assets of a **company/corporation/estate**
net/total/average assets
valuable/tangible assets
acquire/purchase/sell assets
value/invest/freeze assets

▶ **SYNONYMS:** possessions, property, capital

as|sign /əsaɪn/ (assigns, assigning, assigned)

1 VERB If you **assign** a piece of work **to** someone, you give them the work to do. ○ [+ to] The task is sometimes jointly assigned to accounting and engineering departments. ○ Workers felt forced to work late because managers assigned them more work than they could complete in a regular shift. ○ When teachers assign homework, students usually feel an obligation to do it.

2 VERB If you **assign** a particular function or value **to** someone or something, you say they have it. ○ [+ to] Under Mr. Harel's system, each business must assign a value to each job. ○ Assign the letters of the alphabet their numerical values – A equals 1, B equals 2, etc.

▶ **COLLOCATIONS:**
assign something **to** someone/something
assign a **task/chore/duty**
assign **homework**
assign a **value/score/meaning/role**

▶ **SYNONYMS:** allot, allocate

as|sist /əsɪst/ (assists, assisting, assisted)

1 VERB If you **assist** someone, you help them to do a job or task by doing part of the work for them. ○ [+ with] The family decided to assist me with my chores. ○ Dr. Amid was assisted by a young Asian nurse.

2 VERB If you **assist** someone, you give them information, advice, or money. ○ [+ in] The public is urgently requested to assist police in tracing this *man.* ○ [+ *with*] *Officials assisted with transportation and finance problems.*

3 VERB If something **assists in** doing a task, it makes the task easier to do. ○ [+ *in*] *a chemical that assists in the manufacture of proteins* ○ [+ *in*] *an increasing number of techniques to assist people in creating successful strategies* ○ *Salvage operations have been greatly assisted by the good weather conditions.*

▶ **COLLOCATIONS:**
assisted **by** *someone/something*
assist *someone* **with/in** *something*
assist in/with a **search/rescue/investigation/inquiry**
ably/greatly/materially/financially assisted
assisted **suicide/living**
assist a **victim/refugee**
assist the **police**

▶ **SYNONYMS:** help, aid, back

as|sis|tance /əsɪstəns/

NONCOUNT NOUN ○ [+ *of*] *Since 1976 he has been operating the shop with the assistance of volunteers.* ○ [+ *in*] *Employees are being offered assistance in finding new jobs.* ○ *a viable program of economic assistance*

▶ **COLLOCATIONS:**
assistance **with/in** *something*
assistance **from** *someone*
assistance with/in a **matter/investigation/case**
assistance from the **community/police/government**
provide/offer/seek/receive assistance
humanitarian/financial/technical/medical assistance
emergency/disaster/development assistance
an assistance **package/program**

▶ **PHRASES:**
advice and assistance
aid and assistance
with the assistance of

▶ **SYNONYMS:** help, aid

as|sume /əsum/ (assumes, assuming, assumed)

VERB If you **assume that** something is true, you imagine that it is true, sometimes wrongly. ○ [+ *that*] *It is a misconception to assume that the two continents are similar.* ○ [+ *to-inf*] *If mistakes occurred, they were assumed to be the fault of the commander on the spot.*

▶ **COLLOCATIONS:**
wrongly/mistakenly/automatically/safely assume *something*
widely assumed

▶ **SYNONYMS:** presume, expect

as|sump|tion /əsʌmpʃᵊn/ (assumptions)

NOUN If you make an **assumption that** something is true or will happen, you accept that it is true or will happen, often without any real proof. ○ *Dr. Subroto questioned the scientific assumption on which the global warming theory is based.* ○ [+ *of*] *Economists are working on the assumption of an interest rate cut.*

▶ **COLLOCATIONS:**
on an assumption
an assumption **of** *something*
an assumption of **superiority/risk/guilt**
make/challenge/question an assumption
an **underlying/implicit** assumption

▶ **SYNONYMS:** presumption, premise, supposition

---

as|sure /əʃʊər/ (assures, assuring, assured)

1 VERB If you **assure** someone **that** something is true or will happen, you tell them that it is definitely true or will definitely happen, often in order to make them less worried. ○ [+ *that*] *Russia has assured us that it maintains robust command and control arrangements for its nuclear weapons.* ○ [+ *that*] *Assure yourself that the assertion of your paper is both clear and worth supporting.* ○ [+ *of*] *Government officials recently assured Hindus of protection.*

▶ **COLLOCATIONS:**
assure *someone* **of** *something*
assure the **public**

▶ **SYNONYM:** reassure

2 VERB To **assure** someone **of** something means to make certain that they will get it. ○ [+ *of*] *Henry VII's Welsh ancestry assured him of the warmest support in Wales.* ○ *a retraining program to assure laid-off employees new work* ○ *A level of self-containment renders us immune to criticism or disapproval, thus assuring our serenity of mind.*

▶ **COLLOCATIONS:**
assure *someone* **of** *something*
assure the **victory/success** of *something*
assure the **discretion** of *someone*

▶ **SYNONYM:** guarantee

at|tach /ətætʃ/ (attaches, attaching, attached) `COMMUNICATIONS`

1 VERB If you **attach** something **to** an object, you join it or fasten it to the object. ○ [+ to] *The gadget can be attached to any vertical surface.* ○ *For further information, please contact us on the attached form.*

2 VERB In computing, if you **attach** a file **to** a message that you send to someone, you send it with the message but separate from it. ○ [+ to] *It is possible to attach executable program files to e-mail.*

▶ **COLLOCATIONS:**
attach *something* **to** *something*
attach a **rope/wire/cord/device**
attach a **file/chart/form**
firmly/securely/permanently/physically attach *something*

▶ **SYNONYM:** connect

BUSINESS CORRESPONDENCE: *attach or enclose?*

You use **attach** when you send a file or document together with an e-mail message. ○ *I'm attaching a copy of the schedule for the training day.* ○ *Please find attached the schedule for the training day.*

You use **enclose** when you send another document in the same envelope as a letter. ○ *I'm enclosing more information and an application form.*

---

at|tach|ment /ətætʃmənt/ (attachments)

1 NOUN An **attachment** is a device that can be fixed onto a machine in order to enable it to do different jobs. ○ [+ for] *Some models come with attachments for dusting.*

▶ **COLLOCATIONS:**
an attachment **for** *something*
a **camera/hose/shower** attachment

▶ **SYNONYMS:** fixture, fitting, part

2 NOUN An **attachment** is a document or file that is added to another document or an e-mail. ○ [+ to] *Justice Fitzgerald included a 120-page discussion paper as an attachment to the annual report.* ○ *When you send an e-mail you can also send a sound or graphic file as an attachment.*

▶ **COLLOCATIONS:**
an attachment **to** *something*
send *something* **as** an attachment
open an attachment

▶ **SYNONYMS:** appendix, supplement

at|tend|ance /əˈtɛndəns/ (attendances) `OFFICE`

1 **NONCOUNT NOUN** Someone's **attendance** at an event or an institution is the fact that they are present at the event or go regularly to the institution. ○ [+ at] *Her attendance at school was sporadic.* ○ *Church attendance continues to decline.*

2 **NOUN** The **attendance** at an event is the number of people who are present at it. ○ *Average weekly movie attendance in February was 2.41 million.* ○ *This year attendances were 28% lower than forecast.*

▶ **COLLOCATIONS:**
attendance **at** something
attendance at a **meeting/conference/event**
attendance at **school/church**
compulsory/mandatory attendance
average/total/weekly attendance
an attendance **rate/figure/record**
boost/increase attendance

▶ **SYNONYM:** presence

at|trac|tion /əˈtrækʃən/ (attractions)

1 **NONCOUNT NOUN** **Attraction** is a feeling of liking someone, and often of being sexually interested in them. ○ [+ to] *Our level of attraction to the opposite sex has more to do with our inner confidence than how we look.*

▶ **COLLOCATIONS:**
attraction **to** someone
sexual/physical attraction

2 **NOUN** An **attraction** is a feature that makes something interesting or desirable. ○ [+ of] *the attractions of living on the waterfront*

▶ **COLLOCATIONS:**
the attractions **of** something/doing something
a **main/big/major/added** attraction

audi|to|rium /ɔdɪˈtɔriəm/ (auditoriums or auditoria) `OFFICE`

NOUN An **auditorium** is a large room, hall, or building that is used for events such as meetings and concerts. ○ *a high school auditorium*

▶ **COLLOCATIONS:**
a **full/packed** auditorium
a **high-school/civic/open-air** auditorium

▶ **SYNONYMS:** hall, theater

aug|ment /ɔgmɛnt/ (augments, augmenting, augmented)

VERB To **augment** something means to make it larger, stronger, or more effective by adding something to it. [FORMAL] ○ *While searching for a way to augment the family income, she began making dolls.*

▸ **COLLOCATIONS:**
augment **income**
augment the **supply** of *something*

▸ **SYNONYM:** supplement

aug|men|ta|tion /ɔgmənteɪʃ°n/

NONCOUNT NOUN ○ [+ *of*] *the augmentation of the Association's resources to improve the disciplinary process*

▸ **COLLOCATION:** the augmentation **of** *something*

authen|tic /ɔθɛntɪk/

1 ADJECTIVE An **authentic** person, object, or emotion is genuine.
○ *authentic Italian food* ○ *a demand for reliable, authentic information on which to base investment decisions*

2 ADJECTIVE If you describe something as **authentic**, you mean that it is such a good imitation that it is almost the same as or as good as the original. ○ *patterns for making authentic frontier-style clothing*

▸ **COLLOCATIONS:**
authentic **cuisine**
an authentic **portrayal/replica/flavor**
the authentic **voice** of *a group of people*
historically authentic
look/sound/feel authentic

▸ **SYNONYMS:** genuine, real

author|ize /ɔθəraɪz/ (authorizes, authorizing, authorized)

VERB If someone in a position of authority **authorizes** something, they give their official permission for it to happen. [in BRIT, also use **authorise**] ○ *It would certainly be within his power to authorize a police raid like that.*

▸ **COLLOCATIONS:**
authorize the **use** of *something*
authorize an **action/war/strike/payment**
authorize *someone* **to** *do something*

an authorized **biography/signature**
authorized **personnel**

▶ SYNONYM: sanction

---

avail|able /əveɪləbᵊl/

ADJECTIVE If something you want or need is **available**, you can get it. ○ *all the available evidence* ○ *There is a lot of information available on this subject.* ○ *The drug is widely available.* ○ *[+ for] The studio is available for private use.*

▶ COLLOCATIONS:
available **for** *something*
available **from/through/via/in** *somewhere*
widely/freely/readily/easily available
currently/immediately available
commercially/publicly/generally available
the available **information/evidence/space/resources**
make *something* available

▶ PHRASE: available on request

▶ SYNONYM: accessible

---

av|er|age /ævərɪdʒ, ævrɪdʒ/ (averages, averaging, averaged)

1 NOUN An **average** is the result that you get when you add two or more numbers together and divide the total by the number of numbers you added together. ○ *[+ of] Take the average of those ratios and multiply by a hundred.* ○ *The school's results are above the national average.*

▶ COLLOCATIONS:
the average **of** *something*
above/below average
the **national/overall** average
the **monthly/weekly/annual** average

▶ SYNONYM: mean

● **Average** is also an adjective. ○ *The average price of goods rose by just 2.2%.* ○ *The average age for a woman to have her first child was 29.*

▶ COLLOCATIONS:
the average **rate/price/cost**
the average **age/temperature**

▶ SYNONYM: mean

2 ADJECTIVE An **average** person or thing is typical or normal. ○ *The average adult man burns 1,500 to 2,000 calories per day.* ○ *Packaging is about a third* *of what is found in an average American trash can.*

▶ **SYNONYM:** typical

3 NOUN An amount or quality that is **the average** is the normal amount or quality. ○ *Most areas suffered more rain than usual, with our state getting double the average for the month.*

▶ **SYNONYM:** norm

● **Average** is also an adjective. ○ *$6 for a beer is average.* ○ *a woman of average height*

---

aware|ness /əwɛ̱ərnəs/

NONCOUNT NOUN Awareness of something is knowing about it. ○ [+ *of*] *There has been an increasing awareness of environmental issues.* ○ [+ *of*] *We need to raise public awareness of the disease.*

▶ **COLLOCATIONS:**
awareness **of/about** *something*
increase/raise/promote/heighten awareness
an **increasing/growing/heightened** awareness
public awareness
environmental/political awareness

Bb

back|ground /ˈbækɡraʊnd/ (backgrounds)

NOUN The **background** to an event or situation consists of the facts that explain what caused it. ○ [+ of] *The meeting takes place against a background of continuing political violence.* ○ [+ to] *The background to the experience is important.*

▶ **COLLOCATIONS:**
the background **to/of** *something*
background **information/knowledge**
background **report/check/material/reading**

▶ **PHRASE:** against a background of something

▶ **SYNONYM:** context

bag|gage /ˈbæɡɪdʒ/ `TRAVEL`

NONCOUNT NOUN Your **baggage** is all the bags that you take with you when you travel. ○ *Justin's baggage arrived at his parents' home.*

▶ **COLLOCATIONS:**
excess baggage
a baggage **handler/claim/allowance**

▶ **SYNONYM:** suitcases

bal|ance /ˈbæləns/ (balances, balancing, balanced) `BANKING & FINANCE`

1 VERB If you **balance** one thing **with** something different, each of the things has the same strength or importance. ○ *The state has got to find some way to balance these two needs.* ○ [+ with] *If your main occupation is using your brain, balance this with exercise.*

▶ **COLLOCATIONS:**
balance *something* **with** *something*
evenly/finely/carefully balanced

2 NOUN A **balance** is a situation in which all the different parts are equal in strength or importance. ○ [+ between] *We are forever trying to achieve a balance between two opposites.* ○ [+ of] *a way to ensure that people get the right balance of foods* ○ [+ of] *the ecological balance of the forest*

▶ COLLOCATIONS:
a balance **between** *things*
the balance **of** *something*
find/achieve/strike/maintain/restore a balance
redress/tip/upset/shift the balance
a **perfect/right/healthy/delicate/fine** balance

▶ PHRASE: balance of power

▶ SYNONYM: equilibrium

bal|anced /bælənst/

ADJECTIVE A **balanced** way of considering things is fair and reasonable. ○ *Journalists should present balanced reports.*

▶ COLLOCATIONS: a balanced **approach/view/perspective**

▶ PHRASE: fair and balanced

▶ SYNONYM: unbiased

bal|ance sheet /bæləns ʃit/ (balance sheets)

1 NOUN A **balance sheet** is a statement of the amount of money and property that a company has and the amount of money that it owes. ○ *Rolls-Royce needed to produce a strong balance sheet.*

2 NOUN A **balance sheet** is the general financial state of a company. ○ *The strong currency has helped the balance sheets of Brazilian companies with international aspirations.*

▶ COLLOCATION: **draw up** a balance sheet

bank ac|count /bæŋk əkaʊnt/ (bank accounts) `BANKING & FINANCE`

NOUN A **bank account** is an arrangement with a bank that allows you to keep your money in the bank and to take some out when you need it. ○ *Paul had at least 17 different bank accounts.*

▶ COLLOCATIONS:
deposit *money* **into** a bank account
withdraw *money* **from** a bank account

▶ RELATED WORDS: checking account, savings account

bank|rupt /bǽŋkrʌpt/ **BANKING & FINANCE**

ADJECTIVE People or organizations that go **bankrupt** do not have enough money to pay their debts. ○ *If the company cannot sell its products, it will go bankrupt.* ○ *He was declared bankrupt after failing to pay a $114 million loan guarantee.*

▶ **COLLOCATIONS:**
  go/become bankrupt
  be **declared** bankrupt

▶ **SYNONYM:** insolvent

bank|rupt|cy /bǽŋkrʌptsi, -rəpsi/

NONCOUNT NOUN ○ *It is the second airline in two months to file for bankruptcy.* ○ *Many established businesses were facing bankruptcy.*

▶ **COLLOCATIONS:**
  face/file for/avoid/declare bankruptcy
  bankruptcy **law/proceedings/protection**

▶ **SYNONYM:** insolvency

bar code /bɑr koʊd/ **(bar codes)** also **barcode** **MARKETING & SALES**

NOUN A **bar code** is an arrangement of numbers and lines that is printed on a product that can be read by a computer in order to get information about the product. ○ *Although all bar codes contain some common information, such as a general description of the product, they have space for only so much detail.*

▶ **COLLOCATIONS: scan/swipe** a bar code

▶ **SYNONYMS:** Universal Product Code, UPC

bare|ly /bɛ́ərli/

1 **ADVERB** If someone **barely** does something, they only just succeed in doing it. ○ *Spending on services and goods such as food and clothing barely grew.*

2 **ADVERB Barely** is used for emphasizing how quickly one action or event followed another. ○ *She had barely sat down when her name was called.*

▶ **COLLOCATIONS:**
  barely **notice/touch/contain** *something/someone*
  barely **audible/visible**
  barely **speak to** *someone*

▶ **SYNONYM:** scarcely

bar|gain /bɑːrgɪn/ (bargains) `MARKETING & SALES`

NOUN A **bargain** is something that is being sold at a lower price than usual. ○ *At this price, the dress is a real bargain.* ○ *Some are starting to offer wines at bargain prices.*

▶ **COLLOCATIONS:**
   drive/strike/find/offer a bargain
   a **hard/real** bargain
   a bargain **price/hunter/basement**

bar graph /bɑːr græf/ (bar graphs) or bar chart `COMMUNICATIONS`

NOUN A **bar graph** is a graph which uses parallel lines or rectangles to represent changes in the size, value, or rate of something or to compare the amount of something relating to a number of different countries or groups. ○ *The bar graph below shows the huge growth of car exports over the past few years.*

▶ **COLLOCATIONS:**
   a bar graph **shows/illustrates/reflects** *something*
   a bar graph **compares** *things*

EXTEND YOUR VOCABULARY

There are several ways to show information visually. A **graph** shows how two sets of numbers or measurements relate to each other.

Chart is a general word to describe information shown visually.
○ *The chart below shows our top 10 choices.*

A **diagram** is a simple picture showing how something works.
○ *as shown in the diagram of a mechanical fuel pump*

---

ba|si|cal|ly /beɪsɪkli/

ADVERB **Basically** is used for talking about a situation in a general way.
   ○ *Basically, he is a nice man.*

ba|sic wage /beɪsɪk weɪdʒ/ (basic wages) `PERSONNEL`

1 NOUN Your **basic wage** is the amount of money you earn at your job, not including overtime and bonuses. ○ *The basic wage for casino employees is $5.35 an hour plus tips.* ○ *a huge overtime bonus on top of his basic wage*

▶ **COLLOCATIONS:** a **low/high** basic wage

2 **NOUN** The **basic wage** is the lowest amount that an employer is legally allowed to pay an employee. ○ *Our workers are just managing to exist on the basic wage.*

ba|sis /beɪsɪs/ (bases)

NOUN If something is done **on** a particular **basis**, it is done according to that method, system, or principle. ○ *We're going to be meeting there on a regular basis.* ○ *They want all groups to be treated on an equal basis.* ○ *These judges dealt with questions of law on a day-to-day basis.*

▶ **COLLOCATIONS:**
on a *particular* basis
on a **regular/individual/equal** basis
on a **part-time/voluntary/temporary** basis
on a **daily/weekly/monthly/permanent** basis
a **case-by-case/day-to-day/pro rata** basis
a **first-come-first-served/need-to-know** basis

▶ **SYNONYMS:** method, system, footing, principle

bear mar|ket /beər mɑrkɪt/ (bear markets)   `BANKING & FINANCE`

NOUN A **bear market** is when people are selling a lot of shares of stock because they expect the price to drop. Then they make a profit by buying the shares again after a short time. ○ *Is the bear market in equities over?*

▶ **COLLOCATION:** a bear market **in** *something*

▶ **RELATED WORD:** bull market

before|hand /bɪfɔrhænd/

ADVERB If something happens **beforehand**, it happens before a particular event. ○ *How did she know beforehand that I was going to go out?*

▶ **COLLOCATIONS:**
x **hours/days/weeks/months** beforehand
know *something* beforehand

▶ **SYNONYMS:** in advance, already

be|gin|ner /bɪgɪnər/ (beginners)

NOUN A **beginner** is someone who has just started learning to do something. ○ *a course for beginners*

▶ COLLOCATIONS:
a **complete/absolute** beginner
a beginner's **class/course**

▶ SYNONYM: novice

---

be|have /bɪheɪv/ (behaves, behaving, behaved)

1 VERB The way that you **behave** is the way that you do and say things, and the things that you do and say. ○ [+ in] *I couldn't believe these people were behaving in this way.* ○ *He'd behaved badly.*

2 VERB In science, the way that something **behaves** is the things that it does. ○ *Under certain conditions, electrons can behave like waves rather than particles.*

▶ COLLOCATIONS:
behave **in** a *particular way*
behave in a particular **way/manner/fashion**
behave **like** *something*
behave **badly/differently/responsibly**

▶ SYNONYM: act

be|hav|ior /bɪheɪvyər/

1 NONCOUNT NOUN People's or animals' **behavior** is the way that they behave. [in BRIT, use **behaviour**] ○ *Make sure that good behavior is rewarded.* ○ *He frequently exhibited violent behavior.* ○ *human sexual behavior*

▶ COLLOCATIONS:
the behavior **of** *someone*
bad/anti-social/unacceptable/inappropriate behavior
human/sexual/criminal behavior
exhibit/display a type of behavior

▶ PHRASE: attitudes and behavior

▶ SYNONYM: conduct

2 NONCOUNT NOUN In science, the **behavior** of something is the way that it behaves. [in BRIT, use **behaviour**] ○ *It will be many years before anyone can predict a hurricane's behavior with much accuracy.* ○ [+ of] *the behavior of subatomic particles*

▶ COLLOCATION: the behavior **of** *something*

b

be|lieve /bɪliːv/ (believes, believing, believed)

VERB If you **believe** that something is true, you think that it is true, but you are not sure. [FORMAL] ○ [+ that] *Experts believe that the coming drought will be extensive.* ○ *Sleepiness in drivers is widely believed to be an important cause of road traffic injuries.* ○ *The main problem, I believe, lies elsewhere.*

▶ **COLLOCATIONS:**
be **widely** believed
strongly/firmly believe *something*

▶ **SYNONYMS:** think, consider

be|long /bɪlɒŋ/ (belongs, belonging, belonged)

1 VERB If something **belongs to** you, you own it. ○ [+ to] *This handwriting belongs to a male.* ○ *a home he says rightfully belongs to his family*

2 VERB If someone **belongs to** a particular group, they are a member of that group. ○ [+ to] *I used to belong to a youth club.*

3 VERB If something or someone **belongs in** or **to** a particular category, type, or group, they are of that category, type, or group. ○ [+ in] *The judges could not decide which category it belonged in.*

▶ **COLLOCATIONS:**
belong **to** *someone/something*
belong **in** *something*
belong in a **category/class/bracket**
rightfully/rightly/legally belong

bench|mark /bɛntʃmɑːrk/ (benchmarks)   `RGD`

NOUN A **benchmark** is something that is used to assess whether performance has been successful. ○ *The truck industry is a benchmark for the economy.*

▶ **COLLOCATIONS: set/meet/become** a benchmark

▶ **SYNONYMS:** reference point, gauge, standard

be|neath /bɪniːθ/

PREPOSITION If an item is **beneath** something, it is under it. ○ *He sat in the conference room beneath a huge photograph of himself.*

▶ **PHRASE:** up from beneath

▶ **SYNONYM:** under

ben|efit /bɛnɪfɪt/ (benefits, benefiting or benefitting, benefited or benefitted)   `PERSONNEL`

1 **NOUN** The **benefit of** something is the help that you get from it or the advantage that results from it. ○ [+ of] *the benefits of this form of therapy* ○ *For maximum benefit, use your treatment every day.* ○ [+ to] *I hope what I have written will be of benefit to someone else.* ○ [+ of] *This remarkable achievement took place without the benefit of modern telecommunications.*

▶ **COLLOCATIONS:**
the benefit **of** *something*
of benefit **to** *someone*
maximum/potential/additional benefit
health/economic/financial/social benefit
reap the benefit of *something*
bring/provide benefit

▶ **PHRASE:** the benefit of hindsight

▶ **SYNONYMS:** advantage, profit

2 **VERB** If you **benefit from** something or if it **benefits** you, it helps you or improves your life. ○ [+ from] *Both sides have benefited from the talks.* ○ *a variety of government programs benefiting children*

▶ **COLLOCATIONS:**
benefit **from** *something*
greatly/directly/personally/financially benefit *someone*

▶ **SYNONYMS:** profit, gain, help

USAGE: *benefit or profit?*

These words both describe something good that you get as a result of something. A **benefit** can be any positive result for an individual or a group of people. ○ *the potential benefits of the new technology* ○ *a more realistic view of the benefits of globalization*

A **profit** is usually money that a person or a company gets from an activity. ○ *The bank reported a profit of 572 million dollars.* ○ *A senior official profited illegally from smuggling.*

---

ben|efits pack|age /bɛnɪfɪts pækɪdʒ/ (benefits packages)

NOUN A **benefits package** is a set of benefits that some people get from their job in addition to their salary. ○ *New West Consultants has an excellent benefits package.* ○ *They offered a benefits package that included maternity leave, part-time work, and job sharing.*

▶ **COLLOCATIONS:** a **family/employee/medical** benefits package

▶ **PHRASE:** salary and benefits package

---

be|sides /bɪsaɪdz/

PREPOSITION **Besides** something means in addition to it. ○ *They have investments in a whole variety of businesses besides manufacturing.*

▶ **COLLOCATION:** besides **being** something

▶ **SYNONYM:** in addition to

---

best prac|tice /bɛst præktɪs/ (best practices)   `PERSONNEL`

1 **NONCOUNT NOUN** **Best practice** is an agreed process for getting something done in the most efficient way. ○ *a place where people can meet to swap ideas and develop best practice*

2 **PLURAL NOUN** **Best practices** are the best methods to get something done or to accomplish a goal. ○ *As natural-resource funds proliferate, they will have more opportunities to share expertise and best practices.*

▶ **COLLOCATIONS:** **follow/develop/establish** best practice

---

best-seller /bɛstsɛlər/ (best-sellers) or   `MARKETING & SALES`
bestseller

NOUN A **best-seller** is a product that is very popular and that many people buy. ○ *The best-sellers are electronic toys.* ○ *Every book featured on Oprah's monthly book club has made the New York Times best-seller list.*

best-selling /bɛstsɛlɪŋ/

ADJECTIVE ○ *Astrology magazines and booklets are among the best-selling publications at supermarket checkouts.*

▶ **COLLOCATIONS:**
a best-selling **novel/book/album**
a best-selling **author/novelist**
a best-selling **brand**

---

bev|er|age /bɛvərɪdʒ, bɛvrɪdʒ/ (beverages)

NOUN A **beverage** is a drink. [FORMAL] ○ *hot beverages*

▶ **COLLOCATIONS:**
drink/serve/sell a beverage
a **hot/cold/alcoholic/non-alcoholic** beverage

bias /baɪəs/ (biases, biasing, biased)

1 **NOUN** **Bias** is a tendency to prefer one person or thing to another, and to favor that person or thing. ○ [+ against] *Bias against women permeates every level of the judicial system.* ○ *There were fierce attacks on the radio station for alleged political bias.*

2 **NOUN** **Bias** is a concern with or interest in one thing more than others. ○ [+ toward] *The Department has a strong bias toward neuroscience.*

▶ **COLLOCATIONS:**
bias **against/toward** *something*
show/display/perceive/allege bias
eliminate/avoid bias
political/racial/cultural/gender bias

▶ **SYNONYMS:** prejudice, favor

3 **VERB** To **bias** someone means to influence them in favor of a particular choice. ○ *We mustn't allow it to bias our teaching.*

bi|ased /baɪəst/

ADJECTIVE ○ [+ against] *He seemed a bit biased against women in my opinion.* ○ [+ toward] *University funding was tremendously biased toward scientists.* ○ *examples of inaccurate and biased reporting* ○ *politically biased allegations*

▶ **COLLOCATIONS:**
biased **against** *someone/something*
biased **in favor of/toward** *someone/something*
biased **reporting/coverage/research/advice**
a biased **opinion/sample/referee/judge**
racially/culturally/politically biased
heavily biased

▶ **SYNONYM:** prejudiced

bill|able /bɪləbᵊl/ `BANKING & FINANCE`

ADJECTIVE **Billable** hours are the hours that a professional spends doing work for clients and for which the clients will have to pay. ○ *Most law firms expect at least forty billable hours a week.*

bill of lad|ing /bɪl əv leɪdɪŋ/ `LOGISTICS & DISTRIBUTION`
(bills of lading)

NOUN A **bill of lading** is a document containing full details of the goods that are being shipped. ○ *There were bills of lading from a steel mill in Indiana.*

▶ **SYNONYM:** invoice

b

black and white /blæk ənd waɪt/ also **black-and-white**

ADJECTIVE In a **black and white** photograph or film, everything is shown in black, white, and gray. ○ *old black and white films*

blank check /blæŋk tʃɛk/ (blank checks) `BANKING & FINANCE`

NOUN A **blank check** is a signed check on which the amount of money has not been written yet.

▶ **COLLOCATIONS: give/write** *someone* a blank check

blog /blɒg/ (blogs) `COMMUNICATIONS`

NOUN A **blog** is a website that describes the daily life of the person who writes it, and also their thoughts and ideas. ○ *His blog was later published as a book.*

▶ **COLLOCATIONS:**
write/start/run a blog
a blog **entry/site/reader/post**

board of di|rec|tors /bɔrd əv dɪrɛktərz/ (boards of directors) `JOBS`

NOUN A **board of directors** is the group of people elected by a company's shareholders to manage the firm. ○ *The board of directors has approved the decision unanimously.*

▶ **COLLOCATIONS:** the board of directors **decides/approves** *something*

board|room /bɔrdrum/ (boardrooms) also **board room** `OFFICE`

NOUN A **boardroom** is a room where the board of a company meets.
○ *Everyone had already assembled in the boardroom for the 9:00 a.m. session.*

▶ **COLLOCATIONS:**
a **corporate** boardroom
a boardroom **coup/shake-up**
boardroom **pay**

▶ **SYNONYMS:** conference room, meeting room

bond|holder /bɒndhoʊldər/ (bondholders) `BANKING & FINANCE`
also **bond holder**

NOUN A **bondholder** is a person who owns one or more investment bonds.

▶ **COLLOCATIONS:**
pay/owe a bondholder

an **unsecured** bondholder

▸ **SYNONYMS:** investor, shareholder

---

book|keeping /bʊ̠kkipɪŋ/ also **book-keeping** BANKING & FINANCE

b

NONCOUNT NOUN Bookkeeping is the job or activity of keeping an accurate record of the money that is spent and received by a business or other organization.

▸ **COLLOCATIONS:**
  corporate bookkeeping
  single-entry/double-entry bookkeeping
  creative/questionable bookkeeping

▸ **SYNONYM:** accounting

book|keeper /bʊ̠kkipər/ **(bookkeepers)** also **book-keeper**

NOUN A **bookkeeper** is a person whose job is to keep an accurate record of the money that is spent and received by a business.

▸ **SYNONYM:** accountant

---

boom /bu̠m/ **(booms, booming, boomed)** BANKING & FINANCE

1 NOUN If there is a **boom** in the economy, there is an increase in economic activity, for example, in the amount of things that are being bought and sold. ○ [+ in] *An economic boom followed, especially in housing and construction.* ○ *The 1980s were indeed boom years.* ○ *the cycle of boom and bust which has damaged us for 40 years*

2 NOUN A **boom in** something is an increase in its amount, frequency, or success. ○ [+ in] *The boom in the sport's popularity has meant more calls for stricter safety regulations.* ○ *Public transportation has not been able to cope adequately with the travel boom.* ○ *the collapse of the dotcom boom*

▸ **COLLOCATIONS:**
  a boom **in** something
  the boom **of** a period of time
  a boom in **spending/tourism/travel/housing**
  the boom of the **1960s/1990s**
  the boom **years**
  a **consumer/economic** boom
  the **property/dotcom/tech/telecom** boom
  the **baby** boom
  a boom **collapses/subsides/peaks/ends**

▸ **PHRASE:** boom and bust

b

3 VERB If the economy or a business **is booming**, the amount of things being bought or sold is increasing. ○ *By 2008 the economy was booming.* ○ *a booming global consumer electronics market* ○ *It has a booming tourist industry.*

▶ **COLLOCATIONS:**
the **economy** is booming
business is booming
sales are booming
a booming **market/industry/population**

---

bor|row /bɒrəʊ/ (borrows, borrowing, borrowed)   `BANKING & FINANCE`

1 VERB If you **borrow** something that belongs to someone else, you use it for a period of time and then return it. ○ *Can I borrow a pen please?*

2 VERB If you **borrow** money **from** someone or **from** a bank, they give it to you and you agree to pay it back at some time in the future. ○ [+ *from*] *Morgan borrowed $5000 from his father to form the company 20 years ago.* ○ [+ *from*] *It's so expensive to borrow from finance companies.*

▶ **COLLOCATIONS:** borrow **money/cash**

▶ **RELATED WORD:** lend

bor|row|er /bɒrəʊər/ (borrowers)

NOUN ○ *Borrowers with a big mortgage should go for a fixed rate.*

---

bounda|ry /baʊndəri/ (boundaries)

1 NOUN The **boundary of** an area of land is an imaginary line that separates it from other areas. ○ [+ *of*] *The Bow Brook forms the western boundary of the wood.*

▶ **COLLOCATIONS:**
the boundary **of** something
the boundary **between** something and something
beyond a boundary
mark/set/draw a boundary
a boundary **dispute**
a boundary **line**

▶ **SYNONYMS:** border, frontier

2 NOUN The **boundaries of** something such as a subject or activity are the limits that people think that it has. ○ *The boundaries between history and storytelling are always being blurred.*

▶ COLLOCATIONS:
cross/push/blur the boundaries
the boundaries of **knowledge**

---

brand /brænd/ (brands)   `MARKETING & SALES`

NOUN A **brand** of a product is the version of it that is made by one particular manufacturer. ○ [+ of] *another brand of cola* ○ *I bought one of the leading brands.* ○ *a supermarket's own brand*

▶ COLLOCATIONS:
a brand **of** something
create/build/launch a brand
a **leading/own/strong/global** brand

▶ SYNONYM: make

brand loy|al|ty /brænd lɔɪəlti/

NONCOUNT NOUN **Brand loyalty** is the way some people always buy a particular brand of a product, and are not likely to start buying a different brand. ○ *Perfume is becoming an everyday purchase and buyers are no longer showing brand loyalty.*

▶ COLLOCATIONS: **develop/create/build** brand loyalty

brand name /brænd neɪm/ (brand names)

NOUN A **brand name** is the name that a manufacturer gives to a product that it sells. ○ *The drug is marketed under the brand name Viramune.*

▶ COLLOCATION: **under** the brandname

▶ SYNONYM: trademark

brand-new /brændnu/

ADJECTIVE Something **brand-new** is completely new. ○ *a brand-new car*

▶ SYNONYM: unused

brand re|cog|ni|tion /brænd rɛkəgnɪʃən/

NONCOUNT NOUN **Brand recognition** is when a person knows what a product is or knows something about it as soon as they see it or hear its name. ○ *The strategic linchpin of Sun-Rype's marketing plans is the strong brand recognition enjoyed by their products.*

▶ COLLOCATIONS:
strong/poor brand recognition
build/develop brand recognition

b

break|down /ˈbreɪkdaʊn/ (breakdowns)

NOUN A **breakdown** is a situation in which a car or a piece of machinery stops working. ○ *You should be prepared for breakdowns and accidents.*

▶ **COLLOCATIONS:** a **complete/mechanical** breakdown

▶ **SYNONYM:** failure

break|even point /ˈbreɪkivən pɔɪnt/ `BANKING & FINANCE`
(breakeven points) also **break-even point** or **breakeven**

NOUN The **breakeven point** is the point at which the money a company makes from the sale of goods or services is equal to the money it has spent. ○ *"Terminator 2" finally made $200 million, the breakeven point for the movie.* ○ *The bank announced in the final quarter of last year that it had reached breakeven.*

▶ **COLLOCATIONS:**
lower/raise the breakeven point
reach breakeven point

break|through /ˈbreɪkθru/ (breakthroughs) `R&D`

NOUN A **breakthrough** is an important development or achievement.
○ [+ in] *The company looks poised to make a significant breakthrough in China.*
○ *The breakthrough came hours before a U.N. deadline.*

▶ **COLLOCATIONS:**
a breakthrough **in** something
a breakthrough in **technology/research**
make/achieve/represent/produce/expect a breakthrough
a **possible/major/significant/imminent** breakthrough
a **technological/scientific** breakthrough

▶ **SYNONYMS:** development, achievement, advance

bricks and mor|tar /brɪks ən ˈmɔrtər/ `BANKING & FINANCE`
also **bricks-and-mortar**

NONCOUNT NOUN **Bricks and mortar** is a building or buildings that are considered in terms of their value. ○ *He invested in bricks and mortar rather than stocks.*

brief|case /ˈbrifkeɪs/ (briefcases) `OFFICE`

NOUN A **briefcase** is a small case for carrying business papers in. ○ *a middle-aged businessman clutching a battered leather briefcase*

▶ **COLLOCATIONS:**
carry/clutch/open a briefcase
a briefcase **full of/containing** *something*

▶ **SYNONYM:** attaché case

b

bril|liant /brɪlyənt/

1 ADJECTIVE Someone who is **brilliant** is extremely clever or skillful.
○ *She had a brilliant mind.*

2 ADJECTIVE A **brilliant** light or color is extremely bright. ○ *brilliant green eyes*

▶ **COLLOCATIONS:**
a brilliant **mind/color**
brilliant **light/sunshine**

▶ **SYNONYMS:** intelligent, luminous

brink /brɪŋk/

NOUN If you are **on the brink of** something, usually something important, terrible, or exciting, you are just about to do it or experience it. ○ [+ *of*] *Their economy is teetering on the brink of collapse.*

▶ **COLLOCATIONS:**
on the brink of *something*
on the brink of **war/collapse/extinction/bankruptcy/disaster**

▶ **SYNONYM:** verge

broad|en /brɔdᵊn/ (broadens, broadening, broadened)

VERB When you **broaden** something such as your experience or popularity or when it **broadens**, the number of things or people that it includes becomes greater. ○ *We must broaden our appeal.* ○ *The political spectrum has broadened.*

▶ **COLLOCATIONS:**
broaden *someone's* **appeal/base/horizon**
broaden the **scope/range** of *something*

▶ **SYNONYMS:** widen, increase, expand

bro|chure /broʊʃʊər/   **MARKETING & SALES**

NOUN A **brochure** is a thin magazine with pictures that gives you information about a product or a service. ○ *travel brochures*

▶ **COLLOCATIONS:**
produce/publish/distribute a brochure
a **free/glossy/travel** brochure

▶ **SYNONYM:** pamphlet

---

bub|ble /bʌbᵊl/ (bubbles) `BANKING & FINANCE`

NOUN A **bubble** is a situation in which there is a large increase in economic activity. ○ *These hi-tech companies look like the focus of a speculative bubble.*

▶ **COLLOCATIONS:**
the bubble **bursts/collapses**
the **dot-com/Internet/housing** bubble

---

budg|et /bʌdʒɪt/ (budgets, budgeting, budgeted) `BANKING & FINANCE`

1 NOUN Your **budget** is the amount of money that you have available to spend. The **budget** for something is the amount of money that a person, organization, or country has available to spend on it. ○ [+ *for*] *This year's budget for AIDS prevention probably won't be much higher.* ○ *Set goals which you can meet within your budget and resources.* ○ *working on a very tight budget*

▶ **COLLOCATIONS:**
a budget **for** *something*
a **total/annual/overall** budget
a **state/federal** budget
a **marketing/advertising/defense/education** budget
a budget **cut/increase/deficit**

▶ **PHRASES:**
within your budget
on a tight budget

2 VERB If you **budget** certain amounts of money for particular things, you decide that you can afford to spend those amounts on those things. ○ [+ *for*] *The company has budgeted $10 million for advertising.* ○ *I'm learning how to budget.*

▶ **COLLOCATION:** budget **for** *something*

---

bulk /bʌlk/

QUANTIFIER The **bulk of** something is most of it. ○ [+ *of*] *The bulk of the text is essentially a review of these original documents.* ○ [+ *of*] *The vast bulk of imports and exports are carried by ships.*

- **Bulk** is also a pronoun. ○ *They come from all over the world, though the bulk is from the Indian subcontinent.* ○ *from 1992 the bulk came from Bosnia*

▶ **COLLOCATIONS:**
the bulk **of** *something*
the bulk of the **population/funding**
the **vast/main/overwhelming** bulk
constitute/form/comprise the bulk
provide/supply the bulk

EXTEND YOUR VOCABULARY

You talk about **the bulk** or **the majority of** people or things in a group to refer to a large proportion or most of them. ○ *The vast bulk/ majority of people driving in the city are residents.*

You do not use **the majority** when you talk about an amount or part of something. ○ *The bulk of the savings will come from job losses.*

A majority of people or things can also refer more precisely to more than 50% of them. ○ *A majority of delegates voted to approve the change.*

---

bul‖letin board /bʊlɪtɪn bɔrd/ (bulletin boards)   OFFICE

1 **NOUN** A **bulletin board** is a board on a wall for notices giving information. ○ *Her telephone number was pinned to the bulletin board.*

2 **NOUN** In computing, a **bulletin board** is a system that allows users to send and receive messages.

▶ **COLLOCATIONS:**
an **Internet/online/electronic** bulletin board
post *something* **on** a bulletin board

---

bull mar‖ket /bʊl mɑrkɪt/ (bull markets)   BANKING & FINANCE

NOUN A **bull market** is when people are buying a lot of shares of stock because they expect the price to increase. ○ *There was a decline in prices after the bull market peaked in April 2000.*

▶ **COLLOCATION:** a bull market **in** *something*

▶ **RELATED WORD:** bear market

bur|den /bˈɜrdᵊn/ (burdens)

NOUN If you describe a problem or a responsibility as a **burden**, you mean that it causes someone a lot of difficulty, worry, or hard work. ○ [+ of] *The developing countries bear the burden of an enormous external debt.* ○ *The financial burden will be more evenly shared.* ○ [+ on] *Its purpose is to ease the burden on accident and emergency departments by filtering out non-emergency calls.*

▶ COLLOCATIONS:
the burden **of** *something*
a burden **on** *someone/something*
a burden on **society/taxpayers/employers**
the burden of **responsibility/debt/disease**
shoulder/bear/carry a burden
place/impose/shift a burden
ease/lighten/alleviate a burden
a **heavy/financial** burden

bu|reau|cra|cy /byʊrˈɒkrəsi/ `OFFICE`

NONCOUNT NOUN **Bureaucracy** refers to all the rules and procedures followed by government departments and similar organizations, especially when you think that these are complicated and cause long delays. ○ *People usually complain about having to deal with too much bureaucracy.*

▶ COLLOCATIONS:
government bureaucracy
cut/create bureaucracy
excessive/unnecessary bureaucracy

▶ SYNONYMS: red tape, regulations, administration

bu|reau|crat|ic /byʊərəkrˈætɪk/

ADJECTIVE ○ *Diplomats believe that bureaucratic delays are inevitable.* ○ *The department has become a bureaucratic nightmare.*

busi|ness cy|cle /bˈɪznɪs sˈaɪkᵊl/ (business cycles) `R-D`

NOUN A **business cycle** is the periods of growth, depression, and recovery that occur over and over again in the economic activity of a country. ○ *Trade in these goods has always been subject to substantial fluctuations during the business cycle.*

busi|ness mod|el /bɪznɪs mɒdᵊl/ (business models) `R&D`

NOUN A **business model** is the structure of a business, including the relationships between the different parts of the business. ○ *the entirely new business models made possible by the Internet* ○ *There are inefficiencies in traditional business models.*

▶ **COLLOCATIONS:**
a **new/good/sustainable** business model
create/develop a business model

busi|ness ob|jec|tive /bɪznɪs əbdʒɛktɪv/ `R&D`
(business objectives)

NOUN A **business objective** is something that a company is trying to achieve. ○ *The key business objectives of commercial and charitable organizations are to bring in as much money as possible and to make the most effective use of available resources.*

▶ **SYNONYMS:** business aim, business goal

busi|ness plan /bɪznɪs plæn/ (business plans) `R&D`

NOUN A **business plan** is a detailed plan for setting up or developing a business. ○ *She learned how to write a business plan for the catering business she wanted to launch.*

▶ **COLLOCATIONS:** **write/develop/submit/pitch** a business plan

buy|er's mar|ket /baɪəz mɑrkɪt/ `BANKING & FINANCE`

NOUN When there is a **buyer's market** for a particular product, there are more of the products for sale than there are people who want to buy them. In a **buyer's market**, buyers have a lot of choice and can make prices come down. ○ *Real estate remains a buyer's market.*

▶ **RELATED WORD:** seller's market

buy|out /baɪaʊt/ (buyouts) `BANKING & FINANCE`

NOUN A **buyout** is the buying of a firm by its managers or employees. ○ *It is thought that a management buyout is one option.*

▶ **COLLOCATIONS:**
back/consider/offer/propose a buyout
a **$x** buyout
a **leveraged** buyout

Cc

Cabi|net /kæbɪnɪt/ (Cabinets)

NOUN The **Cabinet** is a group of the most senior ministers in a government, who meet regularly to discuss policies. ○ *The announcement came after a three-hour Cabinet meeting in Downing Street.* ○ *a former Cabinet Minister*

▶ **COLLOCATIONS:**
a Cabinet **minister/meeting/reshuffle**
appoint/dissolve a Cabinet
a Cabinet **convenes/votes**
a Cabinet **debates/rejects/decides** *something*
a **two-tier/all-male/civic** Cabinet

caf|eteria /kæfɪtɪəriə/ (cafeterias) `OFFICE`

NOUN In places such as hospitals and offices, a **cafeteria** is a restaurant where you buy a meal and carry it to the table yourself. ○ *My mother worked in a school cafeteria.* ○ *Many schools now offer healthier cafeteria food.*

▶ **COLLOCATIONS:**
a **school/hospital/university** cafeteria
a cafeteria **worker/table/tray**

▶ **SYNONYMS:** café, lunchroom

cal|cu|late /kælkyəleɪt/ (calculates, calculating, calculated) `OFFICE`

VERB If you **calculate** a number or amount, you discover it from information that you already have, by using arithmetic, mathematics, or a special machine. ○ *From this you can calculate the total mass in the Galaxy.* ○ *[+ that] We calculate that the average size farm in Lancaster County is 65 acres.* ○ *A computer calculates by switching currents on or off.*

▶ **COLLOCATIONS:**
a **computer/researcher** calculates *something*
calculate a **rate/cost/amount/value**

▸ **SYNONYM:** work out

▸ **RELATED WORDS:** add, subtract, multiply, divide

cal|cu|la|tion /kælkyəleɪʃ³n/ (calculations)

NOUN ○ *This calculation is made by subtracting the age of death from 65.*
○ *[+ of] the calculation of their assets* ○ *His calculations showed that the price index would go down by half a percent.*

▸ **COLLOCATIONS:**
a calculation **of** *something*
perform/make a calculation
a calculation **shows/suggests/indicates** *something*

▸ **SYNONYM:** sum

cal|cu|la|tor /kælkyəleɪtər/ (calculators)

NOUN A **calculator** is a small electronic machine that you use to calculate numbers. ○ *He reached into his poncho and pulled out a pocket calculator.*

▸ **COLLOCATIONS:**
a **scientific/financial** calculator
a **pocket/hand-held/online** calculator

cal|en|dar /kælɪndər/ (calendars) OFFICE

NOUN A **calendar** is a list of days, weeks, and months for a particular year.
○ *He recorded his charitable contributions in a pocket calendar.* ○ *The calendar turned to January 1, 2000.*

▸ **COLLOCATIONS:**
a **wall/desk/pocket** calendar
someone **turns/changes/flips** a calendar

cali|ber /kælɪbər/

NONCOUNT NOUN The **caliber of** a person or thing is their quality or level of excellence, especially when it is good. [in BRIT, use **calibre**] ○ *[+ of] The caliber of teaching was very high.* ○ *a man of extremely high caliber*

▸ **COLLOCATIONS:**
the caliber **of** *something*
high caliber

cam|paign /kæmpeɪn/

MARKETING & SALES

(campaigns, campaigning, campaigned)

1 **NOUN** A **campaign** is a planned set of activities that people carry out over a period of time in order to achieve something such as social or political change. ○ *During his election campaign he promised to put the economy back on its feet.* ○ [+ to-inf] *Our company has launched a campaign to improve the training of staff.* ○ [+ against] *the campaign against public smoking*

▶ **COLLOCATIONS:**
a campaign **on/for/against** something
a **presidential/election/advertising** campaign
a **nationwide/political** campaign
launch/run/lead a campaign
a campaign on an **issue**

▶ **SYNONYM:** protest

2 **VERB** If someone **campaigns for** something, they carry out a planned set of activities over a period of time in order to achieve their aim.
○ [+ for] *We are campaigning for law reform.* ○ [+ for/against] *Mr. Burns has actively campaigned against a hostel being set up here.* ○ [+ to-inf] *They have been campaigning to improve the legal status of women.*

▶ **COLLOCATIONS:**
campaign **for/against** something
actively/tirelessly campaign
campaign for **independence/reform**

▶ **SYNONYMS:** lobby, protest, advocate, promote

---

can|cel /kæns²l/ (cancels, canceling or cancelling, canceled or cancelled)

VERB If you **cancel** something that has been planned, you stop it from happening. ○ *We canceled our trip to Washington.* ○ *The flight was canceled after the terrorist attacks.*

▶ **COLLOCATIONS:**
cancel a **flight/appointment/meeting/reservation**
cancel something **abruptly/immediately/suddenly/without notice**

▶ **SYNONYM:** annul

can|cel|la|tion /kænsəleɪʃən/ (cancellations)

NOUN ○ *The hotel has agreed to waive the cancellation fee.* ○ [+ of] *The airline announced the abrupt cancellation of six flights.*

▶ **COLLOCATIONS:**
the cancellation **of** something
force/cause/prompt the cancellation of something

demand/order the cancellation of *something*
request/propose/urge the cancellation of *something*
a **last-minute/abrupt/sudden/late** cancellation
a cancellation **fee/charge/penalty**

▸ SYNONYM: annulment

---

can|did /kǽndɪd/

ADJECTIVE When you are **candid** about something or with someone, you speak honestly. ○ [+ *about*] *Natalie is candid about the problems she is having with Steve.* ○ [+ *with*] *I haven't been completely candid with him.*

▸ COLLOCATIONS:
candid **about** *something*
candid **with** *someone*
completely candid

▸ SYNONYM: frank

---

can|di|date /kǽndɪdeɪt, -dɪt/ (candidates) PERSONNEL

NOUN A **candidate** is someone who is being considered for a position, for example, someone who is running in an election or applying for a job. ○ *The Democratic candidate is still leading in the polls.* ○ [+ *for*] *He is a candidate for the office of Governor.* ○ *We all spoke to them and John emerged as the best candidate.*

▸ COLLOCATIONS:
a candidate **for** *something*
a candidate for the **post/presidency/seat/leadership**
a candidate **stands/runs/wins/applies**
a **presidential/parliamentary/mayoral** candidate
a **potential/independent/liberal** candidate
elect/choose/support a candidate
interview/favor/consider a candidate
a candidate **list**

▸ SYNONYMS: applicant, contender, nominee

---

ca|pable /kéɪpəbəl/

ADJECTIVE If a person or thing is **capable of** doing something, they have the ability to do it. ○ [+ *of*] *He appeared hardly capable of conducting a coherent conversation.* ○ [+ *of*] *The kitchen is capable of catering for several hundred people.* ○ [+ *of*] *a man capable of murder*

▶ **COLLOCATIONS:**
capable **of** *something*
capable of **cruelty/greatness**
look/seem/prove capable
perfectly/physically/fully capable

▶ **SYNONYM:** able

ca|pa|bil|ity /keɪpəbɪlɪti/ (capabilities)

NOUN If you have the **capability** or the **capabilities** to do something, you have the ability or the qualities that are necessary to do it. ○ *People experience differences in physical and mental capability depending on the time of day.* ○ *The standards set four years ago in Seoul will be far below the athletes' capabilities now.*

▶ **COLLOCATIONS:**
collaborative/technological/technical capability
organizational/analytical/intellectual capability
wireless/processing/manufacturing capability

▶ **SYNONYMS:** ability, functionality

---

ca|pac|ity /kəpæsɪti/ (capacities)

1 NONCOUNT NOUN The **capacity** of something such as a factory, industry, or region is the quantity of things that it can produce or deliver with the equipment or resources that are available. ○ [+ *in*] *the amount of spare capacity in the economy* ○ *Bread factories are working at full capacity.*

2 NOUN The **capacity** of a piece of equipment or a building is its size, power, or volume. ○ [+ *of*] *an aircraft with a bomb-carrying capacity of 750 lbs.* ○ *a feature which gave the vehicles a much greater fuel capacity than other trucks* ○ [+ *of*] *Each stadium had a seating capacity of about 50,000.*

▶ **COLLOCATIONS:**
capacity **in/of** *something*
increase/reduce/limit *something's* capacity
spare/full capacity
a **limited/excess** capacity
production/storage/generating/fuel capacity
a **crowd/audience/building/stadium** capacity

▶ **PHRASE:** filled to capacity

▶ **SYNONYMS:** ability, size

capi|tal /kæpɪtᵊl/ (capitals)

1 NOUN The **capital** of a country is the city or town where its government or legislature meets. ○ [+ of] *Kathmandu, the capital of Nepal*

▶ **COLLOCATIONS:**
the capital **of** *somewhere*
the capital of a **country/state/province**

2 NONCOUNT NOUN **Capital** is a large sum of money that you use to start a business, or that you invest in order to make more money. ○ *Companies are having difficulty in raising capital.* ○ *A large amount of capital is invested in all these branches.*

3 NONCOUNT NOUN You can use **capital** to refer to buildings or machinery that are necessary to produce goods or to make companies more efficient, but that do not make money directly. ○ *capital equipment that could have served to increase production* ○ *capital investment*

capi|tal|ize /kæpɪtᵊlaɪz/ (capitalizes, capitalizing, capitalized)

1 VERB If you **capitalize on** a situation, you use it to gain some advantage for yourself. [in BRIT, also use **capitalise**] ○ *Car dealers are capitalizing on the expected price increases to generate more showroom traffic.* ○ *Anelka capitalized on a goalkeeping error to score the first goal.*

▶ **COLLOCATIONS:** capitalize on a **mistake/error/opportunity**

▶ **SYNONYMS:** exploit, take advantage of

2 VERB In business, if you **capitalize** something that belongs to you, you sell it to make money. [in BRIT, also use **capitalise**] ○ *Our intention is to capitalize the company by any means we can.*

cap|tive mar|ket /kæptɪv mɑrkɪt/
(captive markets)

NOUN A **captive market** is a group of consumers who give a supplier a monopoly because they are obliged to buy a particular product. ○ *Airlines consider business travelers a captive market.* ○ [+ for] *At that time the colonies were captive markets for Spanish products.*

▶ **COLLOCATIONS:**
a captive market **for** *something*
create/develop a captive market

cap|ture /kæptʃər/ (captures, capturing, captured)

VERB If you **capture** someone or something, you catch them, especially in a war. ○ *The guerrillas shot down one airplane and captured the pilot.*

○ [+ *from*] *The Russians now appear ready to capture more territory from the Chechens.*

▶ **COLLOCATIONS:**
capture *someone/something* **from** *someone*
capture **territory**
fail to capture *someone/something*

• **Capture** is also a noun. ○ [+ *of*] *the final battles which led to the army's capture of the town*

▶ **COLLOCATIONS:**
the capture **of** *someone/something*
avoid/escape capture

---

ca|reer /kəriər/ (careers)   PERSONNEL

NOUN A **career** is the job or profession that someone does for a long period of their life. ○ [+ *as*] *She is now concentrating on a career as a fashion designer.* ○ [+ *in*] *scientists wishing to pursue a career in medicine* ○ *Staff can choose courses based on their career development plans.*

▶ **COLLOCATIONS:**
a career **in/as** *something*
a career in **politics/industry/law/business**
a career as a **writer/actor/teacher**
a **political/managerial/military/academic** career
have/choose/pursue a career
career **prospects/development**
a career **move/opportunity/path**

▶ **SYNONYMS:** profession, work, employment, vocation

---

car pool /kɑr pul/ (car pools, car pooling, car pooled)   TRAVEL
also **carpool** or **car-pool**

NOUN A **car pool** is an arrangement where a group of people take turns driving each other to work, or driving each other's children to school. ○ *He drives the children to school in the car pool.* ○ *a lane reserved for car pools*

▶ **COLLOCATIONS:**
join/arrange/set up/operate a car pool
a car-pool **lane**

• **Car-pool** is also a verb. ○ *Fewer Americans are car-pooling to work.*

cash flow /kæʃ floʊ/ also **cash-flow**   `BANKING & FINANCE`

NONCOUNT NOUN The **cash flow** of a firm or business is the movement of money into and out of it. ○ *The company ran into cash-flow problems and faced liquidation.*

▶ **COLLOCATIONS:**
   operating/negative/positive cash flow
   cash-flow **problems**

---

casu|al|ty /kæʒuəlti/ (casualties)   `HEALTH & FITNESS`

NOUN A **casualty** is a person who is injured or killed in a war or in an accident. ○ *Helicopters bombed the town, causing many casualties.* ○ *It was dangerous work and the casualty rate was high.*

▶ **COLLOCATIONS:**
   inflict/cause casualties
   suffer/sustain/incur casualties
   casualties **mount/rise/continue**
   casualties are **light/low/heavy/high**
   civilian/military/combat casualties

▶ **SYNONYMS:** fatality, victim

---

cata|log (catalogs, cataloging, cataloged)   `MARKETING & SALES`

VERB To **catalog** things means to make a list of them. [in BRIT, use **catalogue**] ○ *The Royal Greenwich Observatory was founded to observe and catalog the stars.* ○ *The report catalogs a long list of extreme weather patterns.*

→ see note at **document**

▶ **COLLOCATIONS:**
   catalog **items**
   a **report** catalogs *things*
   catalog things **carefully/meticulously/properly**

▶ **SYNONYM:** list

---

cat|ego|ry /kætɪgɔri/ (categories)

NOUN If people or things are divided into **categories**, they are divided into groups in such a way that the members of each group are similar to each other in some way. ○ [+ *of*] *This book clearly falls into the category of fictionalized autobiography.* ○ *The tables were organized into six different categories.*

▶ **COLLOCATIONS:**
a category **of** something
in/into a category
fall into a category
a **different/broad/general** category
a **product** category

▶ **SYNONYMS:** class, classification

cat|ego|rize /kǽtɪgəraɪz/ (categorizes, categorizing, categorized)

VERB If you **categorize** people or things, you divide them into sets or you say which set they belong to. [in BRIT, also use **categorise**] ○ *Lindsay, like his films, is hard to categorize.* ○ [+ *as*] *Make a list of your child's toys and then categorize them as sociable or antisocial.* ○ *new ways of categorizing information*

▶ **COLLOCATIONS:**
categorize something **as** something
hard/difficult to categorize

▶ **SYNONYM:** classify

---

cau|tion /kɔʃən/

NONCOUNT NOUN Caution is great care that you take in order to avoid possible danger. ○ *Extreme caution should be exercised when buying used tires.* ○ *The Chancellor is a man of caution.*

▶ **COLLOCATIONS:**
extreme/considerable caution
exercise/advocate/urge caution

▶ **SYNONYMS:** care, prudence

cau|tious /kɔʃəs/

1 **ADJECTIVE** Someone who is **cautious** acts very carefully in order to avoid possible danger. ○ [+ *about*] *The scientists are cautious about using enzyme therapy on humans.* ○ *Many Canadians have become overly cautious when it comes to investing.*

2 **ADJECTIVE** If you describe someone's attitude or reaction as **cautious**, you mean that it is limited or careful. ○ *He has been seen as a champion of a more cautious approach to economic reform.* ○ *There may have been good reasons for this cautious attitude.*

▶ **COLLOCATIONS:**
cautious **about** something
a cautious **attitude/reaction/approach/outlook**

scientists/investors/analysts/experts are cautious
remain/appear cautious
overly/excessively/relatively/understandably cautious

▶ SYNONYMS: careful, circumspect

CD-ROM /si di rɒm/ (CD-ROMs) OFFICE

NOUN A **CD-ROM** is a CD that stores a very large amount of information that you can read using a computer. ○ *The Encyclopedia Britannica is available on CD-ROM and DVD.*

▶ COLLOCATIONS: a CD-ROM **drive/player**

---

cease /siːs/ (ceases, ceasing, ceased)

1 **VERB** If something **ceases**, it stops happening or existing. [FORMAL]
○ *At one o'clock the rain ceased.* ○ *Six years on, his February depressions have ceased.*

2 **VERB** If you **cease to** do something, you stop doing it. [FORMAL]
○ [+ to-inf] *A brain deprived of oxygen ceases to function within a few minutes.*
○ [+ to-inf] *The Church has almost ceased to exist in Albania.*

3 **VERB** If you **cease** something, you stop it from happening or working. [FORMAL] ○ *The Tundra Times ceased publication this week.* ○ [+ v-ing] *A small number of companies have ceased trading.*

▶ COLLOCATIONS:
hostilities cease
cease an **activity**
cease **production/operations/trading**
cease **immediately/abruptly/altogether**
cease to **exist/function/operate**

EXTEND YOUR VOCABULARY

In everyday English, you often say that something **stops**, **ends**, or **finishes**. ○ *soon after the fighting stopped/ended* ○ *The meeting finished/ended just after 6.*

In more formal writing, you can say that someone **ceases** an activity, especially a business activity.

▶ cease **production/activity/operations/trading** ○ *The country's second largest airline ceased operations.*

You can say that a process which people take part in **concludes** to mean that it comes to an end.

▶ a **meeting/conference** concludes ○ *The Group of Seven major industrial countries concluded its annual summit meeting today.*

cel|ebra|tion /sɛlɪbreɪʃən/ (celebrations)

NOUN A **celebration** is a special event that is organized in order to celebrate something. ○ *Eid al-Fitr is a celebration marking the end of Ramadan.* ○ *The company is organizing a weekend of celebrations.*

▶ **COLLOCATIONS:**
a celebration **of** something
a celebration **in honor of** something or someone
a **birthday/anniversary/wedding/victory** celebration

▶ **SYNONYMS:** party, commemoration

ce|leb|rity /sɪlɛbrɪti/ (celebrities)

NOUN A **celebrity** is someone who is famous, especially in areas of entertainment such as movies, music, writing, or sports. ○ *In 1944, at the age of 30, Hersey suddenly became a celebrity.* ○ *a host of celebrities*

▶ **COLLOCATIONS:**
become a celebrity
celebrity **status**
a celebrity **chef/guest/host**

▶ **SYNONYM:** star

cell|phone /sɛlfoʊn/ (cellphones)   COMMUNICATIONS

NOUN A **cellphone** is a telephone that you carry around with you. ○ *The woman called the police on her cellphone.* ○ *She was driving down the freeway when her cellphone rang.*

▶ **COLLOCATIONS:** a cellphone **user/provider/network**

▶ **SYNONYM:** cell

cen|ti|me|ter /sɛntɪmitər/ (centimeters)

NOUN A **centimeter** is a unit of length in the metric system equal to ten millimeters or one-hundredth of a meter. The abbreviation **cm** is used in written notes. ○ *a tiny fossil plant, only a few centimeters high* ○ *Up to 15 centimeters of snow was expected to fall on mainland Nova Scotia.*

▶ **COLLOCATIONS:**
  x centimeters **of** something
  x centimeters **high/tall/long/wide/thick/deep**
  x centimeters **in length/diameter**
  a **square/cubic** centimeter

▶ **RELATED WORDS:** meter, millimeter

CEO /siː iː oʊ/ (CEOs)   `JOBS`

NOUN CEO is an abbreviation for **chief executive officer**. ○ [+ *of*] *Carlzon is the former CEO of the airline SAS.*

▶ **COLLOCATIONS:**
  the CEO **of** something
  name/appoint/hire a CEO
  replace/fire/oust a CEO
  a **former/interim/acting** CEO

cer|emo|ny /sɛrɪmoʊni/ (ceremonies)

NOUN A **ceremony** is a formal event such as a wedding or funeral.
  ○ *They're planning a traditional wedding ceremony.* ○ *Several hundred people attended a prayer ceremony for the victims.*

▶ **COLLOCATIONS:**
  a **solemn/formal/religious** ceremony
  a **lavish/elaborate/glitzy/colorful** ceremony
  a **graduation/wedding/marriage/award** ceremony
  an **induction/initiation** ceremony
  a **closing/opening** ceremony

▶ **SYNONYMS:** ritual, commemoration

cer|ti|fy /sɜrtɪfaɪ/ (certifies, certifying, certified)

VERB If someone **certifies** something, they officially say that it is true.
  ○ *Each year they audit our accounts and certify them as being true and fair.*
  ○ *The secretary of state has four days to certify county election results.*
  ○ *Documents show the pilot was not certified to fly that particular aircraft.*

▶ **COLLOCATIONS:**
  certify a **result**
  a **doctor/inspector/accountant** certifies something

officially/formally/falsely certify *something*

▸ **SYNONYMS:** validate, verify, confirm

cer|tifi|cate /sərtɪfɪkɪt/ **(certificates)**

1 NOUN A **certificate** is an official document that proves that the facts on it are true. ○ *Death and marriage certificates point to her birthplace as Ipswich.* ○ *Police said the certificates were forged.*

▸ **COLLOCATIONS:**
   a **birth/death/marriage** certificate
   a certificate is **valid/void**
   a certificate **shows/confirms/proves/indicates** *something*
   forge/falsify a certificate

▸ **SYNONYM:** document

2 NOUN A **certificate** is an official document that you receive when you have completed a course of study or training. ○ *To the right of the fireplace are various framed certificates.* ○ *He recently obtained a teaching certificate.*

▸ **COLLOCATIONS:**
   a **teaching/graduation** certificate
   issue/award/present/revoke a certificate
   obtain/receive a certificate

▸ **SYNONYMS:** license, diploma

CFO /sɪ ɛf oʊ/ **(CFOs)** `JOBS`

NOUN CFO is an abbreviation of **chief financial officer**. ○ [+ *of*] *the CFO of Bell Atlantic*

▸ **COLLOCATIONS:**
   be named/be appointed CFO
   an **acting/interim** CFO

---

chair|person /tʃɛərpɜrsᵊn/ **(chairpeople)** `JOBS`

NOUN A **chairperson** is the person who controls a meeting or organization. ○ [+ *of*] *She's the chairperson of the planning committee.*

▸ **COLLOCATIONS:**
   the chairperson **of** *something*
   elect/appoint a chairperson
   an **outgoing/acting/interim** chairperson

▸ **SYNONYM:** chair

▸ **RELATED WORDS:** chairman, chairwoman

chal|lenge /tʃælɪndʒ/ (challenges, challenging, challenged)

1 **NOUN** A **challenge** is something new and difficult that requires great effort and determination. ○ *I like a big challenge and they don't come much bigger than this.* ○ *The new government's first challenge is the economy.*

2 **NOUN** A **challenge to** something is a questioning of its truth or value. A **challenge to** someone is a questioning of their authority. ○ [+ to] *The demonstrators have now made a direct challenge to the authority of the government.* ○ [+ to] *Paranormal dreams pose a challenge to current scientific conceptions.*

> ▶ **COLLOCATIONS:**
> a challenge **to** *something*
> **present/pose/accept/face/meet** a challenge
> a **serious/real/major/great** challenge
> a **legal** challenge

> ▶ **SYNONYMS:** question, test, confrontation

3 **VERB** If you **challenge** ideas or people, you question their truth, value, or authority. ○ *Democratic leaders have challenged the president to sign the bill.* ○ [+ on] *I challenged him on the hypocrisy of his political attitudes.*

> ▶ **COLLOCATIONS:**
> challenge *someone* **on/about** *something*
> challenge a **notion/assumption/decision**
> **successfully/seriously** challenge *something*

> ▶ **SYNONYM:** question

cham|pi|on|ship /tʃæmpiənʃɪp/ (championships)

NOUN A **championship** is a competition to find the best player or team in a particular sport. ○ *We need to win our last game to clinch the championship.* ○ [+ of] *The British Open is the unofficial world championship of golf.*

> ▶ **COLLOCATIONS:**
> **win/clinch/capture/secure** a championship
> **host/stage/schedule** a championship
> a championship **match/game/final/qualifier**
> a championship **win/defeat/title/crown**
> a championship **medal/ring/trophy**
> a **world/national/major** championship
> a **hockey/basketball/tennis** championship

> ▶ **SYNONYM:** title

cha|os /keɪɒs/

NONCOUNT NOUN Chaos is when there is no order or organization.
○ *The economy was in chaos.* ○ *Chaos erupted after a bomb went off that killed 24 people.*

▶ **COLLOCATIONS:**
cause/create/spark/trigger chaos
avert/avoid chaos
chaos **erupts/breaks out/descends/spreads**
utter/absolute/total/complete chaos
the **ensuing/resulting** chaos

▶ **SYNONYMS:** disorder, confusion, anarchy

cha|ot|ic /keɪɒtɪk/

ADJECTIVE ○ *My own house feels as filthy and chaotic as a bus terminal.*

▶ **COLLOCATIONS:** a chaotic **scene/situation/world/system/life/condition**

char|ac|ter|is|tic /kærɪktərɪstɪk/ (characteristics)

1 NOUN The **characteristics** of a person or thing are the qualities or features that belong to them and make them recognizable. ○ [+ *of*] *Genes determine the characteristics of every living thing.* ○ *their physical characteristics*

▶ **COLLOCATIONS:**
the characteristics **of** *someone/something*
a **defining/distinguishing** characteristic
a **shared/unique** characteristic
a **physical/fundamental/essential** characteristic

▶ **SYNONYMS:** feature, trait

2 ADJECTIVE A quality or feature that is **characteristic of** someone or something is one that is often seen in them and seems typical of them. ○ [+ *of*] *the absence of strife between the generations that was so characteristic of such societies* ○ *Nehru responded with characteristic generosity.*

▶ **COLLOCATIONS:**
characteristic **of** *someone/something*
characteristic **greed/modesty/wit**

▶ **SYNONYM:** typical

charge /tʃɑrdʒ/ (charges, charging, charged) [BANKING & FINANCE]

1 **VERB** If you **charge** someone an amount of money, you ask them to pay that amount for something that you have sold to them or done for them. ○ *Even local nurseries charge $150 a week.* ○ [+ for] *The hospitals charge the patients for every aspirin.* ○ *Some banks charge if you access your account to determine your balance.*

▶ **COLLOCATIONS:**
charge (*someone*) **for** something
charge a **fee/rate**
charge **$x**
charge a **client/customer**
charge for a **service/purchase**

2 **NOUN** A **charge** is an amount of money that you have to pay for a service. ○ *We can arrange this for a small charge.* ○ [+ of] *When users choose to play games, a monthly charge of $2.50 or less shows up on their phone bill.*

▶ **COLLOCATIONS:**
a charge **of** *x*
face/pay a charge
a **monthly/annual/additional** charge

▶ **SYNONYMS:** fee, cost, price, rate

> **USAGE:** *charge*, *cost*, or *pay*?
>
> These verbs are all used to talk about exchanging money when you buy something. The seller **charges** someone an amount of money **for** a product or service; they ask for this amount. ○ *The company charges customers $1.50 a minute for foreign calls.*
>
> A product or service **costs** an amount; this is the price. ○ *Foreign calls cost $1.50 a minute.*
>
> The customer **pays** an amount **for** a product or service. ○ *Customers pay $1.50 a minute for foreign calls.*

charge card /tʃɑrdʒ kɑrd/ (charge cards)

1 **NOUN** A **charge card** is a plastic card that you use to buy goods on credit from a particular store or group of stores. ○ *Pay with your Nieman's charge card to save an extra five percent.*

▶ **COLLOCATIONS:** a charge card **holder/user**

2 **NOUN** A **charge card** is the same as a **credit card**. ○ *Americans now have on average three charge cards in their wallets.* ○ *a Bank of America charge card*

---

check|ing ac|count /tʃɛkɪŋ əkaʊnt/ `BANKING & FINANCE`
(checking accounts)

NOUN A **checking account** is a bank account that you can take money out of by writing a check. ○ *I have a checking account and a savings account.* ○ *Police say the suspect opened a checking account in another man's name.*

▶ **COLLOCATIONS:**
   open/close a checking account
   a **joint/personal/separate** checking account
   a **free/low-cost** checking account

▶ **RELATED WORD:** savings account

---

chief ex|ecu|tive of|fic|er /tʃif ɪgzɛkyətɪv ɔfɪsər/ `JOBS`
(chief executive officers)

NOUN The **chief executive officer** of a company is the person who has overall responsibility for the management of that company. The abbreviation **CEO** is often used. ○ *The company is seeking to appoint a new chief executive officer.*

---

chief fi|nan|cial of|fic|er /tʃif fɪnænʃˀl ɔfɪsər/ `JOBS`
(chief financial officers)

NOUN The **chief financial officer** of a company is the person who has responsibility for the financial arrangements of that company. The abbreviation **CFO** is often used. ○ *Jeremy Brown has been appointed chief financial officer of the agency.*

---

chron|ic /krɒnɪk/

1 **ADJECTIVE** A **chronic** illness or disability lasts for a very long time. ○ *chronic back pain* ○ *the condition is often chronic*

▶ **COLLOCATIONS:**
   chronic **pain/stress/depression**
   a chronic **illness/disease/condition/disorder**

▶ **PHRASES:**
   chronic and degenerative
   chronic and inflammatory

▶ **SYNONYM:** long-term

▶ **RELATED WORD:** acute

2 ADJECTIVE A **chronic** situation or problem is very severe and unpleasant. ○ *One cause of the artist's suicide seems to have been chronic poverty.* ○ *There is a chronic shortage of patrol cars in this police district.*

▶ **COLLOCATIONS:**
  chronic **poverty**
  a chronic **shortage**

▶ **SYNONYM:** severe

chrono|logi|cal /krɒnəlɒdʒɪkəl/

ADJECTIVE If things are described or shown in **chronological** order, they are described or shown in the order in which they happened. ○ *Such a paper might present a chronological sequence of events.* ○ *The play is in strict chronological order, and attention is paid to demographic and statistical details.*

▶ **COLLOCATIONS:** a chronological **sequence/arrangement**

▶ **PHRASE:** in chronological order

cir|cu|late /sɜrkyəleɪt/ (circulates, circulating, circulated)

VERB When something **circulates**, it moves easily and freely within a closed place or system. ○ [+ *via*] *a virus which circulates via the bloodstream* ○ [+ *through*] *the sound of water circulating through pipes*

▶ **COLLOCATIONS:**
  circulate **around/via/through** something
  blood/water/air circulates

▶ **SYNONYM:** flow

cir|cu|la|tion /sɜrkyəleɪʃən/

NONCOUNT NOUN ○ [+ *of*] *The north pole is warmer than the south and the circulation of air around it is less well contained.* ○ [+ *of*] *the principle of free circulation of goods*

▶ **COLLOCATIONS:**
  the circulation **of** something
  the circulation of **blood/air/goods/money**

▶ **SYNONYM:** flow

cir|cum|stance /sɜrkəmstæns/ (circumstances)

1 NOUN The **circumstances** of a particular situation are the conditions that affect what happens. ○ *Recent opinion polls show that 60 percent favor* abortion under certain circumstances. ○ *The strategy was too dangerous in the explosive circumstances of the times.*

▸ COLLOCATIONS: **certain/similar/different** circumstances

▸ PHRASES:
under the circumstances
under no circumstance

2 PLURAL NOUN The **circumstances** of an event are the way it happened or the causes of it. ○ [+ *of*] *I'm making inquiries about the circumstances of Mary Dean's murder.*

▸ COLLOCATION: the circumstances **of** *something*

▸ PHRASE: a victim of circumstances

cir|cum|stan|tial /sɜrkəmstænʃəl/

ADJECTIVE Circumstantial evidence is evidence that makes it seem likely that something happened, but does not prove it. [FORMAL] ○ *Fast work by the police had started producing circumstantial evidence.*

▸ COLLOCATIONS:
circumstantial **evidence**
a circumstantial **case**
largely/purely circumstantial

---

citi|zen /sɪtɪzⁿn/ (citizens)

1 NOUN A **citizen** is someone who legally belongs to a particular country. ○ *a naturalized citizen* ○ *We are proud to be American citizens.*

▸ COLLOCATIONS: a **British/Saudi/Japanese** citizen

2 NOUN A **citizen** is someone who lives in a particular town or city. ○ *Law-abiding citizens are crying out for the government to do something about crime.* ○ [+ *of*] *the citizens of Buenos Aires*

▸ COLLOCATIONS:
a citizen **of** *something*
a **law-abiding/upstanding/prominent** citizen
a **decent/ordinary/average** citizen

▸ SYNONYM: resident

---

claim /kleɪm/ (claims, claiming, claimed)

1 VERB If you say that someone **claims that** something is true, you mean they say that it is true but you are not sure whether or not they are telling the truth. ○ [+ *that*] *He claimed that it was all a conspiracy against him.*

○ [+ to-inf] *A man claiming to be a journalist threatened to reveal details about her private life.* ○ *He claims a 70 to 80 percent success rate.*

▶ **COLLOCATIONS:** claim **falsely/rightly/wrongly/repeatedly**

▶ **SYNONYMS:** maintain, assert, allege

2 NOUN A **claim** is something that someone says that they cannot prove and that may be false. ○ [+ that] *He repeated his claim that the people of Trinidad and Tobago backed his action.* ○ [+ that] *He rejected claims that he had affairs with six women.*

▶ **COLLOCATIONS:**
reject/investigate a claim
a **true/false** claim

▶ **SYNONYMS:** allegation, assertion

---

clari|fy /ˈklærɪfaɪ/ (clarifies, clarifying, clarified) `COMMUNICATIONS`

VERB To **clarify** something means to make it easier to understand, usually by explaining it in more detail. [FORMAL] ○ *It is important to clarify the distinction between the relativity of values and the relativity of truth.* ○ *A bank spokesman was unable to clarify the situation.* ○ [+ what] *You will want to clarify what your objectives are.*

▶ **COLLOCATIONS:**
clarify a **position/situation/remark/distinction**
clarify the **meaning** of *something*
a **statement/amendment** clarifies *something*
legislation/guidelines clarify *something*

---

clash /klæʃ/ (clashes, clashing, clashed)

VERB When people **clash**, they fight or argue with each other. ○ *He often clashed with his staff.*

▶ **COLLOCATIONS:**
demonstrators/protesters/supporters clash
someone clashes **with** *someone*
people clash **heatedly/angrily/publicly/openly**

▶ **SYNONYM:** fight

● **Clash** is also a noun. ○ *Management clashes between merged companies were blamed.*

▶ **COLLOCATIONS:**
avoid/avert/provoke/spark a clash

a clash **erupts/breaks out/ensues**
a **violent/fierce/stormy** clash

▶ **SYNONYM:** fight

---

clas|si|fy /klǽsɪfaɪ/ (classifies, classifying, classified)

VERB To **classify** things means to divide them into groups or types so that
things with similar characteristics are in the same group. ○ [+ into] *It is
necessary initially to classify the headaches into certain types.* ○ *Rocks can be
classified according to their mode of origin.* ○ [+ as] *The coroner immediately
classified his death as a suicide.*

▶ **COLLOCATIONS:**
classify *something* **as/according to** *something*
classify *something* **into** *things*
classify *something* into **categories/types**
classify *something* **officially/wrongly/correctly**

▶ **SYNONYMS:** categorize, sort

clas|si|fi|ca|tion /klǽsɪfɪkeɪʃ°n/

NONCOUNT NOUN ○ [+ of] *the arbitrary classification of knowledge into fields of
study* ○ *the British Board of Film Classification*

▶ **COLLOCATIONS:**
the classification **of** *something*
the classification of **diseases/drugs/organisms**
a classification **system**

▶ **SYNONYM:** categorization

---

class|room /klǽsrum/ (classrooms)

NOUN A **classroom** is a room in a school where lessons take place. ○ *Many
students are struggling to learn in crowded classrooms.* ○ *The aim is to improve
the quality of classroom teaching using computers.*

▶ **COLLOCATIONS:**
a **kindergarten/second-grade/college** classroom
a **science/biology/reading** classroom
a **crowded/empty/temporary** classroom
classroom **teaching/learning/instruction**

cli|ent /klaɪənt/ (clients)

NOUN A **client** of a professional person or organization is a person or company that receives a service from them in return for payment.
○ *a lawyer and his client* ○ *The company required clients to pay substantial fees in advance.*

▶ **COLLOCATIONS:**
a **firm's** clients
advise/represent a client
a **prospective** client

▶ **SYNONYM:** customer

USAGE: *client or customer?*

In general, someone who uses a professional service, such as a lawyer or an accountant, is a **client**. Someone who buys goods from a store or a company is a **customer**.

Doctors and hospitals have **patients**, while hotels have **guests**. People who travel on public transportation are referred to as **passengers**.

---

cli|mate /klaɪmɪt/ (climates)

NOUN The **climate** of a place is the general weather conditions that are typical of it. ○ [+ of] *the hot and humid climate of Cyprus* ○ *Herbs tend to grow in temperate climates.*

▶ **COLLOCATIONS:**
the climate **of** somewhere
a **temperate/warm/tropical/humid/mild** climate

▶ **PHRASE:** climate change

▶ **SYNONYM:** weather

USAGE: *climate or weather?*

The **climate** of a place refers to the general weather patterns over a long period of time. The **weather** is used to talk about the conditions at a particular time.

---

clock|wise /klɒkwaɪz/

ADVERB When something is moving **clockwise**, it is moving in a circle in the same direction as the hands on a clock. ○ [+ around] *He told the children to start moving clockwise around the room.* ○ [+ around] *In the southern hemisphere winds rotate clockwise around the center of the cyclone.*

▶ **COLLOCATION:** clockwise **around** something

clos|ing price /kloʊzɪŋ praɪs/ (closing prices) `BANKING & FINANCE`

NOUN The **closing price** is the price of a share at the end of a day's business on the stock exchange. ○ *The price is slightly above yesterday's closing price.* ○ [+ of] *a closing price of $61.54 a share*

▶ **COLLOCATIONS:**
the closing price **of** x
a **high/low/record** closing price

coach /koʊtʃ/ (coaches, coaching, coached) `JOBS`

VERB If you **coach** a person or a team, you help them to become better at a particular sport or skill. ○ *She coached a golf team in San José.* ○ *Ella had coached her on what to expect.*

▶ **COLLOCATIONS:**
coach a **football/basketball/hockey** team
coach **tennis/soccer/baseball**

▶ **SYNONYMS:** instruct, train

coast|al /koʊstəl/

ADJECTIVE Coastal is used to refer to things that are in the ocean or on an area of land next to the ocean. ○ *Local radio stations serving coastal areas often broadcast forecasts for yachtsmen.* ○ *The fish are on sale from our own coastal waters.*

▶ **COLLOCATIONS:**
a coastal **area/region/town/city/province**
coastal **waters**

code /koʊd/ (codes)

1 NOUN A **code** is a set of rules about how people should behave or about how something must be done. ○ *Article 159 of the Turkish penal code* ○ [+ of] *The committee agreed to set up a code of conduct on business taxation.* ○ *local building codes*

▶ **COLLOCATIONS:**
  a code **of** something
  a code of **conduct/practice/ethics/honor/behavior**
  a **dress** code
  a **penal/criminal/moral/ethical** code

▶ **SYNONYMS:** rules, laws

2 NOUN A **code** is any system of signs or symbols that has a meaning.
  ○ It will need different microchips to reconvert the digital code back into normal TV signals.

▶ **COLLOCATIONS:** a **binary/numeric/digital** code

---

co|her|ent /koʊhɪ̯ərənt, -hɛrənt/

ADJECTIVE If something is **coherent**, it is well planned, so that it is clear and sensible and all its parts go well with each other. ○ He has failed to work out a coherent strategy for modernizing the service. ○ The President's policy is perfectly coherent.

▶ **COLLOCATIONS:**
  a coherent **strategy/policy/plan**
  a coherent **vision/approach**
  a coherent **presentation/narrative/theory/critique**
  intellectually/perfectly coherent

▶ **SYNONYM:** cohesive

co|her|ence /koʊhɪ̯ərəns, -hɛrəns/

NONCOUNT NOUN ○ The campaign was widely criticized for making tactical mistakes and for a lack of coherence. ○ The three interlocking narratives achieve an overall coherence. ○ The anthology has a surprising sense of coherence.

▶ **COLLOCATIONS:**
  the coherence **of** something
  lack/possess/achieve coherence
  lend/bring coherence to something
  stylistic/thematic/logical/structural coherence

▶ **PHRASES:**
  a sense of coherence
  coherence and consistency

▶ **SYNONYM:** cohesion

co|in|cide /koʊɪnsaɪd/ (coincides, coinciding, coincided)

1 VERB If one event **coincides with** another, they happen at the same time. ○ [+ with] *Although his mental illness had coincided with his war service, it had not been caused by it.* ○ *The beginning of the solar and lunar years coincided every 13 years.*

2 VERB If the ideas or interests of two or more people **coincide**, they are the same. ○ *a case in which public and private interests coincide* ○ [+ with] *He gave great encouragement to his students, especially if their passions happened to coincide with his own.*

▶ **COLLOCATIONS:**
coincide **with** *something*
broadly/conveniently/frequently coincide
rarely coincide

co|in|ci|dence /koʊɪnsɪdəns/ (coincidences)

NOUN A **coincidence** is when two or more similar or related events occur at the same time by chance and without any planning. ○ *It is, of course, a mere coincidence that the author of this piece is also a pathologist.* ○ *It is no coincidence that so many of the romantic poets suffered from tuberculosis.*

▶ **COLLOCATIONS:**
by coincidence
pure/mere/sheer/no coincidence
a **happy/remarkable/strange** coincidence

col|lat|er|al /kəlætərəl/

NONCOUNT NOUN Collateral is money or property that is used as a guarantee that someone will repay a loan. [FORMAL] ○ [+ for] *Many people use personal assets as collateral for small business loans.*

▶ **COLLOCATIONS:**
collateral **for** *something*
collateral for a **loan**
require/hold/furnish/provide collateral
underlying/additional collateral

▶ **SYNONYM:** security

col|league /kɒliːg/ (colleagues) PERSONNEL

NOUN Your **colleagues** are the people you work with, especially in a professional job. ○ *Female academics are still paid less than their male* *colleagues.* ○ *In the corporate world, the best sources of business are your former colleagues.*

▶ COLLOCATIONS:
a **senior/junior** colleague
a **former/close** colleague
male/female colleagues
a **work/professional** colleague

▶ SYNONYM: coworker

col|lec|tion /kəlɛkʃᵊn/ (collections)

1 NOUN A **collection of** things is a group of similar things that you have deliberately acquired, usually over a period of time. ○ [+ *of*] *The Art Gallery of Ontario has the world's largest collection of sculptures by Henry Moore.* ○ *a valuable record collection*

▶ COLLOCATIONS:
a collection **of** *things*
a **large/vast/extensive** collection
a **CD/record/art/stamp** collection
a collection of **paintings/photographs/sculpture**

2 NONCOUNT NOUN **Collection** is the act of collecting something from a place or from people. ○ *Money can be sent to any one of 22,000 agents worldwide for collection.* ○ [+ *of*] *computer systems to speed up collection of information* ○ *new guidelines on online data collection*

▶ COLLOCATIONS:
collection **of** *something*
data/tax/debt collection
collection of **data/information**

▶ SYNONYM: acquisition

col|lege /kɒlɪdʒ/ (colleges)

NOUN A **college** is an institution where students study after they have left secondary school. ○ *She is doing business studies at a local college.* ○ *He is now a professor of economics at Western New England College.* ○ *business programs offered to college graduates*

▶ COLLOCATIONS:
a college **of** *something*
a college of **art/education/commerce**
go to/attend/start/enter/finish college
a **community/private** college

a **technical/art/agricultural** college
a college **graduate/student/professor**

▶ **PHRASE:** college and university

▶ **RELATED WORD:** university

col|lide /kəlaɪd/ (collides, colliding, collided)

VERB If people or vehicles **collide**, they hit each other. ○ *The two cars collided.* ○ [+ with] *He broke his ankle after colliding with a teammate during training.*

▶ **COLLOCATIONS:**
collide **with** *someone/something*
collide **head-on/violently/heavily**

▶ **SYNONYM:** crash

col|li|sion /kəlɪʒ³n/ (collisions)

NOUN A **collision** is an accident in which two moving objects hit each other. ○ *Fifty-three passengers were killed in the collision.* ○ [+ with] *Her car was crushed in a head-on collision with a truck.* ○ [+ between] *a collision between a bus and a train*

▶ **COLLOCATIONS:**
a collision **with** *something*
a collision **between** *things*
a **head-on/fatal/violent** collision
a **minor/high-speed/accidental** collision
avoid/avert/escape a collision

▶ **SYNONYM:** crash

col|umn /kɒləm/ (columns)

1 NOUN A **column** is a tall, solid structure that supports part of a building. ○ *The house has six white columns across the front.* ○ *Two large doors hide the columns supporting the roof.*

▶ **COLLOCATIONS:** columns **support/frame/separate** *something*

▶ **SYNONYMS:** pillar, post

2 NOUN A **column** is a group of short lines of words or numbers on a page. ○ *In the left column you'll see a list of names.*

▶ **COLLOCATIONS:** the **left-hand/right-hand/middle** column

▶ **RELATED WORD:** row

com|bine /kəmbaɪn/ (combines, combining, combined)

1 VERB If you **combine** two or more things or if they **combine**, they exist together. ○ [+ with] *If improved education is combined with other factors, dramatic results can be achieved.* ○ [+ to-inf] *Relief workers say it's worse than ever as disease and starvation combine to kill thousands.*

2 VERB If you **combine** two or more things or if they **combine**, they join together to make a single thing. ○ *They have combined the data from these 19 studies.* ○ [+ to-inf] *Carbon, hydrogen and oxygen combine chemically to form carbohydrates and fats.* ○ [+ with] *Combined with other compounds, they created a massive dynamite-type bomb.*

▶ COLLOCATIONS:
combine **with** something
combine to **form/create/produce** something
combine **ingredients/elements**

▶ SYNONYMS: join, mix, blend

com|bi|na|tion /kɒmbɪneɪʃ³n/ (combinations)

NOUN A **combination of** things is a mixture of them. ○ [+ of] *A combination of circumstances led to the disaster.* ○ [+ of] *a chemical formed by the combination of elements*

▶ COLLOCATIONS:
a combination **of** things
a combination of **factors/circumstances/elements/ingredients**

▶ SYNONYMS: group, mixture, blend

com|fort|able /kʌmftəb³l, -fərtəb³l/

1 ADJECTIVE Something that is **comfortable** makes you feel physically relaxed. ○ *The car's front seats are particularly comfortable.*

▶ COLLOCATIONS: a comfortable **chair/seat/bed**

▶ SYNONYM: relaxing

2 ADJECTIVE **Comfortable** means feeling physically relaxed and having no pain. ○ *Sit down and make yourself comfortable.*

▶ SYNONYM: relaxed

com|ment /kɒmɛnt/ (comments, commenting, commented) COMMUNICATIONS

1 VERB If you **comment on** something, you give your opinion about it or you give an explanation for it. ○ [+ on] *Police refuse to comment on whether*

anyone has been arrested. ○ *"I'm always happy with new developments,"*
he commented. ○ [+ *that*] *Stuart commented that this was very true.*

▶ **COLLOCATIONS:**
comment **on** *something*
comment on a **rumor/allegation/report/matter/incident**
refuse to comment
comment **publicly/directly**

▶ **SYNONYMS:** remark, state, explain

2 NOUN A **comment** is something that you say that expresses your
opinion of something or that gives an explanation of it. ○ *He made his*
comments at a news conference in Amsterdam. ○ [+ *about*] *There's been no*
comment so far from police about the allegations. ○ [+ *on*] *A spokesman*
declined comment on the matter.

▶ **COLLOCATIONS:**
a comment **on/about** *something*
a comment **from** *someone*
make a comment

▶ **PHRASE:** no comment

▶ **COLLOCATIONS:** a **public/written/brief** comment

▶ **SYNONYM:** statement

---

com|merce /kɒmɜrs/   ORGANIZATION

NONCOUNT NOUN **Commerce** is the activities and procedures involved in
buying and selling things. ○ *They have made their fortunes from industry and*
commerce. ○ *The online commerce market is new, rapidly evolving and intensely*
competitive.

▶ **COLLOCATIONS:**
regulate/affect commerce
obstruct/disrupt/facilitate/promote commerce
electronic/online/Internet commerce
global/international/foreign commerce

▶ **SYNONYM:** trade

com|mer|cial /kəmɜrʃ⁰l/

1 ADJECTIVE **Commercial** means involving or relating to the buying and
selling of goods. ○ *The region in its heyday was a major center of industrial*
and commercial activity. ○ *Attacks were reported on police, vehicles, and*
commercial premises.

2 **ADJECTIVE** **Commercial** organizations and activities are concerned with making money or profits, rather than, for example, with scientific research or providing a public service. ○ *Conservationists in Chile are concerned over the effect of commercial exploitation of forests.* ○ *Whether the project will be a commercial success is still uncertain.*

▶ COLLOCATIONS:
increasingly/purely commercial
a commercial **interest/property/use**
a commercial **venture/enterprise/activity/success**
commercial **premises**

▶ SYNONYM: business

---

com|mis|sion /kəmɪʃ°n/ (commissions, commissioning, commissioned)

BANKING & FINANCE

1 **VERB** If you **commission** something or **commission** someone **to** do something, you formally arrange for someone to do a piece of work for you. ○ *The Department of Agriculture commissioned a study into organic farming.* ○ [+ to-inf] *You can commission them to paint something especially for you.* ○ *specially commissioned reports*

▶ COLLOCATIONS:
commissioned **by** *someone*
commission a **study/report/survey**
commission **research**
commission a **composer/architect**
specially commissioned

● **Commission** is also a noun. ○ [+ to-inf] *He approached John Wexley with a commission to write the screenplay of the film.* ○ [+ to-inf] *Armitage won a commission to design the war memorial.*

▶ COLLOCATIONS: **gain/receive/win** a commission

2 **NOUN** **Commission** is a sum of money paid to a salesperson for every sale that he or she makes. If a salesperson is paid **on commission**, the amount they receive depends on the amount they sell. ○ *The salesmen work on commission only.* ○ [+ for] *He also got a commission for bringing in new clients.*

▶ COLLOCATIONS:
on commission
a commission **for** *something*

3 **NONCOUNT NOUN** If a bank or other company charges **commission**, they charge a fee for providing a service, for example for exchanging money or issuing an insurance policy. ○ [+ on] *Travel agents charge 1 percent commission on tickets.* ○ *Sellers pay a fixed commission fee.*

▶ **COLLOCATIONS:**
commission **on** *something*
charge/pay commission
a commission **fee**
x **percent** commission

4 **NOUN** A **commission** is a group of people who have been appointed to find out about something or to control something. ○ [+ to-inf] *The authorities have been asked to set up a commission to investigate the murders.* ○ *the Press Complaints Commission*

▶ **COLLOCATIONS:**
set up/appoint a commission
a **complaints/independent** commission
a **special/electoral** commission

---

com|mit /kəmɪt/ (commits, committing, committed)

1 **VERB** If someone **commits** a crime or a sin, they do something illegal ooor bad. ○ *I have never committed any crime.* ○ *This is a man who has committed murder.*

▶ **COLLOCATIONS:** commit a **crime/offense/atrocity/murder**

2 **VERB** If you **commit** money or resources **to** something, you decide to use them for a particular purpose. ○ [+ to] *They called on Western nations to commit more money to the poorest nations.* ○ [+ toward] *Large telephone companies have committed billions of dollars toward launching video services.*

▶ **COLLOCATIONS:**
commit *something* **to/for** *something*
commit **time/money/troops**

▶ **SYNONYMS:** give, pledge

3 **VERB** If you **commit yourself to** something, you say that you will definitely do it. ○ [+ to] *I would advise people to think very carefully about committing themselves to working Sundays.* ○ [+ to] *You don't have to commit to anything over the phone.*

▶ **COLLOCATIONS:**
commit **to** *something*
fully/totally commit to *something*

▶ **SYNONYM:** promise

com|mit|ment /kəmɪtmənt/ (commitments)

NOUN If you make a **commitment to** do something, you promise that you will do it. [FORMAL] ○ [+ to-inf] *We made a commitment to keep working* *together.* ○ [+ *to*] *They made a commitment to peace.*

▶ COLLOCATIONS:
a commitment **to** *something*
make/honor a commitment
a **long-term/lifelong/long-standing/ongoing** commitment
a **financial/emotional/work/family** commitment

▶ SYNONYMS: pledge, promise

---

com|mit|tee /kəmɪti/ (committees)   `ORGANIZATION`

NOUN A **committee** is a group of people who meet to make decisions or plans for a larger group. ○ *The report was given to the ethics committee for review.* ○ [+ *of*] *He chaired an eight-member committee of outside directors.* ○ [+ *on*] *the Senate committee on banking, trade, and commerce*

▶ COLLOCATIONS:
a committee **investigates/reviews/examines/studies** *something*
a committee **decides/concludes/recommends** *something*
a committee **approves/rejects** *something*
chair/head/steer a committee
a **parliamentary/congressional/legislative** committee

▶ SYNONYMS: group, commission

---

com|mod|ity /kəmɒdɪti/ (commodities)   `BANKING & FINANCE`

NOUN A **commodity** is something that is sold for money. ○ *The government increased prices on several basic commodities like bread and meat.* ○ *Unlike gold, most commodities are not kept solely for investment purposes.*

▶ COLLOCATIONS:
a commodity **market/exchange**
commodity **trading/futures/prices**
a **tradeable/marketable/valuable/rare** commodity
a **basic** commodity

---

com|mu|ni|cate /kəmyuːnɪkeɪt/   `COMMUNICATIONS`
(communicates, communicating, communicated)

VERB If you **communicate with** someone, you share or exchange information with them, for example by speaking, writing, or using equipment. You can also say that two people **communicate**. ○ [+ *with*] *Officials of the CIA depend heavily on electronic mail to communicate with each other.* ○ [+ *by*] *Communicating by text can have disadvantages.*

▶ **COLLOCATIONS:**
communicate **with** someone
communicate **by** something
communicate with **others/the public**
communicate by **e-mail/telephone/letter**
communicate **verbally/wirelessly/electronically/directly**

▶ **SYNONYMS:** converse, correspond

com|mu|ni|ca|tion /kəmyunɪkeɪʃ°n/

1 **NONCOUNT NOUN** ○ [+ between] *There was a tremendous lack of communication between us.* ○ [+ with] *Good communication with people around you could prove difficult.* ○ *Poor communication skills can be a problem in the workplace.*

▶ **COLLOCATIONS:**
communication **with/between** people
communication **skills**
written/verbal/direct/electronic/instant communication

2 **PLURAL NOUN Communications** are the systems and processes that are used to communicate or broadcast information. ○ *In 1962 the USA launched the world's first communications satellite, Telstar.* ○ *advanced communications equipment for emergency workers*

▶ **COLLOCATIONS:**
wireless/satellite/radio communications
a communications **satellite/device/network**
communications **equipment/technology**

---

com|mute /kəmyut/ (commutes, commuting, commuted)   TRAVEL

VERB If you **commute**, you travel a long distance every day between your home and your place of work. ○ [+ to] *Mike commutes to Connecticut every day.* ○ [+ between] *McLaren began commuting between Paris and London.* ○ *He's going to commute.*

▶ **COLLOCATIONS:**
commute **between** places
commute **to** somewhere
commute **by** something
commute to **work**
commute by **train/car/bus**

▶ **SYNONYM:** travel

com|mut|er (commuters)

NOUN ○ *The number of commuters has dropped by 100,000.* ○ *The most desirable properties are in the commuter belt with good transportation links.*

▶ **COLLOCATIONS:**
a commuter **train/plane/bus**
a commuter **town/belt**

---

com|pact /kəmpækt/ OFFICE

ADJECTIVE Something that is **compact** is small and takes up little space.
○ *a compact camera* ○ *a compact sport-utility vehicle*

▶ **COLLOCATIONS:** a compact **sedan/hatchback/pickup**

▶ **SYNONYM:** small

com|pact disc /kəmpækt dɪsk/ (compact discs)

NOUN A **compact disc** is a small disk on which sound, especially music, is recorded. The short form **CD** is also used. ○ *We downloaded the movie from the Internet and burned it onto a compact disc.* ○ *[+ of] compact discs of Iranian pop music*

▶ **COLLOCATIONS:**
record/release a compact disc
a **video/audio/bootleg/pirated** compact disc

---

com|pa|ny /kʌmpəni/ (companies) ORGANIZATION

NOUN A **company** is a business organization that makes money by selling goods or services. ○ *a successful businessman who owned a company that sold coffee machines* ○ *the Ford Motor Company*

▶ **COLLOCATIONS:**
a **software/insurance/oil/investment** company
a **private/public/multinational** company
own/run/operate a company
a company **reports/plans/announces/sells/operates** *things*
a company **executive/director/car**

▶ **SYNONYMS:** business, corporation, enterprise

> **EXTEND YOUR VOCABULARY**
>
> You can talk about a **company**, a **firm**, or a **business** to refer to a particular business organization. ○ *a Chicago-based software company* ○ *a small law firm* ○ *She left to start her own consulting business.*

> You can also talk about more specific types of business organizations.
> A **corporation** is a large company. ○ *a huge multinational corporation*
>
> A **conglomerate** is a large organization consisting of several different companies. ○ *a global media conglomerate*

com|pa|rable /kɒmpərəbᵊl/

ADJECTIVE Things that are **comparable** are similar and able to be compared. ○ *No other company can provide comparable goods or services.* ○ [+ to] *The price of laptop computers is now comparable to desktops.* ○ [+ in] *The two cities are broadly comparable in size.* ○ [+ with] *They could not afford anything comparable with their old home.*

▶ **COLLOCATIONS:**
  comparable **to/in/with** *something*
  a comparable **salary/wage**
  a comparable **level/standard/quality**
  roughly/directly/exactly comparable

▶ **SYNONYMS:** similar, related

com|para|tive /kəmpærətɪv/

1 **ADJECTIVE** You use **comparative** to show that your description of something is accurate only when it is compared to something else, or to what is usual. ○ *those who manage to reach comparative safety* ○ *The task was accomplished with comparative ease.*

▶ **COLLOCATIONS:**
  a comparative **advantage**
  comparative **ease/safety**

▶ **SYNONYM:** relative

2 **ADJECTIVE** A **comparative** study is a study that involves the comparison of two or more things of the same kind. ○ *a comparative study of the dietary practices of people from various regions of India* ○ *a professor of English and comparative literature*

▶ **COLLOCATIONS:**
  a comparative **study/analysis**
  comparative **literature/religion**

com|para|tive|ly /kəmpǽrətɪvli/

ADVERB ○ *a comparatively small nation* ○ *children who find it comparatively easy to make and keep friends*

▶ **COLLOCATIONS:**
comparatively **little/small**
comparatively **rare/modest/mild/inexpensive**

---

com|pare /kəmpέər/ (compares, comparing, compared)

VERB When you **compare** things, you consider them and discover the differences or similarities between them. ○ *Compare the two illustrations in Fig. 60.* ○ [+ with] *Was it fair to compare private schools with public schools?* ○ [+ to] *Note how smooth the skin of the upper arm is, then compare it to the skin on the elbow.*

▶ **COLLOCATIONS:** compare something **with/to** something

▶ **PHRASES:**
compare and contrast
compared with the average

com|pari|son /kəmpǽrɪsən/ (comparisons)

NOUN When you make a **comparison**, you consider two or more things and discover the differences between them. ○ [+ of] *a comparison of the British and German economies* ○ [+ between] *Its recommendations are based on detailed comparisons between the public and private sectors.* ○ *There are no previous statistics for comparison.*

▶ **COLLOCATIONS:**
a comparison **of/between** things
in/by comparison
make/draw a comparison
invite/bear comparison
a **difficult/unfair/valid** comparison
a **direct/inevitable** comparison

---

com|pat|ible /kəmpǽtɪbəl/

1 ADJECTIVE If things, for example, systems, ideas, and beliefs, are **compatible**, they work well together or can exist together successfully. ○ [+ with] *Free enterprise, he argued, was compatible with Russian values and traditions.* ○ *The two aims are not necessarily compatible.*

▶ **COLLOCATIONS:**
compatible **with** something
compatible **aims/ideas/beliefs**

2 **ADJECTIVE** If a brand of computer or equipment is **compatible with** another brand, they can be used together and can use the same software. ○ [+ with] *iTunes is only compatible with the iPod while Microsoft and Sony are offering rival technologies.* ○ [+ with] *Only Windows-based desktop computers less than 4 years old are compatible with the software.*

▸ COLLOCATIONS:
compatible **with** *something*
compatible with a **device/browser/pc/system**
compatible with **software**

com|pel /kəmpɛl/ (compels, compelling, compelled)

VERB If a situation, a rule, or a person **compels** you **to** do something, they force you to do it. ○ [+ to] *the introduction of legislation to compel cyclists to wear a helmet*

▸ COLLOCATIONS:
compel *someone* to **take action/act/respond/make a decision**
compel a **company/witness/people/government**

com|pen|sate /kɒmpənseɪt/ (compensates, compensating, compensated) `LEGAL`

1 **VERB** To **compensate** someone **for** money or things that they have lost means to pay them money or give them something to replace that money or those things. ○ [+ for] *To ease financial difficulties, farmers could be compensated for their loss of subsidies.* ○ *The Anglican Church has pledged to fully compensate sex abuse victims in South Australia.*

▸ COLLOCATIONS:
compensate *someone* **for** *something*
financially compensated
adequately/amply/generously/fully compensated

2 **VERB** Something that **compensates for** something else balances it or reduces its effects. ○ [+ for] *It is crucial that a system is found to compensate for inflation.* ○ [+ for] *The drug may compensate for prostaglandin deficiency.*

▸ COLLOCATIONS:
compensate **for** *something*
compensate for a **deficiency/imbalance**
compensate for a **loss/absence**

com|pen|sa|tion /kɒmpənseɪ∫ᵊn/ (compensations)

NONCOUNT NOUN Compensation is money that someone who has experienced loss or suffering claims from the person or organization responsible, or from the state. ○ [+ for] *He received one year's salary as compensation for loss of employment.* ○ *The Court ordered Dr. Williams to pay $500 compensation and $150 costs after admitting assault.*

▶ **COLLOCATIONS:**
   compensation **for** *something*
   compensation for **unfair dismissal/loss of earnings**
   pay/award/grant/deny/refuse compensation
   demand/seek/claim/receive compensation
   a compensation **payout/package/payment**

---

com|pe|tence /kɒmpɪtəns/   PERSONNEL

NONCOUNT NOUN Competence is the ability to do something well. ○ *No one doubts his competence.* ○ *Employees can acquire the necessary competence through training.* ○ [+ as] *Nobody challenged his competence as a classroom teacher.*

▶ **COLLOCATIONS:**
   develop/achieve/acquire competence
   possess/lack competence
   technical/professional/managerial competence

▶ **SYNONYMS:** ability, skill, proficiency

com|pe|tent /kɒmpɪtənt/

ADJECTIVE Competent means able to do something well. ○ *a highly competent manager* ○ [+ at] *Neither my father nor my mother was very competent at being parents.*

▶ **COLLOCATIONS:**
   highly/fully/extremely competent
   a competent **surgeon/swimmer/professional**

▶ **SYNONYMS:** skilled, proficient

---

com|pe|ti|tion /kɒmpɪtɪ∫ᵊn/   R&D

NONCOUNT NOUN Competition is an activity involving two or more companies, in which each company tries to get people to buy its own goods in preference to the other companies' goods. ○ [+ in] *The deal would have reduced competition in the commuter-aircraft market.* ○ *The farmers have*

been seeking higher prices as better protection from foreign competition.
○ [+ *from*] *Clothing stores also face heavy competition from factory outlets.*

▶ **COLLOCATIONS:**
competition **from** *something*
competition **for/in** *something*
competition from a **rival/supplier/producer**
competition in a **market/marketplace/industry**
face/increase/reduce competition
stiff/heavy/intense competition
international/foreign/domestic competition

com|peti|tor /kəmpɛtɪtər/

1 **NOUN** A **competitor** is a person who takes part in a competition.
○ *One of the oldest competitors won the silver medal.* ○ *Whitlock is one of the fiercest competitors on the track.*

▶ **COLLOCATIONS:** a **fierce/tough/formidable** competitor

▶ **SYNONYMS:** contestant, participant

2 **NOUN** A company's **competitors** are companies who are trying to sell similar goods or services to the same people. ○ *The bank isn't performing as well as some of its competitors.* ○ *Today the company outsells all other competitors in personal computers.*

▶ **COLLOCATIONS:**
a **major/direct/close** competitor
someone's **main/nearest/principal** competitor
lose ground to/see off a competitor
outperform/outbid/outsell a competitor

▶ **SYNONYMS:** rival, competition

com|plaint /kəmpleɪnt/ (complaints)　　　COMMUNICATIONS

NOUN A **complaint** is a statement in which you say that you are not satisfied with something. ○ [+ *about*] *a complaint about abusive behavior from a business rival* ○ [+ *against*] *The number of complaints against the police fell last year.* ○ [+ *from*] *The company has received several complaints from customers.*

▶ **COLLOCATIONS:**
file/lodge/register a complaint
investigate/receive/handle a complaint
dismiss/reject a complaint
resolve/settle/uphold a complaint

a **valid/serious/unfounded** complaint
a **formal/official/criminal** complaint

▶ SYNONYMS: criticism, grievance, accusation

BUSINESS CORRESPONDENCE: Writing about complaints

There are several common expressions used to make complaints in business correspondence. ○ *I am writing to complain about the poor service during my recent visit to your store.* ○ *I am writing to express my dissatisfaction with the service I received from your staff.*

Be careful not to confuse the verb form **complain** and the noun form **complaint**. ○ *We have received a number of complaints about poor service.*

---

com|ple|ment /ˈkɒmplɪmɛnt/ (complements, complementing, complemented)

VERB If people or things **complement** each other, they are different or do something different, which makes them a good combination. ○ *There will be a written examination to complement the practical test.* ○ *Their academic program is complemented by a wide range of sports, recreational, and cultural activities.*

▶ COLLOCATIONS:
   complemented **by** *something*
   complement the **menu/architecture/setting**
   perfectly complement *something*

---

com|plex /ˈkɒmplɛks, kəmˈplɛks/

ADJECTIVE Something that is **complex** has many different parts, and is therefore often difficult to understand. ○ *in-depth coverage of today's complex issues* ○ *a complex system of voting* ○ *complex machines*

▶ COLLOCATIONS:
   a complex **task/calculation/process**
   a complex **relationship/system/issue**

▶ SYNONYMS: complicated, intricate

---

com|pli|cat|ed /ˈkɒmplɪkeɪtɪd/

ADJECTIVE Something that is **complicated** has many parts and is difficult to understand. ○ *The situation is very complicated.* ○ *The operation was an extremely complicated procedure.*

▶ **COLLOCATIONS:**
  something is **extremely/incredibly/immensely** complicated
  a complicated **formula/calculation/equation**
  a complicated **process/procedure/situation**

▶ **SYNONYMS:** complex, elaborate, difficult

com|pli|ment (compliments, complimenting, complimented)

> Pronounce the verb /ˈkɒmplɪmɛnt/. Pronounce the noun
> /ˈkɒmplɪmənt/.

1 **NOUN** A **compliment** is something nice that you say to someone,
for example about their appearance. ○ *He paid me several compliments.*
○ *The two leaders exchanged compliments after their meeting.*

▶ **COLLOCATIONS:**
  pay/offer someone a compliment
  accept/receive/acknowledge/return a compliment
  exchange/trade compliments
  a **great/huge/tremendous** compliment

2 **VERB** If you **compliment** someone, you say something nice to them,
for example about their appearance. ○ *They complimented me on the way
I managed the team.*

▶ **SYNONYM:** praise

com|ply /kəmˈplaɪ/ (complies, complying, complied)   LEGAL

VERB If someone or something **complies with** an order or set of rules, they
are in accordance with what is required or expected. ○ [+ with] *The
commander said that the army would comply with the ceasefire.* ○ [+ with]
Some beaches had failed to comply with water quality standards.

▶ **COLLOCATIONS:**
  comply **with** something
  comply with **requirements/regulations/laws**
  fully/willingly comply

> **EXTEND YOUR VOCABULARY**
>
> You can say that someone **obeys** or **complies with** rules, regulations,
> or the law, if they act according to them. ○ *All employees are expected to
> obey/comply with the rules on safety.*

You can say that someone **obeys** a rule or another person. You can only say that someone **complies with** a rule. ○ *He was charged with failure to obey a police officer.*

You often say that something, such as a product or a system, **complies with** regulations, whereas it is usually a person who **obeys** something. ○ *New vehicles must comply with emission standards.*

---

com|po|nent /kəmpoʊnənt/ (components)

NOUN The **components** of something are the parts that it is made of. ○ [+ of] *Enriched uranium is a key component of a nuclear weapon.* ○ *The management plan has four main components.* ○ *The companies concerned were automotive component suppliers to the car manufacturers.*

▶ COLLOCATIONS:
  a component **of** *something*
  manufacture/supply components
  a **key/major/main** component
  a **vital/essential/critical** component
  a **software/hardware/electronic/electrical** component

---

com|pose /kəmpoʊz/ (composes, composing, composed)

1 **VERB** When someone **composes** a piece of music, they write it. ○ *Vivaldi composed a large number of very fine concertos.* ○ *Cale also uses electronic keyboards to compose.*

▶ COLLOCATIONS:
  compose **music**
  compose a **symphony/song/score**

▶ SYNONYM: write

2 **VERB** The things that something **is composed of** are its parts or members. The separate things that **compose** something are the parts or members that form it. ○ [+ of] *The force would be composed of troops from NATO countries.* ○ *Protein molecules compose all the complex working parts of living cells.* ○ [+ of] *They agreed to form a council composed of leaders of the rival factions.*

▶ COLLOCATIONS:
  composed **of** *something*
  mainly/largely/entirely composed of *something*

com|po|si|tion /kɒmpəzɪʃ°n/

NONCOUNT NOUN When you talk about the **composition** of something, you are referring to the way in which its various parts are put together and arranged. ○ [+ of] *Television has transformed the size and composition of the audience at sports events.* ○ *Forests vary greatly in composition from one part of the country to another.*

▶ COLLOCATIONS:
the composition **of** something
change/study/alter/determine something's composition
something's **exact/chemical/racial** composition

---

com|pre|hend /kɒmprɪhɛnd/ (comprehends, comprehending, comprehended)

VERB If you cannot **comprehend** something, you cannot understand it. [FORMAL] ○ *Patients may not be mentally focused enough to comprehend the full significance of the diagnosis.* ○ *Wilson did not comprehend the intricacies of his own government's policy and decision-making.*

▶ COLLOCATIONS:
fully/adequately/scarcely comprehend
comprehend the **importance/magnitude/meaning**
comprehend the **implications/intricacies/complexities**

▶ SYNONYM: understand

---

com|pre|hen|sive /kɒmprɪhɛnsɪv/

ADJECTIVE Something that is **comprehensive** includes everything that is needed or relevant. ○ *The Rough Guide to Nepal is a comprehensive guide to the region.* ○ *The first step involves a comprehensive analysis of the job.* ○ *a comprehensive investigation*

▶ COLLOCATIONS:
a comprehensive **review/survey**
a comprehensive **plan/strategy/approach**
a comprehensive **package/range/collection**

▶ SYNONYMS: full, thorough, complete

---

com|pro|mise /kɒmprəmaɪz/ (compromises, compromising, compromised)

1 NOUN A **compromise** is a situation in which people accept something slightly different from what they actually want, because of circumstances or because they are considering the wishes of other people. ○ [+ between] *Encourage your child to reach a compromise between what he wants and what you want.* ○ *Every side makes compromises and concessions in order to reach an agreement.* ○ *The government's policy of compromise is not universally popular.*

▶ **COLLOCATIONS:**
a compromise **between** things/people
reach/find a compromise
a **possible/necessary/likely/reasonable** compromise
a compromise **plan/deal/agreement/proposal/solution**
a compromise **candidate/bill**

▶ **SYNONYMS:** agreement, settlement

2 VERB If you **compromise with** someone, you reach an agreement with them in which you both give up something that you originally wanted. You can also say that two people or groups **compromise**. ○ [+ over] *The government has compromised with its critics over monetary policies.* ○ [+ on] *Israel had originally wanted $1 billion in aid, but compromised on the $650 million.*

▶ **COLLOCATIONS:**
compromise **over/on** something
compromise **with** someone

▶ **SYNONYM:** concede

---

comp|trol|ler /kəntroʊlər, kɒmp-/   `BANKING & FINANCE`
(comptrollers)

NOUN A **comptroller** is someone who is in charge of the accounts of a business or a government department. ○ *Robert Clarke, U.S. Comptroller of the Currency*

▶ **COLLOCATIONS:**
the **state/city/county** comptroller
a **deputy/assistant** comptroller

---

com|pul|so|ry /kəmpʌlsəri/

ADJECTIVE If something is **compulsory**, you must do it or accept it, because it is the law or because someone in a position of authority says you must. ○ *Many companies ask workers to accept voluntary retirement as opposed to compulsory retirement.* ○ *Many young men are trying to get away from compulsory military conscription.*

▶ **COLLOCATIONS:**
compulsory **for** someone

make *something* compulsory
compulsory **vaccination/voting/schooling**
compulsory **retirement/layoff**
compulsory **insurance**

▸ SYNONYM: mandatory

---

com|put|er /kəmpyutər/ (computers)   OFFICE

NOUN A **computer** is an electronic machine that can store and deal with
large amounts of information. ○ *The data are then fed into a computer.*
○ *The company installed a $650,000 computer system.* ○ *The car was designed
by computer.*

▸ COLLOCATIONS:
by computer
a **personal/laptop/desktop/notebook** computer
computer **software/hardware/technology**
a computer **system/network/screen/game/program**
a computer **user/programmer**
use/access/program a computer

---

con|ceal /kənsil/ (conceals, concealing, concealed)

1 VERB If you **conceal** a piece of information or a feeling, you do not let
other people know about it. ○ *Politicians accused the police of concealing
information.*

▸ COLLOCATIONS:
conceal **information/evidence/facts/truth/emotions**
conceal the **identity** of *someone/something*

2 VERB If something **conceals** something else, it covers it and prevents it
from being seen. ○ *a pair of carved Indian doors which conceal a built-in
cupboard*

▸ COLLOCATIONS: conceal a **weapon/gun/camera/bomb**

---

con|cede /kənsid/ (concedes, conceding, conceded)

1 VERB If you **concede** something, you admit, often unwillingly, that it is
true or correct. ○ [+ *that*] *The author concedes that some cases of
reincarnation are impressive.* ○ [+ *quote*] *"If we can find no outlet for our
savings, then it would be better to save less," he conceded.*

▸ COLLOCATIONS: **readily/reluctantly** concede

▸ PHRASE: concede the point

2 VERB If you **concede** something **to** someone, you give it away, usually unwillingly. ○ *Poland's Communist government conceded the right to establish independent trade unions.*

▶ **COLLOCATIONS:**
concede a **right/privilege/power**
concede **victory** to *someone*
concede an **election/race** to *someone*

▶ **SYNONYM:** cede

con|ceive /kənsiːv/ (conceives, conceiving, conceived)

1 VERB If you cannot **conceive of** something, you cannot imagine it or believe it. ○ [+ *of*] *Western leaders could not conceive of the idea that there might be traitors at high levels in their own governments.* ○ [+ *of*] *He was immensely ambitious but unable to conceive of winning power for himself.* ○ [+ *that*] *We cannot conceive that he will die at home.*

▶ **COLLOCATIONS:**
conceive **of** *something*
not conceive of *something*
not conceive of a **circumstance/idea/situation/possibility**

2 VERB If you **conceive** something **as** a particular thing, you consider it to be that thing. ○ [+ *as*] *The ancients conceived the Earth as afloat in water.* ○ [+ *of*] *We conceive of the family as being in a constant state of change.* ○ [+ *of*] *She cannot conceive of herself being anything else but a doctor.*

▶ **COLLOCATIONS:**
conceive *something* **as** *something*
conceive **of** *something* as *something*

con|cen|tra|tion /kɒnsᵊntreɪʃᵊn/ (concentrations)

1 NONCOUNT NOUN **Concentration** on something involves giving all your attention, effort, and resources to it. ○ *Neal kept interrupting, breaking my concentration.* ○ [+ *on*] *Changing needs led to a concentration on electricity generation.*

▶ **COLLOCATIONS:**
a concentration **on** *something*
lose/require/need/aid concentration
intense concentration
a concentration **level/span/lapse**

2 NOUN A **concentration of** something is a large amount of it or large numbers of it in a small area. ○ [+ *of*] *The area has one of the world's greatest* *concentrations of wildlife.* ○ [+ *of*] *There's been too much concentration of power in the hands of central authorities.*

▶ **COLLOCATIONS:**
a concentration **of** *something*
a concentration of **power/wealth**
a **high/low/dense/heavy** concentration

3 NOUN The **concentration of** a substance is the proportion of essential ingredients or substances in it. ○ [+ *of*] *pH is a measure of the concentration of free hydrogen atoms in a solution.* ○ *Global ozone concentrations had dropped over the last decade.*

▶ **COLLOCATIONS:**
the concentration **of** *something*
a **high/low** concentration
concentration **levels**

---

con|cept /kɒnsɛpt/ (concepts)

NOUN A **concept** is an idea or abstract principle. ○ [+ *of*] *She added that the concept of arranged marriages is misunderstood in the west.* ○ *basic legal concepts*

▶ **COLLOCATIONS:**
the concept **of** *something*
the concept of **freedom/democracy/justice**
understand/introduce/explain a concept
a **basic/original/abstract/simple/key/underlying** concept
a **marketing/design** concept

---

con|cern /kənsɜːn/ (concerns, concerning, concerned)

1 VERB If something such as a book or a piece of information **concerns** a particular subject, it is about that subject. ○ *The bulk of the book concerns Sandy's two middle-aged children.* ○ *The proceedings concern the fraudulent offer and sale of over $2.1 billion in municipal securities.*

▶ **SYNONYMS:** cover, relate to

2 VERB If a situation, event, or activity **concerns** you, it affects or involves you. ○ *It doesn't concern you at all.* ○ *There are interesting political dimensions to these two duties, but they do not concern us here.*

▶ **COLLOCATIONS:** a **matter/issue/question** concerns *someone*

3 PHRASE You can say **as far as** something **is concerned** to indicate the subject that you are talking about. ○ *As far as starting a family is concerned,* *the trend is for women having their children later in life.* ○ *It's clear that orthodox medicine doesn't have all the answers where cancer is concerned.*

▸ **SYNONYMS:** regarding, as regards, in relation to

con|cerned /kənsɜːrnd/

ADJECTIVE ○ [+ with] *Randolph's work was exclusively concerned with the effects of pollution on health.* ○ *It's a very stressful situation for everyone concerned.*

▸ **COLLOCATIONS:**
concerned **in/with** *something*
primarily/particularly concerned with something
everyone concerned
the **person/people** concerned

▸ **SYNONYMS:** related, involved

con|cern|ing /kənsɜːrnɪŋ/

PREPOSITION You use **concerning** to indicate what a question or piece of information is about. [FORMAL] ○ *a large body of research concerning the relationship between anger and health* ○ *various questions concerning pollution and the environment*

▸ **SYNONYMS:** regarding, about

---

con|ces|sion /kənsɛʃᵊn/ (concessions)

NOUN If you make a **concession to** someone, you agree to let them do or have something, especially in order to end an argument or conflict. ○ *We made too many concessions and we got too little in return.*

▸ **COLLOCATIONS:**
make/offer/grant/give a concession to *someone*
get/demand/extract/win a concession from *someone*

---

con|cise /kənsaɪs/

ADJECTIVE Something that is **concise** says everything that is necessary without using any unnecessary words. ○ *Burton's text is concise and informative.* ○ *Whatever you are writing make sure you are clear, concise, and accurate.*

▸ **COLLOCATIONS:**
a concise **summary/history/description/statement**
a concise **introduction/explanation/guide**

▸ **PHRASE:** clear and concise

▸ **SYNONYMS:** brief, succinct

con|clude /kənkluːd/ (concludes, concluding, concluded)

1 VERB If you **conclude that** something is true, you decide that it is true using the facts you know as a basis. ○ [+ that] *Larry had concluded that he had no choice but to accept Paul's words as the truth.* ○ [+ from] *So what can we conclude from this debate?*

▶ **COLLOCATIONS:**
conclude something **from** something
researchers/investigators/experts conclude
reasonably/reluctantly/unanimously/rightly conclude

▶ **SYNONYMS:** decide, judge

2 VERB When you **conclude**, you say the last thing that you are going to say. [FORMAL] ○ *"It's a waste of time," he concluded.* ○ *I would like to conclude by saying that I do enjoy your magazine.*

▶ **SYNONYMS:** end, close, finish

con|clu|sion /kənkluːʒən/ (conclusions)

1 NOUN When you come to a **conclusion**, you decide that something is true after you have thought about it carefully and have considered all the relevant facts. ○ [+ that] *Over the years I've come to the conclusion that she's a very great musician.* ○ *I have tried to give some idea of how I feel – other people will no doubt draw their own conclusions.*

▶ **COLLOCATIONS:**
come to/draw/reach a conclusion
a **clear/obvious/foregone/inescapable** conclusion

▶ **SYNONYMS:** decision, opinion

2 NOUN The **conclusion** of a piece of academic writing is its last section. ○ *The function of the essay's conclusion is to restate the main argument.* ○ *Your essay lacks only two paragraphs now: the introduction and the conclusion.*

▶ **COLLOCATION:** the conclusion **of** something

▶ **RELATED WORD:** introduction

3 PHRASE You say **in conclusion** to indicate that what you are about to say is the last thing that you want to say. ○ *In conclusion, walking is a cheap, safe, enjoyable and readily available form of exercise.*

con|clu|sive /kənkluːsɪv/

ADJECTIVE **Conclusive** evidence shows that something is certainly true. ○ *Her attorneys claim there is no conclusive evidence that any murders took place.* ○ *Research on the matter is far from conclusive.*

▶ **COLLOCATIONS:**
conclusive **evidence/proof**
conclusive **results/tests**

con|crete /kɒŋkrit, kɒŋkrit/

1 **ADJECTIVE** You use **concrete** to indicate that something is definite and specific. ○ *He had no concrete evidence.* ○ *There were no concrete proposals on the table.*

▶ **COLLOCATIONS:** concrete **evidence/proof**

▶ **SYNONYMS:** specific, precise, definite

2 **ADJECTIVE** A **concrete** object is a real, physical object. ○ *using concrete objects to teach addition and subtraction* ○ *Did we want to discuss abstract or concrete matters?*

▶ **COLLOCATION:** a concrete **object**

▶ **SYNONYMS:** real, material, actual

con|dense /kəndɛns/ (condenses, condensing, condensed)

VERB When a gas or vapor **condenses**, or **is condensed**, it changes into a liquid. ○ [+ to-inf] *Water vapor condenses to form clouds.* ○ [+ into] *The compressed gas is cooled and condenses into a liquid.* ○ [+ out of] *As the air rises it becomes colder and moisture condenses out of it.*

▶ **COLLOCATIONS:**
condense **into/out of** *something*
condense into **rain/liquid/droplets**
vapor/moisture/steam/gas condenses
a **cloud** condenses

con|di|tion /kəndɪʃᵊn/ (conditions)

1 **NOUN** The **condition** of someone or something is the state they are in. ○ *He remains in a critical condition in a California hospital.* ○ *The two-bedroom chalet is in good condition.* ○ *Poor physical condition leaves you prone to injury.*

▶ **COLLOCATIONS:**
the condition **of** *something/someone*
in a condition
in **stable/critical** condition
in **good/excellent/poor** condition
someone's **medical/physical** condition

▶ **SYNONYM:** state

2 **PLURAL NOUN** The **conditions** in which people live or do things are the factors that affect their comfort, safety, or success. ○ *This change has been timed under laboratory conditions.* ○ *The mild winter has created the ideal conditions for an ant population explosion.* ○ *People are living in appalling conditions.*

▶ **COLLOCATIONS:**
weather/trading/market conditions
living/working/employment conditions
economic/financial conditions
poor/appalling/favorable/ideal conditions

▶ **SYNONYMS:** circumstances, situation

3 **NOUN** A **condition** is something that must happen or be done in order for something else to be possible, especially when this is written into a contract or law. ○ *[+ for] economic targets set as a condition for loan payments* ○ *[+ of] terms and conditions of employment* ○ *Egypt had agreed to a summit subject to certain conditions.*

▶ **COLLOCATIONS:**
a condition **for/of** *something*
impose/attach/set a condition
meet/satisfy/fulfill/breach a condition

▶ **SYNONYM:** requirement

---

con|duct /kəndʌkt/ (conducts, conducting, conducted)

1 **VERB** When you **conduct** an activity or task, you organize it and carry it out. ○ *I decided to conduct an experiment.* ○ *He said they were conducting a campaign against Democrats across the country.*

▶ **COLLOCATIONS:**
conduct **business/research**
conduct a **test/experiment/study**
conduct a **poll/survey/review/interview**
conduct a **search/investigation**

▶ **SYNONYMS:** run, direct, manage, organize

2 **VERB** If something **conducts** heat or electricity, it allows heat or electricity to pass through it or along it. ○ *Water conducts heat faster than air.* ○ *The molecule did not conduct electricity.*

▶ **COLLOCATIONS:** conduct **heat/electricity**

con|fer|ence /kɒnfərəns, -frəns/ (conferences) `COMMUNICATIONS`

NOUN A **conference** is a meeting, often lasting a few days, that is organized on a particular subject or to bring together people who have a common interest. ○ [+ on] *The President summoned all the state governors to a conference on education.* ○ *the Republican Party conference* ○ *Last weekend the Roman Catholic Church in Scotland held a conference, attended by 450 delegates.*

▶ **COLLOCATIONS:**
a conference **on** *something*
attend/hold a conference
a **peace/party** conference
a **national/international/annual** conference
a conference **delegate**

▶ **SYNONYM:** meeting

con|fer|ence call /kɒnfərəns kɔl/ (conference calls)

NOUN A **conference call** is a phone call with more than two people. ○ *Mr. Baird is on a conference call and can't be disturbed.* ○ *Officials scheduled a conference call for 5pm Sunday.* ○ [+ with] *There are daily conference calls with Washington.*

▶ **COLLOCATIONS:**
a **half-hour/45-minute** conference call
a **daily/weekly/monthly** conference call
schedule/arrange/set up a conference call
host/attend/join/participate in a conference call

con|fi|den|tial /kɒnfɪdɛnʃ^əl/ `PERSONNEL`

ADJECTIVE Information that is **confidential** is meant to be kept secret or private. ○ *She accused them of leaking confidential information about her private life.*

▶ **COLLOCATIONS:**
confidential **information/advice/details/matters**
a confidential **document/report/file/letter**
a confidential **source/informant**
highly/completely/strictly confidential
keep *something* confidential

▶ **SYNONYMS:** private, restricted

con|fi|den|ti|al|ity /kɒnfɪdɛnʃiælɪti/

NONCOUNT NOUN ○ *Mitchell refused to violate the confidentiality that reporters promise their sources.* ○ [+ of] *the confidentiality of the client-attorney relationship* ○ [+ between] *confidentiality between doctor and patient*

▶ **COLLOCATIONS:**
breach/violate/break confidentiality
complete/absolute/total confidentiality
a confidentiality **agreement/clause/rule**

▶ **SYNONYM:** secrecy

---

con|firm /kənfɜrm/ (confirms, confirming, confirmed) [COMMUNICATIONS]

1 VERB If something **confirms** what you believe, suspect, or fear, it shows that it is definitely true. ○ [+ that] *X-rays have confirmed that he has not broken any bones.* ○ *These new statistics confirm our worst fears about the depth of the recession.* ○ [+ wh] *This confirms what I suspected all along.*

2 VERB If you **confirm** something that has been stated or suggested, you say that it is true because you know about it. ○ [+ that] *The spokesman confirmed that the area was now in rebel hands.* ○ [+ wh] *He confirmed what had long been feared.*

▶ **COLLOCATIONS:**
confirm a **report/diagnosis/finding**
confirm a **rumor/fear/suspicion/impression**
confirm *something's* **existence/presence/identity**
independently/officially confirmed

3 VERB If you **confirm** an arrangement or appointment, you say that it is definite, usually in a letter or on the telephone. ○ *If you make the reservation, I'll confirm it in writing.*

▶ **COLLOCATIONS:**
confirm a **booking/appointment/date**
confirm **details/arrangements**

BUSINESS CORRESPONDENCE: Confirming arrangements

Confirm is used in several common expressions in business correspondence when making arrangements. ○ ***I am writing to confirm*** *your booking for May 15.* ○ ***We can confirm that*** *a meeting room has been reserved for 10:30 am.* ○ *Could you please contact me to confirm your exact flight details nearer the time?*

▶ confirm **an appointment/a booking**

▶ confirm **details/a date**

con|fir|ma|tion /kɒnfərmeɪʃᵊn/

NONCOUNT NOUN ○ [+ *of*] *They took her resignation from Bendix as confirmation of their suspicions.* ○ *She glanced over at James for confirmation.*

▶ **COLLOCATIONS:**
confirmation **of** something
receive/need/get/await/provide confirmation
written/official/independent confirmation
further/final confirmation

▶ **SYNONYMS:** proof, affirmation

---

con|flict (conflicts, conflicting, conflicted)

> The noun is pronounced /kɒnflɪkt/. The verb is pronounced /kənflɪkt/.

1 NONCOUNT NOUN Conflict is serious disagreement and argument about something important. ○ *You must be sure to deal with any conflict immediately.* ○ [+ *with*] *Employees already are in conflict with management over job cuts.* ○ *The two companies came into conflict.*

▶ **COLLOCATIONS:**
conflict **with** someone
resolve/settle conflict
conflict **arises/exists**

▶ **SYNONYM:** disagreement

2 NOUN Conflict is fighting between countries or groups of people. [WRITTEN] ○ *talks aimed at ending four decades of conflict* ○ *The National Security Council has met to discuss ways of preventing a military conflict.*

▶ **COLLOCATIONS:**
end/settle/prevent/avoid conflict
a conflict **begins/erupts**
a **bloody/armed/violent/bitter** conflict
a **military/civil** conflict
a conflict **zone**

▶ **SYNONYMS:** hostility, fighting

3 VERB If two beliefs, ideas, or interests **conflict**, they are very different. ○ *Personal ethics and professional ethics sometimes conflict.* ○ *three powers with conflicting interests*

▶ **COLLOCATIONS:**
conflicting **reports/claims/accounts/messages**

conflicting **interests/signals/feelings/views**
directly/potentially conflict

▶ SYNONYM: clash

---

con|front /kənfrʌnt/ (confronts, confronting, confronted)

1 VERB If you **confront** someone, you move close to them and start to
fight or argue with them. ○ *She confronted him face to face.* ○ *Two rangers
were confronted by a mob who threatened to attack them.*

▶ COLLOCATIONS:
confront a **burglar/intruder**
confront *someone* **directly/head-on/face to face**

▶ SYNONYMS: face, stand up to, challenge

2 VERB If you **confront** someone **with** a fact, you tell them it in order to
accuse them of something. ○ *She decided to confront her boss with the truth.*

▶ COLLOCATIONS:
confront *someone* **with** *something*
confront *someone* with **evidence/the facts/the truth/an allegation**

---

con|fuse /kənfyuz/ (confuses, confusing, confused)

VERB If you **confuse** two things or people, by mistake, you think that one
of them is the other one. ○ *I always confuse my left and my right.* ○ *[+ with]*
She's often confused with her twin sister.

▶ COLLOCATION: confuse *someone* **with** *someone*

▶ SYNONYMS: mix up with, mistake for

con|fused /kənfyuzd/

ADJECTIVE If you are **confused**, you are not able to understand something
because information is not clear. ○ *[+ about] Consumers can become
confused about the type of life insurance to buy.*

▶ COLLOCATIONS:
confused **about** *something*
totally/hopelessly/utterly confused

▶ SYNONYMS: bewildered, puzzled, perplexed

con|fus|ing /kənfyuzɪŋ/

ADJECTIVE Confusing means difficult to understand because information
is not clear. ○ *The financial regulations are really confusing.* ○ *a confusing
instruction manual*

▶ COLLOCATIONS:
rather/somewhat/a little confusing
terribly/thoroughly/extremely confusing

▶ SYNONYMS: bewildering, puzzling, baffling

con|fu|sion /kənfyuʒ⁣ən/

1 NONCOUNT NOUN If there is **confusion** about something, people do not understand something because information is not clear. ○ [+ among] *The new ballots created confusion among voters.* ○ [+ about] *There's still confusion about the scale of their debts.* ○ [+ over] *There was confusion over his grandmother's real date of birth.*

▶ COLLOCATIONS:
confusion **among** *people*
confusion **about/over** *something*
cause/create/provoke confusion
minimize/resolve confusion

▶ SYNONYMS: uncertainty, puzzlement, bewilderment

2 NONCOUNT NOUN **Confusion** is a situation in which a lot of things are happening in a badly organized way. ○ *In the confusion, he managed to escape.* ○ *a scene of utter confusion*

▶ COLLOCATIONS:
widespread/utter/mass confusion
confusion **reigns/arises/ensues**

▶ SYNONYMS: disorder, chaos

con|glom|er|ate /kənglɒmərɪt/ (conglomerates) `ORGANIZATION`

NOUN A **conglomerate** is a large business firm consisting of several different companies. ○ *the world's second-largest media conglomerate* ○ *They bought other companies to create a conglomerate known as Hanson Trust.*

▶ COLLOCATIONS:
create/build/assemble a conglomerate
run/head/lead a conglomerate
a **media/engineering/manufacturing** conglomerate

con|gratu|late /kəngrætʃəleɪt/ (congratulates, congratulating, congratulated) `COMMUNICATIONS`

VERB If you **congratulate** someone, you express pleasure about something good that has happened to them. ○ *She congratulated him on* *his company's impressive results.* ○ *They heartily congratulated Stonewall for their efforts in organizing the rally.*

▶ **COLLOCATIONS:**
congratulate the **winner/victor**
warmly/heartily/personally congratulate *someone*
publicly/privately/quietly congratulate *someone*

▶ **SYNONYM:** compliment

con|gratu|la|tions /kəngrætʃəleɪʃənz/ You say
"**Congratulations**" to someone in order to congratulate them.
○ *The organizers of the Games deserve the warmest congratulations.* ○ [+ *on*]
Congratulations on your new job!

▶ **COLLOCATIONS: hearty/warm/sincere** congratulations

▶ **SYNONYMS:** best wishes, compliments

---

con|nect /kənɛkt/ (connects, connecting, connected)

1 VERB If something or someone **connects** one thing **to** another, or if one thing **connects to** another, the two things are joined together. ○ [+ *to*]
You can connect the machine to your laptop. ○ [+ *to*] *Two cables connect to each corner of the plate.* ○ *a television camera connected to the radio telescope*

2 VERB If a piece of equipment or a place **is connected to** a source of power or water, it is joined to that source so that it has power or water.
○ [+ *to*] *These appliances should not be connected to power supplies.* ○ [+ *to*]
Ischia was now connected to the mainland water supply.

▶ **COLLOCATIONS:**
connect *something* **to** *something*
be connected **to** *something*
be connected **by** *something*
be connected by a **wire/cable**
connect a **computer/device/pipe**
connect **directly/permanently/wirelessly**

▶ **SYNONYM:** attach

con|nec|tion /kənɛkʃən/ (connections)

1 NOUN If there is a **connection** between a piece of equipment and a source of power or water, the piece of equipment is joined to the source so that it receives power or water. ○ *Check all radiators for small leaks, especially around pipework connections.* ○ *a high-speed Internet connection*

▶ **COLLOCATIONS:**
a connection **to** *something*

a **cable/wireless/Internet/broadband/telephone** connection
a **direct/high-speed/fast** connection
connection **speed**

2 **NOUN** A **connection** is a relationship between two things, people, or groups. ○ [+ between] *There was no evidence of a connection between BSE and the brain diseases recently confirmed in cats.* ○ [+ with] *The police say he had no connection with the security forces.* ○ [+ to] *He has denied any connection to the bombing.*

▶ **COLLOCATIONS:**
a connection **between** things
a connection **with/to** something
make/establish/suggest/deny/maintain a connection
a **clear/obvious/direct** connection
a **close/strong/important** connection

▶ **SYNONYMS:** relationship, link, association

---

con|secu|tive /kənsɛkyətɪv/

ADJECTIVE **Consecutive** periods of time or events happen one after the other without interruption. ○ *This is the third consecutive year that these countries achieved economic growth.* ○ *Photographs taken at the same time on two consecutive sunny days can be quite different from one another.*

▶ **COLLOCATIONS:**
consecutive **days/nights/months/years**
the **second/third/fourth** consecutive *day/year*
two/three/four consecutive *days/years*

▶ **SYNONYM:** successive

---

con|sen|sus /kənsɛnsəs/

NOUN A **consensus** is general agreement among a group of people.
○ [+ among] *The consensus among the world's scientists is that the world is likely to warm up over the next few decades.* ○ [+ on] *So far, the Australians have been unable to come to a uniform consensus on the issue.*

▶ **COLLOCATIONS:**
the consensus **among** people
a consensus **on/about** something
reach/build/achieve a consensus
seek/establish a consensus
a **scientific/cross-party/broad/general** consensus

con|sent /kənsɛnt/ **(consents, consenting, consented)**

1 **NONCOUNT NOUN** If you give your **consent to** something, you give someone permission to do it. [FORMAL] ○ [+ to] *Patients must give their signed consent to an operation.* ○ *Can my child be medically examined without my consent?*

▶ **COLLOCATIONS:**
consent **to** *something*
with/without *someone's* consent
seek/solicit/obtain/grant/refuse consent
written/unanimous/mutual/parental consent

2 **VERB** If you **consent to** something, you agree to do it or to allow it to be done. [FORMAL] ○ [+ to-inf] *Doctors failed to fully inform patients before they consented to participate.* ○ [+ to] *She had consented to the conditions of the contract.* ○ *Churchill proposed to Stalin a division of influence in the Balkan states. Stalin readily consented.*

▶ **COLLOCATIONS:**
consent **to** *something*
consent to **marry** *someone*
consent to **allow** *something*

▶ **SYNONYM:** agree

con|se|quence /kɒnsɪkwɛns, -kwəns/ **(consequences)**

1 **NOUN** The **consequences of** something are the results or effects of it. ○ [+ of] *Her lawyer said she understood the consequences of her actions and was prepared to go to jail.* ○ [+ for] *An economic crisis may have tremendous consequences for our global security.*

▶ **COLLOCATIONS:**
a consequence **of** *something*
the consequences **for** *someone/something*
the consequences of **war/action/failure**
the consequences for the **economy/future/region**
suffer/face/accept/consider/understand the consequences
serious/severe/tragic consequences
likely/unintended consequences
health/tax consequences

▶ **SYNONYM:** result

2 **PHRASE** If one thing happens and then another thing happens **in consequence** or **as a consequence**, the second thing happens as a result of the first. ○ *His death was totally unexpected and, in consequence, no* *plans had been made for his replacement.* ○ [+ of] *people who are suffering and dying as a consequence of cigarette smoking*

▶ **PHRASE:** in consequence/as a consequence of something

con|se|quent|ly /kɒnsɪkwɛntli, -kwəntli/

ADVERB Consequently means as a result. [FORMAL] ○ *They said that Freud had not understood women and consequently belittled them.* ○ *Apprehension and stress had made him depressed and consequently irritable with his family.*

▶ **SYNONYMS:** as a result, thus

con|serva|tive /kənsɜːvətɪv/

1 ADJECTIVE Someone who is **conservative** has right-wing views.
○ *counties whose citizens invariably support the most conservative candidate in any election* ○ *the mood of America is turning back to the conservative views of the Ronald Reagan era*

▶ **COLLOCATIONS:**
a conservative **politician/activist/commentator**
a conservative **view/approach/agenda**
fiscally/socially/politically conservative
deeply conservative

▶ **SYNONYMS:** right-wing, traditionalist, conventional, reactionary

2 ADJECTIVE Someone who is **conservative** or has **conservative** ideas is unwilling to accept changes and new ideas. ○ *People tend to be more aggressive when they're young and more conservative as they get older.* ○ *a narrow conservative approach to child care*

3 ADJECTIVE A **Conservative** politician or voter is a member of or votes for the Conservative Party in Britain. ○ *Most Conservative MPs appear happy with the government's reassurances.* ○ *disenchanted Conservative voters*

▶ **COLLOCATIONS:**
a Conservative **voter/MP**
the Conservative **Party**

▶ **SYNONYM:** Tory

con|serve /kənsɜːv/ (conserves, conserving, conserved)

1 VERB If you **conserve** a supply of something, you use it carefully so that it lasts for a long time. ○ *The republic's factories have closed for the weekend to conserve energy.* ○ *We must abandon our wasteful ways and conserve resources.*

2 **VERB** To **conserve** something means to protect it from harm, loss, or change. ○ *aid to help developing countries conserve their forests* ○ *the body responsible for conserving historic buildings*

▶ **COLLOCATIONS:**
conserve **water/electricity/power/fuel**
conserve **energy/resources/heat/wildlife**
conserve a **forest/building/habitat**
conserve the **environment**

▶ **SYNONYMS:** save, protect, preserve

con|sid|er|able /kənsɪdərəbᵊl/

ADJECTIVE **Considerable** means great in amount or degree. [FORMAL] ○ *Other studies found considerable evidence to support this finding.* ○ *Doing it properly makes considerable demands on our time.* ○ *Vets' fees can be considerable.*

▶ **COLLOCATIONS:**
a considerable **amount**
considerable **influence/pressure/demands**
considerable **skill/success**

▶ **SYNONYMS:** substantial, large

con|sid|er|ably /kənsɪdərəbli/

ADVERB ○ *Children vary considerably in the rate at which they learn.* ○ *In the past ethical standards have often been considerably lower.*

▶ **COLLOCATIONS:**
considerably **more/less/higher/lower**
vary/differ/improve considerably

▶ **SYNONYM:** significantly

con|sid|er|ate /kənsɪdərɪt/

ADJECTIVE Someone who is **considerate** is always thinking and caring about the feelings of other people. ○ *He's the most considerate man I know.* ○ *[+ of] She was always polite and considerate of others.*

▶ **COLLOCATION:** considerate **of** *someone*

▶ **SYNONYM:** thoughtful

con|sid|era|tion /kənsɪdəreɪʃ°n/

1 **NONCOUNT NOUN** **Consideration** is careful thought about something.
○ [+ about] *There should be careful consideration about the use of such toxic chemicals.*

▶ **COLLOCATIONS:**
careful/serious consideration
full/due consideration
special/further consideration

▶ **PHRASE:** take into consideration

2 **PHRASE** If something is **under consideration**, it is being discussed.
○ *Several proposals are under consideration by the state assembly.*

con|sist|ent /kənsɪstənt/

1 **ADJECTIVE** Someone who is **consistent** always behaves in the same way, has the same attitudes toward people or things, or achieves the same level of success in something. ○ *Becker has never been the most consistent of players anyway.* ○ *his consistent support of free trade* ○ *a consistent character with a major thematic function*

▶ **COLLOCATIONS:** a consistent **player/performer**

▶ **SYNONYM:** reliable

2 **ADJECTIVE** If one fact or idea is **consistent with** another, they do not contradict each other. ○ [+ with] *This result is consistent with the findings of Garnett & Tobin.* ○ [+ with] *New goals are not always consistent with the existing policies.*

▶ **COLLOCATIONS:**
consistent **with** *something*
consistent with a **finding/hypothesis**
entirely/fairly/broadly/remarkably consistent

▶ **SYNONYM:** compatible

con|sist|ent|ly /kənsɪstəntli/

ADVERB ○ *It's something I have consistently denied.* ○ *Jones and Armstrong maintain a consistently high standard.*

▶ **COLLOCATIONS:**
consistently **deny/argue/oppose**
consistently **maintain/refuse/fail**

▶ **SYNONYM:** constantly

con|sult /kənsʌlt/ **(consults, consulting, consulted)**   `JOBS`

1 **VERB** If you **consult** an expert or someone senior to you or **consult with** them, you ask them for their opinion and advice about what you should do or their permission to do something. ○ *Consult your doctor about how much exercise you should attempt.* ○ [+ with] *He needed to consult with an attorney.* ○ *If you are in any doubt, consult a financial adviser.*

2 **VERB** If a person or group of people **consults with** other people or **consults** them, they talk and exchange ideas and opinions about what they might decide to do. ○ [+ with] *After consulting with her manager she decided to take on the part.* ○ *The two countries will have to consult their allies.* ○ *The umpires consulted quickly.*

▸ **COLLOCATIONS:**
  consult **with** *someone*
  consult a **doctor/lawyer/specialist/adviser/expert**

▸ **SYNONYM:** confer

con|sult|ant /kənsʌltənt/ **(consultants)**

NOUN A **consultant** is a person who gives expert advice to a person or organization on a particular subject. [+ to] ○ *a team of management consultants sent in to reorganize the department*

▸ **COLLOCATIONS:**
  a consultant **to** *someone/something*
  pay/hire a consultant
  a **senior/independent/outside** consultant
  a **technical/environmental/marketing/design** consultant
  a **management/recruitment/property/security** consultant
  a consultant's **report**

▸ **SYNONYMS:** specialist, adviser

EXTEND YOUR VOCABULARY

There are several words used to talk about people that a company works with but does not directly employ. A **consultant** gives expert advice on a particular subject. ○ *The company hired a marketing consultant to revamp its image.*

A **contractor** is a person or company that has a **contract** to do work for another business. The contractor might use a **subcontractor** to do some parts of that work. ○ *The company uses private maintenance contractors.*

A **supplier** is a business who makes or provides a product for another company. ○ *the company's equipment supplier*

con|sul|ta|tion /kɒnsəlteɪʃᵊn/ (consultations)

NOUN A **consultation**, or a **consultation with** someone, is a meeting which is held to discuss something. **Consultation** is discussion about something. ○ [+ with] *The plans were drawn up in consultation with the World Health Organization.* ○ [+ with] *A personal diet plan is devised after a consultation with a nutritionist.*

▶ **COLLOCATIONS:**
a consultation **with** *someone*
in consultation with *someone*
hold/launch/conduct a consultation
public/extensive/further/initial consultation
a consultation **process/period/exercise**

▶ **SYNONYMS:** discussion, meeting, deliberation

con|sum|er be|hav|ior /kənsu:mər bɪheɪvyər/   `MARKETING & SALES`

NONCOUNT NOUN Consumer behavior is the way that groups of consumers typically behave. ○ *Developments in materials, marketing, and styling have all had an effect on consumer behavior.* ○ *Campbell studies consumer behavior at the University of Colorado.*

con|sum|er|ism /kənsuːmərɪzəm/   `MARKETING & SALES`

NONCOUNT NOUN Consumerism is the belief that it is good to buy and use a lot of goods. ○ *They have clearly embraced Western consumerism.*

▶ **COLLOCATIONS:**
American/Western/capitalist consumerism
embrace/promote/reject consumerism

con|tact /kɒntækt/ (contacts, contacting, contacted)   `COMMUNICATIONS`

1 NONCOUNT NOUN Contact involves meeting or communicating with someone, especially regularly. ○ [+ with] *Opposition leaders are denying any contact with the government in Kabul.* ○ [+ between] *He forbade contact between directors and executives outside his presence.*

▶ **COLLOCATIONS:**
contact **with/between** *people*
maintain/establish contact
direct/close/regular/human/social contact
eye/radio/telephone contact
a contact **number/address**

▶ **PHRASES:**
make/have contact with someone
lose contact with someone

▶ **SYNONYM:** communication

2 VERB If you **contact** someone, you telephone them, write to them, or go to see them in order to tell or ask them something. ○ *Contact the Tourist Information Bureau for further details.* ○ *His client was on vacation and couldn't be contacted.*

▶ **COLLOCATIONS:**
contact the **police/authorities**
contact *someone* **immediately**

▶ **SYNONYM:** communicate with

BUSINESS CORRESPONDENCE: Making contact

Contact is used in a number of common expressions in business correspondence. ○ ***Please contact*** *your local agent for further details* ○ ***Don't hesitate to contact me*** *if you have any further questions.* ○ *The orders department can be **contacted by** e-mail at ...* ○ *You can update your **contact details** by logging onto the website.*

---

3 NONCOUNT NOUN When people or things are in **contact**, they are touching each other. ○ [+ with] *They compared how these organisms behaved when left in contact with different materials.* ○ *There was no physical contact.* ○ *This shows where the foot and shoe are in contact.*

▶ **COLLOCATIONS:**
in contact
in contact **with** *something/someone*
direct/physical/sexual contact

---

con|tain|er /kənteɪnər/ (containers)

NOUN A **container** is something such as a box or bottle that is used to hold or store things in. ○ *the plastic containers in which fish are stored and sold*

▶ **COLLOCATIONS:**
a container **of** *something*
a container of **milk/water/chemicals**
a **plastic/glass/metal** container
fill/load/unload/store a container

▶ **SYNONYMS:** receptacle, vessel

con|tem|plate /kɒntəmpleɪt/ (contemplates, contemplating, contemplated)

VERB If you **contemplate** an action, you think about whether to do it or not. ○ *For a time he contemplated a career as an army medical doctor.*

▶ **COLLOCATIONS:**
contemplate **retirement/action/war**
contemplate a **career/move/change**

▶ **SYNONYM:** consider

con|tem|pla|tion /kɒntəmpleɪʃⁿn/

NONCOUNT NOUN ○ *It is a place of quiet contemplation.* ○ [+ of] *He was lost in the contemplation of the landscape for a while.*

▶ **COLLOCATIONS:**
contemplation **of** something
contemplation of **nature**
quiet contemplation

con|tend /kəntɛnd/ (contends, contending, contended)

VERB If you **contend that** something is true, you state or argue that it is true. [FORMAL] ○ [+ that] *The government contends that he is fundamentalist.* ○ [+ that] *The government strongly contends that no student should be compelled to pay a fee to support political activism.*

▶ **COLLOCATIONS:**
seriously/strongly contend
a **prosecutor/attorney/critic/opponent** contends

▶ **SYNONYMS:** state, argue

con|ti|nent /kɒntɪnənt/ (continents)

NOUN A **continent** is a very large area of land, such as Africa or Asia, that consists of several countries. ○ *Conflicts are taking place in nine out of 52 countries in the African continent.* ○ *Dinosaurs evolved when most continents were joined in a single land mass.*

▶ **COLLOCATIONS:**
the **American/European/Antarctic/African** continent
a **whole/entire** continent

con|ti|nen|tal /kɒntɪnɛntᵊl/

ADJECTIVE **Continental** is used to refer to something that belongs to or relates to a continent. ○ *The most ancient parts of the continental crust are 4,000 million years old.*

▶ **COLLOCATIONS:**
continental **drift**
a continental **shelf/crust**

con|tin|gent /kəntɪndʒᵊnt/ (contingents)

NOUN A **contingent** is a group of people representing a country or organization at a meeting or other event. [FORMAL] ○ *The American contingent will stay overnight in London.*

▶ **COLLOCATIONS:**
a **large/small** contingent
send/lead/head a contingent
a contingent of **troops/soldiers/police/peacekeepers**

con|tinu|ation /kəntɪnyueɪʃən/

NONCOUNT NOUN The **continuation of** something is the fact that it continues to happen or to exist. ○ [+ of] *Investors are hoping for a continuation of Monday's 41-point rally.* ○ *a treatment to ensure continuation of good health*

▶ **COLLOCATIONS:** **ensure/guarantee/assure** continuation

con|tract (contracts, contracting, contracted) `PERSONNEL`

> The noun is pronounced /kɒntrækt/. The verb is pronounced /kəntrækt/.

1 **NOUN** A **contract** is a legal agreement, usually between two companies or between an employer and employee, which involves doing work for a stated sum of money. ○ [+ for] *The company won a prestigious contract for work on Europe's tallest building.* ○ [+ with] *He was given a seven-year contract with an annual salary of $150,000.*

▶ **COLLOCATIONS:**
a contract **for** *something*
a contract **with** *someone*
win/give/award/offer/sign a contract
a contract **worth** *an amount*

a **one-year/long-term/new** contract
a **recording/maintenance/employment** contract

▶ **SYNONYMS:** commission, agreement

2 VERB When something **contracts** or when something **contracts** it, it becomes smaller or shorter. ○ *Blood is only expelled from the heart when it contracts.* ○ *New research shows that an excess of meat and salt can contract muscles.*

▶ **COLLOCATIONS:**
the **throat** contracts
the **muscles/ventricles** contract
contract **rhythmically/rapidly**

---

contra|dict /kɒntrədɪkt/ (contradicts, contradicting, contradicted)

VERB If one statement or piece of evidence **contradicts** another, the first one makes the second one appear to be wrong. ○ *Her version contradicted the Government's claim that they were shot after being challenged.* ○ *The result seems to contradict a major U.S. study reported last November.* ○ *Often his conclusions flatly contradicted orthodox medical opinion.*

→ see note at **criticize**

▶ **COLLOCATIONS:**
contradict a **belief/claim/statement**
directly/flatly contradict *something*

contra|dic|tion /kɒntrədɪkʃᵊn/ (contradictions)

NOUN If you describe an aspect of a situation as a **contradiction**, you mean that it is completely different from other aspects, and so makes the situation confused or difficult to understand. ○ [+ *between*] *In my opinion, there is no contradiction between the two types of treatment.* ○ [+ *of*] *The performance seemed to me unpardonable, a contradiction of all that the Olympics is supposed to be.* ○ [+ *in*] *There are various contradictions in the evidence.*

▶ **COLLOCATIONS:**
a contradiction **between** *things*
a contradiction **of/in** *something*
an **apparent** contradiction

▶ **SYNONYMS:** inconsistency, conflict

contra|dic|tory /kɒntrədɪktəri/

ADJECTIVE If two or more facts, ideas, or statements are **contradictory**, they state or imply that opposite things are true. ○ *Customs officials have* *made a series of contradictory statements about the equipment.* ○ *advice that sometimes is contradictory and confusing*

▶ **COLLOCATIONS:**
a contradictory **statement/message**
contradictory **evidence/testimony**
apparently contradictory

▶ **SYNONYMS:** inconsistent, conflicting, incompatible

con|tra|ry /ˈkɒntrɛri/

1 ADJECTIVE Ideas, attitudes, or reactions that are **contrary to** each other are completely different from each other. ○ [+ to] *This view is contrary to the aims of critical social research for a number of reasons.* ○ *Several of those present had contrary information.* ○ *people with contrary interests*

▶ **COLLOCATIONS:**
contrary **to** *something*
run/seem contrary to *something*
a contrary **view/opinion/direction**
contrary **evidence/information**

▶ **SYNONYMS:** opposite, different, opposing

2 PHRASE If you say that something is true **contrary to** other people's beliefs or opinions, you are emphasizing that it is true and that they are wrong. ○ *Contrary to popular belief, moderate exercise actually decreases your appetite.* ○ *Contrary to its popular definition, Shamanism is not a religion: there is no dogma here.*

con|trast (contrasts, contrasting, contrasted)

The noun is pronounced /ˈkɒntrɑːst, -træst/. The verb is pronounced /kənˈtrɑːst, -ˈtræst/.

1 NOUN A **contrast** is a great difference between two or more things that is clear when you compare them. ○ [+ between] *the contrast between city life and country life* ○ [+ in] *The two visitors provided a startling contrast in appearance.*

▶ **COLLOCATIONS:**
a contrast **between** *things*
a contrast **in** *something*
a **stark/sharp/marked/striking/dramatic** contrast

2 PHRASE You say **by contrast** or **in contrast**, or **in contrast to** something, to show that you are mentioning a very different situation from the one you have just mentioned. ○ *The private sector, by contrast, has plenty of money to spend.* ○ *In contrast, the lives of girls in well-to-do families were often very sheltered.* ○ *In contrast to similar services in France and Germany, Intercity rolling stock is very rarely idle.*

3 **PHRASE** If one thing is **in contrast to** another, it is very different from it. ○ [+ to] *His public statements have always been in marked contrast to those of his son.*

4 **VERB** If you **contrast** one thing **with** another, you point out or consider the differences between those things. ○ [+ with] *She contrasted the situation then with the present crisis.* ○ *In this section we contrast four possible broad approaches.*

▶ **COLLOCATIONS:**
contrast *something* **with** *something*
contrast a **view/approach** with *something*

5 **VERB** If one thing **contrasts with** another, it is very different from it. ○ [+ with] *Johnson's easy charm contrasted sharply with the prickliness of his boss.* ○ [V-ing] *Paint the wall in a contrasting color.*

▶ **COLLOCATIONS:**
contrast **with** *something*
a **color/style** contrasts with *something*
contrast **sharply/starkly**

▶ **SYNONYM:** differ

---

con|trib|ute /kəntrɪbyut/ (contributes, contributing, contributed)

1 **VERB** If you **contribute to** something, you say or do things to help to make it successful. ○ [+ to] *The three sons also contribute to the family business.* ○ [+ to] *He believes he has something to contribute to a discussion concerning the uprising.*

2 **VERB** If something **contributes to** an event or situation, it is one of the causes of it. ○ [+ to] *The report says design faults in both the vessels contributed to the tragedy.* ○ [V-ing] *Stress, both human and mechanical, may also be a contributing factor.*

▶ **COLLOCATIONS:**
contribute **to** *something*
a contributing **factor**
contribute **greatly/directly/significantly/substantially**

con|tri|bu|tion /kɒntrɪbyuʃən/ (contributions)

NOUN If you make a **contribution to** something, you do something to help make it successful or to produce it. ○ [+ to] *American economists have made important contributions to the field of financial and corporate economics.* ○ [+ to] *He was awarded a prize for his contribution to world peace.*

▶ COLLOCATIONS:
a contribution **to** something
make a contribution
a **significant/outstanding/major/positive** contribution

---

con|trol /kəntroʊl/ (controls, controlling, controlled)

1 **NONCOUNT NOUN Control of** an organization, place, or system is the power to make all the important decisions about the way that it is run. ○ [+ of] *The restructuring involves Mr. Ronson giving up control of the company.* ○ [+ over] *The first aim of his government would be to establish control over the republic's territory.* ○ *Nobody knows who is in control of the club.* ○ *All the newspapers were taken under government control.*

2 **NONCOUNT NOUN** If you have **control** of something or someone, you are able to make them do what you want them to do. ○ [+ of] *He lost control of his car.* ○ [+ over] *Some teachers have more control over students than their parents have.*

▶ COLLOCATIONS:
control **of/over** something
control of a **situation/territory/city/vehicle**
control over **spending/resources/timing**
have/take/seize/gain/regain control
lose/relinquish/surrender control

▶ PHRASES:
be in control of something
something is under your control

▶ SYNONYMS: power, command

3 **VERB** The people who **control** an organization or place have the power to make all the important decisions about the way that it is run. ○ *He now controls the largest retail development empire in southern California.* ○ *Almost all of the countries in Latin America were controlled by dictators.* ○ [V-ing] *Minebea sold its controlling interest in both firms.*

▶ COLLOCATIONS:
control a **company/organization/country**
tightly/strictly/carefully controlled

▶ SYNONYMS: manage, direct

con|tro|ver|sy /kɒntrəvɜrsi/ (controversies)

NOUN **Controversy** is a lot of discussion and argument about something, often involving strong feelings of anger or disapproval. ○ *The proposed cuts have caused considerable controversy.* ○ [+ over] *a fierce political controversy over human rights abuses*

▶ **COLLOCATIONS:**
a controversy **over/about/surrounding** *something*
considerable/political controversy
cause/spark controversy

▶ **SYNONYMS:** argument, discussion, debate

con|tro|ver|sial /kɒntrəvɜrʃəl/

ADJECTIVE ○ *Immigration is a controversial issue in many countries.* ○ *The changes are bound to be controversial.* ○ *the controversial 19th century politician Charles Parnell*

▶ **COLLOCATIONS:**
a controversial **decision/plan/proposal/issue/figure**
prove controversial
highly controversial

con|veni|ent /kənviːnyənt/

1 ADJECTIVE If a way of doing something is **convenient**, it is easy, or very useful or suitable for a particular purpose. ○ *a flexible and convenient way of paying for business expenses* ○ [+ to-inf] *Customers find it more convenient to participate online.*

▶ **COLLOCATIONS:**
a convenient **way** of *doing something*
find *something* convenient

▶ **SYNONYM:** handy

2 ADJECTIVE If you describe a place as **convenient**, you are pleased because it is near to where you are, or because you can reach another place from there quickly and easily. ○ [+ for] *The town is well placed for easy access to London and convenient for Heathrow Airport.* ○ *the university's convenient city location*

▶ **COLLOCATIONS:**
a convenient **location**
convenient **access**

con|ven|tion|al /kənvɛnʃənᵊl/

1 **ADJECTIVE** Someone who is **conventional** has behavior or opinions that are ordinary and normal. ○ *a respectable married woman with conventional opinions* ○ *this close, fairly conventional English family*

2 **ADJECTIVE** A **conventional** method or product is one that is usually used or that has been in use for a long time. ○ *These disks hold more than 400 times as much information as a conventional computer floppy disk.*

▶ **COLLOCATIONS:**
conventional **wisdom/thinking/treatment/methods**
conventional **forces/weapons**

▶ **SYNONYMS:** standard, traditional

con|vert /kənvɜrt/ (converts, converting, converted)

1 **VERB** If one thing **is converted** or **converts into** another, it is changed into a different form. ○ [+ into] *The signal will be converted into digital code.* ○ [+ into] *naturally occurring substances which the body can convert into vitamins* ○ [+ to] *Spreadsheet data is automatically converted to a table.*

2 **VERB** If you **convert** a quantity **from** one system of measurement **to** another, you calculate what the quantity is in the second system. ○ [+ to] *Converting metric measurements to U.S. equivalents is easy.*

▶ **COLLOCATIONS:** convert **from** something **to/into** something

▶ **SYNONYMS:** change, transform, alter

con|vey /kənveɪ/ (conveys, conveying, conveyed)

VERB To **convey** information or feelings means to cause them to be known or understood by someone. ○ *Semiological analysis sees a sign as any cultural symbol which conveys a meaning.* ○ *In every one of her pictures she conveys a sense of immediacy.* ○ *He also conveyed his views and the views of the bureaucracy.*

▶ **COLLOCATIONS:**
convey a **sense/impression** of something
convey the **meaning** of something
convey something **vividly/powerfully/accurately**
convey **information/emotion**
convey a **message**

▶ **SYNONYM:** communicate

con|vince /kənvɪns/ (convinces, convincing, convinced)

VERB If someone or something **convinces** you **of** something, they make you believe that it is true or that it exists. ○ [+ of] *We remain to be convinced of the validity of some of the research.* ○ [+ that] *The waste disposal industry is finding it difficult to convince the public that its operations are safe.*

▶ **COLLOCATIONS:**
convince *someone* **of** *something*
convinced **by** *something/someone*
convinced by the **argument/evidence**
convinced of the **merit/importance**
convince the **public/electorate/jury**

cooperate (cooperates, cooperating, cooperated)

VERB If you **cooperate with** someone, you work with them or help them for a particular purpose. You can also say that two people **cooperate**. ○ [+ with] *The U.N. had been cooperating with the State Department on a plan to find countries willing to take the refugees.* ○ [+ in] *It was agreed that the two leaders should cooperate in a joint enterprise.* ○ *The French and British are cooperating more closely than they have for years.*

▶ **COLLOCATIONS:**
cooperate **with** *someone*
cooperate **in** *something*
cooperate **fully**

▶ **SYNONYM:** collaborate

cooperation

NONCOUNT NOUN ○ [+ with] *A deal with Japan could indeed open the door to economic cooperation with East Asia.* ○ [+ by] *Scientists claimed there had been a lack of cooperation by food manufacturers.* ○ *The patient's cooperation is of course essential.*

▶ **COLLOCATIONS:**
cooperation **with/by** *someone*
require/increase/strengthen cooperation
economic/regional/international cooperation
close/full cooperation

▶ **SYNONYMS:** teamwork, collaboration

coordinate (coordinates, coordinating, coordinated)

VERB If you **coordinate** an activity, you organize the various people and
things involved in it. ○ *Government officials visited the earthquake zone to*
coordinate the relief effort. ○ *the setting up of an advisory committee to*
coordinate police work

▶ **COLLOCATIONS:**
  a coordinated **effort/response/approach**
  a coordinated **operation/activity/action/attack**
  centrally/nationally/closely/carefully coordinated

▶ **SYNONYMS:** organize, synchronize

coordination

NONCOUNT NOUN ○ [+ between] *the lack of coordination between the civilian*
and military authorities ○ [+ of] *the coordination of economic policy* ○ [+ of]
Coordination of planning was to be the responsibility of the Group Marketing
Director.

▶ **COLLOCATIONS:**
  coordination **between** *people*
  coordination **of** *something*
  poor/close/good coordination
  physical/hand-eye coordination

▶ **SYNONYMS:** organization, synchronization

cope /koʊp/ (copes, coping, coped)

VERB If you **cope with** a problem or task, you deal with it in a successful way.
○ *She suffers from depression but has learned to cope.* ○ [+ with] *The centers*
were started over a decade ago to help America cope with its trade problem.

▶ **COLLOCATIONS:**
  cope **with** *something*
  cope **admirably/magnificently/effectively**

▶ **SYNONYMS:** deal with, manage, handle

copy|right /kɒpiraɪt/ (copyrights)   `LEGAL`

NOUN If someone has **copyright** on a piece of writing or music, it is illegal
to reproduce or perform it without their permission. ○ *To order a book one*
first had to get permission from the monastery that held the copyright. ○ *She*
threatened legal action against the newspaper for breach of copyright.

▶ **COLLOCATIONS:**
a copyright **on** *something*
a copyright **infringement/violation**
copyright **protection/law**
infringe/violate a copyright
hold/protect a copyright

▶ **PHRASE:** breach of copyright

---

cor|po|rate /kɔ̱rpərɪt, -prɪt/ ORGANIZATION

ADJECTIVE Corporate means relating to business corporations or to a particular business corporation. ○ *top U.S. corporate executives* ○ *the U.K. corporate sector* ○ *a corporate lawyer* ○ *This established a strong corporate image.*

▶ **COLLOCATIONS:**
corporate **finance/business**
a corporate **lawyer/executive/image/body**

---

cor|po|ra|tion /kɔ̱rpəre̱ɪʃ°n/ (corporations) ORGANIZATION

NOUN A **corporation** is a large business or company. ○ *multinational corporations* ○ *the Seiko Corporation*

▶ **COLLOCATIONS:**
a **giant/major** corporation
a **multinational/foreign/private/global** corporation
corporation **tax/law**

▶ **SYNONYMS:** business, company, organization

---

cor|rec|tion /kəre̱kʃ°n/ (corrections)

NOUN The **correction of** a problem, mistake, or fault is the act of making it right. ○ [+ *of*] *legislation to require the correction of factual errors* ○ *We will then make the necessary corrections.*

▶ **COLLOCATIONS:**
the correction **of** *something*
make a correction

---

cor|re|spond|ing /kɔ̱rɪspɒ̱ndɪŋ/

ADJECTIVE Corresponding things have a close similarity or connection between them. ○ *March and April sales this year were up 8 percent on the* *corresponding period in 1992.* ○ *[+ to] Older types of meters show the reading on a series of dials, corresponding to different powers of 10.*

▶ **COLLOCATIONS:**
corresponding **to** *something*
a corresponding **figure/period**
a corresponding **increase/decrease**

▶ **SYNONYMS:** equivalent, matching, related

cost-effective /kɔst ɪfɛktɪv/　　BANKING & FINANCE

ADJECTIVE Cost-effective means saving or making a lot of money in comparison with the costs involved. ○ *The bank must be run in a cost-effective way.* ○ *Going to a state university rather than a private one can be very cost-effective.*

▶ **COLLOCATIONS:**
highly/extremely cost-effective
a cost-effective **solution/alternative/option**

▶ **SYNONYMS:** economical, profitable

counter|offer /kaʊntərɔfər/ (counteroffers)　　BANKING & FINANCE

NOUN A **counteroffer** is an offer that someone makes, for example, for a house or business, in response to an offer by another person or group. ○ *Many would welcome a counteroffer from a foreign bidder.*

▶ **COLLOCATIONS: submit/present/reject** a counteroffer

cov|er let|ter /kʌvər lɛtər/ (cover letters)　　COMMUNICATIONS

NOUN A **cover letter** is a letter that you send with a package or with another letter in order to provide extra information. ○ *Your cover letter creates the employer's first impression of you.* ○ *Always send a cover letter with your application.*

▶ **COLLOCATIONS: send/submit/attach** a cover letter

co-worker /koʊwɜrkər/ (co-workers)　　PERSONNEL

NOUN A **co-worker** is a person who works alongside another. ○ *A co-worker of mine mentioned that the deadline was moved back a week.*

▶ **SYNONYM:** colleague

crash /kræʃ/ (crashes, crashing, crashed)

1 VERB If a computer or a computer program **crashes**, it suddenly stops working. ○ *All of his files were lost when his computer crashed.*

2 VERB If a business or financial system **crashes**, it fails suddenly, often with serious effects. ○ *When the market crashed, they assumed the deal would be cancelled.*

▶ **COLLOCATIONS:** a **company/business/market** crashes

▶ **SYNONYM:** collapse

● **Crash** is also a noun. ○ *He predicted correctly that there was going to be a stock market crash.* ○ [+ in] *a crash in the housing market*

▶ **SYNONYM:** collapse

crea|tive /kriˈeɪtɪv/

ADJECTIVE Someone who is **creative** is good at inventing things and having new ideas. ○ *When you don't have much money, you have to be creative.* ○ *the creative genius behind her husband's success*

▶ **COLLOCATIONS:**
a creative **genius/thinker**
highly/truly/wonderfully creative

▶ **SYNONYMS:** imaginative, inventive, ingenious

cred|ible /ˈkrɛdɪbəl/

ADJECTIVE **Credible** means able to be trusted or believed. ○ [+ to] *Baroness Thatcher's claims seem credible to many.* ○ *But in order to maintain a credible threat of intervention, we have to maintain a credible alliance.*

→ see note at **conclusive**

▶ **COLLOCATIONS:**
credible **to** *someone*
appear/look/sound credible
a credible **threat/claim/witness/theory**
scarcely credible

▶ **SYNONYM:** plausible

cred|it /ˈkrɛdɪt/   `BANKING & FINANCE`

NONCOUNT NOUN If you are given **credit**, you are allowed to pay for goods or services several weeks or months after you have received them.

○ *The group can't get credit to buy farming machinery.* ○ *You can ask a dealer for a discount whether you pay cash or buy on credit.*

▶ COLLOCATIONS:
on credit
buy/get *something* on credit
interest-free credit
credit **card/rating**

cred|it card /krɛdɪt kɑrd/ (credit cards)

NOUN A **credit card** is a card that you use to buy something and pay for it later. ○ *Call this number to order by credit card.* ○ *He worked hard to pay off his credit-card debt.* ○ *The most common credit-card purchases are airline tickets, household appliances and groceries.*

▶ COLLOCATIONS:
a credit card **holder/issuer**
a credit card **bill/payment/balance**
a credit card **purchase/transaction**
credit card **debt/fraud**

▶ RELATED WORD: charge card

criti|cal /krɪtɪkəl/

1 ADJECTIVE To be **critical of** someone or something means to criticize them. ○ [+ of] *His report is highly critical of the trial judge.* ○ *He has apologized for critical remarks he made about the referee.*

▶ COLLOCATIONS:
critical **of** *someone/something*
critical of a **government/regime/policy/decision**
highly critical

▶ SYNONYM: disapproving

2 ADJECTIVE A **critical** approach to something involves examining and judging it carefully. ○ *We need to become critical text-readers.* ○ *Marx's work was more than a critical study of capitalist production.* ○ *the critical analysis of political ideas*

▶ COLLOCATIONS: a critical **analysis/report/study**

▶ SYNONYM: analytical

criti|cize /krɪtɪsaɪz/ (criticizes, criticizing, criticized)

VERB If you **criticize** someone or something, you express your disapproval of them by saying what you think is wrong with them. [in BRIT, also use

criticise] ○ *Human rights groups are criticizing the decision.* ○ [+ *for*] *The regime has been harshly criticized for human rights violations.*

▶ COLLOCATIONS:
criticize someone **for** something
criticize the **government/administration/president**
criticize a **decision/policy/proposal**
sharply/harshly/strongly/widely criticized

criti|cism /krɪtɪsɪzəm/ (criticisms)

1 NOUN **Criticism** is the action of expressing disapproval of something or someone. A **criticism** is a statement that expresses disapproval. ○ *This policy had repeatedly come under strong criticism on Capitol Hill.* ○ [+ *of*] *unfair criticism of his tactics* ○ [+ *that*] *The criticism that the English do not truly care about their children was often voiced.*

▶ COLLOCATIONS:
criticism **of** someone/something
draw/attract/face/reject criticism
strong/public/valid/unfair criticism
harsh/widespread/heavy/sharp criticism

▶ SYNONYM: disapproval

2 NONCOUNT NOUN **Criticism** is a serious examination and judgment of something such as a book or play. ○ *She has published more than 20 books including novels, poetry, and literary criticism.* ○ *academic film criticism*

▶ COLLOCATIONS: **literary/film** criticism

---

crowd|ed /kraʊdɪd/

ADJECTIVE If a place is **crowded**, it is full of people or a lot of people live there. ○ *He peered slowly around the small crowded room.* ○ *The street was crowded and noisy.* ○ [+ *with*] *The old town square was crowded with people.* ○ *a crowded city of 2 million*

▶ COLLOCATIONS:
crowded **with** people
a crowded **bus/street/train**

▶ SYNONYMS: busy, congested

---

cru|cial /kruʃ³l/

ADJECTIVE If you describe something as **crucial**, you mean it is extremely important. ○ *He had administrators under him but made the crucial decisions* *himself.* ○ *the most crucial election campaign for years* ○ [+ to] *Improved consumer confidence is crucial to an economic recovery.*

▶ **COLLOCATIONS:**
crucial **to/for** something
crucial for **survival/development**
a crucial **decision/role/point/question**
a crucial **difference/distinction**
a crucial **element/aspect/factor**

EXTEND YOUR VOCABULARY

You describe something as **crucial** or **critical** if the success of something depends on it. ○ *Intellectual-property law is crucial to economic success.* ○ *Interpersonal skills are critical for the successful personnel manager.*

You say that something is **essential** or **vital** if it is necessary for something to exist or continue. ○ *Jordan promised to trim the city budget without cutting essential services.* ○ *Team leaders play vital roles within the group.*

---

cur|ren|cy /kɜrənsi/ (currencies) `BANKING & FINANCE`

NOUN The money used in a particular country is referred to as its **currency**.
○ *Tourism is the country's top earner of foreign currency.* ○ *More people favor a single European currency than oppose it.*

▶ **COLLOCATIONS:**
European/Asian currencies
a **single** currency
a **foreign/local** currency
currency **exchange**

---

cur|rent /kɜrənt/ (currents)

1 ADJECTIVE Current means happening, being used, or being done at the present time. ○ *The current situation is very different to that in 1990.* ○ *He plans to repeal a number of current policies.*

▶ **COLLOCATIONS:**
the current **situation/system/crisis**
the current **level/rate/price**
the current **owner/president**

▶ **PHRASE:** current affairs

▶ **SYNONYMS:** present, present-day

2 NOUN A **current** is a steady and continuous flowing movement of some of the water in a river, lake, or ocean. ○ [+ of] *The ocean currents of the tropical Pacific travel from east to west.* ○ *The couple was swept away by the strong current.*

3 NOUN A **current** is a steady, flowing movement of air. ○ [+ of] *a current of cool air* ○ *The spores are very light and can be wafted by the slightest air current.*

4 NOUN An electric **current** is a flow of electricity through a wire or circuit. ○ *A powerful electric current is passed through a piece of graphite.* ○ [+ of] *the current of electricity from the stun gun*

▶ **COLLOCATIONS:**
a current **of** something
a current of **air/electricity**
a **strong/ocean** current

---

cus|tom|er /kʌstəmər/ **(customers)**　　**MARKETING & SALES**

NOUN A **customer** is someone who buys goods or services, especially from a store. ○ *Our customers have very tight budgets.* ○ *the quality of customer service* ○ *We also improved our customer satisfaction levels.*

→ see note at **client**

▶ **COLLOCATIONS:**
a **happy/satisfied/loyal/regular/potential** customer
a **broadband/banking/mortgage** customer
attract/encourage customers
customer **service/care/management**
customer **loyalty/feedback/satisfaction/correspondence**
a customer **base**

▶ **SYNONYMS:** client, consumer, buyer, shopper

cus|tom|er ser|vice /kʌstəmər sɜrvɪs/

NONCOUNT NOUN Customer service refers to the way that companies behave toward their customers. ○ *a mail-order business with a strong reputation for customer service* ○ *The firm has an excellent customer service department.*

▶ **COLLOCATIONS:**
provide/improve customer service
a customer service **representative/agent/center**

cus|tom|ize /kʌstəmaɪz/ (customizes, customizing, customized)

VERB If you **customize** something, you change its appearance or features to suit your tastes or needs. [in BRIT, also use **customise**] ○ *a control that allows photographers to customize the camera's basic settings* ○ *The software can be customized to fit any building plan.*

▶ **COLLOCATIONS:**
  customize a **machine**
  customize **software/content**

▶ **SYNONYMS:** adapt, revise

cus|toms /kʌstəmz/ LOGISTICS & DISTRIBUTION

NOUN Customs is the official organization responsible for collecting taxes on goods coming into a country and preventing illegal goods from being brought in. ○ *What right does Customs have to search my car?* ○ *a three-hour delay to go through Customs*

cut and paste /kʌt ən peɪst/ (cuts and pastes, COMMUNICATIONS
cutting and pasting, cut and pasted)

VERB When you **cut and paste** words or pictures on a computer, you remove them from one place and copy them to another place. ○ *She had cut and pasted the entire paragraph.*

▶ **RELATED WORD:** copy and paste

Dd

dam|age /dǽmɪdʒ/ **(damages, damaging, damaged)**

1 **VERB** To **damage** an object means to break it, spoil it physically, or stop it from working properly. ○ *He maliciously damaged a car with a baseball bat.* ○ *The sun can damage your skin.*

2 **VERB** To **damage** something means to cause it to become less good, pleasant, or successful. ○ *Jackson doesn't want to damage his reputation as a political personality.* ○ *He warned that the action was damaging the economy.*

▶ **COLLOCATIONS:**
damage a **building/vehicle**
damage **the environment**
damage *someone's* **brain/ligaments/knee/ankle**
damage *someone's* **prospects/reputation/credibility**
badly/severely/seriously/permanently damage *something*

▶ **SYNONYMS:** harm, injure

3 **NONCOUNT NOUN Damage** is physical harm that is caused to an object. ○ [+ *to*] *The blast caused extensive damage to the house.* ○ *Many professional boxers end their careers with brain damage.*

4 **NONCOUNT NOUN Damage** consists of the unpleasant effects that something has on a person, situation, or type of activity. ○ [+ *to*] *Incidents of this type cause irreparable damage to relations with the community.* ○ *Adhering to the new rules meant inflicting serious damage on auto racing.*

▶ **COLLOCATIONS:**
damage **to** *something*
cause/do/inflict damage
suffer/sustain damage
assess/repair damage
prevent/minimize/avoid/limit damage
structural/environmental/criminal damage
brain/ligament/liver/nerve damage
flood/storm/smoke damage

bad/severe/serious/extensive/substantial damage
permanent/irreparable damage

▶ SYNONYMS: harm, injury

USAGE: *damage, harm* or *injure?*

You usually talk about **damaging** an object, a situation, or a relationship, but not a person. ○ *If the goods are damaged, you should contact the company.*

▶ damage a **building/vehicle**

▶ damage **the environment/economy**

▶ damage *someone's* **reputation/credibility**

You can talk about **harming** a person or an animal, a situation, or a relationship, but not normally an object

▶ harm **the environment/wildlife**

▶ harm **relations/a reputation**

You talk about **injuring** a person or a part of the body.

▶ injure a **person/passenger/driver**

▶ injure your **knee/shoulder/ankle**

---

dam|ag|ing /dæmɪdʒɪŋ/

ADJECTIVE ○ *We can see the damaging effects of pollution in cities.*

▶ COLLOCATIONS:
damaging **effects/impact/consequences**
damaging **information/allegations/evidence/revelations**
politically/environmentally damaging
highly/extremely/potentially/particularly damaging

▶ SYNONYM: harmful

---

dan|ger|ous /deɪndʒərəs, deɪndʒrəs/

ADJECTIVE If something is **dangerous**, it is likely to harm you. ○ *We're in a very dangerous situation.* ○ *a dangerous breed of dog*

▶ COLLOCATIONS:
extremely/potentially/particularly dangerous
a dangerous **condition/situation/time/person/place**

a dangerous **weapon/game/job**
dangerous **driving**

▶ **SYNONYM:** hazardous

dar|ing /dɛ̱ərɪŋ/

ADJECTIVE If something is **daring**, it is brave and potentially dangerous.
○ *Mr. McGee had daring plans to triple the size of the airline's fleet.*

▶ **COLLOCATIONS:** a daring **raid/rescue/mission/move/attempt/plan**

▶ **SYNONYM:** bold

da|ta /de̱ɪtə, dæ̱tə/ COMMUNICATIONS

1 NONCOUNT NOUN You can refer to information as **data**, especially when it is in the form of facts or statistics that you can analyze. ○ [+ *from*] *The study was based on data from 2,100 women.*

2 NONCOUNT NOUN Data is information that can be stored and used by a computer program. ○ *You can compress huge amounts of data onto a CD-ROM.*

▶ **COLLOCATIONS:**
data **from** *people/things*
store/collect/collate/analyze/delete data
raw/primary data
data **protection/collection/transmission**
data **suggest/show/indicate** *things*

▶ **SYNONYMS:** information, figures, statistics

day|time /de̱ɪtaɪm/

NOUN The **daytime** is the part of a day between the time when it gets light and the time when it gets dark. ○ *He rarely went anywhere in the daytime.*

▶ **COLLOCATIONS:** daytime **temperatures/traffic/TV/activities**

▶ **RELATED WORD:** nighttime

dead|line /dɛ̱dlaɪn/ (deadlines) OFFICE

NOUN A **deadline** is a time or date before which a particular task must be finished or a particular thing must be done. ○ *We were not able to meet the deadline because of manufacturing delays.*

▶ **COLLOCATIONS:**
  meet/set/miss/extend/impose a deadline
  a deadline **passes/approaches/expires**
  a **tight/final** deadline
  a **filing/registration** deadline
  a **midnight/midday/Friday** deadline

d

deal /dil/ (deals)

NOUN A **deal** is an agreement or arrangement, especially in business.
  ○ *They made a deal to share the money between them.*

▶ **COLLOCATIONS:**
  a **business/financial/licensing/trade** deal
  a **book/record** deal
  make/strike/reach/close/conclude/seal/clinch/cut a deal
  arrange/negotiate a deal
  a **major/great/lucrative/exclusive** deal
  a deal **worth** *x dollars*

▶ **PHRASE:** the terms of the deal

deal|ings /dilɪŋz/

PLURAL NOUN Someone's **dealings with** a person or organization are the
  relations that they have with them or the business that they do with
  them. ○ [+ *with*] *He has learned little in his dealings with the international
  community.*

▶ **COLLOCATIONS:**
  dealings **with** *someone*
  extensive/day-to-day/future dealings
  business/financial/personal dealings

de|bate /dɪbeɪt/ (debates, debating, debated)   COMMUNICATIONS

1 NOUN A **debate** is a discussion about a subject on which people have
  different views. ○ *An intense debate is going on within the Israeli government.*
  ○ [+ *about*] *There has been a lot of debate among scholars about this.*

▶ **COLLOCATIONS:** ·
  a debate **on/over/about/within** *something*
  a debate on a **subject/issue**
  a **heated/lively/intense/ongoing** debate
  a **televised/public/political** debate
  spark/provoke/trigger a debate

▶ **SYNONYMS:** discussion, argument

2 **VERB** If people **debate** a topic, they discuss it fairly formally, putting forward different views. ○ *The United Nations Security Council will debate the issue today.* ○ *[+ whether] Scholars have debated whether or not Yagenta became a convert.*

▶ **COLLOCATIONS:**
debate *something* **with** *someone*
scholars/historians/scientists debate
debate a **matter/topic/issue**
hotly debated

▶ **SYNONYMS:** discuss, argue

---

deb|it /dɛbɪt/ (debits, debiting, debited)   **BANKING & FINANCE**

VERB When your bank **debits** your account, money is taken from it and paid to someone else. ○ *We will always confirm the revised amount to you in writing before debiting your account.*

▶ **COLLOCATIONS:**
debit an **account**
debit an **amount**
money is debited
automatically debit

▶ **RELATED WORD:** credit

deb|it card /dɛbɪt kɑrd/ (debit cards)

NOUN A **debit card** is a bank card that you can use to pay for things.

▶ **COLLOCATIONS:**
a debit card **transaction**
a **bank** debit card
use a debit card

▶ **RELATED WORD:** credit card

---

debt /dɛt/ (debts)   **BANKING & FINANCE**

1 **NOUN** A **debt** is a sum of money that you owe someone. ○ *consumers struggling to repay outstanding debts* ○ *reducing the country's $18 billion foreign debt*

2 **NONCOUNT NOUN** **Debt** is the state of owing money. ○ *Debt is a main reason for stress.* ○ *He was already deeply in debt through gambling losses.*

▶ **COLLOCATIONS:**
a debt **of** $x
in debt

owe/incur/repay/pay off a debt
foreign/long-term/outstanding/crippling debt
gambling/household/mortgage/credit-card debts
debt **repayment/relief/burden**

▶ **SYNONYM:** deficit

---

dec|ade /dɛkeɪd/ (decades)

NOUN A **decade** is a period of ten years, especially one that begins with a year ending in 0, for example 1980 to 1989. ○ *the last decade of the nineteenth century*

▶ **COLLOCATIONS:**
the **last/next** decade
recent/past/previous decades
a decade **later/earlier/ago**
decades **of** *something*
decades of **war/conflict/neglect**

▶ **RELATED WORD:** century

---

de|ceive /dɪsiːv/ (deceives, deceiving, deceived)

1 VERB If you **deceive** someone, you make them believe something that is not true, usually in order to get some advantage for yourself. ○ *He has deceived and disillusioned us all.*

▶ **COLLOCATIONS: cruelly/deliberately** deceive

2 VERB If something **deceives** you, it gives you a wrong impression and makes you believe something that is not true. ○ *Do not be deceived by claims on food labels like "light" or "low fat."*

▶ **COLLOCATION: easily** deceived

▶ **PHRASE:** do not be deceived

▶ **SYNONYM:** mislead

de|cep|tion /dɪsɛpʃⁿn/

NONCOUNT NOUN ○ *He admitted conspiring to obtain property by deception.*

▶ **COLLOCATIONS:**
use deception
deliberate/willful/cruel deception

▶ **PHRASE:** obtain by deception

de|cent /diːsᵊnt/

ADJECTIVE **Decent** is used to describe something that is considered to be of an acceptable standard or quality. ○ *He didn't get a decent explanation.*

▶ **COLLOCATIONS:**
a decent **job/wage/salary/income/price**
a decent **meal**
a decent **player/team/performance**
pretty/perfectly/fairly decent

▶ **SYNONYMS:** acceptable, adequate, passable, reasonable

de|cep|tive /dɪsɛptɪv/

ADJECTIVE If something is **deceptive**, it makes you believe something that is not true. ○ *The organizers claimed that deals worth $1.4 billion had been made, but those figures are deceptive.*

▶ **COLLOCATIONS:**
deceptive **advertising/practices/conduct**
figures are deceptive

▶ **SYNONYM:** misleading

▶ **PHRASE:** appearances can be deceptive

de|cide /dɪsaɪd/ (decides, deciding, decided)

1 VERB If you **decide** to do something, you choose to do it, usually after you have thought carefully about the other possibilities. ○ [+ to-inf] *She decided to take a course in philosophy.* ○ [+ that] *He has decided that he will step down as leader.*

▶ **COLLOCATIONS:** decide **in favor of/against** *something*

2 VERB If a person or group of people **decides** something, they choose what something should be like or how a particular problem should be solved. ○ *The judge would take her age into account when deciding her sentence.* ○ *This is an issue that should be decided by local government.*

▶ **COLLOCATIONS:**
a **court/judge/jury** decides *something*
a **government/board/committee** decides *something*
decide *someone's* **fate/future**
decide the **matter/issue/outcome**
decide a **case/sentence**

3 VERB If you **decide** that something is true, you form that opinion about it after considering the facts. ○ [+ that] *The government decided that the* *company represented a security risk.* ○ [+ whether] *The committee has to decide whether the applicant is trustworthy.*

de|ci|sion /dɪsɪʒ³n/ (decisions)

NOUN ○ [+ to-inf] *A decision was made to discipline Marshall.* ○ *I don't want to make the wrong decision and regret it later.* ○ [+ on] *A final decision on this issue is long overdue.* ○ *The moment of decision cannot be delayed.*

▶ **COLLOCATIONS:**
  a decision **about/on** something
  make/reach a decision
  a **tough/difficult/hard** decision
  a **final/important/major/controversial/unanimous** decision
  the **right/wrong** decision
  the **government's/court's/judge's** decision

▶ **SYNONYMS:** judgment, conclusion, finding

decision-making /dɪsɪʒ³nmeɪkɪŋ/

NONCOUNT NOUN Decision-making is the process of reaching decisions, especially in a large organization or in government. ○ *She wants to see more women involved in decision-making.*

▶ **COLLOCATIONS:**
  corporate decision-making
  effective decision-making
  a decision-making **body**
  the decision-making **process**
  decision-making **ability/powers**

---

de|clare /dɪklɛər/ (declares, declaring, declared)

VERB If you **declare** something, you state officially and formally that it exists or is the case. ○ *The government is ready to declare a permanent ceasefire.* ○ *His lawyers are confident that the judges will declare Mr. Stevens innocent.* ○ *The U.N. has declared it to be a safe zone.*

▶ **COLLOCATIONS:**
  declare a **ceasefire/truce/emergency**
  declare **war**
  declare something **unsafe/illegal/invalid**
  declare someone **dead/bankrupt**
  officially/formally/publicly declare

▶ **SYNONYMS:** assert, state, pronounce

de|cline /dɪklaɪn/ (declines, declining, declined)

1 **VERB** If something **declines**, it becomes less in quantity, importance, or strength. ○ [+ from] *The number of staff has declined from 217,000 to 114,000.* ○ *Hourly output by workers declined 1.3% in the first quarter.* ○ [V-ing] *a declining birthrate*

▶ **COLLOCATIONS:**
   decline **from** *x* **to** *y*
   decline **by** *x*
   decline **in** *something*
   decline in **value/importance/popularity**
   steadily/rapidly/sharply decline

2 **NOUN** If there is a **decline in** something, it becomes less in quantity, importance, or quality. ○ [+ in] *The reasons for the apparent decline in fertility are unclear.* ○ *Rome's decline in the fifth century* ○ *The first signs of economic decline became visible.*

▶ **COLLOCATIONS:**
   a decline **in** *something*
   a decline in **value/sales/revenue/population/fertility**
   experience/suffer/report/reverse a decline
   a **market/economic/population** decline
   a **steep/sharp/rapid/gradual** decline

EXTEND YOUR VOCABULARY

You use **decrease** or **reduce** to talk about things becoming less in size or intensity.

▶ decrease/reduce the **amount/risk/likelihood/incidence**

You use **decline** to talk about something becoming less in size, importance, or quality, often in a way that is considered negative.

▶ **sales/revenues/exports** decline

▶ **popularity/attendance/output** declines

---

deco|rate /dɛkəreɪt/ (decorates, decorating, decorated)

VERB If you **decorate** something, you make it more attractive by adding things to it. ○ [+ with] *He decorated his room with pictures of all his favorite sports figures.*

▶ **COLLOCATIONS:**
   decorate *something* **with** *something*

decorate the **room/walls/house**
decorate a **Christmas tree/cake/gift**
highly/beautifully/tastefully/elaborately decorated

deco|ra|tion

NONCOUNT NOUN ○ *The renovation and decoration took four months.*

▶ **COLLOCATION: interior** decoration

deco|ra|tive /dɛkərətɪv, -əreɪtɪv/

ADJECTIVE ○ *The drapes are only decorative — they don't open or close.*

▶ **COLLOCATIONS:**
decorative **items**
highly/richly decorative
only/purely decorative

---

de|crease (decreases, decreasing, decreased)

The verb is pronounced /dɪˈkriːs/. The noun is pronounced /ˈdiːkriːs/.

1 VERB When something **decreases** or when you **decrease** it, it becomes less in quantity, size, or intensity. ○ [+ by] *Population growth is decreasing by 1.4% each year.* ○ [+ from/to] *The number of independent businesses decreased from 198 to 96.* ○ *Gradually decrease the amount of vitamin C you are taking.*

▶ **COLLOCATIONS:**
decrease **in/by** *something*
decrease **from** *x* **to** *y*
significantly/dramatically decrease
slightly/steadily/gradually decrease
decrease the **risk/likelihood/incidence** of *something*

▶ **SYNONYMS:** lower, reduce, fall, drop, decline

2 NOUN A **decrease in** the quantity, size, or intensity of something is a reduction in it. ○ [+ in] *a decrease in the number of young people out of work* ○ [+ of] *Prime rates have fallen from 10 percent to 6 percent – a decrease of 4 percent.*

▶ **COLLOCATIONS:**
a decrease **in/by** *something*
a decrease **of** *x*
a decrease in *size/value*
a **significant/slight/dramatic/sharp/marked** decrease
see/expect/show/report a decrease

▶ **SYNONYMS:** reduction, fall, drop, decline, loss

EXTEND YOUR VOCABULARY

You use **decrease** and **reduce** to talk about things becoming less or smaller in many different contexts.

▸ decrease/reduce the **amount/risk/likelihood/effectiveness**

You use **fall**, **drop**, and **lower** to talk about a number, rate, or level becoming less.

▸ the **price/rate** falls/drops

▸ **profits/revenues/sales** fall/drop

▸ lower the **price/rate/level/cost/limit**

You use **decline** to talk about something becoming less, usually in a way that is negative. ○ *Sales declined by 2.4% over the month of September.*

---

dedi|cate /dɛdɪkeɪt/ (dedicates, dedicating, dedicated)

VERB If someone **dedicates** a book, a play, or a piece of music **to** you, they say on the first page that they have written it for you. ○ [+ to] *She dedicated her first book to her sons.*

▸ COLLOCATIONS:
  dedicate something **to** someone
  dedicate a **book/poem/song/play/performance/show**

dedi|ca|tion /dɛdɪkeɪʃⁿn/ (dedications)

NOUN ○ *I read the dedication at the beginning of the book.*

▸ COLLOCATION: a **book's** dedication

---

de|duce /dɪdus/ (deduces, deducing, deduced)

VERB If you **deduce** something or **deduce** that something is true, you reach that conclusion because of other things that you know to be true. ○ [+ that] *The observations led the team to deduce that the two clusters approached one another from a different direction.* ○ [+ from] *The date of the document can be deduced from references to the Civil War.* ○ *The researchers have to analyze a huge amount of information in order to deduce any conclusions.*

▸ COLLOCATIONS:
  deduce something **from** something
  deduce something from a **fact/observation**
  deduce a **pattern/hypothesis/conclusion**

deduce the **existence/presence** of *something*
correctly/logically deduce

---

de|duct /dɪdʌkt/ (deducts, deducting, deducted)   BANKING & FINANCE

VERB When you **deduct** an amount from a total, you subtract it from the
total. ○ [+ from] *The company deducted this payment from his compensation.*
○ [+ for] *Up to 5% of grades on the exams will be deducted for spelling mistakes.*

▸ **COLLOCATIONS:**
deduct *something* **from/for** *something*
deduct *something* from a **salary/income/amount/account**
deduct a **cost/amount/fee/point**
deduct **expenses/payment/tax**
automatically/electronically deducted

▸ **SYNONYM:** subtract

---

de|duct|ible /dɪdʌktɪbəl/ (deductibles)   BANKING & FINANCE

1 **ADJECTIVE** **Deductible** is the same as **tax-deductible**. ○ *Part of the
auto-loan interest is deductible as a business expense.*

▸ **COLLOCATIONS:**
a deductible **expense/contribution/amount/loss**
fully deductible

2 **NOUN** A **deductible** is a sum of money that you have to pay toward the
cost of an insurance claim when the insurance company pays the rest.
○ *Each time they go to a hospital, they have to pay a deductible of $628.*

▸ **COLLOCATIONS:**
pay a deductible
a **high/large/low/small** deductible
an **annual** deductible

---

deep|en /diːpən/ (deepens, deepening, deepened)

VERB If an emotion or a feeling **deepens**, it becomes stronger or more
noticeable. ○ *Her feelings for him had deepened in recent months.* ○ *the
deepening conflict in the region*

▸ **COLLOCATIONS:**
emotions/feelings deepen
love/understanding/depression/fear deepens
a **friendship/relationship** deepens
a **crisis/scandal/conflict/recession** deepens

▸ **SYNONYM:** heighten

de|fault /dɪfɔ̱lt/

1 **ADJECTIVE** A **default** situation is what exists or happens unless someone or something changes it. ○ *default passwords installed on commercial machines* ○ *Death, not life, is the default state of cells.*

2 **NONCOUNT NOUN** In computing, the **default** is a particular set of instructions that the computer always uses unless the person using the computer gives other instructions. ○ *The default is usually the setting that most users would probably choose.* ○ *advising consumers to change default settings*

▶ **COLLOCATIONS:**
  a default **password/rate/setting**
  a default **mode/state/option**

▶ **SYNONYM:** standard

de|fec|tive /dɪfɛ̱ktɪv/

ADJECTIVE If something is **defective**, it has faults and is not working properly. ○ *the cost of the defective equipment*

▶ **COLLOCATIONS:**
  defective **equipment/merchandise/goods**
  a defective **part/product/system/car**

▶ **SYNONYM:** faulty

de|fend /dɪfɛ̱nd/ (defends, defending, defended)

VERB When a lawyer **defends** a person who has been accused of something, the lawyer argues on their behalf in a court of law that the charges are not true. ○ *a lawyer who defended political prisoners during the military regime* ○ [+ against] *He has hired a lawyer to defend him against the allegations.*

▶ **COLLOCATIONS:**
  defend *someone* **against** *something*
  defend *someone* against a **charge/allegation/lawsuit**

de|fense /dɪfɛ̱ns/ (defenses)

1 **NOUN** In a court of law, an accused person's **defense** is the process of presenting evidence in their favor. ○ *He has insisted on conducting his own defense.*

2 **NOUN** The **defense** is the case that is presented by a lawyer in a trial for the person who has been accused of a crime. You can also refer to this

person's lawyers as **the defense**. ○ *The defense was that the records of the interviews were fabricated by the police.* ○ *The defense pleaded insanity.*

▶ **COLLOCATIONS:**
the defense **argues/claims/alleges** *something*
conduct *someone's* defense
a defense **lawyer/attorney**

---

de|fi|cien|cy /dɪfɪʃənsi/ (deficiencies) `HEALTH & FITNESS`

NOUN A **deficiency** that someone or something has is a weakness or imperfection in them. ○ *The company was financially liable for any design or manufacturing deficiencies..* ○ [+ in] *a serious deficiency in our air defense*

▶ **COLLOCATIONS:**
a deficiency **in/of** *something*
a deficiency in/of a **system**
a **structural/procedural** deficiency
a **severe/serious/glaring/chronic** deficiency
identify/address a deficiency
remedy/rectify/correct a deficiency

▶ **SYNONYMS:** weakness, imperfection, inadequacy

---

defi|cit /dɛfəsɪt/ (deficits) `BANKING & FINANCE`

NOUN A **deficit** is the amount by which something is less than what is required or expected, especially the amount by which the total money received is less than the total money spent. ○ *They're ready to cut the federal budget deficit for the next fiscal year.* ○ [+ of] *a deficit of 3.275 billion dollars* ○ *The current account of the balance of payments is in deficit.*

▶ **COLLOCATIONS:**
in deficit
a deficit **of** $x
cut/reduce/overcome a deficit
a deficit **rises/grows/widens/narrows**
a **fiscal/federal/budget** deficit
a **trade/current-account** deficit

▶ **SYNONYM:** shortage

---

de|fine /dɪfaɪn/ (defines, defining, defined)

1 VERB If you **define** something, you show, describe, or state clearly what it is and what its limits are, or what it is like. ○ [+ what] *We were unable to define what exactly was wrong with him.* ○ *a musical era when genres were less narrowly defined*

2 **VERB** If you **define** a word or expression, you explain its meaning, for example, in a dictionary. ○ [+ as] Collins English Dictionary defines a workaholic as "a person obsessively addicted to work."

▶ **COLLOCATIONS:**
define something **as/in terms of** something
define a **term/concept**
a **rule/law** defines something
clearly/narrowly/broadly defined

▶ **SYNONYMS:** explain, expound, interpret

defi|nite /dɛfɪnɪt/

1 **ADJECTIVE** If something such as a decision or an arrangement is **definite**, it is firm and clear, and unlikely to be changed. ○ It's too soon to give a definite answer. ○ She made no definite plans for her future.

2 **ADJECTIVE** **Definite** evidence or information is true, rather than being someone's opinion or guess. ○ We didn't have any definite proof. ○ There is no definite conclusion that can be reached from these studies. ○ The police had nothing definite against her.

3 **ADJECTIVE** You use **definite** to emphasize the strength of your opinion or belief. ○ There has already been a definite improvement. ○ That's a very definite possibility.

▶ **COLLOCATIONS:**
definite **proof/evidence**
a definite **answer/conclusion/diagnosis**
a definite **advantage/possibility/improvement**

▶ **SYNONYMS:** certain, definitive, conclusive, real

defi|nite|ly /dɛfɪnɪtli/

ADVERB You use **definitely** to emphasize that something is the case, or to emphasize the strength of your intention or opinion. ○ I'm definitely going to get in touch with these people. ○ While intra-region trade in Asia has definitely improved, the pace of recovery in individual economies has been uneven.

▶ **SYNONYM:** certainly

defi|ni|tion /dɛfɪnɪʃ°n/ (definitions)

NOUN A **definition** is a statement giving the meaning of a word or expression, especially in a dictionary. ○ [+ of] There is no general agreement on a standard definition of intelligence. ○ Human perception is highly imperfect and by definition subjective.

▶ **COLLOCATIONS:**
  by definition
  a definition **of** *something*
  a **dictionary/textbook/legal** definition
  a **precise/broad/narrow/clear** definition
  broaden/clarify/propose/change a definition

▶ **SYNONYMS:** explanation, interpretation

---

de|gree /dɪɡriː/ **(degrees)**

1 **NOUN** A **degree** is a unit of measurement that is used to measure temperatures. It is often written as °, for example, 23°. ○ *It's over 80 degrees outside.* ○ *Pure water sometimes does not freeze until it reaches minus 40 degrees Fahrenheit.*

  ▶ **COLLOCATIONS:** degrees **Fahrenheit/Celsius/centigrade**

2 **NOUN** A **degree** is a unit of measurement that is used to measure angles. It is often written as °, for example, 23°. ○ *It was pointing outward at an angle of 45 degrees.*

3 **NOUN** A **degree** at a university or college is a title or qualification that you get when you have completed a course of study there. ○ *He earned a master's degree in economics at Yale.* ○ *an engineering degree*

  ▶ **COLLOCATIONS:**
    a degree **in** *something*
    a degree **from** a *university*
    earn/get/receive a degree
    award *someone* a degree
    complete/pursue a degree
    an **undergraduate/graduate** degree
    a **college/bachelor's/master's/honorary** degree
    a **law/science/engineering** degree

  ▶ **RELATED WORD:** diploma

4 **NOUN** You use **degree** to indicate the extent to which something happens or is the case, or the amount which something is felt. ○ [+ *of*] *These manmade barriers will ensure a very high degree of protection.* ○ [+ *of*] *Politicians have used television with varying degrees of success.*

  ▶ **COLLOCATIONS:**
    a degree **of** *something*
    a degree of **certainty/accuracy/autonomy/flexibility**
    a **varying/high** degree

  ▶ **SYNONYMS:** amount, extent

5 **PHRASE** You use expressions such as **to some degree**, **to a large degree**, or **to a certain degree** in order to indicate that something is partly true, but not entirely true. ○ *These statements are, to some degree, all correct.* ○ *It is impossible to make these points without generalizing to a certain degree.*

▶ **SYNONYM:** to some extent

6 **PHRASE** You use expressions such as **to what degree** and **to the degree that** when you are discussing how true a statement is, or in what ways it is true. ○ *To what degree would you say you had control over things that went on?* ○ *The valves may scar and thicken to the degree that they may fail to open completely or close properly.*

▶ **SYNONYMS:** to what extent, to the extent that

---

de|lay /dɪleɪ/ (delays, delaying, delayed)

1 **VERB** If you **delay** doing something, you do not do it immediately or at the planned or expected time, but you leave it until later. ○ *The disclosures forced it to delay publication of its annual report.*

2 **VERB** To **delay** someone or something means to make them late or to slow them down. ○ *The therapy is known to delay the onset of osteoporosis.* ○ *Various setbacks and problems delayed production.*

▶ **COLLOCATIONS:**
delay the **onset/start** of *something*
delay the **implementation/introduction** of *something*
delay a **decision/announcement/delivery**
delay **publication/production**
delay **indefinitely**

▶ **SYNONYMS:** postpone, slow

3 **NOUN** If there is a **delay**, something does not happen until later than planned or expected. ○ [+ in] *The delay in the implementation of the law has dismayed businesses.* ○ *Although the tests have caused some delay, flights should be back to normal soon.*

▶ **COLLOCATIONS:**
a delay **in** *something*
a delay in **payment/implementation/completion**
a **flight/traffic** delay
cause/experience/avoid a delay
a **lengthy/further/unnecessary/bureaucratic/slight** delay

▶ **SYNONYM:** setback

del|egate (delegates, delegating, delegated)   `PERSONNEL`

> The noun is pronounced /dɛlɪgɪt/. The verb is pronounced /dɛlɪgeɪt/.

1 NOUN A **delegate** is a person who is chosen to vote or make decisions on behalf of a group of other people, especially at a conference or a meeting. ○ *a meeting attended by delegates from 35 countries*

▶ **COLLOCATIONS: convention/party/union/conference** delegates

▶ **SYNONYM:** representative

2 VERB If you **delegate** duties, responsibilities, or power **to** someone, you give them those duties, those responsibilities, or that power so that they can act on your behalf. ○ [+ to] *He talks of traveling less, and delegating more authority to his deputies.*

▶ **COLLOCATIONS:**
delegate *something* **to** *someone*
delegate **authority/duties/responsibilities/power**

del|ega|tion

NONCOUNT NOUN ○ [+ of] *A key factor in running a business is the delegation of responsibility.*

▶ **COLLOCATIONS:**
delegation **of** *something*
delegation of **power/responsibility**

---

deli|cate /dɛlɪkɪt/

1 ADJECTIVE If something is **delicate**, it is easy to harm, damage, or break, and needs to be handled or treated carefully. ○ *Although the coral looks hard, it is very delicate.*

▶ **COLLOCATIONS:** delicate **flowers/fabrics/skin/hands**

▶ **SYNONYM:** fragile

2 ADJECTIVE You use **delicate** to describe a situation, problem, matter, or discussion that needs to be dealt with carefully and sensitively in order to avoid upsetting things or offending people. ○ *Ottawa and Washington have to find a delicate balance between the free flow of commerce and legitimate security concerns.*

▶ **COLLOCATIONS:**
a delicate **situation/problem/issue/matter/question**
delicate **negotiations/discussions**
a delicate **balance**
delicate **sensibilities**

de|light|ed /dɪlaɪtɪd/

1 **ADJ** If you are **delighted**, you are extremely pleased and excited about something. ○ [+ to-inf] *I know Frank will be delighted to see you.*

2 **ADJ** If someone invites or asks you to do something, you can say that you would be **delighted** to do it, as a way of showing that you are very willing to do it. ○ *"You have to come to Todd's graduation party." — "I'd be delighted."*

▶ **COLLOCATIONS**: **absolutely/genuinely/obviously** delighted

▶ **SYNONYMS**: thrilled, pleased

BUSINESS CORRESPONDENCE: Writing about good news

Several common adjectives are used to talk about good news in business correspondence, including **pleased**, **happy**, **glad**, and **delighted**. ○ *I am happy to tell you that your application has been successful.* ○ *We are pleased to inform you that we have availability for those dates.* ○ *We would be delighted to host your event.* ○ *I'm glad to hear that you found the session useful.*

---

de|liv|er /dɪlɪvər/ (delivers, delivering, delivered)

LOGISTICS & DISTRIBUTION

VERB If you **deliver** something somewhere, you take it there. ○ *Only 90% of first-class mail is delivered on time.*

▶ **COLLOCATIONS**:
deliver *something* **to** *someone/somewhere*
deliver a **package/letter/mail**
a **company/store/messenger** delivers
deliver **daily/direct**

de|liv|ery /dɪlɪvəri/ (deliveries)

NOUN A **delivery** is an occasion when goods or mail are delivered. ○ [+ of] *We are waiting for a delivery of new parts.*

▶ **COLLOCATIONS**:
delivery **of** *something*
delivery of **mail/goods**
fast/overnight/free delivery
a delivery **charge/date/service**
take/accept delivery
make a delivery
expect/receive/arrange a delivery

de|mand /dɪmænd/   `MARKETING & SALES`

NONCOUNT NOUN If you refer to **demand**, or to the **demand for**
something, you are referring to how many people want to have it, do it,
or buy it. ○ *Another flight would be arranged if sufficient demand arose.*
○ [+ *for*] *Demand for coal is down.*

▸ **COLLOCATIONS:**
  demand **for** *something*
  demand for **goods/electricity/housing**
  domestic/global demand
  high/strong/sluggish/growing demand
  stimulate/boost/fuel/create/reduce/dampen demand
  meet/satisfy demand
  demand **soars/slows/grows**
  demand **exceeds/outstrips** *something*

▸ **PHRASE:** supply and demand

de|mo|graph|ic /dɛməgræfɪk/   `MARKETING & SALES`
(demographics)

1 ADJECTIVE Demographic means relating to or concerning the people
who live in an area. ○ *The final impact of industrialization on the family was
demographic.* ○ *the relationship between economic and demographic change*

▸ **COLLOCATIONS:**
  a demographic **change/shift/trend/transition**
  a demographic **profile**

2 PLURAL NOUN The **demographics** of a place or society are the statistics
relating to the people who live there. ○ [+ *of*] *the changing demographics of
the United States*

▸ **COLLOCATIONS:**
  the demographics **of** *something/somewhere*
  changing/shifting demographics

3 NOUN In business, a **demographic** is a group of people in a society,
especially people in a particular age group. ○ *Most of our listeners are in the
25-39 demographic.* ○ *well-read individuals, the target demographic of this
newspaper section*

▸ **COLLOCATIONS:**
  the **key/target/core** demographic
  the **consumer/audience/age** demographic

de|mol|ish /dɪmɒlɪʃ/ (demolishes, demolishing, demolished)

VERB To **demolish** something such as a building means to destroy it completely. ○ *A storm moved directly over the island, demolishing buildings and flooding streets.*

▶ **COLLOCATIONS:** demolish a **building/house/wall**

demo|li|tion /dɛməlɪʃⁿn/ (demolitions)

NOUN The **demolition** of a structure, for example, a building, is the act of deliberately destroying it, often in order to build something else in its place. ○ [+ of] *The project required the total demolition of the old bridge.*

▶ **COLLOCATIONS:**
the demolition **of** something
the demolition of a **building/house/bridge/structure**

▶ **PHRASE:** due for demolition

dem|on|strate /dɛmənstreɪt/ (demonstrates, demonstrating, demonstrated)

1 VERB To **demonstrate** a fact means to make it clear to people.
○ *The study also demonstrated a direct link between obesity and mortality.*
○ [+ that] *His experiments demonstrated that plants alter their shape at night.*
○ [+ to] *They are anxious to demonstrate to the voters that they have practical policies.*

2 VERB If you **demonstrate** something, you show people how it works or how to do it. ○ *The BBC has just successfully demonstrated a new digital radio transmission system.* ○ [+ to] *He demonstrated the prototype to a group of senior officers.*

▶ **COLLOCATIONS:**
demonstrate something **to** someone
a **study/experiment** demonstrates something
amply/conclusively/convincingly/clearly demonstrate

▶ **SYNONYMS:** show, prove, display

dem|on|stra|tion /dɛmənstreɪʃⁿn/ (demonstrations)

1 NOUN A **demonstration** of something is a talk by someone who shows you how to do it or how it works. ○ *a cooking demonstration* ○ [+ of] *demonstrations of new products*

2 NOUN A **demonstration of** a fact or situation is a clear proof of it. ○ [+ of] *This is a clear demonstration of how technology has changed.*

▶ **COLLOCATIONS:**
a demonstration **of** *something*
a demonstration of **support/power/unity/commitment**
a **practical/hands-on** demonstration

▶ **SYNONYMS:** explanation, proof

---

d

dense /dɛns/ (denser, densest)

1 ADJECTIVE Something that is **dense** contains a lot of things or people in a small area. ○ *Where Bucharest now stands, there once was a large, dense forest.* ○ *an area of dense immigrant population*

▶ **COLLOCATIONS:**
a dense **forest/jungle/thicket/rainforest**
a dense **population/crowd/area/network**
dense **foliage/undergrowth**

▶ **SYNONYM:** compressed

2 ADJECTIVE In science, a **dense** substance is very heavy in relation to its volume. ○ *a small, dense star* ○ *The densest ocean water is the coldest and most saline.*

den|sity /dɛnsɪti/ (densities)

1 NOUN Density is the extent to which something is filled or covered with people or things. ○ [+ *of*] *a law which restricts the density of housing* ○ *The region has a very high population density.*

2 NOUN In science, the **density** of a substance or object is the relation of its mass or weight to its volume. ○ *Jupiter's moon Io, whose density is 3.5 grams per cubic centimeter, is all rock.* ○ [+ *of*] *assessing the temperature, heat capacity, density, and hardness of Mercury's surface*

▶ **COLLOCATIONS:**
the density **of** *something*
population/housing/traffic density
bone density
high/low/maximum density

▶ **SYNONYMS:** mass, hardness

---

dent /dɛnt/ (dents, denting, dented)

VERB If you **dent** the surface of something, you make a hollow area in it by hitting it. ○ *The stone dented the car's fender.*

▶ COLLOCATIONS:
dent a **fender/door/car**
slightly/badly dented
dented **cans/aluminum/steel/armor**

---

deny /dɪnaɪ/ (denies, denying, denied)

VERB When you **deny** something, you state that it is not true. ○ *Official advice denies the existence of any link between the MMR vaccine and autism.* ○ [+ that] *The government has denied that there was a plot to assassinate the president.* ○ [+ v-ing] *They all denied ever having seen her.*

▶ COLLOCATIONS:
deny a **claim/allegation/charge/suggestion**
deny **murdering/killing/assaulting** *someone*
vehemently/strenuously/categorically deny *something*

▶ SYNONYM: refute

---

de|part|ment /dɪpɑrtmənt/ (departments) `PERSONNEL`

NOUN A **department** is one of the sections in an organization such as a government, business, or school. ○ [+ of] *the U.S. Department of Health* ○ *He moved to the sales department.* ○ *the geography department of Moscow University*

▶ COLLOCATIONS:
a department **of** *something*
a department of **medicine/biology/agriculture**
a **sales/finance/planning/human resources** department
a **fire/police/health/government** department

▶ SYNONYMS: section, division

de|part|men|tal /dɪpɑrtmɛntəl/

ADJECTIVE **Departmental** is used to describe the activities, responsibilities, or possessions of a department in a government, company, or other organization. ○ *cuts in departmental budgets*

▶ COLLOCATIONS:
a departmental **head/budget**
departmental **spending**

de|par|ture /dɪpɑrtʃər/ (departures) `TRAVEL`

NOUN Departure is the act of leaving somewhere. ○ [+ *for*] *Illness delayed the president's departure for Helsinki.*

▶ **COLLOCATIONS:**
departure **for** *somewhere*
a **sudden/abrupt/delayed/early** departure
schedule/delay/postpone/announce a departure

▶ **PHRASE:** arrivals and departures

de|pend|ent /dɪpɛndənt/

ADJECTIVE To be **dependent on** something or someone means to need them in order to succeed or be able to survive. ○ [+ *on*] *The local economy is overwhelmingly dependent on oil and gas extraction.* ○ *Just 26 percent of households are married couples with dependent children.*

▶ **COLLOCATIONS:**
dependent **on/upon** *something/someone*
dependent on/upon **aid/exports/tourism**
heavily/totally/entirely dependent
financially/economically/chemically dependent

▶ **SYNONYM:** reliant

de|pend|ence /dɪpɛndəns/

NONCOUNT NOUN Your **dependence on** something or someone is your need for them in order to succeed or be able to survive. ○ [+ *on*] *the city's traditional dependence on tourism* ○ [+ *on*] *efforts to encourage bicycle use and reduce dependence on the car*

▶ **COLLOCATIONS:**
dependence **on** *something/someone*
dependence on **oil/tourism/aid/drugs**
physical/emotional/psychological dependence
economic/financial/mutual dependence
heavy/excessive/continued/growing dependence
reduce/lessen/increase dependence

▶ **SYNONYM:** reliance

de|plete /dɪplit/ (depletes, depleting, depleted)

VERB To **deplete** a stock or amount of something means to reduce it. [FORMAL] ○ *substances that deplete the ozone layer* ○ *Most native mammal species have been severely depleted.*

> ▶ **COLLOCATIONS:**
> **severely/seriously/rapidly** depleted
> deplete the **ozone layer**
> deplete **reserves** of *something*

> ▶ **SYNONYMS:** reduce, diminish, augment

---

de|pos|it /dɪpɒzɪt/ **(deposits, depositing, deposited)** `BANKING & FINANCE`

d

1 NOUN A **deposit** is a sum of money that is part of the full price of something, and that you pay when you agree to buy it. ○ *A $50 deposit is required when ordering, and the balance is due upon delivery.*

> ▶ **COLLOCATIONS:**
> a deposit **of** $x
> **require/request/pay/refund** a deposit

> ▶ **SYNONYM:** security

2 NOUN A **deposit** is a sum of money that is in a bank account or savings account, especially a sum that will be left there for some time. ○ *Bank customers are able to make deposits and withdraw money from automatic teller machines.*

> ▶ **COLLOCATIONS:**
> a **bank** deposit
> a deposit **slip/account**
> **make** a deposit

3 NOUN A **deposit** is an amount of a substance that has been left somewhere as a result of a chemical or geological process. ○ *After 10 minutes the surplus material is washed away and any remaining deposit examined with ultraviolet light.* ○ *[+ of] underground deposits of gold and diamonds*

> ▶ **COLLOCATIONS:**
> a deposit **of** *something*
> a **mineral/nickel/gold/glacial** deposit
> a **fatty/calcium** deposit

> ▶ **SYNONYMS:** sediment, silt

4 VERB If a substance **is deposited** somewhere, it is left there as a result of a chemical or geological process. ○ *The phosphate was deposited by the decay of marine microorganisms.*

> ▶ **COLLOCATIONS:**
> deposited **by** *something*
> **sediment/silt** is deposited
> a **layer/mineral** is deposited

de|pre|ci|ate /dɪpriːʃieɪt/ (depreciates, depreciating, depreciated)

BANKING & FINANCE

VERB If something such as a currency **depreciates** or if something **depreciates** it, it loses some of its original value. ○ *Inflation is rising rapidly; the yuan is depreciating.* ○ *The demand for foreign currency depreciates the real value of local currencies.*

▶ COLLOCATIONS:
currency/property depreciates
a depreciating **asset**

de|pre|cia|tion /dɪpriːʃieɪʃⁿn/ (depreciations)

NOUN ○ *miscellaneous costs, including machinery depreciation and wages*

▶ COLLOCATIONS:
the depreciation **of** something
the depreciation of **assets/property**
currency depreciation

de|pressed /dɪprɛst/

BANKING & FINANCE

ADJECTIVE A **depressed** place or industry does not have enough business or employment to be successful. ○ *legislation to encourage investment in depressed areas* ○ *The construction industry is no longer as depressed as it was.*

▶ COLLOCATIONS:
economically depressed
a depressed **region/area**
a depressed **market/sector**

de|prive /dɪpraɪv/ (deprives, depriving, deprived)

VERB If you **deprive** someone **of** something that they want or need, you take it away from them, or you prevent them from having it. ○ [+ *of*] *They've been deprived of the fuel necessary to heat their homes.*

▶ COLLOCATIONS:
deprive *someone/yourself* **of** *something*
deprive *someone* of **food/sleep/rights/opportunities**

dep|ri|va|tion /dɛprɪveɪʃⁿn/ (deprivations)

NOUN ○ *Millions more suffer from serious sleep deprivation caused by long work hours.*

▶ COLLOCATIONS:
suffer/experience deprivation
sleep/sensory/emotional/economic deprivation

the deprivations **of** something
the deprivations of **war/childhood/prison**

---

depth /dɛpθ/ (depth)

NOUN The **depth** of something such as a river or hole is the distance downward from its top surface, or between its upper and lower surfaces. ○ *The smaller lake ranges from five to fourteen feet in depth.* ○ *The depth of the shaft is 520 yards.*

▶ **COLLOCATIONS:**
the depth **of** something
x yards **in** depth

▶ **RELATED WORDS:** width, height, breadth

---

de|regu|late /diːrɛgyəleɪt/ (deregulates, deregulating, deregulated) [LEGAL]

VERB To **deregulate** something means to remove controls and regulations from it. ○ *the need to deregulate the U.S. airline industry*

▶ **COLLOCATIONS:**
deregulate a **market/sector/industry/economy**
deregulate **prices/rates/fees**

de|regu|la|tion /diːrɛgyəleɪʃən/

NONCOUNT NOUN ○ *Since deregulation, banks are permitted to set their own interest rates.*

▶ **COLLOCATIONS:**
deregulation **of** something
industry/energy/market/airline deregulation

---

de|scribe /dɪskraɪb/ (describes, describing, described)

VERB If you **describe** a person, object, event, or situation, you say what they are like or what happened. ○ [+ what] *We asked her to describe what kind of things she did in her spare time.* ○ *She read a poem by Carver which describes their life together.*

▶ **COLLOCATIONS:**
describe something/someone **as** something
describe a **scene/situation/incident/process**
describe something/someone **accurately/vividly/briefly**

▶ **SYNONYMS:** relate, express, depict

de|scrip|tion /dɪskrɪpʃ°n/ (descriptions)

NOUN A **description** of someone or something is an account that explains what they are or what they look like. ○ [+ of] *Police have issued a description of the man who was aged between fifty and sixty.* ○ *a detailed description of the movements and battle plans of Italy's fleet*

▶ **COLLOCATIONS:**
  a description **of** *something/someone*
  provide/give/issue a description
  match/fit a description
  a **detailed/brief/accurate/vivid/full** description
  a **job** description

▶ **SYNONYMS:** account, representation, depiction

des|ert /dɪzɜrʃ°n/ (deserts)

NOUN A **desert** is a large area of land, usually in a hot region, where there is almost no water, rain, trees, or plants. ○ *the Sahara Desert* ○ *The vehicles have been modified to suit conditions in the desert.*

de|serve /dɪzɜrv/ (deserves, deserving, deserved)

VERB If someone **deserves** something, they should receive it because of their actions or qualities. ○ *He works hard – he deserves a promotion.*

▶ **COLLOCATIONS:**
  deserve **to** *do something*
  deserve to **win/lose/live/die**
  deserve **credit/praise/recognition/respect/attention/support**
  deserve an **award/reward/medal**
  fully/definitely/truly deserve

▶ **SYNONYM:** merit

de|sir|able /dɪzaɪərəb°l/

ADJECTIVE If something is **desirable**, you want to have it or do it because it is useful or attractive. ○ *a desirable neighborhood*

▶ **COLLOCATIONS:**
  a desirable **place/location/area/neighborhood**
  a desirable **thing/quality/trait/feature**
  highly/very/socially desirable

des|per|ate /dɛspərɪt/

ADJECTIVE A **desperate** situation is very difficult, serious, or dangerous.
○ Conditions in the hospitals are desperate.

▶ COLLOCATIONS:
a desperate **situation/need/shortage**
a desperate **struggle/attempt/measure/bid/effort/search**
get/feel/look/sound/seem desperate

des|per|ate|ly /dɛspərɪtli/

ADVERB ○ Thousands of people are desperately trying to leave the country.

▶ COLLOCATIONS:
try desperately
desperately **need/want/seek/search/struggle**
desperately **poor/ill**

de|stroy /dɪstrɔɪ/ (destroys, destroying, destroyed)

VERB To **destroy** something means to cause so much damage to it that it is completely ruined or does not exist anymore. ○ That's a sure recipe for destroying the economy and creating chaos. ○ No one was injured in the explosion, but the building was completely destroyed.

▶ COLLOCATIONS:
destroy a **house/home/building/document**
destroy **evidence**
a **fire/earthquake/missile/blast/explosion** destroys something
completely/totally/nearly destroy something

▶ SYNONYM: ruin

de|struc|tion /dɪstrʌkʃən/

NONCOUNT NOUN **Destruction** is the act of destroying something, or the state of being destroyed. ○ [+ of] an international agreement aimed at halting the destruction of the ozone layer ○ weapons of mass destruction

▶ COLLOCATIONS:
the destruction **of** something
cause/prevent the destruction of something
total/massive/complete/widespread destruction
environmental/habitat destruction

de|tail /ˈdiːteɪl, dɪˈteɪl/ (details)

1 NOUN The **details of** something are its individual features or elements. ○ [+ of] *The details of the plan are still being worked out.* ○ *I recall every detail of the party.*

2 PLURAL NOUN Details about someone or something are facts or pieces of information about them. ○ [+ of] *See the bottom of this page for details of how to apply for this exciting offer.* ○ *Full details will be announced soon.*

▶ **COLLOCATIONS:**
   details **of/about** *something*
   details of a **plan/proposal/agreement**
   full/exact/precise/specific details
   further/more details
   announce/give/provide/release/reveal details

▶ **SYNONYMS:** information, facts, specifics

de|tect /dɪˈtɛkt/ (detects, detecting, detected)

VERB To **detect** something means to find it or discover that it is present somewhere by using equipment or making an investigation. ○ *a sensitive piece of equipment used to detect radiation* ○ *Most skin cancers can be cured if detected and treated early.*

▶ **COLLOCATIONS:**
   detect a **virus/abnormality/tumor**
   detect **cancer/radiation**
   detect a **trace/signal/sign**
   a **sensor/radar/test** detects *things*

▶ **SYNONYMS:** discover, reveal

de|tec|tion /dɪˈtɛkʃən/

NONCOUNT NOUN Detection is the act of noticing or sensing something. ○ [+ of] *the early detection of breast cancer*

▶ **COLLOCATIONS:**
   the detection **of** *something*
   early detection
   radar/radiation/cancer/fraud detection
   a detection **device/method/system**

▶ **PHRASE:** detection and prevention

▶ **SYNONYM:** discovery

de|terio|rate /dɪtɪəriəreɪt/ (deteriorates, deteriorating, deteriorated)

VERB If something **deteriorates**, it becomes worse in some way. ○ [+ into] *There are fears that the situation might deteriorate into full-scale war.* ○ [V-ing] *Surface transportation has become less and less viable with deteriorating road conditions.* ○ *Relations between the two countries steadily deteriorated.*

▶ **COLLOCATIONS:**
deteriorate **into** *something*
a **condition/situation** deteriorates
someone's **health** deteriorates
a deteriorating **situation/condition**
deteriorating **relations**
quickly/rapidly/sharply/steadily deteriorate

▶ **SYNONYM:** worsen

de|terio|ra|tion

NONCOUNT NOUN ○ [+ in] *concern about the rapid deterioration in relations between the two countries* ○ [+ of] *the slow steady deterioration of a patient with Alzheimer's disease*

▶ **COLLOCATIONS:**
deterioration **in/of** *something/someone*
rapid/gradual/marked/significant deterioration
further/continued deterioration
physical/mental/bone deterioration
accelerate/reverse/prevent deterioration

▶ **SYNONYMS:** decline, decay, degeneration

de|ter|mine /dɪtɜrmɪn/ (determines, determining, determined)

1 VERB If a particular factor **determines** the nature of a thing or event, it causes it to be of a particular kind. [FORMAL] ○ *IQ is strongly determined by genetic factors.* ○ [+ whether] *What determines whether you are a career success or a failure?*

▶ **COLLOCATIONS:**
determined **by** *something*
determine *something's* **outcome/fate/future/value**
genetically/biologically determined

▶ **SYNONYMS:** dictate, decide

2 VERB To **determine** a fact means to discover it as a result of investigation. [FORMAL] ○ [+ what] *The investigation will determine what* *actually happened.* ○ *Testing needs to be done to determine the long-term effects on humans.* ○ [+ *that*] *Science has determined that the risk is very small.*

▶ **COLLOCATIONS:**
determine the **cause/extent** of *something*
determine **precisely/conclusively/exactly**

▶ **SYNONYMS:** identify, discover, ascertain

de|ter|mi|na|tion /dɪtɜrmɪneɪʃ°n/

NONCOUNT NOUN ○ *Everyone concerned acted with great courage and determination.*

▶ **COLLOCATIONS:**
fierce/great/dogged/steely determination
show/require determination

▶ **PHRASES:**
with determination
courage and determination
strength and determination

de|ter|mined /dɪtɜrmɪnd/

ADJECTIVE If you are **determined to** do something, you have made a firm decision to do it and will not let anything stop you. ○ [+ *to*] *His enemies are determined to ruin him.*

▶ **COLLOCATIONS:** a determined **effort/opponent/leader**

---

de|vel|op /dɪvɛləp/ (develops, developing, developed)   `RG-D`

1 VERB When something **develops**, it grows or changes over a period of time and usually becomes more advanced, complete, or severe. ○ *It's hard to say at this stage how the market will develop.* ○ [+ *into*] *These clashes could develop into open warfare.* ○ [V-ing] *Society begins to have an impact on the developing child.*

2 VERB If you say that a country **develops**, you mean that it changes from being a poor agricultural country to being a rich industrial country.

3 VERB If you **develop** a business or industry, or if it **develops**, it becomes bigger and more successful. ○ *She won a grant to develop her own business.* ○ *Over the last few years tourism here has developed considerably.*

▶ **COLLOCATIONS:**
develop **into** *something*
a **child/baby/fetus/brain** develops
a **country/nation/company** develops

develop **rapidly/gradually/slowly**
highly/fully/newly developed

▶ **SYNONYMS:** build, grow, expand

→ see note at **acquire**

de|vel|oped /dɪvɛləpt/

ADJECTIVE If you talk about **developed** countries or the **developed** world, you mean the countries or the parts of the world that are wealthy and have many industries. ○ *The developed nations have to recognize the growing gap between rich and poor around the world.* ○ *This scarcity is inevitable in less developed countries.*

▶ **COLLOCATIONS:**
the developed **world**
a developed **nation/country/society/economy/market**

▶ **SYNONYMS:** prosperous, industrialized

de|vel|op|ing /dɪvɛləpɪŋ/

ADJECTIVE If you talk about **developing** countries or the **developing** world, you mean the countries or the parts of the world that are poor and have few industries. ○ *In the developing world cigarette consumption is increasing.* ○ *Income disparities between industrial and developing countries will continue to grow.*

▶ **COLLOCATIONS:**
the developing **world**
a developing **nation/country**

▶ **SYNONYMS:** emergent, Third World

de|vel|op|ment /dɪvɛləpmənt/ **(developments)**

NOUN ○ [+ *of*] *an ideal system for studying the development of the embryo* ○ *Education is central to a country's economic development.*

▶ **COLLOCATIONS:**
the development **of** something
the development of **technology/weapons/products**
a **recent/future** development
economic/commercial/industrial/sustainable development
promote/encourage/monitor development
a development **program/project**

▶ **PHRASE:** research and development

▶ **SYNONYMS:** growth, expansion

de|vel|op|men|tal /dɪvɛləpmɛntəl/

ADJECTIVE Developmental means relating to the development of someone or something. ○ *the emotional, educational, and developmental needs of the child* ○ *adults with developmental disabilities*

▶ **COLLOCATIONS:** a developmental **stage/disorder/disability**

de|vi|ate /dɪvieɪt/ (deviates, deviating, deviated)

VERB To **deviate from** something means to start doing something different or not planned, especially in a way that causes problems for others. ○ [+ *from*] *They stopped you as soon as you deviated from the script.* ○ [+ *from*] *wage levels that deviate significantly from international norms* ○ [+ *from*] *behavior that deviates markedly from the expectations of the individual's culture*

▶ **COLLOCATIONS:**
deviate **from** *something*
deviate from a **norm/standard/path/script**
deviate **markedly/significantly/slightly**

▶ **SYNONYM:** depart

de|vice /dɪvaɪs/ (devices) RG-D

NOUN A **device** is an object that has been invented for a particular purpose, for example, for recording or measuring something. ○ [+ *that*] *an electronic device that protects your vehicle 24 hours a day* ○ *An explosive device had been left inside a container.*

▶ **COLLOCATIONS:**
a **mechanical/electronic/nuclear/explosive** device
a **handheld/wireless/portable/storage** device
a **communication/safety/medical/tracking** device
use/install/attach a device

▶ **SYNONYMS:** machine, instrument, gadget

de|vise /dɪvaɪz/ (devises, devising, devised) RG-D

VERB If you **devise** a plan, you have the idea for it. ○ *We devised a strategy to protect profits.*

▶ **COLLOCATIONS:**
devise a **plan/strategy/way/solution**
devise a **formula/system/method/program/policy**

de|vot|ed /dɪvoʊtɪd/

ADJECTIVE Someone who is **devoted** to a person or thing loves that person or thing very much. ○ [+ to] He was devoted to his wife.

▶ COLLOCATIONS:
devoted **to** someone
a devoted **wife/husband/spouse**
seem/remain devoted

di|ag|nose /daɪəgnoʊs/ (diagnoses, diagnosing, diagnosed) [HEALTH & FITNESS]

VERB If someone or something **is diagnosed as** having a particular illness or problem, their illness or problem is identified. If an illness or problem **is diagnosed**, it is identified. ○ [+ with] Almost a million people are diagnosed with colon cancer each year. ○ [+ as] In 1894 her illness was diagnosed as cancer.

▶ COLLOCATIONS:
someone is diagnosed **with** something
someone/something is diagnosed **as** something
diagnosed with **cancer/diabetes/leukemia**
diagnosed with a **disorder/disease/tumor**
diagnosed as **epileptic/diabetic**

di|ag|no|sis /daɪəgnoʊsɪs/ (diagnoses)

NOUN **Diagnosis** is the discovery and naming of what is wrong with someone who is ill or with something that is not working properly. ○ I need to have a second test to confirm the diagnosis. ○ [+ of] The technique could allow earlier and more accurate diagnosis of conditions ranging from ME to Alzheimer's disease.

▶ COLLOCATIONS:
a diagnosis **of** something
a diagnosis of **cancer/schizophrenia/autism**
make/confirm/give a diagnosis
a **correct/accurate/inaccurate/initial/early** diagnosis

▶ RELATED WORD: prognosis

dia|gram /daɪəgræm/ (diagrams) [COMMUNICATIONS]

NOUN A **diagram** is a simple drawing that consists mainly of lines and is used, for example, to explain how a machine works. ○ Each tube enters the muscle wall of the uterus (see diagram on page 20).

▶ **COLLOCATIONS:**
a diagram **illustrates/shows** *something*
draw a diagram
a **schematic/explanatory/simple/complex** diagram

▶ **SYNONYM:** illustration

▶ **RELATED WORD:** graph

d

dial /daɪəl/ (dials)

1 NOUN A **dial** is the part of a machine or instrument such as a clock or watch that shows you the time or a measurement that has been recorded. ○ *The luminous dial on the clock showed five minutes to seven.*

2 NOUN A **dial** is a control on a device or piece of equipment that you can move in order to adjust the setting, for example, to select or change the frequency on a radio or the temperature of a heater. ○ *He turned the dial on the radio.*

▶ **COLLOCATIONS:** **turn/set/move/read/adjust** the dial

di|am|eter /daɪæmɪtər/ (diameters)

NOUN The **diameter** of a round object is the length of a straight line that can be drawn across it, passing through the middle of it. ○ [+ *of*] *a tube less than a fifth of the diameter of a human hair* ○ *a length of 12-in. diameter steel pipe*

▶ **COLLOCATIONS:**
a diameter **of** *x* in.
x in. **in** diameter

▶ **RELATED WORDS:** radius, circumference

dia|mond /daɪmənd, daɪə-/ (diamonds)

NOUN A **diamond** is the shape ◆. ○ *Leave the pie to cool for 10–15 minutes before cutting into diamonds.*

▶ **COLLOCATIONS:**
form a diamond
a diamond **shape**

▶ **RELATED WORD:** square

dia|ry /daɪəri/ (diaries)   OFFICE

NOUN A **diary** is a book for writing things in, with a separate space for each day of the year. ○ *I read the entry from his diary for July 10, 1940.*

▶ COLLOCATIONS:
write in/put in/record in a diary
keep a diary
a diary **entry**
a **pocket/electronic/desk/appointment/travel** diary
a **private/personal/secret** diary
a **daily/monthly** diary

di|choto|my /daɪkɒtəmi/ (dichotomies)

NOUN If there is a **dichotomy** between two things, there is a very great difference or opposition between them. [FORMAL] ○ [+ *between*] *There is dichotomy between the academic world and the industrial world.*

▶ COLLOCATION: a dichotomy **between** *something* and *something*

dic|tate /dɪkteɪt/ (dictates, dictating, dictated)   COMMUNICATIONS

1 VERB If one thing **dictates** another, the first thing causes or influences the second thing. ○ *The film's budget dictated a tough schedule.* ○ *Of course, a number of factors will dictate how long an apple tree can survive.*

▶ COLLOCATIONS:
circumstances/factors/rules dictate *something*
tradition/convention dictates *something*
dictate a **choice/pace/policy/course/outcome**

2 VERB You say that logic or common sense **dictates that** a particular thing is the case when you believe strongly that it is the case and that logic or common sense will cause other people to agree. ○ *Logic dictates that our ancestors could not have held a yearly festival until they figured what a year was.*

▶ COLLOCATIONS: **logic/common sense** dictates *something*

dic|tion|ary /dɪkʃənɛri/ (dictionaries)

NOUN A **dictionary** is a book in which the words and phrases of a language are listed, together with their meanings. ○ *We checked the spelling in the dictionary.*

▶ COLLOCATIONS:
an **electronic/online** dictionary

a **business/medical/biographical** dictionary
a **Spanish/English/German** dictionary
write/edit/publish a dictionary

---

diet /daɪt/ (diets)

NOUN Your **diet** is the type and range of food that you regularly eat.
○ *It's never too late to improve your diet.* ○ *a healthy diet rich in fruit and vegetables* ○ *Poor diet and excess smoking will seriously damage the health of your hair.*

▶ **COLLOCATIONS:**
a diet **of** *something*
follow/eat a diet
improve *your* diet
feed *someone* a diet
a diet **contains/consists of** *something*
a **poor/healthy/balanced** diet
a **low-fat/vegetarian** diet
your **daily** diet
a diet **high/rich/low/deficient** in *something*

▶ **PHRASES:**
diet and exercise
diet and lifestyle

---

dif|fer /dɪfər/ (differs, differing, differed)

VERB If two or more things **differ**, they are unlike each other in some way.
○ [+ *from*] *The story he told police differed from the one he told his mother.*
○ *Management styles differ.*

▶ **COLLOCATIONS:**
differ **from** *something*
differ **significantly/considerably/widely/sharply/markedly**
opinions/views differ

▶ **SYNONYMS:** vary, contrast with

dif|fer|ence /dɪfərəns, dɪfrəns/ (differences)

1 NOUN The **difference** between two things is the way in which they are unlike each other. ○ [+ *between*] *That is the fundamental difference between the two societies.* ○ *There is no difference between the sexes.* ○ [+ *in*] *the vast difference in size*

▶ **COLLOCATIONS:**
the difference **between** *things*

a difference **in** something
tell/notice the difference
a **significant/big/huge/real/fundamental** difference
the **main/major/only** difference
little/not much/no difference
a difference in **quality/size/attitude/approach**

▶ **SYNONYMS:** contrast, variation, distinction

2 **NOUN** A **difference** between two quantities is the amount by which one quantity is less than the other. ○ *The difference between 49 and 100 is 51.*

▶ **COLLOCATION:** the difference **between** *x* and *y*

dif|fer|ent /dɪfərənt, dɪfrənt/

1 **ADJECTIVE** If two people or things are **different**, they are not like each other in one or more ways. ○ [+ from] *London was different from most European capitals.* ○ *We have totally different views.*

2 **ADJECTIVE** You use **different** to indicate that you are talking about two or more separate and distinct things of the same kind. ○ *Different countries specialized in different products.* ○ *The number of calories in different brands of drinks varies enormously.*

▶ **COLLOCATIONS:**
different **from** something
very/completely/totally/entirely different
a different **type/kind/part/thing**
a different **way/approach/view**
be/look/seem/sound/feel different

▶ **SYNONYMS:** contrasting, dissimilar, distinct

dif|fer|en|ti|ate /dɪfərɛnʃieɪt/ (differentiates, differentiating, differentiated)

1 **VERB** If you **differentiate between** things or if you **differentiate** one thing **from** another, you recognize or show the difference between them. ○ [+ between] *A child may not differentiate between his imagination and the real world.* ○ [+ from] *At this age your baby cannot differentiate one person from another.*

2 **VERB** A quality or feature that **differentiates** one thing **from** another makes the two things different. ○ [+ from] *distinctive policies that differentiate them from the other parties* ○ [+ from] *features which differentiate the pygmy elephant from the forest elephant* ○ [V-ing] *The brand did not have a differentiating factor.*

▶ **COLLOCATIONS:**
differentiate **between** things
differentiate something **from** something
a differentiated **product/brand**
a differentiating **factor**

▶ **SYNONYM:** distinguish

d

dif|fi|cult /dɪfɪkʌlt, -kəlt/

ADJECTIVE Something that is **difficult** is not easy to do, understand, or deal with. ○ [+ for] The lack of childcare provisions made it difficult for single mothers to get jobs. ○ [+ to-inf] It was a very difficult decision to make.

▶ **COLLOCATIONS:**
be difficult **for** someone
make/find something difficult
be/become/prove difficult
very/extremely/increasingly/particularly difficult
a difficult **life/task/time/job**
a difficult **situation/question/position/issue**
a difficult **decision/choice**

▶ **SYNONYMS:** challenging, complex, demanding, hard

dig|it /dɪdʒɪt/ **(digits)**

NOUN A **digit** is a written symbol for any of the ten numbers from 0 to 9. ○ Her telephone number differs from mine by one digit. ○ Inflation is still in double digits.

▶ **COLLOCATIONS:**
a **single** digit
binary/double/triple digits

▶ **SYNONYMS:** number, figure

digi|tal /dɪdʒɪtəl/

ADJECTIVE **Digital** systems record or transmit information in the form of thousands of very small signals. ○ The new digital technology would allow a rapid expansion in the number of TV channels.

▶ **COLLOCATIONS:**
a digital **camera/channel/television/radio/photo**
digital **technology**

▶ **RELATED WORDS:** terrestrial, analog

dig|ni|tary /dɪgnɪteri/ (dignitaries)

NOUN **Dignitaries** are people who are considered to be important because they have a high rank in government or in a church. ○ *an office fund used to entertain visiting dignitaries*

▶ COLLOCATIONS:
visiting/foreign dignitaries
church/political dignitaries

di|lem|ma /dɪlɛmə/ (dilemmas)

NOUN A **dilemma** is a difficult situation in which you have to choose between two or more alternatives. ○ *Many Muslim women face the terrible dilemma of having to choose between employment and their Islamic garb.* ○ *The issue raises a moral dilemma.*

▶ COLLOCATIONS:
pose/raise/face/solve a dilemma
a **moral/ethical/policy/workplace** dilemma

▶ SYNONYMS: difficulty, problem, predicament

dili|gent /dɪlɪdʒ³nt/

ADJECTIVE Someone who is **diligent** works hard in a careful and thorough way. ○ *Meyers is a diligent and prolific worker.*

▶ COLLOCATIONS: a diligent **worker/employee/student/researcher**

di|men|sion /dɪmɛnʃ³n, daɪ-/ (dimensions)

1 **NOUN** A particular **dimension** of something is a particular aspect of it. ○ [+ to] *There is a political dimension to the accusations.* ○ [+ to] *This adds a new dimension to our work.*

▶ COLLOCATIONS:
a dimension **of/to** *something*
a **moral/spiritual** dimension
a **different/important/added/extra** dimension
bring/add a dimension

▶ SYNONYM: aspect

2 **NOUN** A **dimension** is a measurement such as length, width, or height. If you talk about the **dimensions** of an object or place, you are referring to its size and proportions. ○ [+ of] *Drilling will continue on the site to assess the dimensions of the new oilfield.* ○ [+ of] *the grandiose dimensions of the building*

▶ SYNONYMS: scale, size, extent, measurement

di|min|ish /dɪmɪnɪʃ/ (diminishes, diminishing, diminished)

VERB When something **diminishes**, or when something **diminishes** it, it becomes reduced in size, importance, or intensity. ○ *The threat of nuclear war has diminished.* ○ *Federalism is intended to diminish the power of the central state.* ○ [V-ing] *Universities are facing grave problems because of diminishing resources.* ○ *This could mean diminished public support for the war.*

▶ **COLLOCATIONS:**
diminish **in** *something*
diminish in **importance/size/number**
rapidly/gradually diminish
greatly/drastically/considerably diminished

▶ **SYNONYMS:** lessen, decrease

di|plo|ma /dɪploʊmə/ (diplomas)

NOUN A **diploma** is a qualification that a student who has completed a course of study may receive. ○ *He was awarded a diploma in social work.*

▶ **COLLOCATIONS:**
a diploma **in** *something*
a **high-school/college/professional** diploma
award/earn a diploma

dip|lo|mat /dɪpləmæt/ (diplomats) JOBS

NOUN A **diplomat** is a senior official whose job is to discuss international affairs with officials from other countries. ○ *Japanese and Russian diplomats have urged the North Koreans to return to the negotiating table.* ○ *a senior American diplomat*

▶ **COLLOCATIONS:**
a **foreign/career/retired/experienced** diplomat
a **Russian/American** diplomat

di|rect /dɪrɛkt, daɪ-/

1 ADJECTIVE Direct means moving toward a place or object, without changing direction and without stopping, for example, in a trip. ○ *They'd come on a direct flight from Athens.* ○ *the direct route from Amman to Bombay*

• **Direct** is also an adverb. ○ *You can fly direct to Amsterdam from most British airports.*

▶ **COLLOCATIONS:** a direct **flight/route**

▶ **PHRASE:** have direct access to something

2 **ADJECTIVE** You use **direct** to describe an experience, activity, or system that only involves the people, actions, or things that are necessary to make it happen. ○ *He has direct experience of the process of privatization.* ○ *He seemed to be in direct contact with the Boss.*

• **Direct** is also an adverb. ○ *the advantage of farmers selling direct to consumers*

▶ **COLLOCATIONS:** direct **contact/experience**

▶ **PHRASE:** in direct contact with *someone*

▶ **SYNONYMS:** close, immediate

3 **ADJECTIVE** You use **direct** to emphasize the closeness of a connection between two things. ○ *They were unable to prove that she died as a direct result of his injection.* ○ *His visit is direct evidence of the improvement in their relationship.*

▶ **COLLOCATIONS:**
a direct **link/involvement/result**
a direct **connection/impact/consequence**

▶ **PHRASE:** as a direct result of *something*

▶ **SYNONYMS:** close, immediate

---

di|rec|tor /dɪrɛktər, daɪ-/ (directors) JOBS

NOUN The **directors** of a company are its most senior managers, who meet regularly to make important decisions about how it will be run. ○ [+ *of*] *He served on the board of directors of a local bank.* ○ *Karl Uggerholt, the financial director of Braun U.K.*

▶ **COLLOCATIONS:**
a director **of** *something*
a **managing/executive/nonexecutive** director
a **deputy/assistant/associate** director
a **finance/marketing/operations** director
the **acting** director
appoint/elect/name a director
a director **agrees/decides/recommends/approves** *something*

▶ **PHRASES:**
the board of directors
director and founder

▶ **SYNONYMS:** manager, executive, CEO

di|rec|tory /dɪrɛktəri, daɪ-/ (directories)

NOUN A **directory** is a book or website containing a list of people's names, addresses, and telephone numbers. ○ *a telephone directory* ○ *Look at our state-by-state directory, and click on your state to find your airport.*

▶ **COLLOCATIONS:** a **telephone/business/shopping/trade** directory

dis|ad|vant|age /dɪsədvæntɪdʒ/ (disadvantages)

NOUN A **disadvantage** is a factor that makes someone or something less useful, acceptable, or successful than other people or things. ○ [+ of] *His two main rivals suffer the disadvantage of having been long-term political exiles.* ○ [+ of] *the advantages and disadvantages of allowing priests to marry*

▶ **COLLOCATIONS:**
the disadvantages **of** something
suffer/face/experience/overcome a disadvantage
a **distinct/competitive** disadvantage

▶ **PHRASE:** the advantages and disadvantages of something

▶ **SYNONYMS:** drawback, inconvenience, downside

dis|agree /dɪsəgriː/ (disagrees, disagreeing, disagreed)

1 VERB If you **disagree with** someone or **disagree with** what they say, you do not accept that what they say is true or correct. You can also say that two people **disagree**. ○ [+ with] *You must continue to see them no matter how much you may disagree with them.* ○ *They can communicate even when they strongly disagree.*

2 VERB If you **disagree with** a particular action or proposal, you disapprove of it and believe that it is wrong. ○ [+ with] *I respect the president but I disagree with his decision.*

▶ **COLLOCATIONS:**
disagree **with** someone/something
disagree **on/about** something
disagree with a **statement/assessment/decision/view**
disagree about a **point/issue**
strongly/vehemently/totally/completely/publicly disagree

▶ **SYNONYM:** differ

dis|agree|ment /dɪsəgrimənt/ (disagreements)

1 **NONCOUNT NOUN** **Disagreement** means objecting to something such
as a proposal. ○ [+ with] *Britain and France have expressed some disagreement
with the proposal.*

▶ **COLLOCATIONS:**
disagreement **with/over/on/about** *something*
disagreement **continues/remains/exists/arises**
considerable disagreement
express disagreement

▶ **SYNONYMS:** opposition, dissent

2 **NOUN** When there is **disagreement** about something, people disagree
or argue about what should be done. ○ [+ over] *Congress and the president
are still locked in disagreement over proposals.* ○ *My instructor and I had a brief
disagreement.*

▶ **COLLOCATIONS:**
a disagreement **with** *someone*
a disagreement **between** *people*
disagreement **over/on/about** *something*
express/cause disagreement
resolve/settle a disagreement
overcome/avoid a disagreement
a **fundamental/profound/sharp/bitter/serious** disagreement

▶ **SYNONYMS:** dispute, argument, conflict, dissent

---

dis|ap|point /dɪsəpɔɪnt/ (disappoints, disappointing, disappointed)

VERB If something **disappoints** you, it is not as good as you hoped.
○ *The new proposal is likely to disappoint some banks.*

▶ **COLLOCATIONS:**
be disappointed **with** *someone/something*
be disappointed **about** *something*
very/extremely/bitterly/deeply/slightly disappointed

dis|ap|point|ment /dɪsəpɔɪntmənt/ (disappointments)

NONCOUNT NOUN **Disappointment** is the feeling of being slightly sad
because something has not happened or because something is not as
good as you hoped. ○ [+ with] *Business leaders have expressed
disappointment with the slow pace of progress.*

▶ **COLLOCATIONS:**
disappointment **with** *something/someone*
to *someone's* disappointment

a **bitter/great/major/obvious/deep** disappointment
express/conceal/hide *your* disappointment

▶ **PHRASES:**
a feeling of disappointment
a sense of disappointment

---

dis|ap|prove /dɪsəpruːv/ (disapproves, disapproving, disapproved)

VERB If you **disapprove of** something or someone, you do not like them, or do not approve of them. ○ [+ *of*] *He disapproved of the way they dealt with the situation.*

▶ **COLLOCATIONS:**
disapprove **of** *something/someone/doing something*
strongly/thoroughly disapprove

dis|ap|prov|al /dɪsəpruːvᵊl/

NONCOUNT NOUN If you feel or show **disapproval of** something or someone, you feel or show that you do not approve of them. ○ *His action had been greeted with almost universal disapproval.*

▶ **COLLOCATIONS:**
feel/show/express/voice disapproval
strong/mild/public/official disapproval

▶ **PHRASE:** shake your head in disapproval

---

dis|as|ter /dɪzæstər/ (disasters)

NOUN If you refer to something as a **disaster**, you are emphasizing that it is a complete failure. ○ *The launch was a total disaster.*

▶ **COLLOCATIONS:**
a **total/complete** disaster
a **financial/global/national/political** disaster
a **natural/environmental/ecological/nuclear** disaster
avoid/avert/suffer/face/cause/survive a disaster
a disaster **occurs/strikes/looms/threatens**

▶ **SYNONYM:** catastrophe

dis|as|trous /dɪzæstrəs/

ADJECTIVE A **disastrous** event causes great problems or is very unsuccessful. ○ *The country suffered a disastrous earthquake in July.* ○ *their disastrous performance in the election*

▶ **COLLOCATIONS:**
a disastrous **event/earthquake/flood/storm**
financially disastrous

▶ **SYNONYM:** catastrophic

---

dis|card /dɪskɑrd/ (discards, discarding, discarded)

VERB If you **discard** something, you get rid of it because you no longer
want it or need it. ○ *Read the manufacturer's guidelines before discarding the box.*

▶ **COLLOCATIONS:**
discard **clothing/trash**
discarded **materials**

▶ **SYNONYM:** dispose of

---

dis|charge (discharges, discharging, discharged)

The verb is pronounced /dɪstʃɑrdʒ/. The noun is pronounced
/dɪstʃɑrdʒ/.

VERB When someone **is discharged from** somewhere, they are officially
allowed to leave, or told that they must leave. ○ [+ *from*] *He has a broken
nose but may be discharged from the hospital today.*

▶ **COLLOCATIONS:**
discharge a **prisoner/employee/soldier**
dishonorably/honorably discharged

● **Discharge** is also a noun. ○ *He was given a conditional discharge and ordered
to pay Miss Smith $500 compensation.*

▶ **COLLOCATIONS:**
a discharge **from** somewhere
a discharge from the **military/army**
a discharge from **employment**
a **conditional/honorable/military** discharge

---

dis|con|nect /dɪskənɛkt/ (disconnects, 　　COMMUNICATIONS
disconnecting, disconnected)

VERB If you **disconnect** a piece of equipment, you stop electricity or water
from going into it. ○ *Try disconnecting the modem for a while.*

▶ **COLLOCATIONS:**
disconnect the **power supply/electricity/cord/pipe**
disconnect a **phone/printer/TV**

▶ **SYNONYM:** unplug

dis|count /dɪskaʊnt/ (discounts, discounting, discounted) `MARKETING & SALES`

VERB If you **discount** an idea, fact, or theory, you consider that it is not true, not important, or not relevant. ○ *However, traders tended to discount the rumor.*

▶ **COLLOCATIONS:**
discount a **rumor/report/idea/fact/theory**
discount a **possibility/threat**
discount the **importance** of *something*

▶ **SYNONYM:** disregard

dis|cour|age /dɪskɜrɪdʒ/ (discourages, discouraging, discouraged)

VERB If someone or something **discourages** you, they make you feel that you do not want to do a particular activity anymore. ○ *Learning a language is difficult at first but don't let this discourage you.*

▶ **COLLOCATIONS:**
discourage *someone* **from** doing something
easily discouraged
strongly/actively discourage

dis|cov|ery /dɪskʌvəri/ (discoveries) `R&D`

NOUN If someone makes a **discovery**, they are the first person to find or become aware of a place, substance, or scientific fact that no one knew about before. ○ *In that year, two momentous discoveries were made.* ○ [+ of] *the discovery of the ozone hole over the South Pole*

▶ **COLLOCATIONS:**
the discovery **of** *something*
make/announce/report a discovery
a **scientific/archaeological** discovery
a **momentous/exciting/remarkable/recent** discovery

▶ **PHRASES:**
discovery and invention
discovery and exploration

dis|cuss /dɪskʌs/ (discusses, discussing, discussed) `COMMUNICATIONS`

1 VERB If people **discuss** something, they talk about it, often in order to reach a decision. ○ *I will be discussing the situation with colleagues tomorrow.* ○ [+ how] *The cabinet met today to discuss how to respond to the ultimatum.*

2 VERB If you **discuss** something, you write or talk about it in detail.
○ *I will discuss the role of diet in cancer prevention in Chapter 7.*

▶ **COLLOCATIONS:**
discuss *something* **with** *someone*
discuss a **matter/issue/topic/situation**
discuss a **proposal/plan/idea/problem/case**
discuss the **possibility/details** of *something*
openly/publicly discuss *something*
discuss *something* **at length**

▶ **PHRASE:** discuss and debate

▶ **SYNONYMS:** consider, debate, examine

dis|cus|sion /dɪskʌʃ^ən/ (discussions)

1 NOUN If there is **discussion** about something, people talk about it, often
in order to reach a decision. ○ [+ of/about/on] *There was a lot of discussion
about the wording of the report.* ○ *Council members are due to have informal
discussions later on today.*

2 NOUN A **discussion of** a subject is a piece of writing or a lecture in which
someone talks about it in detail. ○ [+ of] *For a discussion of biology and
sexual politics, see chapter 4.*

▶ **COLLOCATIONS:**
discussion **of/about/on/over** *something*
discussion **with** *someone*
discussion **among/between** *people*
discussion on a **topic/issue/subject/matter**
hold/initiate a discussion
a discussion **concerns/focuses on** *something*
detailed/preliminary/frank discussions
lengthy/further/informal discussions
a discussion **group/paper/forum**

▶ **PHRASES:**
discussion and debate
discussion and negotiation

▶ **SYNONYMS:** debate, argument, examination, analysis

disk /dɪsk/ (disks)   OFFICE

NOUN A **disk** is a flat, circular shape or object. ○ *Most shredding machines
are based on a revolving disk fitted with replaceable blades.* ○ [+ of] *a small disk
of metal*

► **COLLOCATIONS:**
  a disk **of** something
  a **revolving/spinning** disk

USAGE: Spelling

In American English, the spelling **disk** is used to describe both a round, flat object and the part of a computer where information is stored, although the spelling **disc** is used to talk about a CD or phonograph record.

In British English, the spelling **disc** is usually used to describe a round, flat object and the spelling **disk** is used to talk about the part of a computer where information is stored.

---

disk drive /dɪsk draɪv/ (disk drives)

NOUN The **disk drive** on a computer is the part that holds a disk. ○ *all-in-one cases that incorporate the processors, disk drives and screen in a box about two inches thick*

► **COLLOCATIONS:**
  external disk drive
  hard/floppy disk drive

---

dis|miss /dɪsmɪs/ (dismisses, dismissing, dismissed)   `PERSONNEL`

VERB If you **dismiss** something, you decide or say that it is not important enough for you to think about or consider. ○ [+ *as*] *Mr. Wakeham dismissed the reports as speculation.*

► **COLLOCATIONS:**
  dismiss something **as** something
  dismiss a **matter/idea/objection/suggestion**
  dismiss a **possibility**
  dismiss a **case/charge/accusation**

► **PHRASE:** not easy to dismiss

► **SYNONYMS:** discount, reject

dis|mis|sal /dɪsmɪsəl/

NONCOUNT NOUN ○ *bureaucratic indifference to people's rights, and high-handed dismissal of public opinion*

► **SYNONYM:** rejection

dis|par|ity /dɪspæ̱rɪti/ (disparities)

NOUN If there is a **disparity between** two or more things, there is a noticeable difference between them. [FORMAL] ○ [+ between] *the health disparities between ethnic and socioeconomic groups in the U.S.*

▶ COLLOCATIONS:
economic/regional/racial disparities
a **huge/great/wide** disparity
disparity **between** *something* and *something*
a disparity **in** *something*
a disparity in **income/wealth/size/price**

▶ SYNONYMS: difference, inequality

dis|play /dɪsple̱ɪ/ (displays, displaying, displayed)

VERB If you **display** a characteristic, quality, or emotion, you behave in a way that shows that you have it. ○ *Researchers have found that women can display symptoms of a heart attack up to a month in advance.* ○ *He has displayed remarkable courage in his efforts to reform the party.*

▶ COLLOCATIONS:
display a **symptom/sign/attitude/tendency**
display a **lack** of *something*
display **emotion/talent/courage**

▶ SYNONYM: show

● **Display** is also a noun. ○ [+ of] *a public display of unity*

▶ COLLOCATIONS:
a display **of** *something*
a display of **emotion/affection/unity/solidarity**

▶ SYNONYM: show

dis|pose /dɪspo̱ʊz/ (disposes, disposing, disposed)

VERB If you **dispose of** something that you no longer want or need, you throw it away. ○ [+ of] *the safest means of disposing of nuclear waste*

▶ COLLOCATIONS:
dispose **of** *something*
dispose of **waste/trash/property/assets**

dis|pos|able /dɪspo̱ʊzəbəl/

ADJECTIVE ○ *lightweight vinyl disposable gloves*

▶ COLLOCATIONS: a disposable **camera/diaper/razor/syringe/cup**

dis|pos|al /dɪspoʊzᵊl/

NONCOUNT NOUN ○ [+ of] methods for the permanent disposal of radioactive wastes

▶ **COLLOCATIONS:**
disposal **of** something
disposal of **waste/trash/sewage/property**

---

dis|pute /dɪspyut/ (disputes, disputing, disputed)

1 **NOUN** A **dispute** is an argument or disagreement between people or groups. ○ [+ with] They have won previous pay disputes with the government. ○ [+ between] a bitter dispute between the European Community and the United States over subsidies to farmers

▶ **COLLOCATIONS:**
a dispute **over** something
a dispute **with** someone
a dispute **between** groups
a **pay/custody/border** dispute
settle/resolve/solve/end/win a dispute
a **bitter/ongoing/long-running** dispute

▶ **SYNONYMS:** argument, disagreement, debate

2 **VERB** If you **dispute** a fact, statement, or theory, you say that it is incorrect or untrue. ○ He disputed the allegations. ○ [+ that] No one disputes that vitamin C is of great value in the treatment of scurvy. ○ [+ whether] Some economists disputed whether consumer spending is as strong as the figures suggest.

▶ **COLLOCATIONS:**
dispute a **claim/assertion/allegation**
dispute **figures/facts**
hotly/vigorously/bitterly disputed

▶ **SYNONYMS:** argue, contest, refute

---

dis|quali|fy /dɪskwɒlɪfaɪ/ (disqualifies, disqualifying, disqualified)

VERB When someone **is disqualified**, they are stopped from taking part in a competition. ○ [+ from] Thomson was disqualified from the race.

▶ **COLLOCATIONS:**
disqualify someone **from** something
disqualify someone from a **race/competition/office**

dis|re|gard /dɪsrɪgɑːd/ (disregards, disregarding, disregarded)

VERB If you **disregard** something, you ignore it or do not take account of it. ○ *He disregarded the advice of his executives.*

▶ **COLLOCATIONS:** disregard **advice/suggestions/rules/laws/facts/evidence**

● **Disregard** is also a noun. ○ [+ *for*] *Whoever planted the bomb showed a total disregard for the safety of the public.*

▶ **COLLOCATIONS:**
disregard **for** *something*
show disregard
total/complete/utter/reckless disregard

dis|rupt /dɪsrʌpt/ (disrupts, disrupting, disrupted)

VERB If someone or something **disrupts** an event, system, or process, they cause difficulties that prevent it from continuing or operating in a normal way. ○ *Antiwar protesters disrupted the debate.* ○ *The drought has severely disrupted agricultural production.*

▶ **COLLOCATIONS:**
disrupt **supplies/production/traffic/proceedings**
severely/seriously disrupt *something*

▶ **SYNONYM:** interrupt

dis|rup|tion /dɪsrʌpʃən/ (disruptions)

NOUN ○ [+ *to*] *The strike is expected to cause delays and disruption to flights.* ○ [+ *in*] *A stroke is the result of a disruption in the blood supply to the brain.*

▶ **COLLOCATIONS:**
a disruption **to/in/of** *something*
a disruption in/of **supply/production/activity**
cause/avoid/minimize disruption
severe/widespread disruption

▶ **SYNONYM:** interruption

dis|tance /dɪstəns/ (distances)

NOUN The **distance between** two points or places is the amount of space between them. ○ [+ *between*] *the distance between the island and the nearby shore* ○ *Everything is within walking distance.*

▶ **COLLOCATIONS:**
the distance **between** *x* **and** *y*

the distance **from** *somewhere*
a distance **of** *x miles*
walk/travel/cover/drive/measure a distance
a **short/long/considerable/vast/great** distance

▸ **PHRASE:** within walking distance

▸ **SYNONYM:** space

---

dis|tinct /dɪstɪŋkt/

ADJECTIVE If something is **distinct from** something else of the same type, it is different or separate from it. ○ [+ *from*] *Engineering and technology are disciplines distinct from one another and from science.* ○ *This book is divided into two distinct parts.*

▸ **COLLOCATIONS:**
distinct **from** *something*
a distinct **category/type/species/entity**

▸ **SYNONYMS:** separate, discrete, diverse

dis|tinc|tion /dɪstɪŋkʃ°n/ (distinctions)

NOUN A **distinction between** similar things is a difference. ○ [+ *between*] *There are obvious distinctions between the two wine-making areas.*
○ [+ *between*] *We have drawn an important distinction between the market value and the intrinsic value of a company.*

▸ **COLLOCATIONS:**
a distinction **between** *things*
draw/make a distinction
a **clear/sharp/subtle** distinction

▸ **SYNONYMS:** difference, differentiation, separation

dis|tinc|tive /dɪstɪŋktɪv/

ADJECTIVE Something that is **distinctive** has a special quality or feature that makes it easily recognizable and different from other things of the same type. ○ *the distinctive odor of chlorine* ○ *Thompson's distinctive prose style*

▸ **COLLOCATIONS:**
a distinctive **style/characteristic/feature**
a distinctive **flavor/aroma/voice**
highly/visually distinctive

▸ **SYNONYMS:** unique, characteristic, idiosyncratic

dis|tin|guish /dɪstɪŋgwɪʃ/ (distinguishes, distinguishing, distinguished)

VERB If you can **distinguish** one thing **from** another or **distinguish between** two things, you can see or understand how they are different.
○ [+ from] *Asteroids are distinguished from meteorites in terms of their visibility.*
○ [+ between] *Research suggests that babies learn to see by distinguishing between areas of light and dark.*

▶ **COLLOCATIONS:**
distinguish **between** *things*
distinguish *something* **from** *something*
reliably/easily/clearly distinguish

▶ **SYNONYM:** differentiate

dis|tract /dɪstrækt/ (distracts, distracting, distracted)

VERB If something **distracts** you, it takes your attention away from what you are doing. ○ *I'm easily distracted by noise.*

▶ **COLLOCATIONS:**
distract a **player/driver/audience**
distract *someone's* **attention/mind**
easily/momentarily/slightly distracted

dis|trac|tion /dɪstrækʃən/ (distractions)

NOUN ○ [+ for] *DVD players in cars are a dangerous distraction for drivers.*

▶ **COLLOCATIONS:**
a distraction **for** *someone*
a distraction **from** *something*
a **welcome/unwanted/major/unnecessary** distraction
become/provide/need a distraction

dis|trib|ute /dɪstrɪbjut/ (distributes, distributing, distributed) [LOGISTICS & DISTRIBUTION]

1 VERB If you **distribute** things, you hand them or deliver them to a number of people. ○ *Students shouted slogans and distributed leaflets.*
○ [+ to] *Soldiers are working to distribute food to the refugees.* ○ [+ among] *Profits are distributed among the policyholders.*

2 VERB When a company **distributes** goods, it supplies them to the stores or businesses that sell them. ○ *We didn't understand how difficult it was to distribute a national paper.* ○ *companies that manufacture and distribute DVDs*

▶ **COLLOCATIONS:**
distribute *something* **to/among** *people*

distribute **leaflets/flyers/pamphlets/copies/aid/food**

▸ SYNONYMS: disseminate, issue

dis|tri|bu|tion /dɪstrɪbyuˌʃⁿn/ (distributions)

1 NONCOUNT NOUN The **distribution** of things involves giving or delivering them to a number of people or places. ○ [+ of] *the council which controls the distribution of foreign aid* ○ *emergency food distribution*

2 NOUN The **distribution** of something is how much of it there is in each place or at each time, or how much of it each person has. ○ [+ of] *a more equitable distribution of wealth* ○ [+ of] *the geographical distribution of parasitic diseases such as malaria*

▸ COLLOCATIONS:
the distribution **of** something
the distribution of **wealth/income/aid/resources**
rigid/unequal/equitable distribution
income/capital/cash/food distribution
a distribution **channel/system/network**

▸ SYNONYMS: allocation, dissemination, spread

dis|trict /dɪstrɪkt/ (districts)

NOUN A **district** is a particular area of a city or country. ○ *I drove around the business district.*

▸ COLLOCATIONS:
a **business/financial/residential/shopping** district
an **electoral/administrative/Congressional** district
a **historic** district
a **school** district
the **theater/garment** district

dis|turb /dɪstɜrb/ (disturbs, disturbing, disturbed)

1 VERB If something **is disturbed**, its position or shape is changed. ○ *He'd placed his notes in the brown envelope. They hadn't been disturbed.*

▸ COLLOCATIONS:
disturb a **desk/room**
disturb **papers**

2 VERB If something **disturbs** a situation or atmosphere, it spoils it or causes trouble. ○ *What could possibly disturb such tranquillity?*

▸ COLLOCATIONS:
disturb someone's **sleep**

disturb the **pattern/balance/equilibrium/order/routine**
disturb the **silence**

▶ **PHRASE:** disturb the peace

dis|turb|ance /dɪstɜːbəns/

NONCOUNT NOUN ○ *Successful breeding requires quiet, peaceful conditions with as little disturbance as possible.*

▶ **COLLOCATIONS:**
cause/create/prevent disturbance
considerable/serious disturbance

---

di|ver|si|fy /dɪvɜːsɪfaɪ/ (diversifies, diversifying, diversified) `R&D`

VERB When an organization or person **diversifies** into other things, or **diversifies** their range of something, they increase the variety of things that they do or make. ○ [+ *into*] *The company's troubles started only when it diversified into new products.* ○ *Manufacturers have been encouraged to diversify.* ○ *These companies have been given a tough lesson in the need to diversify their markets.*

▶ **COLLOCATIONS:**
diversify **into** *something*
diversify into a **field/area/sector**
diversify the **economy**
diversify a **company/market**
diversify **assets**

▶ **SYNONYM:** expand

di|ver|si|fi|ca|tion (diversifications)

NOUN ○ [+ *of*] *The seminar was to discuss diversification of agriculture.* ○ *These strange diversifications could have damaged or even sunk the entire company.*

▶ **COLLOCATIONS:**
diversification **into/of** *something*
diversification into an **area**
promote/encourage/increase diversification
international/geographic/economic diversification

▶ **SYNONYM:** expansion

---

di|vide /dɪvaɪd/ (divides, dividing, divided)

1 VERB When people or things **are divided** or **divide into** smaller groups or parts, they become separated into smaller parts. ○ [+ *into*] *The physical* *benefits of exercise can be divided into three factors.* ○ [+ into] *It will be easiest if we divide them into groups.* ○ [+ in] *Divide the pastry in half and roll out each piece.*

▶ **COLLOCATIONS:**
divide *something* **into** *something*
divide *something* **between** *people*
divide a **nation/community/society/country**
divide *something* **evenly/equally/roughly/broadly**
divide *something* into **categories/sections/segments**
racially/geographically/politically divided

▶ **SYNONYMS:** split, separate, segregate

2 VERB If you **divide** a larger number **by** a smaller number or **divide** a smaller number **into** a larger number, you calculate how many times the smaller number can fit exactly into the larger number. ○ [+ by/into] *Measure the floor area of the greenhouse and divide it by six.*

▶ **COLLOCATION:** divide *something* **by/into** *something*

▶ **RELATED WORDS:** multiply, add, subtract

---

divi|dend /dˈɪvɪdɛnd/ (dividends) `BANKING & FINANCE`

NOUN A **dividend** is an amount of a company's profits that is paid to people who own shares in the company. ○ *The first quarter dividend has been increased by nearly 4 percent.*

▶ **COLLOCATIONS:**
earn/receive/pay/distribute/declare a dividend
increase/cut a dividend
a **stock/shareholder/cash** dividend

---

docu|ment (documents, documenting, documented) `OFFICE`

The noun is pronounced /dˈɒkyəmənt/. The verb is pronounced /dˈɒkyəmɛnt/.

1 NOUN A **document** is a piece of text or graphics, for example, a letter, that is stored as a file on a computer and that you can access in order to read it or change it. ○ *When you are finished typing, remember to save your document.*

▶ **COLLOCATIONS:** **prepare/scan/save/send** a document

2 VERB If you **document** something, you make a detailed record of it in writing or on film or tape. ○ *The book represents the first real attempt to* *accurately document the history of the entire area.* ○ *The effects of smoking have been well documented.*

▶ **COLLOCATIONS:**
document the **history** of *something*
document **instances** of *something*
well/meticulously/extensively documented
documented **cases/proof/evidence**

dodge /dɒdʒ/ (dodges, dodging, dodged)

VERB If you **dodge**, you move suddenly, especially to avoid something. ○ *I dodged back behind the tree and waited.*

▶ **COLLOCATIONS:**
dodge **behind** *something*
dodge **between** *something*
dodge **through** *something*

dol|lar /dɒlər/ (dollars)   BANKING & FINANCE

NOUN The **dollar** ($) is the unit of money that is used in the U.S., Canada, and some other countries. There are 100 cents in a **dollar**. ○ *She earns twelve dollars an hour.*

▶ **PHRASE:** dollars and cents

do|mes|tic /dəmɛstɪk/   MARKETING & SALES

1 ADJECTIVE Domestic political activities, events, and situations happen or exist within one particular country. ○ *over 100 domestic flights a day to 15 U.K. destinations* ○ *sales in the domestic market*

▶ **COLLOCATIONS:**
domestic **politics/demand/production/competition**
the domestic **market/economy**
a domestic **issue/flight**

▶ **SYNONYM:** internal

2 ADJECTIVE Domestic means relating to or concerned with the home and family. ○ *a plan for sharing domestic chores* ○ *the sale of furniture and domestic appliances* ○ *victims of domestic violence*

▶ **COLLOCATIONS:**
a domestic **chore/servant/appliance**
domestic **violence**

▶ **SYNONYM:** household

domestic market /dəmɛstɪk mɑrkɪt/ **(domestic markets)**

NOUN A **domestic market** is a market that exists within a particular country. ○ *The domestic market is worth 24 percent of the tourism earnings.*

▶ **COLLOCATIONS:**
the **American/Canadian/British** domestic market
a **large/small/weak/strong** domestic market

▶ **PHRASES:**
international and domestic markets
the foreign and domestic markets

---

domi|nate /dɒmɪneɪt/ **(dominates, dominating, dominated)** `R&D`

VERB To **dominate** a situation means to be the most powerful or important person or thing in it. ○ *Microsoft's products dominate the global market for computer operating systems.* ○ *countries where life is dominated by war*

▶ **COLLOCATIONS:**
dominated **by** *someone/something*
dominate a **conversation/discussion**
dominate a **market/campaign/agenda**

▶ **SYNONYMS:** lead, overshadow, govern

domi|nant /dɒmɪnənt/

ADJECTIVE Someone or something that is **dominant** is more powerful, successful, influential, or noticeable than other people or things. ○ *a change which would maintain his party's dominant position* ○ *She was a dominant figure in the French film industry.*

▶ **COLLOCATIONS:**
a dominant **theme/ideology/feature**
a dominant **position/role/culture**
politically/economically/socially/overwhelmingly dominant

▶ **SYNONYMS:** preeminent, leading, powerful

---

do|nate /doʊneɪt/ **(donates, donating, donated)** `BANKING & FINANCE`

VERB If you **donate** your blood or a part of your body, you allow doctors to use it to help someone who is ill. ○ *people who are willing to donate their organs for use after death* ○ *All donated blood is screened for HIV.*

▶ **COLLOCATIONS:**
donate **blood/sperm/eggs**
donate a **kidney/organ**
donate *something* **anonymously**

do|na|tion /dooneɪʃ°n/ (donations)

NOUN ○ *measures aimed at encouraging organ donation* ○ *routine screening of blood donations*

▶ COLLOCATIONS: **organ/blood** donation

Dow Jones av|er|age /daʊ dʒoʊnz ævərɪdʒ, `BANKING & FINANCE` ævrɪdʒ/ or **Dow Jones industrial average**

NOUN **The Dow Jones average** is a daily index of stock-exchange prices based on the average price of a selected number of securities. ○ *The Dow Jones plummeted by 508.32 points.*

▶ COLLOCATIONS:
The Dow Jones average **falls/slides/climbs/soars**
The Dow Jones average **closes/opens**
The Dow Jones average is **up/down**

down|grade /daʊngreɪd/ (downgrades, downgrading, `PERSONNEL` downgraded)

VERB If someone **is downgraded**, their job or status is changed so that they become less important or receive less money. ○ *There was no criticism of her work until after she was downgraded.*

▶ COLLOCATIONS:
a **soldier/employee** is downgraded
a **job** is downgraded

down|load /daʊnloʊd/ (downloads, downloading, `OFFICE` downloaded)

1 VERB If you **download** information, you move it to your computer from a bigger computer or network. ○ *You can download the software from the Internet.*

▶ COLLOCATIONS:
download **software/files/programs**
download **songs/ringtones/images/movies**

2 NOUN **Download** is the process of downloading information. ○ *SpeedBit has managed to slash download times for a full-length feature film to 40 minutes.*

▶ COLLOCATIONS:
high-speed download
download **time/speed**

▶ PHRASE: available for download

d

3 **NOUN** A **download** is a computer file that has been downloaded. ○ *The Adobe ActiveShare software is also available as a free download.*

▶ **COLLOCATIONS:**
a **free** download
software/music downloads

▶ **RELATED WORD:** upload

d

down pay|ment /daʊn peɪmənt/ BANKING & FINANCE
(down payments) also **downpayment**

NOUN If you make a **down payment on** something, you pay part of the total cost when you buy it and the rest in regular payments later. ○ [+ *on*] *Celeste asked for the money as a down payment on an old farmhouse.*

▶ **COLLOCATIONS:**
a down payment **on** *something*
a down payment **for** *something*
a down payment **of** *x dollars*
make/give/require a down payment

down|size /daʊnsaɪz/ **(downsizes, downsizing, downsized)** PERSONNEL

VERB To **downsize** something such as a business or industry means to make it smaller. ○ *American manufacturing organizations have been downsizing their factories.* ○ *today's downsized economy*

▶ **COLLOCATIONS:**
downsize a **company/business/department/industry**
downsize a **factory/hospital**
downsize **employees/jobs**

down|siz|ing /daʊnsaɪzɪŋ/

NONCOUNT NOUN ○ *a trend toward downsizing in the personal computer market*

▶ **COLLOCATIONS:**
a **corporate** downsizing
announce/undergo a downsizing

down|turn /daʊntɜrn/ **(downturns)** BANKING & FINANCE

NOUN If there is a **downturn** in the economy or in a company or industry, it becomes worse or less successful than it had been. ○ *They predicted a severe economic downturn.*

▶ **COLLOCATIONS:**
weather/experience/suffer a downturn

a **global/sharp/severe** downturn
a **market/economic/housing** downturn

---

doz|en /dˈʌzᵊn/ (dozens)

QUANTIFIER **Dozens of** things or people means a lot of them. ○ [+ of] *The storm destroyed dozens of buildings.*

▶ **COLLOCATION:** dozens **of** *things/people*

---

draft /drˈæft/ (drafts) `COMMUNICATIONS`

NOUN A **draft** is an early version of a piece of writing. ○ *a draft report from a major U.S. university* ○ [+ of] *a final draft of an essay*

▶ **COLLOCATIONS:**
a draft **of** *something*
a draft of a **paper/manuscript/chapter/essay**
a draft **report/bill/document**
a **rough/first/final** draft
write/type/prepare/compose/revise a draft

▶ **SYNONYM:** version

---

drain /drˈeɪn/ (drains, draining, drained)

VERB If you **drain** something or if something drains, liquid flows out of it or off it. ○ *They built the tunnel to drain water out of the mines.* ○ *Drain the pasta well.*

▶ **COLLOCATIONS:**
drain *something* **from** *something*
drain the **pipes/well**
drain **fat/grease/water**

---

dra|mat|ic /drəmˈætɪk/

ADJECTIVE A **dramatic** change or event happens suddenly and is very noticeable and surprising. ○ *A fifth year of drought is expected to have dramatic effects on the California economy.* ○ *This policy has led to a dramatic increase in our prison populations.*

▶ **COLLOCATIONS:**
a dramatic **effect/impact/change/shift/improvement**
a dramatic **increase/rise/decrease/decline/fall**

▶ **SYNONYMS:** sudden, striking

dra|mati|cal|ly

ADVERB ○ *At speeds above 50 mph, serious injuries dramatically increase.*
○ *the construction of a dam which will dramatically alter the landscape*

▶ **COLLOCATIONS:**
increase/rise/vary/grow dramatically
change/alter/reduce/improve *something* dramatically

▶ **SYNONYMS:** suddenly, strikingly

EXTEND YOUR VOCABULARY

There are a range of different adjectives and adverbs you can use to
describe changes and trends. You use **dramatic/dramatically** to
describe a big change that happens very suddenly. ○ *a dramatic
improvement in aviation safety*

You can use **rapid/rapidly** to emphasize that something changes
very quickly. ○ *a rapidly expanding company*

You can use **significant/significantly**, **noteable/notably** or
marked/markedly to describe a change that is big enough to be
important or to have an effect. ○ *a way to significantly reduce unwanted
e-mail* ○ *a marked improvement in standards of living*

You can describe a sudden increase or decrease, especially as shown
on a graph, as **sharp** or **steep**. ○ *a sharp/steep rise in unemployment*

---

dras|tic /ˈdræstɪk/

1 ADJECTIVE If you have to take **drastic** action in order to solve a problem,
you have to do something extreme and basic to solve it. ○ *Drastic
measures are needed to clean up the profession.* ○ *He's not going to do anything
drastic about economic policy.*

2 ADJECTIVE A **drastic** change is a very great change. ○ *a drastic reduction in
the numbers of people dying*

▶ **COLLOCATIONS:**
drastic **measures/steps/cutbacks/action**
a drastic **change/reduction/decline**

▶ **SYNONYMS:** radical, severe, extreme

drawer /drɔr/ (drawers) `OFFICE`

NOUN A **drawer** is a part of a desk or other piece of furniture that you can pull out and put things in. ○ *She opened her desk drawer and took out the report.*

▶ COLLOCATIONS:
a **desk/kitchen** drawer
the **top/middle/bottom** drawer
a **locked** drawer
open/close a drawer

dress code /drɛs koʊd/ (dress codes) `PERSONNEL`

NOUN The **dress code** of a place is the rules about what kind of clothes people are allowed to wear there. ○ *There was a rigid dress code (jeans, no short hair).*

▶ COLLOCATIONS:
a **strict/rigid/relaxed/formal/casual** dress code
adhere to a dress code

driv|er's li|cense /draɪvərz laɪsəns/ (driver's licenses) `TRAVEL`

NOUN A **driver's license** is a card that shows that you have passed a driving test and that you are allowed to drive. ○ *In Montana, a driver's license is the only identification required to purchase a rifle.*

▶ COLLOCATIONS:
a **valid/expired** driver's license
a **New York** driver's license
renew/apply for a driver's license

due /du/

PHRASE If an event is **due to** something, it happens or exists as a direct result of that thing. ○ *The country's economic problems are largely due to the weakness of the recovery.*

▶ COLLOCATIONS:
partly/primarily due to *something*
largely/mainly/mostly due to *something*

du|ra|tion /dʊəreɪʃⁿn/

NONCOUNT NOUN The **duration of** an event or state is the time during which it happens or exists. ○ [+ of] *The result was an increase in the average duration of prison sentences.* ○ *Courses are of two years' duration.*

▸ **COLLOCATIONS:**
the duration **of** *something*
the duration of a **war**
x **hours'/minutes'/years'** duration
a **long/short/average/maximum** duration

▸ **SYNONYMS:** extent, period, term

---

d

duty /dˈuti/ (duties)   `BANKING & FINANCE`

NOUN A **duty** is a tax imposed by a government. ○ [+ *on*] *Proton pays only half the normal excise duty on imported components.*

▸ **COLLOCATIONS:**
import/export/excise/customs duties
impose/assess/levy/collect/pay duty

DVD /di vi di/ (DVDs)   `OFFICE`

NOUN A **DVD** is a disk on which a movie or music is recorded. **DVD** is short for "digital video disk." ○ *The DVD digs up even more history on the film's impact.*

▸ **COLLOCATIONS:**
a DVD **player**
a **movie/music** DVD

▸ **PHRASE:** available on DVD

Ee

---

ecol|ogy /ɪkɒlədʒi/ **(ecologies)**

NONCOUNT NOUN Ecology is the study of the relationships between plants, animals, people, and their environment, and the balances between these relationships. ○ *a senior lecturer in ecology* ○ *a growing interest in conservation and ecology*

---

econo|my /ɪkɒnəmi/ **(economies)**   **BANKING & FINANCE**

NOUN The **economy** of a country or region is the system by which money, industry, and trade are organized. ○ *Zimbabwe boasts Africa's most industrialized economy.* ○ *The Japanese economy grew at an annual rate of more than 10 percent.* ○ *the region's booming service economy*

▶ **COLLOCATIONS:**
the economy **of** *somewhere*
a **modern/industrial/service/market** economy
a **booming/strong/weak** economy
the **global/world/local/domestic** economy
the **American/Canadian/Japanese/British** economy
stimulate/revive/boost the economy
the economy **grows/recovers/shrinks/slows down**

eco|nomi|cal /ɛkənɒmɪkəl, ik-/

ADJECTIVE Something that is **economical** does not require a lot of money to operate. For example a car that only uses a small amount of gas is **economical**. ○ *the most economical method of extracting essential oils from plant materials*

▶ **COLLOCATIONS:** an economical **method/solution/alternative**

▶ **PHRASE:** efficient and economical

▶ **SYNONYMS:** cost-effective, inexpensive

USAGE: *economic* or *economical*?

Be careful not to confuse these two adjectives. **Economic** describes something related to the economy. ○ *the government's economic policies*

Something that is **economical** is cost-effective. ○ *the most effective and economical use of resources*

---

e

eco|nomi|cal|ly

ADVERB ○ *an economically depressed area* ○ *Small English orchards can hardly compete economically with larger French ones.*

▶ **COLLOCATIONS:**
prosper/benefit/grow/survive economically
suffer/struggle/develop economically
economically **viable/feasible/sustainable**
economically **dependent/disadvantaged/depressed/inefficient**

---

edi|tion /ɪdɪʃən/ **(editions)**

NOUN An **edition** is a particular version of a book, magazine, or newspaper that is printed at one time. ○ *A paperback edition is now available at bookstores.* ○ [+ of] *They brought out a special edition of The Skulker.*

▶ **COLLOCATIONS:**
an edition **of** something
a **special/new/limited/revised** edition
the **first/second/latest** edition
a **print/online/electronic** edition
a **collector's/paperback/hardcover** edition

---

ef|fect /ɪfɛkt/ **(effects)**

NOUN The **effect of** one thing **on** another is the change that the first thing causes in the second thing. ○ [+ of/on] *The Internet could have a significant effect on trade in the next few years.* ○ *The housing market is feeling the effects of the increase in interest rates.* ○ *Even minor head injuries can cause long-lasting psychological effects.*

→ see note at **affect**

▶ **COLLOCATIONS:**
the effect **of** something
the effect **on** something/someone

a **profound/dramatic/significant** effect
a **negative/harmful/adverse/devastating** effect
a **positive/beneficial/desired** effect
a **long-term/lasting/immediate** effect
a **psychological/health/knock-on** effect
have an effect on *something/someone*
feel the effects of *something*

▶ PHRASE: cause and effect

▶ SYNONYMS: influence, impact

ef|fec|tive /ɪfɛktɪv/

ADJECTIVE Something that is **effective** works well and produces the
results that were intended. ○ [+ in] *The project looks at how we could be more
effective in encouraging students to enter teacher training.* ○ [+ against] *Simple
antibiotics are effective against this organism.* ○ *an effective public
transportation system*

▶ COLLOCATIONS:
effective **in/against** *something*
highly/extremely/particularly effective
an effective **manner/strategy**
an effective **method/means/way**

▶ SYNONYM: successful

ef|fec|tive|ly /ɪfɛktɪvli/

ADVERB ○ *the team roles which you believe to be necessary for the team to
function effectively* ○ *Services need to be more effectively organized than they are
at present.*

▶ COLLOCATIONS:
function/work/operate effectively
communicate effectively

ef|fi|cient /ɪfɪʃ°nt/

ADJECTIVE If something or someone is **efficient**, they are able to do tasks
successfully, without wasting time or energy. ○ *With today's more efficient
contraception, women can plan their families and careers.* ○ *Technological
advances allow more efficient use of labor.* ○ *an efficient way of testing
thousands of compounds*

▶ COLLOCATIONS:
an efficient **use** of *something*
an efficient **way** of *doing something*

an efficient **manner**
highly/extremely efficient
fuel/energy efficient

▶ SYNONYMS: systematic, organized

ef|fi|cient|ly

ADVERB ○ *Enzymes work most efficiently within a narrow temperature range.*
○ *the ability to run a business efficiently*

▶ COLLOCATIONS:
function/work/operate/run efficiently
run/manage/organize *something* efficiently

---

e.g. /ˌiː ˈdʒiː/

ADVERB **e.g.** is an abbreviation that means "for example". It is used before a
noun, or to introduce another sentence. ○ *We need helpers of all types,
engineers, scientists (e.g. geologists), and teachers.* ○ *Or consider how you can
acquire these skills, e.g. by taking extra courses.*

▶ SYNONYMS: for example, for instance, such as

---

eight|een /eɪˈtiːn/

NUMBER **Eighteen** is the number 18. ○ *She will be eighteen in November.*

▶ COLLOCATIONS:
someone **is** eighteen
eighteen **dollars/pounds**
eighteen **yards/meters**
eighteen **months/years**

---

eighty /ˈeɪti/

NUMBER **Eighty** is the number 80. ○ *My grandmother is eighty.*

▶ COLLOCATIONS:
someone **is** eighty
eighty **dollars/euros**
eighty **miles/kilometers**
eighty **minutes/seconds**

elabo|rate (elaborates, elaborating, elaborated)

> The adjective is pronounced /ɪlæbərɪt/. The verb is pronounced /ɪlæbəreɪt/.

1 ADJECTIVE You use **elaborate** to describe something that is very complex because it has a lot of different parts. ○ *an elaborate research project*

> ▶ COLLOCATIONS:
> an elaborate **ceremony/ritual/network/costume/design**
> elaborate **detail**

> ▶ SYNONYM: complicated

2 ADJECTIVE **Elaborate** plans, systems, and procedures are complicated because they have been planned in very great detail, sometimes too much detail. ○ *elaborate efforts at the highest level to conceal the problem*

> ▶ COLLOCATIONS: an elaborate **effort/plan/system/procedure/ hoax/scam**

> ▶ SYNONYM: complicated

3 VERB If you **elaborate** a plan or theory, you develop it by making it more complicated and more effective. ○ *His task was to elaborate policies that would make a market economy compatible with a clean environment.*

> ▶ COLLOCATIONS:
> elaborate a **plan/theory/policy/idea**
> elaborate **on** *something*
> elaborate on a **statement/idea**

> ▶ PHRASES:
> refuse to elaborate
> elaborate further

elect /ɪlɛkt/ (elects, electing, elected)

VERB When people **elect** someone, they choose that person to represent them, by voting for them. ○ *The people of the Philippines have voted to elect a new president.* ○ *[+ as] Pelton was elected as mayor.* ○ *the newly elected prime minister*

> ▶ COLLOCATIONS:
> be elected **as** *something*
> elect a **president/leader/government**
> **democratically/newly/directly** elected

> ▶ SYNONYMS: choose, vote

e

elec|tion /ɪlɛkʃⁿn/ (elections)

NOUN An **election** is a process in which people vote to choose a person or group of people to hold an official position. ○ *his decision to hold the first general election in Nepal's history* ○ *During his election campaign he promised to increase economic growth.*

▶ **COLLOCATIONS:**
  a **presidential/mayoral/parliamentary** election
  a **general/local** election
  hold/call/win/lose an election
  vote in an election
  an election **campaign/manifesto/day/result**

▶ **SYNONYMS:** vote, poll, ballot

---

elec|tric|ity /ɪlɛktrɪsɪti, ilɛk-/ JOBS

NONCOUNT NOUN **Electricity** is energy that is used for heating and lighting, and to provide power for machines. ○ *Competition has brought electricity prices down in the short term.*

▶ **COLLOCATIONS:**
  generate/produce/use/provide/supply electricity
  restore/connect/cut off/lose electricity
  conduct electricity
  save/conserve electricity
  electricity **flows**

▶ **PHRASES:**
  water and electricity
  gas and electricity

elec|tri|cal /ɪlɛktrɪkᵊl/

ADJECTIVE ○ *shipments of electrical equipment* ○ *The study found that small electrical appliances consume a fifth of the electricity used in a typical American home.*

▶ **COLLOCATIONS:**
  electrical **equipment/appliances/goods**
  electrical **engineer/engineering**

elec|tri|cian /ɪlɛktrɪʃən, ilɛk-/ (electricians)

NOUN An **electrician** is a person whose job is to install and repair electrical equipment. ○ *Have the wiring checked by an electrician to make sure that it is safe.*

▶ **COLLOCATIONS:** a **qualified/licensed** electrician

el|ement /ɛlɪmənt/ (elements)

1 **NOUN** The different **elements** of a situation, activity, or process are the different parts of it. ○ [+ of] *The exchange of prisoners of war was one of the key elements of the U.N.'s peace plan.* ○ [+ of] *The plot has all the elements not only of romance but of high drama.*

▶ **COLLOCATIONS:**
an element **of** *something*
an element of **surprise/truth/luck/danger/uncertainty/risk**
contain/include/add an element
a **key/important/essential/main/vital/basic** element
certain/core elements

▶ **SYNONYMS:** part, constituent, component

2 **NOUN** An **element** is a substance such as gold, oxygen, or carbon that consists of only one type of atom. ○ *an essential trace element for animals and man* ○ *the minerals and elements in sea water*

▶ **COLLOCATIONS:** a **trace/chemical/radioactive** element

▶ **RELATED WORD:** compound

el|eva|tor /ɛlɪveɪtər/ (elevators) OFFICE

NOUN An **elevator** is a machine that carries people or things up and down inside tall buildings. ○ *We took the elevator to the fourteenth floor.*

▶ **COLLOCATIONS:**
take/ride the elevator
the elevator **opens/stops**

eli|gible /ɛlɪdʒɪbəl/

ADJECTIVE Someone who is **eligible to** do something is qualified or able to do it, for example, because they are old enough. ○ [+ to-inf] *Almost half the population are eligible to vote in today's election.* ○ [+ for] *You could be eligible for a university scholarship.*

▶ **COLLOCATIONS:**
eligible **for** *something*
eligible for **parole/release/compensation/assistance**
eligible for a **grant/refund/bonus/benefit**
eligible to **vote/apply/enter/play/participate/compete**
automatically/potentially/currently eligible
an eligible **voter/employee/patient**

▶ **SYNONYMS:** entitled, qualified

eli|gibil|ity /ɛlɪdʒəbɪlɪti/

NONCOUNT NOUN ○ [+ for] *The rules covering eligibility for benefits changed in the 1980s.* ○ *Each worker must meet various eligibility requirements.*

▶ **COLLOCATIONS:**
  eligibility **for** *something*
  eligibility for **credit/benefit/parole**
  an eligibility **requirement/criterion/rule**
  determine/establish *someone's* eligibility

elimi|nate /ɪlɪmɪneɪt/ (eliminates, eliminating, eliminated)

VERB To **eliminate** something, especially something you do not want or need, means to remove it completely. [FORMAL] ○ *The Sex Discrimination Act has not eliminated discrimination in employment.* ○ [+ from] *If you think you may be allergic to a food or drink, eliminate it from your diet.*

▶ **COLLOCATIONS:**
  eliminate *something* **from** *something*
  eliminate a **need/risk/requirement/deficit/threat/possibility**
  eliminate **waste**
  effectively eliminate *something*

▶ **SYNONYMS:** remove, abolish

elimi|na|tion /ɪlɪmɪneɪʃᵊn/

NONCOUNT NOUN ○ [+ of] *the prohibition and elimination of chemical weapons* ○ [+ of] *Complete elimination of the infection is usually possible.*

▶ **COLLOCATIONS:**
  the elimination **of** *something*
  the elimination of **weapons/discrimination/waste**
  the elimination of **subsidies/taxes/poverty**

▶ **SYNONYMS:** removal, abolition, eradication

else|where /ɛlswɛər/

ADVERB **Elsewhere** means in other places or to another place. ○ *80 percent of the state's residents were born elsewhere.*

▶ **COLLOCATIONS:**
  look/go/happen elsewhere
  lie elsewhere

▶ **PHRASE:** here and elsewhere

email /iˈmeɪl/ (emails, emailing, emailed) also **e-mail** `COMMUNICATIONS`

1 NONCOUNT NOUN Email is a system of sending written messages from one computer to another. **Email** is short for "electronic mail." ○ *You can contact us by email.*

▶ COLLOCATIONS:
   by email
   an email **address/system/account/service**
   use email

2 NOUN An **email** is a message sent from one computer to another. ○ *I got an email from Paul Cassidy this morning.*

▶ COLLOCATIONS:
   get/send/read/delete/reply to/forward an email
   a **personal/unsolicited** email

3 VERB If you **email** someone, you send them an email. ○ *Jamie emailed me to say he couldn't come.*

em|bas|sy /ˈɛmbəsi/ (embassies) `ORGANIZATION`

NOUN An **embassy** is a group of people who represent their government in a foreign country, or the building in which they work. ○ *The embassy advised British nationals to leave the country immediately.* ○ *The embassy was surrounded by the FBI.*

▶ COLLOCATIONS:
   the **American/British** embassy
   a **foreign** embassy
   an embassy **spokesman/official**
   close/contact the embassy

▶ RELATED WORD: consulate

emerge /ɪˈmɜrdʒ/ (emerges, emerging, emerged) `MARKETING & SALES`

1 VERB To **emerge** means to come out from an enclosed or dark space such as a room or a vehicle, or from a position where you could not be seen. ○ [+ *from*] *like a butterfly emerging from a chrysalis* ○ [V-ing] *holes made by the emerging adult beetle*

▶ COLLOCATIONS:
   emerge **from** *somewhere*
   emerge from **obscurity/hibernation/darkness**
   emerge from a **chrysalis/cocoon**

▶ SYNONYM: appear

2 VERB If a fact or result **emerges** from a period of thought, discussion, or investigation, it becomes known as a result of it. ○ *the growing corruption that has emerged in the past few years* ○ [+ that] *It soon emerged that neither the July nor August mortgage repayment had been collected.*

▶ **COLLOCATIONS:**
   details emerge
   evidence emerges
   a **pattern/picture** emerges

3 VERB If someone or something **emerges as** a particular thing, they become recognized as that thing. ○ [+ as] *Vietnam has emerged as the world's third-biggest rice exporter.* ○ *New leaders have emerged.*

▶ **COLLOCATIONS:**
   emerge **as** *something*
   emerge as a **favorite/victor/winner/candidate/contender**

emerg|ing mar|ket /ɪmɜ́rdʒɪŋ mɑ́rkɪt/ (emerging markets)

NOUN An **emerging market** is a financial or consumer market in a newly developing country or former communist country. ○ *Many emerging markets have outpaced more mature markets, such as the U.S. and Japan.*

▶ **COLLOCATION: invest in** an emerging market

---

em|pha|sis /ɛ́mfəsɪs/ (emphases)

NOUN Emphasis is special or extra importance that is given to an activity or to a part or aspect of something. ○ [+ on] *Too much emphasis is placed on research.* ○ [+ on] *Grant puts a special emphasis on weather in his paintings.*

▶ **COLLOCATIONS:**
   an emphasis **on** *something*
   place/put/add emphasis
   great/particular emphasis
   heavy/strong/special emphasis

▶ **SYNONYMS:** importance, attention, weight

em|pha|size /ɛ́mfəsaɪz/ (emphasizes, emphasizing, emphasized)

VERB To **emphasize** something means to indicate that it is particularly important or true, or to draw special attention to it. [in BRIT, also use **emphasise**] ○ [+ that] *But it's also been emphasized that no major policy changes can be expected.* ○ [+ how] *Discuss pollution with your child, emphasizing how nice a clean street, lawn, or park looks.*

▶ **COLLOCATIONS:**
emphasize the **importance/need**
repeatedly/strongly emphasize *something*

▶ **PHRASE:** cannot emphasize enough

▶ **SYNONYM:** stress

---

em|ploy /ɪmplɔɪ/ (employs, employing, employed)　　`PERSONNEL`

1 VERB If you **employ** certain methods, materials, or expressions, you use them. ○ *the vocabulary that she employs* ○ [+ *in*] *the approaches and methods employed in the study*

▶ **COLLOCATIONS:**
employ *something* **in/as** *something*
employ a **technique/method/strategy**

▶ **SYNONYMS:** use, utilize

2 VERB If a person or company **employs** you, they pay you to work for them. ○ *The company employs 18 staff.* ○ [+ *in*] *More than 3,000 local workers are employed in the tourism industry.*

▶ **COLLOCATIONS:**
employ *someone* **as** *something*
be employed **in** an industry
a **company/corporation** employs *someone*
staff/workers/people are employed
be employed **full-time/part-time**

▶ **SYNONYMS:** hire, recruit

em|ployee /ɪmplɔɪi/ (employees)

NOUN An **employee** is a person who is paid to work for an organization or for another person. ○ [+ *of*] *He is an employee of Fuji Bank.* ○ *Many of its employees are women.*

▶ **COLLOCATIONS:**
an employee **of/at** *something*
hire/recruit/dismiss employees
a **full-time/part-time** employee
a **government/state** employee
an employee of a **company/department**
an employee at a **factory/hospital**

▶ **SYNONYMS:** worker, staff

e

EXTEND YOUR VOCABULARY

Employee is a general word to talk about someone who works for a company. You can also talk about **workers** especially to describe people who do manual jobs, for example in a factory, or when you are comparing them to the management. ○ *The union represents nearly 3,400 workers at the Wichita plant.*

Worker is also often used in compounds to talk about the type of work someone does.

▶ a **construction/healthcare/postal** worker

▶ a **skilled/part-time/temporary** worker

▶ a **farm/office/factory** worker

You can talk about **staff** or **personnel** to refer to employees collectively. You can also talk about an individual **staff member**. ○ *Security staff conducted a search of the building.* ○ *The hotel recently hired a new chef and other key personnel.* ○ *The memo was sent to four other staff members.*

em|ploy|ment /ɪmplɔɪmənt/

NONCOUNT NOUN **Employment** is the fact of having or giving someone a paid job. ○ *Many graduates are unable to find employment.* ○ *[+ of] the employment of children under nine* ○ *96% of immigrants are in full-time employment.* ○ *economic policies designed to secure full employment*

▶ **COLLOCATIONS:**
the employment **of** *someone*
seek/find/provide employment
paid/full-time/part-time employment
employment **opportunities/prospects/law/rights**
an employment **agency**

▶ **SYNONYMS:** work, job, occupation

emp|ty /ɛmpti/ (emptier, emptiest)

ADJECTIVE An **empty** place, vehicle, or container has no people or things inside. ○ *an empty office* ○ *an empty glass*

▶ **COLLOCATIONS:**
an empty **room/house/restaurant/hotel/store**
an empty **glass/tank**

completely/nearly/fairly empty

▶ **SYNONYM:** vacant

---

en|close /ɪnklouz/ (encloses, enclosing, enclosed)

VERB If you **enclose** something with a letter, you put it in the same envelope as the letter. ○ *I have enclosed a check for $100.*

▶ **COLLOCATIONS:**
enclose a **check/payment/coupon/form/card/photograph**
enclose a **self-addressed envelope**
the enclosed **postage-paid envelope/reply envelope**

▶ **PHRASE:** I am enclosing *something*

▶ **SYNONYM:** insert

---

en|coun|ter /ɪnkaʊntər/ (encounters, encountering, encountered)

VERB If you **encounter** problems or difficulties, you experience them.
○ *Every day of our lives we encounter stresses of one kind or another.*
○ *Environmental problems they found in Poland were among the worst they encountered.*

▶ **COLLOCATIONS:**
encounter **resistance/opposition**
encounter a **difficulty/problem**

▶ **SYNONYMS:** meet, experience, face

---

en|cour|age /ɪnkɜrɪdʒ/ (encourages, encouraging, encouraged)

VERB If you **encourage** someone **to** do something, you try to persuade them to do it. ○ [+ to] *The plan is to encourage people to sell their assets and pay taxes at the lower rate.*

▶ **COLLOCATIONS:**
encourage **people/children/students**
encourage **companies/businesses/investors**
encourage **customers/users/employees**
strongly/actively encourage

▶ **SYNONYM:** urge

en|cour|age|ment /ɪnkɜrɪdʒmənt/

NONCOUNT NOUN ○ *Friends and colleagues gave me a lot of encouragement.*

▶ **COLLOCATIONS: give/need/offer/receive/provide** encouragement

▶ **PHRASES:**
support and encouragement
given the slightest encouragement

en|cour|ag|ing /ɪnkɜːrɪdʒɪŋ/

ADJECTIVE ○ *These are very encouraging sales figures.*

▶ **COLLOCATIONS:**
extremely/very/tremendously encouraging
encouraging **results/data/news/signs**
encouraging **words**
an encouraging **start/performance/development**

---

en|dorse /ɪndɔːrs/ (endorses, endorsing, endorsed) [MARKETING & SALES]

1 VERB If you **endorse** someone or something, you say publicly that you support or approve of them. ○ *I can endorse their opinion wholeheartedly.* ○ *policies endorsed by the electorate*

▶ **COLLOCATIONS:**
endorsed **by** *someone*
endorsed by the **electorate/voters/state**
endorse a **candidate/plan/idea/treaty**
overwhelmingly/unanimously/heartily endorse *something*

▶ **SYNONYMS:** support, approve

2 VERB If you **endorse** a product or company, you appear in advertisements for it. ○ *The twins endorsed a line of household cleaning products.* ○ *The report also warned people to be wary of diets which are endorsed by celebrities.*

▶ **COLLOCATIONS:**
endorsed **by** *someone*
endorsed by a **celebrity**
endorse a **product/brand/company**

▶ **SYNONYMS:** promote, advertise

en|dorse|ment /ɪndɔːrsmənt/ (endorsements)

1 NOUN An **endorsement** is a statement or action that shows that you support or approve of something or someone. ○ [+ *of*] *That adds up to an endorsement of the status quo.* ○ [+ *for*] *This is a powerful endorsement for his softer style of government.*

▶ **COLLOCATIONS:**
an endorsement **by** *someone*

an endorsement **of/for** *something/someone*
a **ringing/resounding/glowing** endorsement

▶ **SYNONYM:** approval

2 NOUN An **endorsement for** a product or company involves appearing in advertisements for it or showing support for it. ○ *Fashion designers still value celebrity endorsements.* ○ *Bryant has earned millions of dollars in product endorsements.*

▶ **COLLOCATIONS:**
an endorsement **by** *someone*
an endorsement **of/for** *something*
an endorsement of/for a **product/brand/company**
a **celebrity/product/lucrative** endorsement
an endorsement **deal/contract/opportunity**

▶ **PHRASE:** a multimillion dollar endorsement

---

en|er|get|ic /ɛnərdʒɛtɪk/

ADJECTIVE An **energetic** person has a lot of energy. **Energetic** activities require a lot of energy. ○ *Mr. Jones was an inspired and energetic leader.*
○ *an energetic daily exercise regimen of brisk walking, bicycle riding, sports, or aerobics*

▶ **COLLOCATIONS:**
an energetic **woman/man/child**
an energetic **performance/show**
feel energetic

▶ **SYNONYMS:** lively, vigorous

---

en|force /ɪnfɔrs/ (enforces, enforcing, enforced) `LEGAL`

VERB If people in authority **enforce** a law or a rule, they make sure that it is obeyed, usually by punishing people who do not obey it. ○ *Until now, the government has only enforced the ban with regard to American ships.*
○ *The measures are being enforced by Interior Ministry troops.* ○ *A strict curfew was enforced.*

▶ **COLLOCATIONS:**
enforced **by** *someone*
strictly/aggressively/effectively enforce *something*
enforce a **law/regulation/ban/curfew**
a **court/regulator/law** enforces *something*
the **police/army/government** enforce *something*

en|force|ment /ɪnfɔ̱rsmənt/

NONCOUNT NOUN If someone carries out the **enforcement of** an act or rule, they enforce it. ○ [+ of] *The doctors want stricter enforcement of existing laws, such as those banning sales of cigarettes to children.* ○ *Interpol is liaising with all the major law enforcement agencies around the world.*

▶ COLLOCATIONS:
the enforcement **of** *something*
strict/tough/effective/lax/inadequate enforcement
enforcement of a **law/regulation/ban/agreement**
law/traffic/drug enforcement
an enforcement **agency/authority/official**
oversee/relax/tighten/strengthen enforcement

en|gage /ɪngeɪdʒ/ (engages, engaging, engaged)

VERB If you **engage in** an activity, you do it. [FORMAL] ○ [+ in] *He has never engaged in criminal activities.*

▶ COLLOCATIONS:
engage **in** *something*
engage in **activities/acts/practices/crime**
engage in a **discussion/conversation/debate**
engage in **talks/negotiations/business**

en|gi|neer /ɛ̱ndʒɪnɪ̱ər/ (engineers)   JOBS

NOUN An **engineer** is a person who uses scientific knowledge to design, construct, and maintain engines and machines or structures such as roads, railroads, and bridges. ○ *Structural engineers assessed the damage to the building.* ○ *one of the engineers who designed the railroad*

▶ COLLOCATIONS:
a **mechanical/electrical/structural** engineer
an engineer **designs/invents** *something*
an engineer **surveys/inspects** *something*

en|large /ɪnlɑ̱rdʒ/ (enlarges, enlarging, enlarged)

VERB When you **enlarge** something or when it **enlarges**, it becomes bigger. ○ *The college plans to enlarge its stadium.* ○ *The glands in the neck may enlarge.* ○ *the use of silicone to enlarge the breasts*

▶ COLLOCATIONS:
enlarge the **breasts/penis**
enlarge a **hole/image**

an enlarged **heart/organ/prostate**
digitally/greatly/significantly enlarged

---

en|roll /ɪnrоʊl/ (enrolls, enrolling, enrolled)

VERB If you **enroll in** a class or **at** a school, you officially join it. ○ [+ at] He
has already enrolled at the university.

▶ **COLLOCATIONS:**
  enroll **in** something
  enroll **at** a place
  enroll in a **class/program/course**
  enroll at a **school/university/college**
  a **student/child** enrolls

▶ **SYNONYM:** register

---

en|ter|prise /ɛntərpraɪz/ (enterprises) 　ORGANIZATION

NOUN An **enterprise** is a company or business, often a small one. ○ There
are plenty of small industrial enterprises. ○ Many small and relatively primitive
enterprises flourish under laissez-faire. ○ one of Japan's most profitable
enterprises

▶ **COLLOCATIONS:**
  a **commercial/industrial/state** enterprise
  a **profitable/profit-making/loss-making** enterprise
  an enterprise **flourishes/succeeds/collapses**
  an enterprise **produces/supplies** something

▶ **PHRASE:** small-to-medium enterprises

▶ **SYNONYMS:** business, company

---

en|thu|si|asm /ɪnθuziæzəm/

NONCOUNT NOUN **Enthusiasm** is the feeling that you have when you
really enjoy something or want to do something. ○ [+ for] This probably
reflects our enthusiasm for foreign cars and continuing dissatisfaction with
American vehicles.

▶ **COLLOCATIONS:**
  show/generate/dampen enthusiasm
  a **shared/real/genuine/renewed/growing** enthusiasm
  great/infectious/youthful enthusiasm

en|tire|ly /ɪntaɪərli/

ADVERB **Entirely** means completely and not just partly. ○ *an entirely new approach* ○ *The two operations achieve entirely different results.* ○ *Their price depended almost entirely on their scarcity.*

▶ **COLLOCATIONS:**
entirely **new/different**
entirely **predictable/convincing/understandable**
consist/depend entirely
almost entirely

▶ **SYNONYMS:** completely, totally

---

en|trance /ɛntrəns/ (entrances) `OFFICE`

NOUN The **entrance to** a place is the way into it, for example a door or gate. ○ [+ *to/into/of*] *the entrance to the church* ○ *A marble entrance hall leads to a sitting room.*

▶ **COLLOCATIONS:**
an entrance **to/into/of** *something*
a **side/main/front/back** entrance
an entrance **hall/gate**

▶ **SYNONYM:** entry

---

en|tre|pre|neur /ɒntrəprənɜr, -nʊər/ (entrepreneurs) `JOBS`

NOUN An **entrepreneur** is a person who sets up businesses and business deals. ○ *The two Sydney-based entrepreneurs founded the company in 1995.* ○ *the financial incentives for successful entrepreneurs to innovate and invest*

▶ **COLLOCATIONS:**
an entrepreneur **founds/invents/launches** *something*
a **budding/successful/visionary** entrepreneur
an entrepreneur **owns/builds/founds/starts** *something*

en|tre|pre|neur|ial /ɒntrəprənɜriəl, -nʊər-/

ADJECTIVE **Entrepreneurial** means having the qualities that are needed to succeed as an entrepreneur. ○ *her prodigious entrepreneurial flair* ○ *His initial entrepreneurial venture was setting up Britain's first computer-dating agency.* ○ *Germany's entrepreneurial culture is less vigorous than it was.*

▶ **COLLOCATIONS:**
entrepreneurial **flair/spirit/skill**
an entrepreneurial **culture/mind-set/venture**

highly entrepreneurial

▸ SYNONYM: business

---

entry-level /ɛntrɪlɛvəl/ `PERSONNEL`

ADJECTIVE **Entry-level** jobs are suitable for people who do not have previous experience or qualifications in a particular area of work.
○ *Many entry-level jobs were filled by high school grads.*

▸ COLLOCATIONS:
an entry-level **job/position/post**
entry-level **workers/wages**

---

en|velope /ɛnvəloʊp, ɒn-/ (envelopes) `OFFICE`

NOUN An **envelope** is a paper cover in which you put a letter before you send it to someone.

▸ COLLOCATIONS:
a **fat/bulky/thin/thick/padded/manila/plain/business** envelope
a **self-addressed/postage-paid/reply/return** envelope
a **sealed** envelope
address/open/stuff an envelope

---

en|vi|ron|ment /ɪnvaɪrənmənt, -vaɪərn-/ (environments)

1 NOUN Someone's **environment** is their surroundings, especially the conditions in which they grow up, live, or work. ○ *Students are taught in a safe, secure environment.* ○ *His method is based on observing the animal in its natural environment.*

▸ COLLOCATIONS:
a **safe/secure/supportive** environment
a **work/business/learning** environment
a **natural** environment

▸ SYNONYMS: surroundings, setting, background

2 NOUN The **environment** is the natural world of land, sea, air, plants, and animals. ○ *the need to protect the environment* ○ *Their aim is to increase income from tourism without damaging the environment.*

▸ COLLOCATIONS:
protect/preserve/conserve the environment
damage/pollute/harm the environment
an environment **spokesman/department**

▸ SYNONYMS: the wild, the natural world, the countryside

> **USAGE:** *the* + **environment**
> Remember that when you use **the environment** to talk about the natural world, you always need the definite article **the**.

en|vi|ron|men|tal /ɪnvaɪrənmɛntəl, -vaɪərn-/

ADJECTIVE ○ *the environmental impact of buildings and transportation systems* ○ *It protects against environmental hazards such as wind and sun.*

▶ **COLLOCATIONS:**
an environmental **group/problem/issue**
environmental **protection/impact**

---

equal /ikwəl/ (equals, equaling, equaled) [in BRIT, use **equalling, equalled**]

1 ADJECTIVE If two things are **equal** or if one thing is **equal to** another, they are the same in size, number, standard, or value. ○ [+ *to*] *Investors can borrow an amount equal to the property's purchase price.* ○ *in a population having equal numbers of men and women* ○ *Research and teaching are of equal importance.*

2 ADJECTIVE If people are **equal**, they all have the same rights and are treated in the same way. ○ [+ *in*] *We are equal in every way.* ○ *At any gambling game, everyone is equal.*

▶ **COLLOCATIONS:**
an equal **amount/proportion/quantity**
equal **importance/status/value**
equal **pay/treatment/rights**
roughly/approximately/almost equal

▶ **PHRASE:** equal opportunities

▶ **SYNONYMS:** the same, identical, equivalent

3 VERB If something **equals** a particular number or amount, it is the same as that amount or the equivalent of that amount. ○ *9 percent interest less 7 percent inflation equals 2 percent.* ○ *The average pay raise equaled 1.41 times inflation.*

▶ **COLLOCATIONS:** equal a **sum/total/amount**

equali|ty /ɪkwɒlɪti/

NONCOUNT NOUN Equality is the same status, rights, and responsibilities for all the members of a society, group, or family. ○ [+ *of*] *equality of* the sexes ○ *Women had not achieved full legal and social equality in America by the 1930s.*

▶ **COLLOCATIONS:**
equality **of** something
racial/sexual/social equality
equality of **opportunity/status/rights**

▶ **SYNONYMS:** fairness, equity

---

equip|ment /ɪkwɪpmənt/ `OFFICE`

NONCOUNT NOUN Equipment consists of the things that are used for a particular purpose, for example, a hobby or job. ○ *computers, electronic equipment, and machine tools* ○ *a shortage of medical equipment and medicine*

▶ **COLLOCATIONS:**
electrical/electronic/medical/military equipment
computer/telecommunications equipment
modern/state-of-the-art/high-tech equipment

▶ **SYNONYMS:** machinery, supplies, tools

> **USAGE: Noncount noun**
>
> Remember, **equipment** is a noncount noun, so you do **not** talk about "equipments" or "an equipment". ○ *The company supplies schools with computer equipment.*
>
> You can talk about a **piece of equipment**. ○ *You can connect up to eight pieces of equipment to a single line.*

---

er|rand /ɛrənd/ (errands)

NOUN An **errand** is a short trip to do a job, for example, when you go to a store to buy something. ○ *We ran errands and brought her meals when she was sick.*

▶ **COLLOCATIONS:**
run/do/go on errands
a **simple/little/important** errand

▶ **PHRASE:** chores and errands

es|ca|la|tor /ɛskəleɪtər/ (escalators)　`OFFICE`

NOUN An **escalator** is a set of moving stairs. ○ *Take the escalator to the third floor.*

▶ COLLOCATIONS: **ride/take** the escalator

es|sen|tial /ɪsɛnʃ°l/ (essentials)

1 **ADJECTIVE** Something that is **essential** is extremely important or absolutely necessary to a particular subject, situation, or activity. ○ [+ to-inf] *It was absolutely essential to separate crops from the areas that animals used as pasture.* ○ *Jordan promised to trim the city budget without cutting essential services.*

2 **ADJECTIVE** The **essential** aspects of something are its most basic or important aspects. ○ *Most authorities agree that play is an essential part of a child's development.* ○ *Tact and diplomacy are two essential ingredients in international relations.*

▶ COLLOCATIONS:
essential **for** *something*
absolutely essential
essential **services/information**
an essential **ingredient/element/part/component**
an essential **requirement/feature**

▶ SYNONYMS: crucial, vital, fundamental, basic

es|tab|lish /ɪstæblɪʃ/ (establishes, establishing, established)　`ORGANIZATION`

1 **VERB** If someone **establishes** something such as an organization, a type of activity, or a set of rules, they create it or introduce it in such a way that it is likely to last for a long time. ○ *The U.N. has established detailed criteria for who should be allowed to vote.* ○ *The School was established in 1989 by an Italian professor.*

→ see note at **launch**

▶ SYNONYM: found

2 **VERB** If you **establish that** something is true, you discover facts that show that it is definitely true. [FORMAL] ○ [+ that] *Medical tests established that she was not their own child.* ○ [+ how] *It will be essential to establish how the money is being spent.* ○ *An autopsy was being done to establish the cause of death.*

▶ **COLLOCATIONS:**
establish a **link/relationship**
firmly/quickly establish *something*

▶ **SYNONYMS:** ascertain, prove, confirm

es|tab|lish|ment /ɪstˈæblɪʃmənt/ **(establishments)**

1 NOUN The **establishment of** an organization or system is the act of creating it or beginning it. [FORMAL] ○ [+ *of*] *His ideas influenced the establishment of National Portrait Galleries in London and Edinburgh.* ○ [+ *of*] *the establishment of diplomatic relations*

▶ **COLLOCATIONS:**
the establishment **of** *something*
announce/support/propose the establishment of *something*
oppose the establishment of *something*
the establishment of a **state**
the establishment of **relations**

▶ **SYNONYMS:** creation, formation

2 NOUN An **establishment** is a store, business, or organization occupying a particular building or place. [FORMAL] ○ *a scientific research establishment* ○ *stores and other commercial establishments*

▶ **COLLOCATIONS:**
a **political/medical/educational** establishment
a **literary/scientific/religious** establishment

▶ **SYNONYMS:** office, building

---

euro /yʊ̯ərˈoʊ/ **(euros)** `BANKING & FINANCE`

NOUN The **euro** is a unit of money that is used by most countries in the European Union.

▶ **COLLOCATIONS:**
adopt/use/introduce/reject the euro
the euro **zone/area**
euro **notes/coins**
a **strong/weak** euro

---

evalu|ate /ɪvˈælyueɪt/ **(evaluates, evaluating, evaluated)**

VERB If you **evaluate** something or someone, you consider them in order to make a judgment about them, for example about how good or bad they are. ○ *They will first send in trained nurses to evaluate the needs of the individual situation.* ○ *The market situation is difficult to evaluate.* ○ [+ how] *We evaluate how well we do something.*

▶ **COLLOCATIONS:**
evaluate a **situation/impact/risk**
evaluate the **effectiveness** of *something*
evaluate the **performance** of *someone*
carefully evaluate *something*

▶ **SYNONYMS:** assess, analyze

evalu|ation /ɪvælyueɪʃªn/ (evaluations)

NOUN Evaluation is the act of considering someone or something in order to make a judgment about them, for example, about how good or bad they are. ○ [+ of] *the opinions and evaluations of college students* ○ *Evaluation is standard practice for all training arranged through the school.*

▶ **COLLOCATIONS:**
evaluation **of** *something*
undergo/provide evaluation
performance/job/psychiatric/psychological evaluation
thorough/careful/formal evaluation
evaluation **process/team/system/report**

▶ **SYNONYMS:** analysis, appraisal, assessment, review

even|tu|al|ly /ɪvɛntʃuəli/

1 **ADVERB Eventually** means in the end, especially after a lot of delays, problems, or arguments. ○ *Eventually, the army caught up with him in Latvia.* ○ *The flight eventually got away six hours late.*

▶ **SYNONYM:** finally

2 **ADVERB Eventually** means at the end of a situation or process or as the final result of it. ○ *Dehydration eventually leads to death.* ○ *researchers who hope eventually to create insulin-producing cells*

▶ **SYNONYM:** ultimately

evi|dent /ɛvɪdənt/

ADJECTIVE If something is **evident**, you notice it easily and clearly. ○ *His footprints were clearly evident in the heavy dust.* ○ [+ in] *The threat of inflation is already evident in bond prices.*

▶ **COLLOCATIONS:**
evident **from** *something*
evident **to** *someone*
become/seem evident
clearly evident

▶ **SYNONYM:** noticeable

---

ex|ag|ger|ate /ɪgzædʒəreɪt/ (exaggerates, exaggerating, exaggerated)

VERB If something **exaggerates** a situation, quality, or feature, it makes the situation, quality, or feature appear greater, more obvious, or more important than it really is. ○ *These figures exaggerate the loss of competitiveness.*

▶ **COLLOCATIONS:**
exaggerate a **situation/quality/feature**
exaggerate a **threat/problem/risk**
exaggerate the **importance/extent** of *something*
exaggerate a **claim/case**
greatly/grossly exaggerate

ex|ag|gera|tion /ɪgzædʒəreɪʃən/

NOUN (exaggerations) ○ *He's completely incompetent — and that's no exaggeration.*

▶ **COLLOCATIONS:** a **gross/slight** exaggeration

▶ **PHRASES:**
say without exaggeration
it is no exaggeration to say *something*

▶ **SYNONYM:** overstatement

---

ex|am|ine /ɪgzæmɪn/ (examines, examining, examined)

1 VERB If you **examine** something, you look at it carefully. ○ *He examined her passport and stamped it.* ○ *Forensic scientists are examining the bombers' car.*

▶ **COLLOCATIONS:**
examine **evidence**
a **scientist/investigator/expert** examines *something*
examine **forensically/closely**

▶ **SYNONYMS:** study, inspect

2 VERB If a doctor **examines** you, he or she looks at your body, feels it, or does simple tests in order to check how healthy you are. ○ *Another doctor examined her and could still find nothing wrong.*

example | 254

▶ **COLLOCATIONS:**
a **doctor/psychiatrist/specialist** examines *someone*
examine a **patient**
examine *someone* **carefully**

3 **VERB** If an idea, proposal, or plan **is examined**, it is considered very carefully. ○ *I have given the matter much thought, examining all the possible alternatives.* ○ *The plans will be examined by E.U. environment ministers.*
○ [+ *how*] *Psychologists have been examining how we make sense of events.*

▶ **COLLOCATIONS:**
examined **by** *someone*
examine a **possibility/proposal/implication**
examine an **issue/effect/aspect**
examine *something* **critically/systematically**

▶ **SYNONYMS:** consider, investigate

ex|ami|na|tion /ɪgzæmɪneɪʃᵊn/ (examinations)

NOUN ○ [+ *of*] *The Navy is to carry out an examination of the wreck tomorrow.* ○ *He was later discharged after an examination at the local hospital.* ○ *The proposal requires careful examination and consideration.*

▶ **COLLOCATIONS:**
an examination **of** *something*
conduct/undergo/perform an examination
a **forensic/physical/medical** examination
a **careful/internal/postmortem** examination
a **detailed/close** examination
an examination **reveals/shows/finds** *something*

▶ **SYNONYMS:** inspection, consideration

exam /ɪgzæm/ (exams)

NOUN An **exam** is a formal test that you take to show your knowledge of a subject. ○ *I don't want to take any more exams.*

▶ **COLLOCATIONS:**
a **difficult/easy** exam
a **math/history** exam
a **written/oral** exam
take/pass/fail an exam

ex|am|ple /ɪgzæmpᵊl/ (examples)

1 **NOUN** An **example of** something is a particular situation, object, or person that shows that what is being claimed is true. ○ [+ *of*] *The doctors* *gave numerous examples of patients being expelled from the hospital.* ○ *The following example illustrates the change that took place.*

▶ COLLOCATIONS:
  an example **of** something
  cite/provide/give an example
  an example **illustrates** something
  a **good/classic/perfect** example
  a **specific/typical/concrete** example

2 PHRASE You use **for example** to introduce and emphasize something that shows that something is true. The abbreviation **e.g.** is used in written notes. ○ *"educational toys" that are designed to promote the development of, for example, children's spatial ability* ○ *A few simple precautions can be taken, for example, ensuring that desks are the right height.*

▶ SYNONYMS: for instance, such as

ex|ceed /ɪksiːd/ (exceeds, exceeding, exceeded)

VERB If something **exceeds** a particular amount or number, it is greater or larger than that amount or number. [FORMAL] ○ *Its research budget exceeds $700 million a year.* ○ *The demand for places at some schools exceeds the supply.* ○ *His performance exceeded all expectations.*

▶ COLLOCATIONS:
  exceed a **limit/expectation/target/supply**
  far/greatly/easily exceed something

▶ SYNONYM: surpass

ex|cess /ɪksɛs/ (excesses)

1 NOUN An **excess of** something is a larger amount than is needed, allowed, or usual. ○ *Large doses of vitamin C are not toxic, since the body will excrete any excess.*

▶ COLLOCATION: an excess **of** something

▶ SYNONYMS: surfeit, surplus

2 PHRASE **In excess of** means more than a particular amount. [FORMAL] ○ *Avoid deposits in excess of $20,000 in any one account.* ○ *The energy value of dried fruits is considerably in excess of that of fresh items.*

ex|ces|sive /ɪksɛsɪv/

ADJECTIVE If you describe the amount or level of something as **excessive**, you disapprove of it because it is more or higher than is necessary or reasonable. ○ *the alleged use of excessive force by police* ○ *The government says that local authority spending is excessive.*

▸ **COLLOCATIONS:**
an excessive **punishment/sentence/fine**
manifestly/grossly excessive
excessive **consumption/drinking/use/intake**
excessive **noise/speed/heat/force**

▸ **PHRASE:** excessive and disproportionate

▸ **SYNONYMS:** inordinate, undue, exorbitant

---

ex|cept /ɪksɛpt/

1 PREPOSITION You use **except** to introduce the only thing or person that a statement does not apply to, or a fact that prevents a statement from being completely true. ○ *No illness, except malaria, has caused as much death as smallpox.*

● **Except** is also a conjunction. ○ *Physical examination was normal, except that her blood pressure was high.*

2 PHRASE You use **except for** to introduce the only thing or person that prevents a statement from being completely true. ○ *Elephant shrew are found over most of Africa, except for the west.*

▸ **SYNONYMS:** apart from, excluding

ex|cep|tion /ɪksɛpʃ°n/ (exceptions)

NOUN An **exception** is a particular thing, person, or situation that is not included in a general statement, judgment, or rule. ○ [+ *of*] *The trees there are older than any other trees in the world, with the exception of the Californian redwoods.* ○ *The law makes no exceptions.*

▸ **COLLOCATIONS:**
make an exception
a **notable/obvious/possible/rare** exception
the **sole/only** exception

▸ **PHRASE:** with the exception of

ex|cep|tion|al /ɪksɛpʃən°l/

1 ADJECTIVE You use **exceptional** to describe someone or something that has a particular quality, usually a good quality, to an unusually high degree. ○ *children with exceptional ability*

▸ **COLLOCATIONS:**
exceptional **talent/ability/skill**
an exceptional **student/child**
an exceptional **performance**
exceptional **service**

▸ **SYNONYM:** extraordinary

2 **ADJECTIVE Exceptional** situations and incidents are unusual and only likely to happen infrequently. [FORMAL] ○ *A review panel concluded that there were no exceptional circumstances that would warrant a lesser penalty for him.*

▸ **COLLOCATIONS:** an exceptional **situation/circumstance/case**

▸ **SYNONYM:** unusual

e

ex|change /ɪkstʃeɪndʒ/ (exchanges, exchanging, exchanged) BANKING & FINANCE

VERB If you **exchange** something, you replace it with a different thing, especially something that is better or more satisfactory. ○ *the chance to sell back or exchange goods* ○ [+ for] *If the car you have leased is clearly unsatisfactory, you can always exchange it for another.*

▸ **COLLOCATIONS:**
exchange *something* **for** *something*
exchange *something* for **cash/goods**

▸ **SYNONYMS:** change, trade

ex|change rate /ɪkstʃeɪndʒ reɪt/ (exchange rates)

NOUN The **exchange rate** is the amount of one country's money that you can buy with another country's money. ○ *The exchange rate is around 3.7 pesos to the dollar.*

▸ **COLLOCATIONS:**
the **official** exchange rate
the **dollar's** exchange rate
stabilize/destabilize exchange rates
high/falling/fluctuating exchange rates

ex|clude /ɪksklud/ (excludes, excluding, excluded)

VERB If you **exclude** something that has some connection with what you are doing, you deliberately do not use it or consider it. ○ [+ from] *They eat only plant foods, and take care to exclude animal products from other areas of their lives.* ○ *In some schools, Christmas carols are being modified to exclude any reference to Christ.*

▸ **COLLOCATIONS:**
exclude *something* **from** *something*
deliberately/unfairly/temporarily exclude

▸ **SYNONYMS:** omit, reject

ex|clud|ing /ɪkˈskluːdɪŋ/

PREPOSITION You use **excluding** before mentioning a person or thing to show that you are not including them in your statement. ○ *The families questioned, excluding those on Medicaid, have a net income of $500 a week.* ○ *Excluding water, half of the body's weight is protein.*

▶ **SYNONYMS:** except, without

ex|clu|sion /ɪkˈskluːʒən/ (exclusions)

NOUN The **exclusion of** something is the act of deliberately not using, allowing, or considering it. ○ [+ *of*] *It calls for the exclusion of all commercial lending institutions from the college loan program.* ○ *Certain exclusions and limitations apply.*

▶ **COLLOCATIONS:**
the exclusion **of** *someone/something*
exclusion **from** *something*
social exclusion
permanent/temporary/automatic exclusion
an exclusion **zone/order/clause**

▶ **SYNONYM:** ban

ex|clu|sive /ɪkˈskluːsɪv/

1 ADJECTIVE Something that is **exclusive** is available only to people who are rich or powerful. ○ *It's marketed very much as an exclusive product.*

▶ **COLLOCATIONS:**
an exclusive **product**
an exclusive **school/resort/hotel**
socially/racially exclusive

▶ **SYNONYM:** select

2 ADJECTIVE If a person or company has an **exclusive** contract or agreement with another person or company, they only do business with that person or company. ○ *the cable industry's exclusive deals with high-speed Internet services*

▶ **COLLOCATIONS:** an exclusive **contract/agreement/deal**

---

ex|ecute /ˈɛksɪkyut/ (executes, executing, executed)

VERB If you **execute** a plan, you carry it out. [FORMAL] ○ *We are going to execute our campaign plan to the letter.* ○ *the expertly executed break-in in which three men overpowered and tied up a detective*

▶ **COLLOCATION:** **brilliantly** executed

ex|ecu|tion

NONCOUNT NOUN ○ [+ of] *U.S. forces are fully prepared for the execution of any action once the order is given by the president.* ○ *the need for first-class customer care and flawless execution*

▶ **COLLOCATIONS:**
the execution **of** *something*
the execution of a **plan/strategy/agreement**

---

ex|ecu|tive /ɪɡzɛ̱kyətɪv/ **(executives)**   `JOBS`

1 NOUN An **executive** is someone who is employed by a business at a senior level. Executives decide what the business should do, and ensure that it is done. ○ *an advertising executive* ○ *Her husband is a senior bank executive.*

▶ **COLLOCATIONS:**
appoint an executive
a **chief/senior/top** executive
a **marketing/advertising/television/industry** executive

▶ **SYNONYMS:** director, official, manager

> **EXTEND YOUR VOCABULARY**
>
> Business organizations have different management structures and the titles of the members of the **top management** are different from company to company. The people making decisions at a senior level may be called **executives** or **directors**, and there may be a **board of directors**.
>
> The most senior person in a business organization may be called the **CEO** (chief executive officer), the **president**, or the **chairman**.
>
> A person who is responsible for running part of a business, such as a department, is usually called a **manager**.

2 NOUN The **executive** is the part of the government of a country that is concerned with carrying out decisions or orders, as opposed to the part that makes laws or the part that deals with criminals. ○ *The executive, the legislature, and the judiciary are supposed to be separate.*

▶ **COLLOCATIONS:** a **national/power-sharing** executive

▶ **SYNONYMS:** administration, government

ex|er|cise /ˈɛksərsaɪz/ (exercises)

NOUN An **exercise** is an activity that you do in order to practice a skill.
○ *a writing exercise*

▶ **COLLOCATIONS:**
a **writing/training/military** exercise
an exercise **book**

---

ex|hib|it /ɪgˈzɪbɪt/ (exhibits, exhibiting, exhibited)   MARKETING & SALES

VERB If someone or something shows a particular quality, feeling, or type of behavior, you can say that they **exhibit** it. [FORMAL] ○ *He has exhibited symptoms of anxiety and overwhelming worry.* ○ *Two cats or more in one house will also exhibit territorial behavior.* ○ *The economy continued to exhibit signs of decline in September.*

▶ **COLLOCATIONS:**
exhibit **behavior/signs/symptoms**
exhibit **characteristics/similarities/variation**
typically/commonly exhibit *something*

▶ **SYNONYM:** show

ex|hi|bi|tion /ˌɛksɪˈbɪʃᵊn/ (exhibitions)

NOUN An **exhibition** is a public event at which pictures, sculptures, or other objects of interest are displayed, for example at a museum or art gallery. ○ [+ of] *an exhibition of expressionist art*

▶ **COLLOCATIONS:**
an exhibition **of** *something*
an exhibition of **paintings/photographs/art**

---

ex|pand /ɪkˈspænd/ (expands, expanding, expanded)   R&D

1 VERB If something **expands** or **is expanded**, it becomes larger.
○ *Engineers noticed that the pipes were not expanding as expected.* ○ *The money supply expanded by 14.6 percent in the year to September.* ○ [V-ing] *a rapidly expanding universe*

2 VERB If something such as a business, organization, or service **expands**, or if you **expand** it, it becomes bigger and includes more people, goods, or activities. ○ *The popular ceramics industry expanded toward the middle of the 19th century.* ○ *Health officials are proposing to expand their services by organizing counseling.*

▶ **COLLOCATIONS:**
expanded **by** *an amount*

an expanding **universe/economy/population**
expand **capacity/coverage/production**
expand the **scope/range** of *something*
expand **rapidly/dramatically**

▶ **SYNONYMS:** increase, grow, enlarge, develop

ex|pan|sion /ɪkspænʃ°n/

NONCOUNT NOUN Expansion is the process of becoming greater in size, number, or amount. ○ [+ *of*] *the rapid expansion of private health insurance* ○ *a new period of economic expansion*

▶ **COLLOCATIONS:**
the expansion **of** *something*
rapid/further/future expansion
economic/global/major expansion
an expansion **plan/program/project/team**

▶ **SYNONYMS:** growth, spread, increase, development

---

ex|pect /ɪkspɛkt/ (expects, expecting, expected)

1 VERB If you **expect** something **to** happen, you believe that it will happen. ○ [+ *to-inf*] *a worker who expects to lose his job in the next few weeks* ○ [+ *to-inf*] *The talks are expected to continue until tomorrow.* ○ *They expect a gradual improvement in sales of new cars.*

▶ **COLLOCATIONS:**
expect **growth/returns/earnings/profits/results**
be **widely** expected

▶ **SYNONYM:** anticipate

2 VERB If you **expect** something, or **expect** a person **to** do something, you believe that it is your right to have that thing, or the person's duty to do it for you. ○ *He wasn't expecting our hospitality.* ○ [+ *to-inf*] *I do expect to have some time to myself in the evenings.*

▶ **COLLOCATIONS:**
expect *something* **of** *someone*
reasonably/realistically/normally expect *something*

ex|pec|ta|tions /ɛkspɛkteɪʃ°nz/

PLURAL NOUN Your **expectations** are your strong hopes or beliefs that something will happen or that you will get something that you want. ○ *Students' expectations were as varied as their expertise.* ○ *The car has been General Motors' most visible success story, with sales far exceeding expectations.*

▶ **COLLOCATIONS:**
  lower/raise expectations
  meet/exceed/surpass expectations
  realistic/reasonable/unrealistic/high expectations

▶ **SYNONYMS:** hope, prediction, forecast

---

ex|pendi|ture /ɪkspɛndɪtʃər/ BANKING & FINANCE

NONCOUNT NOUN Expenditure is the spending of money on something, or the money that is spent on something. [FORMAL] ○ *Policies of tax reduction must lead to reduced public expenditure.* ○ [+ on] *They should cut their expenditure on defense.*

▶ **COLLOCATIONS:**
  expenditure **on** *something*
  reduce/cut expenditure
  rising/falling/total expenditure
  advertising/health/public/government expenditure

▶ **SYNONYMS:** spending, costs

---

ex|pense /ɪkspɛns/ (expenses) BANKING & FINANCE

1 NONCOUNT NOUN Expense is the cost or price of something. ○ *He bought a big television at great expense.*

2 PLURAL NOUN Expenses are amounts of money that you spend while doing something in the course of your work, which will be paid back to you afterward. ○ *As a member of the International Olympic Committee her fares and hotel expenses were paid by the IOC.* ○ *Can you claim this back on expenses?*

▶ **COLLOCATIONS:**
  operating/business expenses
  hotel/travel/work-related expenses
  legitimate/out-of-pocket expenses
  incur/claim/claim back/deduct expenses
  cover/pay/refund expenses

▶ **PHRASE:** all expenses paid

▶ **SYNONYM:** costs

ex|pen|sive /ɪkspɛnsɪv/

ADJECTIVE If something is **expensive**, it costs a lot of money. ○ *an expensive restaurant*

▶ COLLOCATIONS:
   very/prohibitively/extremely/quite expensive
   an expensive **car/restaurant/item/home/drug**

▶ SYNONYM: costly

ex|pense ac|count /ɪkspɛns əkaʊnt/ (expense accounts)

NOUN An **expense account** is an arrangement between an employer and an employee that allows the employee to spend the company's money on things relating to their job, such as traveling or dealing with clients.
   ○ *He put Elizabeth's motel bill and airfare on his expense account.*

▶ COLLOCATIONS:
   a **generous** expense account
   pad an expense account

---

ex|peri|ence /ɪkspɪəriəns/ (experiences, experiencing, PERSONNEL experienced)

1 NONCOUNT NOUN **Experience** is knowledge or skill in a particular job or activity, that you have gained because you have done that job or activity for a long time. ○ *He has also had managerial experience on every level.*
   ○ [+ *in/of/with*] *three years of relevant experience in stem-cell research*

▶ COLLOCATIONS:
   experience **of/in/with/as** *something*
   have/gain/lack experience
   work/office/managerial/professional experience
   relevant/previous/essential/valuable experience

2 NONCOUNT NOUN **Experience** is used to refer to the past events, knowledge, and feelings that make up someone's life or character.
   ○ *I should not be in any danger here, but experience has taught me caution.*
   ○ *She had learned from experience to take little rests in between her daily routine.*

▶ COLLOCATIONS:
   life/past/personal/first-hand experience
   learn from experience
   experience **teaches/shows** *something*

3 NOUN An **experience** is something that you do or that happens to you, especially something important that affects you. ○ [+ *of*] *His only experience of gardening so far proved immensely satisfying.* ○ *Many of his clients are very nervous, usually because of a bad experience in the past.*

▶ COLLOCATIONS:
   an experience **of/with** *something*
   have/enjoy/describe an experience

a **good/bad/painful/wonderful** experience
the **whole** experience

▶ SYNONYMS: event, incident

USAGE: **Count and noncount uses**

As a noncount noun, you use **experience** to talk generally about the skills and knowledge that someone has gained over time. You do not talk about "work experiences" or "some experiences of dealing with customers." ○ *They gain practical, hands-on experience.*

As a count noun, an **experience** is a particular event or situation that you go through. ○ *We're trying to create a positive experience for our customers.* ○ *The whole experience was really worthwhile.*

---

4 VERB If you **experience** a particular situation, you are in that situation or it happens to you. ○ *British business is now experiencing a severe recession.*

▶ COLLOCATIONS:
experience a **difficulty/problem/loss**
experience **growth/decline**

ex|pe|ri|enced /ɪkspɪəriənst/

ADJECTIVE If you are **experienced**, you have knowledge or skill in a particular job or activity because you have done it for a long time. ○ *These were experienced investors.*

▶ COLLOCATIONS:
experienced **at** *something/doing something*
experienced **in** *something/doing something*
very/vastly/highly/quite experienced
an experienced **player/teacher/pilot/driver**
an experienced **professional/worker/manager**

▶ PHRASE: skilled and experienced

---

ex|pert /ɛkspɜrt/ (experts)   JOBS

NOUN An **expert** is a person who is very skilled at doing something or who knows a lot about a particular subject. ○ *Health experts warn that the issue is a global problem.* ○ [+ on] *an expert on trade in that area*

▶ COLLOCATIONS:
an expert **in/on** *something*
a **leading/acknowledged** expert

a **legal/medical/health/security** expert
experts **warn/predict/say**

▶ SYNONYM: specialist

ex|per|tise /ˈɛkspɜrtiːz/

NONCOUNT NOUN **Expertise** is special skill or knowledge that is acquired by training, study, or practice. ○ [+ to-inf] *The problem is that most local authorities lack the expertise to deal sensibly in this market.* ○ [+ in] *students with expertise in forensics* ○ *a pooling and sharing of knowledge and expertise*

▶ COLLOCATIONS:
expertise **in** *something*
lack/possess/acquire/bring expertise
technical/managerial/scientific expertise
marketing/engineering/computer expertise

▶ PHRASE: knowledge and expertise

USAGE: *expert* or *expertise*?

An **expert** is a person with special knowledge or skills in a particular area. ○ *Experts are predicting that inflation will start to rise again next year.*
Expert can also be used as an adjective. ○ *expert medical advice*

Expertise is a noncount noun that is used to talk about the specialized knowledge or skills that an **expert** has. ○ *employees with less technical expertise*

---

ex|plain /ɪkspleɪn/ (explains, explaining, explained)   COMMUNICATIONS

1 VERB If you **explain** something, you give details about it or describe it so that it can be understood. ○ *Not every judge, however, has the ability to explain the law in simple terms.* ○ [+ how] *Professor Griffiths explained how the drug appears to work.*

2 VERB If you **explain** something that has happened, you give people reasons for it, especially in an attempt to justify it. ○ [+ why] *Explain why you didn't telephone.* ○ [+ that] *The receptionist apologized for the delay, explaining that it had been a hectic day.*

▶ COLLOCATIONS:
explain the **meaning/significance** of *something*
explain the **circumstances/situation/reason**
explain the **difference**
explain a **phenomenon/concept**

▶ **SYNONYMS:** describe, account for

→ see note at **describe**

ex|pla|na|tion /ɛkspləneɪʃ⁰n/ (explanations)

NOUN ○ [+of] *The researchers offer two possible explanations of this.* ○ [+ for] *an explanation for the different results*

▶ **COLLOCATIONS:**
an explanation **of/for** *something*
give/provide/offer an explanation
a **plausible/satisfactory** explanation

▶ **SYNONYMS:** reason, description

---

ex|port (exports, exporting, exported)   `LOGISTICS & DISTRIBUTION`

The verb is pronounced /ɪkˈspɔːt/. The noun is pronounced /ˈekspɔːt/.

1 **VERB** To **export** products or raw materials means to sell them to another country. ○ *The nation also exports beef.* ○ [+ to] *They expect the antibiotic products to be exported to Southeast Asia and Africa.* ○ *To earn foreign exchange we must export.*

▶ **COLLOCATIONS:**
export *something* **to** *somewhere*
export *something* **worldwide/overseas**
export **oil/goods/products**
illegally export *something*

2 **NOUN** **Exports** are goods that are sold to another country and sent there. ○ *He did this to promote American exports.* ○ *Ghana's main export is cocoa.*

▶ **COLLOCATIONS:**
exports **of** *something*
exports of **goods/products/commodities**
halt/boost/ban/increase exports
exports **rise/fall/grow**
cheap/expensive/illegal exports
total/net exports
oil/arms/agricultural/live exports
the export **market/trade**

ex|po|sure /ɪkspoʊʒər/

NONCOUNT NOUN **Exposure to** something dangerous means being in a situation where it might affect you. ○ [+ to] *Exposure to lead is known to damage the brains of young children.* ○ [+ to] *the potential exposure of people to nuclear waste*

▶ **COLLOCATIONS:**
  exposure **to** *something*
  sun/radiation/asbestos exposure
  risk/limit/reduce/increase/measure/cause exposure
  prolonged/repeated/excessive/constant exposure
  low-level/minimal/accidental exposure

▶ **SYNONYMS:** subjection, contact, experience

ex|press /ɪkspres/ (expresses, expressing, expressed) COMMUNICATIONS

VERB When you **express** an idea or feeling, or **express yourself**, you show what you think or feel. ○ *He expressed grave concern at American attitudes.* ○ *He expresses himself easily in English.* ○ [+ what] *groping for some way to express what she felt*

▶ **COLLOCATIONS:**
  express a **feeling/view/opinion/idea**
  express **concern/disapproval/disappointment/regret**
  express **interest/doubt/hope**
  express *something* **clearly/openly/publicly/privately**

▶ **SYNONYMS:** communicate, convey

ex|tend /ɪkstend/ (extends, extending, extended)

1 VERB If you **extend** something, you make it longer or bigger. ○ *This year they have introduced three new products to extend their range.* ○ *The building was extended in 1500.* ○ *an extended exhaust pipe*

▶ **SYNONYM:** lengthen

2 VERB If you **extend** something, you make it last longer than before or end at a later date. ○ [+ by] *They have extended the deadline by twenty-four hours.* ○ *an extended contract*

▶ **COLLOCATIONS:**
  extend *something* **for/by** *a period*
  extend a **deadline/ban/loan**
  an extended **contract/welcome**
  extend *something* **indefinitely**

▶ **SYNONYMS:** continue, stretch, lengthen

ex|ten|sion /ɪkstɛnʃ°n/

NONCOUNT NOUN **Extension** is the process of making something bigger or making something continue for a longer period of time. ○ [+ to] *I was given a two-year extension to my contract* ○ *The space was large enough to build an extension.*

▶ **COLLOCATIONS:**
an extension **of/to** something
an extension of a **ban/deadline/lease/benefit**
negotiate/approve/announce/offer an extension
build/open an extension
a **one-year/two-year** extension

ex|ten|sive /ɪkstɛnsɪv/

ADJECTIVE Something that is **extensive** covers a wide range of details, ideas, or items. ○ *She recently completed an extensive study of elected officials who began their political careers before the age of 35.* ○ *The security forces have extensive powers of search and arrest.*

▶ **COLLOCATIONS:**
an extensive **study/investigation/network/collection**
extensive **knowledge/powers/experience/training**
extensive **damage/repairs**
extensive **testing/tests/work/research**

ex|tent /ɪkstɛnt/

1 **NOUN** If you are talking about how great, important, or serious a difficulty or situation is, you can refer to **the extent of** it. ○ [+ of] *The government itself has little information on the extent of industrial pollution.* ○ [+ of] *The full extent of the losses was disclosed yesterday.*

▶ **COLLOCATIONS:**
the extent **of** something
assess/determine/gauge the extent
reveal/realize/discover/appreciate the extent
the extent of the **damage/problem/injury**
the **full** extent

▶ **PHRASE:** the nature and extent of something

▶ **SYNONYMS:** magnitude, amount, degree, scale

2 **PHRASE** You use expressions such as **to a large extent, to some extent,** or **to a certain extent** in order to indicate that something is partly true, but not entirely true. ○ *It was and, to a large extent, still is a good show.* ○ *To some extent this was the truth.* ○ *To a certain extent it's* *easier for men to get work.* ○ *This also endangers American interests in other regions, although to a lesser extent.*

3 **PHRASE** You use expressions such as **to what extent**, **to that extent**, or **to the extent that** when you are discussing how true a statement is, or in what ways it is true. ○ *It's still not clear to what extent this criticism is originating from within the ruling party.* ○ *To that extent they helped bring about their own destruction.* ○ *We may not be able to do it to the extent that we would like.*

ex|ter|nal /ɪkstɜrnəl/

ADJECTIVE **External** is used to indicate that something is on the outside of a surface or body, or that it exists, happens, or comes from outside. ○ *a much reduced heat loss through external walls* ○ *internal and external allergic reactions*

▶ **COLLOCATIONS:** external **factors/affairs/stimuli/influences**

▶ **PHRASE:** for external use

▶ **SYNONYM:** outside

ex|tra /ɛkstrə/

ADJECTIVE An **extra** amount, person, or thing is more than is usual, necessary, or expected. ○ *The company now has a chance to sell an extra 40,000 cars a year.*

▶ **COLLOCATIONS:**
an extra **charge**
extra **days/time**
extra **money/costs/spending/revenue/income**
extra **work/effort/help/support**

▶ **SYNONYM:** additional

extraor|di|nary /ɪkstrɔrdənɛri/

ADJECTIVE If you describe something or something as **extraordinary**, you mean that they have an extremely good or special quality. ○ *My advice is to work for someone who is an extraordinary leader and watch how he does it.*

▶ **COLLOCATIONS:**
an extraordinary **achievement/ability/talent**
extraordinary **efforts/measures**
extraordinary **circumstances/events**
quite/truly/most extraordinary

▶ **PHRASE:** go to extraordinary lengths

ex|trava|gant /ɪkstrǽvəgənt/

ADJECTIVE Something that is **extravagant** costs more money than you can afford or uses more of something than is reasonable. ○ *The royal family's lifestyle looks extravagant in a country where most people are dirt-poor.*

▶ **COLLOCATIONS:**
an extravagant **lifestyle**
an extravagant **gift/party**
look/seem extravagant

▶ **SYNONYM:** lavish

ex|treme /ɪkstrím/

ADJECTIVE **Extreme** means very great in degree or intensity. ○ *people living in extreme poverty* ○ *the author's extreme reluctance to generalize*

▶ **COLLOCATIONS:**
extreme **poverty/danger/difficulty**
extreme **heat/cold/caution**

▶ **SYNONYM:** great

ex|treme|ly /ɪkstrímli/

ADVERB You use **extremely** in front of adjectives and adverbs to emphasize that the specified quality is present to a very great degree. ○ *These headaches are extremely common.* ○ *Three of them are working extremely well.*

▶ **COLLOCATIONS:**
extremely **difficult/dangerous/important/rare/common**
extremely **useful/helpful/popular/well**

▶ **SYNONYMS:** exceedingly, highly, greatly, very

Ff

fa|cil|ity /fəsɪlɪti/ (facilities)

OFFICE

NOUN A **facility** is a room, building, or piece of equipment that is used for a particular purpose. ○ *The hotel has no conference facilities.*

▶ **COLLOCATIONS:**
  a **military/waste/industrial/tourist** facility
  good/excellent/adequate/poor facilities

fa|cili|tate /fəsɪlɪteɪt/ (facilitates, facilitating, facilitated)

VERB To **facilitate** an action or process, especially one that you would like to happen, means to make it easier or more likely to happen. ○ *The new airport will facilitate the development of tourism.* ○ *He argued that the economic recovery had been facilitated by his tough stance.* ○ *the facilitated diffusion of glucose in red blood cells*

▶ **COLLOCATIONS:**
  facilitated **by** *something*
  facilitate **communication/interaction/dialogue**
  facilitate **cooperation/integration/access**
  greatly facilitate

▶ **SYNONYMS:** assist, aid

fac|to|ry /fæktəri, -tri/ (factories)

ORGANIZATION

NOUN A **factory** is a large building where machines are used to make large quantities of goods. ○ *He owned furniture factories in New York State.*

▶ **COLLOCATIONS:**
  a factory **makes/produces** *something*
  a factory **opens/closes**
  a **car/chemical/weapons** factory
  a factory **worker/owner**
  factory **jobs**

▶ **SYNONYM:** plant

fade /feɪd/ (fades, fading, faded)

VERB When something **fades**, it slowly becomes lighter in color or less bright. ○ *The light was fading.*

▶ COLLOCATIONS:
daylight/ink/paintwork fades
hope/optimism fades

▶ SYNONYM: disappear

fad|ed /feɪdɪd/

ADJECTIVE ○ *He was wearing faded jeans and a T-shirt.*

▶ COLLOCATIONS:
faded **jeans**
a faded **photograph**

▶ SYNONYM: bleached

fail /feɪl/ (fails, failing, failed)

1 VERB If you **fail** to do something that you were trying to do, you do not succeed in doing it. ○ [+ to-inf] *He narrowly failed to qualify.* ○ [+ in] *He failed in his attempt to take control of the company.*

2 VERB If an activity, attempt, or plan **fails**, it is not successful. ○ *We tried to develop plans for them to get along, which all failed miserably.* ○ *He was afraid the revolution they had started would fail.* ○ *After a failed military offensive, all government troops and police were withdrawn from the island.*

3 VERB If someone or something **fails** to do a particular thing that they should have done, they do not do it. [FORMAL] ○ [+ to-inf] *Some schools fail to assign any homework.* ○ [+ to-inf] *The bomb failed to explode.*

▶ COLLOCATIONS:
fail **in** *something*
fail in a **bid/attempt**
narrowly/completely/consistently/repeatedly fail
fail **miserably/dismally**

fail|ure /feɪlyər/ (failures)

NOUN Failure is a lack of success in doing or achieving something. ○ *Three attempts on the British 200-meter record also ended in failure.* ○ *feelings of failure* ○ *The program was a complete failure.*

▶ COLLOCATIONS:
a **complete/total** failure

dismal/abject/spectacular failure

▶ **PHRASE:** end in failure

---

fa|mili|ar /fəmɪlyər/

ADJECTIVE If someone or something is **familiar**, you have seen them or heard of them before. ○ *His face looks familiar.* ○ *The slogan may sound familiar to consumers with long memories.*

▶ **COLLOCATIONS:**
   a familiar **person/face/name**
   a familiar **sound/story**
   vaguely/strangely/oddly familiar

▶ **SYNONYM:** well-known

---

fa|mous /feɪməs/

ADJECTIVE Someone or something that is **famous** is very well known by a lot of people. ○ *a famous actor* ○ *The famous mail-order company prides itself on its service.*

▶ **COLLOCATIONS:**
   a famous **singer/actor/artist/writer**
   internationally/hugely/deservedly famous

▶ **SYNONYMS:** well-known, celebrated

---

fare /fɛər/ (fares, faring, fared)

VERB If you say that someone or something **fares** well or badly, you are referring to the degree of success they achieve in a particular situation or activity. ○ *It is unlikely that the marine industry will fare any better in September.*

▶ **COLLOCATIONS:**
   fare **in** *something*
   fare in an **election**
   fare **well/badly/poorly**
   fare **better/best/worse/worst**

▶ **SYNONYM:** do

---

fa|vor|able /feɪvərəbᵊl/

ADJECTIVE If your opinion or your reaction is **favorable** to something, you agree with it and approve of it. ○ *The president's speech received favorable reviews.*

▶ **COLLOCATIONS:** a favorable **reaction/review/outcome**

▶ **SYNONYM:** encouraging

---

fax /fæks/ (faxes)   `COMMUNICATIONS`

NOUN A **fax** is a copy of a document that you send or receive using a special machine that is joined to a telephone line. ○ *I have to go to the office early tomorrow to send a fax to the company in Milan.*

▶ **COLLOCATIONS:**
   send/receive/read a fax
   an **urgent/unsolicited/anonymous** fax

---

fea|sible /fizəbᵊl/

ADJECTIVE If something is **feasible**, it can be done, made, or achieved. ○ [+ to-inf] *She questioned whether it was feasible to stimulate investment in these regions.* ○ *Supporters argue that the plan is now technically and economically feasible.*

▶ **COLLOCATIONS:**
   perfectly feasible
   economically/financially/technically/politically feasible

▶ **SYNONYMS:** practicable, possible

fea|sibil|ity /fizəbɪlɪti/

NONCOUNT NOUN ○ [+ of] *The committee will study the feasibility of setting up a national computer network.*

▶ **COLLOCATIONS:**
   the feasibility **of** something
   study/examine/assess the feasibility of something
   a feasibility **study/report**

---

fea|ture /fitʃər/ (features)

NOUN A **feature of** something is an interesting or important part or characteristic of it. ○ [+ of] *The key feature of terrorists is their total disregard for the lives of innocent civilians.* ○ *Italian democracy's unique feature is that government has not alternated between two parties.* ○ *The ships have built-in safety features including specially-strengthened hulls.*

▶ **COLLOCATIONS:**
   a feature **of** something
   a **key/important/central** feature

a **special/unique/striking/distinctive/distinguishing** feature
a **safety/security/design** feature

▶ **SYNONYMS:** characteristic, quality

---

feed|back /fiːdbæk/ `COMMUNICATIONS`

NONCOUNT NOUN Feedback is written or spoken remarks on how well you
do something. ○ *He said the company was encouraged by feedback it received
from selected customers.*

▶ **COLLOCATIONS:**
give/provide/receive feedback
positive/constructive/negative feedback

---

fif|teen /fɪftiːn/

NUMBER Fifteen is the number 15. ○ *She will be fifteen in April.* ○ *a class of
fifteen students*

▶ **COLLOCATIONS:**
someone **is** fifteen
fifteen **dollars/euros**
fifteen **miles/kilometers**
fifteen **minutes/years**

▶ **PHRASE:** fourteen or fifteen

---

fif|ty /fɪfti/

NUMBER Fifty is the number 50. ○ *He will be fifty in May.* ○ *He earned around
fifty dollars a month.*

▶ **COLLOCATIONS:**
someone **is** fifty
fifty **dollars/euros**
fifty **miles/kilometers**
fifty **minutes/years**

▶ **PHRASE:** forty or fifty

---

fig|ure /fɪgyər/ **(figures)** `BANKING & FINANCE`

1 NOUN A **figure** is a particular amount expressed as a number, especially
a statistic. ○ *Norway is a peaceful place with low crime figures.* ○ *Government
figures show that one in three marriages end in divorce.*

▶ **COLLOCATIONS:**
figures **show/reveal/suggest/indicate** *something*
publish/release figures
official/government/crime/unemployment figures
trade/profit/inflation figures
the latest figures

▶ **PHRASE:** facts and figures

▶ **SYNONYM:** statistic

2 NOUN A **figure** is any of the ten written symbols from 0 to 9 that are used to represent a number. ○ *In business writing, all numbers over ten are usually written as figures.*

▶ **COLLOCATIONS:**
in/as figures
in **single/double** figures

▶ **SYNONYMS:** digit, number

3 NOUN In a piece of writing, the diagrams that help to show or explain information are referred to as **figures**. ○ *If you look at a world map (see Figure 1) you can identify the major wine-producing regions.* ○ *Figure 1.15 shows which provinces lost populations between 1910 and 1920.*

---

file /faɪl/ **(files)**　　　　　　　　　　　　OFFICE

NOUN In computing, a **file** is a set of related data that has its own name. ○ *Now that you have loaded WordPerfect, it's easy to create a file.*

▶ **COLLOCATIONS:**
a **computer/digital** file
a **video/music/audio/image/text** file
a **zip/MP3/PDF** file
create/open/delete a file
send/share/store/retrieve a file
file **format/size/sharing**

▶ **RELATED WORD:** folder

---

fi|nal|ist /faɪnəlɪst/ **(finalists)**

NOUN A **finalist** is someone who reaches the final stage of a competition. ○ *He was chosen from a set of ten short-listed finalists.* ○ *an Olympic finalist*

▶ **COLLOCATIONS:** a **short-listed/defeated/beaten** finalist

fi|nal|ly /faɪnəli/

1 **ADVERB** You use **finally** to indicate that something is last in a series of actions or events. ○ *The action slips from comedy to melodrama and finally to tragedy.*

▶ **SYNONYM:** lastly

2 **ADVERB** You use **finally** in speech or writing to introduce a final point, question, or topic. ○ *Finally, and perhaps most importantly, Project Challenge has raised awareness of the issue.*

▶ **SYNONYMS:** in conclusion, lastly

fi|nance /faɪnæns, fɪnæns/ `BANKING & FINANCE`

NONCOUNT NOUN **Finance** is the management of money. ○ *the principles of corporate finance* ○ *We looked at three common problems in international finance.* ○ *During his 40 years in education, he's served as a teacher, finance director, and superintendent.*

▶ **COLLOCATIONS:**
corporate/personal/public/international finance
a finance **director/committee/department**

▶ **PHRASES:**
banking and finance
finance and economics

fi|nan|cial /faɪnænʃl, fɪn-/

ADJECTIVE ○ *The company is in financial difficulties.* ○ *There has been an improvement in the company's financial position.* ○ *the government's financial advisers*

▶ **COLLOCATIONS:**
a financial **crisis**
financial **difficulties/problems**
financial **help/aid/assistance/performance**
a financial **institution/adviser/officer**
someone's financial **position**

▶ **SYNONYMS:** monetary, economic

USAGE: *financial* **or** *economic*?

You use **financial** to describe things involving the money that a person or an organization has or earns. It also describes organizations that work with money, such as banks. ○ *You should seek independent financial advice.*

f

You use **economic** to describe things involving the whole economy of a country; the money, business, political policies, etc. ○ *policies to promote economic growth*

---

firm /fɜ̱rm/ (firms)

ORGANIZATION

NOUN A **firm** is an organization that sells or produces something or that provides a service that people pay for. ○ *The firm's employees were expecting large bonuses.* ○ [+ of] *a firm of heating engineers*

▶ **COLLOCATIONS:**
a firm **of** *something*
a **small/large** firm
a **law/consulting/accounting** firm
a **research/brokerage/technology** firm

▶ **SYNONYM:** company

---

first-class /fɜ̱rstklæ̱s/ also first class

1 **ADJECTIVE** If you describe someone or something as **first-class**, you mean that they are of the highest quality. ○ *The service was first class.*

▶ **COLLOCATIONS:** a first-class **degree/facility**

▶ **RELATED WORD:** second-class

2 **ADJECTIVE** **First-class** seats are the most expensive seats on a train or airplane. ○ *He won two first-class tickets to fly to Dublin.*

▶ **COLLOCATIONS:** a first-class **compartment/cabin/carriage**

• **First-class** is also an adverb. ○ *The company directors always travel first-class.*

▶ **COLLOCATIONS:** **travel/fly** first-class

---

fis|cal /fɪ̱skəl/

BANKING & FINANCE

ADJECTIVE **Fiscal** is used to describe something that relates to government money or public money, especially taxes. ○ *The government has tightened fiscal policy.* ○ *in a climate of increasing fiscal austerity*

▶ **COLLOCATIONS:**
a fiscal **policy/deficit/year/crisis**
fiscal **restraint/prudence/autonomy/austerity**

flash drive /flæʃ draɪv/ (flash drives) OFFICE

NOUN A **flash drive** is a small object for storing computer information that you can carry with you and use in different computers. ○ *I keep my flash drive on my keychain.*

▶ **COLLOCATIONS:**
  plug in a flash drive
  a **portable/removable/compact** flash drive

▶ **SYNONYM:** memory stick

flaw /flɔ/ (flaws)

1 NOUN A **flaw in** something such as a theory or argument is a mistake in it, that causes it to be less effective or valid. ○ [+ in] *There were, however, a number of crucial flaws in his monetary theory.* ○ *Almost all of these studies have serious flaws.*

▶ **COLLOCATIONS:**
  a flaw **in** *something*
  a **serious/critical/obvious/inherent/fatal** flaw
  a **methodological/technical/structural/procedural** flaw
  correct/fix/discover a flaw
  overlook/exploit/expose a flaw

▶ **SYNONYM:** mistake

2 NOUN A **flaw in** something such as a pattern or material is a fault in it that should not be there. ○ *lenses containing flaws and imperfections* ○ *a special kind of glass that was treasured for its flaws rather than its perfection*

▶ **COLLOCATION:** a flaw **in** *something*

▶ **SYNONYM:** imperfection

flex|ible /flɛksɪbəl/

1 ADJECTIVE A **flexible** object or material can be bent easily without breaking. ○ *brushes with long, flexible bristles* ○ *Air is pumped through a flexible tube.*

▶ **SYNONYM:** pliable

2 ADJECTIVE Something or someone that is **flexible** is able to change easily and adapt to different conditions and circumstances. ○ *more flexible arrangements to allow access to services after normal working hours* ○ *We encourage flexible working hours.*

▶ **COLLOCATIONS:**
a flexible **approach/system/arrangement**
flexible **working hours**
a flexible **rate/market**

▶ **SYNONYM:** adaptable

flexi|bil|ity /flɛksɪbɪlɪti/

NONCOUNT NOUN ○ [+ of] *The flexibility of distance learning would be particularly suited to busy managers.* ○ [+ of] *The flexibility of the lens decreases with age.*

▶ **COLLOCATIONS:**
the flexibility **of** something
offer/provide/increase/show flexibility

▶ **SYNONYM:** adaptability

flop|py disk /flɒpi dɪsk/ (floppy disks)　　OFFICE

NOUN A **floppy disk** is a small plastic computer disk that is used for storing information. ○ *Mrs Aitcheson had made back-up copies of all her accounts on floppy disks.*

fluc|tu|ate /flʌktʃueɪt/ (fluctuates, fluctuating, fluctuated)

VERB If something **fluctuates**, it changes a lot in an irregular way. ○ *The temperature fluctuates very little between daytime and night-time.* ○ *Share prices have fluctuated wildly in recent weeks.* ○ [V-ing] *the fluctuating price of oil*

▶ **COLLOCATIONS:**
a **price/rate/value** fluctuates
the **temperature/weight** fluctuates
fluctuate **wildly/significantly**

fluc|tua|tion /flʌktʃueɪʃⁿn/ (fluctuations)

NOUN ○ [+ in] *Much of the seasonal fluctuation in death rates was caused by cold, the researchers concluded.* ○ [+ in] *daily fluctuations in core body temperature*

▶ **COLLOCATIONS:**
a fluctuation **in** something
a **currency/price/market** fluctuation
a **short-term/seasonal** fluctuation

> **EXTEND YOUR VOCABULARY**
>
> You can use **fluctuate/fluctuation** and **vary/variation** to describe something that changes frequently. If the level of something **fluctuates**, it goes up and down a lot over a period of time. ○ *Wheat prices fluctuated between $230 and $280 a ton.*
>
> If something **varies**, it changes or is different depending on the situation. ○ *The price varies according to your airport and time of arrival.*

flu|ent /flu̱ənt/

ADJECTIVE Someone who is **fluent in** a particular language can speak the language easily and correctly. You can also say that someone speaks **fluent** French, Chinese, or some other language. ○ [+ in] *She studied eight foreign languages but is fluent in only six of them.* ○ *He speaks fluent Russian.*

▶ **COLLOCATIONS:**
  fluent **in** something
  fluent **English/Japanese/German**
  a fluent **speaker** of something

fol|low|ing /fɒ̱loʊɪŋ/

1 ADJECTIVE You use **following** to refer to something that you are about to mention. ○ *Write down the following information: name of product, type, date purchased, and price.* ○ *The method of helping such patients is explained in the following chapters.*

● **The following** is also a pronoun. ○ *The following is a paraphrase of what was said.* ○ *One serving of any of the following would provide an adult's complete daily requirement of salt.*

2 PREPOSITION Following a particular event means after that event. ○ *In the centuries following Christ's death, Christians genuinely believed the world was about to end.* ○ *Following a day of medical research, the conference focused on educational practices.*

▶ **SYNONYM:** after

3 ADJECTIVE The **following** day, week, or year is the day, week, or year after the one you have just mentioned. ○ *He had a speech to make the following day.* ○ *The following year she joined the Royal Opera House.*

▶ **SYNONYM:** next

fore|cast /fɔrkæst/ (forecasts, forecasting, forecasted) `R&D`

> The forms **forecast** and **forecasted** can both be used for the past tense and past participle.

1 NOUN A **forecast** is a statement of what is expected to happen in the future, especially in relation to a particular event or situation. ○ [+ *of*] *a forecast of a 2.25 percent growth in the economy* ○ *He gave his election forecast.* ○ *The weather forecast is better for today.*

▶ **COLLOCATIONS:**
  a forecast **of** *something*
  make/give/revise a forecast
  a **growth/economic/earnings/profit** forecast
  a **weather/gloomy/optimistic** forecast

▶ **SYNONYM:** prediction

2 VERB If you **forecast** future events, you say what you think is going to happen in the future. ○ *They forecast a humiliating defeat for the Prime Minister.* ○ [+ *that*] *He forecasts that average salary increases will remain around 4 percent.*

▶ **COLLOCATIONS:**
  forecast the **weather**
  forecast an **increase**
  forecast **growth**

▶ **SYNONYM:** predict

fore|clo|sure /fɔrklouʒər/ (foreclosures) `BANKING & FINANCE`

NOUN A **foreclosure** is an occasion when a lender takes a person's property because that person did not pay back the money they borrowed to buy it. ○ *If homeowners can't keep up the payments, they face foreclosure.* ○ *The bank was threatening foreclosure on her house.*

▶ **COLLOCATIONS:**
  threaten/initiate foreclosure
  a **mortgage** foreclosure

for|eign /fɔrɪn/ `BANKING & FINANCE`

1 ADJECTIVE Something or someone that is **foreign** comes from or relates to a country that is not your own. ○ *This was his first experience in a foreign country.* ○ *a foreign language* ○ *It is the largest ever foreign investment in the Bolivian mining sector.*

▶ **COLLOCATIONS:**
a foreign **country/language/currency/vacation**
foreign **workers/students**

▶ **SYNONYMS:** overseas, international

2 ADJECTIVE In politics and journalism, **foreign** is used to describe people, jobs, and activities relating to countries that are not the country of the person or government concerned. ○ *the German foreign minister* ○ *the foreign correspondent in Washington of La Tribuna newspaper of Honduras* ○ *the effects of U.S. foreign policy*

▶ **COLLOCATIONS:**
foreign **policy/aid/debt**
the foreign **minister/secretary**
a foreign **correspondent**

▶ **SYNONYMS:** overseas, international

for|eign ex|change /fɔrɪn ɪkstʃeɪndʒ/ (foreign exchanges)

1 PLURAL NOUN Foreign exchanges are the institutions or systems involved with changing one currency into another. ○ *On the foreign exchanges, the U.S. dollar is up point forty-five.*

2 NONCOUNT NOUN Foreign exchange is foreign currency that is obtained through the foreign exchanges. ○ *an important source of foreign exchange*

▶ **COLLOCATIONS:**
a foreign exchange **dealer/trader**
the foreign exchange **market**

form /fɔrm/ (forms, forming, formed)

1 NOUN A **form of** something is a type or kind of it. ○ [+ *of*] *He contracted a rare form of cancer.* ○ *I am against hunting in any form.* ○ *In its present form, the law could lead to new injustices.*

▶ **COLLOCATION:** a form **of** *something*

▶ **SYNONYMS:** type, kind, sort

2 NOUN The **form** of something is its shape. ○ *the form of the body*

▶ **SYNONYM:** shape

3 VERB If something consists of particular things, people, or features, you can say that they **form** that thing. ○ *This idea formed the basis of his entire philosophy.* ○ *Cereals form the staple diet of an enormous number of people around the world.*

▶ **COLLOCATION:** form the **basis** of *something*

▶ **SYNONYM:** constitute

4 VERB If you **form** an organization, group, or company, you start it.
○ *Threadneedle is a company formed in 1994 with the merger of Allied Dunbar and Eagle Star.* ○ [+ into] *They formed themselves into teams.*

→ see note at **launch**

▶ **COLLOCATIONS:**
form **into** *something*
form a **government/coalition/committee**
form a **partnership/alliance/group/band**

▶ **SYNONYMS:** start, create

5 VERB When something natural **forms** or **is formed**, it begins to exist and develop. ○ *The stars must have formed 10 to 15 billion years ago.* ○ *Huge ice sheets were formed.*

▶ **COLLOCATIONS:**
a **planet/star/galaxy** forms
a **cell/clot** forms
cloud/ice forms

▶ **SYNONYM:** develop

---

for|mal /fɔrmᵊl/

1 ADJECTIVE Formal speech or behavior is very correct and serious rather than relaxed and friendly, and is used especially in official situations.
○ *He wrote a very formal letter of apology to Douglas.* ○ *Business relationships are necessarily a bit more formal.*

2 ADJECTIVE A **formal** action, statement, or request is an official one.
○ *U.N. officials said a formal request was passed to American authorities.*
○ *No formal announcement had been made.*

▶ **COLLOCATIONS:**
a formal **investigation**
a formal **announcement/statement/agreement**
a formal **offer/request/proposal/complaint**
formal **talks/negotiations**

▶ **SYNONYM:** official

---

for|mat /fɔrmæt/ (formats)

NOUN The **format** of something is the way or order in which it is arranged and presented. ○ [+ of] *He explained the new format and policy of the paper.*

○ *music available in a digital format* ○ [+ of] *You all know the format of the show.*
○ *a large-format book*

▶ **COLLOCATIONS:**
the format **of** something
in a format
a **different/traditional/digital/electronic/online** format

▶ **SYNONYMS:** style, form

for|mer /fɔrmər/

1 ADJECTIVE Former is used to describe what someone or something used to be in the past. ○ *He pleaded not guilty to murdering his former wife.* ○ *the former Soviet Union* ○ *the former home of Sir Christopher Wren*

▶ **COLLOCATIONS:**
a former **president**
someone's former **husband/wife/boyfriend/girlfriend**
someone's former **career/home**

▶ **SYNONYM:** ex-

▶ **RELATED WORD:** current

2 ADJECTIVE Former is used to describe a situation or period of time that came before the present one. [FORMAL] ○ *He would want you to remember him as he was in former years.*

▶ **PHRASE:** in former times

▶ **SYNONYM:** previous

3 PRONOUN When two people, things, or groups have just been mentioned, you can refer to the first of them as **the former**. ○ *He writes about two series of works: the Caprichos and the Disparates. The former are a series of etchings done by Goya.* ○ *The wife may choose the former and the husband the latter.*

for|mer|ly /fɔrmərli/

ADVERB If something happened or was true **formerly**, it happened or was true in the past. ○ *He had formerly been in the Navy.* ○ *East Germany's formerly state-controlled companies*

for|mu|la /fɔrmyələ/ (formulae or formulas) `R&D`

1 NOUN A **formula** is a group of letters, numbers, or other symbols that represents a scientific or mathematical rule. ○ *He developed a mathematical formula describing the distances of the planets from the Sun.* ○ *using a standard scientific formula*

▶ **COLLOCATIONS:**
develop a formula
a **mathematical/scientific** formula

2 NOUN In science, the **formula** for a substance is a list of the amounts of various substances that make up that substance, or an indication of the atoms that it is composed of. ○ *Water's chemical formula is H2O.* ○ [+ for] *NO is the formula for nitric oxide.*

▶ **COLLOCATIONS:**
the formula **for** *something*
the **chemical** formula

for|mu|late /fɔ̱rmyəleɪt/ (formulates, formulating, formulated)

VERB If you **formulate** something such as a plan or proposal, you invent it, thinking about the details carefully. ○ *Detectives tend to formulate one hypothesis and then try to confirm it.* ○ *a scientifically formulated supplement recommended for dogs and cats* ○ *Formulate a strategy for long term business development.*

▶ **COLLOCATIONS:**
formulate a **strategy/policy/proposal/plan/response**
formulate a **hypothesis/theory**
scientifically/specially/carefully formulated

▶ **SYNONYMS:** invent, devise

for|tune /fɔ̱rtʃən/ (fortunes) `BANKING & FINANCE`

1 NOUN You can refer to a large sum of money as **a fortune** or **a** small **fortune** to emphasize how large it is. ○ *He made a small fortune in the property boom.*

▶ **COLLOCATIONS:**
a **small/vast** fortune
make/amass/earn/lose/save/inherit a fortune
something **costs** a fortune
pay a fortune for *something*

2 NOUN Someone who has a **fortune** has a very large amount of money. ○ *He made his fortune in car sales.*

▶ **COLLOCATIONS:**
make/spend/invest/lose a fortune
a **personal** fortune

for|ty /fɔ̱rti/

NUMBER **Forty** is the number 40. ○ *She will be forty next birthday.* ○ *Forty planes have been grounded.*

▶ **COLLOCATIONS:**
  someone **is** forty
  forty **dollars/euros**
  forty **miles/kilometers**
  forty **minutes/years**

▶ **PHRASE:** thirty or forty

for|ward /fɔ̱rwərd/ (forwards, forwarding, forwarded) `COMMUNICATIONS`

VERB If you **forward** a letter or an email **to** someone, you send it to them after you have received it.

▶ **COLLOCATIONS:** forward a **letter/email/request/invoice**

found|er /fa̱ʊndər/ (founders) `ORGANIZATION`

NOUN The **founder** of an institution, organization, or building is the person who got it started or caused it to be built, often by providing the necessary money. ○ [+ of] *He was one of the founders of the university's medical faculty.* ○ [+ of] *the founder of the Zionist movement* ○ *Hsin Tao, the organization's founder and leader*

▶ **COLLOCATIONS:**
  the founder **of** *something*
  the founder of a **company/movement/museum/website/charity**
  the **original/joint** founder

four|teen /fɔ̱rti̱n/

NUMBER **Fourteen** is the number 14. ○ *Her son is fourteen.* ○ *They paid me fourteen dollars.*

▶ **COLLOCATIONS:**
  someone **is** fourteen
  fourteen **dollars/euros**
  fourteen **miles/kilometers**
  fourteen **years**

▶ **PHRASE:** thirteen or fourteen

f

frame|work /freɪmwɜrk/ **(frameworks)**

NOUN A **framework** is a particular set of rules, ideas, or beliefs that you use in order to deal with problems or to decide what to do. ○ [+ *for*] *The purpose of the chapter is to provide a framework for thinking about why exchange rates change.* ○ *Doctors need a clear legal framework to be able to deal with difficult clinical decisions.*

▶ **COLLOCATIONS:**
within a framework
a framework **of/for** *something*
agree on/develop/establish/set a framework
a **legal/regulatory/legislative/political** framework
a **conceptual/theoretical** framework

fran|chise /fræntʃaɪz/ **(franchises, franchising,** `ORGANIZATION`
franchised)

1 NOUN A **franchise** is an authority that is given by an organization to someone, allowing them to sell its goods or services or to take part in an activity that the organization controls. ○ *fast-food franchises* ○ [+ *to-inf*] *the franchise to build and operate the tunnel* ○ *Talk to other franchise holders and ask them what they think of the parent company.*

▶ **COLLOCATIONS:**
a **fast-food/pizza/banking/railroad** franchise
a franchise **holder/outlet/operator/chain/store**
operate/own/secure/buy/run a franchise

2 VERB If a company **franchises** its business, it sells franchises to other companies, allowing them to sell its goods or services. ○ *She has recently franchised her business.* ○ *Though the service is available only in California, its founder Michael Cane says he plans to franchise it in other states.* ○ *It takes hundreds of thousands of dollars to get into the franchised pizza business.*

▶ **COLLOCATIONS:**
franchise a **service/operation/business**
franchise a **store/outlet**

fre|quent|ly /frikwəntli/

ADVERB If something happens **frequently**, it happens often. ○ *Iron and folic acid supplements are frequently given to pregnant women.* ○ *the most frequently asked question*

▶ **SYNONYMS:** often, regularly

func|tion /fˈʌŋkʃən/ (functions, functioning, functioned)

1 NOUN The **function** of something or someone is the useful thing that they do or are intended to do. ○ *This enzyme serves various functions.* ○ [+ *of*] *The main function of the merchant banks is to raise capital for industry.*

▶ **COLLOCATIONS:**
the function **of** *something/someone*
perform/serve a function
the **primary** function
a **basic/important/useful** function

▶ **SYNONYMS:** purpose, role

2 VERB If a machine or system **is functioning**, it is working or operating. ○ *The authorities say the prison is now functioning normally.* ○ *Conservation programs cannot function without local support.*

▶ **COLLOCATIONS:**
function **effectively/efficiently/smoothly**
barely function

▶ **SYNONYMS:** operate, work

func|tion|al /fˈʌŋkʃənᵊl/

ADJECTIVE Functional means relating to the way in which something works or operates, or relating to how useful it is. ○ *Every new employee starts with a fully functional workspace and a full day of training in desktop tools.*

▶ **SYNONYM:** operational

fund /fˈʌnd/ (funds, funding, funded) BANKING & FINANCE

1 PLURAL NOUN Funds are amounts of money that are available to be spent, especially money that is given to an organization or person for a particular purpose. ○ [+ *for*] *The concert will raise funds for research into AIDS.* ○ *Funds are allocated according to regional needs.*

▶ **COLLOCATIONS:**
funds **for** *something*
raise/use/receive/provide/allocate/invest funds
public/federal/government/private funds

▶ **SYNONYMS:** money, finances

2 VERB When a person or organization **funds** something, they provide money for it. ○ *The Bush Foundation has funded a variety of faculty development programs.* ○ *The airport is being privately funded by a construction group.* ○ *a new, privately funded program*

▶ **COLLOCATIONS:**
funded **by** *someone*
publicly/privately/federally funded
largely/adequately/partly/jointly funded

▶ **SYNONYM:** finance

---

fun|da|men|tal /fʌndəmɛntəl/

ADJECTIVE You use **fundamental** to describe things, activities, and principles that are very important, basic, or essential. ○ *Our Constitution embodies all the fundamental principles of democracy.* ○ *The fundamental problem lies in their inability to distinguish between reality and invention.* ○ *But on this question, the two leaders have very fundamental differences.*

▶ **COLLOCATIONS:**
a fundamental **principle/value/right**
a fundamental **change/shift/difference**
a fundamental **problem/question/issue/flaw**

▶ **SYNONYM:** basic

Gg

gadg|et /ˈɡædʒɪt/ (gadgets)   `R&D`

NOUN A **gadget** is a small machine or useful object. ○ *electronic gadgets*

▶ **COLLOCATIONS:**
buy/use a gadget
a **high-tech/electronic** gadget

▶ **PHRASES:**
gadgets and gizmos
the latest gadget

▶ **SYNONYM:** device

gap /ɡæp/ (gaps)

NOUN A **gap** is a big difference between two things, people, or ideas.
○ *America's trade gap widened.* ○ [+ between] *the gap between rich and poor*
○ [+ between] *The overall pay gap between men and women narrowed slightly.*

▶ **COLLOCATIONS:**
a gap **between** *things*
a **huge/widening** gap
a **gender/generation/pay/age** gap
a gap **widens/narrows/exists/remains**
bridge/close/narrow/reduce the gap

▶ **SYNONYM:** difference

gath|er /ˈɡæðər/ (gathers, gathering, gathered)

1 **VERB** If you **gather** things, you collect them together so that you can use them. ○ *The expedition gathered samples of animal and plant life.*
○ *Search teams spent weeks gathering thousands of pieces of wreckage.*

2 **VERB** If you **gather** information or evidence, you collect it, especially over a period of time and after a lot of hard work. ○ *The organization gathers information on the dangers of smoking.* ○ *The commission began to*

gather evidence for the forthcoming trial. ○ [+ together] *The book gathers together all the short stories in a single volume.*

▶ **COLLOCATIONS:**
gather *things* **together**
gather **samples/information/evidence/data/material**

▶ **SYNONYM:** collect

GDP /dʒiː diː piː/ (GDPs)   `BANKING & FINANCE`

NOUN In economics, a country's **GDP** is the total value of goods and services produced within a country in a year, not including its income from investments in other countries. **GDP** is an abbreviation for "gross domestic product". ○ *That is 2.6 percent of total GDP.* ○ *Per capita GDP has increased, at today's rates, from 12,637 to 17,096.*

▶ **COLLOCATIONS:**
annual/national/per capita GDP
a **high/low** GDP

▶ **RELATED WORD:** GNP

---

gen|er|al|ly /dʒɛnrəli/

1 ADVERB You use **generally** to give a summary of a situation, activity, or idea without referring to the particular details of it. ○ *Teachers generally have admitted a lack of enthusiasm.* ○ *Generally speaking, standards have improved.* ○ *a generally positive economic outlook*

▶ **COLLOCATIONS:**
generally **positive/supportive/upbeat**
generally **unwell/weak/hostile**

▶ **PHRASE:** generally speaking

▶ **SYNONYM:** mainly

2 ADVERB You use **generally** to say that something happens or is used on most occasions but not on every occasion. ○ *As women we generally say and feel too much.* ○ *It is generally true that the darker the fruit the higher its iron content.* ○ *Blood pressure less than 120 over 80 is generally considered ideal.*

▶ **COLLOCATIONS:** generally **true/accepted/considered/regarded**

▶ **SYNONYMS:** usually, normally, mostly, commonly

gen|er|al|ize /dʒɛnərəlaɪz/ (generalizes, generalizing, generalized)

VERB If you **generalize**, you say something that seems to be true in most situations or for most people, but that may not be completely true in all cases. [in BRIT, also use **generalise**] ○ *"In my day, children were a lot better behaved." — "It's not true, you're generalizing."* ○ [+ *about*] *It is still possible to generalize about regional styles.*

▶ COLLOCATION: generalize **about** something

▶ SYNONYMS: stereotype, hypothesize

gen|er|ali|za|tion /dʒɛnərəlɪzeɪʃ°n/ (generalizations)

NOUN ○ *He is making sweeping generalizations to get his point across.* ○ [+ *about*] *It's dangerous to make generalizations about education.*

▶ COLLOCATIONS:
a generalization **about** something
make generalizations
a **broad/abstract/simplistic/sweeping** generalization
a **negative/unfair** generalization

---

gen|er|ate /dʒɛnəreɪt/ (generates, generating, generated)

1 VERB To **generate** something means to cause it to begin and develop. ○ *He said the reforms would generate new jobs.* ○ *the excitement generated by the changes in Eastern Europe*

▶ COLLOCATIONS:
generated **by** something
generate **excitement/publicity/controversy/enthusiasm**
generate **wealth/income/profit**

▶ SYNONYMS: create, cause

2 VERB To **generate** a form of energy or power means to produce it. ○ *The company, New England Electric, burns coal to generate power.*

▶ COLLOCATIONS: generate **electricity/energy/heat/power**

▶ SYNONYM: produce

---

genu|ine /dʒɛnyuɪn/

ADJECTIVE If something is **genuine**, it is true and real. ○ *a genuine American hero*

▶ COLLOCATIONS:
genuine **concern/fear**
a genuine **attempt**
be/appear genuine

▶ PHRASE: the genuine article

▶ SYNONYM: authentic

glob|al /ɡloʊbᵊl/ MARKETING & SALES

ADJECTIVE You can use **global** to describe something that happens in all parts of the world or affects all parts of the world. ○ *a global ban on nuclear testing* ○ *On a global scale, AIDS may well become the leading cause of infant death.*

▶ **COLLOCATIONS:**
   a global **scale/reach**
   a global **recession/downturn/recovery**
   a global **brand/trend**
   the global **economy/marketplace**
   global **trade/growth/capitalism/poverty/terrorism**
   increasingly global

▶ **PHRASE:** global warming

▶ **SYNONYMS:** worldwide, international

glob|al mar|ket /ɡloʊbᵊl mɑrkɪt/ **(global markets)** or **global marketplace**

NOUN A **global market** is a market for something that exists throughout the world. ○ *Producers are giving a high priority to efforts to build cars which can meet the needs of a global market.*

glut /ɡlʌt/ **(gluts)** LOGISTICS & DISTRIBUTION

NOUN A **glut** is so much of something that it cannot all be sold or used. ○ *Exports have become increasingly important to wineries as they battle a global wine glut.*

▶ **COLLOCATIONS:** a **global/worldwide/current** glut

▶ **SYNONYM:** surplus

GNP /dʒi ɛn pi/ **(GNPs)** BANKING & FINANCE

NOUN A country's **GNP** is the total value of all the goods produced and services provided by that country in one year. **GNP** is an abbreviation for **gross national product**. Compare with **GDP**. ○ *By 1973 the government deficit equaled thirty percent of GNP.*

▶ **COLLOCATIONS:**
   real/potential GNP
   a GNP **of** $x

goal /gəʊl/ (goals)

NOUN Something that is your **goal** is something that you hope to achieve, especially when much time and effort will be needed. ○ *Be realistic and set goals that are within reach.* ○ *Their goals are ambitious: to nearly double federal money for Down syndrome research.* ○ *[+ of] the Nationalist goal of independence*

▶ **COLLOCATIONS:**
the goal **of** *something*
set/accomplish/achieve/reach a goal
the **ultimate/main/key/stated** goal
an **achievable/ambitious/unrealistic** goal

▶ **SYNONYMS:** aim, objective, ambition

gov|ern|ment /gʌvərnmənt/ (governments)

NOUN The **government** of a country is the group of people who are responsible for governing it. ○ *The government has insisted that confidence is needed before the economy can improve.* ○ *[+ of] the governments of 12 European countries* ○ *the government's foreign policy*

▶ **COLLOCATIONS:**
the government **of** *a country*
federal/state/local government
the **British/Chinese/Canadian** government
a government **official/department/policy**

grade /greɪd/ (grades, grading, graded)

1 **VERB** If something **is graded**, its quality is judged, and it is often given a number or a name that indicates how good or bad it is. ○ *Dust masks are graded according to the protection they offer.* ○ *South Point College does not grade the students' work.*

▶ **COLLOCATIONS:**
a grading **system/structure**
grade an **exam/exercise/assignment**

▶ **SYNONYMS:** mark, categorize

2 **NOUN** Your **grade** on an examination or piece of written work is the mark you get, usually in the form of a letter or number, that indicates your level of achievement. ○ *Results show a 0.8 percentage point increase in candidates achieving a grade of A.*

▶ **COLLOCATIONS:**
get/obtain/attain/achieve a grade
a **good/high/low** grade
school/exam grades
grade **of A/B/C**

▶ **SYNONYMS:** mark, score

---

grad|ual /ˈɡrædʒuəl/

ADJECTIVE A **gradual** change or process occurs in small stages over a long period of time, rather than suddenly. ○ *Losing weight is a slow, gradual process.* ○ *You can expect her progress at school to be gradual.*

▶ **COLLOCATIONS:** a gradual **process/decline/improvement/change**

▶ **SYNONYM:** slow

gradu|al|ly /ˈɡrædʒuəli/

ADVERB If something changes **gradually**, it changes in small stages over a long period of time, rather than suddenly. ○ *The slope gradually decreased.* ○ *Start slowly and gradually increase the number of steps.* ○ *Gradually we learned to cope.*

▶ **COLLOCATIONS:**
gradually **increase/evolve/accumulate**
gradually **decrease/fade/diminish**

▶ **SYNONYMS:** slowly, gently, steadily

---

graph|ics /ˈɡræfɪks/

PLURAL NOUN Graphics are drawings, pictures, or symbols, especially when they are produced by a computer.

▶ **COLLOCATIONS:**
use/feature/provide graphics
3-D/computer graphics
a graphics **card/chip**

---

guar|an|tee /ˈɡærənti/ (guarantees, guaranteeing, guaranteed)

1 VERB If one thing **guarantees** another, the first is certain to cause the second thing to happen. ○ *Surplus resources alone do not guarantee growth.* ○ *[+ that] one of the few ways to virtually guarantee that a fraudster cannot open an account in your name*

2 VERB If you **guarantee** something, you promise that it will definitely happen, or that you will do or provide it for someone. ○ *Most states guarantee the right to free and adequate education.* ○ *All students are guaranteed campus accommodations.*

▶ COLLOCATIONS:
guarantee **freedom/security/rights/access**
guarantee **safety/success/satisfaction**
guarantee a **return/income**
virtually/almost guarantee

▶ SYNONYMS: ensure, promise

3 NOUN A **guarantee** is a promise that something will definitely happen or that you will do or provide it. ○ [+ *that*] *The Editor can give no guarantee that they will fulfill their obligations.* ○ [+ *of*] *California's state Constitution includes a guarantee of privacy.*

▶ COLLOCATIONS:
a guarantee **of** *something*
a guarantee of **freedom/success/safety/quality**
a **written/constitutional/cast-iron** guarantee
seek/require a guarantee
supply/offer/provide/obtain/secure a guarantee

▶ SYNONYMS: promise, pledge

g

Hh

hand|shake /ˈhændʃeɪk/ (handshakes) COMMUNICATIONS

NOUN A **handshake** is the act of holding someone's hand and moving it up and down, for example as a greeting. ○ *a firm handshake*

▶ **COLLOCATIONS:**
exchange handshakes
give/offer/receive a handshake
a **warm/hearty/limp/firm** handshake

▶ **PHRASES:**
a golden handshake
a smile and a handshake

hard drive /ˈhɑrd draɪv/ (hard drives) OFFICE

NOUN A **hard drive** is the part of a computer that contains the hard disk. ○ *You can download the file to your hard drive.*

▶ **COLLOCATIONS:**
a **computer/internal/external/portable** hard drive
store/retrieve/install *something* **on** a hard drive

haz|ard|ous /ˈhæzərdəs/

ADJECTIVE Something that is **hazardous** is dangerous, especially to people's health or safety. ○ *They have no way to dispose of the hazardous waste they produce.* ○ *The pollution of ground water by hazardous wastes has resulted in the closing of wells.*

▶ **COLLOCATIONS:** hazardous **waste/material/substances**

▶ **SYNONYMS:** dangerous, toxic

health care /ˈhɛlθ kɛər/ also **healthcare** HEALTH & FITNESS

NONCOUNT NOUN **Health care** is services for preventing and treating illnesses and injuries. ○ *I believe that one of the great changes we shall see in* *health care will come in the treatment of mental illness.*

▶ COLLOCATIONS:
preventative/general/natural/alternative health care
children's/women's health care
a health care **provider/professional/system/industry/routine**

---

height|en /ˈhaɪtᵊn/ (heightens, heightening, heightened)

VERB If something **heightens** a feeling or if the feeling **heightens**, the feeling increases in degree or intensity. ○ *The move has heightened tension in the state.* ○ *Recent changes in economic policy will heighten the tensions.*

▶ COLLOCATIONS: heighten **tension/fear/concern**

▶ SYNONYM: intensify

---

high|light /ˈhaɪlaɪt/ (highlights, highlighting, highlighted)

VERB If someone or something **highlights** a point or problem, they emphasize it or make you think about it. ○ *This incident highlights the care needed when disposing of unwanted plants.* ○ *Once again, the "Free Press" prefers not to highlight these facts.*

▶ COLLOCATIONS:
highlight the **importance/need/danger/lack** of *something*
a **report/survey/incident** highlights *something*
clearly/dramatically highlighted

▶ SYNONYMS: emphasize, draw attention to, illustrate, expose

---

high-tech /ˈhaɪ tɛk/ also **high tech** or **hi tech**   R&D

ADJECTIVE **High-tech** activities or equipment use the most modern technology. ○ *Taiwan's high-tech industry* ○ *New high-tech equipment allows doctors to magnify a section of your skin and project it on to a computer screen.*

▶ COLLOCATIONS:
a high-tech **company/industry**
high-tech **equipment**
a high-tech **job/system**

▶ SYNONYMS: state-of-the-art, cutting edge

---

host /ˈhoʊst/ (hosts)

NOUN The **host** of a parasite is the plant or animal that it lives on or inside and from which it gets its food. ○ *When the eggs hatch the larvae eat the*

living flesh of the host animal. ○ [+ for] *Farmed fish are perfect hosts for parasites.*

▶ **COLLOCATIONS:**
a host **for** *something*
a host for a **parasite**
a host **organism/ant/species**
a **susceptible/intermediate** host

---

ho|tel /hoʊtɛl/ (hotels) `TRAVEL`

NOUN A **hotel** is a building where people pay to sleep and eat meals. ○ *Janet stayed the night in a small hotel near the harbor.*

▶ **COLLOCATIONS:**
build/operate/own/book a hotel
a **luxury/boutique/resort/airport** hotel

▶ **SYNONYMS:** inn, guest house

---

how|ever /haʊɛvər/

1 ADVERB You use **however** when you are adding a comment that is surprising or that contrasts with what has just been said. ○ *This was not an easy decision. It is, however, a decision that we had to make.* ○ *Some of the food crops failed. However, the cotton did quite well.* ○ *Higher sales have not helped profits, however.*

2 ADVERB You use **however** before an adjective or adverb to emphasize that the degree or extent of something cannot change a situation.
○ *You should always try to achieve more, however well you have done before.*
○ *However hard she tried, nothing seemed to work.* ○ *However much it hurt, he could do it.*

▶ **SYNONYM:** no matter how

---

hu|man re|sources /hyumən risɔrsız/ `PERSONNEL`

NONCOUNT NOUN In a company or other organization, the department of **human resources** is the department with responsibility for the recruiting, training, and welfare of the staff. The abbreviation **HR** is often used. ○ *The firm's head of human resources is on vacation.*

▶ **COLLOCATION:** human resources **planning**

hy|brid /haɪbrɪd/ (hybrids) `RG·D`

1 **NOUN** A **hybrid** is an animal or plant that has been bred from two different species of animal or plant. ○ *All these brightly colored hybrids are so lovely in the garden.* ○ [+ between] *a hybrid between water mint and spearmint*

• **Hybrid** is also an adjective. ○ *hybrid corn* ○ *You can cheat by buying a disease-resistant hybrid tea.*

2 **NOUN** You can use **hybrid** to refer to anything that is a mixture of other things, especially two other things. ○ [+ of] *a hybrid of solid and liquid fuel* ○ [+ of] *a hybrid of psychological thriller and sci-fi mystery*

• **Hybrid** is also an adjective. ○ *a hybrid system* ○ *incredible, strange, hybrid nonfiction*

▶ **COLLOCATIONS:**
a hybrid **between/of** things
breed/produce/create a hybrid
a hybrid **tea/rose/berry**
a hybrid **vehicle/sedan**

Ii

iden|ti|fy /aɪdɛntɪfaɪ/ (identifies, identifying, identified)

1 VERB If you can **identify** someone or something, you are able to recognize them or distinguish them from others. ○ *There are a number of distinguishing characteristics by which you can identify a Hollywood epic.*

▶ **COLLOCATIONS:**
correctly/incorrectly identify *someone/something*
positively identify *someone/something*

▶ **SYNONYMS:** recognize, distinguish

2 VERB If you **identify** something, you discover or notice its existence. ○ *Scientists claim to have identified natural substances with cancer-combating properties.* ○ [+ as] *It was not until the twentieth century that mosquitoes were identified as the carriers of malaria.*

▶ **COLLOCATIONS:**
identify *something* **as** *something*
identify a **cause/factor/need/gene/virus**

▶ **SYNONYM:** discover

iden|ti|fi|ca|tion /aɪdɛntɪfɪkeɪʃ°n/

NONCOUNT NOUN The **identification** of something is the recognition that it exists, is important, or is true. ○ [+ of] *Early identification of a disease can prevent death and illness.* ○ [+ of] *the identification of training needs*

▶ **COLLOCATIONS:**
the identification **of** *something*
the identification of a **gene/protein/factor/need**

▶ **SYNONYM:** recognition

il|legal /ɪliːg°l/ LEGAL

ADJECTIVE If something is **illegal**, the law says that it is not allowed. ○ [+ to-inf] *It is illegal to intercept radio messages.* ○ *Birth control was illegal there until 1978.* ○ *illegal drugs*

▶ **COLLOCATIONS:**
become illegal
declare/make/consider *something* illegal
an illegal **drug/activity/weapon/trade**
illegal **immigration/immigrants**

▶ **PHRASE:** be illegal for someone to do something

▶ **SYNONYM:** unlawful

il|lus|trate /ɪləstreɪt/ (illustrates, illustrating, illustrated)

1 VERB If you say that something **illustrates** a situation that you are drawing attention to, you mean that it shows that the situation exists. ○ *The example of the United States illustrates this point.* ○ [+ how] *The incident graphically illustrates how difficult their position is.* ○ [+ that] *The case also illustrates that some women are now trying to fight back.*

2 VERB If you use an example, story, or diagram to **illustrate** a point, you use it to show that what you are saying is true or to make your meaning clearer. ○ *To illustrate this point, Wolf gives an example from the car production sector in America.* ○ [+ with] *Throughout, she illustrates her analysis with excerpts from discussions.*

▶ **COLLOCATIONS:**
illustrate *something* **with/by** *something*
illustrate *something* by a **story/fact/example/case**
illustrate a **point/principle/difficulty**
illustrate the **importance/extent/complexity** of *something*
graphically/perfectly/vividly illustrate

▶ **SYNONYMS:** demonstrate, exemplify

il|lus|tra|tion /ɪləstreɪʃ³n/ (illustrations)

NOUN ○ *This can best be described by way of illustration.* ○ [+ of] *a perfect illustration of the way Britain absorbs and adapts external influences*

▶ **COLLOCATIONS:**
an illustration **of** *something*
an illustration of a **fact/effect/principle/difference**

▶ **PHRASE:** by way of illustration

▶ **SYNONYMS:** demonstration, example

im|age /ɪmɪdʒ/ (images)   `MARKETING & SALES`

1 NOUN The **image** of a person, group, or organization is the way that they appear to other people. ○ [+ of] *He has cultivated the image of an elder* statesman. ○ *The tobacco industry has been trying to improve its image.*

▶ COLLOCATIONS:
create/improve/project an image
public/corporate/your image
body/self- image
a **negative/positive** image

▶ SYNONYMS: impression, reputation

2 NOUN An **image** is a picture of someone or something. [FORMAL] ○ [+ *of*] *photographic images of young children* ○ *A computer in the machine creates an image on the screen.*

▶ COLLOCATIONS:
display an image
a **full-size/mirror** image
produce/feature/capture an image

▶ SYNONYM: picture

im|ag|ine /ɪmˈædʒɪn/ (imagines, imagining, imagined)

VERB If you **imagine** something, you form a picture or idea of it in your mind. ○ *I can't imagine doing my job without the Internet.*

▶ COLLOCATIONS:
hardly/scarcely imagine *something/doing something*
easily imagine *something*

▶ PHRASES:
it's hard to imagine *something*
try to imagine *something*

▶ SYNONYMS: envisage, envision

im|agi|na|tion /ɪmædʒɪneɪʃən/ (imaginations)

NOUN Your **imagination** is your ability to invent pictures or ideas in your mind. ○ *Designers need to use creativity and imagination.* ○ *I had to come up with a presentation that would capture the wholesalers' imaginations.*

▶ COLLOCATIONS:
capture/catch/fire/stir the imagination
lack/show imagination
a **vivid/fertile** imagination
stretch the imagination
the **public/popular** imagination

▶ PHRASE: creativity and imagination

imi|tate /ˈɪmɪteɪt/ (imitates, imitating, imitated)

VERB If you **imitate** someone, you copy what they do or produce. ○ *It's a genuine German musical which does not try to imitate the American model.* ○ *an American style of architecture that has been widely imitated in Europe*

▶ **COLLOCATIONS: widely/much/often/slavishly** imitated

▶ **SYNONYMS:** copy, recreate

imi|ta|tion /ˌɪmɪteɪʃ°n/ (imitations)

NOUN An **imitation** of something is a copy of it. ○ [+ of] *the most accurate imitation of Chinese architecture in Europe* ○ [+ of] *Then the British invasion of Spanish beaches created the Euro-pub, albeit a pale imitation of the real thing.*

▶ **COLLOCATIONS:**
  an imitation **of** *something*
  a **poor/pale/cheap** imitation
  a **passable/fair/good** imitation

▶ **SYNONYMS:** copy, replica

---

im|medi|ate|ly /ɪˈmiːdiːtli/

ADVERB Immediately is used to emphasize that something comes next, or without any delay. ○ *I answered his email immediately.*

▶ **COLLOCATIONS:**
  begin/return/respond/follow/know immediately
  immediately **after/before**

▶ **SYNONYM:** at once

---

im|pact (impacts, impacting, impacted)

> The noun is pronounced /ˈɪmpækt/. The verb is pronounced /ɪmˈpækt/ or /ˈɪmpækt/.

1 NOUN The **impact** that something has **on** a situation, process, or person is a sudden and powerful effect that it has on them. ○ [+ on] *the mining industry's devastating impact on the environment* ○ *an area where technology can make a real impact*

▶ **COLLOCATIONS:**
  an impact **on** *something*
  an impact on the **environment/economy**
  an impact on **society/health/earnings/tourism**
  a **historical/economic/environmental** impact

a **significant/important/major/profound** impact
a **lasting/immediate/negative/adverse/positive** impact
an impact **statement/assessment/study**

▶ SYNONYMS: effect, mark, impression

2 VERB To **impact on** a situation, process, or person means to affect them. ○ [+ *on*] *That would impact on inflation and competition.* ○ *the potential for women to impact the political process*

▶ COLLOCATIONS:
impact **on/upon** *something*
impact on/upon **growth/industry**
negatively/adversely/directly impact

▶ SYNONYM: affect

---

im|par|tial /ɪmpɑːrʃ^əl/

ADJECTIVE Someone who is **impartial** is not directly involved in a particular situation, and is therefore able to give a fair opinion or decision about it. ○ *Citizens have the right to a speedy and public trial before an impartial jury.* ○ *Career advisers offer impartial advice to all students.*

▶ COLLOCATIONS:
impartial **advice**
an impartial **jury/tribunal/judge**
an impartial **analysis/investigation/manner**

▶ SYNONYMS: unbiased, neutral, objective, disinterested

im|par|tial|ity /ɪmpɑːrʃiælɪti/

NONCOUNT NOUN ○ *a justice system lacking impartiality by democratic standards*

▶ COLLOCATIONS:
judicial/political impartiality
ensure/maintain impartiality

▶ SYNONYMS: neutrality, objectivity

---

im|pa|tient /ɪmpeɪʃənt/

1 ADJECTIVE If you are **impatient**, you are annoyed because you do not want to wait for something. ○ *People are impatient for the war to be over.*

2 ADJECTIVE If you are **impatient**, you are often annoyed by people making mistakes or by things happening too slowly. ○ [+ *with*] *Try not to be impatient with your staff.*

> ▶ **COLLOCATIONS:**
> impatient **with** *someone/something*
> impatient **for** *something*
> **grow** impatient
> an impatient **crowd/driver**

▶ **PHRASE:** angry and impatient

im|pa|tience

NONCOUNT NOUN ○ *Start-ups are driven by the zeal and the impatience of the entrepreneur.*

> ▶ **COLLOCATIONS:**
> impatience **with** *someone/something*
> **growing** impatience

▶ **PHRASE:** a sigh of impatience

---

im|pede /ɪmpiːd/ (impedes, impeding, impeded)

VERB If you **impede** someone or something, you make their movement, development, or progress difficult. [FORMAL] ○ *Debris and fallen rock are impeding the progress of the rescue workers.*

> ▶ **COLLOCATIONS:**
> impede **progress/effort/growth**
> impede the **airflow/recovery/circulation**

▶ **SYNONYMS:** hinder, hamper

im|pedi|ment /ɪmpɛdɪmənt/ (impediments)

NOUN Something that is an **impediment to** a person or thing makes their movement, development, or progress difficult. [FORMAL] ○ *There was no legal impediment to the marriage.* ○ *a major impediment to achieving their objects*

> ▶ **COLLOCATIONS:**
> an impediment **to** *something*
> a **major/significant/big** impediment
> a **structural/regulatory/bureaucratic** impediment
> **remove/overcome/eliminate** an impediment

▶ **SYNONYM:** obstacle

im|ple|ment /ˈɪmplɪmɛnt, -mənt/ (implements, implementing, implemented)

RGD

VERB If you **implement** something such as a plan, you ensure that what has been planned is done. ○ *The government promised to implement a new system to control financial loan institutions.* ○ *The report sets out strict inspection procedures to ensure that the recommendations are properly implemented.*

▶ **COLLOCATIONS:**
implement a **plan/policy/program/change**
implement a **recommendation/directive**
successfully/poorly implement *something*

im|ple|men|ta|tion /ˌɪmplɪmənˈteɪʃᵊn, -mɛn-/

NONCOUNT NOUN ○ [+ *of*] *Very little has been achieved in the implementation of the peace agreement.* ○ [+ *of*] *Full implementation of the ban was deferred until 2012.*

▶ **COLLOCATIONS:**
the implementation **of** *something*
the implementation of a **plan/policy/agreement**
oversee/monitor/delay/defer implementation
full/effective/successful implementation

im|ply /ɪmˈplaɪ/ (implies, implying, implied)

VERB If an event or situation **implies** that something is the case, it makes you think it likely that it is the case. ○ [+ *that*] *Exports in June rose 1.5%, implying that the economy was stronger than many investors had realized.* ○ *A "frontier-free" Europe implies a greatly increased market for all economic operators.*

▶ **COLLOCATIONS:** **not necessarily/clearly/strongly** imply *something*

▶ **SYNONYMS:** suggest, indicate, point to

im|port (imports, importing, imported)

LOGISTICS & DISTRIBUTION

The verb is pronounced /ɪmˈpɔrt/ or /ˈɪmpɔrt/. The noun is pronounced /ˈɪmpɔrt/.

1 VERB To **import** products or raw materials means to buy them from another country for use in your own country. ○ *Britain spent nearly £5000 million more on importing food than selling abroad.* ○ [+ *from*] *imported goods from Mexico*

▶ **COLLOCATIONS:**
import *something* **from** *somewhere*
import **goods/products/oil/steel/beef**
import *x* **tons** of *something*

▶ **PHRASE:** importing and exporting

• **Import** is also a noun. ○ [+ *of*] *Germany, however, insists on restrictions on the import of Polish coal.* ○ *import duties on cars*

▶ **COLLOCATIONS:**
the import **of** *something*
import **tariffs/duty/restrictions**

2 NOUN Imports are products or raw materials bought from another country for use in your own country. ○ *farmers protesting about cheap imports* ○ *Exports fell 3 percent while imports rose 1 percent.*

▶ **COLLOCATIONS:**
cheap/expensive/illegal imports
beef/oil/steel imports
ban/restrict/allow imports
imports **rise/fall**

---

im|por|tant /ɪmpɔːrtᵊnt/

ADJECTIVE Something that is **important** is very significant, is highly valued, or is necessary. ○ *The planned general strike represents an important economic challenge to the government.* ○ [+ *to-inf*] *It's important to answer her questions as honestly as you can.*

▶ **COLLOCATIONS:**
an important **role/part/issue/question/decision**
an important **factor/element/aspect/point**
extremely/particularly/vitally important
equally/increasingly important

▶ **PHRASE:** the single most important thing

▶ **SYNONYMS:** significant, critical, essential

im|por|tance /ɪmpɔːrtᵊns/

NONCOUNT NOUN ○ [+ *of*] *We have always stressed the importance of economic reform.* ○ *Safety is of paramount importance.* ○ *Institutions place great importance on symbols of corporate identity.*

▶ **COLLOCATIONS:**
be **of** importance
the importance **of** *something*

place importance **on** *something*
recognize/stress/emphasize the importance of *something*
understand/know the importance of *something*
of **great/critical/enormous/growing/increasing** importance

▶ **SYNONYM:** significance

---

im|pose /ɪmpoʊz/ (imposes, imposing, imposed)

VERB If you **impose** something **on** people, you use your authority to force them to accept it. ○ [+ on] *Britain imposed fines on airlines which bring in passengers without proper papers.* ○ *Many companies have imposed a pay freeze.*

▶ **COLLOCATIONS:**
impose *something* **on** *someone/something*
impose **restrictions/sanctions**
impose a **fine/tax/penalty/sentence/ban/limit**
a **judge/authority/government** imposes *something*
externally/unilaterally/centrally imposed

▶ **SYNONYMS:** dictate, enforce

im|po|si|tion /ɪmpəzɪʃᵊn/

NONCOUNT NOUN ○ [+ of] *the imposition of a ban on biking in the city center* ○ [+ of] *The key factor is that there is no imposition of locally unpopular development.*

▶ **COLLOCATIONS:**
the imposition **of** *something*
the imposition of **sanctions/tariffs/taxes**
the imposition of a **penalty/law**

▶ **SYNONYM:** enforcement

---

im|pos|sible /ɪmpɒsɪbᵊl/

ADJECTIVE Something that is **impossible** cannot be done or cannot happen. ○ *It's impossible for me to get another job at my age.*

▶ **COLLOCATIONS:**
impossible **for** *someone*
impossible **to** *do something*
almost/virtually/nearly impossible
an impossible **task/dream/situation**

im|prac|ti|cal /ɪmpræktɪkəl/

ADJECTIVE If you describe an object, idea, or course of action as **impractical**, you mean that it is not sensible or realistic. ○ *It's an interesting idea but it's rather impractical.*

▶ **COLLOCATIONS:**
highly/totally/rather impractical
an impractical **proposal/suggestion/solution**

▶ **SYNONYM:** unworkable

im|prove /ɪmpruv/ (improves, improving, improved)   RGD

VERB If something **improves** or if you **improve** it, it gets better. ○ *Both the texture and condition of your hair should improve.* ○ *Time won't improve the situation.*

▶ **COLLOCATIONS:**
dramatically/significantly improve
improve **slightly**
continue/expect/need/try to improve

im|prove|ment /ɪmpruvmənt/ (improvements)

NOUN ○ [+ in] *the dramatic improvements in organ transplantation in recent years* ○ *There is considerable room for improvement in state facilities for treating the mentally handicapped.*

▶ **COLLOCATIONS:**
improvement **in** something
an improvement **over** time
an improvement in **relations/quality/performance**
show/see/make an improvement
a **gradual/big/dramatic/marked/significant/slight** improvement
home/self- improvement

in|ac|ces|sible /ɪnəksɛsɪbəl/

ADJECTIVE If something is **inaccessible**, you are unable to see, use, or buy it. ○ *Ninety-five percent of its magnificent collection will remain inaccessible to the public.* ○ *the remote and inaccessible areas*

▶ **COLLOCATIONS:**
an inaccessible **area/region/place**
virtually/largely/almost inaccessible

▶ **SYNONYM:** unavailable

in|ac|cu|rate /ɪnˈækyərɪt/

ADJECTIVE If a statement or measurement is **inaccurate**, it is not accurate or correct. ○ *These figures are inaccurate and misleading.* ○ *The reports were based on inaccurate information.*

▶ **COLLOCATIONS:**
inaccurate **information/reporting**
an inaccurate **description/portrayal**
factually/historically/wildly/grossly inaccurate
figures/results are inaccurate
a **claim/report** is inaccurate

▶ **SYNONYMS:** wrong, incorrect

in|ac|cu|ra|cy /ɪnˈækyərəsi/ (inaccuracies)

NOUN The **inaccuracy** of a statement or measurement is the fact that it is not accurate or correct. ○ [+ of] *He was disturbed by the inaccuracy of the answers.* ○ *The report contains serious factual inaccuracies.*

▶ **COLLOCATIONS:**
the inaccuracy **of** *something*
factual/historical/glaring inaccuracy
contain/correct an inaccuracy

▶ **SYNONYMS:** incorrectness, mistakes

in|ac|tive /ɪnˈæktɪv/

ADJECTIVE Someone or something that is **inactive** is not doing anything or is not working. ○ *He certainly was not politically inactive.*

▶ **COLLOCATIONS:**
physically/politically/economically inactive
inactive **ingredient/substance**

▶ **SYNONYM:** idle

in|ad|equate /ɪnˈædɪkwɪt/

ADJECTIVE If something is **inadequate**, there is not enough of it or it is not good enough. ○ *Supplies of food and medicines are inadequate.* ○ *The problem goes far beyond inadequate staffing.*

▶ **COLLOCATIONS:**
inadequate to **deal with/meet** *something*
inadequate **funding/training/staffing/supervision**
an inadequate **supply/response**

woefully/grossly inadequate

▸ SYNONYM: deficient

---

in|ca|pable /ɪnkeɪpəbəl/

ADJECTIVE Someone who is **incapable** of doing something is not able to do it. ○ *She's incapable of making sensible decisions.*

▸ COLLOCATIONS:
incapable **of** *something/doing something*
quite/totally/utterly incapable
physically incapable

---

in|cen|tive /ɪnsɛntɪv/ (incentives)

NOUN If something is an **incentive to** do something, it encourages you to do it. ○ [+ to-inf] *There is little or no incentive to adopt such measures.* ○ [+ for] *Many companies are keen on the idea of tax incentives for R&D.*

▸ COLLOCATIONS:
an incentive **for** *something/someone*
provide/offer/give/create an incentive
a **financial/economic/added/extra/additional** incentive
a **tax/cash/strong/powerful/perverse** incentive

▸ SYNONYMS: inducement, enticement

---

in|ci|dent /ɪnsɪdənt/ (incidents)

NOUN An **incident** is something that happens, often something that is unpleasant. [FORMAL] ○ *These incidents were the latest in a series of disputes between the two nations.* ○ *The attack on Liquica was the worst in a series of violent incidents in East Timor.* ○ *The voting went ahead without incident.*

▸ COLLOCATIONS:
a **serious/unfortunate/tragic/alleged** incident
a **terrorist/friendly-fire/isolated** incident
investigate/witness an incident
an incident **happens/occurs/takes place**
an incident **involves** *someone/something*

---

in|con|clu|sive /ɪnkənklusɪv/

ADJECTIVE If research or evidence is **inconclusive**, it has not proved anything. ○ *Research has so far proved inconclusive.* ○ *The judge ruled that the medical evidence was inconclusive.*

▶ **COLLOCATIONS:**
prove inconclusive
an inconclusive **result/test**
inconclusive **evidence**

in|con|ven|ient /ɪnkənvi̱nyənt/

ADJECTIVE Something that is **inconvenient** causes problems or difficulties for someone. ○ *Can you come at 10:30? I know it's inconvenient, but I have to see you.*

▶ **COLLOCATIONS: very/extremely** inconvenient

in|crease (increases, increasing, increased)

> The verb is pronounced /ɪnkri̱s/. The noun is pronounced /ɪ̱nkris/.

1 VERB If something **increases** or you **increase** it, it becomes greater in number, level, or amount. ○ *The population continues to increase.* ○ [+ by/from/to] *Japan's industrial output increased by 2%.*

▶ **COLLOCATIONS:**
increase **by/from/to** *x*
increase **in** *something*
increase **dramatically/rapidly**

▶ **SYNONYMS:** rise, raise

2 NOUN If there is an **increase in** the number, level, or amount of something, it becomes greater. ○ [+ in] *a sharp increase in productivity* ○ *The city is considering a tax increase of more than five percent.*

▶ **COLLOCATIONS:**
an increase **of/from/to** *x*
an increase **in** *something*
an increase in **crime/demand/spending**
an increase in **size/temperature/value**
a **population/price/salary** increase
a **big/marked/sharp** increase

▶ **SYNONYM:** rise

in|creas|ing|ly /ɪnkri̱sɪŋli/

ADVERB You can use **increasingly** to indicate that a situation or quality is becoming greater in intensity or more common. ○ *He was finding it increasingly difficult to make decisions.* ○ *The U.S. has increasingly relied on Japanese capital.*

▶ **COLLOCATIONS:**
become increasingly…
increasingly **difficult/popular/important**
increasingly **clear/common/complex**

▶ **SYNONYM:** more

---

in|deed /ɪndiːd/

1 ADVERB You use **indeed** to confirm or agree with something that has just been said. ○ *Later, he admitted that the payments had indeed been made.* ○ *"Did you know him?" — "I did indeed."*

2 ADVERB You use **indeed** to introduce a further comment or statement that strengthens the point you have already made. ○ *We have nothing against diversity; indeed, we want more of it.*

3 ADVERB You use **indeed** at the end of a clause to give extra force to the word "very," or to emphasize a particular word. ○ *The results are often strange indeed.* ○ *We are very pleased indeed.*

▶ **COLLOCATIONS: fortunate/true** indeed

---

in|de|pend|ent /ɪndɪpɛndənt/

1 ADJECTIVE If one thing or person is **independent of** another, they are separate and not connected, so the first one is not affected or influenced by the second. ○ [+ *of*] *Your questions should be independent of each other.* ○ *Two independent studies have been carried out.*

2 ADJECTIVE If someone is **independent**, they do not need help or money from anyone else. ○ [+ *of*] *Phil was now much more independent of his parents.* ○ *She would like to be financially independent.*

3 ADJECTIVE Independent countries and states are not ruled by other countries but have their own government. ○ *a fully independent state* ○ [+ *from*] *Papua New Guinea became independent from Australia in 1975.*

▶ **COLLOCATIONS:**
independent **of/from** *someone/something*
fully/financially independent
an independent **adviser/inquiry/state**

▶ **SYNONYMS:** self-reliant, self-supporting, liberated, self-governing

---

in|dex /ɪndɛks/ (indexes)

NOUN An **index** is an alphabetical list that is printed at the back of a book and tells you on which pages important topics are referred to.

○ *There's even a special subject index.*

▶ **COLLOCATION:** an **alphabetical** index

▶ **RELATED WORD:** table of contents

---

in|di|cate /ˈɪndɪkeɪt/ (indicates, indicating, indicated)

VERB If one thing **indicates** another thing, the first thing shows that the second is true. ○ *The report indicates that most people agree.*

▶ **COLLOCATIONS:**
seem to/appear to indicate
a **report/study/poll/research** indicates
figures/records indicate

▶ **SYNONYMS:** show, imply

in|di|ca|tion /ˌɪndɪkeɪʃ°n/ (indications)

NOUN An **indication** is a sign that suggests that something exists or is going to happen. ○ *All the indications are that we are going to receive reasonable support from abroad.* ○ [+ of] *These numbers give an indication of the extent of the disease.*

▶ **COLLOCATIONS:**
an indication **of** *something*
an indication of **strength/importance/progress**
a **clear/strong/early/initial** indication

▶ **SYNONYM:** sign

in|di|ca|tor /ˈɪndɪkeɪtər/ (indicators)

NOUN An **indicator** is a measurement or value that gives you an idea of what something is like. ○ *vital economic indicators, such as inflation, growth, and the trade gap* ○ [+ of] *The number of wells is a fair indicator of the demand for water.*

▶ **COLLOCATIONS:**
an indicator **of** *something*
an indicator **suggests/shows/points to** *something*
a **key/reliable/broad/leading** indicator
a **performance/stock/economic** indicator

---

in|di|rect /ˌɪndaɪrɛkt, -dɪr-/

ADJECTIVE An **indirect** result or effect is not caused immediately and obviously by a thing or person, but happens because of something else that they have done. ○ *Businesses are feeling the indirect effects from the* *recession that's going on elsewhere.* ○ *Millions could die of hunger as an indirect result of the war.*

▶ **COLLOCATIONS:**
indirect **taxation/taxes/costs**
an indirect **effect**

---

in|dis|pen|sable /ˌɪndɪspɛnsəbᵊl/

ADJECTIVE If you say that someone or something is **indispensable**, you mean that they are absolutely essential and other people or things cannot function without them. ○ *She was becoming indispensable to him.* ○ *He considered proletarian philosophy an indispensable part of the revolutionary socialist education.*

▶ **COLLOCATIONS:**
an indispensable **tool/part**
an indispensable **requirement/component/ingredient/element**

▶ **SYNONYM:** essential

---

in|di|vid|ual /ˌɪndɪvɪdʒuᵊl/ (individuals)

1 ADJECTIVE Individual means relating to one person or thing, rather than to a large group. ○ *They wait for the group to decide rather than making individual decisions.* ○ *Aid to individual countries is linked to progress towards democracy.*

▶ **COLLOCATIONS:** individual **freedom/responsibility/members**

▶ **SYNONYM:** single

2 NOUN An **individual** is a person. ○ *anonymous individuals who are doing good things within our community* ○ *the rights and responsibilities of the individual*

▶ **COLLOCATIONS:**
a **private/wealthy/healthy** individual
a **particular/certain** individual
an individual's **right/need**

▶ **SYNONYMS:** human being, person

EXTEND YOUR VOCABULARY

You can use **people** to refer to a large group or to everyone in a society. You can also talk about **the public** to refer to the ordinary people in a society or country. ○ *issues affecting young people* ○ *The public increasingly demands more choice.*

You talk about **individuals** to refer to people when each one is considered separately rather than as a group. ○ *a small group of wealthy individuals*

in|doors /ɪndɔ̱rz/

ADVERB If something happens **indoors**, it happens inside a building.
○ *They warned us to close the windows and stay indoors.*

▶ **COLLOCATIONS: stay/remain/go/play** indoors

▶ **RELATED WORD:** outdoors

in|dus|try /ɪ̱ndəstri/ (industries)

ORGANIZATION

1 **NONCOUNT NOUN Industry** is the work and processes involved in making things in factories. ○ *The changes will boost jobs and benefit Australian industry.* ○ *in countries where industry is developing rapidly*

2 **NOUN** A particular **industry** consists of all the people and activities involved in making a particular product or providing a particular service. ○ *the motor vehicle and textile industries* ○ *the American tourist industry*

▶ **COLLOCATIONS:**
a **booming/thriving** industry
heavy/high-tech industry
the **pharmaceutical/tourism/airline/oil** industry

▶ **PHRASES:**
trade and industry
industry and commerce

▶ **SYNONYM:** business

EXTEND YOUR VOCABULARY

There are several words to describe a general area of business. You can talk about a **business** or an **industry**. Both words are often used in compounds to name a particular field of work. ○ *In 1982, about 35,000 people were working in the advertising business in New York City.*

▶ the **music/tourism/advertising** business/industry
▶ the **airline/auto/insurance** industry

You can also use the more specialized term **sector**. ○ *The technology sector is still showing growth.*

Trade and **commerce** are used to talk generally about the business of buying and selling goods. ○ *the regulation of interstate commerce*

in|dus|trial /ɪndʌstriəl/

1 **ADJECTIVE** ○ *industrial machinery and equipment* ○ *a link between industrial chemicals and cancer*

▶ **COLLOCATIONS:** industrial **machinery/products/production**

▶ **PHRASES:**
industrial action
an industrial park
industrial relations

2 **ADJECTIVE** An **industrial** city or country is one in which industry is important or highly developed. ○ *ministers from leading Western industrial countries*

▶ **COLLOCATIONS:** an industrial **area/city/country**

▶ **SYNONYMS:** industrialized, developed

in|fe|ri|or /ɪnfɪəriər/

ADJECTIVE Something that is **inferior** is not as good as something else.
○ *the inferior nutritional quality of foods which have been heavily processed*
○ [+ to] *If children were made to feel inferior to other children, their confidence declined.*

▶ **COLLOCATIONS:**
inferior **to** *something/someone*
inferior **quality/status**
an inferior **product**
vastly/intellectually inferior

▶ **SYNONYM:** worse

in|fla|tion /ɪnfleɪʃⁿn/ BANKING & FINANCE

NONCOUNT NOUN Inflation is a general increase in the prices of goods and services in a country. ○ *rising unemployment and high inflation* ○ *an inflation rate of only 2.2%*

▶ COLLOCATIONS:
control/reduce inflation
high/low/underlying/house/wage inflation
inflation **rises/falls**
inflation **runs at** *x%*
the inflation **rate/figures**

---

in|flu|ence /ɪnˈfluəns/ (influences, influencing, influenced)

1 NOUN To have an **influence on** people or situations means to affect what they do or what happens. ○ [+ on] *Van Gogh had a major influence on the development of modern painting.* ○ *Many other medications have an influence on cholesterol levels.*

▶ COLLOCATIONS:
the influence **of** *someone/something*
influence **on/over** *someone/something*
the influence of **alcohol/drugs**
have/exert influence on *someone/something*
considerable/powerful/positive/political influence
a **major/important/strong/good/bad** influence

▶ SYNONYM: effect

2 VERB If someone or something **influences** a person or situation, they have an effect on that person's behavior or that situation. ○ *We became the best of friends and he influenced me deeply.* ○ *What you eat may influence your risk of getting cancer.* ○ *Leadership means influencing the organization to follow the leader's vision.*

▶ COLLOCATIONS:
influence **behavior/opinion/people**
influence a **decision/policy/development**
heavily/strongly influence *someone/something*

▶ SYNONYM: affect

in|flu|en|tial /ɪnˈfluɛnʃ°l/

ADJECTIVE Someone or something that is **influential** has a lot of influence over people or events. ○ *the influential position of chairman of the finance committee* ○ [+ in] *He had been influential in shaping economic policy.* ○ *one of the most influential books ever written*

▶ COLLOCATIONS:
influential **in** *something*
an influential **figure/voice/magazine**
an influential **cleric/critic/politician**

▶ SYNONYMS: effective, powerful

in|form /ɪnfɔrm/ (informs, informing, informed)   `COMMUNICATIONS`

VERB If you **inform** someone **of** something, you tell them about it. ○ [+ of]
They would inform him of any progress they had made. ○ [+ that] *contracts that
inform customers that their details will be passed to a third party*

▶ **COLLOCATIONS:**
   inform *someone* **of/about** *something*
   inform *someone* of **developments/progress/findings**
   inform **parents/readers/patients/customers**
   inform the **public/police**
   reliably/fully/officially informed

EXTEND YOUR VOCABULARY

Tell is a common verb in everyday English to describe
communication between two or more people. In more formal
writing, you can use the verbs **inform** and **notify** to talk about
passing on information in a formal or official context. You **notify**
someone about a specific fact. You can **inform** someone about a
fact or about a subject more generally.

Remember that all these verbs are transitive and must be followed
by an object - **tell/inform/notify** + *someone*. ○ *Have you informed the
local authorities?*

Tell can be followed by two objects - **tell** *someone something*.
○ *He called a meeting to tell everyone the good news.*

To use two objects (the person and the information) with **inform**
or **notify** you use a preposition - **inform/notify** *someone* **of/about**
something. ○ *They posted signs in their stores to inform customers about
the problem.* ○ *Policyholders will be notified of the changes by mail.*

---

in|for|mal /ɪnfɔrməl/

ADJECTIVE **Informal** speech or behavior is relaxed and friendly rather than
serious or official. ○ *She is refreshingly informal.* ○ *This was an informal,
unofficial investigation.* ○ *This door leads to the informal living area.*

▶ **COLLOCATIONS:** an informal **discussion/meeting/talk**

▶ **SYNONYMS:** relaxed, casual, unofficial

in|for|ma|tion /ɪnfərmeɪʃ°n/

NONCOUNT NOUN Information about someone or something consists of facts about them. ○ [+ *about*] *The tables gave background information about each school.* ○ [+ *on*] *Each center would provide information on technology and training.* ○ *For further information contact the number below.* ○ *an important piece of information*

▸ **COLLOCATIONS:**
information **about/on** *something*
additional/further/detailed/background/personal information
give/provide information
gather/collect/obtain information
contain information

▸ **SYNONYMS:** facts, data, details

> **USAGE: Noncount noun**
>
> Remember that **information** is a noncount noun. You do **not** say "an information" or "informations", and it is followed by a singular verb. ○ *The information is stored in a database.*
>
> You can talk about a **piece of information** or an **item of information**. ○ *His article contains several pieces of incorrect information.*
>
> You can also talk about a **fact** or a **detail**. ○ *His article contains several incorrect details.*

in|forma|tive /ɪnfɔrmətɪv/

ADJECTIVE Something that is **informative** gives you useful information. ○ *The meeting was friendly and informative.*

▸ **COLLOCATIONS: very/highly** informative

▸ **PHRASE:** entertaining and informative

infra|struc|ture /ɪnfrəstrʌktʃər/   `LOGISTICS & DISTRIBUTION`
(infrastructures)

NOUN The **infrastructure** of a country, society, or organization consists of the basic facilities such as transportation, communications, power supplies, and buildings, that enable it to function. ○ *investment in infrastructure projects* ○ *a focus on improving existing infrastructure*

▸ **COLLOCATIONS:**
the infrastructure **of** *something*
have infrastructure **in place**

build/rebuild/improve/destroy infrastructure
existing/basic infrastructure
transportation/rail/telecommunications/security infrastructure
infrastructure **improvement/spending/investment**

---

in|hab|it|ant /ɪnhæbɪtənt/ (inhabitants)

NOUN The **inhabitants** of a place are the people who live there. ○ [+ of] *the inhabitants of Glasgow* ○ *Jamaica's original inhabitants were the Arawak Indians.*

▶ **COLLOCATIONS:**
the inhabitants **of** *somewhere*
indigenous/native/original/local inhabitants

▶ **SYNONYMS:** resident, citizen

---

in|her|it /ɪnhɛrɪt/ (inherits, inheriting, inherited)

1 VERB If you **inherit** money or property, you receive it from someone who has died. ○ *He has no son to inherit his land.* ○ [+ from] *paintings that he inherited from his father*

▶ **COLLOCATIONS:** inherit a **fortune/estate/legacy**

2 VERB If you **inherit** a characteristic or quality, you are born with it, because your parents or ancestors also had it. ○ [+ from] *We inherit many of our physical characteristics from our parents.* ○ *All sufferers from asthma have inherited a gene that makes them susceptible to the disease.* ○ *Stammering is probably an inherited defect.*

▶ **COLLOCATIONS:**
inherit *something* **from** *someone*
inherit a **trait/predisposition/characteristic/gene**
an inherited **defect/disorder**

---

in-house /ɪnhaʊs/ LOGISTICS & DISTRIBUTION

ADJECTIVE In-house work or activities are done by employees of an organization or company, rather than by workers outside the organization or company. ○ *A lot of companies do in-house training.*

▶ **COLLOCATIONS:** in-house **training/publications**

● **In-house** is also an adverb. ○ *The magazine is still produced in-house.*

▶ **COLLOCATIONS:** **produce/design/develop** *something* in-house

ini|tial /ɪnɪʃªl/

ADJECTIVE You use **initial** to describe something that happens at the beginning of a process. ○ *The initial reaction has been excellent.* ○ *The aim of this initial meeting is to clarify the issues.*

▶ **COLLOCATIONS:**
an initial **reaction/response/impression/diagnosis**
an initial **offering/purchase/investment/meeting**
the initial **stages/results/success**

▶ **SYNONYMS:** first, preliminary

ini|tial|ly /ɪnɪʃəli/

ADVERB **Initially** means soon after the beginning of a process or situation, rather than in the middle or at the end of it. ○ *Forecasters say the gales may not be as bad as they initially predicted.*

▶ **COLLOCATIONS:**
initially **refuse/deny/oppose/reject** *something*
initially **propose/plan/schedule/predict** *something*

▶ **SYNONYM:** originally

in|ju|ry /ɪndʒəri/ (injuries)　　　　`HEALTH & FITNESS`

NOUN An **injury** is damage caused to the body of a person or animal. ○ *Four police officers sustained serious injuries in the explosion.* ○ *The two other passengers escaped serious injury.* ○ [+ to] *a serious injury to his left leg*

▶ **COLLOCATIONS:**
an injury **to** *something*
suffer/cause/escape injury
a **bodily/minor/internal/life-threatening** injury
a **personal/serious/severe** injury
a **knee/shoulder/ankle** injury

▶ **SYNONYM:** wound

in|no|va|tion /ɪnəveɪʃªn/ (innovations)　　　　`R&D`

1 NOUN An **innovation** is a new thing or a new method of doing something. ○ *The vegetarian burger was an innovation which was rapidly exported to Britain.* ○ [+ of] *the transformation wrought by the technological innovations of the industrial age*

2 NONCOUNT NOUN **Innovation** is the introduction of new ideas, methods, or things. ○ *We must promote originality and encourage innovation.*

▶ COLLOCATIONS:
the innovations **of** a period
technological/technical/product innovation
foster/encourage/stifle innovation

▶ SYNONYMS: novelty, creativity

in|no|va|tive /ɪnəveɪtɪv/

ADJECTIVE ○ products which are more innovative than those of their competitors
○ He was one of the most creative and innovative engineers of his generation.

▶ COLLOCATIONS:
an innovative **design/approach/solution/idea**
an innovative **method/project/product**
technologically innovative

▶ SYNONYMS: new, original, state-of-the-art, creative

in|or|di|nate /ɪnɔːrdᵊnɪt/

ADJECTIVE If you describe something as **inordinate**, you are emphasizing
that it is unusually or excessively great in amount or degree. [FORMAL]
○ They spend an inordinate amount of time talking.

▶ COLLOCATIONS: an inordinate **amount/number**

in|put /ɪnpʊt/ (inputs, inputting)

The form **input** is used in the present tense and is also the past tense
and past participle.

1 NOUN **Input** is information that is put into a computer. An **input** is a
connection where information enters a computer or other device.
○ an error in data input ○ an amplifier with an input socket

▶ COLLOCATIONS:
an input **jack/socket/device**
stereo/audio/video/data input

2 VERB If you **input** information into a computer, you feed it in, for
example, by typing it on a keyboard. ○ [+ into] All this information had to be
input into the computer.

▶ COLLOCATIONS:
input something **into** something
input **data/information**

▶ SYNONYMS: type, enter

in|quire /ɪnkwaɪər/ (inquires, inquiring, inquired)   `COMMUNICATIONS`

VERB If you **inquire** about something, you ask for information about it.
[FORMAL] [in BRIT, also use **enquire**] ○ *"What are you doing there?"*
she inquired. ○ [+ *about*] *He called them several times to inquire about job*
possibilities.

▶ **COLLOCATIONS: politely/directly** inquire

▶ **SYNONYM:** ask

in|quiry /ɪnkwaɪəri, ɪŋkwɪri/ (inquiries) also **enquiry**

1 **NOUN** An **inquiry** is a question you ask in order to get some information.
○ *He made some inquiries and discovered she had gone to Connecticut.*

▶ **COLLOCATIONS:**
further inquiries
make an inquiry

▶ **SYNONYM:** question

2 **NOUN** An **inquiry** is an official investigation. ○ *a crucial witness in the*
murder inquiry ○ [+ *into*] *The Democratic Party has called for an independent*
inquiry into the incident.

▶ **COLLOCATIONS:**
an inquiry **into** something
an inquiry into a **murder/death/affair/incident**
a **judicial/public/independent/police/murder/corruption** inquiry
conduct/hold/launch/order/adjourn/reopen an inquiry
an inquiry **concludes/reveals/investigates/hears** something

▶ **SYNONYM:** investigation

in|sert /ɪnsɜrt/ (inserts, inserting, inserted)

VERB If you **insert** an object **into** something, you put the object inside it.
○ [+ *into*] *tubes that are inserted into diseased arteries*

▶ **COLLOCATIONS:**
insert something **into** something
insert a **needle/pin/tube/catheter**
surgically/carefully/gently insert

in-service /ɪnsɜrvɪs/   `PERSONNEL`

ADJECTIVE If people working in a particular profession are given **in-service**
training, they attend special courses to improve their skills or to learn

about new developments in their field. ○ *in-service courses for people such as doctors, teachers, and civil servants*

▶ **COLLOCATIONS:** in-service **training/courses**

---

in|sig|nifi|cant /ɪnsɪgnɪfɪkənt/

ADJECTIVE Something that is **insignificant** is unimportant, especially because it is very small. ○ *The data were based on statistically insignificant samples.* ○ *In 1949 Bonn was a small, insignificant city.*

▶ **COLLOCATIONS:**
an insignificant **sum/amount/difference**
an insignificant **piece/detail/matter**
statistically/relatively/seemingly insignificant

▶ **SYNONYM:** unimportant

---

in|spect /ɪnspɛkt/ (inspects, inspecting, inspected)

1 **VERB** If you **inspect** something, you look at every part of it carefully in order to find out about it or check that it is all right. ○ *Safety engineers will periodically inspect the boiler and other machinery for structural defects.*

2 **VERB** When an official **inspects** a place or a group of people, they visit it and check it carefully, for example, in order to find out whether regulations are being obeyed. ○ *Each hotel is inspected and, if it fulfills certain criteria, is recommended.* ○ *U.N. nuclear officials inspected four suspected nuclear weapons sites.*

▶ **COLLOCATIONS:**
inspect **damage**
inspect a **site/facility/property**
visually/carefully/periodically/regularly inspect *something*

▶ **SYNONYMS:** examine, check

in|spec|tion /ɪnspɛkʃ°n/ (inspections)

NOUN ○ [+ of] *He had completed his inspection of the doors.* ○ [+ of] *Officers making a routine inspection of the vessel found fifty kilograms of the drug.* ○ *demands for weapons inspections*

▶ **COLLOCATIONS:**
an inspection **of** *something*
an inspection of a **site/plant/vehicle/facility**
resume/conduct/pass an inspection
a **weapons/arms/safety** inspection

a **routine/close** inspection
an inspection **team/regime/report**
an inspection **reveals** *something*

▶ **SYNONYMS:** examination, check, inquiry

---

in|spi|ra|tion /ɪnspɪreɪʃᵊn/

NONCOUNT NOUN Inspiration is a feeling of enthusiasm you get from
someone or something, that gives you new and creative ideas.
○ *My inspiration comes from poets like Baudelaire and Jacques Prévert.*

▶ **COLLOCATIONS: find/seek/take/draw** inspiration

▶ **PHRASE:** a source of inspiration

---

in|stall|ment /ɪnstɔːlmənt/ (installments) [BANKING & FINANCE]

NOUN If you pay for something in **installments**, you pay for it in many
small regular payments. ○ *She is repaying the loan in monthly installments
of $300.*

▶ **COLLOCATIONS:**
in installments
pay an installment
annual/monthly installments
the **first/final** installment

---

in|stance /ɪnstəns/ (instances)

1 **PHRASE** You use **for instance** to introduce a particular event, situation,
or person that is an example of what you are talking about. ○ *There are a
number of improvements; for instance, both mouse buttons can now be used.*
○ *TB is an infinitely bigger problem than, for instance, AIDS.*

▶ **SYNONYM:** for example

2 **NOUN** An **instance** is a particular example or occurrence of something.
○ *The committee reported numerous instances where key information was not
shared.* ○ [+ of] *an investigation into a serious instance of corruption*

▶ **COLLOCATIONS:**
an instance **of** *something*
a **rare/isolated/particular/specific/reported/recorded** instance
numerous/several instances
document/cite/record/report an instance

▶ **SYNONYMS:** example, case, occurrence

in|stant mes|sag|ing /ɪnstənt mɛsɪdʒɪŋ/ `COMMUNICATIONS`

NONCOUNT NOUN Instant messaging is the activity of sending written messages from one computer to another so that they appear immediately. ○ *College students are about twice as likely as average Internet users to use instant messaging.*

in|stinct /ɪnstɪŋkt/ (instincts)

NOUN Instinct is the natural tendency that a person or animal has to behave or react in a particular way. ○ *A woman's maternal instincts are stimulated when there are children around.* ○ *He always knew what time it was, as if by instinct.*

▶ COLLOCATIONS:
  a **basic/natural/gut/survival** instinct
  a **killer/animal/maternal/competitive** instinct

▶ SYNONYMS: intuition, sense

in|sti|tute /ɪnstɪtut/ (institutes) `ORGANIZATION`

NOUN An **institute** is an organization set up to do a particular type of work, especially research or teaching. You can also use **institute** to refer to the building the organization occupies. ○ *the National Cancer Institute* ○ *an elite research institute devoted to computer software*

▶ COLLOCATIONS:
  found/establish an institute
  a **research/training** institute

▶ SYNONYMS: organization, foundation

in|sti|tu|tion /ɪnstɪtuʃən/ (institutions)

NOUN An **institution** is a large important organization such as a university, church, or bank. ○ [+ *of*] *the Institution of Civil Engineers* ○ *Class size varies from one type of institution to another.* ○ *The Hong Kong Bank is Hong Kong's largest financial institution.*

▶ COLLOCATIONS:
  the institution **of** *something*
  a **financial/banking/lending** institution
  a **research/educational/academic/cultural/religious** institution

▶ SYNONYMS: organization, establishment

in|struc|tor /ɪnstrʌktər/ (instructors)   `JOBS`

NOUN An **instructor** is someone whose job is to teach a skill or an activity.
○ *a swimming instructor*

▶ **COLLOCATIONS:**
   a **fitness/dance/ski/driving** instructor
   a **qualified/experienced** instructor

▶ **SYNONYM:** teacher

in|stru|ment /ɪnstrəmənt/ (instruments)   `R&D`

NOUN An **instrument** is a tool or device that is used to do a particular task, especially a scientific task. ○ [+ *for*] *instruments for cleaning and polishing teeth* ○ *The environment will be measured by about 60 scientific instruments.*

▶ **COLLOCATIONS:**
   an instrument **for** *something*
   a **scientific/surgical** instrument
   a **sensitive/blunt/sharp** instrument
   design/sterilize an instrument

▶ **SYNONYMS:** tool, device, mechanism

in|suf|fi|cient /ɪnsəfɪʃ°nt/

ADJECTIVE Something that is **insufficient** is not large enough in amount or degree for a particular purpose. [FORMAL] ○ *He decided there was insufficient evidence to justify criminal proceedings.* ○ *These efforts were insufficient to contain the crisis.*

▶ **COLLOCATIONS:**
   insufficient **for** *something*
   insufficient **evidence/funds**

▶ **SYNONYM:** inadequate

in|sur|ance /ɪnʃʊərəns/   `BANKING & FINANCE`

NONCOUNT NOUN Insurance is an arrangement in which you pay money to a company, and they pay money to you if something unpleasant happens to you, for example if your property is stolen or damaged, or if you get a serious illness. ○ *The insurance company paid out for the stolen jewelry and silver.* ○ [+ *on*] *We recommend that you take out travel insurance on all vacations.* ○ *regulation of the insurance industry*

▶ **COLLOCATIONS:**
insurance **on** *something*
an insurance **company/policy/premium/claim**
the insurance **industry**
health/medical/life/home/car/travel insurance
buy/purchase/take out/sell/carry insurance

▶ **SYNONYM:** cover

---

in|te|grate /ɪntɪɡreɪt/ (integrates, integrating, integrated)

1 VERB If someone **integrates** into a social group, or **is integrated** into it, they behave in such a way that they become part of the group or are accepted into it. ○ [+ *into*] *reforms to help immigrants integrate better into British society* ○ [+ *with*] *Integrating the kids with the community, finding them a role, is essential.*

▶ **COLLOCATIONS:**
integrate **into/with** *something*
integrate into **society**
integrate with a **community**

2 VERB If you **integrate** one thing **with** another, or one thing **integrates with** another, the two things become closely linked or form part of a whole idea or system. You can also say that two things **integrate**. ○ [+ *with*] *Integrating the pound with other European currencies could cause difficulties.* ○ [+ *into*] *Little attempt was made to integrate the parts into a coherent whole.*

▶ **COLLOCATIONS:**
integrate *something* **with/into** *something*
integrate a **component/application/system/database**
integrate **data/information/knowledge/efforts**

▶ **SYNONYMS:** fuse, incorporate, merge, assimilate, combine

in|te|gra|tion /ɪntɪɡreɪʃ°n/

NONCOUNT NOUN ○ [+ *of*] *the integration of disabled people into mainstream society* ○ *an aim to promote racial integration* ○ *closer European integration*

▶ **COLLOCATIONS:**
integration **of/with/into** *something*
racial/economic/European integration
close/further integration
facilitate/promote/achieve integration
an integration **process/issue**

▶ **SYNONYMS:** fusion, incorporation, assimilation

in|tel|li|gent /ɪntɛlɪdʒ³nt/

ADJECTIVE A person or animal that is **intelligent** has the ability to think, understand, and learn things quickly and well. ○ *Susan's a very bright and intelligent woman.* ○ *lively and intelligent conversation* ○ *the opinion that whales are as intelligent as human beings*

▶ **COLLOCATIONS:**
an intelligent **reader/audience/class/being**
highly intelligent

▶ **SYNONYMS:** bright, clever, sharp, smart

in|tend /ɪntɛnd/ (intends, intending, intended)

1 VERB If you **intend** to do something, you have decided or planned to do it. ○ [+ to-inf] *an opinion poll on how people intend to vote* ○ [+ v-ing] *I didn't intend coming to Germany to work.* ○ [+ that] *We had always intended that the new series would be live.*

▶ **SYNONYMS:** mean, plan

2 VERB If something **is intended** for a particular purpose, it has been planned to fulfill that purpose. If something **is intended** for a particular person, it has been planned to be used by that person or to affect them in some way. ○ [+ for] *This money is intended for the development of the tourist industry.* ○ [+ to-inf] *Columns are usually intended in architecture to add grandeur and status.* ○ [+ as] *Originally, Hatfield had been intended as a leisure complex.*

▶ **COLLOCATIONS:**
intended **for/as** *something*
originally/primarily intended

in|tent /ɪntɛnt/ (intents)

1 ADJECTIVE If you are **intent on** doing something, you are eager and determined to do it. ○ *The rebels are obviously intent on keeping up the pressure.*

▶ **COLLOCATIONS:**
intent **on** *something*
intent on **revenge**

▶ **SYNONYMS:** bent, set

2 NOUN A person's **intent** is their intention to do something. [FORMAL] ○ *a strong statement of intent on arms control*

▶ **COLLOCATIONS: malicious/criminal/evil** intent

in|ten|tion|al /ɪntɛnʃənəl/

ADJECTIVE Something that is **intentional** is deliberate. ○ *Women who are the victims of intentional discrimination will be able to get compensation.*

▶ **COLLOCATIONS:** intentional **killing/discrimination/wrongdoing**

▶ **SYNONYMS:** deliberate, planned

---

in|tense /ɪntɛns/

ADJECTIVE **Intense** is used to describe something that is very great or extreme in strength or degree. ○ *He was sweating from the intense heat.* ○ *His threats become more intense, agitated, and frequent.*

▶ **COLLOCATIONS:**
intense **heat/pain/pressure/scrutiny/fighting**
intense **debate/speculation/negotiations**
intense **competition/rivalry**

▶ **SYNONYM:** extreme

---

inter|act /ɪntərækt/ (interacts, interacting, interacted)

1 VERB When people **interact with** each other or **interact**, they communicate as they work or spend time together. ○ *While the other children interacted and played together, Ted ignored them.* ○ [+ *with*] *rhymes and songs to help parents interact with their babies*

▶ **COLLOCATIONS:**
interact **with** *someone*
interact **directly/socially/easily**

▶ **SYNONYM:** communicate

2 VERB When people **interact with** computers, or when computers **interact with** other machines, information, or instructions are exchanged. ○ [+ *with*] *Millions of people want new, simplified ways of interacting with a computer.* ○ *There will be a true global village in which telephones, computers, and televisions interact.*

▶ **COLLOCATION:** interact **with** *something*

3 VERB When one thing **interacts with** another or two things **interact**, the two things affect each other's behavior or condition. ○ *You have to understand how cells interact.* ○ [+ *with*] *Atoms within the fluid interact with the minerals that form the grains.*

▶ **COLLOCATIONS:**
interact **with** *something*
interact with a **protein/environment/object**

inter|ac|tive /ɪntərˈæktɪv/

ADJECTIVE An **interactive** computer program or television system is one that allows direct communication between the user and the machine. ○ *This will make video games more interactive than ever.* ○ *high-speed Internet services and interactive television*

▶ **COLLOCATIONS:**
 interactive **television**
 an interactive **presentation/map/guide/display**

inter|change|able /ɪntərˈtʃeɪndʒəbəl/

ADJECTIVE Things that are **interchangeable** can be exchanged with each other without it making any difference. ○ *His greatest innovation was the use of interchangeable parts.*

▶ **COLLOCATIONS:**
 virtually/almost/otherwise interchangeable
 interchangeable **parts/components**

in|ter|est /ˈɪntrɪst, -tərɪst/ (interests, interesting, `BANKING & FINANCE` interested)

1 **NOUN** If you have an **interest in** something, you want to learn or hear more about it. ○ [+ in] *There has been a lively interest in the elections in the last two weeks.* ○ [+ in] *His parents tried to discourage his interest in music, but he persisted.* ○ [+ to] *material which was of immense interest to the press*

▶ **COLLOCATIONS:**
 an interest **in** *something*
 be **of** interest
 of interest **to** *someone*
 a **level/conflict/place** of interest
 attract/express/lose interest
 great/little/strong/self interest

2 **VERB** If something **interests** you, it attracts your attention so that you want to learn or hear more about it or continue doing it. ○ *a collection of documents they seem to think might interest us* ○ [+ to-inf] *It may interest you to know that Miss Woods, the housekeeper, witnessed the attack.*

▶ **COLLOCATIONS:**
 interest *someone* **in** *something*
 interest a **reader/buyer**

3 **NOUN** If something is in the **interests** of a particular person or group, it will benefit them in some way. ○ [+ of] *Did those directors act in the best interests of their club?* ○ *The media were required to act in the public interest.*

▶ COLLOCATIONS:
  be **in** *someone's* interests
  in the interests **of** *someone*
  in the interests of **consumers/shareholders**
  in the **public/national** interest
  someone's **best** interests

4 NOUN If a person, country, or organization has an **interest in** a possible event or situation, they want that event or situation to happen because they are likely to benefit from it. ○ [+ *in*] *The West has an interest in promoting democratic forces in Eastern Europe.*

▶ COLLOCATIONS:
  an interest **in** *something*
  a **vested/particular/keen** interest

5 NONCOUNT NOUN **Interest** is extra money that you receive if you have invested a sum of money. **Interest** is also the extra money that you pay if you have borrowed money or are buying something on credit. ○ *a current account which pays interest* ○ *This is an important step toward lower interest rates.*

▶ COLLOCATIONS:
  pay/lose/accrue/earn interest
  interest **rates/charges**

6 PHRASE If you do something **in the interests of** a particular result or situation, you do it in order to achieve that result or maintain that situation. ○ *a call for all businessmen to work together in the interests of national stability*

▶ COLLOCATIONS: in the interests of **fairness/justice/safety**

in|ter|est rate /ɪntrɪst reɪt/ (interest rates)

NOUN The **interest rate** is the amount of interest that must be paid on a loan or investment, expressed as a percentage of the amount that is borrowed or gained as profit. ○ *The Federal Reserve lowered interest rates by half a point.*

▶ COLLOCATIONS:
  rising/falling interest rates
  interest rates **go up/come down/drop**

inter|fere /ɪntərfɪər/ (interferes, interfering, interfered)

1 VERB If you say that someone **interferes in** a situation, you mean they get involved in it although it does not concern them and their involvement is not wanted. ○ [+ *in*] *The U.N. cannot interfere in the internal affairs of any country.*

▶ **COLLOCATIONS:**
interfere **in** *something*
interfere in a **matter/process/affair**
the **right/ability** to interfere

▶ **SYNONYM:** intervene

2 VERB Something that **interferes with** a situation, activity, or process has a damaging effect on it. ○ [+ *with*] *Smoking and drinking interfere with your body's ability to process oxygen.*

▶ **COLLOCATIONS:**
interfere **with** *something*
interfere with **digestion/absorption/function**

▶ **SYNONYMS:** inhibit, obstruct

inter|fer|ence /ɪntərfɪ̱ərəns/

NONCOUNT NOUN ○ [+ *in*] *The parliament described the decree as interference in the republic's internal affairs.* ○ [+ *from*] *Airlines will be able to set cheap fares without interference from the government.*

▶ **COLLOCATIONS:**
interference **in/with** *something*
interference **from** *someone*
interference in a **matter/process/affair**
unwarranted/undue/outside/political interference

▶ **SYNONYMS:** intervention, meddling

---

in|ter|im /ɪ̱ntərɪm/

1 ADJECTIVE Interim is used to describe something that is intended to be used until something permanent is done or established. ○ *She was sworn in as head of an interim government in March.* ○ *These interim reports provide an outline of the problem and a general idea of the work being carried out.*

▶ **COLLOCATIONS:**
an interim **government/constitution/administration/authority**
an interim **president/minister/coach/chairman/report**
interim **results**

2 PHRASE In the interim means until a particular thing happens or until a particular thing happened. [FORMAL] ○ *But, in the interim, we obviously have a duty to maintain law and order.* ○ *He was to remain in jail in the interim.*

▶ **SYNONYMS:** in the meantime, meanwhile

inter|medi|ate /ɪntərmiːdiɪt/

ADJECTIVE An **intermediate** stage, level, or position is one that occurs between two other stages, levels, or positions. ○ *a process commencing at the primitive stage and leading, through an intermediate stage, to modernity* ○ *hourly trains to Perugia, Assisi, and intermediate stations*

▶ **COLLOCATION:** an intermediate **stage**

▶ **SYNONYM:** middle

inter|mit|tent /ɪntərmɪtᵊnt/

ADJECTIVE Something that is **intermittent** happens occasionally rather than continuously. ○ *After three hours of intermittent rain, the game was abandoned.* ○ *The constant movement of cables can easily damage the fragile wires inside, causing intermittent problems that are hard to detect.*

▶ **COLLOCATIONS:**
intermittent **rain/showers**
an intermittent **problem/fault**

▶ **SYNONYM:** sporadic

in|tern (interns, interning, interned)   PERSONNEL

The verb is pronounced /ɪntɜrn/. The noun is pronounced /ɪntɜrn/.

NOUN An **intern** is an advanced student or a recent graduate who is being given practical training under supervision. ○ *a summer intern at a New York industrial design firm*

▶ **COLLOCATIONS:**
a **medical** intern
a **summer** intern

● **Intern** is also a verb. ○ *He will intern with a company interested in international timber ventures.*

▶ **COLLOCATION:** intern **with** *a company*

in|tern|ship /ɪntɜrnʃɪp/ (internships)

NOUN An **internship** is the position held by an intern, or the period of time when someone is an intern. ○ *The high internship success rate has led to a number of job offers.*

▶ **COLLOCATIONS:**
a **summer** internship
a **medical/legal** internship

in|ter|nal /ɪntɜːnᵊl/

1 **ADJECTIVE Internal** is used to describe things that exist or happen inside a country or organization. ○ *The country stepped up internal security.* ○ *We now have a Europe without internal borders.* ○ *an internal mailbox*

▶ **COLLOCATIONS:**
internal **affairs/security/politics**
an internal **inquiry/investigation/review/flight**

▶ **SYNONYM:** domestic

2 **ADJECTIVE Internal** is used to describe things that exist or happen inside a particular person, object, or place. ○ *massive internal bleeding* ○ *disorders which affected the skin and internal organs alike*

▶ **COLLOCATIONS:**
an internal **organ**
internal **bleeding**

inter|na|tion|al /ɪntərnæʃᵊnᵊl/

ADJECTIVE International means between or involving different countries. ○ *an international agreement against exporting arms to that country* ○ *Kuwait International Airport* ○ *emergency aid from the international community*

▶ **COLLOCATIONS:** international **community/law/pressure/effort**

In|ter|net /ɪntərnɛt/ also **internet**   COMMUNICATIONS

NOUN The Internet is the network that allows computer users to connect with computers all over the world, and that carries email. ○ *Opportunities exist, and are being exploited, in selling fast-moving consumer goods over the Internet.*

▶ **COLLOCATIONS:**
over/via the Internet
browse/surf/access/go on the Internet
an Internet **site/portal**
Internet **access**
wireless Internet

in|ter|pret /ɪntɜːprɪt/ (interprets, interpreting, interpreted)

VERB If you **interpret** something in a particular way, you decide that this is its meaning or significance. ○ [+ *as*] *The whole speech might well be interpreted as a coded message to the Americans.* ○ *methods of gathering and interpreting data*

▶ **COLLOCATIONS:**
  interpreted **as** *something*
  interpret **data/results/meaning**
  widely/correctly interpreted

▶ **SYNONYM:** understand

in|ter|pre|ta|tion /ɪntɜrprɪteɪʃ°n/ (interpretations)

NOUN An **interpretation** of something is an opinion about what it means.
  ○ *The opposition put a different interpretation on the figures.* ○ [+ *of*]
  a disagreement on the interpretation of scientific data

▶ **COLLOCATIONS:**
  an interpretation **of** *something*
  an interpretation of **data**
  an interpretation of a **law/rule/event**
  a **literal/strict/subjective** interpretation
  differing/conflicting/varying interpretations
  offer/reject an interpretation
  put an interpretation **on** *something*

▶ **PHRASE:** interpretation and analysis

▶ **SYNONYMS:** understanding, reading

in|ter|rup|tion /ɪntərʌpʃən/

NONCOUNT NOUN **Interruption** is the stopping of an activity for a period
of time. ○ *The meeting continued without interruption.*

▶ **COLLOCATIONS:**
  without interruption
  the interruption **of** *something*
  interruption **from** *something*
  constant interruption

in|ter|val /ɪntərvəl/ (intervals)

1 NOUN An **interval** between two events or dates is the period of time
between them. ○ [+ *of*] *The ferry service has restarted after an interval of 12
years.* ○ [+ *of*] *There was a long interval of silence.*

▶ **COLLOCATIONS:**
  an interval **of** *something/time*
  an interval **between** *things*

▶ **SYNONYM:** gap

2 **PHRASE** If something happens **at intervals**, it happens several times with gaps or pauses in between. ○ *The subjects were monitored at intervals during their adult life.*

▶ **SYNONYMS:** regularly, periodically

---

inter|view /ɪntərvyu/ (interviews, interviewing, interviewed)

`PERSONNEL`

1 **NOUN** An **interview** is a formal meeting at which someone is asked questions in order to find out information about them. ○ *Not everyone who writes in can be invited for an interview.* ○ [+ with] *The three-year study is based on interviews with judges, lawyers, and parents.*

▶ **COLLOCATIONS:**
an interview **with** *someone*
a **job** interview
a **telephone/phone** interview
conduct an interview

2 **VERB** If you **are interviewed**, someone asks you questions about yourself to find out information about you. ○ [+ for] *He was among the three candidates interviewed for the job.* ○ *The resident doctor interviewed her and prepared a case history.*

▶ **COLLOCATIONS:**
interview *someone* **for** *something*
interview *someone* for a **story/article/job**
interview a **witness/candidate/sample**
police/investigators/detectives/researchers interview *someone*
interviewed by a **reporter/journalist/researcher**

---

in|tri|cate /ɪntrɪkət/

ADJECTIVE You use **intricate** to describe something that has many small parts or details. ○ *their intricate pattern of markings*

▶ **COLLOCATIONS:**
an intricate **pattern/design**
incredibly/highly/extremely intricate

---

intro|duc|tion /ɪntrədʌkʃn/ (introductions)

1 **NOUN** The **introduction** of something is the process of bringing it into a place or system for the first time. ○ [+ of] *He is best remembered for the introduction of the moving assembly-line.* ○ [+ of] *the introduction of a privacy bill*

▶ **COLLOCATIONS:**
the introduction **of** *something*
the introduction of **legislation/technology**
the introduction of a **fee/scheme**
propose/oversee/delay the introduction

▶ **SYNONYMS:** establishment, launch

2 NOUN The **introduction to** a book, essay, or talk is the part that comes at the beginning and tells you what the rest of the book, essay, or talk is about. ○ [+ *to*] *Ellen Malos, in her introduction to "The Politics of Housework," provides a summary of the debates.* ○ *An essay's introduction usually indicates what the topic and thesis are and why the topic is of some importance.*

▶ **COLLOCATIONS:**
an introduction **to** *something*
a **brief/concise** introduction
write an introduction

▶ **SYNONYM:** preface

intro|duc|tory /ɪntrədʌktəri/

ADJECTIVE An **introductory** offer or price on a new product is something such as a free gift or a low price that is meant to attract new customers. ○ *a special introductory offer*

▶ **COLLOCATIONS:**
an introductory **offer/rate/discount**
an introductory **course/session/class**
an introductory **remark/chapter/paragraph**

▶ **SYNONYM:** initial

in|va|lid /ɪnvælɪd/

1 ADJECTIVE If an action, procedure, or document is **invalid**, it cannot be accepted, because it breaks the law or some official rule. ○ *The trial was stopped and the results declared invalid.* ○ *He tried to leave for the Philippines on an invalid passport.*

2 ADJECTIVE An **invalid** argument or conclusion is wrong because it is based on a mistake. ○ *We think that those arguments are rendered invalid by the hard facts on the ground.* ○ *The paper lacked a coherent method and was statistically invalid.*

▶ **COLLOCATIONS:**
an invalid **election/result/marriage/vote**
an invalid **claim/argument**

an invalid **passport/signature/ticket/contract**
declare/deem/render *something* invalid

▶ **SYNONYMS:** null, false

---

in|vent /ɪnvɛnt/ **(invents, inventing, invented)** `R&D`

VERB If you **invent** something such as a machine or process, you are the
first person to think of it or make it. ○ *He invented the first electric clock.*
○ *Writing had not been invented then.*

▶ **SYNONYMS:** come up with, devise

in|ven|tion /ɪnvɛnʃən/ **(inventions)**

NOUN ○ *The spinning wheel was a Chinese invention.* ○ [+ *of*] *the invention of
the telephone*

▶ **COLLOCATIONS:**
the invention **of** *something*
technological/computer-assisted invention
develop/patent an invention
a **mechanical/revolutionary** invention

---

in|ven|tory /ɪnvəntɔːri/ **(inventories)** `LOGISTICS & DISTRIBUTION`

NOUN The **inventory** of a business is the amount or value of its raw
materials, work in progress, and finished goods. ○ *Second-quarter growth
slowed because distributors had too much inventory.* ○ *Business inventories rose
at a $22 billion annual rate.*

▶ **COLLOCATIONS:**
a **complete/full** inventory
take/manage/track/reduce inventory
excess/low inventory
inventory **management/levels**
inventories **rise/fall/grow**

▶ **SYNONYM:** stock

---

in|vest /ɪnvɛst/ **(invests, investing, invested)** `BANKING & FINANCE`

1 VERB If you **invest in** something, or if you **invest** a sum of money,
you use your money in a way that you hope will increase its value,
for example, by paying it into a bank, or buying stocks or property.
○ [+ *in*] *He invested all our profits in gold stocks.*

2 **VERB** When a government or organization **invests in** something, it gives or lends money for a purpose that it considers useful or profitable.
○ [+ in] *the government's failure to invest in an integrated transportation system*
○ *Why does Japan invest, on average, twice as much capital per worker per year than the United States?*

▶ **COLLOCATIONS:**
invest **in** *something*
invest in **stocks/bonds/securities/equities**
invest in **infrastructure/technology/equipment**
invest **money/capital/assets**
invest a **sum/amount**
primarily/principally/heavily/directly invest

in|vest|ment /ɪnvɛstmənt/ (investments)

1 **NONCOUNT NOUN** **Investment** is the activity of investing money.
○ *The government must introduce tax incentives to encourage investment.*

2 **NOUN** An **investment** is an amount of money that you invest, or the thing that you invest it in. ○ [+ of] *an investment of twenty-eight million dollars* ○ [+ in] *Total foreign investment in America still constitutes only about 5% of U.S. assets.*

▶ **COLLOCATIONS:**
investment **in** *something/somewhere*
an investment **of** *$x*
investment in **stocks/bonds/infrastructure/technology**
attract/encourage/stimulate investment
foreign/private/direct/capital/property investment
an investment **bank/strategy/banker/adviser/dealer**
investment **banking/income**

▶ **PHRASE:** savings and investments

in|ves|tor /ɪnvɛstər/ (investors)

NOUN An **investor** is a person or organization that buys stocks or bonds, or pays money into a bank in order to receive a profit. ○ [+ in] *The main investor in the project is the French bank Credit National.*

▶ **COLLOCATIONS:**
an investor **in** *something*
a **foreign/private/retail/individual** investor

▶ **SYNONYMS:** banker, lender

in|ves|ti|gate /ɪnvɛstɪgeɪt/ (investigates, investigating, investigated)

VERB If you investigate something, you study or examine it carefully to find out the truth about it. ○ *Research is now investigating a possible link between endometriosis and the immune system.* ○ [+ how] *Police are still investigating how the accident happened.*

▸ **COLLOCATIONS:**
investigate a **link/case/incident/complaint/allegation**
thoroughly/fully/properly investigate

▸ **SYNONYMS:** examine, explore, study, analyze

in|volve /ɪnvɒlv/ (involves, involving, involved)

1 VERB If a situation or activity **involves** something, that thing is a necessary part or consequence of it. ○ [+ v-ing] *Nicky's job as a public relations director involves spending quite a lot of time with other people.* ○ *the risks involved in the procedure*

▸ **COLLOCATIONS:** involve **risk/work/money**

▸ **SYNONYM:** entail

2 VERB If a situation or activity **involves** someone, they are taking part in it. ○ *If there was a cover-up, it involved people at the very highest levels of government.* ○ *a riot involving a hundred inmates*

▸ **COLLOCATIONS:**
be involved **in** *something*
be **actively/directly/heavily** involved
deeply/emotionally involved

▸ **SYNONYM:** include

iso|late /aɪsəleɪt/ (isolates, isolating, isolated)

1 VERB If you **isolate** something such as an idea or a problem, you separate it from others that it is connected with, so that you can concentrate on it or consider it on its own. ○ *attempts to isolate a single factor as the cause of the decline of Britain*

2 VERB To **isolate** a substance means to obtain it by separating it from other substances using scientific processes. ○ *We can use genetic engineering techniques to isolate the gene that is responsible.* ○ [+ from] *Researchers have isolated a new protein from the seeds of poppies.*

3 VERB To **isolate** a sick person or animal means to keep them apart from other people or animals, so that their illness does not spread.

○ [+ from] *Patients will be isolated from other people for between three days and one month after treatment.*

▶ **COLLOCATIONS:**
isolate *something/someone* **from** *something*
isolate *something/someone* from **the world/society**
isolate a **gene/virus/protein/cell**

▶ **SYNONYM:** separate

iso|la|tion /aɪsəleɪʃᵊn/

NONCOUNT NOUN **Isolation** is when someone or something is separated from other people or things. ○ [+ of] *The epidemic finally stopped in mid-2003, due to stringent isolation of cases.*

Jj

jeop|ardy /dʒɛpərdi/

PHRASE If someone or something is **in jeopardy**, they are in a dangerous situation where they might fail, be lost, or be destroyed. ○ *A series of setbacks have put the whole project in jeopardy.*

▶ **COLLOCATIONS:** in **serious/great/real** jeopardy

▶ **SYNONYM:** danger

jeop|ard|ize /dʒɛpərdaɪz/ (jeopardizes, jeopardizing, jeopardized)

VERB To **jeopardize** a situation or activity means to do something that may destroy it or cause it to fail. [in BRIT, also use **jeopardise**] ○ *He has jeopardized his future career.*

▶ **COLLOCATIONS:** jeopardize *someone's* **safety/security/health**

▶ **SYNONYMS:** threaten, endanger

jet lag /dʒɛt læg/ `TRAVEL`

NONCOUNT NOUN If you have **jet lag**, you feel tired after a long trip by airplane. ○ *We were tired because we still had jet lag.*

▶ **COLLOCATIONS:** **suffer/beat/prevent** jet lag

job de|scrip|tion /dʒɒb dɪskrɪpʃᵊn/ (job descriptions) `PERSONNEL`

NOUN A **job description** is a written statement of all the duties involved in a particular job. ○ *This is the job description for the position of division general manager.*

▶ **COLLOCATIONS:** a **full/written/clear** job description

▶ **PHRASE:** part of the job description

joint /dʒɔɪnt/ `ORGANIZATION`

ADJECTIVE Joint means shared by or belonging to two or more people. ○ *The two leaders issued a joint statement.*

▶ **COLLOCATIONS:**
  a joint **bid/agreement/decision**
  a joint **statement/account**

▶ **SYNONYMS:** shared, collective

joint ven|ture /dʒɔɪnt vɛntʃər/ (joint ventures)

NOUN A **joint venture** is a business set up by two or more companies or people. ○ *a commercial joint venture between the BBC and Flextech* ○ *It will be sold to a joint venture created by Dow Jones and Westinghouse Broadcasting.*

▶ **COLLOCATIONS:**
  a joint venture **between** things
  set up/arrange a joint venture **with** someone

junk mail /dʒʌŋk meɪl/ [COMMUNICATIONS]

NONCOUNT NOUN **Junk mail** is publicity materials in your mail that you have not asked for. ○ *We still get junk mail for the previous occupants.*

▶ **COLLOCATIONS: get/send/stop** junk mail

Ll

la|bel /léɪbᵊl/ (labels, labeling, labeled) [in BRIT, use labelling, labelled]

VERB If you **label** a diagram, chart, picture, etc., you write information saying what each part is or what each part represents. ○ *You could be asked to label diagrams.* ○ *There is a map, with key targets circled in red and clearly labeled.*

▸ **COLLOCATION: clearly** labeled

● **Label** is also a noun. ○ *The pattern is obvious as we look at all of the pictures and their labels in Figure 7.3.*

la|bor /léɪbər/   **PERSONNEL**

NONCOUNT NOUN Labor is used to refer to the workers of a country or industry, considered as a group. [in BRIT, use **labour**] ○ *Latin America lacked skilled labor.* ○ *Immigrants arrived in the 1950s to deal with postwar labor shortages.*

▸ **COLLOCATIONS:**
    skilled/semiskilled/unskilled/cheap labor
    the labor **market**
    a labor **shortage/dispute**
    labor **relations**

la|bor force /léɪbər fɔrs/ (labor forces)

NOUN The labor force is all the people who are able to work in a country or area, or all the people who work for a particular company. ○ *Unemployment rose to 8.1% of the labor force.* ○ *The number of young people entering the labor force is growing.*

▸ **COLLOCATIONS:**
    enter/join/leave the labor force
    the labor force **shrinks/falls/grows**
    a **declining/shrinking/growing** labor force

▸ **SYNONYM:** workforce

labor-intensive /ˈleɪbərɪntɛnsɪv/

ADJECTIVE **Labor-intensive** industries or methods of producing things involve a lot of workers. ○ *Construction remains a relatively labor-intensive industry.*

▶ **COLLOCATIONS:**
   a labor-intensive **industry/business**
   a labor-intensive **process/task/method**

▶ **RELATED WORD:** capital-intensive

---

la|bora|tory /ˈlæbrətɔri/ (laboratories)   `R&D`

NOUN A **laboratory** is a building or a room where scientific experiments and research are carried out. **Lab** is also used in informal and spoken English. ○ *The two scientists tested the idea in laboratory experiments.* ○ *a medical research laboratory*

▶ **COLLOCATIONS:**
   a laboratory **conducts** *experiments*
   equip a laboratory
   laboratory **conditions/equipment**
   a laboratory **test/experiment/technician**
   a **well-equipped/mobile/research** laboratory
   a **forensic/biological/clinical/research** laboratory

---

lack /læk/ (lacks, lacking, lacked)

1 NONCOUNT NOUN If there is a **lack of** something, there is not enough of it or it does not exist at all. ○ [+ *of*] *Despite his lack of experience, he got the job.* ○ [+ *of*] *The charges were dropped for lack of evidence.*

▶ **COLLOCATIONS:**
   a lack **of** *something*
   a lack of **experience/interest/knowledge**
   a lack of **resources/support/evidence/progress**
   a lack of **sleep/confidence**
   show/cite/perceive a lack
   a **complete/total/distinct** lack
   a **relative/apparent** lack

▶ **SYNONYMS:** shortage, absence, deficiency

2 VERB If you say that someone or something **lacks** a particular quality or that a particular quality **is lacking** in them, you mean that they do not have any or enough of it. ○ *It lacked the power of the Italian cars.* ○ *Certain vital information is lacking in the report.*

▸ **COLLOCATIONS:**
be lacking **in** *something*
lacking in **confidence**
lack **resources/skills/credibility**
lack **confidence/courage/ability**
sorely/sadly/totally/often lacking

large|ly /lɑrdʒli/

1 **ADVERB** You use **largely** to say that a statement is not completely true but is mostly true. ○ *The fund is largely financed through government borrowing.*

2 **ADVERB** **Largely** is used to introduce the main reason for a particular event or situation. ○ *Retail sales dipped 6/10ths of a percent last month, largely because Americans were buying fewer cars.* ○ *[+ through] The French empire had expanded, largely through military conquest.*

▸ **COLLOCATIONS:** largely **because of/through** *something*

▸ **SYNONYMS:** mainly, mostly

▸ **RELATED WORD:** partly

late|ly /leɪtli/

ADVERB **Lately** means recently. ○ *The regulators have gotten extremely tough lately.* ○ *The stock market has lately begun to recover.*

lat|ter /lætər/

PRONOUN When two people, things, or groups have just been mentioned, you can refer to the second of them as **the latter**. ○ *At school, he enjoyed football and boxing; the latter remained a lifelong hobby.* ○ *without hesitation they chose the latter*

▸ **COLLOCATIONS:** **choose/prefer** the latter

● **Latter** is also an adjective. ○ *Private share holdings exist in the UK, Italy, and Portugal and plans are underway to increase the level of private investment in the latter two countries.* ○ *Adrienne heard nothing of the latter part of this speech.*

▸ **COLLOCATIONS:** the latter **stage/part/category**

launch /lɔːntʃ/ (launches, launching, launched)   `MARKETING & SALES`

VERB If a company **launches** a new product, it makes it available to the public. ○ *Crabtree & Evelyn has just launched a new jam, Worcesterberry Preserve.* ○ *Talbots recently hired model Linda Evangelista to launch its new range.*

▶ **COLLOCATIONS:** launch a **product/model/brand/book/magazine**

▶ **SYNONYM:** unveil

● **Launch** is also a noun. ○ [+ *of*] *The company's spending has also risen following the launch of a new Sunday magazine.* ○ [+ *of*] *legal wrangling threatens to delay the launch of the product*

▶ **COLLOCATIONS:**
the launch **of** *something*
a **product/book** launch
an **official** launch
announce/delay/postpone a launch

law of sup|ply and de|mand   `BANKING & FINANCE`

/lɔr əv səplaɪ ən dɪmænd/

NONCOUNT NOUN **The law of supply and demand** is the theory that prices are set by the relationship between the amount of goods that are available and the amount of goods that people want to buy. ○ *Under the law of supply and demand, the greater the supply of a product, the lower the price you can charge for it.*

law|yer   /lɔɪər, lɔyər/ **(lawyers)**   `LEGAL`

NOUN A **lawyer** is a person who is qualified to advise people about the law and represent them in court. ○ *Prosecution and defense lawyers are expected to deliver closing arguments next week.*

▶ **COLLOCATIONS:**
  hire/consult/appoint a lawyer
  a lawyer **argues/claims** something
  a lawyer **represents/acts for/advises/defends** someone
  a **defense/divorce/immigration** lawyer
  a **human rights/civil rights/criminal/corporate** lawyer
  a **prominent/top** lawyer

▶ **SYNONYM:** attorney

lay|off   /leɪɔf/ **(layoffs)**   `PERSONNEL`

NOUN A **layoff** is a situation when a company tells its workers to leave their job, usually because there is no more work for them to do. ○ *It will close more than 200 stores nationwide resulting in the layoffs of an estimated 2,000 employees.*

▶ **COLLOCATIONS:**
  mass/widespread/large-scale layoffs
  avoid/prevent/avert layoffs

▶ **SYNONYM:** discharge

lead|er|ship   /lidərʃɪp/ **(leaderships)**   `PERSONNEL`

NOUN You refer to people who are in control of a group or organization as the **leadership**. ○ *He is expected to hold talks with both the Croatian and Slovenian leaderships.* ○ *[+ of] Later he advised the leadership of the party to dissolve it.*

▶ **COLLOCATIONS:**
  the leadership **of** something
  liberal/communist leadership

union/party/church leadership
the leadership **decides/agrees/rejects** something

---

lead|ing edge /li̲dɪŋ ɛdʒ/ `RGD`

NOUN The **leading edge of** an area of research or development is the most advanced area of it. ○ [+ of] I think Israel tends to be at the leading edge of technological development. ○ [+ in] The school will have a leading edge in education when its science facility is completed this year.

▶ **COLLOCATIONS:**
the leading edge **of** something
a leading edge **in** something

▶ **SYNONYMS:** cutting edge, forefront, vanguard

---

leave of ab|sence /li̲v əv æbsəns/ **(leaves of absence)** `PERSONNEL`

NOUN A **leave of absence** is permission to be away from work for a certain period. ○ [+ from] Morris will be taking a leave of absence from the newspaper.

▶ **COLLOCATIONS:**
a leave of absence **from** something
be on/take a leave of absence
ask for/request a leave of absence
be granted/be given/obtain a leave of absence
a **temporary/extended/indefinite** leave of absence
a **paid/unpaid** leave of absence

▶ **SYNONYMS:** leave, sabbatical

---

le|gal /li̲gᵊl/ `LEGAL`

1 ADJECTIVE **Legal** is used to describe things that relate to the law. ○ He vowed to take legal action. ○ the American legal system ○ I sought legal advice on this.

▶ **COLLOCATIONS:**
legal **action/advice/fees/costs**
a legal **battle/challenge/expert/adviser**
legal **rights/proceedings**
the legal **profession/system**

2 ADJECTIVE An action or situation that is **legal** is allowed or required by law. ○ What I did was perfectly legal. ○ drivers who have more than the legal limit of alcohol

▶ **COLLOCATIONS:**
perfectly/entirely legal
the legal **limit**
a legal **requirement**

▶ **SYNONYMS:** lawful, permissible

le|gal|ize /ˈliːɡəlaɪz/ (legalizes, legalizing, legalized)

VERB If something **is legalized**, it is made legal by a law being passed.
[in BRIT, also use **legalise**] ○ *Divorce was legalized in 1981.* ○ *a proposal to legalize same-sex marriage*

▶ **COLLOCATIONS:**
a **decision/ruling/law/legislation** legalizing *something*
to legalize **abortion/gambling/marijuana**

▶ **SYNONYMS:** authorize, decriminalize, approve

---

le|giti|mate /lɪˈdʒɪtɪmɪt/ `LEGAL`

1 ADJECTIVE Something that is **legitimate** is acceptable according to the law. ○ *The French government has condemned the coup in Haiti and has demanded the restoration of the legitimate government.* ○ *The government will not seek to disrupt the legitimate business activities of the defendant.*

▶ **COLLOCATIONS:**
perfectly/wholly/democratically legitimate
a legitimate **heir/ruler/marriage**

▶ **SYNONYMS:** legal, authentic, valid

2 ADJECTIVE If you say that something such as a feeling or claim is **legitimate**, you think that it is reasonable and justified. ○ *That's a perfectly legitimate fear.* ○ *The New York Times has a legitimate claim to be a national newspaper.*

▶ **COLLOCATIONS:** a legitimate **claim/concern/excuse/expectation**

▶ **SYNONYMS:** reasonable, justified

---

length /lɛŋθ/ (lengths)

1 NOUN The **length** of something is the amount that it measures from one end to the other along the longest side. ○ *It is about a yard in length.* ○ [+ *of*] *the length of the field* ○ [+ *of*] *The plane had a wing span of 34 ft and a length of 22 ft.*

2 NOUN The **length** of something such as a piece of writing is the amount of writing that is contained in it. ○ *a book of at least 100 pages in length* ○ [+ *of*] *The length of a paragraph depends on the information it conveys.*

3 **NOUN** The **length** of an event, activity, or situation is the period of time from beginning to end for which something lasts or during which something happens. ○ [+ of] *The exact length of each period may vary.* ○ *His film, over two hours in length, is a subtle study of family life.*

▶ **COLLOCATIONS:**
be *x* **in** length
the length **of** *something*
the length of a **prison sentence/stay**
something **stretches/extends** the length of *something*
have a length of *x*
measure/run/walk/travel the length of *something*
a **considerable/exact/average/short/maximum** length
the **entire/full/whole/total/overall** length of *something*

▶ **PHRASES:**
length of time
of varying lengths
the length and breadth of something
at arm's length
focal length

▶ **RELATED WORDS:** breadth, width, height, depth

lengthy /lɛŋθi/ (lengthier, lengthiest)

ADJECTIVE **Lengthy** means lasting for a long time. ○ *a lengthy meeting* ○ *Ellis faces a lengthy prison sentence if convicted.*

▶ **COLLOCATIONS:**
a lengthy **suspension/sentence/ban**
a lengthy **discussion/negotiation/investigation/process**
a lengthy **delay/wait**
quite/rather/very/fairly lengthy

▶ **SYNONYMS:** long, prolonged

---

let|ter of cred|it /lɛtər əv krɛdɪt/ (letters of credit) BANKING & FINANCE

NOUN A **letter of credit** is a written promise from a bank stating that they will repay bonds to lenders if the borrowers are unable to pay them. ○ *The project is being backed by a letter of credit from Lasalle Bank.*

▶ **COLLOCATIONS:**
provide/submit/issue/obtain a letter of credit
a **$50 million/£30 million** letter of credit
open/post a letter of credit

lev|er|age /lɛvərɪdʒ, lɛvrɪdʒ/ `BANKING & FINANCE`

NONCOUNT NOUN Leverage is the ability to influence situations or people so that you can control what happens. ○ *His job as mayor affords him the leverage to get things done by attending committee meetings.* ○ *Sam's Club has tremendous leverage with suppliers.*

▶ COLLOCATIONS:
considerable/enormous/significant/substantial leverage
increase/gain/reduce/lose leverage

lia|bil|ity /laɪəbɪlɪti/ `BANKING & FINANCE`

NONCOUNT NOUN Liability is legal responsibility for something. ○ *He is claiming damages from London Underground, which has admitted liability but disputes the amount of his claim.* ○ [+ for] *This covers your legal liability for injury or damage which you may cause to others and their property.*

▶ COLLOCATIONS:
liability **for** *something*
accept/admit/deny liability
legal/personal liability

▶ SYNONYM: responsibility

li|cense /laɪsᵊns/ (licenses)

NOUN A **license** is an official document that gives you permission to do, use, sell, or own something. [in BRIT, use **licence**] ○ *Payne lost his driver's license a year ago for drunk driving.* ○ [+ to-inf] *It gained a license to operate as a bank in 1981.*

▶ COLLOCATIONS:
issue/grant/revoke/suspend a license
a **driver's/fishing/gun** license
a **software/entertainment/gaming/liquor** license
a **radio/marriage** license
a **valid** license
a license **application/fee/holder**

▶ SYNONYM: permit

life|time /laɪftaɪm/ (lifetimes)

NOUN A **lifetime** is the length of time that someone is alive. ○ *During my lifetime I haven't gotten around to much traveling.* ○ [+ of] *an extraordinary lifetime of achievement*

▶ **COLLOCATIONS:**
 a lifetime **of** *something*
 a lifetime of **experience/achievement**
 spend/last a lifetime
 a lifetime **award/achievement/ban/guarantee**
 lifetime **employment**
 a **whole/entire** lifetime

▶ **PHRASE:** during your lifetime

like|li|hood /laɪklihʊd/

NONCOUNT NOUN The **likelihood of** something happening is how probable it is that it will happen. ○ [+ *of*] *The likelihood of infection is minimal.* ○ [+ *of*] *concerns that these changes would increase the likelihood of wrongful conviction*

▶ **COLLOCATIONS:**
 the likelihood **of** *something*
 lessen/decrease/reduce the likelihood of *something*
 a **strong/great/high/reasonable/substantial** likelihood
 little/less likelihood

▶ **SYNONYMS:** probability, possibility, chance

like|wise /laɪkwaɪz/

ADVERB You use **likewise** when you are comparing two methods, states, or situations and saying that they are similar. ○ *All attempts by the Socialists to woo him back were spurned. Similar overtures from the right have likewise been rejected.* ○ *The V2 was not an ordinary weapon: it could only be used against cities. Likewise the atom bomb.*

▶ **SYNONYM:** similarly

lim|it /lɪmɪt/ (limits, limiting, limited)

1 NOUN A **limit** is the greatest amount, extent, or degree of something that is possible. ○ *warnings that hospitals are being stretched to the limit* ○ [+ *to*] *There is no limit to how much fresh fruit you can eat in a day.*

▶ **COLLOCATIONS:**
 to the limit
 a limit **to** *something*
 the limits **of** *something*
 the limits of **endurance/tolerance**

push/stretch/test *something* to the limit
put a limit on *something*

▶ **PHRASE:** there is no limit to something

▶ **SYNONYM:** utmost

2 NOUN A **limit** of a particular kind is the largest or smallest amount of something such as time or money that is allowed because of a rule, law, or decision. ○ *The three month time limit will be up in mid-June.* ○ [+ on] *The secretary of commerce announced limits on gas sales.*

▶ **COLLOCATIONS:**
a limit **on** *something*
a limit **of** x
impose/set/place/put a limit on *something*
reach/exceed/break/raise/reduce a limit
a limit on a **number/amount** of *something*
a limit on **emissions/size/spending/investment**
a **speed/credit/age/time** limit
a **strict/legal/daily/reasonable/absolute** limit
a **maximum/upper/minimum** limit
a **spending/alcohol** limit

▶ **SYNONYM:** restriction

3 VERB If you **limit** something, you prevent it from becoming greater than a particular amount or degree. ○ *He limited payments on the country's foreign debt.* ○ [+ to] *The view was that the economy would grow by 2.25 percent. This would limit unemployment to around 2.5 million.*

▶ **COLLOCATIONS:**
limit *something* **to** x
limit the **amount/number/size** of *something*
limit the **use** of *something*
limit **damage**
severely/strictly limit *something*

▶ **SYNONYM:** restrict

lim|it|ed /lɪmɪtɪd/

ADJECTIVE Something that is **limited** is not very great in amount, range, or degree. ○ *They may only have a limited amount of time to get their points across.* ○ *The bike will be produced in extremely limited quantities.*

▶ **COLLOCATIONS:**
rather/quite/pretty limited
strictly/severely/extremely/highly limited

limited **options/opportunities/chances/resources**
a limited **amount/supply/quantity**

▶ **SYNONYMS:** minimal, reduced, restricted

---

line of cred|it /laɪn əv krɛdɪt/ (lines of credit) `BANKING & FINANCE`

NOUN A **line of credit** is the amount of debt a person or company is allowed by a creditor. ○ *The company is negotiating a new line of credit agreement with the Bank of Tokyo-Mitsubishi.* ○ [+for] *Mexicans are seeking lines of credit for everything from cars to apartments.*

▶ **COLLOCATIONS:**
a **home equity/bank/personal** line of credit
a **revolving/established/existing** line of credit
establish/extend/provide a line of credit
negotiate/secure a line of credit

---

link /lɪŋk/ (links, linking, linked)

1 **NOUN** If there is a **link between** two things or situations, there is a relationship between them, for example because one thing causes or affects the other. ○ [+ between] *the link between smoking and lung cancer* ○ [+ with] *Police are investigating potential links with the bombing of a car on Monday.*

▶ **COLLOCATIONS:**
a link **between** *things*
a link **with** *something*
uncover/investigate a link
a **direct/close/possible/strong** link

▶ **SYNONYMS:** connection, relationship, association

2 **VERB** If someone or something **links** two things or situations, there is a relationship between them, for example because one thing causes or affects the other. ○ [+ with] *The study further strengthens the evidence linking smoking with early death.* ○ *The detention raised two distinct but closely linked questions.*

▶ **COLLOCATIONS:**
link *something* **with/to** *something*
closely/directly/inextricably/intimately/allegedly linked
evidence/speculation/rumor links *things*
a **study** links *things*
link a **death/murder/incident/suspect/group** to *something*

liq|ui|date /lɪkwɪdeɪt/ (liquidates, liquidating, liquidated) BANKING & FINANCE

1 **VERB** To **liquidate** a company is to close it down and sell all its assets, usually because it is in debt. ○ *A unanimous vote was taken to liquidate the company.* ○ *The High Court has appointed an official receiver to liquidate a bankrupt travel company.*

▸ **COLLOCATION:** liquidate a **company**

▸ **SYNONYMS:** sell, close down

2 **VERB** If a company **liquidates** its assets, its property such as buildings or machinery is sold in order to get money. ○ *The company closed down operations and began liquidating its assets in January.*

▸ **COLLOCATIONS:**
liquidate **assests/merchandise/securities**
gradually/periodically/systematically liquidate *something*

▸ **SYNONYM:** sell

liq|ui|da|tion /lɪkwɪdeɪʃən/ (liquidations)

NOUN ○ *The company went into liquidation.* ○ *The number of company liquidations rose 11 percent.*

▸ **COLLOCATIONS:**
the liquidation **of** *something*
the liquidation of a **company/corporation**
the liquidation of **assets/shares**
voluntary/compulsory liquidation
avoid/force/face liquidation

list price /lɪst praɪs/ (list prices) MARKETING & SALES

NOUN The **list price** is the price that the manufacturer of an item suggests that a store should charge for it. ○ *[+ of] a small car with a list price of $18,000* ○ *Why pay list price when you can get a 75% discount?*

▸ **COLLOCATIONS:**
sell something for/pay list price
the **official/suggested/published** list price
above/below list price

▸ **SYNONYMS:** sticker price, retail price

liv|ing wage /lɪvɪŋ weɪdʒ/ (living wages) PERSONNEL

NOUN A **living wage** is a wage that is just enough to allow you to buy food, clothing, and other necessary things. ○ *Many farmers have to depend on subsidies to make a living wage.* ○ *The law ensures a living wage for construction workers.*

▶ COLLOCATIONS:
earn/make/get a living wage
pay/provide a living wage

lob|by /lɒbi/ (lobbies) `OFFICE`

NOUN A **lobby** is the large area that is just inside the entrance of a public building. ○ *I met her in the lobby of the museum.*

▶ COLLOCATIONS:
hotel/entrance/elevator lobby
a **crowded** lobby

▶ SYNONYMS: hall, corridor, entrance

lo|cal /loʊkəl/

ADJECTIVE **Local** means existing in or belonging to the area where you live, or to the area that you are talking about. ○ *a copy of the local newspaper* ○ *Some local residents joined the students' protest.* ○ *encouraging children to use the local library*

▶ COLLOCATIONS:
a local **school/shop/hospital/newspaper/bar/library**
a local **resident/community/population**

▶ SYNONYMS: regional, provincial

lo|cate /loʊkeɪt/ (locates, locating, located)

VERB If you **locate** something or someone, you find out where they are. ○ *They couldn't locate the missing ship.* ○ *The police are asking for the public's help locating the suspect.*

▶ COLLOCATIONS:
have difficulty/have trouble locating *something/someone*
need help locating *something/someone*

▶ SYNONYM: discover

lo|cat|ed /loʊkeɪtɪd/

ADJECTIVE [FORMAL] ○ *The restaurant is located near the cathedral.* ○ *[+ within] A boutique and beauty salon are conveniently located within the grounds.*

> ▶ **COLLOCATIONS:**
> located **in/near/within** *a place*
> **conveniently/centrally** located

▶ **SYNONYM:** situated

lo|ca|tion /loʊkeɪʃᵊn/ **(locations)**

NOUN A **location** is the place where something happens or is situated. ○ *The first thing he looked at was his office's location.* ○ *Macau's newest small luxury hotel has a beautiful location.* ○ [+ of] *finding the exact location of the church*

▶ **COLLOCATIONS:**
the location **of** *something*
a location **for** *something*
reveal/identify/pinpoint/determine the location of *something*
a **different/specific/exact/remote/geographical** location
a **prime/central/ideal/exotic** location
a **secret/undisclosed/seaside/waterfront** location

▶ **PHRASES:**
location and size
location and name
location and date
locations around the world
locations across the country

▶ **SYNONYMS:** setting, place, situation

log|ic /lɒdʒɪk/

NONCOUNT NOUN **Logic** is a method of reasoning that involves a series of statements, each of which must be true if the statement before it is true. ○ *Apart from criminal investigation techniques, students learn forensic medicine, philosophy, and logic.* ○ *to prove God's existence by means of deductive logic*

logo /loʊgoʊ/ **(logos)**   MARKETING & SALES

NOUN The **logo** of a company or organization is the special design or way of writing its name that it puts on all its products, notepaper, or advertisements. ○ *Staff should wear uniforms, and vehicles should bear company logos.* ○ *a red T-shirt with a logo on the front*

▶ **COLLOCATIONS:**
a logo **on** *something*
design/feature/display/bear a logo

a **corporate/company/famous/new** logo
a logo **appears** *somewhere*
a logo **features** *something*
a logo on the **front/back/side/cover** of *something*

▶ **PHRASE:** name and logo

▶ **SYNONYM:** emblem

---

long-distance /lɒŋdɪstəns/

ADJECTIVE Long-distance means traveling or covering large distances.
○ *The company also owns a regional long-distance carrier.* ○ *Stacey makes a lot of long-distance calls on her cellphone.*

▶ **COLLOCATIONS:**
a long-distance **call/carrier**
a long-distance **runner/swimmer/walker**
long-distance **running/swimming/cycling**

---

loom /luːm/ (looms, looming, loomed)

VERB If a worrying or threatening situation or event **is looming**, it seems likely to happen soon. ○ *Another government spending crisis is looming in the United States.* ○ *The threat of renewed civil war looms ahead.* ○ *a looming deadline*

▶ **COLLOCATIONS:** a **deadline/crisis** is looming

---

loose /luːs/ (looser, loosest)

ADJECTIVE Loose means not firmly fixed. ○ *One of Hannah's top front teeth is loose.* ○ *She idly pulled at a loose thread on her skirt.*

▶ **COLLOCATIONS:**
a loose **tooth/thread/screw**
slightly/rather/extremely loose

---

loose|ly /luːsli/

ADVERB ○ *He held the gun loosely in his hand.* ○ *A scarf hung loosely around his neck.*

▶ **COLLOCATIONS:** loosely **tied/knotted/draped/clasped**

---

lose /luːz/ (loses, losing, lost)　　BANKING & FINANCE

1 VERB You say that you **lose** something when you no longer have it because it has been taken away from you or destroyed. ○ *I lost my job*

when the company moved to another state. ○ *He lost his license for six months.*
○ *She was terrified they'd lose their home.*

2 VERB If a business **loses** money, it earns less money than it spends and
is therefore in debt. ○ *His stores stand to lose millions of dollars.* ○ *$1 billion
a year may be lost.*

▶ **COLLOCATIONS:**
lose your **job/license/home**
nearly/completely/almost lose *something*
lose **money/$x**

loss /lɒs/ (losses)

1 NOUN Loss is the fact of no longer having something or having less of it
than before. ○ [+ *of*] *Wildlife is under threat from hunting, pollution, and loss
of habitat.* ○ *The job losses will reduce the total workforce to 7,000.*

2 NOUN If a business reports a **loss**, it earns less than it spends. ○ [+ *of*]
The company suffered a loss of $270 million. ○ *Both businesses reported pretax
losses in the first half.*

▶ **COLLOCATIONS:**
the loss **of** *something*
the loss of **jobs/earnings/income/revenue/$x**
take/incur/post/report a loss
suffer/sustain/cause a loss
a **net/pretax/full-year/quarterly** loss
a **heavy/significant/total/huge** loss
a **financial/annual/operating** loss
job losses

▶ **PHRASES:**
profit and loss
losses and gains

USAGE: *lose, loss or loose?*

Lose is a verb, and it has the irregular past tense form **lost**.
○ *The project began to lose money.* ○ *300 workers lost their jobs when
the factory closed.*

Loss is a noun. ○ *The factory closed with the loss of 300 jobs.*

Loose is an adjective to describe something that is not tight or firm.
It has no connection with the two words above. ○ *Wear loose,
comfortable clothing.*

---

lot|tery /lɒtəri/ (lotteries)

NOUN A **lottery** is a game in which many people buy tickets with numbers on them. The person whose number is later chosen wins a prize. ○ *the national lottery*

▶ **COLLOCATIONS:**
  a lottery **ticket/jackpot/winner**
  win/play/enter the lottery
  run/operate/organize a lottery
  a **national/state-run/online** lottery

▶ **SYNONYMS:** sweepstake, raffle

lounge /laʊndʒ/ (lounges)   `TRAVEL`

NOUN A **lounge** is a room in a hotel or an airport where people can sit. ○ *an airport lounge* ○ *We met for drinks at the hotel lounge.*

▶ **COLLOCATIONS:** a **departure/airport/transit/hotel** lounge

lucki|ly /lʌkɪli/

ADVERB **Luckily** is used for saying that it is good that something happened. ○ *Luckily, nobody was seriously injured in the accident.* ○ *Motloung was assaulted by five gang members but luckily survived.*

▶ **SYNONYMS:** fortunately, happily

lu|cra|tive /luːkrətɪv/   `BANKING & FINANCE`

ADJECTIVE A **lucrative** activity, job, or business deal is very profitable. ○ *Thousands of ex-army officers have found lucrative jobs in private security firms.* ○ *a highly lucrative career*

▶ **COLLOCATIONS:**
  a lucrative **contract/career/offer**
  a lucrative **deal/trade**

▶ **SYNONYMS:** profitable, worthwhile

lug|gage /lʌɡɪdʒ/   `TRAVEL`

NONCOUNT NOUN **Luggage** is the bags that you take with you when you travel. ○ *"Do you have any luggage?" — "Just my briefcase."* ○ *His job was to screen all luggage for explosives.* ○ *A loaded handgun was found in Donaldson's carry-on luggage.*

▶ **COLLOCATIONS:**
screen/scan/inspect/search luggage
unattended/unaccompanied/lost/left luggage
carry-on/hand luggage
a luggage **rack/cart/compartment/belt**

▶ **SYNONYM:** baggage

---

lump sum /lʌmp sʌm/ (lump sums)   **BANKING & FINANCE**

NOUN A **lump sum** is an amount of money that is paid as a large amount at one time rather than as smaller amounts at separate times. ○ *a tax-free lump sum of $50,000*

▶ **COLLOCATIONS:**
a lump sum **of** *x*
a lump sum **payment/payout/settlement**
a lump sum **investment/withdrawal**
pay/award *someone* a lump sum
receive/take a lump sum

Mm

ma|chin|ery /məʃɪnəri/ OFFICE

NONCOUNT NOUN You can use **machinery** to refer to machines in general, or machines that are used in a factory or on a farm. ○ *quality tools and machinery* ○ *hi-tech packaging machinery*

▶ **COLLOCATIONS:**
agricultural/industrial machinery
farm/factory/garden/textile machinery
mining/printing/manufacturing/harvesting machinery
electrical/solar-powered/hydraulic machinery
state-of-the-art/high-tech machinery
lubricate/oil/repair machinery
install/operate/manufacture/supply machinery

▶ **PHRASE:** machinery and equipment

▶ **SYNONYMS:** equipment, hardware, technology

maga|zine /mægəzɪn, -zin/ (magazines)

NOUN A **magazine** is a thin book with stories and pictures that you can buy every week or every month. ○ *a fashion magazine*

▶ **COLLOCATIONS:**
read/publish/buy/edit a magazine
a magazine **reports/covers/publishes/features** *something*
a **weekly/monthly/quarterly/bimonthly** magazine
a **trade/fashion/literary/lifestyle** magazine
a magazine **cover/article/editor/subscription/interview**

▶ **SYNONYMS:** journal, periodical

mag|net|ic /mægnɛtɪk/

ADJECTIVE If something metal is **magnetic**, it attracts iron to it. ○ *The moon exerts a magnetic pull on the Earth's water levels.* ○ *a material consisting of magnetic particles*

▶ **COLLOCATIONS:**
a magnetic **field/pull**
a magnetic **strip/compass**
magnetic **particles**

---

mag|ni|fy /mægnɪfaɪ/ (magnifies, magnifying, magnified)

VERB To **magnify** an object means to make it appear larger than it really is, by means of a special lens or mirror. ○ *This version of the Digges telescope magnifies images 11 times.* ○ *A lens would magnify the picture so it would be like looking at a large TV screen.* ○ [V-ing] *magnifying lenses*

▶ **COLLOCATIONS:**
a magnifying **lens/glass**
magnify **images/pictures**
highly magnified

▶ **SYNONYM:** enlarge

mag|ni|fi|ca|tion /mægnɪfikeɪʃᵊn/ (magnifications)

1 NONCOUNT NOUN Magnification is the act or process of magnifying something. ○ *Pores are visible without magnification.* ○ [+ of] *the magnification of minute sounds through a computer*

▶ **COLLOCATIONS:**
magnification **of** something
magnification of **sound/light/images**

2 NOUN Magnification is the degree to which a lens, mirror, or other device can magnify an object, or the degree to which the object is magnified. ○ *The electron microscope uses a beam of electrons to produce images at high magnifications.* ○ *The magnification is 833,333 times the original size.*

▶ **COLLOCATIONS: low/high/maximum** magnification

---

mag|ni|tude /mægnɪtud/

NONCOUNT NOUN If you talk about the **magnitude** of something, you are talking about its great size, scale, or importance. ○ *An operation of this magnitude is going to be difficult.* ○ *These are issues of great magnitude.* ○ [+ of] *No one seems to realize the magnitude of this problem.*

▶ **COLLOCATIONS:**
the magnitude **of** something
the magnitude of the **problem/change/task/disaster**
the **sheer** magnitude

a **similar/preliminary/unprecedented** magnitude
measure/grasp/realize the magnitude of *something*

▶ **SYNONYMS:** immensity, extent, enormity

---

mail or|der /meɪl ɔrdər/ MARKETING & SALES

NONCOUNT NOUN **Mail order** is a system of buying goods by mail.
○ *The toys are available by mail order.* ○ *Many of them also offer a mail-order service.*

▶ **COLLOCATIONS:**
a mail-order **catalog/service**
a mail-order **company/business/firm**

---

main|stream /meɪnstrim/ (mainstreams)

NOUN People, activities, or ideas that are part of the **mainstream** are regarded as the most typical, normal, and conventional because they belong to the same group or system as most others of their kind. ○ *people outside the economic mainstream* ○ [+ of] *This was the company's first step into the mainstream of scientific and commercial computing.* ○ *The show wanted to attract a mainstream audience.*

▶ **COLLOCATIONS:**
the mainstream **of** *something*
infiltrate/enter/join/penetrate the mainstream
the **scientific/literary/academic/political** mainstream
mainstream **politicians/republicans/feminists**
mainstream **sociology/cinema/politics**
a mainstream **audience**

▶ **SYNONYMS:** typical, average

---

main|tain /meɪnteɪn/ (maintains, maintaining, maintained)

1 VERB If you **maintain** something, you continue to have it and do not let it stop or grow weaker. ○ *The Department maintains close contacts with the chemical industry.* ○ *Such extroverted characters try to maintain relationships no matter how damaging these relationships may be.* ○ *emergency powers to try to maintain law and order*

2 VERB If you **maintain** something **at** a particular rate or level, you keep it at that rate or level. ○ [+ at] *The government was right to maintain interest rates at a high level.* ○ [+ at] *action is required to ensure standards are maintained at as high a level as possible*

m

▶ **COLLOCATIONS:**
maintain *something* **at** *a level*
maintain **standards/interest/levels/discipline/control/silence**
maintain **contacts/relationships**

▶ **PHRASE:** maintain law and order

EXTEND YOUR VOCABULARY

In everyday English, you use **keep** or **continue** to talk about something not stopping or staying the same. ○ *They planned to keep working through the weekend.* ○ *Oil consumption will continue at the same level.*

In more formal writing, you can use **maintain** or **sustain** to talk about keeping something the same. **Sustain** is often used to talk about keeping something at a high level, especially when this is difficult. ○ *The company encourages employees to maintain a healthy balance between their work and personal lives.* ○ *Successive governments were unable to sustain economic growth.*

You use **retain** to talk about keeping something you already have and not losing it. ○ *This will help us to attract and retain qualified staff.*

---

main|te|nance /ˈmeɪntɪnəns/

NONCOUNT NOUN If you ensure the **maintenance of** a state, process, or object, you make sure that they remain in a good or favorable condition. ○ [+ of] *the maintenance of peace and stability in Asia* ○ [+ of] *the importance of natural food to the maintenance of health*

▶ **COLLOCATIONS:**
the maintenance **of** *something*
the maintenance of **peace/standards/order/health**
the maintenance of the **equipment/building/facility**

▶ **SYNONYMS:** upkeep, continuation

---

ma|jor /ˈmeɪdʒər/

ADJECTIVE You use **major** when you want to describe something that is more important, serious, or significant than other things in a group or situation. ○ *The major factor in the decision to stay or to leave was usually professional.* ○ *Drug abuse is a major problem in the city.* ○ *Exercise has a major part to play in preventing disease.*

▶ **COLLOCATIONS:**
a major **event/concern/project**
a major **problem/factor/change**

▶ **PHRASE:** play a major part in *something*

▶ **SYNONYMS:** key, crucial, central, primary

ma|jor|ity /mədʒɔ̱rɪti, -dʒɒ̱r-/

NOUN The **majority** of people or things in a group is more than half of them. ○ *Before the war a majority opposed invasion, yet 51% now think it was justified.* ○ *[+ of] The vast majority of our cheeses are made with pasteurized milk.*

▶ **COLLOCATIONS:**
the majority **of** *something*
the majority of **voters/people/citizens/members**
the majority of the **population/electorate**
a **vast/great/overwhelming/slim** majority
the majority **support/favor/endorse/reject/oppose** *something*

▶ **PHRASE:** in the majority

---

make|up /me̱ɪkʌp/ or **make-up**

NONCOUNT NOUN Makeup is the creams and powders that people put on their face to make themselves look more attractive. Actors also wear makeup. ○ *I don't wear much makeup.*

▶ **COLLOCATIONS:**
wear/apply/put on/use makeup
makeup **covers** *something*
heavy/eye/stage makeup

▶ **PHRASE:** hair and makeup

▶ **SYNONYM:** cosmetics

---

man|age /mæ̱nɪdʒ/ (manages, managing, managed) `JOBS`

1 VERB If someone **manages** an organization, business, or system, they are responsible for controlling it. ○ *Within two years he was managing the store.* ○ *The factory was badly managed.* ○ *the government's ability to manage the economy*

2 VERB If you **manage** time, money, or other resources, you deal with them carefully and do not waste them. ○ *In a busy world, managing your time is increasingly important.* ○ *We are trying to manage water resources effectively.*

▶ **COLLOCATIONS:**
manage a **business/system/organization**
manage **time/money/resources**
manage *something* **badly/poorly/aggressively**
manage *something* **successfully/well/carefully/effectively**

▶ **SYNONYMS:** organize, run, direct

man|ag|ing /mǽnədʒɪŋ/

ADJECTIVE ○ *Eric Shaw, the law firm's managing partner*

▶ **COLLOCATIONS:** a managing **editor/director/partner**

man|age|ment /mǽnɪdʒmənt/ (managements)

1 NONCOUNT NOUN Management is the control and organizing of a business or other organization. ○ *The zoo needs better management.*
○ *[+ of] the management of the mining industry* ○ *the responsibility for its day-to-day management*

▶ **COLLOCATIONS:**
the management **of** *something*
business/fiscal/economic management
day-to-day/operational/sustainable management
a management **consultant/structure/system/style**

▶ **PHRASE:** management and administration

▶ **SYNONYMS:** organization, control, directorship

2 NOUN You can refer to the people who control and organize a business or other organization as the **management**. ○ *The management is doing its best to improve the situation.* ○ *We need to get more women into top management.*

▶ **COLLOCATIONS:** **top/senior/middle** management

▶ **SYNONYM:** staff

man|ag|er /mǽnɪdʒər/ (managers)

NOUN A **manager** is a person who is responsible for running part of or the whole of a business organization. ○ *The chef, staff, and managers are all Chinese.* ○ *a retired bank manager*

▶ **COLLOCATIONS:**
a **bank/business/accounts/general** manager
appoint/recruit/hire/sack/fire a manager

▶ **SYNONYMS:** director, head, executive, leader

mana|gerial /mænɪdʒɪəriəl/

ADJECTIVE ○ his managerial skills ○ a managerial career

▶ **COLLOCATIONS:** a managerial **skill/position/career**

▶ **SYNONYM:** administrative

---

ma|nipu|late /mənɪpyəleɪt/ (manipulates, manipulating, manipulated)

1 VERB If you say that someone **manipulates** an event or situation, you disapprove of them because they use or control it for their own benefit, or cause it to develop in the way they want. ○ He said that the state television was trying to manipulate the election outcome. ○ They felt he had been cowardly in manipulating the system to avoid the draft.

▶ **COLLOCATIONS:**
manipulate an **outcome/opinion**
manipulate the **media**
skilfully/easily/fraudulently/cynically manipulate something

2 VERB If you **manipulate** something that requires skill, such as a complicated piece of equipment or a difficult idea, you operate it or process it. ○ The technology uses a pen to manipulate a computer. ○ The puppets are expertly manipulated by Liz Walker. ○ His mind moves in quantum leaps, manipulating ideas and jumping on to new ones as soon as he can.

▶ **COLLOCATIONS:**
manipulate a **puppet/gadget/object**
deftly/skilfully manipulate something

▶ **SYNONYMS:** work, handle

---

man|power /mænpaʊər/ `PERSONNEL`

NONCOUNT NOUN Workers are sometimes referred to as **manpower**.
○ the shortage of skilled manpower in the industry

▶ **COLLOCATIONS:**
need/provide/lack/require manpower
enough/extra/more/additional/skilled/military manpower

▶ **SYNONYMS:** personnel, workers

---

manu|al /mænyuəl/ `JOBS`

ADJECTIVE Manual work is work in which you use your hands or your physical strength rather than your mind. ○ skilled manual workers ○ They work in factory or manual jobs.

▶ **COLLOCATIONS:**
manual **work/labor**
a manual **job/worker/laborer**

▶ **SYNONYMS:** blue-collar, physical

---

manu|fac|ture /mænyəfæktʃər/ (manufactures, ORGANIZATION
manufacturing, manufactured)

VERB To **manufacture** something means to make it in a factory, usually in
large quantities. ○ *They manufacture the class of plastics known as
thermoplastic materials.* ○ *The first three models are being manufactured at the
factory in Detroit.* ○ *The company imports foreign manufactured goods.*

▶ **COLLOCATIONS:**
manufacture **products/components**
manufacture **worldwide/overseas/abroad/locally**
synthetically/genetically/artificially manufactured
manufactured **goods**

▶ **SYNONYM:** produce

manu|fac|tur|er /mænyəfæktʃərər/ (manufacturers)

NOUN A **manufacturer** is a business or company that makes goods in
large quantities to sell. ○ *the world's largest doll manufacturer* ○ *major
manufacturers and retailers of woodworking tools*

▶ **COLLOCATIONS:**
a **PC/hardware/equipment/clothing/automobile** manufacturer
a **Japanese/Italian/Swedish** manufacturer
a **major/rival** manufacturer
manufacturers **produce/supply/export** *something*

▶ **SYNONYM:** producer

manu|fac|tur|ing /mænyəfæktʃərɪŋ/

NONCOUNT NOUN ○ [+ *of*] *the manufacturing of a luxury type automobile*

▶ **COLLOCATIONS:**
the manufacturing **of** *something*
the manufacturing of **equipment/products/components**
a manufacturing **plant/facility**
the manufacturing **sector/industry**

mar|gin /mɑ́rdʒɪn/ (margins)

1 **NOUN** A **margin** is the difference between two amounts, especially the difference in the number of votes or points between the winner and the loser in an election or other contest. ○ *They could end up with a 50-point winning margin.* ○ *The Wall Street Journal remains the brand leader by a huge margin.* ○ *The margin in favor was 280-to-153.*

▶ COLLOCATIONS:
a margin **of** x
a **gross/winning/narrow/slim/wide** margin
a **profit** margin

2 **NOUN** The **margin** of a written or printed page is the empty space at the side of the page. ○ *She added her comments in the margin.* ○ [+ *of*] *The wood-eating insects also don't like the taste of ink and prefer the binding and the margin of the pages.*

3 **NOUN** The **margin** of a place or area is the extreme edge of it. ○ *the low coastal plain along the western margin* ○ [+ *of*] *These islands are on the margins of human habitation.*

▶ COLLOCATIONS:
the margin **of** *something*
in the margin
on the margins

▶ SYNONYMS: edge, periphery

mar|gin|al /mɑ́rdʒɪnəl/

1 **ADJECTIVE** If you describe something as **marginal**, you mean that it is small or not very important. ○ *This is a marginal improvement on October.* ○ *The role of the opposition party proved marginal.*

→ see note at **negligible**

▶ COLLOCATIONS:
a marginal **rate/cost/increase**
a marginal **seat/constituency**

▶ SYNONYM: slight

2 **ADJECTIVE** If you describe people as **marginal**, you mean that they are not involved in the main events or developments in society because they are poor or have no power. ○ *The tribunals were established for the well-integrated members of society and not for marginal individuals.* ○ *I don't want to call him marginal, but he's not a major character.*

▶ COLLOCATION: **socially** marginal

mark|down /ˈmɑrkdaʊn/ (markdowns) `MARKETING & SALES`

NOUN A **markdown** is a reduction in the price of something. ○ *Customers know that our sales offer genuine markdowns across the store.*

---

mar|ket /ˈmɑrkɪt/ (markets, marketing, marketed) `MARKETING & SALES`

1 NOUN The **market** for a particular type of thing is the number of people who want to buy it, or the area of the world in which it is sold. ○ *the markets targeted by global chains* ○ *[+ for] the Russian market for personal computers* ○ *[+ in] There is no youth market in cars.*

▶ **COLLOCATIONS:**
a market **for/in** *something*
the **stock/currency/housing/labour/property** market
a **volatile/booming/buoyant/competitive** market
market **share/value/research**
penetrate/manipulate/target/test a market

2 VERB To **market** a product means to organize its sale, by deciding on its price, where it should be sold, and how it should be advertised. ○ *the company that markets the drug* ○ *The devices are being marketed in America this year.* ○ *[+ as] The soap is marketed as an anti-acne product.*

▶ **COLLOCATIONS:**
market *something* **as** *something*
market *something* **to** *someone*
market a **product/brand/drug/device**

▶ **SYNONYMS:** advertise, promote, sell

mar|ket|able /ˈmɑrkɪtəbᵊl/

ADJECTIVE Something that is **marketable** is able to be sold because people want to buy it. ○ *What began as an attempt at artistic creation has turned into a marketable commodity.*

▶ **COLLOCATIONS:**
readily/highly marketable
a marketable **skill/product**

▶ **SYNONYMS:** in demand, sought after

market|place /ˈmɑrkɪtpleɪs/ (marketplaces)

NOUN A **marketplace** is a place or situation where products may be bought and sold. ○ *We hope to play a greater role in the marketplace and, therefore, supply more jobs.*

▶ **COLLOCATIONS:**
enter/create/dominate a marketplace
a **changing/competitive/global/international** marketplace

▶ **PHRASE:** in today's marketplace

mar|ket re|search /mɑ̱rkɪt rɪsɜ̱rtʃ/

NONCOUNT NOUN **Market research** is the activity of collecting and studying information about what people want, need, and buy.
○ *Market research showed that customers want both online and telephone banking.*

▶ **COLLOCATIONS:**
conduct/carry out market research
a market research **company/firm**

mar|ket sec|tor /mɑ̱rkɪt sɛktər/ (market sectors)

NOUN A **market sector** is one part of a market consisting of related products or services. ○ *It achieved this growth by identifying a market sector, and moving quickly to become the leader in that sector.*

mar|ket value /mɑ̱rkɪt væ̱lyu/ (market values)

NOUN The **market value** of an item is the price that it can be sold at depending on how many of the items are available and how many people want to buy them. ○ *He must sell the house for the current market value.*

▶ **COLLOCATIONS:**
current/true/fair/original/full market value
below/above market value

---

mass-produce /mæ̱sprədu̱s/ (mass-produces, mass-producing, mass-produced)

VERB If someone **mass-produces** something, they make it in large quantities by machine. ○ *the invention of machinery to mass-produce footwear*

mass-produced /mæ̱sprədu̱st/

ADJECTIVE ○ *In 1981 it launched the first mass-produced mountain bike.*

▶ **COLLOCATIONS:**
mass-produced **copies**
commercially mass-produced

mass pro|duc|tion /mæs prədʌkʃ°n/

NONCOUNT NOUN ○ [+ of] *This equipment will allow the mass production of baby food.*

▶ **COLLOCATIONS:**
enable/allow mass production
the mass production **of** *something*

ma|terial /mətɪəriəl/ (materials)

1 **NOUN** A **material** is a solid substance. ○ *electrons in a conducting material such as a metal* ○ *the design of new absorbent materials* ○ *recycling of all materials*

▶ **COLLOCATIONS:**
import/produce/recycle materials
a **raw/synthetic/toxic/recycled** material

▶ **SYNONYM:** substance

2 **PLURAL NOUN Materials** are the things that you need for a particular activity. ○ *The builders ran out of materials.* ○ *sewing materials*

▶ **COLLOCATIONS: sewing/building/art** materials

▶ **SYNONYM:** supplies

3 **ADJECTIVE Material** things are related to possessions or money, rather than to more abstract things such as ideas or values. ○ *Every room must have been stuffed with material things.* ○ *his descriptions of their poor material conditions*

▶ **COLLOCATIONS:**
material **assistance/support**
a material **possession/resource**

maxi|mum /mæksɪməm/

1 **ADJECTIVE** You use **maximum** to describe an amount that is the largest that is possible, allowed, or required. ○ *The maximum sentence for supplying illegal drugs is life imprisonment.* ○ *China took the lead with maximum points.*

● **Maximum** is also a noun. ○ [+ of] *The law provides for a maximum of two years in prison.*

▶ **COLLOCATION:** a maximum **of** *an amount*

2 **ADJECTIVE** You use **maximum** to indicate how great an amount is. ○ *the maximum amount of information* ○ *It was achieved with minimum fuss and maximum efficiency.* ○ *a maximum security prison*

▶ COLLOCATIONS:
maximum **efficiency/security/flexibility**
the maximum **sentence/penalty/speed/amount/height/weight**

max|im|ize /mˈæksɪmaɪz/ (maximizes, maximizing, maximized)

VERB If you **maximize** something, you make it as great in amount or importance as you can. [in BRIT, also use **maximise**] ○ *In order to maximize profit, the company would seek to maximize output.* ○ *They were looking for suitable ways of maximizing their electoral support.*

▶ COLLOCATIONS: maximize **profit/revenue/appreciation/efficiency**

mean|time /mˈiːntaɪm/

PHRASE **In the meantime** is used for talking about the period of time between two events. ○ *This panic will soon be over but in the meantime investors have become very sensitive to risk.*

mean|while /mˈiːnwaɪl/

1 ADVERB **Meanwhile** means while a particular thing is happening. ○ *Brush the eggplant with oil, add salt and pepper, and bake till soft. Meanwhile, heat the remaining oil in a heavy pan.*

2 ADVERB **Meanwhile** means in the period of time between two events. ○ *You needn't worry; I'll be ready to greet them. Meanwhile, I'm off to discuss the Fowler's party with Felix.*

3 ADVERB You use **meanwhile** to introduce a different aspect of a particular situation, especially one that is completely opposite to the one previously mentioned. ○ *Meanwhile in the US, forecasts confirm that climate change will have a very real impact on the country.*

meas|ure /mˈɛʒər/ (measures, measuring, measured)

1 VERB If you **measure** the quality, value, or effect of something, you discover or judge how great it is. ○ *The college measures student progress against national standards.* ○ *The school's success was measured in terms of the number of students who got into a good college.* ○ *It was difficult to measure the impact of the war.*

▶ COLLOCATIONS:
measure *something* **in terms of/against** *something*
measure the **success/progress/impact/quality** of *something*

2 VERB If you **measure** a quantity that can be expressed in numbers, such as the length of something, you discover it using a particular instrument or device, for example a ruler. ○ *Measure the length and width of the gap.* ○ *He measured the speed at which ultrasonic waves travel along the bone.*

▶ **COLLOCATIONS:**
measure the **length/width/height/temperature** of *something*
measure *something* **carefully/accurately**

▶ **PHRASE:** weigh and measure

3 VERB If something **measures** a particular length, width, or amount, that is its size or intensity, expressed in numbers. ○ *The house is twenty yards long and measures six yards in width.* ○ *This dinner plate measures 12 inches across.*

▶ **COLLOCATIONS:**
measure *x* in **width/length/height**
measure *x* **across**

▶ **SYNONYM:** be

4 PLURAL NOUN When someone, usually a government or other authority, takes **measures** to do something, they carry out particular actions in order to achieve a particular result. [FORMAL] ○ [+ to-inf] *The government warned that police would take tougher measures to contain the trouble.* ○ [+ against] *He said stern measures would be taken against the killers.*

▶ **COLLOCATIONS:**
measures **against** *someone/something*
take/employ measures
precautionary/preventative/practical measures
health/safety/security measures

▶ **SYNONYM:** actions

meas|ure|ment /mɛʒərmənt/ (measurements)

NOUN ○ *We took lots of measurements.* ○ *The measurements are very accurate.* ○ [+ of] *Measurement of blood pressure can be undertaken by nurses.* ○ [+ of] the *measurement of output in the non-market sector*

▶ **COLLOCATIONS:**
a measurement **of** *something*
the measurement of **pressure/distance/temperature**
the measurement of **output/productivity/effectiveness**
take a measurement
a **precise/accurate/exact** measurement

mecha|nism /mɛkənɪzəm/ (mechanisms)

NOUN In a machine or piece of equipment, a **mechanism** is a part, often consisting of a set of smaller parts, that performs a particular function. ○ the locking mechanism ○ A bomb has been detonated by a special mechanism.

▶ **COLLOCATIONS:**
operate/trigger a mechanism
a **locking/release/firing** mechanism

▶ **SYNONYM:** device

me|chani|cal /mɪkænɪkᵊl/

1 ADJECTIVE A **mechanical** device has moving parts and uses power in order to do a particular task. ○ a small mechanical device ○ the oldest working mechanical clock in the world

2 ADJECTIVE **Mechanical** means relating to machines and engines and the way they work. ○ mechanical engineering ○ The train had stopped due to a mechanical problem.

▶ **COLLOCATIONS:**
a mechanical **device/digger/pump/engineer**
mechanical **engineering**
a mechanical **problem/failure/fault**

▶ **RELATED WORDS:** electrical, electronic

m

me|dia /miːdiə/   COMMUNICATIONS

NOUN You can refer to television, radio, newspapers, and magazines as **the media**. ○ It is hard work and not a glamorous job as portrayed by the media. ○ bias in the news media ○ the intensive media coverage of the issue

▶ **COLLOCATIONS:**
in the media
the **foreign/local/international** media
the **mass/mainstream/news** media
the **Western/American/British** media
the media **report/cover/portray** something
media **attention/coverage/reports**
a media **correspondent/mogul/analyst**

▶ **PHRASE:** in/under the media spotlight

▶ **SYNONYM:** press

→ see note at **medium**

me|dio|cre /mi̱dioʊkər/

ADJECTIVE If you describe something as **mediocre**, you mean that it is of average quality but you think it should be better. ○ *His school record was mediocre.*

▶ **COLLOCATIONS:**
a mediocre **performance/season**
decidedly/pretty/fairly mediocre

me|dium /mi̱diəm/ (mediums, media)   `COMMUNICATIONS`

1 NOUN A **medium** is a way or means of expressing your ideas or of communicating with people. ○ [+ *of*] *In Sierra Leone, English is used as the medium of instruction for all primary education.* ○ *But Artaud was increasingly dissatisfied with film as a medium.*

▶ **COLLOCATIONS:**
a medium **of** *something*
a medium of **instruction/exchange/communication**
the medium of **television/film/radio**

▶ **SYNONYM:** means

2 NOUN A **medium** is a substance or material which is used for a particular purpose or in order to produce a particular effect. ○ *Blood is the medium in which oxygen is carried to all parts of the body.* ○ *Hyatt has found a way of creating these qualities using the more permanent medium of oil paint.*

▶ **SYNONYMS:** material, substance

USAGE: Plural forms

In everyday language, we often talk about **the media** to refer to television, radio, newspapers, etc. together. This is actually the plural form of the noun **medium**, meaning a means of communication. ○ *The launch got a lot of coverage in the media.*

The plural of the noun **medium** can be **media** or **mediums**.
○ *More and more companies are turning to technological mediums such as the internet.*

---

meet|ing /mi̱tɪŋ/ (meetings)   `OFFICE`

NOUN A **meeting** is an event in which a group of people come together to discuss things or to make decisions. ○ *Can we have a meeting to discuss that?*

▶ **COLLOCATIONS:**
hold/attend/schedule a meeting
a meeting **begins/starts/ends**
a **general/annual/public/private/emergency** meeting

▶ **SYNONYMS:** assembly, gathering

---

melt|down /mɛltdaʊn/ `BANKING & FINANCE`

NONCOUNT NOUN The **meltdown** of a company or system is its sudden and complete failure. ○ *There have been urgent talks to prevent the market going into financial meltdown.*

▶ **COLLOCATIONS:**
cause/suffer/avoid a meltdown
a **financial/economic/market** meltdown

▶ **SYNONYM:** break down

---

mem|ber /mɛmbər/ (members)

1 NOUN A **member** of a group is one of the people, animals, or things belonging to that group. ○ [+ *of*] *He refused to name the members of staff involved.* ○ *a sunflower or a similar member of the daisy family* ○ *the brightest members of a dense cluster of stars*

2 NOUN A **member** of an organization such as a club or a political party is a person who has officially joined the organization. ○ *The support of our members is of great importance to the Association.* ○ *The United States is a full member of NATO.* ○ [+ *of*] *He was a member of the British parliament.*

▶ **COLLOCATIONS:**
a member **of** something
a **family/crew/staff/gang** member
a **club/party** member
a **permanent/prominent/key/full** member
members **approve/refuse/support/oppose** something

▶ **PHRASES:**
a member of the public
a member of the staff
a member of Congress

mem|ber|ship /mɛmbərʃɪp/ (memberships)

NONCOUNT NOUN **Membership** in an organization is the state of being a member of it. ○ [+ *in*] *The country has been granted membership in the World Trade Organisation.* ○ *He sent me a membership form.*

▶ **COLLOCATIONS:**
membership **in** *something*
a membership **form/card/fee/application**
permanent/full/voluntary membership
expand/increase/limit/restrict membership
award/grant/deny *someone* membership

---

memo /mɛmoʊ/ **(memos)**   COMMUNICATIONS

NOUN A **memo** is a short note that you send to a person who works with you. ○ *He sent a memo to everyone in his department.*

▶ **COLLOCATIONS:**
write/send/leak/issue a memo
a **confidential/internal** memo

▶ **SYNONYMS:** note, memorandum

---

memo|ry /mɛməri/   OFFICE

1 NOUN Your **memory** is your ability to remember things. ○ *All the details of the meeting are fresh in my memory.* ○ *[+ for] He had a good memory for faces.* ○ *He suffers from poor memory and concentration.*

▶ **COLLOCATIONS:**
in *someone's* memory
a memory **for** *something*
a **good/bad/poor** memory for *something*
a **short/long** memory

▶ **SYNONYM:** recollection

2 NOUN A computer's **memory** is the part of the computer where information is stored, especially for a short time before it is transferred to disks or magnetic tapes. ○ *The device has 32GB of built-in memory.* ○ *Flash memory is used in digital cameras.* ○ *You can upgrade your computer's memory.*

▶ **COLLOCATIONS:**
a memory **card/chip**
built-in/on-board/internal/flash memory
a **computer's/device's** memory

memo|ry stick /mɛməri stɪk/ **(memory sticks)**

NOUN A **memory stick** is a small object for storing computer information that you can carry with you and use in different computers. ○ *Using a memory stick you can store tens of thousands of songs.*

▶ COLLOCATION: **save** *something* **on** a memory stick

▶ SYNONYM: flash drive

men|tion /mɛnʃⁿn/ (mentions, mentioning, mentioned)

VERB If you **mention** something, you say something about it, usually briefly. ○ *She did not mention her mother's absence.* ○ [+ that] *He mentioned that his father had been an attaché at the German Embassy in London.* ○ *For example, Sydney University's Professor of Medicine did not even mention insulin when lecturing on diabetes in 1923.*

▶ COLLOCATIONS: mention *something* **briefly/frequently/casually**

mer|chan|dise /mɜrtʃəndaɪz, -daɪs/ `MARKETING & SALES`

NONCOUNT NOUN **Merchandise** is products that are bought, sold, or traded. [FORMAL] ○ *a mail-order company that provides merchandise for people suffering from allergies* ○ *The official website offers merchandise.*

▶ COLLOCATIONS:
counterfeit/stolen/defective/unofficial merchandise
official/licensed/exclusive merchandise

▶ SYNONYM: goods

mer|chant /mɜrtʃənt/ (merchants) `LOGISTICS & DISTRIBUTION`

NOUN A **merchant** is a person who buys or sells goods in large quantities. ○ *Any knowledgeable wine merchant would be able to advise you.*

▶ COLLOCATIONS: a **wealthy/rich/online** merchant

▶ SYNONYMS: vendor, seller

merge /mɜrdʒ/ (merges, merging, merged) `ORGANIZATION`

VERB If one thing **merges with** another, or **is merged with** another, they combine or come together to make one whole thing. You can also say that two things **merge**, or **are merged**. ○ [+ with] *Bank of America merged with a rival bank.* ○ *The rivers merge just north of a vital irrigation system.* ○ [+ into] *The two countries merged into one.*

▶ COLLOCATIONS:
merge **with/into** *something*
merge with a **rival/bank/company**
a **bank/company** merges with *something*

merge into the **traffic/background/crowd**
merge **together/successfully/recently**

▶ SYNONYM: join

mer|ger /mɜrdʒər/ (mergers)

NOUN A **merger** is the joining together of two separate companies or organizations so that they become one. ○ [+ between] *a merger between two of Britain's biggest trades unions* ○ [+ of] *the proposed merger of two Japanese banks*

▶ COLLOCATIONS:
a merger **between/of** *things*
a merger between/of **companies/banks/parties**
propose/approve/complete/announce a merger
a merger **forms/fails/succeeds**
a **planned/three-way/friendly/bank** merger
a merger **talk/proposal/agreement**

▶ SYNONYMS: union, amalgamation

---

mes|sage /mɛsɪdʒ/ (messages)   COMMUNICATIONS

NOUN The **message** that someone is trying to communicate, for example in a book or play, is the idea or point that they are trying to communicate. ○ *The film has a very powerful antiwar message.* ○ *The clear message from this research is that children do not benefit from this.*

▶ COLLOCATIONS:
get/understand/send/convey/deliver a message
the **main/general** message of *something*
a **clear/powerful/strong/positive** message

▶ SYNONYMS: idea, point

---

mes|sen|ger /mɛsɪndʒər/ (messengers)   JOBS

NOUN A **messenger** is a person whose job is to take messages or packages to people. ○ *A messenger delivered a large envelope to his office.*

▶ COLLOCATIONS:
send a messenger
a messenger **boy/service**

▶ SYNONYM: courier

meth|od /mɛθəd/ (methods)

NOUN A **method** is a particular way of doing something. ○ [+ of] *The pill is the most efficient method of birth control.* ○ *new teaching methods* ○ *Experts will use a variety of scientific methods to measure fatigue levels.*

▶ **COLLOCATIONS:**
a method **of** *something*
a method of **teaching/execution/calculation/communication**
a **scientific/proven/statistical/efficient** method
a **preferred/usual/conventional/traditional** method
devise/employ/adopt/test a method
a **teaching/cooking/testing/detection** method

▶ **SYNONYMS:** manner, procedure

met|ro|poli|tan /mɛtrəpɒlɪtən/

ADJECTIVE **Metropolitan** means belonging to or typical of a large, busy city. ○ *the metropolitan district of Miami* ○ *a dozen major metropolitan hospitals*

▶ **COLLOCATIONS:** a metropolitan **area/center/region**

micro|phone /maɪkrəfoʊn/ (microphones) `OFFICE`

NOUN A **microphone** is a piece of electronic equipment that you use to make sounds louder or to record them onto a machine. ○ *I stood on the stage in front of a microphone, spoke for thirty minutes or so, and then answered questions.*

▶ **COLLOCATIONS:**
grab/attach a microphone
a **hidden/directional/built-in/wireless** microphone

middle|man /mɪdəlmæn/ (middlemen) `LOGISTICS & DISTRIBUTION`

NOUN A **middleman** is a person or company that buys things from the people who produce them and sells them to the people who want to buy them. ○ *Why don't they cut out the middleman and let us do it ourselves?*

▶ **COLLOCATIONS:** **cut out/eliminate** the middleman

▶ **SYNONYM:** intermediary

minia|ture /mɪniətʃər, -tʃʊər/ (miniatures)

ADJECTIVE **Miniature** is used to describe something that is very small, especially a smaller version of something which is normally much bigger. ○ *a miniature version of the real thing* ○ *a miniature remote-control aircraft*

▶ COLLOCATIONS: a miniature **replica/version**

mini|mal /mɪnɪməl/

ADJECTIVE Something that is **minimal** is very small in quantity, value, or degree. ○ *The co-operation between the two is minimal.* ○ *One aim of these reforms is effective defense with minimal expenditure.*

▶ COLLOCATIONS: minimal **impact/effect/damage/risk/ expenditure**

mini|mize /mɪnɪmaɪz/ (minimizes, minimizing, minimized)

VERB If you **minimize** a risk, problem, or unpleasant situation, you reduce it to the lowest possible level, or prevent it from increasing beyond that level. [in BRIT, also use **minimise**] ○ *Concerned people want to minimize the risk of developing cancer.* ○ *Many of these problems can be minimized by sensible planning.*

▶ COLLOCATIONS:
minimize a **risk/impact/effect**
minimize **damage**

mini|mum /mɪnɪməm/ `PERSONNEL`

ADJECTIVE You use **minimum** to describe an amount which is the smallest that is possible, allowed, or required. ○ *If found guilty, she faces a minimum sentence of ten years and 30 lashes.* ○ *a rise in the minimum wage*

● **Minimum** is also a noun. ○ [+ of] *This will take a minimum of one hour.* ○ *To provide welfare at a level greater than this bare minimum discourages self-reliance.*

▶ COLLOCATIONS:
a minimum **of** *something/an amount*
the minimum **amount/height/requirement/wage/sentence**
a **bare/absolute/required/stated** minimum

mini|mum wage /mɪnɪməm weɪdʒ/

NOUN A **minimum wage** is the lowest wage that an employer is allowed to pay an employee. ○ *Some of them earn below the minimum wage.*

▶ COLLOCATIONS:
earn/raise/provide/introduce the minimum wage
a **national/daily** minimum wage

---

mi|nor /ˈmaɪnər/

ADJECTIVE You use **minor** when you want to describe something that is less important, serious, or significant than other things in a group or situation. ○ *She had a minor role in the film.* ○ *Officials say the problem is minor, and should be quickly overcome.*

▶ COLLOCATIONS:
a minor **problem/matter/incident/setback**
minor **things/details/surgery/damage**
a minor **ailment/injury/wound/accident**
a minor **road/league/role**

▶ SYNONYMS: unimportant, small

mi|nor|ity /mɪˈnɒrɪti, maɪ-, -ˈnɔːr-/ (minorities)

1 NOUN If you talk about a **minority** of people or things in a larger group, you are referring to a number of them that forms less than half of the larger group, usually much less than half. ○ [+ of] *Childcare covers only a tiny minority of working mothers.* ○ *These children are only a small minority.* ○ *In the past conservatives have been in the minority.*

▶ COLLOCATIONS:
a minority **of** *people/things*
in a/the minority
the minority of the **population**
the minority of **voters/individuals/citizens**
a **small/tiny/sizeable/significant** minority

2 NOUN A **minority** is a group of people of the same race, culture, or religion who live in a place where most of the people around them are of a different race, culture, or religion. ○ *the region's ethnic minorities* ○ *Students have called for greater numbers of women and minorities on the faculty.*

▶ COLLOCATIONS:
ethnic/racial/religious minorities
Christian/Muslim minorities
minority **rights**

mi|nus /maɪnəs/

1 **CONJUNCTION** You use **minus** to show that one number or quantity is being subtracted from another. ○ *One minus one is zero.* ○ *They've been promised their full July salary minus the hardship payment.*

> ▸ **SYNONYM:** less

2 **ADJECTIVE** **Minus** before a number or quantity means that the number or quantity is less than zero. ○ *The aircraft was subjected to temperatures of minus 65 degrees and plus 120 degrees.* ○ *What's the square root of minus 1?*

> ▸ **COLLOCATIONS:** minus **one/two/50/300**

mi|nute /maɪnuːt/ (minutest)

ADJECTIVE If something is **minute**, it is very small. ○ *minute particles of dirt and grime* ○ *minute traces of chemical or biological residue* ○ *We can't work out every minute logistical detail in advance.*

> ▸ **COLLOCATIONS:** minute **details/particles/traces**

> ▸ **SYNONYMS:** small, tiny

mis|cel|la|neous /mɪsəleɪniəs/

ADJECTIVE A **miscellaneous** collection of people or things consists of many different kinds of things or people that are difficult to put into one particular category. ○ *They questioned the rise in the company's miscellaneous expenses.*

> ▸ **COLLOCATIONS:** miscellaneous **items/deductions**

> ▸ **SYNONYM:** mixed

mis|take /mɪsteɪk/ (mistakes, mistaking, mistook, mistaken)

1 **NOUN** A **mistake** is something that is not correct. ○ *a spelling mistake*

2 If you do something **by mistake**, you do something that you did not want or plan to do. ○ *They gave us the wrong figures by mistake.*

3 **VERB** If you **mistake** one person **for** another person, you wrongly think that they are the other person. ○ *People are always mistaking Lauren for her sister.*

> ▸ **COLLOCATION:** mistake *something* **for** *something*

> ▸ **PHRASE:** there is no mistaking

> ▸ **SYNONYMS:** error, oversight

mis|tak|en /mɪsteɪkən/

ADJECTIVE If you are **mistaken about** something, you are wrong about it.
○ *I think that you must be mistaken — Jackie wouldn't do a thing like that.*

▶ **COLLOCATIONS:**
seriously/sadly mistaken
a mistaken **belief/impression**

▶ **PHRASE:** mistaken identity

▶ **SYNONYM:** wrong

mis|under|stand /mɪsʌndərstænd/ (misunderstands, misunderstanding, misunderstood)

VERB If you **misunderstand** someone or something, you do not understand them correctly. ○ *I think you've misunderstood me.*

▶ **COLLOCATIONS: completely/frequently** misunderstand *something*

▶ **PHRASES:**
misunderstand the nature of something
misunderstand the question

▶ **SYNONYM:** misinterpret

m

mo|bile /moʊbəl/

ADJECTIVE You use **mobile** to describe something large that can be moved easily from place to place. ○ *mobile laboratories in six-wheel-drive vehicles* ○ *more of a mobile home than a caravan*

▶ **COLLOCATIONS:** a mobile **home/laboratory**

▶ **SYNONYMS:** movable, portable

mod|el /mɒdəl/ (models, modeling, modeled) [in BRIT, use modelling, modelled]   R&D

1 NOUN A **model** is a system that is being used and that people might want to copy in order to achieve similar results. [FORMAL] ○ [+ *of*] *We believe that this is a general model of managerial activity.* ○ [+ *of*] *the European model of social responsibility*

▶ **COLLOCATIONS:**
a model **of** *something*
a model of **efficiency/consistency/excellence**
introduce/adopt/follow a model

▶ **SYNONYMS:** system, example

2 **NOUN** A **model** of a system or process is a theoretical description that can help you understand how the system or process works, or how it might work. [FORMAL] ○ [+ of] *Darwin eventually put forward a model of biological evolution.*

▸ **COLLOCATIONS:**
a model **of** *something*
a model of the **universe**
a model of **evolution**
propose a model

▸ **SYNONYM:** theory

3 **VERB** If someone such as a scientist **models** a system or process, they make an accurate theoretical description of it in order to understand or explain how it works. [FORMAL] ○ *the mathematics needed to model a nonlinear system like an atmosphere* ○ *It is no surprise that we find such processes hard to model mathematically.*

---

mod|er|ate /mɒdərɪt/

1 **ADJECTIVE** You use **moderate** to describe something that is neither large nor small in amount or degree. ○ *While a moderate amount of stress can be beneficial, too much stress can exhaust you.* ○ *Heavy drinkers die earlier than moderate drinkers.*

▸ **COLLOCATIONS:**
a moderate **amount/extent**
moderate **weather/heat/exercise/drinking**

▸ **SYNONYM:** reasonable

2 **ADJECTIVE** A **moderate** change in something is a change that is not great. ○ *Most drugs offer either no real improvement or, at best, only moderate improvements.* ○ *House prices are still quite moderate in relation to personal incomes.*

▸ **COLLOCATIONS:** a moderate **increase/growth/decline**

▸ **SYNONYM:** slight

mod|er|ate|ly /mɒdərɪtli/

ADVERB ○ *Both are moderately large insects.* ○ *Share prices on the Tokyo Exchange declined moderately.*

▸ **COLLOCATIONS:**
drink/exercise/eat moderately
moderately **attractive/overweight/successful**

increase/rise/fall moderately

▶ SYNONYMS: reasonably, slightly

---

mod|ern /mɒdərn/ `R&D`

1 ADJECTIVE **Modern** means relating to the present time, for example the present decade or present century. ○ *the problem of materialism in modern society* ○ *the alienation of the modern world*

2 ADJECTIVE Something that is **modern** is new and involves the latest ideas or equipment. ○ *Modern technology has opened our eyes to many things.* ○ *It was a very modern school for its time.*

▶ COLLOCATIONS:
modern **society/living**
fairly/quite/relatively modern
very/thoroughly/strikingly modern
modern **technology/design/medicine**
a modern **kitchen/bathroom/house/appliance**

▶ PHRASE: the modern world

▶ SYNONYMS: contemporary, current, present, advanced, up-to-date, state-of-the-art

mod|ern|ize /mɒdərnaɪz/ (modernizes, modernizing, modernized)

VERB To **modernize** something such as a system or a factory means to change it by replacing old equipment or methods with new ones. [in BRIT, also use **modernise**] ○ *plans to modernize the curriculum* ○ *We need to modernise our electoral system.* ○ *the cost of modernizing the economy*

▶ COLLOCATIONS:
rapidly/radically/extensively modernize
modernize the **economy/military/curriculum**
modernize **infrastructure/agriculture/production**

▶ SYNONYM: update

---

modi|fy /mɒdɪfaɪ/ (modifies, modifying, modified)

VERB If you **modify** something, you change it slightly, usually in order to improve it. ○ *The club members did agree to modify their recruitment policy.* ○ *The plane was a modified version of the C-130.*

→ see note at **adapt**

▶ COLLOCATIONS:
modify **food/crops/ingredients**

genetically/chemically modified
extensively/significantly modified

▸ SYNONYM: alter

modi|fi|ca|tion /mɒdɪfɪkeɪʃən/ (modifications)

NOUN ○ *Relatively minor modifications were required.* ○ *behavior modification techniques*

▸ COLLOCATIONS:
genetic/evolutionary/dietary/behavior modification
a **minor/slight** modification

▸ SYNONYMS: alteration, change

---

mo|ment /moʊmənt/ (moments)

NOUN A **moment** is a very short period of time. ○ *In a moment he was gone.*
○ *"Please take a seat. Mr. Garcia will see you in a moment."*

▸ COLLOCATIONS:
enjoy/seize/capture a moment
a **defining/brief/fleeting/key** moment
a moment **comes/arrives/goes/passes**

▸ SYNONYM: instant

---

mon|etary /mɑnɪtɛri/ [BANKING & FINANCE]

ADJECTIVE **Monetary** means relating to the total amount of money in a country. ○ *Some countries tighten monetary policy to avoid inflation.*

▸ COLLOCATIONS: a monetary **policy/union/committee/value**

▸ SYNONYM: financial

---

money-maker /mʌnimeɪkər/ (money-makers) [MARKETING & SALES]

NOUN A **money-maker** is a business or product that makes a lot of money.
○ *This car is the group's biggest money-maker.*

▸ COLLOCATIONS: a **guaranteed/big** money-maker

---

moni|tor /mɒnɪtər/ (monitors, monitoring, monitored)

1 VERB If you **monitor** something, you regularly check its development or progress, and sometimes comment on it. ○ *Officials had not been allowed to monitor the voting.* ○ *Senior managers can then use the budget as a control document to monitor progress against the agreed actions.*

▶ **COLLOCATIONS:**
  closely/strictly/regularly/carefully monitored
  monitor **progress/activity/effectiveness**
  monitor the **situation**

▶ **SYNONYMS:** observe, oversee

2 NOUN A **monitor** is a machine that is used to check or record things, for example processes or substances inside a person's body. ○ *The heart monitor shows low levels of consciousness.* ○ *A blood glucose monitor at a local drug store costs around $25.*

▶ **COLLOCATIONS:** a **heart/heart-rate/glucose** monitor

---

mo|nopo|lize /mənɒpəlaɪz/ (monopolizes, monopolizing, monopolized)   `MARKETING & SALES`

VERB If you say that someone **monopolizes** something, you mean that they have a very large share of it and prevent other people from having a share. [in BRIT, also use **monopolise**] ○ *They are controlling so much cocoa that they are virtually monopolizing the market.* ○ *He himself is pushing quite aggressively to try to monopolize power in the government.*

▶ **COLLOCATIONS:**
  monopolize a **conversation/market**
  monopolize **power/trade**

▶ **SYNONYMS:** control, dominate

---

month|ly /mʌnθli/

ADJECTIVE Something that occurs **monthly** happens or appears every month. ○ *Monthly payments will be $143.47.*

▶ **COLLOCATIONS:** a monthly **payment/fee/meeting/bill/income**

---

moon|light /muːnlaɪt/ (moonlights, moonlighting, moonlighted)   `PERSONNEL`

VERB If someone **moonlights**, they have a second job in addition to their main job, often without informing their main employers or the tax authorities. ○ *an engineer who was moonlighting as a taxi driver*

▶ **COLLOCATION:** moonlight **as** *something*

▶ **SYNONYM:** work

moon|lighting /muːnlaɪtɪŋ/

NONCOUNT NOUN ○ *He was fired for moonlighting.*

more|over /mɔrouvər/

ADVERB You use **moreover** to introduce a piece of information that adds to or supports the previous statement. [FORMAL] ○ *The young find everything so simple. The young, moreover, see it as their duty to be happy and do their best to be so.* ○ *A new species, it was unique to Bali - moreover, it is this island's only endemic bird.*

▶ **SYNONYMS:** furthermore, in addition

mort|gage /mɔrgɪdʒ/ (mortgages)　　　　BANKING & FINANCE

NOUN A **mortgage** is a loan of money that you get from a bank or building society in order to buy a house. ○ *an increase in mortgage rates* ○ *the borrower was free to repay the mortgage at any time*

▶ **COLLOCATIONS:**
repay/pay the mortgage
mortgage **repayments/rates**

mort|gage rate /mɔrgɪdʒ reɪt/ (mortgage rates)

NOUN A **mortgage rate** is the level of interest that a bank charges people who borrow money to buy a house. ○ *The bank has cut its variable mortgage rate by 0.14%.*

▶ **COLLOCATIONS:**
rising/base/low/high mortgage rates
mortgage rates **rise/fall**

mo|tion /mouʃ°n/ (motions)

1 NONCOUNT NOUN **Motion** is the activity or process of continually changing position or moving from one place to another. ○ *the laws governing light, sound, and motion* ○ *One group of muscles sets the next group in motion.*

▶ **COLLOCATIONS:**
planetary/slow/perpetual/constant motion
motion **sickness/detection**
a motion **detector/sensor**

▶ **SYNONYM:** movement

2 PHRASE If you say that someone **is going through the motions**, you think they are only saying or doing something because it is expected of them without being interested, enthusiastic, or sympathetic. ○ *The startled actors went through the motions of the rest* *of the script.* ○ *The Home Office is "merely going through the motions so that they can come back with a compulsory scheme," he said.*

---

mo|ti|vate /ˈmoʊtɪveɪt/ (motivates, motivating, motivated)

1 VERB If you **are motivated** by something, especially an emotion, it causes you to behave in a particular way. ○ *They are motivated by a need to achieve.* ○ *The crime was not politically motivated.*

▶ **COLLOCATIONS:**
be motivated **by** something
be motivated by **fear/money/greed/friendship/ideals**

2 VERB If someone **motivates** you to do something, they make you feel determined to do it. ○ [+ to-inf] *How do you motivate people to work hard and efficiently?* ○ *Never let it be said that the manager doesn't know how to motivate his players.*

▶ **COLLOCATIONS:** motivate **employees/students**

▶ **SYNONYM:** inspire

mo|ti|vat|ed /ˈmoʊtɪveɪtɪd/

ADJECTIVE ○ *We are looking for a highly motivated professional.*

▶ **COLLOCATIONS:**
economically/politically/commercially motivated
highly motivated
a motivated **individual/workforce/student**

▶ **SYNONYM:** inspired

mo|ti|va|tion /ˌmoʊtɪveɪʃ°n/

NONCOUNT NOUN Your **motivation** for doing something is what causes you to want to do it or is the act or process of someone making you feel determined to do something. ○ *His poor performance may be attributed to lack of motivation.* ○ *Gross's skill in motivation looked in doubt when his side began the second half badly.*

▶ **COLLOCATIONS:**
a **lack** of motivation
personal/political motivation
lack/provide motivation
staff/employee motivation

▶ **SYNONYMS:** inspiration, determination

m

move|ment /mˈuvmənt/ (movements)

1 NOUN Movement involves changing position or going from one place to another. ○ *They monitor the movement of the fish going up river.* ○ *There was movement behind the window.* ○ [+ of] *the movements of a large removal van* ○ *Her hand movements are becoming more animated.*

▶ COLLOCATIONS:
the movement **of** *something*
a **sudden/quick/jerky/animated** movement
a **slow/sluggish/painful** movement
a **fluid/graceful/smooth** movement
track/follow/monitor *someone's* movements
restrict/control/detect *someone's* movements

▶ SYNONYM: motion

2 NOUN Movement is a gradual development or change of an attitude, opinion, or policy. ○ [+ towards/away from] *the movement towards democracy in Latin America* ○ *Participants at the peace talks believed movement forward was possible.*

▶ COLLOCATIONS:
a movement **towards/away from/from/to** *something*
a **slow/gradual/rapid/sudden** movement
movement **forward**

▶ SYNONYMS: shift, change, development, progress

3 NOUN A **movement** is a group of people who share the same beliefs, ideas, or aims. ○ *It's part of a broader Hindu nationalist movement.* ○ *the women's movement*

▶ COLLOCATIONS:
a **separatist/union/independence/democracy** movement
the **youth/peace/women's** movement

multi|media /mˈʌltimidiə/ `COMMUNICATIONS`

NONCOUNT NOUN Multimedia is the use of sound, pictures, and film, as well as text. ○ *Most teachers use multimedia in the classroom.*

● **Multimedia** is also an adjective. ○ *a series of multimedia presentations for scientists and engineers*

▶ COLLOCATIONS:
a multimedia **application**
a multimedia **presentation/exhibit**

multi|na|tion|al /mʌltinæʃənəl/ (multinationals) `ORGANIZATION`
also **multi-national**

ADJECTIVE A **multinational** company has branches or owns companies in many different countries. ○ *The multinational company is increasingly becoming a worldwide phenomenon.* ○ *Not a single multinational firm operates in that country.*

● **Multinational** is also a noun. ○ *multinationals such as Ford and IBM* ○ *Large multinationals are also realizing that they can become more efficient.*

▶ **COLLOCATIONS:**
a multinational **corporation/company/firm**
a **foreign-based/European/American** multinational

▶ **SYNONYM:** international

multi|ple /mʌltɪpəl/

ADJECTIVE You use **multiple** to describe things that consist of many parts, involve many people, or have many uses. ○ *He died of multiple injuries.* ○ *The most common multiple births are twins, two babies born at the same time.*

▶ **COLLOCATIONS:** multiple **fractures/injuries/births/personality**

m

multi|ply /mʌltɪplaɪ/ (multiplies, multiplying, multiplied)

VERB If you **multiply** one number by another, you add the first number to itself as many times as is indicated by the second number. For example, 2 multiplied by 3 equals 6. ○ *[+ by] What do you get if you multiply six by nine?* ○ *The frequency was multiplied by the distance to find the speed of sound at each temperature.*

▶ **COLLOCATIONS:**
multiply *x* **by** *y*
multiply *x* **tenfold/exponentially**

mu|nici|pal /myunɪsɪpəl/

ADJECTIVE A **municipal** building or committee is a structure or group relating to a city or a town and its local government. ○ *a municipal building*

▶ **SYNONYMS:** civic, public

mu|tu|al /myu̱tʃuəl/

ADJECTIVE You use **mutual** to describe a situation, feeling, or action that is experienced, felt, or done by both of two people mentioned. ○ *The East and the West can work together for their mutual benefit and progress.*

▶ **COLLOCATIONS:**
  mutual **trust/attraction/benefit**
  mutual **suspicion/dislike/hostility**

▶ **SYNONYMS:** shared, reciprocal

m

Nn

name|ly /nˈeɪmli/

ADVERB You use **namely** to introduce detailed information about the subject you are discussing, or a particular aspect of it. ○ *One group of people seems to be forgotten, namely retirees.* ○ *They were hardly aware of the challenge facing them, namely, to re-establish prosperity.*

▶ **SYNONYMS:** that is (to say), specifically

na|tion|al /nˈæʃənəl/

ADJECTIVE **National** means relating to the whole of a country or nation rather than to part of it or to other nations. ○ *national and local elections* ○ *major national and international issues* ○ *a member of the U.S. national team*

▶ **COLLOCATIONS:**
a national **park/treasure/anthem**
a national **champion/championship/hero/team/stadium**
national **unity/interest/identity/security**
a national **newspaper/assembly/election**

▶ **PHRASES:**
local and national
national and international

na|tion|al|ity /nˌæʃənˈælɪti/ (nationalities)

NOUN If you have the **nationality** of a particular country, you were born there or have the legal right to be a citizen. ○ *The crew are of different nationalities and have no common language.* ○ *a resident who held dual Iranian-Canadian nationality*

▶ **COLLOCATIONS:**
dual nationality
different/other nationalities

▶ **SYNONYMS:** ethnicity, background, origin

nation|wide /ˈneɪʃənwaɪd/

ADJECTIVE If something is **nationwide**, it happens or exists in all parts of a country. ○ *Car crime is a nationwide problem.* ○ *a nationwide network of wholesalers*

▶ **COLLOCATIONS:**
a nationwide **strike/search/survey/campaign/poll/tour/network**
open *something* nationwide

▶ **SYNONYM:** national

na|tive /ˈneɪtɪv/

1 ADJECTIVE Your **native** language or tongue is the first language that you learned to speak when you were a child. ○ *She spoke not only her native language, Swedish, but also English and French.* ○ *French is not my native tongue.*

▶ **COLLOCATIONS:** a native **speaker/language/tongue**

▶ **SYNONYM:** mother

2 ADJECTIVE Plants or animals that are **native to** a particular region live or grow there naturally and were not brought there. ○ *a project to create a 50 acre forest of native Caledonian pines* ○ [+ to] *Many of the plants are native to Brazil.*

▶ **COLLOCATIONS:**
native **to** *somewhere*
native **trees/vegetation/forest**
a native **species/bird/animal/plant**
native **land/habitat/flora/fauna**
native **population/culture**

▶ **SYNONYM:** indigenous

na|ture /ˈneɪtʃər/ (natures)

1 NONCOUNT NOUN **Nature** is all the animals, plants, and other things in the world that are not made by people, and all the events and processes that are not caused by people. ○ *The most amazing thing about nature is its infinite variety.* ○ *grasses that grow wild in nature* ○ *the ecological balance of nature*

▶ **COLLOCATIONS:**
in nature
understand/reflect/explain nature
change/explore/examine nature

love/preserve nature
mother nature
a nature **reserve/trail**
nature **conservation**

▶ SYNONYM: the environment

2 NOUN The **nature** of something is its basic quality or character. ○ [+ *of*] *the nature of the issues being investigated* ○ [+ *of*] *the ambitious nature of the program* ○ *The protests had been nonpolitical by nature.*

▶ COLLOCATIONS:
the nature **of** *something*
in/by nature
the nature of the **relationship/threat/crime**
the nature of **politics/reality/society**
the nature of the **regime/allegation/conflict**

natu|ral /nætʃərəl, nætʃrəl/

ADJECTIVE Natural things exist or occur in nature and are not made or caused by people. ○ *The typhoon was the worst natural disaster in South Korea in many years.* ○ *a gigantic natural harbor*

▶ COLLOCATIONS:
perfectly/completely natural
a natural **disaster/resource**
natural **light/gas/beauty**

nec|es|sary /nɛsɪsɛri/

ADJECTIVE Something that is **necessary** is needed in order for something else to happen. ○ [+ *to-inf*] *I kept the engine running because it might be necessary to leave fast.* ○ *We will do whatever is necessary to stop them.* ○ [+ *for*] *the skills necessary for writing*

▶ COLLOCATIONS:
necessary **for** *something*
a necessary **action/step/measure/change**
necessary **skills/equipment/precautions**
find/feel/think *something* is necessary
absolutely/wholly/medically necessary

▶ SYNONYMS: essential, obligatory, required

nec|es|sari|ly /nɛsɪsɛrɪli/

ADVERB If you say that something is **not necessarily** the case, you mean that it may not be the case or is not always the case. ○ *Anger is not* *necessarily the most useful or acceptable reaction to such events.* ○ *Brown bread doesn't necessarily mean whole wheat.*

▶ **PHRASE:** not necessarily

ne|ces|sity /nɪsɛsɪti/ (necessities)

NOUN Necessities are things that you must have to live. ○ *Water is a basic necessity of life.*

▶ **COLLOCATIONS:**
a **basic/absolute/economic** necessity
the necessity **of** *something*

▶ **PHRASES:**
driven by necessity
a necessity of life

---

nega|tive /nɛgətɪv/

ADJECTIVE A fact, situation, or experience that is **negative** is unpleasant, depressing, or harmful. ○ *The news from overseas is overwhelmingly negative.* ○ *All this had an extremely negative effect on the criminal justice system.*

▶ **COLLOCATIONS:**
a negative **effect/impact/reaction/feeling/attitude**
a negative **image/experience/comment**
a negative **reaction/response**
negative **publicity/thoughts**
overwhelmingly/wholly/predominantly negative

▶ **SYNONYM:** adverse

nega|tive|ly /nɛgətɪvli/

ADVERB ○ *This will negatively affect the result over the first half of the year.*

▶ **COLLOCATIONS:**
negatively **affect/impact/influence** *something*
negatively **view/portray** *something*

▶ **SYNONYM:** adversely

---

ne|glect /nɪglɛkt/ (neglects, neglecting, neglected)

VERB If you **neglect** someone or something, you fail to look after them properly. ○ *The woman denied that she had neglected her child.* ○ *an ancient and neglected church*

▶ **COLLOCATIONS:**
unjustly/sadly/largely/shamefully neglected

neglect a **child/issue/need/area**
a **parent/government/authority** neglects *something*

▶ SYNONYM: disregard

● **Neglect** is also a noncount noun. ○ *The town's old quayside is collapsing after years of neglect.* ○ *Niwano's business began to suffer from neglect.*

▶ COLLOCATIONS:
neglect **of** *something*
neglect of a **child**
willful/parental/gross neglect

▶ PHRASE: neglect and abuse

▶ SYNONYM: disregard

---

neg|li|gible /nɛglɪdʒɪbəl/

ADJECTIVE An amount or effect that is **negligible** is so small that it is not worth considering or worrying about. ○ *The pay that the soldiers received was negligible.* ○ *Senior managers are convinced that the strike will have a negligible impact.* ○ *cut down to negligible proportions*

▶ COLLOCATIONS:
a negligible **impact/effect/contribution**
a negligible **amount/level/risk/cost**
almost/essentially negligible

EXTEND YOUR VOCABULARY

In everyday English, you often say that an amount or an effect is **small** or **slight**.

In more formal writing, you can describe a very small amount or effect as **marginal** or **minimal**. Both adjectives can be used with a positive or a negative meaning, depending on the context. ○ *The audit found only marginal improvements in services.* ○ *Necessary work was completed causing minimal disruption.*

You use **negligible** to say that something is so small that it is not worth considering. ○ *The suggestion would have a negligible effect on gasoline prices.*

You use **trivial** or **insignificant** to say that something is so small and unimportant that it is not worth serious attention. **Trivial** especially expresses disapproval. ○ *Most of the checks are for insignificant amounts.* ○ *Fierce debates erupt over the most trivial issues.*

ne|go|ti|ate /nɪɡoʊʃieɪt/ (negotiates, negotiating, negotiated)

VERB If people **negotiate with** each other or **negotiate** an agreement, they talk about a problem or a situation such as a business arrangement in order to solve the problem or complete the arrangement. ○ [+ with] *It is not clear whether the president is willing to negotiate with the Democrats.* ○ *The local government and the army negotiated a truce.* ○ [+ to-inf] *Three companies were negotiating to market the drug.*

▶ COLLOCATIONS:
negotiate **with** someone
negotiate **for** something
agree to/fail to/refuse to negotiate
a **government/company/union** negotiates
officials/mediators/representatives negotiate
negotiate a **settlement/deal/agreement/treaty/contract**
the negotiating **table**
successfully/directly negotiate

▶ SYNONYMS: discuss, hold talks, settle

ne|go|tiable /nɪɡoʊʃiəbᵊl, -ʃəbᵊl/

ADJECTIVE ○ *He warned that his economic program for the country was not negotiable.*

▶ SYNONYM: debatable

ne|go|tia|tion /nɪɡoʊʃieɪʃᵊn/ (negotiations)

NOUN ○ *We have had meaningful negotiations, and I believe we are very close to a deal.* ○ *After 10 years of negotiation, the Senate ratified the strategic arms reduction treaty.*

▶ COLLOCATIONS:
negotiation **between** people
under negotiation
conclude negotiations
negotiations **stall/fail/resume/restart/reopen**
government/peace/trade/political negotiations
intense/formal/direct/protracted negotiations
the **process of/basis for** negotiation

▶ SYNONYMS: bargaining, discussion, mediation, arbitration

nei|ther /niðər, naɪ-/

ADJECTIVE If something is **neither** this nor that, it is not one or the other of two things or people. ○ *Neither company would benefit from a merger.*

▶ **COLLOCATION:** neither **of** *us/you/them/something*

▶ **PHRASES:**
neither *something* nor *something*
neither for or against
neither here nor there

---

net|work /nɛtwɜrk/ (networks)　ORGANIZATION

1 NOUN A **network of** lines, roads, veins, or other long thin things is a
large number of them that cross each other or meet at many points.
○ [+ of] *Strasbourg, with its rambling network of medieval streets* ○ [+ of] *a rich
network of blood vessels and nerves*

▶ **COLLOCATIONS:**
a network **of** *something*
a network of **tunnels/rivers/canals/pipelines**

▶ **SYNONYMS:** web, grid

2 NOUN A **network of** people or institutions is a large number of them
that have a connection with each other and work together as a system.
○ [+ of] *a network of local church people and other volunteers* ○ *He is keen to
point out the benefits which the family network can provide.*

▶ **COLLOCATIONS:**
a network **of** *people/things*
a **terrorist/corporate/operator** network
create/build/establish/expand a network

▶ **SYNONYM:** system

3 NOUN A particular **network** is a system of things that are connected and
that operate together. ○ *a computer network with 154 terminals* ○ *Huge
sections of the rail network are out of action.*

▶ **COLLOCATIONS:**
install/operate a network
a **wireless/cellular/cable** network
a **television/computer/radio/telephone** network
a **broadcasting/storage/communications** network
a **rail/railroad/transportation/distribution** network
a network **provider/connection**
network **equipment/infrastructure/capacity**

▶ **SYNONYM:** system

neu|tral /nu̱trəl/

1 ADJECTIVE If a person or country adopts a **neutral** position or remains **neutral**, they do not support anyone in a disagreement, war, or contest. ○ *They'll meet on neutral territory.* ○ [+ in] *Those who had decided to remain neutral in the struggle now found themselves required to take sides.*

▶ **COLLOCATIONS:**
neutral **in** *something*
remain neutral
a neutral **stance/position/zone**
neutral **territory/ground**
politically neutral

▶ **SYNONYMS:** impartial, unbiased

2 ADJECTIVE Neutral is used to describe something that is neither negative nor positive. ○ *Pure water is neutral with a pH of 7.* ○ *ICI is making a profit of $190m on the sale, which will have a neutral impact on its earnings.*

never|the|less /ne̱vərðəle̱s/

ADVERB You use **nevertheless** when saying something that contrasts with what has just been said. [FORMAL] ○ *Most marriages fail after between five and nine years. Nevertheless, people continue to get married.* ○ *There had been no indication of any loss of mental faculties. His whole life had nevertheless been clouded with a series of illnesses.*

▶ **SYNONYMS:** nonetheless, even so, still, yet

news|letter /nu̱zletər/ **(newsletters)** `COMMUNICATIONS`

NOUN A **newsletter** is a report giving information about an organization that is sent regularly to its members. ○ *All members receive a free monthly newsletter.*

▶ **COLLOCATIONS:**
publish/design/send/receive a newsletter
a **free/monthly/weekly/quarterly/online/industry** newsletter

news|paper /nu̱zpeɪpər, nu̱s-/ **(newspapers)** `COMMUNICATIONS`

NOUN A **newspaper** is a number of large sheets of folded paper with news, advertisements, and other information printed on them. ○ *They read about it in the newspaper.*

▶ **COLLOCATIONS:**
read/publish/sell/buy a newspaper
a newspaper **reports/says/publishes** *something*

a **leading/daily/weekly/national/local** newspaper
a newspaper **article/editor/ad**

---

niche mar|ket /nɪtʃ mɑrkɪt, niʃ/ ◼ MARKETING & SALES

(niche markets)

NOUN A **niche market** is a specialized area for which particular products are made. ○ *In soft drink niche markets, being second is being nowhere.*

▶ **COLLOCATIONS:**
 develop/create/secure/target/find a niche market
 a **new/small/potential** niche market

Nik|kei Stock Av|er|age ◼ BANKING & FINANCE

/nɪkeɪ stɒk ævərɪdʒ, ævrɪdʒ/

NONCOUNT NOUN The **Nikkei Stock Average** is an index of prices on the Tokyo Stock Exchange. ○ *The Nikkei Stock Average momentarily hit 23,100 yen in afternoon trading.*

---

nine|teen /naɪntin/

NUMBER **Nineteen** is the number 19. ○ *He was a senior manager for nineteen years.*

▶ **COLLOCATIONS:**
 someone **is** nineteen
 nineteen **dollars/euros**
 nineteen **miles/kilometers**
 nineteen **minutes/seconds**

▶ **PHRASE:** eighteen or nineteen

---

nine-to-five job /naɪntəfaɪv dʒɒb/ **(nine-to-five jobs)** ◼ PERSONNEL

NOUN A **nine-to-five job** is a job in which the working day lasts from nine o'clock in the morning to five o'clock in the evening. ○ *Coco won't be able to work five days a week in a nine-to-five job.*

▶ **COLLOCATIONS:**
 work/do/hold down a nine-to-five job
 a **regular/normal** nine-to-five job

---

nine|ty /naɪnti/

NUMBER **Ninety** is the number 90. ○ *The Boston hospital was only open for ninety days.*

nomi|nal /nɒmɪnᵊl/

1 **ADJECTIVE** You use **nominal** to indicate that someone or something is supposed to have a particular identity or status, but in reality does not have it. ○ *As he was still not allowed to run a company, his wife became its nominal head.*

▶ COLLOCATIONS: a nominal **leader/ruler/head**

2 **ADJECTIVE** A **nominal** price or sum of money is very small in comparison with the real cost or value of the thing that is being bought or sold. ○ *I am prepared to sell my shares at a nominal price.*

▶ COLLOCATIONS: a nominal **fee/charge/sum**

▶ SYNONYM: token

3 **ADJECTIVE** In economics, the **nominal** value, rate, or level of something is the one expressed in terms of current prices or figures, without taking into account general changes in prices that take place over time. ○ *Inflation would be lower and so nominal rates would be more attractive in real terms.*

▶ COLLOCATIONS: a nominal **rate/value/amount**

nomi|nate /nɒmɪneɪt/ (nominates, nominating, nominated)

VERB If you **nominate** someone, you formally suggest their name for a job, a position, or a prize. ○ [+ *for*] *He was nominated for the presidency.*

▶ COLLOCATIONS:
nominate a **candidate/film/director/president**
be nominated **by** *someone*

▶ SYNONYM: propose

nomi|na|tion /nɒmɪneɪʃən/ (nominations)

NOUN A **nomination** is an official suggestion that someone should be considered for a job, a position, or a prize. ○ [+ *for*] *a nomination for best actor*

▶ **COLLOCATIONS:**
  win/accept/receive/seek/announce a nomination
  a **presidential/Democratic/Republican/judicial/Oscar**
  nomination
  a nomination **for** something

▶ **SYNONYM:** proposal

---

none|the|less /nʌnðəlɛs/

ADVERB **Nonetheless** means "although something is true." [FORMAL]
  ○ There is still a long way to go. Nonetheless, some progress has been made.

▶ **COLLOCATIONS:** nonetheless **true/real/important**

▶ **SYNONYM:** however

---

non|re|fund|able /nɒnrifʌndəbᵊl/   MARKETING & SALES

ADJECTIVE If you pay for something that is **nonrefundable**, you will not get
  your money back if you want to cancel the purchase. ○ Tickets must be
  purchased by August 11 and are nonrefundable.

▶ **COLLOCATIONS:** a nonrefundable **ticket/deposit/fee/reservation**

---

norm /nɔrm/ (norms)

1 **NOUN** **Norms** are ways of behaving that are considered normal in a
  particular society. ○ [+ of] the commonly accepted norms of democracy
  ○ [+ that] a social norm that says drunkenness is inappropriate behavior

▶ **SYNONYMS:** average, rule, value

2 **NOUN** A **norm** is an official standard or level that organizations are
  expected to reach. ○ an agency which would establish European norms and
  coordinate national policies to halt pollution

▶ **COLLOCATIONS:**
  a norm **of** something
  the norms of **behavior**
  a **cultural/democratic/social/accepted** norm
  accept/establish/meet the norms of something

▶ **SYNONYMS:** standard, rule

nor|mal|ly /nɔrməli/

ADVERB If you say that something **normally** happens or that you
  normally do a particular thing, you mean that it is what usually happens
  or what you usually do. ○ All airports in the country are working normally

today. ○ *Social progress is normally a matter of struggles and conflicts.*
○ *Normally, the transportation system in Paris carries 950,000 passengers a day.*

▶ COLLOCATIONS:
function/behave/operate/develop normally
eat/breathe/act normally

▶ SYNONYMS: as normal, as usual

---

note /noʊt/ (notes, noting, noted)

1 NOUN A **note** is something that you write down to remind yourself of something. ○ *I knew that if I didn't make a note I would lose the thought.*
○ *Take notes during the consultation.*

▶ COLLOCATIONS:
a note **of** *something*
write/take/leave/make a note
scribble/jot down a note
a **handwritten** note
a note **pad/book**

▶ SYNONYM: reminder

2 VERB If you **note** something, you mention it in order to draw people's attention to it. ○ [+ that] *The report notes that export and import volumes picked up in leading economies.* ○ *The yearbook also noted a sharp drop in reported cases of sexually transmitted disease.* ○ [+ how] *Note how the average level of job performance increases as the self-regulation decreases.*

▶ COLLOCATIONS:
a **report/observer/analyst** notes *something*
note a **difference/increase/improvement/similarity**

▶ PHRASES:
please note
note with interest

▶ SYNONYM: observe

no|table /noʊtəbᵊl/

ADJECTIVE Someone or something that is **notable** is important or interesting. ○ [+ for] *The proposed new structure is notable not only for its height, but for its shape.* ○ *With a few notable exceptions, doctors are a pretty sensible bunch.*

→ see note at **dramatic**

▶ COLLOCATIONS:
notable **for** something
a notable **exception/example/difference**
a notable **achievement/success/contribution**

▶ SYNONYMS: noteworthy, remarkable, marked, striking

---

no|tice /nˈoʊtɪs/ (notices, noticing, noticed)

VERB If you **notice** something or someone, you become aware of them.
○ Did you notice anything unusual about him?

▶ COLLOCATIONS:
notice a **difference/change/improvement/increase**
nobody/somebody/anyone/everyone notices something

▶ SYNONYM: pay attention to

no|tice|able /nˈoʊtɪsəbªl/

ADJECTIVE Something **noticeable** is obvious and easy to see. ○ The difference in quality is noticeable.

▶ COLLOCATIONS:
a noticeable **effect/difference/improvement**
barely/particularly/hardly noticeable

▶ SYNONYM: obvious

---

nov|ice /nˈɒvɪs/ (novices)

NOUN A **novice** is someone who has been doing a job or other activity for only a short time and so is not experienced at it. ○ For expert and novice alike, it's a foolproof system. ○ Business novices learn the entrepreneurial ropes fast.

▶ COLLOCATIONS: a **complete/relative/comparative** novice

▶ SYNONYM: beginner

---

nowa|days /nˈaʊədeɪz/

ADVERB **Nowadays** means at the present time, in contrast with the past.
○ Nowadays it's acceptable for women to be ambitious. But it wasn't then.
○ This method is seldom used nowadays.

→ see note at **current**

▶ SYNONYMS: at the present time, currently, these days

nu|clear /ˈnuːkliər/

1 **ADJECTIVE** **Nuclear** means relating to the nuclei of atoms, or to the energy released when these nuclei are split or combined. ○ *a nuclear power plant* ○ *nuclear energy* ○ *nuclear physics*

▶ **COLLOCATIONS:**
  a nuclear **power plant/station/facility**
  nuclear **power/energy/waste/material**
  nuclear **physics**

2 **ADJECTIVE** **Nuclear** means relating to weapons that explode by using the energy released when the nuclei of atoms are split or combined. ○ *They rejected a demand for the removal of all nuclear weapons from U.S. soil.* ○ *nuclear testing*

▶ **COLLOCATIONS:** a nuclear **weapon/test/program**

▶ **SYNONYM:** atomic

---

nu|mer|ous /ˈnuːmərəs/

ADJECTIVE If people or things are **numerous**, they exist or are present in large numbers. ○ *Sex crimes were just as numerous as they are today.* ○ *Numerous tests had been made, but no physical cause for her symptoms could be found.*

▶ **COLLOCATIONS:**
  numerous **attempts/examples/occasions/times**
  numerous **problems/studies**

> **EXTEND YOUR VOCABULARY**
>
> You use **a lot of**, **lots of**, or **loads of** in informal and spoken English to describe a large number of something. ○ *I've been there loads of times.*
>
> You use **many** in more formal writing, especially to talk about a large proportion of a group. ○ *Many experts believe that the system needs major modifications.*
>
> You use **numerous** in formal writing to describe a large, but unknown number. ○ *There are numerous examples from other parts of the world.*
>
> You can also use **innumerable** and **countless** to emphasize a number too large to count. ○ *The new system could save travelers countless hours in airport lounges.*

Oo

ob|ject (objects, objecting, objected)

> The noun is pronounced /ˈɒbdʒɪkt/. The verb is pronounced /əbˈdʒɛkt/.

1 NOUN An **object** is anything that has a fixed shape or form, that you can touch or see, and that is not alive. ○ *an object the shape of a coconut* ○ *In the cozy consulting room the children are surrounded by familiar objects.* ○ *household objects such as lamps and ornaments*

▶ **COLLOCATIONS:**
an object **such as**...
a **heavy/metal/small/sharp/solid** object
a **familiar/everyday** object
an **inanimate** object

▶ **SYNONYM:** thing

2 NOUN The **object** of what someone is doing is their aim or purpose. ○ [+ *of*] *The object of the exercise is to raise money for the charity.* ○ [+ *in*] *He made it his object in life to find the island.* ○ *My object was to publish a scholarly work on Peter Mourne.*

▶ **COLLOCATIONS:**
the object **of/in** *something*
the object of the **exercise**
someone's object in **life**

▶ **SYNONYMS:** purpose, aim, point

3 VERB If you **object** to something, you express your dislike or disapproval of it. ○ [+ *to*] *A lot of people will object to the book.* ○ [+ *that*] *Cullen objected that his small staff would be unable to handle the added work.* ○ *We objected strongly but were outvoted.*

▶ **COLLOCATIONS:**
object **to** *something*
object to the **idea/notion/use**
object **strongly**

▶ **SYNONYMS:** protest, argue

ob|jec|tion /əbdʒɛkʃ°n/ (objections)

NOUN If you make or raise an **objection to** something, you say that you do not like it or agree with it. ○ [+ to] *Some general managers have recently raised objections to the NFL's handling of these negotiations.* ○ [+ by] *Despite objections by the White House, the Senate voted today to cut off aid.*

▶ **COLLOCATIONS:**
an objection **to** *something*
an objection **by** *someone*
raise/dismiss/overrule an objection
a **moral/religious** objection

▶ **SYNONYMS:** protest, opposition, complaint

ob|jec|tive /əbdʒɛktɪv/ (objectives)

1 NOUN Your **objective** is what you are trying to achieve. ○ *Our main objective was the recovery of the child safe and well.* ○ *Our objective is to become the number one digital corporation.*

▶ **COLLOCATIONS:**
the **primary/key** objective
achieve/set/meet an objective

▶ **SYNONYMS:** purpose, aim, goal

2 ADJECTIVE Objective information is based on facts. ○ *He had no objective evidence that anything extraordinary was happening.* ○ *It is futile to look for objective causes of drug addiction.*

▶ **COLLOCATIONS:** objective **evidence/truth/reality**

▶ **SYNONYM:** factual

▶ **RELATED WORD:** subjective

3 ADJECTIVE If someone is **objective**, they base their opinions on facts rather than on their personal feelings. ○ *I believe that a journalist should be completely objective.* ○ *I would really like to have your objective opinion on this.*

▶ **COLLOCATIONS:**
completely/supposedly/truly objective
an objective **opinion/account**

▶ **SYNONYMS:** impartial, unbiased, unprejudiced, open-minded

---

ob|li|ga|tion /ɒblɪɡeɪʃən/ (obligations)

NOUN If you have an **obligation to** do something, you should do it.
○ *Directors do not have an obligation to present alternatives to shareholders.*

○ *He made no attempt to meet his financial obligations.* ○ *the rights and obligations of marriage*

▶ **COLLOCATIONS:**
fulfill/meet/satisfy/honor an obligation
a **financial/legal/contractual/moral** obligation

▶ **PHRASES:**
a duty and obligation
rights and obligations

▶ **SYNONYM:** duty

---

oblige /əblaɪdʒ/ (obliges, obliging, obliged)

VERB If you **are obliged to** do something, a situation, rule, or law makes it necessary for you to do that thing. ○ [+ to-inf] *You are not obliged to say anything unless you wish to do so.*

▶ **COLLOCATIONS:**
legally/contractually/duly obliged
morally/ethically obliged
obliged to **inform/resign/accept/disclose**

▶ **SYNONYM:** compel

ob|liga|tory /əblɪgətɔri/

ADJECTIVE If something is **obligatory**, you must do it because of a rule or a law. ○ *Medical tests are usually not obligatory.* ○ *Essays of this kind include obligatory references to emperors of Rome.*

▶ **COLLOCATIONS:** an obligatory **test/class**

▶ **SYNONYM:** compulsory

---

ob|serve /əbzɜrv/ (observes, observing, observed)

VERB If you **observe** a person or thing, you watch them carefully, especially in order to learn something about them. ○ *Stern also studies and observes the behavior of babies.* ○ [+ how] *I got a chance to observe how a detective actually works.*

▶ **COLLOCATIONS:**
scientists/researchers observe *something*
observe **behavior**
closely observe

▶ **SYNONYMS:** study, monitor

ob|ser|va|tion /ˌɒbzərˈveɪʃən/

NONCOUNT NOUN **Observation** is the action or process of carefully watching someone or something. ○ [+ *of*] *careful observation of the movement of the planets* ○ *In the hospital she'll be under observation all the time.*

▶ **COLLOCATIONS:**
observation **of** *something*
under observation
observation of the **nature/behavior** of *something*
careful observation
astronomical/scientific observation

▶ **SYNONYMS:** study, surveillance

---

ob|so|lete /ˈɒbsəliːt/   `RGD`

ADJECTIVE Something that is **obsolete** is no longer needed because something better has been invented. ○ *So much equipment becomes obsolete almost as soon as it's made.* ○ *obsolete technologies such as vinyl records*

▶ **COLLOCATIONS:**
obsolete **equipment/technology**
become/grow obsolete
render *something* obsolete
functionally/technologically obsolete

▶ **SYNONYM:** outdated

---

ob|struct /əbˈstrʌkt/ **(obstructs, obstructing, obstructed)**

1 VERB To **obstruct** someone or something means to make it difficult for them to move forward by blocking their path. ○ *A number of local people have been arrested for trying to obstruct trucks loaded with logs.* ○ *Drivers who park their cars illegally, particularly obstructing traffic flow, deserve to be punished.*

▶ **COLLOCATIONS:**
obstruct **traffic**
obstruct a **highway/sidewalk/artery/airway**
obstruct the **flow/passage** of *something*

▶ **SYNONYM:** block

2 VERB To **obstruct** progress or a process means to prevent it from happening properly. ○ *The authorities are obstructing a United Nations* *investigation.* ○ *He was convicted of obstructing justice for trying to evade a DNA test.*

▶ **COLLOCATIONS:**
obstruct **justice/progress**
obstruct an **investigation**
deliberately/willfully obstruct *something*

▶ **SYNONYMS:** prevent, hinder

ob|tain /əbteɪn/ (obtains, obtaining, obtained)

VERB To **obtain** something means to get it or achieve it. [FORMAL] ○ *Evans was trying to obtain a fake passport.* ○ *The perfect body has always been difficult to obtain.*

→ see note at **acquire**

▶ **COLLOCATIONS:**
obtain **help/approval/permission**
obtain **information/documents/financing**
obtain *something* **easily/fraudulently/illegally**

▶ **SYNONYMS:** get, acquire, achieve

ob|vi|ous /ɒbviəs/

ADJECTIVE If something is **obvious**, it is easy to see or understand.
○ *the need to rectify what is an obvious injustice* ○ *More and more healthy troops were dying for no obvious reason.* ○ *The answer is obvious.*

▶ **COLLOCATIONS:**
an obvious **choice/answer/question/solution**
an obvious **flaw/danger**
obvious **reasons/differences**
blindingly/glaringly/painfully/patently obvious

▶ **SYNONYMS:** clear, plain

ob|vi|ous|ly /ɒbviəsli/

ADVERB ○ *As a private hospital, it obviously needs to balance its budget each year.* ○ *They were obviously disappointed about the decision.*

▶ **COLLOCATIONS:** obviously **disappointed/pleased/upset**

▶ **SYNONYMS:** clearly, of course

oc|ca|sion /əkeɪʒ³n/ (occasions)

NOUN An **occasion** is a time when something happens, or a case of it happening. ○ *The team repeated the experiment on three separate occasions with the same results.* ○ *Mr. Davis has been asked on a number of occasions.*

▶ **COLLOCATIONS:**
  on an occasion
  a **number of** occasions
  numerous/several/many occasions
  a **previous/separate** occasion

EXTEND YOUR VOCABULARY

In everyday English, you often talk about a **time** when something happens. ○ *I've met him several times, and each time he forgot my name.*

In more formal writing, you can use **occasion** to talk about something that happens at a particular time. You say that something happened on **several occasions** to refer to similar events that happened at different times. ○ *The site was visited on several occasions.*

You can also use **case** to talk about something that happens. You talk about **several cases** to refer to different examples of the same type of event, when the time is not important. ○ *In many cases, the solution is relatively simple.*

---

oc|ca|sion|al /əkeɪʒən³l/

ADJECTIVE Something that is **occasional** happens sometimes but not often. ○ *I get occasional headaches.* ○ *Apart from an occasional television appearance, he doesn't work much now.*

▶ **COLLOCATIONS:** an occasional **appearance/visit**

▶ **SYNONYMS:** infrequent, rare, periodic

oc|ca|sion|al|ly /əkeɪʒən³li/

ADVERB ○ *Importers have occasionally rejected their shipments.*

▶ **SYNONYMS:** sometimes, periodically

---

oc|cu|pa|tion /ɒkyəpeɪʃ³n/ (occupations)   PERSONNEL

NOUN Your **occupation** is your job or profession. ○ *I suppose I was looking for an occupation which was going to be an adventure.* ○ *Occupation: administrative assistant.*

▶ **SYNONYMS:** profession, work

oc|cu|pa|tion|al /ˌɒkyəpeɪʃənᵊl/

ADJECTIVE Occupational means relating to a person's job or profession.
 ○ *Catching frequent colds is unfortunately an occupational hazard in this profession.*

▶ **COLLOCATIONS:**
 an occupational **hazard**
 an occupational **therapist**
 occupational **health**

▶ **SYNONYM:** job-related

---

oc|cu|py /ˈɒkyəpaɪ/ (occupies, occupying, occupied)

1 VERB The people who **occupy** a building or a place are the people who live or work there. ○ *There were over 40 tenants, all occupying one wing of the hospital.* ○ *Land is, in most instances, purchased by those who occupy it.*

▶ **COLLOCATIONS:**
 occupy **land**
 occupy a **building/floor**

▶ **SYNONYM:** inhabit

2 VERB If someone or something **occupies** a particular place in a system, process, or plan, they have that place. ○ *We occupy a quality position in the marketplace.* ○ *Men still occupy more positions of power than women.*

▶ **COLLOCATION:** occupy a **position**

▶ **SYNONYM:** hold

3 VERB If something **occupies** a particular area or place, it fills or covers it, or exists there. ○ *Even very small aircraft occupy a lot of space.* ○ *Bookshelves occupied most of the living room walls.*

▶ **COLLOCATIONS:**
 occupy **space**
 occupy a **wall/floor**

oc|cu|pied /ˈɒkyəpaɪd/

ADJECTIVE Someone or something that is **occupied** is being kept busy by something. ○ *Keep your brain occupied.* ○ *The women were kept fully occupied caring for the sick.*

▶ **COLLOCATIONS:**
 keep/remain/stay occupied
 fully occupied

oc|cu|pan|cy /ɒkyəpənsi/

NONCOUNT NOUN Occupancy is the act of using a room, building, or area of land, usually for a fixed period of time. [FORMAL] ○ *Hotel occupancy has been as low as 40%.* ○ *Room rates start at $179 a night, single or double occupancy.*

  ▶ COLLOCATIONS: **single/double/multiple** occupancy

  ▶ SYNONYM: occupation

oc|cu|pant /ɒkyəpənt/ (occupants)

NOUN The **occupants** of a building or room are the people who live or work there. ○ *Most of the occupants had left before the fire broke out.* ○ *The filing cabinets had all gone with the previous occupants.*

  ▶ COLLOCATIONS: a **previous/sole/original/future** occupant

  ▶ SYNONYM: occupier

---

oc|cur /əkɜr/ (occurs, occurring, occurred)

1 VERB When something **occurs**, it happens. ○ [+ at] *If headaches only occur at night, lack of fresh air and oxygen is often the cause.* ○ [+ when] *The crash occurred when the crew shut down the wrong engine.*

  ▶ COLLOCATIONS:
  occur **at** *a time*
  changes/problems/incidents occur
  accidents/deaths/diseases/injuries occur
  naturally/normally occur

> **EXTEND YOUR VOCABULARY**
>
> In everyday English, you say often that something **happens** or **takes place**. ○ *The accident happened/took place in heavy rain.*
>
> In more formal writing, you can say that something **occurs**. ○ *The incident occurred on June 28.*
>
> You can also say that some types of things **arise**. ○ *Some problems arose that required outside expertise.*
>
>   ▶ a **problem/complication/difficulty** arises
>
>   ▶ a **question/issue/opportunity** arises

2 VERB When something **occurs** in a particular place, it exists or is present there. ○ *The cattle disease occurs more or less anywhere in Africa where the fly* *occurs.* ○ [+ *on*] *These snails do not occur on low-lying coral islands.*

▶ **COLLOCATIONS:**
occur **in/on** *somewhere*
frequently/naturally/normally occur

▶ **SYNONYM:** exist

oc|cur|rence /əkɜːrəns/ (occurrences)

NOUN An **occurrence** is something that happens. [FORMAL] ○ *Complaints seemed to be an everyday occurrence.* ○ [+ *of*] *There is no generally agreed explanation for the occurrence of hallucinations.*

▶ **COLLOCATIONS:**
the occurrence **of** *something*
prevent/reduce/increase the occurrence of *something*
a **common/rare/daily/everyday** occurrence

▶ **SYNONYMS:** incident, happening, event, phenomenon

ocean /oʊʃ°n/ (oceans)

1 NOUN The ocean is the salty water that covers much of the Earth's surface. ○ *new technology used to explore the deep ocean* ○ *a fish's habitat on the ocean floor*

▶ **COLLOCATIONS:**
the **vast/deep/open** ocean
an ocean **current/wave**
the ocean **floor**

▶ **SYNONYM:** the sea

2 NOUN An **ocean** is one of the five very large areas of salt water on the Earth's surface. ○ *a small island in the Indian ocean*

▶ **COLLOCATIONS:** the **Indian/Pacific/Atlantic/Antarctic/Arctic** Ocean

▶ **SYNONYM:** a sea

o'clock /əklɒk/

ADVERB O'clock is used after numbers to say what time it is. ○ *ten o'clock* ○ *When Frank woke it was nearly six o'clock in the evening.*

▶ **COLLOCATIONS:**
two/four/seven o'clock
x o'clock in the **morning/afternoon/evening**

odd /ɒd/

ADJECTIVE Odd numbers, such as 3 and 17, are those which cannot be divided exactly by the number two. ○ *Multiplying an odd number by an odd number always gives an odd number.* ○ *There's an odd number of candidates.*

▶ COLLOCATION: an odd **number**

of|fense /əfɛns/ (offenses)

1 NOUN An **offense** is a crime that breaks a particular law and requires a particular punishment. [in BRIT, use **offence**] ○ *Thirteen people have been charged with treason – an offense which can carry the death penalty.* ○ [+ to-inf] *In America the Consumer Product Safety Act makes it a criminal offense to sell goods that are unsafe.*

▶ COLLOCATIONS:
   commit/admit an offense
   a **criminal/serious/punishable** offense
   a **drug/sex/traffic** offense

▶ SYNONYM: crime

2 NOUN Offense or an **offense** is behavior that causes people to be upset or embarrassed. [in BRIT, use **offence**] ○ *He said he didn't mean to give offense.*

▶ COLLOCATIONS: **give/cause/create** offense

3 PHRASE If someone **takes offense at** something you say or do, they feel upset, often unnecessarily, because they think you are being rude to them. [in BRIT, use **offence**] ○ *Instead of taking offense, the woman smiled.*

▶ COLLOCATION: take **serious** offense

▶ SYNONYMS: insult, put-down, snub

of|fen|sive /əfɛnsɪv/ (offensives)

1 ADJECTIVE Something that is **offensive** upsets or embarrasses people because it is rude or insulting. ○ *Some friends of his found the play extremely offensive.*

▶ COLLOCATIONS: offensive **language/behavior**

2 NOUN A military **offensive** is a carefully planned attack made by a large group of soldiers. ○ *Its latest military offensive against rebel forces is aimed at re-opening important trade routes.* ○ *In May 1940, the Germans launched the western offensive.*

▶ SYNONYMS: assault, onslaught

▶ COLLOCATIONS: a **military/ground/air** offensive

3 **NOUN** If you conduct an **offensive**, you take strong action to show how angry you are about something or how much you disapprove of something. ○ *Republicans acknowledged that they had little choice but to mount an all-out offensive on the Democratic nominee.*

▶ **COLLOCATIONS:** **launch/mount** an offensive

▶ **SYNONYMS:** attack, campaign

of|fend /əfɛnd/ (offends, offending, offended)

VERB If someone **offends**, they commit a crime. [FORMAL] ○ *In Western countries girls are far less likely to offend than boys.* ○ *Victims wanted assurances their attackers would never offend again.*

▶ **PHRASE:** likely to offend

▶ **SYNONYM:** break the law

of|fer /ɔfər/ (offers, offering, offered)

1 **VERB** If you **offer** something to someone, you ask them if they would like to have it. ○ *She offered him a cup of coffee.* ○ *Patients are offered dietary advice.*

▶ **COLLOCATIONS:** offer **help/assistance/advice**

▶ **SYNONYM:** present with

2 **VERB** If you **offer to** do something, you say that you are willing to do it. ○ *They offered to buy the company for $110 a share.* ○ *I offered to help her with the garden.* ○ *Howard offered to resign, and the mayor accepted.*

▶ **COLLOCATIONS:**
offer **to** *do something*
offer to **help/assist**
offer to **resign/surrender**
offer to **buy/purchase/sell** *something*

3 **NOUN** An **offer** is something that someone says they will give you or do for you. ○ [+ *of*] *The company accepted a takeover offer of $29.835 a share.* ○ *Five bidders have submitted offers.* ○ *This offer is valid until August 28.*

▶ **COLLOCATIONS:**
an offer **of** *something*
an offer of **help/assistance**
submit/make/extend/withdraw an offer
reject/decline/refuse an offer
accept/receive/consider an offer
an offer **expires/is valid**
a **special/final/introductory** offer
a **job/contract/scholarship** offer

4 **VERB** If you **offer** goods, you present them for sale. ○ *The paintings were initially offered as three separate lots.* ○ *All our books are offered at a discount of 25%.*

▶ **COLLOCATIONS:**
offer *something* for **sale**
offer *something* at a **discount**
offer *something* at **auction**

▶ **SYNONYM:** put up for sale

5 **VERB** If you **offer** something, you propose to give it as payment. ○ *They offered $21.50 a share in cash for 49.5 million shares.* ○ *The Nets offered him $102 million over seven years.*

▶ **SYNONYM:** propose

---

of|fice /ɔfɪs, ɒf-/ (offices) `OFFICE`

1 **NOUN** An **office** is a room or a part of a building where people work sitting at desks. ○ *He had an office big enough for his desk and chair, plus his computer.* ○ *At about 4:30 p.m. Audrey arrived at the office.* ○ *Call their main office for more details.*

▶ **COLLOCATIONS:**
be **at** the office
leave the office
a **main/branch/regional** office
an office **block/building/complex/worker**
office **equipment/hours/space**

2 **NOUN** An **office** is a department of an organization, especially the government, where people deal with a particular kind of administrative work. ○ *Thousands have registered with unemployment offices.* ○ *the White House press office* ○ *the Congressional Budget Office*

▶ **COLLOCATION:** a **press** office

▶ **SYNONYM:** department

---

of|fi|cial /əfɪʃᵊl/ (officials) `PERSONNEL`

1 **ADJECTIVE** **Official** means approved by the government or by someone in authority. ○ *According to the official figures, over one thousand people died during the revolution.* ○ *A report in the official police newspaper gave no reason for the move.*

▶ **COLLOCATIONS:**
official **figures/statistics**

an official **announcement/statement/policy/visit**

▶ **SYNONYM:** authorized

2 NOUN An **official** is a person who holds a position of authority in an organization. ○ *A senior U.N. official hopes to visit Baghdad this month.* ○ *Local officials say the shortage of water restricts the kind of businesses they can attract.*

▶ **COLLOCATIONS:**
a **senior/government/military/health** official
officials **say/warn/confirm** *things*

---

of|ten /ˈɔfⁿn/

ADVERB **Often** means many times or much of the time. ○ *Investors often borrow heavily to buy their holdings.* ○ *That doesn't happen very often.* ○ *She believes if she says something often enough it becomes true.*

▶ **COLLOCATIONS:** **fairly/quite/very** often

▶ **SYNONYM:** frequently

---

okay /ˈoʊkeɪ/ also **OK**, **O.K.** or **ok**

ADJECTIVE or **ADVERB** If something is **okay**, it is acceptable. [INFORMAL] ○ *Is it okay if I go by myself?* ○ *We seemed to manage okay.*

▶ **COLLOCATIONS:** **perfectly/reasonably/quite** okay

▶ **SYNONYM:** all right

---

old-fashioned /ˈoʊldfæʃənd/

1 ADJECTIVE Something such as a style, method, or device that is **old-fashioned** is no longer used, done, or admired by most people, because it has been replaced by something that is more modern. ○ *The house was dull, old-fashioned, and in bad condition.* ○ *There are some traditional farmers left who still make cheese the old-fashioned way.*

2 ADJECTIVE **Old-fashioned** ideas, customs, or values are the ideas, customs, and values of the past. ○ *She has some old-fashioned values and can be a strict disciplinarian.* ○ *good old-fashioned cooking*

▶ **COLLOCATIONS:**
an old-fashioned **way/style**
good old-fashioned…
old-fashioned **values/notions**

▶ **SYNONYM:** traditional

omit /oʊmɪt/ **(omits, omitting, omitted)**

VERB If you **omit** something, you do not include it in an activity or piece of work, deliberately or accidentally. ○ [+ *from*] *Some details of the initial investment were inadvertently omitted from the financial statements.*
○ [+ *from*] *Our apologies to David Pannick for omitting his name from last week's article.*

▶ **COLLOCATIONS:**
  omit *something* **from** *something*
  omit **information**
  omit a **word/fact/name/reference**
  inadvertently/deliberately/carefully omit *something*

▶ **SYNONYM:** leave out

on|going /ɒnɡoʊɪŋ/

ADJECTIVE An **ongoing** situation has been happening for quite a long time and seems likely to continue for some time in the future. ○ *There is an ongoing debate on the issue.* ○ *That research is ongoing.*

▶ **COLLOCATIONS:**
  an ongoing **debate/process/effort/war**
  an ongoing **investigation/dispute/discussion/debate**
  ongoing **research**

▶ **SYNONYM:** continuing

on|line /ɒnlaɪn/ also **on-line**   〔MARKETING & SALES〕

ADJECTIVE **Online** means available on or connected to the Internet.
  ○ *an online recruitment service* ○ *Approximately 90 percent of households are now online.*

● **Online** is also an adverb. ○ *The study was published online.*

▶ **COLLOCATIONS:**
  an online **retailer/buyer/store/service**
  an online **journal/newsletter**
  online **banking/shopping/learning/access**
  shop/register online
  buy/sell/find/access/publish/order *something* online

▶ **SYNONYMS:** on the Internet, web-based

on|line shop|ping /ɒnlaɪn ʃɒpɪŋ/

NONCOUNT NOUN **Online shopping** is the activity of buying goods and services via the Internet. ○ *Flextech owns a string of websites and provides interactive services such as online shopping.*

---

on-the-job trai|ning /ɒnðədʒɒb treɪnɪŋ/ PERSONNEL

NONCOUNT NOUN **On-the-job training** is training that is given to employees while they are at work. ○ *Japanese companies provide on-the-job training as well as access to technical education.* ○ *Their on-the-job training program lasts for a year.*

▸ **COLLOCATIONS:** **provide/offer** on-the-job training

---

op|er|ate /ɒpəreɪt/ (operates, operating, operated) LOGISTICS & DISTRIBUTION

1 VERB If you **operate** a business or organization, you work to keep it running properly. If a business or organization **operates**, it carries out its work. ○ *Until his death in 1986, Greenwood owned and operated an enormous pear orchard.* ○ *allowing commercial banks to operate in the country* ○ [V-ing] *Operating costs jumped from $85.3m to $95m.*

2 VERB The way that something **operates** is the way that it works or has a particular effect. ○ *Ceiling and wall lights can operate independently.* ○ *The world of work doesn't operate that way.*

3 VERB When you **operate** a machine or device, or when it **operates**, you make it work. ○ *accidents from driving or operating machinery* ○ *The number of these machines operating around the world has now reached ten million.*

▸ **COLLOCATIONS:**
  operating **costs/expenses/profit/loss**
  a **company/firm/organization/airline** operates
  operate **efficiently/profitably**
  operate **machinery**
  manually/remotely/independently operated

▸ **SYNONYMS:** run, work, function

op|era|tion|al /ɒpəreɪʃənˀl/

ADJECTIVE **Operational** means in use or ready for use. ○ *The whole system will be fully operational by December.*

▸ **COLLOCATIONS:** **partly/fully** operational

▸ **SYNONYMS:** working, functioning

op|er|at|ing budg|et /ˈɒpəreɪtɪŋ bˈʌdʒɪt/ (operating budgets)

NOUN An **operating budget** is a forecast of the costs and profits of an organization, used to monitor its trading activities, usually for one year.
○ [+ of] *The division's annual operating budget of about $245 million is under constant strain.* ○ [+ for] *a $2.55 billion operating budget for the coming school year*

▶ **COLLOCATIONS:**
an operating budget **of** *something*
an operating budget **for** *something*
annual/yearly/total operating budget
the **county's/school's/museum's** operating budget
cut/increase an operating budget

opin|ion /əpˈɪnyən/ (opinions)

NOUN Your **opinion** about something is what you think or believe about it.
○ *He held the opinion that a government should think before introducing a tax.*
○ *Most who expressed an opinion spoke favorably of Thomas.*

▶ **COLLOCATIONS:**
an opinion **about/on** *something*
an opinion about/on a **subject/issue/matter**
have/hold/express/voice/offer/form an opinion
a **personal/strong/favorable** opinion

▶ **PHRASE:** a matter of opinion

▶ **SYNONYMS:** feeling, belief, view, point of view

op|por|tu|nity /ˌɒpərtˈuːnɪti/ (opportunities)

NOUN An **opportunity** is a situation in which it is possible for you to do something that you want to do. ○ [+ to-inf] *Participants must have the opportunity to take part in the discussion.* ○ [+ for] *I want to see more opportunities for young people.* ○ [+ in] *equal opportunities in employment*

▶ **COLLOCATIONS:**
an opportunity **in** *something*
an opportunity **for** *something/someone*
an opportunity for **growth/advancement/expansion**
take/have/seize/miss/waste an opportunity
give/offer *someone* an opportunity
a **golden/unique/rare/ideal/perfect** opportunity
a **career/business/investment** opportunity
an opportunity **arises**

▶ **PHRASES:**
equal opportunities
the opportunity of a lifetime

▶ **SYNONYM:** chance

---

op|pose /əpo͞uz/ (opposes, opposing, opposed)

VERB If you **oppose** someone or **oppose** their plans or ideas, you disagree
with what they want to do and try to prevent them from doing it.
○ *Mr. Taylor was not bitter towards those who had opposed him.* ○ *Many parents
oppose bilingual education.*

▶ **COLLOCATIONS:**
oppose a **plan/move/view/idea/war/bill**
strongly oppose *something*

op|posed /əpo͞uzd/

ADJECTIVE If you **are opposed to** something, you disagree with it or
disapprove of it. ○ [+ to] *I am utterly opposed to any form of terrorism.*
○ [+ to] *We are strongly opposed to the presence of America in this region.*

▶ **COLLOCATIONS:**
opposed **to** *something*
opposed to **abortion/violence**

▶ **SYNONYM:** against

op|pos|ing /əpo͞uzɪŋ/

1 **ADJECTIVE Opposing** ideas or tendencies are totally different from each
other. ○ *I have a friend who has the opposing view and felt that the war was
immoral.*

2 **ADJECTIVE Opposing** groups of people disagree about something or are
in competition with one another. ○ *The Georgian leader said that he still
favored dialogue between the opposing sides.* ○ *the opposing team*

▶ **COLLOCATIONS:**
an opposing **view**
an opposing **faction/camp/force/side/player**

op|po|si|tion /ɒpəzɪʃⁿn/

1 **NONCOUNT NOUN Opposition** is strong, angry, or violent disagreement
and disapproval. ○ *The government is facing a new wave of opposition in the
form of a student strike.* ○ [+ to] *Much of the opposition to this plan has come
from the media.*

▶ **COLLOCATIONS:**
  opposition **to** *something*
  face opposition
  strong/stiff/fierce/political/official opposition

▶ **SYNONYMS:** hostility, resistance

2 NONCOUNT NOUN The opposition is the political parties or groups that are opposed to a government. ○ *The main opposition parties boycotted the election, saying it would not be conducted fairly.* ○ *the opposition refused to disarm its militia*

▶ **COLLOCATIONS:**
  an opposition **party/group/politician/spokesman**
  the opposition **boycotts/claims/demands** *something*
  the opposition **accuses/attacks/criticizes** *someone*

---

opt /ɒpt/ (opts, opting, opted)

VERB If you **opt for** something, or **opt to** do something, you choose it or decide to do it in preference to anything else. ○ [+ *for*] *Depending on your circumstances, you may wish to opt for one method or the other.* ○ [+ *to-inf*] *Our students can also opt to stay in a residence hall.*

▶ **COLLOCATION:** opt **for** *something*

> **EXTEND YOUR VOCABULARY**
>
> In everyday English, you often use the verb **choose** to talk about making **choices**. ○ *Customers choose from a menu of packages.*
>
> In more formal writing, you can use **select** especially to talk about the action of choosing as part of a process. ○ *They surveyed a thousand randomly selected Americans.*
>
> You use **opt** or **decide** especially to talk about the outcome of your choice, your **decision**. ○ *An executive meeting last week opted for a more long-term approach.*

---

op|ti|mize /ɒptɪmaɪz/ (optimizes, optimizing, optimized)

VERB To **optimize** a plan, system, or machine means to arrange or design it so that it operates as smoothly and efficiently as possible. [FORMAL] [in BRIT, also use **optimise**] ○ *Doctors are concentrating on understanding the disease better, and on optimizing the treatment.* ○ [+ *for*] *The new systems have been optimized for running Microsoft Windows.*

▶ **COLLOCATIONS:**
optimize *something* **for** *something*
optimize a **process/system/setting**

op|tion /ˈɒpʃ³n/ (options)

NOUN An **option** is something that you can choose to do in preference to one or more alternatives. ○ *He's argued from the start that America and its allies are putting too much emphasis on the military option.* ○ *What other options do you have?*

▶ **COLLOCATIONS:**
the **preferred/viable** option
a **military/strategic** option

▶ **SYNONYMS:** alternative, choice

op|tion|al /ˈɒpʃən³l/

ADJECTIVE If something is **optional**, you can choose whether or not you do it or have it. ○ *Finally, it becomes economical to offer the customer optional extras.* ○ *The violin part is more than an optional accompaniment.*

▶ **COLLOCATION:** an optional **extra**

or|der /ˈɔrdər/ (orders, ordering, ordered)

1 PHRASE If you do something **in order to** achieve a particular thing or **in order that** something can happen, you do it because you want to achieve that thing. ○ *Most schools are extremely unwilling to cut down on staff in order to cut costs.* ○ *There are increased funds available in order that these targets are met.*

▶ **SYNONYM:** so that

2 NOUN If a set of things are arranged or done **in** a particular **order**, they are arranged or done so one thing follows another, often according to a particular factor such as importance. ○ *The table shows the factors ranked in order of importance.* ○ *Sources should be arranged in alphabetical order by the last name of the author.*

▶ **COLLOCATIONS:**
in/into order
in order **of** *something*
in **alphabetical/chronological/reverse** order
in order of **importance/priority/preference**

3 VERB The way that something **is ordered** is the way that it is organized and structured. ○ *a society which is ordered by hierarchy* ○ *We know the*

French order things differently. ○ *a carefully ordered system in which everyone has his place*

▶ **COLLOCATIONS:** be ordered **alphabetically/logically/neatly**

▶ **SYNONYMS:** organize, structure

---

or|di|nary /ˈɔrdᵊnɛri/

ADJECTIVE **Ordinary** people or things are normal and not special or different in any way. ○ *the impact that technology will have on ordinary people* ○ *It has 25 calories less than ordinary ice cream.*

▶ **COLLOCATIONS:**
   ordinary **people/citizens**
   just/perfectly/quite ordinary

▶ **SYNONYMS:** normal, everyday

---

or|gan|ize /ˈɔrgənaɪz/ (organizes, organizing, organized) ORGANIZATION

1 VERB If you **organize** an event or activity, you make sure that the necessary arrangements are made. [in BRIT, also use **organise**]
○ *The Commission will organize a conference on rural development.*
○ *a two-day meeting organized by the United Nations* ○ *The initial mobilization was well organized.*

2 VERB If you **organize** a set of things, you arrange them in an ordered way or give them a structure. [in BRIT, also use **organise**] ○ *a method of organizing a file* ○ *the way in which the Army is organized*

▶ **COLLOCATIONS:**
   organize *things* **by/into** *something*
   organize *things* by **group/topic**
   organize *things* into **units/sections/chapters**
   organize a **topic/essay**
   organize a **meeting/conference/event/demonstration**
   well/poorly/highly organized
   neatly/logically/loosely organized

▶ **SYNONYMS:** plan, arrange, order, structure

or|gan|ized /ˈɔrgənaɪzd/

ADJECTIVE Someone who is **organized** plans their work and activities well. [in BRIT, also use **organised**] ○ *Managers need to be very organized.* ○ *Keep your room neat and organized.* ○ *a well organized program*

▶ **COLLOCATIONS:** **well/highly/poorly** organized

▶ **PHRASES:**
organized and efficient
neat and organized

or|gani|za|tion /ɔːɡənaɪzeɪʃ³n/ (organizations)

1 NOUN An **organization** is an official group of people, for example a political party, a business, a charity, or a club. [in BRIT, also use **organisation**] ○ *Most of these specialized schools are provided by voluntary organizations.* ○ *the World Health Organization of the United Nations*

▶ **COLLOCATIONS:**
a **charitable/voluntary/nongovernmental** organization
a **news** organization
form/join an organization

▶ **PHRASE:** organizations and individuals

▶ **SYNONYM:** group

2 NONCOUNT NOUN The **organization** of an event or activity involves making all the necessary arrangements for it. [in BRIT, also use **organisation**] ○ [+ of] *the exceptional attention to detail that goes into the organization of this event* ○ *Several projects have been delayed by poor organization.*

▶ **COLLOCATIONS:**
the organization **of** something
effective/efficient/poor organization

3 NONCOUNT NOUN The **organization of** something is the way in which its different parts are arranged or relate to each other. [in BRIT, also use **organisation**] ○ [+ of] *I am aware that the organization of the book leaves something to be desired.* ○ *The economic organization of a society is critical to the society's success or failure.*

▶ **COLLOCATIONS:**
the organization **of** something
the organization of **society/work/industry**

▶ **SYNONYMS:** structure, arrangement

---

ori|gin /ɒrɪdʒɪn, ɔːr-/ (origins) `R&D`

NOUN You can refer to the beginning, cause, or source of something as its **origin** or **origins**. ○ [+ of] *theories about the origin of life* ○ [+ in] *The disorder in military policy had its origins in Truman's first term.* ○ *Most of the thickeners are of plant origin.*

▶ **COLLOCATIONS:**
the origin **of** *something*
an origin **in** *something*
trace/explain the origin

▶ **PHRASE:** of unknown origin

▶ **SYNONYMS:** beginning, source

origi|nal /ərɪdʒɪnᵊl/ (originals)

ADJECTIVE You use **original** when referring to something that existed at the beginning of a process or activity, or the characteristics that something had when it began or was made. ○ *The original plan was to hold an indefinite stoppage.* ○ *The inhabitants have voted overwhelmingly to restore the city's original name of Chemnitz.* ○ *the ancient history of Australia's original inhabitants*

▶ **COLLOCATIONS:**
the original **plan/intention/idea/purpose**
original **inhabitants**

▶ **SYNONYMS:** first, early

origi|nal|ly /ərɪdʒɪnᵊli/

ADVERB When you say what happened or was the case **originally**, you are saying what happened or was the case when something began or came into existence, often to contrast it with what happened later. ○ *The plane has been kept in service far longer than originally intended.* ○ *The castle was originally surrounded by a triple wall, only one of which remains.*

▶ **COLLOCATIONS:** originally **intended/planned/scheduled**

▶ **SYNONYM:** initially

origi|nate /ərɪdʒɪneɪt/ (originates, originating, originated)

VERB When something **originates** or when someone **originates** it, it begins to happen or exist. [FORMAL] ○ [+ *in*] *The disease originated in Africa.* ○ [+ *from*] *All carbohydrates originate from plants.* ○ *No one has any idea who originated the story.*

▶ **COLLOCATIONS:**
originate **in/from** *something/somewhere*
originate in the **16th century/19th century**

▶ **SYNONYMS:** begin, start, invent, create

ortho|dox /ˈɔːθədɒks/

ADJECTIVE Orthodox beliefs, methods, or systems are ones that are accepted or used by most people. ○ *Payne gained a reputation for sound, if orthodox, views.* ○ *Many of these ideas are now being incorporated into orthodox medical treatment.* ○ *orthodox police methods*

▶ **COLLOCATIONS:**
strictly/fairly/religiously orthodox
orthodox **medicine/theology/religion/economics**

▶ **SYNONYM:** conventional

other|wise /ˈʌðəwaɪz/

1 ADVERB You use **otherwise** before stating the general condition or quality of something, when you are also mentioning an exception to this general condition or quality. ○ *The decorations for the games have lent a splash of color to an otherwise drab city.*

▶ **PHRASE:** otherwise known as

2 ADVERB You use **otherwise** to refer in a general way to actions or situations that are very different from, or the opposite to, your main statement. [WRITTEN] ○ *Take approximately 60 mg up to four times a day, unless advised otherwise by a doctor.* ○ *There is no way anything would ever happen between us, and believe me I've tried to convince myself otherwise.*

▶ **COLLOCATIONS: think/suggest/state** otherwise

▶ **SYNONYM:** differently

3 ADVERB You use **otherwise** to indicate that other ways of doing something are possible in addition to the way already mentioned. ○ *The studio could punish its players by keeping them out of work, and otherwise controlling their lives.*

out|come /ˈaʊtkʌm/ (outcomes)

NOUN The **outcome** of an activity, process, or situation is the situation that exists at the end of it. ○ *Mr. Singh said he was pleased with the outcome.* ○ [+ of] *It's too early to know the outcome of her illness.* ○ *a successful outcome*

▶ **COLLOCATIONS:**
the outcome **of** *something*
await/predict/decide/affect/influence the outcome
the **likely** outcome
a **successful** outcome

▶ **SYNONYMS:** result, conclusion

out|let /aʊtlɛt, -lɪt/ (outlets)

1 **NOUN** An **outlet** is a store that sells the goods made by a particular manufacturer at a low price. ○ *a factory outlet* ○ *Vegas boasts several outlet malls a short taxi ride from the strip hotels.*

▶ **COLLOCATIONS:**
a **retail/factory/discount** outlet
an outlet **mall/store/center**

2 **NOUN** An **outlet** is a market for a product or service. ○ *He took a new tack to find outlets for the computers he was selling.*

▶ **COLLOCATIONS:** **find/develop/create** an outlet

out|line /aʊtlaɪn/ (outlines, outlining, outlined)

NOUN An **outline** is a general explanation or description of something.
○ *Charlie Chaplin wrote the outline of the film in 1938.* ○ *Can you give me a rough outline of what transpired?* ○ *[+ of] an outline of the plan*

▶ **COLLOCATIONS:**
an outline **of** *something*
provide/write/present an outline
a **brief/rough/basic** outline
a **broad/detailed** outline

▶ **SYNONYMS:** summary, synopsis

out|look /aʊtlʊk/ (outlooks)

NOUN The **outlook** for something is what people think will happen in relation to it. ○ *The economic outlook is one of rising unemployment.*
○ *[+ for] the uncertain outlook for the automobile industry*

▶ **COLLOCATIONS:**
the outlook **for** *something*
the outlook for **growth/industry**
the **economic/short-term/long-term** outlook
a **bleak/gloomy/positive/optimistic/cautious/uncertain** outlook

▶ **SYNONYMS:** prospect, forecast

out|put /aʊtpʊt/

1 **NONCOUNT NOUN** **Output** is used to refer to something that a person or thing produces. ○ *Government statistics show the largest drop in industrial output for ten years.* ○ *[+ of] The gland enlarges in an attempt to increase the output of hormone.*

▶ COLLOCATIONS:
the output **of** *something*
boost/increase/reduce/cut output
output **rises/falls**
industrial/agricultural/economic/manufacturing output
oil/power output
total/annual output

2 NONCOUNT NOUN The **output** of a computer or other device is the information or signals that it displays on a screen or prints on paper as a result of a particular program. ○ [+ *from*] *You run the software, you look at the output, you make modifications.*

▶ COLLOCATIONS:
the output **from** *something*
digital/computer output
an output **device**

---

out|source /aʊtsɔːs/ (outsources, outsourcing, outsourced)

LOGISTICS & DISTRIBUTION

VERB If a company **outsources** work or things, it pays workers from outside the company and often outside the country to do the work or supply the things. ○ *companies that outsource I.T. functions* ○ *The company began looking for ways to cut costs, which led to the decision to outsource.*

▶ COLLOCATION: a **company** outsources

---

out|stand|ing /aʊtstændɪŋ/

ADJECTIVE Outstanding means extremely good. ○ *She is an outstanding athlete.* ○ *In every restaurant we found ourselves in, the food was outstanding.* ○ *The film features an outstanding performance from Jim Carrey.*

▶ COLLOCATIONS:
quite/absolutely/truly outstanding
an outstanding **performance/achievement/display**
outstanding **talent/ability**

▶ SYNONYMS: excellent, great, exceptional

---

out|weigh /aʊtweɪ/ (outweighs, outweighing, outweighed)

VERB If one thing **outweighs** another, the first thing is of greater importance, benefit, or significance than the second thing. [FORMAL] ○ *The medical benefits of x-rays far outweigh the risk of having them.* ○ *The advantages of this deal largely outweigh the disadvantages.*

▶ **COLLOCATIONS:**
outweigh the **benefits/risk/disadvantages/cost**
the **advantages** outweigh *something*
far outweigh *something*

▶ **SYNONYMS:** override, cancel out, balance out

---

over|all /ˈoʊvərɔl/

ADJECTIVE You use **overall** to indicate that you are talking about a situation in general or about the whole of something. ○ *the overall rise in unemployment* ○ *A company must have both an overall strategy and local strategies for each unit.* ○ *It is usually the woman who assumes overall care of the baby.*

● **Overall** is also an adverb. ○ *The review omitted some studies. Overall, however, the evidence was persuasive.* ○ *The college has few ways to assess the quality of education overall.*

▶ **COLLOCATIONS:**
overall **spending/revenue**
an overall **impression/strategy/performance**
an overall **majority/increase**

▶ **SYNONYM:** general

---

over|ca|pac|ity /ˈoʊvərkəpæsɪti/ 　LOGISTICS & DISTRIBUTION

NONCOUNT NOUN If there is **overcapacity** in a particular industry or area, more goods have been produced than are needed. ○ *There is huge overcapacity in the world car industry.*

▶ **COLLOCATIONS:**
an overcapacity **in** *something*
a **huge/global/chronic** overcapacity

---

over|charge /ˈoʊvərtʃɑrdʒ/ (overcharges, overcharging, overcharged) 　MARKETING & SALES

VERB If someone **overcharges** you, they charge you too much for their goods or services. ○ *If you feel a taxi driver has overcharged you, say so.* ○ *The dispute involved allegations that the law firm had grossly overcharged its client.*

▶ **COLLOCATIONS:**
overcharge **customers/clients/taxpayers**
grossly overcharge

over|come /oʊvərkʌm/ (overcomes, overcoming, overcame)

VERB If you **overcome** a problem or a feeling, you successfully deal with it and control it. ○ *Molly had fought and overcome her fear of flying.* ○ *One way of helping children to overcome shyness is to boost their self-confidence.*

▶ **COLLOCATIONS:** overcome a **problem/difficulty/injury/obstacle**

▶ **SYNONYMS:** defeat, beat, conquer, survive

---

over|draft /oʊvərdræft/ (overdrafts)　　　**BANKING & FINANCE**

NOUN If you have an **overdraft**, you have spent more money than you have in your bank account. ○ *Her bank warned that unless she repaid the overdraft she could face legal action.* ○ *Your savings account provides overdraft protection for your checking account.*

▶ **COLLOCATIONS:**
   reduce/cover/repay an overdraft
   an overdraft **limit/fee/charge**

---

over|due /oʊvərdu/　　　**LOGISTICS & DISTRIBUTION**

1 ADJECTIVE If you say that a change or an event is **overdue**, you mean that you think it should have happened before now. ○ *This debate is long overdue.* ○ *Total revision of the law in this area is long overdue.*

▶ **COLLOCATIONS:**
   an overdue **change/reform**
   long overdue

▶ **SYNONYM:** belated

2 ADJECTIVE Overdue sums of money have not been paid, even though it is later than the date on which they should have been paid. ○ *Teachers have joined a strike aimed at forcing the government to pay overdue salaries and allowances.* ○ *Companies can claim up to $100 compensation for each overdue bill.*

▶ **COLLOCATIONS:** an overdue **payment/bill**

▶ **SYNONYM:** unpaid

---

over|head /oʊvərhɛd/　　　**LOGISTICS & DISTRIBUTION**

NONCOUNT NOUN Overhead is the regular and essential expenses of running a business, such as salaries, rent, and bills. ○ *We had to reduce overhead to remain competitive.* ○ *When did you last review overhead expenditure?*

> ▶ **COLLOCATIONS:**
> **low/high/minimal** overhead
> overhead **expenses/expenditure**
> **reduce/increase** overhead

> ▶ **SYNONYM:** expenses

---

over|look /oʊvərlʊk/ (overlooks, overlooking, overlooked)

VERB If you **overlook** a fact, problem, or a person's bad behavior, you do not notice it, or do not realize how important it is. ○ *We overlook all sorts of warning signals about our own health.*

> ▶ **COLLOCATIONS:**
> overlook a **fact/problem**
> **conveniently/deliberately/inadvertently** overlook

> ▶ **SYNONYM:** ignore

---

over|quali|fied /oʊvərkwɒlɪfaɪd/   `PERSONNEL`

ADJECTIVE If you are **overqualified** for a job, you have more experience or qualifications than are needed for that job. ○ *Many of those employed in India's remote-services business would be deemed overqualified in the West.*

> ▶ **RELATED WORD:** underqualified

---

over|seas /oʊvərsiz/   `TRAVEL`

1 ADJECTIVE You use **overseas** to describe things that involve or are in foreign countries, usually across an ocean. ○ *He has returned to South Africa from his long overseas trip.* ○ *overseas trade figures*

> ▶ **COLLOCATIONS:**
> an overseas **trip/travel/tour/market/operation**
> overseas **aid**

> ▶ **SYNONYM:** foreign

> ▶ **RELATED WORD:** domestic

2 ADJECTIVE An **overseas** student or visitor comes from a foreign country, usually across an ocean. ○ *Every year nine million overseas visitors come to London.* ○ *firmly targeted at overseas buyers*

> ▶ **COLLOCATIONS:** an overseas **student/visitor/investor/buyer**

> ▶ **SYNONYM:** foreign

over|staffed /oʊvərstæft/ `PERSONNEL`

ADJECTIVE If a company or an organization is **overstaffed**, too many staff have been employed to work there. ○ *The personnel department is grossly overstaffed.*

▶ **COLLOCATIONS**: **chronically/grossly/hugely** overstaffed

over|time /oʊvərtaɪm/ `PERSONNEL`

ADVERB If you work **overtime**, you spend extra time doing your job. ○ *He worked overtime to finish the job.*

own|er /oʊnər/ **(owners)** `ORGANIZATION`

NOUN The **owner** of something is the person to whom it belongs. ○ [+ *of*] *Owners of property will lose financially if their property is damaged.* ○ *New owners will have to wait until September before moving in.*

▶ **COLLOCATIONS:**
the owner **of** *something*
the **rightful/previous/original/current** owner
a **property/home/business/pet** owner

own|er|ship /oʊnərʃɪp/

NONCOUNT NOUN Ownership of something is the state of owning it. ○ *rules on the foreign ownership of its airlines* ○ *the growth of home ownership*

▶ **COLLOCATIONS:**
home/land ownership
pet/gun ownership
joint/private/sole ownership

o

Pp

pace /peɪs/ (paces)

NOUN The **pace** of something is the speed at which it happens or is done.
- ○ [+ of] *Many people are not satisfied with the pace of economic reform.*
- ○ *Interest rates would come down as the recovery picked up pace.*

▶ **COLLOCATIONS:**
the pace **of** *something*
the pace of **change/reform/growth/expansion**
pick up the pace
a **brisk/fast/record/slow** pace

▶ **SYNONYM:** speed

pack|age /pækɪdʒ/ (packages, packaging, packaged)

`MARKETING & SALES`

1 NOUN A **package** is something wrapped in paper, or in a box or an envelope in order to be sent somewhere. ○ *I tore open the package.*

▶ **COLLOCATIONS:**
offer/deliver/receive/give a package
a package **includes/contains** *something*
a **suspicious/surprise** package

▶ **SYNONYM:** container

2 VERB If you **package** goods, you design and produce wrapping or a box for them. ○ *The factory will produce the plastic used to package products such as snack foods and tobacco.*

▶ **COLLOCATIONS:**
package **food/products/goods**
neatly/beautifully packaged

pam|phlet /pæmflɪt/ (pamphlets)

`COMMUNICATIONS`

NOUN A **pamphlet** is a thin book with a paper cover that gives information about something. ○ *There are numerous pamphlets on how to deal with interviews.*

▶ COLLOCATIONS: **distribute/write/publish** a pamphlet

▶ SYNONYM: booklet

---

paper|work /ˈpeɪpərwɜrk/ `OFFICE`

NONCOUNT NOUN **Paperwork** is work that involves dealing with letters, reports, and records. ○ *The case will not officially be dismissed until both sides file the necessary paperwork.*

▶ COLLOCATIONS:
  file/complete/require/process paperwork
  the **necessary/relevant/extra** paperwork

---

para|graph /ˈpærəgræf/ (paragraphs) `COMMUNICATIONS`

NOUN A **paragraph** is a section of a piece of writing which begins on a new line. ○ *a short introductory paragraph*

▶ COLLOCATIONS:
  read/write/add/revise a paragraph
  the **introductory/preceding/following/final** paragraph

---

par|al|lel /ˈpærəlɛl/

ADJECTIVE If two lines, two objects, or two lines of movement are **parallel**, they are the same distance apart along their whole length. ○ *Sometimes the crystals join together in parallel lines.* ○ [+ with] *The Andes form a mountain range parallel with the coast.*

▶ COLLOCATIONS:
  parallel **with/to** something
  parallel **lines**

---

par|ent com|pa|ny /ˈpɛərənt kʌmpəni/ `ORGANIZATION`
(parent companies)

NOUN A **parent company** is a company that owns more than half the shares of another company. ○ *Workers fear that the job cuts announced by its American parent company may hit Scotland.*

---

park|ing lot /ˈpɑrkɪŋ lɒt/ (parking lots) `OFFICE`

NOUN A **parking lot** is an area of ground where people can leave their cars. ○ *I found a parking lot one block up the street.*

▶ COLLOCATIONS: a **full/empty/deserted** parking lot

par|tial /ˈpɑːʃˀl/

ADJECTIVE You use **partial** to refer to something that is not complete or whole. ○ *He managed to reach a partial agreement with both republics.* ○ *The government has introduced a partial ban on the use of cars in the city.*

▶ **COLLOCATIONS:**
partial **blindness/amnesia/paralysis**
a partial **agreement/solution/explanation**
partial **deregulation/nationalization/privatization**

▶ **SYNONYM:** incomplete

par|tial|ly /ˈpɑːʃəli/

ADVERB If something happens or exists **partially**, it happens or exists to some extent, but not completely. ○ *He was born with a rare genetic condition which has left him partially sighted.* ○ *partially hydrogenated oils*

▶ **COLLOCATIONS:**
partially **sighted/blind/deaf/paralyzed**
partially **responsible/attributable**

▶ **SYNONYM:** partly

---

par|tici|pate /pɑːˈtɪsɪpeɪt/ (participates, participating, participated)　　　[OFFICE]

VERB If you **participate in** an activity, you take part in it. ○ [+ in] *Hundreds of faithful Buddhists participated in the annual ceremony.* ○ [+ in] *Over half the population of this country participate in sports.* ○ [V-ing] *lower rates for participating corporations*

▶ **COLLOCATIONS:**
participate **in** *something*
participate in a **discussion/activity/debate/process**
participate **equally/willingly/effectively**

▶ **SYNONYM:** take part

par|tici|pa|tion /pɑːˌtɪsɪˈpeɪʃˀn/

NONCOUNT NOUN ○ [+ in] *participation in religious activities* ○ [+ of] *a higher level of participation of women in the labor force*

▶ **COLLOCATIONS:**
participation **in** *something*
participation **of/by** *someone*
participation in a **discussion/activity/debate/process**

▶ **SYNONYMS:** involvement, inclusion

par|tici|pant /pɑrtɪsɪpənt/ (participants)

NOUN The **participants** in an activity are the people who take part in it.
○ *Forty of the course participants are offered employment with the company.*
○ *Conference participants agreed that Canada faces an urgent situation with respect to health care provision.*

▶ COLLOCATIONS:
a participant **in** *something*
a participant in a **discussion/activity/debate/process**
a **willing/active/enthusiastic** participant

par|ticu|lar /pərtɪkyələr/

ADJECTIVE You use **particular** to emphasize that you are talking about one thing or one kind of thing rather than other similar ones. ○ *People with a particular blood type (HLA B27) are much more at risk.* ○ *I have to know exactly why it is I'm doing a particular job.*

▶ COLLOCATIONS: a particular **type/brand/kind/case/problem**

▶ SYNONYM: specific

par|ticu|lar|ly /pərtɪkyələrli/

1 **ADVERB** You use **particularly** to indicate that what you are saying applies especially to one thing or situation. ○ *Keep your office space looking good, particularly your desk.* ○ *More local employment will be created, particularly in service industries.*

2 **ADVERB** **Particularly** means more than usual or more than other things. ○ *Progress has been particularly disappointing.* ○ *I particularly liked the wooden chests and chairs.*

▶ COLLOCATIONS:
particularly **in/among** *something*
particularly **useful/important/interesting/relevant**
particularly **vulnerable/sensitive/difficult**
particularly **concerned/pleased/impressed**

▶ SYNONYM: especially

part|ner /pɑrtnər/ (partners) `ORGANIZATION`

NOUN A **partner** is the person you are doing something with, for example, dancing, playing a sport or running a business. ○ *One business partner can insure the life of the other partner.*

p

▶ **COLLOCATIONS:**
  become/find/seek/choose a partner
  a **business/managing/senior/junior** partner

▶ **SYNONYMS:** companion, associate

part|ner|ship /pɑrtnərʃɪp/ (partnerships)

NOUN **Partnership** or a **partnership** is a relationship in which two or more people, organizations, or countries work together as partners.
  ○ [+ between] the partnership between Germany's banks and its businesses
  ○ [+ between] a new partnership between universities and the private sector

▶ **COLLOCATIONS:**
  a partnership **between** people
  a partnership **with** someone
  in partnership
  a **private/strategic/creative/successful/important** partnership
  form/forge/create/strengthen a partnership

▶ **SYNONYMS:** relationship, association, collaboration

part time /pɑrttaɪm/   PERSONNEL

The adjective is spelled **part-time**.

1 ADVERB If you work **part time**, you work for only part of each day or week. ○ I want to work part time.

2 ADJECTIVE **part-time** is also an adjective. ○ She has a part-time job.

▶ **COLLOCATIONS:**
  a part-time **job/worker/employee**
  part-time **work/employment**

▶ **PHRASE:** on a part-time basis

par|ty /pɑrti/ (parties)

NOUN A **party** is a political organization whose members have similar aims and beliefs. Usually the organization tries to get its members elected to the government of a country. ○ a member of the Republican party ○ India's ruling party ○ her resignation as party leader

▶ **COLLOCATIONS:**
  a **political/opposition/governing/ruling** party
  the **Democratic/Republican** party
  a party **leader/member/official/conference**
  party **leadership**
  vote for/support a party

pas|sage /ˈpæsɪdʒ/ (passages)

NOUN A **passage** in a book, speech, or piece of music is a section of it that you are considering separately from the rest. ○ [+ from] *He reads a passage from Milton.* ○ *the passage in which Blake spoke of the world of imagination*

▶ **COLLOCATIONS:**
a passage **from/in** something
quote/recite/read a passage
a **biblical/lyrical** passage

▶ **SYNONYMS:** excerpt, extract, section

pass|port /ˈpæspɔːt/ (passports) `TRAVEL`

NOUN A **passport** is an official document that you have to show when you enter or leave a country. ○ *You should take your passport with you when you change your money.*

▶ **COLLOCATIONS:**
carry/hold/obtain/forge/issue a passport
a **valid/expired/fake** passport
a passport **photo/holder/application/office**

pa|tent /ˈpætᵊnt/ (patents, patenting, patented) `RGD`

1 NOUN A **patent** is an official right to be the only person or company allowed to make or sell a new product for a certain period of time. ○ [+ on] *P&G applied for a patent on its cookies.* ○ [+ for] *He held a number of patents for his many innovations.* ○ *It sued Centrocorp for patent infringement.*

▶ **COLLOCATIONS:**
a patent **on/for** something
grant/issue/own/infringe a patent
a patent **pends/expires**
a **questionable/exclusive/worldwide/existing** patent
a **drug/product/software** patent
patent **infringement/protection**
a patent **application/dispute/attorney**

▶ **RELATED WORD:** copyright

2 VERB If you **patent** something, you obtain a patent for it. ○ *He patented the idea that the atom could be split.* ○ *The invention has been patented by the university.* ○ *a patented machine called the VCR II*

p

> ▶ **COLLOCATIONS:**
> patent a **method/technique/design**
> patent a **device/invention**

> ▶ **PHRASE:** invent and patent something

---

pa|tient /peɪʃᵊnt/ (patients)

HEALTH & FITNESS

NOUN A **patient** is a person who is receiving medical treatment from a doctor or hospital. A **patient** is also someone who is registered with a particular doctor. ○ *The earlier the treatment is given, the better the patient's chances.* ○ *He specialized in treatment of cancer patients.*

> ▶ **COLLOCATIONS:**
> a patient **with** an illness
> **treat/diagnose/cure/help** patients
> patients **undergo/receive** treatment
> a **cancer/MS/cardiac/stroke/mental health** patient
> a **sick/ill/elderly** patient
> patient **care/records**

> ▶ **SYNONYMS:** case, invalid

---

pat|tern /pætərn/ (patterns)

NOUN A **pattern** is the repeated or regular way in which something happens or is done. ○ *All three attacks followed the same pattern.* ○ *[+ of] A change in the pattern of his breathing became apparent.*

> ▶ **COLLOCATIONS:**
> the pattern **of** something
> a pattern of **behavior/activity**
> a **clear/familiar/normal/typical/usual** pattern
> the **same** pattern
> a **behavior/sleep/eating/weather** pattern
> **repeat/follow/establish/change** a pattern
> a pattern **emerges/changes**

> ▶ **SYNONYMS:** arrangement, order

---

pay|able /peɪəbᵊl/

BANKING & FINANCE

ADJECTIVE If an amount of money is **payable**, it has to be paid or it can be paid. ○ *The money is not payable until January 31.*

> ▶ **SYNONYM:** due

pay|check /ˈpeɪtʃɛk/ (paychecks) `PERSONNEL`

NOUN A **paycheck** is the money that your employer gives you for your work. ○ *I get a small paycheck every month.*

▶ **COLLOCATIONS:**
get/earn/collect/draw/receive a paycheck
a **steady/regular/weekly/monthly/large/small** paycheck

pay|day /ˈpeɪdeɪ/ (paydays) `PERSONNEL`

NOUN **Payday** is the day of the week or month on which you receive your wages or salary. ○ *Until next payday, I was literally without any money.*

▶ **COLLOCATIONS:**
miss a payday
a **big/huge** payday

pay|ment /ˈpeɪmənt/ (payments) `BANKING & FINANCE`

1 NOUN A **payment** is an amount of money that is paid to someone.
○ *You will receive 13 monthly payments.*

2 NONCOUNT NOUN **Payment** is the act of paying money. ○ *Players now expect payment for interviews.*

▶ **COLLOCATIONS:**
receive/make/demand/accept a payment
a payment **totals** $x
a payment **is due**
a **monthly/annual/minimum/principal/direct/regular** payment
a **mortgage/interest/debt/welfare/bonus** payment

pay|roll /ˈpeɪroʊl/ (payrolls) `PERSONNEL`

NOUN The people **on** the **payroll** of a company are the people who work for it and are paid by it. ○ *They had 87,000 employees on the payroll.*

▶ **COLLOCATIONS:**
cut/expand/reduce/meet payroll
a payroll **grows/rises/falls/increases**
a **high/annual/public/government** payroll

pe|des|trian /pɪˈdɛstriən/

ADJECTIVE If you describe something as **pedestrian**, you mean that it is ordinary and not at all interesting. ○ *His style is so pedestrian that the book becomes a real bore.*

> ▶ COLLOCATIONS: **rather/fairly/somewhat** pedestrian

> ▶ SYNONYMS: mundane, ordinary

---

pen|al|ty /pɛnˀlti/ (penalties) `LEGAL`

NOUN A **penalty** is a punishment that someone is given for doing something that is against a law or rule. ○ *One of those arrested could face the death penalty.* ○ *The maximum penalty is up to 7 years' imprisonment or an unlimited fine.*

> ▶ COLLOCATIONS:
> the penalty **for** something
> the **maximum/minimum/death** penalty
> a **harsh/severe/tough** penalty
> **award/impose/face** a penalty

> ▶ SYNONYM: punishment

---

pend|ing /pɛndɪŋ/

ADJECTIVE If something is **pending**, it is due to be dealt with or granted. [FORMAL] ○ *The company has ten patents pending in foreign countries.*

> ▶ COLLOCATIONS:
> a pending **notification/outcome/investigation/appeal**
> **still/now/currently** pending

> ▶ SYNONYMS: forthcoming, undecided

---

pen|etrate /pɛnɪtreɪt/ (penetrates, penetrating, penetrated)

VERB If a company **penetrates** a market, it becomes successful in that market. ○ *Manufacturing companies have been successful in penetrating overseas markets in recent years.*

> ▶ SYNONYM: enter

pen|etra|tion /pɛnɪtreɪʃən/

NONCOUNT NOUN The **penetration** of a market by a company is when that company starts being successful in that market. ○ *[+ of] These factors were major elements in the successful foreign penetration of the UK market.*

> ▶ COLLOCATIONS: **increased/low-price** penetration

> ▶ SYNONYM: entry

pen|sion /pɛnʃᵊn/ (pensions)   PERSONNEL

NOUN Someone who has a **pension** receives a regular sum of money from a company or the government because they have retired or because they are widowed or disabled. ○ *struggling by on a pension* ○ *a company pension plan*

> ▶ **COLLOCATIONS:**
> **on** a pension
> **receive** a pension
> a pension **fund/plan**
> a **basic/annual/private/government** pension

> ▶ **SYNONYMS:** allowance, support

pen|sion plan /pɛnʃən plæn/ (pension plans) or **pension scheme**

NOUN A **pension plan** is an arrangement to receive a pension from an organization in return for making regular payments to them over a number of years. ○ *I would have been much wiser to start my own pension plan when I was younger.*

> ▶ **COLLOCATIONS:**
> **contribute to** a pension plan
> a **personal/employee** pension plan

> ▶ **SYNONYMS:** retirement plan, annuity

per capi|ta /pər kæpɪtə/   BANKING & FINANCE

ADJECTIVE The **per capita** amount of something is the total amount of it in a country or area divided by the number of people in that country or area. ○ *They have the world's largest per capita income.* ○ *The per capita consumption of alcohol has dropped over the past two years.*

> ▶ **COLLOCATIONS:** the per capita **income/output/GDP/consumption**

● **Per capita** is also an adverb. ○ *Ethiopia has almost the lowest oil consumption per capita in the world.* ○ *This year Americans will eat about 40% more fresh apples per capita than the Japanese.*

> ▶ **SYNONYM:** per head

per|ceive /pərsiːv/ (perceives, perceiving, perceived)

VERB If you **perceive** someone or something **as** doing or being a particular thing, it is your opinion that they do this thing or that they are that thing. ○ [+ *as*] *Stress is widely perceived as contributing to coronary heart disease.* ○ [+ *as*] *Bioterrorism is perceived as a real threat in the United States.*

→ see note at **regard**

▶ **COLLOCATIONS:**
perceive *something/someone* **as** *something*
perceive *something* as a **threat/risk/challenge**
commonly/widely/generally/traditionally perceived

▶ **SYNONYMS:** believe, consider

per|cep|tion /pərsɛpʃ°n/ (perceptions)

NOUN Your **perception of** something is the way that you think about it or the impression you have of it. ○ [+ *of*] *He is interested in how our perceptions of death affect the way we live.* ○ [+ *among*] *There was still a perception among the public that the city was unsafe.*

▶ **COLLOCATIONS:**
a perception **of** *something*
a perception **among** *people*
a **common/growing/general** perception
reinforce/heighten/foster/counter/alter/challenge a perception

▶ **SYNONYMS:** impression, understanding

---

percent /pəsɛnt/ (percent) also **per cent**

NOUN You use **percent** to talk about amounts. For example, if an amount is 10 percent (10%) of a larger amount, it is equal to 10 hundredths of the larger amount. ○ [+ *of*] *20 to 40 percent of the voters are undecided.* ○ *We aim to increase sales by 10 percent.*

● **Percent** is also an adjective. ○ *There has been a ten percent increase in the number of new students arriving at community colleges this year.*

● **Percent** is also an adverb. ○ *its prediction that house prices will fall 5 percent over the year*

▶ **COLLOCATION:** *x* percent **of** *something*

▶ **SYNONYMS:** percentage, proportion, fraction

BUSINESS CORRESPONDENCE: *Numbers and abbreviations*

In written notes, charts, diagrams, etc., you often use numbers (5, 48) and symbols (%, $, =). You also use words and phrases that are not in full sentences. ○ *62% workers = female; 48% workers = male*

In more formal writing, you can use numbers and some symbols for statistics, but you need to put these into full sentences. All three versions below are acceptable. ○ *62% of the workers are female and 48% are male.* ○ *62 percent of the workers are female and 48 percent are male.*

○ *Sixty-two percent of the workers are female and forty-eight percent are male.*

It is common to write small numbers in words (four, ten, twelve), but large numbers are usually written in numbers (478, 256).

per|cent|age /pərsɛntɪdʒ/ (percentages)

NOUN A **percentage** is a fraction of an amount expressed as a particular number of hundredths of that amount. ○ [+ of] *Only a few vegetable-origin foods have such a high percentage of protein.* ○ [+ of] *A large percentage of the population speaks fluent English.*

▶ **COLLOCATIONS:**
a percentage **of** something
a percentage of the **population/workforce/household**
a **large/high/sizable/significant/small/tiny/low** percentage

▶ **SYNONYMS:** proportion, amount

USAGE: *percent* or *percentage?*

You use **percent** after a number to express an exact amount.
○ *10%/ten percent of customers*

You use **percentage** to talk more generally about a proportion of a group or amount. ○ *We found a higher percentage of women were being accepted.*

P

per|fect /pɜrfɪkt/

ADJECTIVE Something that is **perfect** is as good as it could possibly be.
○ *He spoke perfect English.*

▶ **COLLOCATIONS:**
perfect **timing/picture/condition**
nearly/absolutely/almost perfect
a perfect **example/solution/opportunity/start**

▶ **SYNONYM:** faultless

per|form /pərfɔrm/ (performs, performing, performed)

1 VERB When you **perform** a task or action, especially a complicated one, you do it. ○ *A robot capable of performing the most complex brain surgery was* *unveiled by scientists yesterday.* ○ *Several grafts may be performed at one operation.*

2 **VERB** If something **performs** a particular function, it has that function.
○ *A complex engine has many separate components, each performing a different function.* ○ *Software can be run on a computer to enable it to perform various tasks.*

▶ **COLLOCATIONS:** perform a **task/action/act/function**

▶ **SYNONYMS:** carry out, undertake

3 **VERB** If someone or something **performs well**, they work well or achieve a good result. If they **perform badly**, they work badly or achieve a poor result. ○ *He had not performed well on his exams.* ○ *State-owned industries will always perform poorly.*

▶ **COLLOCATIONS:**
perform **well/strongly/admirably/consistently**
perform **badly/poorly/dismally**

▶ **SYNONYM:** work

4 **VERB** If you **perform** a play, a piece of music, or a dance, you do it in front of an audience. ○ *Gardiner has pursued relentlessly high standards in performing classical music.* ○ *This play was first performed in 411 BC.*
○ *He began performing in the early fifties, singing and playing guitar.*

▶ **COLLOCATIONS:**
perform **at** *something*
performed **by** *someone*
perform a **concert/dance/song/play/routine**
perform at a **concert/wedding/reception**
perform **live**
performed by **a musician/orchestra/choir**

▶ **SYNONYMS:** act, present

per|for|mance /pərfɔ̱rməns/ (performances)

1 **NOUN** Someone's or something's **performance** is how successful they are or how well they do something. ○ [+ *of*] *That study looked at the performance of 18 surgeons.* ○ *The job of the new director-general was to ensure that performance targets were met.*

▶ **COLLOCATIONS:**
the performance **of** *someone/something*
good/strong/solid/poor/disappointing performance
financial/economic performance
improve/enhance/measure performance
performance **targets/indicators/criteria/standards**

2 NOUN The **performance of** a task is the fact or action of doing it.
○ [+ of] *He devoted in excess of seventy hours a week to the performance of his duties.* ○ [+ of] *The people believe that the performance of this ritual is the will of the Great Spirit.*

▶ COLLOCATIONS:
the performance **of** *something*
the performance of a **procedure/task/operation/duty**
the performance of a **ritual/ceremony/rite**

3 NOUN A **performance** involves entertaining an audience by doing something such as singing, dancing, or acting. ○ [+ of] *Inside the theater, they were giving a performance of Bizet's Carmen.* ○ [+ as] *her performance as the betrayed Medea*

▶ COLLOCATIONS:
a performance **of** *something*
a performance **as** *someone*
a **live/good/outstanding/poor** performance
give a performance

▶ SYNONYMS: production, show

---

per|haps /pərhæps, præps/

ADVERB **Perhaps** is used for showing that you are not sure whether something is true or possible. ○ *Perhaps, in time, they will understand.*

▶ SYNONYM: maybe

---

per|ma|nent /pɜrmənənt/   PERSONNEL

1 ADJECTIVE Something that is **permanent** lasts forever. ○ *Heavy drinking can cause permanent damage to the brain.* ○ *The ban is intended to be permanent.*

2 ADJECTIVE A **permanent** employee is one who is employed for an unlimited length of time. ○ *At the end of the probationary period you will become a permanent employee.* ○ *a permanent job*

▶ COLLOCATIONS:
permanent **residence/status/employment**
a permanent **job/position/vacancy/employee/worker**
permanent **damage/disability**

▶ SYNONYMS: ongoing, lasting

per|mit (permits, permitting, permitted)

> The verb is pronounced /pərmɪt/. The noun is pronounced /pɜrmɪt/.

1 VERB If someone **permits** something, they allow it to happen. If they **permit** you **to** do something, they allow you to do it. [FORMAL] ○ *He can let the court's decision stand and permit the execution.* ○ [+ to-inf] *Employees are permitted to use the golf course during their free hours.* ○ [+ into] *No outside journalists have been permitted into the country.*

▶ **COLLOCATIONS:**
   be permitted **into** somewhere
   be permitted to **visit/enter/travel**
   a **law/rule** permits something
   permit **smoking/access/use**
   expressly/legally/knowingly permit

▶ **SYNONYMS:** allow, let

2 NOUN A **permit** is an official document which says that you may do something. For example you usually need a **permit** to work in a foreign country. ○ *The majority of foreign nationals working here have work permits.*

▶ **COLLOCATIONS:**
   issue/grant/obtain/require a permit
   a **work/residence/building** permit
   a **special/temporary/necessary** permit
   a permit **holder/application/request/fee**

▶ **SYNONYMS:** warrant, license

per|mis|sion /pərmɪʃⁿn/

NONCOUNT NOUN If someone who has authority over you gives you **permission to** do something, they say that they will allow you to do it. ○ *He asked permission to leave the room.* ○ [+ for] *Police said permission for the march had not been granted.* ○ *They cannot leave the country without permission.*

▶ **COLLOCATIONS:**
   with/without permission
   permission **for** something
   ask/receive permission
   give/grant/refuse permission
   written/special/official/government permission

▶ **SYNONYMS:** authorization, consent

per|sis|tent /pərsɪstənt/

ADJECTIVE Something that is **persistent** continues to exist or happen for a long time; used especially about bad or undesirable states or situations. ○ *Her position as national leader has been weakened by persistent fears of another coup attempt.* ○ *The public has to be reassured that children are safe from persistent predatory offenders.*

▶ **COLLOCATIONS:**
a persistent **rumor/offender**
a persistent **infection/cough/headache**
persistent **speculation/refusal/rain**
more/increasingly/stubbornly persistent

▶ **SYNONYMS:** continuous, constant, relentless, perpetual, incessant

per|son|al /pɜrsənᵊl/ `OFFICE`

1 ADJECTIVE A **personal** opinion, quality, or thing belongs or relates to one particular person rather than to other people. ○ *In addition to being clear and simple, survey questions should never convey your personal opinions.* ○ *books, furniture, and other personal belongings* ○ *an estimated personal fortune of almost seventy million dollars*

2 ADJECTIVE Personal matters relate to your feelings, relationships, and health. ○ *teaching young people about marriage and personal relationships* ○ *Mr. Knight said that he had resigned for personal reasons.*

▶ **COLLOCATIONS:**
a personal **opinion/belief/experience/reason/matter/choice**
a personal **relationship/life**
personal **effects/belongings/property/fortune/wealth**
deeply/intensely/highly/strictly personal

▶ **SYNONYMS:** private, individual

per|son|al com|put|er /pɜrsənəl kəmpyutər/ (personal computers)

NOUN A **personal computer** is a computer that you use at work, school, or home. ○ *The personal computer has created an explosion of opportunities for changes in when and where work is done.*

per|son|nel /pɜrsənɛl/ `PERSONNEL`

PLURAL NOUN The **personnel** of an organization are the people who work for it. ○ *military personnel*

▶ **COLLOCATIONS:**
  train/involve personnel
  personnel **serve/work**
  military/medical/civilian/armed/key personnel

▶ **SYNONYM:** workers

per|spec|tive /pərspɛktɪv/ (perspectives)

NOUN A particular **perspective** is a particular way of thinking about something, especially one that is influenced by your beliefs or experiences: ○ [+ on] *two different perspectives on the nature of adolescent development* ○ [+ of] *Most literature on the subject of immigrants in France has been written from the perspective of the French themselves.* ○ *I would like to offer a historical perspective.*

▶ **COLLOCATIONS:**
  a perspective **on** *something*
  the perspective **of** *someone*
  from the perspective of *someone/something*
  a **historical/feminist/sociological** perspective
  a **different/new/fresh** perspective

▶ **SYNONYMS:** viewpoint, position

per|suade /pərsweɪd/ (persuades, persuading, persuaded)

VERB If you **persuade** someone **to** do something, you cause them to do it by giving them good reasons for doing it. ○ [+ to-inf] *We're trying to persuade manufacturers to sell them here.* ○ [+ to-inf] *They were eventually persuaded by the police to give themselves up.*

▶ **COLLOCATIONS:**
  be persuaded **by** *something/someone*
  try/attempt/fail to persuade
  eventually/finally/successfully persuade
  easily persuaded
  persuaded by an **argument**
  persuade *someone* to **stay/reconsider/join**

▶ **SYNONYMS:** convince, cajole, urge

pe|ti|tion /pətɪʃ°n/ (petitions, petitioning, petitioned)

1 NOUN A **petition** is a document signed by a lot of people that asks a government or other official group to do a particular thing. ○ *a petition signed by 4,500 people·*

▶ COLLOCATIONS:
sign/support/challenge a petition
circulate/present/organize a petition
a **public-interest/anti-war** petition
a **formal/written/online** a petition

2 NOUN A **petition** is a formal request made to a court of law for some legal action to be taken. ○ *His lawyers filed a petition for all charges to be dropped.* ○ *a petition asking Congress to reconsider the law*

3 VERB If you **petition** someone in authority, you make a formal request to them. ○ [+ *for*] *couples petitioning for divorce* ○ *All the attempts to petition Congress had failed.*

▶ COLLOCATIONS:
petition *someone* **for** *something*
petition for **divorce/citizenship/custody**

---

phase /feɪz/ (phases)

NOUN A **phase** is a particular stage in a process or in the gradual development of something. ○ [+ *of*] *This autumn, 6,000 residents will participate in the first phase of the project.* ○ *The crisis is entering a crucial, critical phase.*

▶ COLLOCATIONS:
a phase **of** *something*
enter/commence/begin/undergo a phase
mark/herald/signal a phase
a **first/initial/early** phase
a **transitional/experimental/developmental** phase
a **crucial/critical/decisive** phase

▶ SYNONYMS: stage, period

---

phe|nom|enon /fɪnɒmɪnɒn/ (phenomena)

NOUN A **phenomenon** is something that is observed to happen or exist. [FORMAL] ○ *scientific explanations of natural phenomena*

▶ COLLOCATIONS:
explain/study/describe a phenomenon
a **strange/unexplained/natural** phenomenon

P

phone call /foʊn kɔl/ (phone calls)

COMMUNICATIONS

NOUN If you make a **phone call**, you enter a number into a telephone and speak to someone who is in another place. ○ *I'll make the right phone calls to set it up.*

▶ **COLLOCATIONS:**
a phone call **to/from** someone
make/receive a phone call

photo|copy /foʊtəkɒpi/ (photocopies, photocopying, photocopied)

OFFICE

1 NOUN A **photocopy** is a copy of a document that you make using a special machine (= a photocopier). ○ *He gave me a photocopy of the letter.*

2 VERB If you **photocopy** a document, you make a copy of it using a photocopier.

▶ **COLLOCATIONS:**
a photocopy **of** something
send/accept a photocopy
a photocopy **machine**
photocopy a **page/sheet/letter**

photo|graph /foʊtəgræf/ (photographs, photographing, photographed)

1 NOUN A **photograph** is a picture that you take with a camera. ○ *He wants to take some photographs of the house.*

▶ **COLLOCATIONS:**
take/frame/publish/release/carry a photograph
a photograph **shows/depicts/captures** something
a **black-and-white/aerial/digital/indecent** photograph

2 VERB When you **photograph** someone or something, you use a camera to take a picture of them. [FORMAL] ○ *She photographed the designs.*

▶ **COLLOCATIONS:**
photograph a **scene/landscape**
beautifully/secretly/rarely photographed

physi|cal /fɪzɪkəl/

ADJECTIVE Physical qualities, actions, or things are connected with a person's body, rather than with their mind. ○ *the physical and mental problems caused by the illness* ○ *Physical activity promotes good health.*

▶ **COLLOCATIONS:**
physical **activities/exercise/exertion**

physical **strength/fitness**
a physical **symptom/disability/illness**
physical **contact/pain/abuse/attraction**
purely physical

▸ SYNONYM: bodily

---

pink slip /pɪŋk slɪp/ (pink slips) PERSONNEL

NOUN A **pink slip** is a form given to employees to inform them that they
are no longer needed to do the job that they have been doing.
[INFORMAL] ○ *It was his fourth pink slip in two years.*

▸ COLLOCATIONS:
get/receive/issue a pink slip
hand *someone* a pink slip

---

plat|form /plætfɔrm/ (platforms) OFFICE

NOUN A **platform** is a flat raised structure on which someone or
something can stand. ○ *He walked toward the platform to begin his speech.*

▸ COLLOCATIONS: **build/raise/provide** a platform

---

plum|met /plʌmɪt/ (plummets, plummeting, plummeted)

VERB If an amount, rate, or price **plummets**, it decreases quickly by
a large amount. ○ *Temperatures plummeted as a cold front swept in from the
North Pole.* ○ [+ from/to/by] *The shares have plummeted from 130p to 2.25p in
the past year.*

▸ COLLOCATIONS:
plummet **to** *something*
plummet **from/by/to** *x*
weight/temperature plummets
stocks/shares/share prices plummet
someone's **popularity/confidence/self-esteem** plummets

▸ PHRASE: plummet to an all-time low

▸ SYNONYMS: plunge, drop, fall

---

poli|cy /pɒlɪsi/ (policies) BANKING & FINANCE

NOUN A **policy** is a set of ideas or plans that is used as a basis for making
decisions, especially in politics, economics, or business. ○ *plans which
include changes in foreign policy and economic reforms* ○ *the U.N.'s policy-
making body*

▶ **COLLOCATIONS:**
foreign/monetary/economic/fiscal/social/public policy
defense/energy/transport/immigration policy
a **new/official** policy
policy **making**
a policy **maker/adviser/committee/analyst**
a policy **shift/change**

▶ **PHRASE:** policy and procedure

▶ **SYNONYMS:** procedure, approach, protocol

policy|holder /pɒlɪsihoʊldər/ (policyholders)

NOUN A **policyholder** is a person who has an insurance policy with an insurance company. ○ *The first 10 percent of legal fees will be paid by the policyholder.*

▶ **COLLOCATIONS:**
protect/represent a policyholder
a **long-suffering/existing/individual** policyholder

pol|lu|tion /pəluʃⁱn/

1 NONCOUNT NOUN Pollution is the process of polluting water, air, or land, especially with poisonous chemicals. ○ [+ *of*] *The fine was for the company's pollution of the air near its plants.* ○ *Recycling also helps control environmental pollution by reducing the need for waste dumps.*

2 NONCOUNT NOUN Pollution is poisonous or dirty substances that are polluting the water, air, or land somewhere. ○ *The level of pollution in the river was falling.*

▶ **COLLOCATIONS:**
pollution **of** *something*
pollution of the **ocean/air/environment**
air/noise/water/light pollution
atmospheric/environmental/industrial pollution
curb/cut/reduce/combat/cause pollution
pollution **control**
a pollution **level/problem**

▶ **SYNONYMS:** emissions, contamination

pon|der /pɒndər/ (ponders, pondering, pondered)

VERB If you **ponder** something, you think about it carefully. ○ *I found myself constantly pondering the question: "How could anyone do these things?"*

○ [+ over] *He pondered over the difficulties involved.*

▶ **COLLOCATIONS:**
ponder the **question/possibility/meaning**
ponder **aloud/quietly/deeply/seriously**
ponder **how/what/why**

▶ **SYNONYM:** think

popu|lar /pɒpyələr/

ADJECTIVE Something that is **popular** is enjoyed or liked by a lot of people.
○ *This is the most popular ball game ever devised.* ○ *These courses have proved very popular with students.*

▶ **COLLOCATIONS:**
popular **among/with** *people*
popular among/with **tourists/locals/the public/students**
popular among/with **voters/consumers/users/buyers**
hugely/wildly/immensely/extremely popular
a popular **destination/resort/pastime/song/choice**
prove/become/remain popular

▶ **SYNONYMS:** well-liked, sought-after

popu|la|tion /pɒpyəleɪʃⁿn/ (populations)

1 NOUN The **population** of a country or area is all the people who live in it.
○ [+ of] *Bangladesh now has a population of about 110 million.* ○ *the annual rate of population growth*

▶ **COLLOCATIONS:**
a population **of** *x*
population **density/size/growth/increase/decline**
the **local/entire** population
population **control**

2 NOUN If you refer to a particular type of **population** in a country or area, you are referring to all the people or animals of that type there.
[FORMAL] ○ *75.6 percent of the male population over sixteen* ○ *areas with a large black population* ○ *the elephant populations of Tanzania and Kenya*

▶ **COLLOCATIONS:**
a **male/female/elderly/aging/working-age** population
a **black/white/Muslim/Jewish/Asian/minority** population
a **deer/elephant/bird/fox** population

port|fo|lio /pɔrtfóʊlioʊ/ (portfolios)　[PERSONNEL]

NOUN A **portfolio** is a collection of examples of someone's work. ○ *After dinner that evening, Edith showed them a portfolio of her own political cartoons.*

▶ **COLLOCATIONS:**
  manage/build a portfolio
  a **diversified/balanced/free** portfolio
  a **property/investment/stock/product** portfolio

por|tion /pɔrʃ°n/ (portions)

NOUN A **portion of** something is a part of it. ○ [+ *of*] *Damage was confined to a small portion of the castle.* ○ [+ *of*] *The protein portion of the enzyme is referred to as an apoprotein.* ○ [+ *of*] *the verbal and mathematics portions of the test*

▶ **COLLOCATIONS:**
  a portion **of** *something*
  a **large/major/sizable/small** portion
  a **substantial/significant/considerable** portion

▶ **SYNONYM:** part

po|si|tion /pəzíʃ°n/ (positions)　[PERSONNEL]

1 **NOUN** The **position** of someone or something is the place where they are in relation to other things. ○ *The ship was identified, and its name and position were reported to the coast guard.* ○ *This conservatory enjoys an enviable position overlooking a leafy expanse.*

▶ **COLLOCATIONS:**
  the position **of** *something*
  occupy/hold/enjoy a position
  a position **overlooking** *something*

▶ **SYNONYMS:** location, setting, place

2 **NOUN** Your **position** in society is the role and the importance that you have in it. ○ [+ *of*] *the position of older people in society* ○ [+ *of*] *the profoundly radical changes to the position of women in Great Britain brought about by the Divorce Act of 1857*

▶ **SYNONYMS:** standing, role

3 **NOUN** A **position** in a company or organization is a job. [FORMAL] ○ [+ *with*] *He left a career in teaching to take up a position with the Arts Council.* ○ *Hyundai said this week it is scaling back its U.S. operations by eliminating 50 positions.*

▶ **COLLOCATIONS:**
the position **of** something/someone
a position **in/with/as** something
a position in/with a **company/organization/firm**
a position as **chairman/president/director**
the position of **clerk/assistant/consultant**
occupy/accept/advertise/vacate a position

▶ **SYNONYM:** post

EXTEND YOUR VOCABULARY

In everyday English, you talk about someone's **job** to refer to the work they do. ○ *He got a job at the local supermarket stacking shelves.*

In a business context, you can talk about a specific job with a **job title** and a **job description** as a **position**, a **post**, or a **role**. ○ *She has moved to a part-time position as an editorial consultant.* ○ *More women are moving into management roles.*

When an organization needs new staff, they advertise a **vacancy**.
○ *a list of current vacancies*

---

4 NOUN Your **position on** a particular matter is your attitude toward it or your opinion of it. [FORMAL] ○ [+ *on*] *He could be depended on to take a moderate position on most of the key issues.* ○ [+ *on*] *Mr. Howard is afraid to state his true position on the republic, which is that he is opposed to it.*

▶ **COLLOCATIONS:**
a position **on** something
take/assume/adopt a position on something
a **moderate/clear/understandable** position

▶ **SYNONYMS:** stance, opinion, attitude

---

posi|tive /pɒzɪtɪv/

ADJECTIVE A **positive** fact, situation, or experience is pleasant and helpful to you in some way. ○ *The project will have a positive impact on the economy.* ○ *Working abroad should be an exciting and positive experience for all concerned.*

● **The positive** in a situation is the good and pleasant aspects of it.
○ *Work on the positive, creating beautiful, loving, and fulfilling relationships.*

▶ **COLLOCATIONS:**
a positive **experience/outcome/effect/result/influence/impact**

overwhelmingly/extremely/generally positive

▶ **SYNONYMS:** beneficial, advantageous

posi|tive|ly /pɒzɪtɪvli/

ADVERB ○ *You must try to start thinking positively.*

▶ **COLLOCATIONS: respond/react/think** positively

▶ **SYNONYM:** definitely

---

pos|sess /pəzɛs/ (possesses, possessing, possessed)

1 VERB If you **possess** something, you have it or own it. ○ *He was then arrested and charged with possessing an offensive weapon.* ○ *He is said to possess a fortune of more than two-and-a-half-thousand million dollars.*

▶ **COLLOCATIONS:**
illegally/unlawfully possess *something*
possess a **weapon**
possess **drugs/pornography**

▶ **SYNONYMS:** own, have

2 VERB If someone or something **possesses** a particular quality, ability, or feature, they have it. [FORMAL] ○ *individuals who are deemed to possess the qualities of sense, loyalty, and discretion* ○ *This figure has long been held to possess miraculous power.*

▶ **COLLOCATIONS:**
possess a **quality/skill/talent**
possess **power/knowledge/strength**

EXTEND YOUR VOCABULARY

Have is a very common verb in everyday English and can be used in many contexts. ○ *She has a big house, lots of money and a great job.*

You can say that someone **owns** something or that it **belongs to** them if it is their property. ○ *All the directors own shares in the company.* ○ *The land belongs to a local farmer.*

In more formal writing, and in legal contexts, you can say that someone **possesses** something. ○ *He was convicted of illegally possessing firearms.*

You can also say that someone **possesses** a quality or an ability. ○ *Candidates should possess good communication skills.*

pos|ses|sion /pəzɛʃ°n/ (possessions)

1 **NONCOUNT NOUN** If you are **in possession of** something, you have it, because you have obtained it or because it belongs to you. [FORMAL]
○ [+ of] *Those documents are now in the possession of theWashington Post.*
○ [+ of] *There is no legal remedy for her to gain possession of the house.*
○ *Religious pamphlets were found in their possession.*

▶ COLLOCATIONS:
possession **of** *something*
in *someone's* possession
gain/lose/surrender/retain possession of *something*
illegal/unlawful possession of *something*
possession of a **weapon**
possession of **drugs/pornography**

▶ SYNONYM: ownership

2 **NOUN** Your **possessions** are the things that you own or have with you at a particular time. ○ *People had lost their homes and all their possessions.* ○ *the acquisition of material possessions*

▶ COLLOCATIONS: **prized/treasured/material/personal** possessions

▶ SYNONYM: belongings

---

pos|sible /pɒsɪb°l/

1 **ADJECTIVE** If it is **possible to** do something, it can be done. ○ [+ to-inf] *If it is possible to find out where your brother is, we shall.* ○ *Everything is possible if we want it enough.* ○ *anesthetics which have made modern surgery possible*

2 **ADJECTIVE** A **possible** event is one that might happen. ○ *He referred the matter to the Attorney General for possible action against several newspapers.* ○ *Her family is discussing a possible move to America.* ○ *One possible solution, if all else fails, is to take legal action.*

3 **ADJECTIVE** If you say that it is **possible that** something is true or correct, you mean that although you do not know whether it is true or correct, you accept that it might be. ○ *It is possible that there's an explanation for all this.*

▶ COLLOCATIONS:
a possible **explanation/cause/link/motive**
a possible **scenario/outcome/solution/exception**
make *something* possible
everything/anything is possible
possible to **imagine/identify/avoid** *something*

perfectly/humanly/entirely/remotely possible
physically/technically possible

▶ **SYNONYMS:** potential, conceivable, likely

EXTEND YOUR VOCABULARY

You can use words like **possible/possibly**, **probable/probably**, **likely**, and **unlikely** to show how certain you are about what you are saying and to avoid making statements that may not be true.
○ *Some checks were returned undelivered, possibly due to wrong addresses.*
○ *the probable/likely cause of the crisis* ○ *Such restrictions seem unlikely to have much effect.*

---

pos|sibil|ity /pɒsɪbɪlɪti/ (possibilities)

NOUN If you say there is a **possibility that** something is the case or **that** something will happen, you mean that it might be the case or it might happen. ○ [+ that] *We were not in the least worried about the possibility that candy could rot the teeth.* ○ *Tax on food has become a very real possibility.*

▶ **COLLOCATIONS:**
the possibility **of** something
explore/discuss/raise/consider a possibility
a **distinct/remote/real** possibility

▶ **SYNONYMS:** chance, likelihood

pos|sibly /pɒsɪbli/

ADVERB You use **possibly** to indicate that you are not sure whether something is true or might happen. ○ *Exercise will not only lower blood pressure but possibly protect against heart attacks.* ○ *a painful and possibly fatal operation* ○ *Do you think that he could possibly be right?*

▶ **COLLOCATIONS:**
quite/just possibly
possibly **harmful/illegal/fatal**

▶ **SYNONYM:** perhaps

---

post|pone /poʊstpoʊn, poʊspoʊn/ (postpones, postponing, postponed)

VERB If you **postpone** an event, you delay it or arrange for it to take place at a later time than was originally planned. ○ *The President is postponing the referendum, due to have been held in October, until August next year.*

○ *The visit has now been postponed indefinitely.*

▶ **COLLOCATIONS:**
  postpone *something* **indefinitely/temporarily**
  postpone *something* **until** *something*
  postpone a **decision/event/election/visit**

▶ **SYNONYM:** delay

post|pone|ment /poʊstpoʊnmənt, poʊspoʊn-/ (postponements)

NOUN ○ *The postponement was due to a dispute over where the talks should be held.* ○ [+ of] *Mandela agreed to the postponement of undiluted one-man, one-vote majority rule.*

▶ **COLLOCATIONS:**
  the postponement **of** something
  the postponement of a **meeting/election**
  force/cause/request/announce a postponement

▶ **SYNONYM:** delay

po|ten|tial /pətɛnʃˀl/

NONCOUNT NOUN If you say that someone or something has **potential**, you mean that they have the necessary abilities or qualities to become successful or useful in the future. ○ *The boy has great potential.* ○ *The school strives to treat students as individuals and to help each one to achieve their full potential.*

▶ **COLLOCATIONS:**
  realize/recognize potential
  have/possess/offer potential
  fulfill/maximize *your* potential
  enormous/tremendous/considerable/great potential
  untapped/future/long-term potential

po|ten|tial|ly /pətɛnʃəli/

ADVERB ○ *Clearly this is a potentially dangerous situation.* ○ *Potentially this could damage the reputation of the whole industry.*

▶ **COLLOCATIONS:**
  potentially **dangerous/lethal/fatal**
  potentially **damage/contaminate/harm** *someone/something*

▶ **SYNONYM:** possibly

prac|ti|cal /ˈpræktɪkᵊl/

ADJECTIVE Practical things involve real situations rather than ideas or theories. ○ *practical suggestions on how to increase the fiber in your diet* ○ *We don't know any practical ways to prevent cancer.*

▶ **COLLOCATIONS:**
practical **advice**
a practical **suggestion**
a practical **application/use**

▶ **SYNONYMS:** useful, pragmatic, realistic

prac|ti|cal|ly /ˈpræktɪkli/

ADVERB Practically means almost. ○ *He's known the old man practically all his life.*

▶ **COLLOCATIONS:** practically **impossible/non-existent/identical**

▶ **PHRASE:** practically all

prac|tice /ˈpræktɪs/ (practices, practicing, practiced)

1 VERB When people **practice** something such as a custom, craft, or religion, they take part in the activities associated with it. [in BRIT, use **practise**] ○ *countries which practice multi-party politics* ○ *Acupuncture was practiced in China as long ago as the third millennium BC.*

▶ **COLLOCATIONS:**
practice a **custom/craft/religion**
practice **yoga/meditation/acupuncture**
commonly/routinely/widely practiced

2 NOUN You can refer to something that people do regularly as a **practice**. ○ *Some firms have cut workers' pay below the level set in their contract, a practice that is illegal in Germany.* ○ *The prime minister demanded a public inquiry into bank practices.*

▶ **COLLOCATIONS:**
the practice **of** *something*
the practice of **medicine/yoga/meditation**
a **corrupt/controversial/illegal** practice
common/normal/accepted practice

▶ **SYNONYMS:** custom, habit, procedure, system

---

pre|cede /prɪsiːd/ (precedes, preceding, preceded)

VERB If one event or period of time **precedes** another, it happens before it.
[FORMAL] ○ *Intensive negotiations between the main parties preceded the vote.*
○ [+ by] *The earthquake was preceded by a loud roar and lasted 20 seconds.*
○ [V-ing] *Industrial orders had already fallen in the preceding months.*

▶ COLLOCATIONS:
immediately/usually/always/often precede *something*
precede a **date/chapter/arrival**
a **period/month/warning** precedes *something*

prec|edent /prɛsɪdənt/ (precedents)

NOUN If there is a **precedent for** an action or event, it has happened before, and this can be regarded as an argument for doing it again.
[FORMAL] ○ [+ for] *The trial could set an important precedent for dealing with large numbers of similar cases.* ○ *There are plenty of precedents in Hollywood for letting people out of contracts.*

▶ COLLOCATIONS:
a precedent **for** *something*
set/establish/create/follow a precedent
a **dangerous/historical/legal** precedent

---

pre|cious /prɛʃəs/

1 **ADJECTIVE** If you say that something such as a resource is **precious**, you mean that it is valuable and should not be wasted or used badly. ○ *After four months in foreign parts, every hour at home was precious.* ○ *A family break allows you to spend precious time together.*

▶ COLLOCATIONS: a precious **commodity/resource/moment**

▶ SYNONYM: valuable

2 **ADJECTIVE** **Precious** objects and materials are worth a lot of money because they are rare. ○ *jewelry and precious objects belonging to her mother*

▶ **COLLOCATIONS:**
a precious **jewel/gem/stone**
a precious **artefact/heirloom/belonging/possession**

▶ **SYNONYM:** valuable

---

pre|cise /prɪsaɪs/

1 **ADJECTIVE** You use **precise** to emphasize that you are referring to an exact thing, rather than something vague. ○ *The precise location of the wreck was discovered in 1988.* ○ *He was not clear on the precise nature of his mission.* ○ *We will never know the precise details of his death.*

2 **ADJECTIVE** Something that is **precise** is exact and accurate in all its details. ○ *They speak very precise English.* ○ *His comments were precise and to the point.*

▶ **COLLOCATIONS:**
precise **details/figures/English**
the precise **moment/nature/location**
precise **information/instructions/measurements**
a precise **definition/description**

▶ **PHRASE:** precise and to the point

▶ **SYNONYMS:** exact, accurate

pre|cise|ly /prɪsaɪsli/

1 **ADVERB** **Precisely** means accurately and exactly. ○ *Nobody knows precisely how many people are still living in the camp.* ○ *The meeting began at precisely 4:00 p.m.*

▶ **COLLOCATIONS:**
at precisely *x o'clock*
know/ascertain/calculate *something* precisely
measure/specify/define *something* precisely

▶ **PHRASE:** precisely and accurately

▶ **SYNONYMS:** exactly, accurately

2 **ADVERB** You can use **precisely** to emphasize that a reason or fact is the only important one there is, or that it is obvious. ○ *Children come to zoos precisely to see captive animals.* ○ *That is precisely the result the system is designed to produce.*

pre|ci|sion /prɪsɪʒ³n/

NONCOUNT NOUN **Precision** is the quality of being exact and accurate in every detail. ○ *The interior is planned with military precision.*

▶ COLLOCATIONS:
with precision
military/surgical/geometric/absolute precision

▶ SYNONYMS: exactness, accuracy

---

pre|de|ces|sor /prɛdɪsɛsər/ (predecessors) `PERSONNEL`

1 NOUN Your **predecessor** is the person who had your job before you. ○ *He learned everything he knew from his predecessor.*

2 NOUN The **predecessor** of an object or machine is the object or machine that came before it in a sequence or process of development. ○ *Although the car is some 2 inches shorter than its predecessor*

▶ COLLOCATIONS:
a **legendary/long-serving/better-known** predecessor
a **medieval/18th-century** predecessor

▶ SYNONYM: forerunner

---

pre|dict /prɪdɪkt/ (predicts, predicting, predicted)

VERB If you **predict** an event, you say that it will happen. ○ *Chinese seismologists have predicted earthquakes this year in Western China.* ○ [+ that] *Some analysts were predicting that online sales during the holiday season could top $10 billion.* ○ [+ when] *tests that accurately predict when you are most fertile*

▶ COLLOCATIONS:
predict an **event/outcome**
predict a **fall/drop/decline/rise/recovery/upturn**
a **forecaster/economist/analyst** predicts *something*
predict *something* **accurately/confidently/correctly**
impossible/difficult/possible to predict
widely/rightly/wrongly predicted

▶ SYNONYMS: forecast, foresee

pre|dict|able /prɪdɪktəbəl/

ADJECTIVE ○ *This was a predictable reaction, given the bitter hostility between the two countries.* ○ *The result was entirely predictable.*

▶ COLLOCATIONS:
a predictable **reaction/outcome/consequence**
entirely/wholly/fairly predictable

▶ PHRASE: predictable and formulaic

pre|dic|tion /prɪdɪkʃⁿn/ (predictions)

NOUN ○ [+ about] *He was unwilling to make a prediction about which books would sell in the coming year.* ○ *Weather prediction has never been a perfect science.*

▶ **COLLOCATIONS:**
   a prediction **about/of** *something*
   make/confirm/defy/dismiss a prediction
   weather/climate/earthquake prediction
   a **reliable/accurate** prediction

▶ **SYNONYMS:** forecast, prophecy

---

pre|fer /prɪfɜr/ (prefers, preferring, preferred)

VERB If you **prefer** someone or something, you like that person or thing better than another, and so you are more likely to choose them if there is a choice. ○ *Centipedes are nocturnal and generally prefer moist conditions such as forests or woodlands.* ○ [+ to] *I became a teacher because I preferred books and people to politics.* ○ [+ to-inf] *Many would prefer to go to Canada and elsewhere.*

▶ **COLLOCATIONS:**
   prefer *something* **to** *something*
   prefer to **stay/remain** *somewhere*
   prefer to **focus/concentrate/rely** on *something*
   prefer to **avoid/forget/ignore** *something*
   generally/still/much prefer
   prefer an **approach**

▶ **SYNONYMS:** favor, choose

pref|er|able /prɛfərəbᵊl, prɛfrə-, prɪfɜrə-/

ADJECTIVE When one thing is **preferable to** another, it is better or more suitable. ○ [+ to] *For many, a trip to the supermarket is preferable to buying food on the Internet.*

▶ **SYNONYM:** better

pref|er|ence /prɛfərəns/ (preferences)

NOUN If you have a **preference for** something, you would like to have or do that thing rather than something else. ○ [+ for] *Parents can express a preference for the school their child attends.* ○ [+ to] *Many of these products were bought in preference to their own.*

▶ **COLLOCATIONS:**
a preference **for** something
in preference **to** something
a **personal/individual/sexual** preference
a **consumer/customer/voter/patient** preference
express/give/show a preference

▶ **SYNONYMS:** choice, selection

---

pre|limi|nary /prɪlɪmɪnɛri/

ADJECTIVE Preliminary activities or discussions take place at the beginning of an event, often as a form of preparation. ○ *Preliminary results show the Republican party with 11 percent of the vote.* ○ *Preliminary talks on the future of the bases began yesterday.*

▶ **COLLOCATIONS:**
a preliminary **report/hearing/agreement**
preliminary **results/talks/discussions**

▶ **SYNONYM:** initial

---

pre|mium /prɪmiəm/ (premiums)   BANKING & FINANCE

NOUN A **premium** is a sum of money that you have to pay for something in addition to the normal cost. ○ *Even if customers want "solutions," most are not willing to pay a premium for them.*

▶ **COLLOCATIONS:**
pay/charge/reduce/receive a premium
a **low/high/payable/monthly/annual/hefty** premium
a **health/auto/insurance** premium

---

pre|pared /prɪpɛərd/

ADJECTIVE If you are **prepared to** do something, you are willing to do it. ○ *Are you prepared to help if we need you?*

▶ **SYNONYMS:** willing, ready

prepa|ra|tion /prɛpəreɪʃən/ (preparations)

1 NONCOUNT NOUN Preparation is the process of getting something ready for use or for a particular purpose or making arrangements for something. ○ [+ for/of] *Rub the surface of the wood in preparation for the varnish.* ○ *Behind any successful event lay months of preparation.*

▶ **COLLOCATIONS:**
preparation **for/of** *something*
be in preparation
thorough/careful/meticulous preparation

▶ **SYNONYM:** arrangement

2 **PLURAL NOUN** **Preparations** are all the arrangements that are made for a future event. ○ [+ *for*] *The United States is making preparations for a large-scale airlift of 1,200 American citizens.* ○ *Final preparations are underway for celebrations to mark German unification.*

▶ **COLLOCATIONS:**
preparations **for** *something*
preparations for **war/invasion**
make/finalize preparations
final preparations
preparations are **underway**
preparations **begin/continue**

▶ **SYNONYM:** arrangements

---

pre|scrip|tion /prɪskrɪpʃən/ (prescriptions) HEALTH & FITNESS

NOUN A **prescription** is a piece of paper on which a doctor writes an order for medicine. ○ *He gave me a prescription for some cream.*

▶ **COLLOCATIONS:**
write/give/issue a prescription
prescription **medicine/medication/painkillers**

▶ **PHRASE:** on prescription

---

pres|ent (presents, presenting, presented) OFFICE

The adjective and noun are pronounced /prɛzᵊnt/. The verb is pronounced /prɪzɛnt/.

1 **ADJECTIVE** You use **present** to describe things and people that exist now, rather than those that existed in the past or those that may exist in the future. ○ *He has brought much of the present crisis on himself.* ○ *It has been skillfully renovated by the present owners.* ○ *No statement can be made at the present time.*

→ see note at **current**

▶ **COLLOCATIONS:**
present **circumstances/arrangements/difficulties**

the present **crisis/situation/climate/time**

the present **value** of *something*

▶ SYNONYM: current

2 NOUN **The present** is the period of time that we are in now and the things that are happening now. ○ *his struggle to reconcile the past with the present* ○ *continuing right up to the present*

3 ADJECTIVE If someone is **present at** an event, they are there. ○ [+ *at*] *The president was not present at the meeting.* ○ [+ *at*] *Nearly 85 percent of men are present at the birth of their children.* ○ *The whole family was present.*

▶ COLLOCATIONS:

present **at** *something*

present at a **meeting/birth/ceremony**

4 ADJECTIVE If something, especially a substance or disease, is **present in** something else, it exists within that thing. ○ [+ *in*] *This special form of vitamin D is naturally present in breast milk.* ○ *If the gene is present, a human embryo will go on to develop as a male.*

▶ COLLOCATIONS:

present **in** *someone/something*

present in **saliva/tissue/fluid**

naturally/commonly/rarely present

a **molecule/enzyme/bacterium/gene** is present

5 VERB When you **present** information, you give it to people in a formal way. ○ *We spend the time collating and presenting the information in a variety of chart forms.* ○ [+ *to*] *We presented three options to the unions for discussion.* ○ [+ *with*] *In effect, Parsons presents us with a beguilingly simple outline of social evolution.*

▶ COLLOCATIONS:

present *something* **to** *someone*

present *someone* **with** *something*

present **information/evidence/options**

present a **check/trophy/petition**

formally/annually/proudly present

▶ SYNONYMS: offer, provide, submit

pres|ence /ˈprɛzᵊns/

1 NONCOUNT NOUN Someone's **presence** in a place is the fact that they are there. ○ [+ *in*] *They argued that his presence in the village could only stir up trouble.* ○ [+ *at*] *The President later honored the principal with his presence at lunch.*

► **COLLOCATIONS:**
presence **in/at** somewhere/something
someone's presence at a **ceremony/dinner/conference/meeting**

2 NONCOUNT NOUN If you refer to the **presence** of a substance in another thing, you mean that it is in that thing. ○ [+ of] The somewhat acid flavor is caused by the presence of lactic acid. ○ [+ of] the presence of a carcinogen in the water ○ Although the fluid presents no symptoms to the patient, its presence can be detected by a test.

► **COLLOCATIONS:**
the presence **of** something
the presence of something **in** something
detect/indicate/confirm the presence of something

pres|en|ta|tion /priːzɛnteɪʃ°n, prɛzən-/ (presentations)

NOUN ○ [+ of] in his first presentation of the theory to the Berlin Academy ○ [+ of] a fair presentation of the facts to a jury

► **COLLOCATIONS:**
a presentation **of** something
a presentation of **data/information/facts**
a **multimedia/video/PowerPoint** presentation
a **formal/detailed/elaborate** presentation

---

pre|serve /prɪzɜrv/ (preserves, preserving, preserved)

1 VERB If you **preserve** a situation or condition, you make sure that it remains as it is, and does not change or end. ○ We will do everything to preserve peace. ○ in order to preserve the integrity of the Gospel

► **COLLOCATIONS:**
preserve the **integrity/unity** of something
preserve **peace/standards**

► **SYNONYMS:** maintain, protect

2 VERB If you **preserve** something, you take action to save it or protect it from damage or decay. ○ the Government's aim of preserving biodiversity ○ The current administration has done little to preserve forest ecosystems.

► **COLLOCATIONS:**
preserve a **building/house/habitat/ecosystem**
well/perfectly/beautifully preserved

► **SYNONYMS:** maintain, save, protect

pres|sure /prɛʃər/

1 NONCOUNT NOUN Pressure is force that you produce when you press hard on something. ○ *She kicked at the door with her foot, and the pressure was enough to open it.* ○ *The best way to treat such bleeding is to apply firm pressure.*

▶ COLLOCATIONS:
apply/exert/maintain/withstand/resist/relieve pressure
upward/downward/intense pressure

2 NONCOUNT NOUN The **pressure** in a place or container is the force produced by the quantity of gas or liquid in that place or container. ○ *Warm air is now being drawn in from another high pressure area over the North Sea.*

▶ COLLOCATIONS:
high/low pressure
blood/air/atmospheric pressure
pressure **drops/rises/intensifies**
raise/lower the pressure

pres|tige /prɛstiʒ, -stidʒ/

NONCOUNT NOUN If a person, a country, or an organization has **prestige**, they are admired and respected because of the position they hold or the things they have achieved. ○ *efforts to build up the prestige of the United Nations*

▶ COLLOCATIONS:
gain/enjoy/carry prestige
social/national/international/personal prestige
great/immense prestige

▶ SYNONYM: renown

pres|tig|ious /prɛstɪdʒəs, -stidʒəs/

ADJECTIVE ○ *It's one of the best equipped and most prestigious schools in the country.*

▶ COLLOCATIONS: a prestigious **award/trophy**

pre|sume /prɪzum/ (presumes, presuming, presumed)

VERB If you **presume that** something is the case, you think that it is the case, although you are not certain. ○ *I presume you're here on business.* ○ *In Madagascar, nearly half of 176 indigenous palm species are endangered or*

presumed extinct. ○ [+ to-inf] *areas that have been presumed to be safe*
○ [+ that] *It is presumed that the hormone melatonin is involved.*

▶ **COLLOCATIONS:**
presume **guilt/innocence**
presumed **dead/extinct/deceased/guilty/innocent/responsible**
wrongly/safely/widely/commonly presumed

▶ **SYNONYM:** assume

pre|sum|ably /prɪzuˈməbli/

ADVERB If you say that something is **presumably** the case, you mean that
you think it is very likely to be the case, although you are not certain.
○ *The spear is presumably the murder weapon.*

▶ **COLLOCATIONS:** presumably **intend/mean/explain**

---

pre|vail /prɪveɪl/ (prevails, prevailing, prevailed)

1 VERB If a proposal, principle, or opinion **prevails**, it gains influence or is
accepted, often after a struggle or argument. ○ *We hoped that common
sense would prevail.* ○ *Rick still believes that justice will prevail.*

2 VERB If one side in a battle, contest, or dispute **prevails**, it wins.
○ *He appears to have the votes he needs to prevail.*

▶ **COLLOCATIONS:**
common sense/justice prevails
something **ultimately/eventually/finally/still** prevails

▶ **SYNONYMS:** win, triumph

preva|lent /prɛvələnt/

ADJECTIVE A condition, practice, or belief that is **prevalent** is common.
○ *This condition is more prevalent in women than in men.* ○ *Smoking is
becoming increasingly prevalent among younger women.*

▶ **COLLOCATIONS:**
a prevalent **belief/view/attitude**
a prevalent **problem/disease**

preva|lence /prɛvələns/

NONCOUNT NOUN ○ *the increased prevalence of autism*

▶ **COLLOCATIONS:**
the prevalence **of** *something*
increase/decrease/reduce the prevalence

pre|vent /prɪvɛnt/ (prevents, preventing, prevented)

VERB To **prevent** something means to ensure that it does not happen.
○ *These methods prevent pregnancy.* ○ [+ *from*] *Further treatment will prevent cancer from developing.* ○ [+ v-ing] *We recognized the possibility and took steps to prevent it happening.*

▶ **COLLOCATIONS:**
prevent *something* **from** *happening*
prevent a **disease/attack/tragedy**
prevent **pregnancy/cancer/damage/abuse/infection/war**
prevent **overheating/swelling/aging**
prevent **the spread of** *something*
prevent **a repeat of** *something*
thereby/thus prevent *something*

▶ **SYNONYMS:** stop, hinder

pre|ven|tion /prɪvɛnʃᵊn/

NONCOUNT NOUN ○ [+ *of*] *the prevention of heart disease* ○ *crime prevention*

▶ **COLLOCATIONS:**
the prevention **of** *something*
the prevention of **disease/cancer/crime**
crime/suicide prevention
cancer/disease prevention

▶ **PHRASE:** treatment and prevention

pre|vi|ous /prɪviəs/

1 ADJECTIVE A **previous** event or thing is one that happened or existed before the one that you are talking about. ○ *She has a teenage daughter from a previous marriage.* ○ *Previous studies have shown that organic farming methods can benefit the wildlife around farms.*

▶ **COLLOCATIONS:**
a **previous government/marriage/occasion**
previous **convictions/studies/estimates/experience**

▶ **SYNONYMS:** earlier, former

2 ADJECTIVE You refer to the period of time or the thing immediately before the one that you are talking about as the **previous** one. ○ *It was a surprisingly dry day after the rain of the previous week.*

▶ **COLLOCATIONS:** the previous **day/week/month/year**

▶ **SYNONYM:** preceding

pre|vi|ous|ly /prɪviəsli/

ADVERB If an event or thing has happened or existed **previously**, it has happened or existed before the one that you are talking about.
○ *Guyana's railroads were previously owned by private companies.* ○ *a collection of previously unpublished poems* ○ *Previously, the company's advertising had been handled by HDM.*

▶ **COLLOCATIONS:**
previously **unknown/unseen/unpublished/undisclosed**
previously **reported/announced/stated/forecast**
previously **owned/held**

▶ **SYNONYMS:** earlier, formerly

pri|ma|ry /praɪmɛri, -məri/

1 ADJECTIVE You use **primary** to describe something that is very important. [FORMAL] ○ *His misunderstanding of language was the primary cause of his other problems.* ○ *The family continues to be the primary source of care and comfort for people as they grow older.*

▶ **COLLOCATIONS:** a primary **aim/concern/focus/cause/source**

2 ADJECTIVE Primary is used to describe something that occurs first. ○ *It is not the primary tumor that kills, but secondary growths elsewhere in the body.*

▶ **COLLOCATIONS:** a primary **tumor/election/ballot/school**

▶ **SYNONYMS:** main, principal

▶ **RELATED WORD:** secondary

pri|mari|ly /praɪmɛrɪli/

ADVERB You use **primarily** to say what is mainly true in a particular situation. ○ *a book aimed primarily at high-energy physicists* ○ *Public order is primarily an urban problem.*

▶ **COLLOCATIONS:**
primarily **because of** *something*
primarily **aimed at/designed for** *someone*
primarily **focused on/concerned with** *something*

▶ **SYNONYMS:** mainly, principally, chiefly

prime /praɪm/

BANKING & FINANCE

ADJECTIVE You use **prime** to describe something that is most important in a situation. ○ *Political stability, meanwhile, will be a prime concern.* ○ *It could* *be a prime target for guerrilla attacks.* ○ *The prime objective of the organization is to increase profit.*

▶ COLLOCATIONS: a prime **concern/target/objective/candidate**

▶ SYNONYMS: main, principal

prime rate /praɪm reɪt/ (prime rates)

NOUN A bank's **prime rate** is the lowest rate of interest that it charges at a particular time and that is offered only to certain customers. ○ *At least one bank cut its prime rate today.*

▶ COLLOCATIONS:
fix/cut/raise/increase/offer the prime rate
the prime rate **rises/falls**
a **high/low/unchanged/annual/current** prime rate

---

prin|ci|pal /prɪnsɪpəl/

ADJECTIVE **Principal** means first in order of importance. ○ *the country's principal source of foreign exchange earnings* ○ *Their principal concern is bound to be that of winning the next general election.*

▶ COLLOCATIONS:
a principal **concern/aim/objective/cause**
a principal **architect/dancer/conductor/speaker/adviser/analyst**

▶ SYNONYMS: main, chief

---

prin|ci|ple /prɪnsɪpəl/ (principles)

1 NOUN The **principles of** a particular theory or philosophy are its basic rules or laws. ○ [+ *of*] *a violation of the basic principles of Marxism* ○ *The doctrine was based on three fundamental principles.*

2 NOUN Scientific **principles** are general scientific laws that explain how something happens or works. ○ *These people lack all understanding of scientific principles.* ○ [+ *of*] *the principles of quantum theory*

▶ COLLOCATIONS:
the principles **of** *something*
scientific/universal/basic/fundamental/democratic principles
apply/uphold/accept principles
violate/undermine/abandon principles

▶ SYNONYMS: rule, law

3 PHRASE If you agree with something, or believe that something is possible, **in principle**, you agree in general terms to the idea of it, although you do not yet know if it will be possible. ○ *I agree with it in principle but I doubt if it will happen in practice.* ○ *Even assuming this to be in principle possible, it will not be achieved soon.*

▶ COLLOCATIONS:
agree/approve in principle
accept *something* in principle
possible in principle

▶ SYNONYM: in theory

→ see note at **principal**

---

print|er /prɪntər/ (printers) `OFFICE`

NOUN A **printer** is a machine for printing copies of computer documents. ○ *paper that can be printed by computer printers*

▶ COLLOCATIONS: a **color/inkjet/laser/commercial** printer

---

pri|or|ity /praɪɔrɪti, -ɒr-/ (priorities)

NOUN If something is a **priority**, it is the most important thing you have to do or deal with, or must be done or dealt with before everything else you have to do. ○ *You may be surprised to find that your priorities change after having a baby.* ○ *The government's priority is to build more power plants.*

▶ COLLOCATIONS:
a priority **for** *someone*
a **first/top/high/low** priority
a **budget/funding/research/policy** priority
set/establish/identify/change a priority

▶ PHRASES:
give priority to *something*
take/have priority over *something*

pri|ori|tize /praɪɔrɪtaɪz, -ɒr-/ (prioritizes, prioritizing, prioritized)

VERB If you **prioritize** something, you treat it as more important than other things. [in BRIT, also use **prioritise**] ○ *The government is prioritizing the service sector, rather than investing in industry and production.* ○ *put emotion aside to prioritize spending*

---

pri|va|cy /praɪvəsi/

NONCOUNT NOUN **Privacy** is the freedom to do things without other people knowing what you are doing. ○ *We have changed the names to* *protect the privacy of those involved.*

▶ **COLLOCATIONS:**
   invade/respect/protect/ensure *someone's* privacy
   personal/complete/individual privacy

▶ **SYNONYM:** seclusion

pri|vate com|pa|ny /praɪvɪt kʌmpəni/ (private companies) (private ORGANIZATION)

NOUN A **private company** is a limited company that does not issue shares for the public to buy. Compare with **public company**. ○ *It is Jamaica's largest private company and the country's biggest earner of foreign exchange.*

pri|vate sec|tor /praɪvɪt sɛktər/ ORGANIZATION

NOUN The **private sector** is the part of a country's economy that consists of industries and commercial companies that are not owned or controlled by the government. ○ *small firms in the private sector*

▶ **RELATED WORD:** public sector

pri|vat|ize /praɪvətaɪz/ (privatizes, privatizing, privatized) ORGANIZATION

VERB If a company, industry, or service that is owned by the state **is privatized**, the government sells it and makes it a private company. [in BRIT, also use **privatise**] ○ *The water boards are about to be privatized.* ○ *a pledge to privatize the railroad and coal industries* ○ *the newly privatized FM radio stations*

▶ **COLLOCATIONS:**
   privatize a **plan/company/industry/utility**
   newly/partially/fully privatized

prob|able /prɒbəbəl/

ADJECTIVE If you say that something is **probable**, you mean that it is likely to be true or likely to happen. ○ [+ *that*] *It is probable that the medication will suppress the symptom without treating the condition.* ○ *An airline official said a bomb was the incident's most probable cause.*

▶ **COLLOCATIONS:**
   a probable **cause/explanation/case**
   highly/quite/very probable

▶ **SYNONYM:** likely

P

prob|abil|ity /prɒbəbɪlɪti/ (probabilities)

NOUN The **probability of** something happening is how likely it is to happen, sometimes expressed as a fraction or a percentage. ○ [+ *of*] *Without a transfusion, the victim's probability of dying was 100 percent.* ○ [+ *of*] *The probabilities of crime or victimization are higher with some situations than with others.*

▶ COLLOCATIONS:
   the probability **of** *something*
   calculate/compute/estimate/assess the probability
   the **estimated/statistical/mathematical** probability
   a **significant/reasonable/high/low/tiny** probability

▶ SYNONYMS: chance, likelihood, possibility

prob|lem /prɒbləm/ (problems)

NOUN A **problem** is a situation that is unsatisfactory and causes difficulties for people. ○ [+ *of*] *the economic problems of the inner city* ○ *The main problem is unemployment.* ○ *He told Americans that solving the energy problem was very important.*

▶ COLLOCATIONS:
   the problem **of/with** *something*
   the problem of **homelessness/poverty/unemployment**
   a **major/serious/real** problem
   a **health/drug/security/crime** problem
   a **financial/economic/medical/environmental** problem
   the **main/biggest** problem
   cause/have/face a problem
   solve/tackle/address/resolve a problem
   a problem **arises/occurs/emerges**
   a problem **lies in** *something*

▶ SYNONYMS: difficulty, concern

pro|cedure /prəsiːdʒər/ (procedures)

NOUN A **procedure** is a way of doing something, especially the usual or correct way. ○ *A biopsy is usually a minor surgical procedure.* ○ [+ *in*] *Police insist that Michael did not follow the correct procedure in applying for a visa.*

▶ COLLOCATIONS:
   the procedure **for/in** *something*
   a **standard/normal/simple/correct** procedure
   a **surgical/medical/cosmetic** procedure

a **complaints/grievance/selection** procedure
perform/undergo/review/explain a procedure

▶ **SYNONYMS:** method, process

pro|cedur|al /prəsi̲dʒərəl/

ADJECTIVE [FORMAL] ○ *A Spanish judge rejected the suit on procedural grounds.* ○ *The Paris talks will mainly be about procedural matters.*

▶ **COLLOCATIONS:** procedural **matters/issues/rules**

---

pro|ceeds /prou̲sidz/   BANKING & FINANCE

PLURAL NOUN The proceeds of an activity or the sale of something is the money that is made from it. ○ [+ *from*] *He uses the proceeds from his photographs to finance his productions.*

▶ **COLLOCATIONS:**
the proceeds **from** *something*
donate/invest the proceeds
the proceeds **benefit/fund** *something*

▶ **SYNONYMS:** profit, income

---

pro|cess /prɒsɛs/ (processes)

1 **NOUN** A **process** is a series of actions that are carried out in order to achieve a particular result. ○ *There was total agreement to start the peace process as soon as possible.* ○ [+ *of*] *The best way to proceed is by a process of elimination.*

2 **NOUN** A **process** is a series of things that happen naturally and result in a biological or chemical change. ○ *It occurs in elderly men, apparently as part of the aging process.*

▶ **COLLOCATIONS:**
a process **of** *something*
a process of **elimination/reconciliation/consultation/integration**
a **learning/selection/decision making** process
the **peace/reform** process
a **political/democratic/legal** process
the **healing/aging** process
a **gradual/long/slow/complicated** process
start/begin/repeat/accelerate/complete a process
put/have a process **in place**

▶ **SYNONYMS:** course, procedure

pro|duce /prədus/ (produces, producing, produced) `MARKETING & SALES`

VERB To **produce** something means to cause it to happen. ○ *The drug is known to produce side-effects in women.* ○ *Talks aimed at producing a new world trade treaty have been under way for six years.*

▸ **COLLOCATIONS:** produce a **result/effect**

▸ **SYNONYMS:** cause, induce

VERB If you **produce** something, you make or create it. ○ *The company produced circuitry for communications systems.* ○ *locally produced vegetables*

▸ **COLLOCATIONS:**
produce **goods/products/crops/wine/weapons**
a **factory/plant/manufacturer/company/farmer** produces *things*
mass/locally/domestically produced

▸ **SYNONYMS:** make, manufacture, create

prod|uct /prɒdʌkt/ (products)

1 NOUN A **product** is something that is produced and sold in large quantities, often as a result of a manufacturing process. ○ *Try to get the best product at the lowest price.* ○ *South Korea's imports of consumer products increased by 33% this year.*

▸ **COLLOCATIONS:**
a **new/finished/commercial** product
consumer/dairy/beef/tobacco/food products
manufacture/produce/develop/market/launch a product
import/buy/purchase a product
export/sell/deliver a product
product **development/marketing**
a product **line**

▸ **SYNONYM:** goods

2 NOUN If you say that someone or something is a **product of** a situation or process, you mean that the situation or process has had a significant effect in making them what they are. ○ [+ *of*] *We are all products of our time.* ○ [+ *of*] *The bank is the product of a 1971 merger of two Japanese banks.*

▸ **COLLOCATIONS:**
a product **of** *something*
a product of a **culture/upbringing/era**

pro|duc|tion /prədʌkʃən/

1 NONCOUNT NOUN Production is the process of manufacturing or growing something in large quantities. ○ *That model won't go into* *production before late 1990.* ○ [+ *of*] *tax incentives to encourage domestic production of oil*

2 NONCOUNT NOUN Production is the amount of goods manufactured or grown by a company or country. ○ *We needed to increase the volume of production.*

▶ **COLLOCATIONS:**
in/into production
production **of** *something*
production of **goods/commodities**
go into production
increase/boost/stimulate production
industrial/agricultural/commercial/mass production
oil/gas/steel/food/energy production
production **costs/capacity**

▶ **SYNONYMS:** manufacturing, output

prod|uc|tiv|ity /prɒdʊktɪvɪti/

NONCOUNT NOUN Productivity is the rate at which goods are produced.
○ *The third-quarter results reflect continued improvements in productivity.*

▶ **COLLOCATIONS: improve/increase/boost/raise/lose** productivity

▶ **SYNONYM:** output

---

pro|fes|sion|al /prəfɛʃənəl/   `JOBS`

1 ADJECTIVE Professional means relating to a person's work, especially work that requires special training. ○ *His professional career started at Cornell University.*

2 ADJECTIVE Professional people have jobs that require advanced education or training. ○ *highly qualified professional people like doctors and engineers*

● **Professional** is also a noun. ○ *My father wanted me to become a professional and have more stability.*

▶ **COLLOCATIONS:**
a professional **career/qualification**
professional **development/help/advice**
thoroughly/highly professional

▶ **SYNONYM:** qualified

prof|it /prɒfɪt/ (profits, profiting, profited) `BANKING & FINANCE`

1 NOUN A **profit** is an amount of money that you gain when you are paid more for something than it cost you to make, get, or do it. ○ *The bank made pretax profits of $3.5 million.* ○ *You can improve your chances of profit by sensible planning.*

▶ **COLLOCATIONS:**
a profit **of** x
make/earn/turn/yield a profit
maximize/increase profits
report/forecast/expect profits
profits **rise/soar/fall**
pretax/net/gross profits
quarterly/annual/corporate profits
a profit **margin**

▶ **PHRASE:** profit and loss

▶ **SYNONYM:** income

2 VERB If you **profit from** something, you earn a profit from it. ○ [+ from/by] *Departmental managers are accustomed to profiting handsomely from bonuses.* ○ [+ from/by] *He has profited by selling his holdings to other investors.*

▶ **COLLOCATIONS:**
profit **from/by** *something*
profit from a **boom/upturn/invention**
profit **handsomely/enormously**

prof|it|able /prɒfɪtəbᵊl/

ADJECTIVE A **profitable** organization or practice makes a profit. ○ *Drug manufacturing is the most profitable business in America.* ○ [+ for] *It was profitable for them to produce large amounts of food.*

▶ **COLLOCATIONS:**
profitable **for** *someone*
a profitable **business/enterprise/operation/niche/venture**
highly profitable

▶ **SYNONYM:** lucrative

pro|gram /prougræm, -grəm/ (programs, programming, programmed)

1 NOUN A **program** is a set of instructions that a computer follows in order to perform a particular task. ○ *The chances of an error occurring in a computer program increase with the size of the program.*

▶ COLLOCATIONS:
a **computer/software** program
design/develop/create/run a program

▶ SYNONYMS: software, code

2 VERB When you **program** a computer, you give it a set of instructions to make it able to perform a particular task. ○ [+ to-inf] *He programmed his computer to compare all the possible combinations.* ○ *a computer programmed to translate a story given to it in Chinese*

▶ COLLOCATIONS:
program a **computer/machine/robot**
digitally/remotely programmed

---

pro|gress (progresses, progressing, progressed)

The noun is pronounced /ˈprɒgrɛs/. The verb is pronounced /prəˈgrɛs/.

1 NONCOUNT NOUN Progress is the process of gradually improving or getting nearer to achieving or completing something. ○ [+ in] *The medical community continues to make progress in the fight against cancer.* ○ [+ toward] *The two sides made little if any progress toward agreement.*

2 NONCOUNT NOUN The progress of a situation or action is the way in which it develops. ○ [+ of] *The Chancellor is reported to have been delighted with the progress of the first day's talks.*

▶ COLLOCATIONS:
the progress **of** *something*
progress **on/in/toward** *something*
progress toward **peace/democracy/unity**
progress toward a **solution/agreement**
economic/academic progress
good/slow/rapid/remarkable/real/steady progress
make progress

▶ SYNONYMS: advancement, development

3 VERB To **progress** means to move over a period of time to a stronger, more advanced, or more desirable state. ○ *He will visit once every two weeks to see how his new staff are progressing.* ○ [+ to] *He started with sketching and then progressed to painting.* ○ *A company spokesman said that talks were progressing well.*

▶ COLLOCATIONS:
progress **to** *something*

a **disease/pregnancy/career** progresses
talks/negotiations progress
progress **smoothly/rapidly/satisfactorily/nicely**

---

pro|hib|it /prouhɪbɪt/ (prohibits, prohibiting, prohibited)

VERB If a law or someone in authority **prohibits** something, they forbid it or make it illegal. [FORMAL] ○ *a law that prohibits tobacco advertising in newspapers and magazines* ○ *Fishing is prohibited.* ○ [+ from] *Federal law prohibits foreign airlines from owning more than 25 percent of any U.S. airline.*

▶ **COLLOCATIONS:**
prohibited **from** *doing something*
the **constitution/law/government** prohibits *something*
prohibit **discrimination/smoking/drugs**
strictly/expressly/currently prohibited

▶ **SYNONYM:** forbid

---

proj|ect (projects, projecting, projected) RG-D

> The noun is pronounced /prɒdʒɛkt/. The verb is pronounced /prədʒɛkt/.

1 NOUN A **project** is a task that requires a lot of time and effort. ○ *Money will also go into local development projects in Vietnam.* ○ *a research project on alternative medicine*

▶ **COLLOCATIONS:**
a **research/development/construction/conservation** project
a **major/massive/innovative/long-term** project
fund/finance/support a project
approve/launch/start/undertake/complete a project
a project **manager/director**

▶ **SYNONYM:** scheme

2 VERB If something **is projected**, it is planned or expected. ○ [+ to-inf] *The population is projected to more than double by 2025.* ○ *The government had been projecting a 5 percent consumer price increase for the entire year.* ○ *a projected deficit of $1.5 million*

▶ **COLLOCATIONS:**
project a **decrease/deficit/shortfall/growth/increase/turnover**
a **forecaster/economist/analyst** projects *something*

▶ **SYNONYMS:** forecast, expect, estimate

pro|jec|tion /prədʒɛkʃ°n/ (projections)

NOUN A **projection** is an estimate of a future amount. ○ [+ of] *the company's projection of 11 million visitors for the first year* ○ *sales projections*

▶ **COLLOCATIONS:**
a projection **of/for** *something*
projections for **growth/inflation/profits**
sales/economic/profit projections

▶ **SYNONYMS:** forecast, estimate

promi|nent /prɒmɪnənt/

1 ADJECTIVE Someone who is **prominent** is important. ○ *a prominent member of the legal community* ○ *the children of very prominent or successful parents*

▶ **COLLOCATIONS:**
a prominent **role/figure/member/politician/businessman**
especially/increasingly/socially/nationally prominent

▶ **SYNONYM:** well-known

2 ADJECTIVE Something that is **prominent** is very noticeable or is an important part of something else. ○ *Here the window plays a prominent part in the design.* ○ *Romania's most prominent independent newspaper*

▶ **COLLOCATIONS:**
a prominent **feature/landmark**
prominent **cheekbones**

prom|ise /prɒmɪs/ (promises, promising, promised)

VERB If you **promise that** you will do something, you say that you will certainly do it. ○ *They have promised to invest $45 million over five years in the three companies.* ○ *Promise me you'll come to the party.*

● **Promise** is also a noun. ○ *James broke every promise he made.*

▶ **COLLOCATIONS:**
make/break/show/keep/offer/hold a promise
a **vague/false/empty** promise

▶ **SYNONYM:** guarantee

pro|mote /prəmoʊt/ (promotes, promoting, promoted)   `PERSONNEL`

1 VERB If people **promote** something, they help or encourage it to happen, increase, or spread. ○ *You don't have to sacrifice environmental*

P

protection to promote economic growth.

▶ **COLLOCATIONS:**
promote **awareness/growth/tourism**
actively/vigorously/strongly promote *something*

▶ **SYNONYM:** encourage

2 VERB If a firm **promotes** a product, it tries to increase the sales or popularity of that product. ○ *He has announced a national tour to promote his second solo album.* ○ *[+ as] a special St. Lucia week where the island could be promoted as a tourist destination*

▶ **COLLOCATIONS:**
promote *something* **as** *something*
a **retailer/ad/billboard/website** promotes *something*
promote a **product**
heavily/vigorously/aggressively promote *something*

▶ **PHRASE:** promote and market

pro|mo|tion /prəmoʊʃᵊn/

NONCOUNT NOUN ○ *[+ of] The government has pledged to give the promotion of democracy higher priority.* ○ *disease prevention and health promotion*

▶ **COLLOCATIONS:**
the promotion **of** *something*
the promotion of **democracy/equality/diversity**
health/trade/tourism/product promotion

▶ **PHRASES:**
promotion and advertising
promotion and marketing

---

prompt /prɒmpt/ (prompts, prompting, prompted)

VERB To **prompt** someone **to** do something means to make them decide to do it. ○ *[+ to-inf] Japan's recession has prompted consumers to cut back on buying cars.* ○ *The need for villagers to control their own destinies has prompted a new plan.*

▶ **COLLOCATIONS:**
prompt *someone* to **write/ask** *something*
prompt *someone* to **act**

▶ **SYNONYM:** encourage

prompt|ly /ˈprɒmptli/

ADVERB immediately ○ *They announced an investment plan which promptly pushed the company's share price up 7%.*

▸ **COLLOCATIONS: respond/act/order/arrive** promptly

▸ **SYNONYM:** immediately

---

pro|pel /prəˈpɛl/ (propels, propelling, propelled)

VERB To **propel** something in a particular direction means to cause it to move in that direction. ○ *The tiny rocket is attached to the spacecraft and is designed to propel it toward Mars.* ○ *the club propels the ball forward rather than up*

● **-propelled** combines with nouns to form adjectives which indicate how something, especially a weapon, is propelled. ○ *rocket-propelled grenades* ○ *the first jet-propelled airplane*

▸ **COLLOCATIONS:**
rocket-/jet-/wind-/engine-propelled
propel a **grenade/rocket/vehicle/ball**
propel *something* **forward/onwards**

▸ **SYNONYMS:** drive, launch, thrust

---

prop|er|ty /ˈprɒpərti/ (properties)

1 NONCOUNT NOUN Someone's **property** is all the things that belong to them or something that belongs to them. [FORMAL] ○ *Richard could easily destroy her personal property to punish her for walking out on him.* ○ *Security forces searched thousands of homes, confiscating weapons and stolen property.*

▸ **COLLOCATIONS:**
personal property
stolen/valuable/damaged property

▸ **SYNONYMS:** belongings, possessions

2 NOUN A **property** is a building and the land belonging to it. [FORMAL] ○ *She inherited a family property near Stamford.* ○ *privately owned properties*

▸ **COLLOCATIONS:**
private property
a **rental/beachfront/four-bedroom** property
own/buy/purchase/rent/lease a property
a property **developer/owner**
the property **market**

▸ **SYNONYMS:** house, building

P

3 **NOUN** The **properties** of a substance or object are the ways in which it behaves in particular conditions. ○ *A radio signal has both electrical and magnetic properties.* ○ [+ *of*] *the electromagnetic properties of electrons*

▶ **COLLOCATIONS:**
the properties **of** *something*
the properties of a **substance/liquid/object**
the properties of a **molecule/electron/atom**
magnetic/electrical/antibacterial properties

---

pro|por|tion /prəpɔːʃ³n/ (proportions)

1 **NOUN** A **proportion of** a group or an amount is a part of it. [FORMAL] ○ [+ *of*] *A large proportion of the dolphins in that area will eventually die.* ○ [+ *of*] *A proportion of the rent is paid in advance.*

2 **NOUN** The **proportion of** one kind of person or thing in a group is the number of people or things of that kind compared to the total number of people or things in the group. ○ [+ *of*] *The proportion of women in the profession had risen to 17.3 percent.* ○ [+ *of*] *A growing proportion of the population is living alone.*

▶ **COLLOCATIONS:**
a proportion **of** *something*
a **large/high/substantial/significant/small/tiny** proportion
a proportion of the **population/workforce/electorate**
a proportion of the **rent/budget/income**

▶ **SYNONYMS:** amount, part, percentage

3 **PHRASE** If something is small or large **in proportion to** something else, it is small or large when compared with that thing. ○ *Children tend to have relatively larger heads than adults in proportion to the rest of their body.* ○ *Japan's contribution to the U.N. budget is much larger in proportion to its economy than that of almost any other country.*

▶ **COLLOCATIONS:** **small/large** in proportion to *something*

▶ **SYNONYM:** in relation to

---

pro|pose /prəpoʊz/ (proposes, proposing, proposed)

1 **VERB** If you **propose** something such as a plan or an idea, you suggest it for people to think about and decide upon. ○ *Britain is about to propose changes to some institutions.* ○ [+ *that*] *It was George who first proposed that we dry clothes in that locker.*

2 **VERB** If you **propose** a theory or an explanation, you state that it is possibly or probably true, because it fits in with the evidence that you have considered. [FORMAL] ○ *This highlights a problem faced by people proposing theories of ball lightning.* ○ *[+that] Newton proposed that heavenly and terrestrial motion could be unified with the idea of gravity.*

▶ COLLOCATIONS:
a **committee/government/theorist/scientist** proposes *something*
propose **changes/talks/plans/reform**
propose a **theory/explanation/solution**
first/originally/initially proposed

EXTEND YOUR VOCABULARY

There are several verbs you can use to report new ideas. ○ *Can anyone **propose** a solution to the timing problem?* ○ *Many commenters **suggested** alternative approaches to achieving those goals.* ○ *Let's look at the various ideas that have been **put forward**.*

---

pro|po|sal /prəpoʊzəl/ (proposals)

NOUN A **proposal** is a plan or an idea, often a formal or written one, that is suggested for people to think about and decide upon. ○ *[+ for] The President is to put forward new proposals for resolving the country's constitutional crisis.* ○ *the British government's proposals to abolish free health care*

▶ COLLOCATIONS:
a proposal **for** *something*
a **government/new/peace** proposal
put forward/reject/compromise a proposal

▶ SYNONYMS: plan, idea

propo|si|tion /prɒpəzɪʃən/ (propositions)

NOUN A **proposition** is a statement or an idea that people can consider or discuss to decide whether it is true. [FORMAL] ○ *The proposition that democracies do not fight each other is based on a tiny historical sample.*

▶ COLLOCATIONS:
a **basic/realistic/feasible/doubtful** proposition
put forward/advance/accept a proposition

▶ SYNONYMS: statement, idea

pros|pect /prɑspɛkt/ (prospects)

1 NOUN If there is a **prospect of** something happening, there is a possibility that it will happen. ○ [+ of] *The prospect of finding a job is slim at present.* ○ [+ for] *The prospects for peace in the country's eight-year civil war are becoming brighter.*

▶ **COLLOCATIONS:**
the prospect **of** *something*
the prospects **for** *something*
the prospect of **war/survival/recession/employment**
the prospects for **peace/recovery/growth/success**

2 NOUN A particular **prospect** is something that you expect or know is going to happen. ○ [+ of] *They now face the prospect of having to wear a bicycle helmet by law.* ○ *Starting up a company may be a daunting prospect.*

▶ **COLLOCATIONS:**
the prospect **of** *something*
relish/welcome/savor/face/dread/contemplate the prospect
a **pleasant/promising/attractive/bleak/daunting/grim** prospect

pro|spec|tive /prəspɛktɪv/

1 ADJECTIVE You use **prospective** to describe someone who wants to be the thing mentioned or who is likely to be the thing mentioned. ○ *The story should act as a warning to other prospective buyers.* ○ *his prospective employers*

▶ **COLLOCATIONS:** a prospective **buyer/student/employer/customer**

▶ **SYNONYMS:** future, would-be

2 ADJECTIVE You use **prospective** to describe something that is likely to happen soon. ○ *the terms of the prospective deal* ○ *prospective economic growth*

▶ **COLLOCATIONS:** a prospective **deal/sale**

▶ **SYNONYM:** anticipated

pros|per|ous /prɒspərəs/

ADJECTIVE Prosperous people, places, and economies are rich and successful. [FORMAL] ○ *the youngest son of a relatively prosperous British family* ○ *The place looks more prosperous than ever.*

▶ **COLLOCATIONS:**
relatively/moderately/economically prosperous
a prosperous **nation/economy/town/businessman/farmer**

EXTEND YOUR VOCABULARY

You often describe people or countries with a lot of money as being **rich** or **wealthy**. ○ *There are rich countries where most people have enough and some have untold wealth, while in the poor countries desperate poverty is widespread.*

Both of these words often suggest a judgment about whether the wealth is positive, unfair, or unequal. In more formal writing, you can use the words **prosperous** and **affluent** to describe areas where people have a relatively high income and a good standard of living. ○ *Australia's economy is prosperous and stable.* ○ *This occurs twice as much in the inner city area as compared with the more affluent suburbs.*

---

pro|vide /prəvaɪd/ (provides, providing, provided)

VERB If you **provide** something that someone needs or wants, or if you **provide** them **with** it, you give it to them or make it available to them. ○ *I'll be glad to provide a copy of this.* ○ *They would not provide any details.* ○ [+ with] *The government was not in a position to provide them with food.*

▶ **COLLOCATIONS:**
provide *someone* **with** *something*
provide *someone* with **food/accommodation/information**
provide **details/evidence/support/assistance**
provide a **service/answer**

EXTEND YOUR VOCABULARY

Give is a very common verb in everyday English. In more formal English, you can use more specific verbs. You can use **provide** with a wide range of nouns; physical objects, services, information, help, etc. Remember to use **with** when you mention who something is given to. ○ *We are focused on providing the best customer service.* ○ *She will provide you with all the information you need.*

You use **supply** especially to talk about products and services that a business gives to a customer. ○ *The company supplies equipment for the oil industry.*

pro|vid|ed /prəvaɪdɪd/

CONJUNCTION If something will happen **provided** that something else happens, the first thing will happen only if the second thing also happens. ○ *He can go running at his age, provided that he is sensible.*

▶ **SYNONYM:** on condition that

prox|im|ity /prɒksɪmɪti/

NONCOUNT NOUN Proximity to a place or person is nearness to that place or person. [FORMAL] ○ [+ *to*] *Part of the attraction is Darwin's proximity to Asia.* ○ [+ *of*] *He became aware of the proximity of the Afghans.* ○ [+ *to*] *Families are no longer in close proximity to each other.*

▶ **COLLOCATIONS:**
proximity **to/of** *something/someone*
close/geographical/physical proximity

pub|li|ca|tion /pʌblɪkeɪʃᵊn/ (publications)   COMMUNICATIONS

1 NONCOUNT NOUN The **publication** of a book or magazine is the act of printing it and sending it to stores to be sold. ○ [+ *of*] *the publication of an article in a physics journal* ○ [+ *of*] *the online publication of the census*

▶ **COLLOCATIONS:**
the publication **of** *something*
the publication of a **book/report/journal/article**
online/weekly/monthly publication
prohibit/delay/ban/await/resume publication

2 NOUN A **publication** is a book or magazine that has been published. ○ *the ease of access to scientific publications on the Internet* ○ *The magazine, which will be a quarterly publication, has received sponsorship from companies in the U.S.*

▶ **COLLOCATIONS:**
a publication **on** *something*
a publication on a **topic/subject**
a **weekly/monthly/quarterly** publication
a **digital/online/scientific/specialist** publication

pub|lic|ity /pʌblɪsɪti/   MARKETING & SALES

NONCOUNT NOUN Publicity means advertising or information about a person, or a product. ○ *A lot of publicity was given to the talks.* ○ *a publicity campaign*

▶ COLLOCATIONS:
   generate/attract/gain/avoid/receive/seek/give publicity
   publicity **surrounding** *something*
   adverse/negative/widespread/bad/free publicity

▶ SYNONYM: advertising

---

pub|lish /pˈʌblɪʃ/ (publishes, publishing, published) `COMMUNICATIONS`

VERB When a company **publishes** a book or magazine, it prints copies of it, which are sent to stores to be sold. If someone **publishes** a book or an article that they have written, they arrange to have it published.
○ *Dr. Peters published the findings of his detailed studies last year.* ○ *The research was published online in the latest British Medical Journal.*

▶ COLLOCATIONS:
   publish *something* **on/in** *something*
   published **by** *someone*
   published in a **journal/newspaper/report/article**
   published **online/on a website/on the Internet**
   publish a **book/report/article/paper**
   publish **findings/figures/research**

pub|lish|er /pˈʌblɪʃər/ (publishers)

NOUN A **publisher** is a person or a company that publishes books, newspapers, magazines, or websites. ○ *The publishers planned to produce the journal on a weekly basis.*

▶ COLLOCATIONS:
   a **magazine/educational/book/newspaper** publisher
   a **Chicago-based/regional/online** publisher
   an **rival/established** publisher

P

---

pur|chase /pˈɜrtʃɪs/ (purchases, purchasing, purchased) `MARKETING & SALES`

1 VERB When you **purchase** something, you buy it. [FORMAL] ○ *Nearly three out of every 10 new car buyers are purchasing their vehicles online.*
○ [+ from] *Most of those shares were purchased from brokers.*

→ see note at **acquire**

▶ COLLOCATIONS:
   purchase *something* **from/through** *someone/somewhere*
   a **customer/buyer/consumer** purchases *something*
   purchase **shares/property/land**
   purchase *something* **online**

> **EXTEND YOUR VOCABULARY**
>
> You can use **purchase** as an alternative to **buy** in more formal writing. ○ *the cost of purchasing equipment*
>
> You can also use **acquire** when you talk about a business buying some types of things.
>
> ▶ a company acquires **assets/shares/property**

2 **NOUN** A **purchase** is something that you buy. [FORMAL] ○ *The latest data reveals that nine in every 10 Internet users have made a purchase online.* ○ *Discounts are available for bulk purchases.*

▶ **COLLOCATIONS:**
   make/complete/refund a purchase
   online/bulk purchase

---

pur|sue /pərsu̱/ (pursues, pursuing, pursued)

1 **VERB** If you **pursue** an activity, interest, or plan, you carry it out or follow it. If you **pursue** a particular topic, you try to find out more about it by asking questions. [FORMAL] ○ *He said Japan would continue to pursue the policies laid down at the London summit.* ○ *If your original request is denied, don't be afraid to pursue the matter.*

▶ **COLLOCATIONS:**
   pursue a **policy/interest/career**
   pursue a **matter/question/claim**

▶ **SYNONYMS:** follow, follow up

2 **VERB** If you **pursue** a particular aim or result, you make efforts to achieve it, often over a long period of time. [FORMAL] ○ *The implication seems to be that it is impossible to pursue economic reform and democracy simultaneously.* ○ *Europe must pursue aggressively its program of economic reform.*

▶ **COLLOCATIONS:**
   pursue a **result/aim/objective/agenda**
   pursue **reform/diplomacy/business**
   aggressively/actively/vigorously pursue *something*

pur|suit /pərsu̱t/

NONCOUNT NOUN The **pursuit of** something is the process of trying to achieve it. The **pursuit of** an activity, interest, or plan consists of all the things that you do when you are carrying it out. ○ [+ *of*] *a young man whose relentless pursuit of excellence is conducted with single-minded determination* ○ [+ *of*] *The vigorous pursuit of policies is no guarantee of success.*

▶ **COLLOCATIONS:**
the pursuit **of** *something*
the pursuit of a **plan/activity/project**
the pursuit of **truth/excellence/perfection/knowledge**

▶ **PHRASE:** in (the) pursuit of *something*

p

Qq

quali|fy /kwɒlɪfaɪ/ (qualifies, qualifying, qualified)   PERSONNEL

VERB When someone **qualifies**, they pass the courses or examinations that they need to be able to work in a particular job. ○ *When I'd qualified and started teaching, it was a different story.* ○ *[+ as/in] I qualified as a lifeguard over 30 years ago.*

> ▶ **COLLOCATIONS:**
> qualify **as/in** *something*
> qualify as a **teacher/trainer/instructor**
> **fail to** qualify

quali|fi|ca|tion /kwɒlɪfɪkeɪʃ°n/ (qualifications)

NOUN ○ *I believe I have all the qualifications to be a good teacher.*

> ▶ **COLLOCATIONS: academic/educational** qualifications

> ▶ **PHRASE:** the proper qualifications

qual|ity /kwɒlɪti/ (qualities)

1 NONCOUNT NOUN The **quality** of something is how good or bad it is. ○ *[+ of] Patients reported a substantial improvement in their symptoms and their quality of life.* ○ *Other services vary dramatically in quality.* ○ *high-quality paper and plywood*

> ▶ **COLLOCATIONS:**
> the quality **of** *something*
> quality of **life/services/care/teaching**
> **improve/enhance/affect** quality
> **poor/sound/high/superior** quality
> **air/water/image** quality
> quality **control/assurance/standards**

> ▶ **PHRASE:** quality and quantity

> ▶ **SYNONYM:** standard

2 **NOUN** You can describe a particular characteristic of a person or thing as a **quality**. ○ *a childlike quality* ○ [+ *of*] *the pretentious quality of the poetry* ○ *Thyme tea can be used by adults for its antiseptic qualities.*

▶ **SYNONYM:** characteristic

---

quar|ter /kwɔrtər/ (quarters)   `BANKING & FINANCE`

1 **NOUN** A **quarter** is one of four equal parts of something. ○ [+ *of*] *A quarter of the residents are over 55 years old.* ○ [+ *of*] *a quarter of an hour* ○ *a unique "four-in-one" channel that splits your screen into quarters*

▶ **COLLOCATIONS:**
   a quarter **of** *something*
   into quarters
   a quarter of a **century/pound**
   cut/split/fold *something* into quarters

▶ **RELATED WORD:** half

2 **NOUN** A **quarter** is a fixed period of three months. Companies often divide their financial year into four quarters. ○ *The group said results for the third quarter are due on October 29.* ○ *PeopleSoft announced yesterday that it had performed better than expected in its current financial quarter.*

▶ **COLLOCATIONS:**
   the **first/second/third/fourth** quarter
   the **previous/final/consecutive/current** quarter
   a **fiscal/financial** quarter

quar|ter|ly /kwɔrtərli/

ADJECTIVE A **quarterly** event happens four times a year, at intervals of three months. ○ *the latest Bank of Japan quarterly survey of 5,000 companies* ○ *The software group last night announced record quarterly profits of $1.98 billion.*

● **Quarterly** is also an adverb. ○ *It makes no difference whether dividends are paid quarterly or annually.* ○ *The list will be updated quarterly by the nonprofit Direct Marketing Association.*

▶ **COLLOCATIONS:**
   a quarterly **survey/report/loss**
   quarterly **profits/earnings/revenue/results**
   update/measure/sample *something* quarterly

q

quick /kwɪk/ (quicker, quickest)

1 ADJECTIVE If something is **quick**, it moves or does things with great speed. ○ *You'll have to be quick.*

2 ADJECTIVE Something **quick** lasts only a short time or happens in a short time. ○ *He took a quick look around the room.* ○ *We are hoping for a quick end to the strike.*

▶ **COLLOCATIONS:**
very/real/pretty/too/relatively quick
a quick **fix/glance/look/trip**

▶ **PHRASES:**
quick as lightning
in quick succession
quick and easy

▶ **SYNONYM:** fast

quick|ly /kwɪkli/

ADVERB ○ *Cussane worked quickly.* ○ *Their job is to bring this information to the market as quickly as possible.*

▶ **COLLOCATIONS:**
move/act/happen/grow quickly
quickly **become/add/follow/learn**

▶ **PHRASES:**
quickly and efficiently
quickly and effectively

▶ **SYNONYM:** swiftly

quit /kwɪt/ (quits, quitting, quit) `PERSONNEL`

VERB If you **quit** something, you stop doing it. [INFORMAL] ○ *Quit talking now and do some work.* ○ *That's enough! I quit!*

▶ **COLLOCATIONS:**
quit **smoking/drinking**
quit **politics/football**

▶ **SYNONYMS:** resign, stop

quo|ta /kwoʊtə/ (quotas) `LOGISTICS & DISTRIBUTION`

1 NOUN A **quota** is the limited number or quantity of something that is officially allowed. ○ [+ *of*] *The quota of four tickets per person had been* *reduced to two.* ○ [+ on] *South Korea now imposes quotas on beef imports to protect its weak farm industry.*

▶ COLLOCATIONS:
a quota **of/on** *something*
a quota of *x* **barrels/tons**
a quota on **imports**
impose/allocate/assign a quota

2 **NOUN** A **quota** is a fixed maximum or minimum proportion of people from a particular group who are allowed to do something, such as come and live in a country or work for the government. ○ *The bill would force employers to adopt a quota system when recruiting workers.* ○ *The court, on a 5-4 vote, outlawed racial quotas in university admissions.*

▶ COLLOCATIONS:
racial/race-based/gender quotas
a quota **system**

---

quote /kwˈout/ (quotes, quoting, quoted)

1 **VERB** If you **quote** someone as saying something, you repeat what they have written or said. ○ [+ as] *He quoted Mr. Polay as saying that peace negotiations were already underway.* ○ *Mawby and Gill (1987) quote this passage from the Home Office White Paper, 1964.* ○ [+ from] *O'Regan cites one exception, quoting from a paper on cancer of the cervix.*

▶ COLLOCATIONS:
quoted **as** *saying something*
quote **from** *something*
quote from a **book/report**
quote a **passage/verse/source**

▶ SYNONYMS: cite, reference

▶ RELATED WORD: paraphrase

2 **NOUN** A **quote from** a book, poem, play, or speech is a passage or phrase from it. ○ [+ from] *The article starts with a quote from an unnamed member of the Cabinet.* ○ *The quote is attributed to the Athenian philosopher Socrates.*

▶ COLLOCATIONS:
a quote **from** *something/someone*
attribute a quote

▶ SYNONYMS: quotation, citation

▶ RELATED WORD: paraphrase

Rr

---

radi|cal /ˈrædɪkᵊl/

ADJECTIVE **Radical** changes and differences are very important and great in degree. ○ *The country needs a period of calm without more surges of radical change.* ○ *Major League Baseball has announced its proposals for a radical reform of the way baseball is run.*

▶ **COLLOCATIONS:**
a radical **departure/overhaul/change/reform**
truly/politically/genuinely radical

▶ **SYNONYM:** fundamental

radi|cal|ly /ˈrædɪkᵊli/

ADVERB ○ *The power of the presidency may be radically reduced in certain circumstances.* ○ *two large groups of people with radically different beliefs and cultures* ○ *proposals for radically new models*

▶ **COLLOCATIONS:**
change/alter/overhaul *something* radically
radically **different/new**

▶ **SYNONYM:** fundamentally

---

raise /ˈreɪz/ (raises, raising, raised)

1 **VERB** If you **raise** the rate or level of something, you increase it. ○ *The Republic of Ireland is expected to raise interest rates.* ○ *Two incidents in recent days have raised the level of concern.* ○ *a raised body temperature*

▶ **COLLOCATIONS:**
raise **taxes/fares**
raise the **rate/level/price** of *something*

▶ **SYNONYM:** increase

2 **VERB** If an event **raises** a particular emotion or question, it makes people feel the emotion or consider the question. ○ *The agreement has raised hopes that the war may end soon.* ○ *The accident again raises questions* *about the safety of the building.*

▶ **COLLOCATIONS:**
raise a **question/issue**
raise **concern/awareness/hopes/doubts**

▶ **SYNONYM:** highlight

USAGE: *raise* or *rise*?

You say that *someone* **raises** something - it is a transitive verb and is usually followed by an object. ○ *The government was forced to raise taxes.* ○ *some of the questions raised by the report*

But you say that *something* **rises** - it is an intransitive verb, so it is not followed by an object and cannot be used in the passive. **Rose** is the past tense form of **rise**. ○ *Car sales rose by nearly 10% in October.*

---

ran|dom /ˈrændəm/

ADJECTIVE A **random** sample or method is one in which all the people or things involved have an equal chance of being chosen. ○ *The survey used a random sample of two thousand people across the United States.* ○ *The competitors will be subject to random drug testing.*

▶ **COLLOCATIONS:**
a random **sample/check/selection/test**
random **testing**

---

range /reɪndʒ/ (ranges, ranging, ranged)

1 NOUN A **range of** things is a number of different things of the same general kind. ○ [+ *of*] *Office workers face a wide range of health and safety problems.* ○ [+ *of*] *The two men discussed a range of issues.*

▶ **COLLOCATIONS:**
a range **of** *things*
a range of **products/services/activities**
a range of **issues/options/colors**
a **wide/broad/limited/narrow** range
offer/cover/provide a range

▶ **SYNONYMS:** variety, selection, collection

2 NOUN A **range** is the complete group that is included between two points on a scale of measurement or quality. ○ *The average age range is*

r

between 35 and 55. ○ *products available in this price range*

▶ **COLLOCATIONS:**
a range **between** *x* **and** *y*
age/price/product range
the **full/normal/whole** range

3 VERB If things **range between** two points or **range from** one point **to** another, they vary within these points on a scale of measurement or quality. ○ *They range in price from $3 to $15.* ○ *The cars were all new models and ranged from sports cars to Cadillacs.* ○ *[+ between] temperatures ranging between 5°F and 20°F*

▶ **COLLOCATIONS:**
range **from** *something* **to** *something*
range **between** *something* **and** *something*
things range **widely**
temperatures/prices/ages/products range widely

▶ **SYNONYM:** vary

---

rap|id /ˈræpɪd/

1 ADJECTIVE A **rapid** change is one that happens very quickly. ○ *the country's rapid economic growth in the 1980's* ○ *the rapid decline in the birth rate in Western Europe*

→ see note at **dramatic**

▶ **COLLOCATIONS:**
a rapid **growth/rise/expansion/decline/change**
extremely/relatively/fairly rapid

2 ADJECTIVE A **rapid** movement is one that is very fast. ○ *He walked at a rapid pace.* ○ *The tunnel will provide more rapid car transport than ferries.*

▶ **COLLOCATIONS:**
a rapid **pace/heartbeat**
rapid **breathing/transit**

rap|id|ly /ˈræpɪdli/

ADVERB ○ *countries with rapidly growing populations* ○ *"Operating profit is rising more rapidly," he said.* ○ *He was moving rapidly around the room.*

→ see note at **dramatic**

▶ **COLLOCATIONS:**
grow/change/spread/expand/rise rapidly
breathe/pace rapidly

▶ **SYNONYMS:** quickly, swiftly

rare /rɛər/ (rarer, rarest)

1 **ADJECTIVE** Something that is **rare** is not common and is therefore interesting or valuable. ○ *the black-necked crane, one of the rarest species in the world* ○ *She collects rare plants.* ○ *Do you want to know about a particular rare stamp or rare stamps in general?*

2 **ADJECTIVE** An event or situation that is **rare** does not occur very often. ○ *those rare occasions when he ate alone* ○ *Heart attacks were extremely rare in babies, he said.* ○ *I think it's very rare to have big families nowadays.*

> ▶ **COLLOCATIONS:**
> rare **for** *someone to do something*
> rare **in** *people*
> rare in **humans/adults/babies**
> **extremely/relatively/increasingly/quite** rare
> a rare **breed/species/bird/plant**
> a rare **condition/disease/disorder**
> a rare **occasion/instance/exception**

> ▶ **SYNONYMS:** scarce, exceptional, uncommon

> ▶ **RELATED WORD:** unique

rate /reɪt/ (rates)

1 **NOUN** The **rate** at which something happens is the speed with which it happens. ○ *The rate at which hair grows can be agonizingly slow.* ○ *The world's tropical forests are disappearing at an even faster rate than experts had thought.*

> ▶ **COLLOCATIONS:**
> a **fast/slow/alarming/normal** rate
> **growth/metabolic** rate

> ▶ **SYNONYMS:** speed, pace

2 **NOUN** The **rate** at which something happens is the number of times it happens over a period of time. ○ [+ *of*] *New diet books appear at a rate of nearly one a week.* ○ *His heart rate was 30 beats per minute slower.* ○ *the highest divorce rate in Europe*

> ▶ **COLLOCATIONS:**
> a rate **of** *x*
> **birth/mortality/death/divorce/survival/success** rates
> *someone's* **heart** rate
> a rate **rises/falls**

3 **NOUN** The **rate** of taxation or interest is the amount of tax or interest that needs to be paid. It is expressed as a percentage of the amount that is earned, gained as profit, or borrowed. ○ *The government insisted that it*

r

would not be panicked into interest rate cuts. ○ [+ *of*] *The card has a fixed annual rate of 9.9% and no annual fee.*

▶ **COLLOCATIONS:**
a rate **of** *x*
fix/cut/raise/charge a rate
a **fixed/variable/standard/base** rate
a **mortgage/interest/tax/lending** rate
a rate **increase/reduction**

▶ **SYNONYM:** percentage

---

ra|ther than /ræðər ðən/

PREPOSITION Rather than means "instead of." ○ *The new advertisements will focus on product and features, rather than image.*

● **Rather than** is also a conjunction. ○ *The cash is being reinvested rather than being handed to shareholders as dividends.*

---

ra|tio /reɪʃoʊ, -ʃioʊ/ (ratios)

NOUN A **ratio** is a relationship between two things when it is expressed in numbers or amounts. For example, if there are ten boys and thirty girls in a room, the ratio of boys to girls is 1:3, or one to three. ○ [+ *of*] *In 1978 there were 884 students at a lecturer/student ratio of 1:15.* ○ [+ *of*] *The bottom chart shows the ratio of personal debt to personal income.* ○ *The adult to child ratio is 1 to 6.*

▶ **COLLOCATIONS:**
a ratio **of** *something*
a ratio of *x* **to** *y*
calculate/adjust a ratio
a **high/constant/low** ratio
a **price-earnings/power-to-weight/pupil-teacher** ratio

▶ **SYNONYM:** proportion

---

ra|tion|al /ræʃənᵊl/

ADJECTIVE Rational decisions and thoughts are based on reason rather than on emotion. ○ *He's asking you to look at both sides of the case and come to a rational decision.* ○ *Mary was able to short-circuit her stress response by keeping her thoughts calm and rational.*

▶ **COLLOCATIONS:**
a rational **decision/argument/explanation/approach**

rational **thought/analysis/debate**
perfectly rational

▶ **PHRASE:** calm and rational

▶ **SYNONYMS:** sensible, logical

---

raw ma|terials /rɔ mətɪəriəlz/ LOGISTICS & DISTRIBUTION

PLURAL NOUN **Raw materials** are materials that are in their natural state, before they are processed or used in manufacturing. ○ *ships bringing the raw materials for the ever-expanding textile industry* ○ *Villages became associated with different trades, depending on the availability of raw materials in the area.*

▶ **COLLOCATIONS:**
provide/lack raw materials
import/extract/purchase/secure/transform raw materials
essential/cheap raw materials

---

reach /riːtʃ/ (reaches, reaching, reached)

VERB If someone or something has **reached** a certain stage, level, or amount, they are at that stage, level, or amount. ○ *The process of political change in South Africa has reached the stage where it is irreversible.* ○ *We're told the figure could reach 100,000 next year.*

▶ **COLLOCATIONS:**
reach a **stage/level/point**
reach **agreement**
reach a **conclusion/settlement/decision**
reach a **temperature/age**
finally/eventually/easily reach *something*
already/almost/never reach *something*

▶ **SYNONYMS:** attain, arrive at

r

---

re|act /riːækt/ (reacts, reacting, reacted)

1 VERB When you **react to** something that has happened to you, you behave in a particular way because of it. ○ [+ *to*] *They reacted violently to the news.* ○ *It's natural to react with disbelief if your child is accused of bullying.*

▶ **COLLOCATIONS:**
react **to/with** *something*
react to **news/information/situation/announcement/decision**
react with **fury/anger/horror/disbelief**

markets/investors/fans react
react **angrily/swiftly/strongly/positively**

▶ SYNONYM: respond

2 VERB When one chemical substance **reacts with** another, or when two chemical substances **react**, they combine chemically to form another substance. ○ [+ with] *Calcium reacts with water.* ○ *Under normal circumstances, these two gases react readily to produce carbon dioxide and water.*

▶ COLLOCATIONS:
react **with** *something*
react **readily/quickly/slowly/normally**

re|ac|tion /riˈækʃᵊn/ (reactions)

1 NOUN Your **reaction** to something that has happened or something that you have experienced is what you feel, say, or do because of it. ○ [+ to] *Reaction to the visit is mixed.* ○ [+ of] *The initial reaction of most participants is fear.*

▶ COLLOCATIONS:
a reaction **to** *something*
the reaction **of** *someone*
provoke/trigger/cause/prompt a reaction
a **positive/negative/mixed/adverse** reaction
an **emotional/angry** reaction
a **knee-jerk/initial/immediate/gut** reaction

▶ SYNONYM: response

2 NOUN A chemical **reaction** is a process in which two substances combine together chemically to form another substance. ○ [+ between] *Ozone is produced by the reaction between oxygen and ultra-violet light.* ○ *Catalysts are materials which greatly speed up chemical reactions.*

▶ COLLOCATIONS:
a reaction **between** *things*
a **chemical/chain** reaction
speed up/slow down/monitor/observe/cause a reaction

read|ily /ˈrɛdɪli/

ADVERB You use **readily** to say that something can be done or obtained quickly and easily. For example, if you say that something can be readily understood, you mean that people can understand it quickly and easily. ○ *The components are readily available in hardware stores.* ○ *Haemoglobin combines with carbon monoxide even more readily than oxygen.*

▶ COLLOCATIONS:
readily **accept/admit/agree**
readily **apparent**
readily **available**

▶ SYNONYM: easily

---

real es|tate /rɪl ɪsteɪt/

NONCOUNT NOUN Real estate is property in the form of land and
buildings. ○ *This is what should you be aware of when you invest in real estate.*

▶ COLLOCATIONS:
sell/buy real estate
a real estate **agent/broker/deal/investment**
real estate **prices**

---

re|al|ity /riælɪti/

1 NONCOUNT NOUN You use **reality** to refer to real things or the real
nature of things rather than imagined, invented, or theoretical ideas.
○ *Fiction and reality were increasingly blurred.* ○ *Psychiatrists become too
caught up in their theories to deal adequately with reality.*

▶ COLLOCATIONS:
harsh/virtual/grim reality
political/economic/commercial reality
face/reflect/distort/understand reality

▶ SYNONYMS: fact, actuality

2 PHRASE You can use **in reality** to introduce a statement about the real
nature of something, when it contrasts with something incorrect that
has just been described. ○ *He came across as streetwise, but in reality he was
not.* ○ *For convenience, we can classify these differences into three groups,
although in reality they are innumerable.*

▶ SYNONYMS: in fact, actually, in truth

re|al|is|tic /riəlɪstɪk/

ADJECTIVE If you are **realistic** about a situation, you recognize and accept
its true nature and try to deal with it in a practical way. ○ [+ *about*] *Police
have to be realistic about violent crime.* ○ *a realistic view of what we can afford*

▶ COLLOCATIONS:
realistic **about** something
a realistic **view/approach/assessment/option**
a realistic **expectation/goal/chance**

re|al|ize /ríəlaɪz/ (realizes, realizing, realized)

VERB If you **realize** something, you become aware of it or understand it. [in BRIT, also use **realise**] ○ [+ that] *Bankers have realized that they will face a lot of loan defaults.* ○ [+ how] *People don't realize how serious the situation is.*

▸ **COLLOCATIONS:**
realize **that/how/what/why**
fully/finally realize

re|al|ly /ríəli/

ADVERB You use **really** to give a sentence a stronger meaning. [SPOKEN] ○ *I'm very sorry. I really am.*

▸ **COLLOCATIONS:**
really **need/hate/like**
really **good/bad/nice**
should really *do something*

rea|son /ríz³n/ (reasons)

1 **NOUN** The **reason for** something is a fact or situation that explains why it happens or what causes it to happen. ○ [+ for] *There is a reason for every important thing that happens.* ○ *Who would have a reason to want to kill her?* ○ *the reason why Italian tomatoes have so much flavor* ○ *My parents came to Germany for business reasons.*

▸ **COLLOCATIONS:**
a reason **for** *something*
for a reason
give/find/have a reason
the **main/obvious/real/only** reason
a **major/good/wrong/simple** reason
for **personal/family/tax/health** reasons
for **safety/security** reasons

▸ **PHRASES:**
for no reason (at all)
for some reason
see no reason why (not)

▸ **SYNONYMS:** grounds, cause, excuse, motive, justification

2 **NONCOUNT NOUN** The ability that people have to think and to make sensible judgments can be referred to as **reason**. ○ *a conflict between emotion and reason* ○ *Never underestimate their powers of reason and logic.* ○ *the man of madness and the man of reason*

▶ **PHRASES:**
the voice of reason
listen to reason
it stands to reason

rea|son|able /ríːzənəbəl/

1 **ADJECTIVE** If you say that a decision or action is **reasonable**, you mean that it is fair and sensible. ○ *a perfectly reasonable decision* ○ *At the time, what he'd done had seemed reasonable.* ○ *reasonable grounds for complaint*

2 **ADJECTIVE** If you say that an expectation or explanation is **reasonable**, you mean that there are good reasons why it may be correct. ○ *It seems reasonable to expect rapid urban growth.* ○ *There must be some other reasonable answer.*

▶ **COLLOCATIONS:**
a reasonable **expectation/assumption/compromise/request**
reasonable **grounds/doubt**
sound/seem reasonable
perfectly reasonable
reasonable to **assume/expect**

▶ **PHRASE:** beyond a reasonable doubt

▶ **SYNONYM:** sensible

rea|son|ing /ríːzənɪŋ/

NONCOUNT NOUN **Reasoning** is the process by which you reach a conclusion after thinking about all the facts. ○ [+ behind] *the reasoning behind the decision* ○ *She was not really convinced by this line of reasoning.*

▶ **COLLOCATIONS:**
the reasoning **behind** *something*
understand/use/explain/follow the reasoning
moral/practical/logical/deductive reasoning
reasoning **ability/skill/power**
the reasoning **process**

▶ **PHRASE:** a line of reasoning

▶ **SYNONYMS:** thinking, logic

---

re|assure /ríːəʃʊər/ (reassures, reassuring, reassured)

VERB If you **reassure** someone, you say or do things to make them stop worrying. ○ [+ that] *I reassured her that the article had given a misleading impression.*

▶ **COLLOCATIONS:**
reassure *someone* **about** *something*
quickly/constantly/gently reassure
try to reassure

▶ **PHRASE:** it is reassuring

re|assur|ance /riəʃʊərəns/

NONCOUNT NOUN ○ [+ *that*] *Suppliers need reassurance that they will be paid.*

▶ **COLLOCATIONS:**
need/want/seek/receive reassurance
give/offer/provide reassurance

---

re|bate /ríːbeɪt/ (rebates)   BANKING & FINANCE

NOUN A **rebate** is an amount of money that is returned to you after you have paid for goods or services or after you have paid tax or rent. ○ [+ *on*] *Citicorp will guarantee its credit card customers a rebate on a number of products.*

▶ **COLLOCATIONS:**
a rebate **on** *something*
claim/receive/get/offer a rebate
eligible for/entitled to a rebate
a **mail-in/online** rebate
a **product/tax/rent/rate** rebate

▶ **SYNONYM:** refund

---

re|ceive /rɪsíːv/ (receives, receiving, received)   BANKING & FINANCE

VERB When you **receive** something, you get it after someone gives it to you or sends it to you. ○ *They will receive their awards at a ceremony in Stockholm.* ○ *I received your letter from November 7th.*

▶ **COLLOCATIONS:**
receive *something* **from** *someone*
receive a **letter/call/complaint/payment/message**
receive **treatment/attention/support/information**
receive a **gift/award/benefit**
receive **compensation/funding**

EXTEND YOUR VOCABULARY

Get is a very common verb in everyday English and can sometimes be informal. In more formal writing, you often use more specific verbs. You use **receive** when you get something because someone gives it to you. ○ *Users receive text messages with regular updates.*

You can use **obtain** when you get something, especially by searching for it or trying to get it. ○ *Market researchers obtained information using detailed questionnaires.*

---

re|ceipt /rɪsiːt/ (receipts)

NOUN A **receipt** is a piece of paper that shows that you have received goods or money. ○ *I gave her a receipt for the money.*

▶ **COLLOCATIONS:**
get/give/issue/ask for/require a receipt
make out/write/sign a receipt

▶ **SYNONYM:** sales slip

---

re|cent /riːsᵊnt/

ADJECTIVE A **recent** event or period of time happened only a short while ago. ○ *In the most recent attack one man was shot dead and two others were wounded.* ○ *Sales have fallen by more than 75 percent in recent years.*

▶ **COLLOCATIONS:**
recent **days/weeks/months/years**
a recent **survey/study/report**
recent **history**
fairly/relatively/comparatively recent

---

re|cep|tion|ist /rɪsɛpʃənɪst/ (receptionists)   [JOBS]

NOUN A **receptionist** is a person in a hotel or a business whose job is to answer the telephone and deal with visitors. ○ [+ *in*] *I was working as a receptionist in my college.*

▶ **COLLOCATIONS:**
a receptionist **in/at** *somewhere*
a **hotel/dental/doctor's** receptionist

re|ces|sion /rɪsɛʃ°n/ (recessions) `BANKING & FINANCE`

NOUN A **recession** is a period when the economy of a country is doing badly, for example because industry is producing less and more people are becoming unemployed. ○ *The recession caused sales to drop off.* ○ *We should concentrate on sharply reducing interest rates to pull the economy out of recession.* ○ *The oil price increases sent Europe into deep recession.*

▶ **COLLOCATIONS:**
avoid/survive/escape/enter a recession
a **global/deep/severe/economic/mild** recession

▶ **PHRASE:** recession and unemployment

▶ **SYNONYMS:** depression, slump

rec|og|nize /rɛkəgnaɪz/ (recognizes, recognizing, recognized)

1 VERB If someone says that they **recognize** something, they acknowledge that it exists or that it is true. [in BRIT, also use **recognise**] ○ [+ *that*] *We recognized that the situation was becoming increasingly dangerous.* ○ [+ *that*] *Well, of course I recognize that evil exists.*

▶ **SYNONYM:** acknowledge

2 VERB If people or organizations **recognize** something as valid, they officially accept it or approve of it. [in BRIT, also use **recognise**] ○ [+ *as*] *Most doctors appear to recognize homeopathy as a legitimate form of medicine.* ○ *a nationally recognized expert on psychology*

▶ **COLLOCATIONS:**
recognize *something* **as** *something*
recognize the **importance/need/danger/reality/value**
a **court/award** recognizes *someone/something*
internationally/widely/officially recognized

▶ **SYNONYM:** accept

rec|og|ni|tion /rɛkəgnɪʃ°n/

NONCOUNT NOUN Recognition of something is an understanding and acceptance of it. ○ [+ *of*] *The CBI welcomed the Chancellor's recognition of the recession.* ○ [+ *of*] *This agreement was a formal recognition of an existing state of affairs.*

▶ **COLLOCATIONS:**
recognition **of** *something*
recognition of a **fact/need/qualification**
recognition of **independence/sovereignty**

formal/official/diplomatic/international recognition
belated/widespread recognition

▶ synonym: acknowledgement

---

rec|om|mend /rɛkəmɛnd/ (recommends, recommending, recommended)

1 verb If someone **recommends** a person or thing to you, they suggest that you would find that person or thing good or useful. ○ [+ *for*] *foods that are recommended for diabetics* ○ *Ask your doctor to recommend a suitable therapist.* ○ [+ *as*] *Brenda came highly recommended as a hard-working manager.*

2 verb If you **recommend** that something is done, you suggest that it should be done. ○ [+ *that*] *The judge recommended that he serve 20 years in prison.* ○ [+ *v-ing*] *We strongly recommend reporting the incident to the police.*

▶ COLLOCATIONS:
recommend *something* **to** *someone*
recommend *something/someone* **for/as** *something*
recommend for **use/children**
highly/strongly recommended
a **doctor/expert/report/committee** recommends *something*
guidelines recommend *something*

▶ SYNONYMS: put forward, suggest, commend, advise, advocate

rec|om|men|da|tion /rɛkəmɛndeɪʃən/ (recommendations)

NOUN ○ *The committee's recommendations are unlikely to be made public.* ○ [+ *of*] *The decision was made on the recommendation of the Interior Secretary.*

▶ COLLOCATIONS:
the recommendation **of** *someone*
on *someone's* recommendation

▶ SYNONYMS: suggestion, advice

---

rec|ord (records, recording, recorded)

(The noun is pronounced /rɛkərd/. The verb is pronounced /rɪkɔrd/.)

1 NOUN If you keep a **record of** something, you keep a written account or photographs of it so that it can be referred to later. ○ [+ *of*] *Keep a record of all the payments.* ○ *There's no record of any marriage or children.* ○ *The result will go in your medical records.*

▶ **COLLOCATIONS:**
a record **of** *something*
keep/check/enter a record
medical/dental/criminal/military records
a **written/historical/official** record

▶ **PHRASES:**
for the record
off the record
on record
set/put the record straight

▶ **SYNONYMS:** document, journal, database, register, file

2 VERB If you **record** a piece of information or an event, you write it down, photograph it, or put it into a computer so that in the future people can refer to it. ○ *Up to five wives are recorded in some tribes.* ○ *a place which has rarely suffered a famine in its recorded history*

▶ **COLLOCATIONS:**
record a **verdict/conviction**
record a **victory/gain/profit/loss**
faithfully/accurately/dutifully/duly record *something*
automatically/officially record *something*

▶ **SYNONYMS:** document, report

▶ **RELATED WORD:** transcribe

re|cov|er /rɪkʌvər/ (recovers, recovering, recovered) `HEALTH & FITNESS`

1 VERB When you **recover from** an illness or an injury, you become well again. ○ [+ *from*] *He is recovering from a knee injury.* ○ *A policeman was recovering in the hospital last night after being stabbed.* ○ *He is fully recovered from the virus.*

▶ **COLLOCATIONS:**
recover **from** *something*
recover from a **virus/infection/illness/injury/operation**
a **patient** recovers
a recovering **addict/alcoholic**
fully/completely/quickly recover

▶ **SYNONYM:** recuperate

2 VERB If something **recovers from** a period of weakness or difficulty, it improves or gets stronger again. ○ *The stock market index fell by 80% before it began to recover.* ○ [+ *from*] *He recovered from a 4-2 deficit to reach the quarter-finals.*

▶ **COLLOCATIONS:**
recover **from** something
recover from a **recession/slump/setback/downturn**
a **market/economy** recovers

▶ **SYNONYM:** rally

re|cov|ery /rɪkʌvəri/ **(recoveries)**

1 NOUN If a sick person makes a **recovery**, he or she becomes well again.
○ [+ from] He made a remarkable recovery from a shin injury. ○ He had been given less than a one in 500 chance of recovery by his doctors.

▶ **COLLOCATIONS:**
recovery **from** something
a **rapid/remarkable/miraculous/full/complete** recovery
a recovery **process/room/rate**

2 NOUN When there is a **recovery** in a country's economy, it improves.
○ Interest-rate cuts have failed to bring about economic recovery. ○ In many sectors of the economy the recovery has started.

▶ **COLLOCATIONS:**
recovery **from** something
predict/expect a recovery
economic recovery
a **slow/steady/sustainable/uncertain** recovery
a recovery **plan/program**

---

rec|rea|tion /rɛkrieɪʃən/

NONCOUNT NOUN Recreation is things that you do in your spare time to relax. ○ Saturday afternoon is for recreation.

▶ **COLLOCATIONS:**
outdoor/indoor/physical recreation
recreation **facilities**
a recreation **center/room/area/building**

▶ **PHRASES:**
rest and recreation
sports and recreation

---

re|cruit /rɪkrut/ **(recruits, recruiting, recruited)**   `PERSONNEL`

VERB If you **recruit** people for an organization, you ask them to join it.
○ We need to recruit and train more skilled workers.

▶ **COLLOCATIONS:**
recruit **as/for/into/to** something
recruit **workers/staff/athletes/players/students**
recruit a **team/crew/army**
recruit **members/volunteers**
a **company/army/school/team** recruits

▶ **SYNONYM:** hire

re|cruit|ment /rɪkrutmənt/

NONCOUNT NOUN ○ [+ of] There has been a drop in the recruitment of soldiers.

▶ **COLLOCATIONS:**
recruitment **of**
recruitment of **workers/soldiers**
executive/staff recruitment
a recruitment **strategy/program/process/policy**

---

re|cur /rɪkɜr/ (recurs, recurring, recurred)

VERB Something that **recurs** happens more than once. ○ a recurring dream

▶ **COLLOCATIONS:**
recur **throughout** something
constantly/frequently/never recur
a recurring **dream/nightmare/thought/headache**
an **event/dream/nightmare** recurs

---

re|cy|cle /risaɪkəl/ (recycles, recycling, recycled)

VERB If you **recycle** things that have already been used, such as bottles or sheets of paper, you process them so that they can be used again. ○ The objective is to recycle 98 percent of domestic waste. ○ All glass bottles which can't be refilled can be recycled. ○ printed on recycled paper

▶ **COLLOCATIONS:**
recycle **cans/glass/plastic/paper/packaging**
recycled **waste/trash/tires/containers**

▶ **SYNONYM:** reuse

▶ **RELATED WORD:** compost

---

re|duce /rɪdus/ (reduces, reducing, reduced)

VERB If you **reduce** something, you make it smaller in size or amount, or less in degree. ○ It reduces the risks of heart disease. ○ Consumption is being *reduced by 25 percent.* ○ *The reduced consumer demand is also affecting company profits.*

→ see note at **decline**

▶ COLLOCATIONS:
   reduce *something* **by** *x*
   reduce *something* by **half/a third**
   reduce the **number/rate/level/size** of *something*
   reduce **costs/debt/spending/taxes**
   reduce **anxiety/pain/stress/violence**
   reduce **waste/emissions**
   dramatically/significantly/substantially reduce *something*

▶ SYNONYMS: decrease, lessen, lower

re|duc|tion /rɪdʌkʃ°n/ (reductions)

NOUN ○ [+ *of*] *This morning's inflation figures show a reduction of 0.2 percent from 5.8 percent to 5.6.* ○ [+ *in*] *Many companies have announced dramatic reductions in staff.* ○ [+ *of*] *the reduction of inflation and interest rates*

▶ COLLOCATIONS:
   a reduction **of** *x*
   a reduction **in** *something*
   the reduction **of** *something*
   a reduction in **mortality/emissions/size/rates**
   cost/deficit/tax/debt/poverty reduction
   weight/noise/stress reduction
   achieve/propose/announce/mean a reduction
   a **significant/further/substantial/dramatic** reduction

▶ SYNONYMS: decrease, lowering

---

re-evaluate /riːɪvælyueɪt/ (re-evaluates, re-evaluating, re-evaluated)

VERB If you **re-evaluate** a plan or an idea, you consider it again in order to decide how good or bad it is. ○ *We are currently re-evaluating our strategy to increase the profile of this campaign.*

▶ COLLOCATIONS: re-evaluate a **plan/idea/strategy/progress**

---

re|fer /rɪfɜr/ (refers, referring, referred)

1 VERB If you **refer to** a particular subject or person, you talk about them or mention them. ○ [+ *to*] *In his speech, he referred to a recent trip to Canada.* ○ *"What precisely is your interest in the patient referred to here?"*

▶ **COLLOCATIONS:**
refer **to** *something/someone*
refer to a **memo/paragraph/article/document**
refer to a **word/phrase/term/statistic**

▶ **SYNONYMS:** mention, cite

2 VERB If you **refer to** someone or something **as** a particular thing, you use a particular word, expression, or name to mention or describe them. ○ [+ to] *Marcia had referred to him as a dear friend.* ○ *Our economy is referred to as a free market.*

▶ **COLLOCATIONS:**
refer **to** *something/someone*
refer to *something/someone* **as** *something*
often/repeatedly/frequently/constantly referred to as *something*
commonly/jokingly/affectionately referred to as *something*

▶ **SYNONYMS:** allude, call, describe

3 VERB If a word **refers to** a particular thing, situation, or idea, it describes it in some way. ○ [+ to] *The term electronics refers to electrically-induced action.* ○ *English prefers nouns to verbs — that is, words which refer to objects rather than words which refer to actions.*

▶ **COLLOCATION:** refer **to** *something/someone*

▶ **SYNONYMS:** describe, relate to, apply to

ref|er|ence /rɛfərəns, rɛfrəns/ (references)

NOUN A **reference** is a word, phrase, or idea that comes from something such as a book, poem, or play and that you use when making a point about something. ○ [+ from] *a reference from the Quran* ○ *historical references* ○ [+ to] *In Doyle's prison file there's a reference to a military intelligence report.*

▶ **COLLOCATIONS:**
a reference **from/to** *something*
make/include/find a reference
quote/cite a reference

▶ **SYNONYMS:** quote, allusion

re|fi|nanc|ing /riːfənænsɪŋ, rifaɪnæn-/ `BANKING & FINANCE`

NONCOUNT NOUN **Refinancing** is the act or process of paying a debt by borrowing money from another lender. ○ *The proceeds will be used for general corporate purposes, which may include debt refinancing.*

▶ **COLLOCATIONS:**
debt/mortgage/loan refinancing

seek/secure/approve refinancing
a refinancing **plan/deal/package/boom**

---

re|flect /rɪflɛkt/ **(reflects, reflecting, reflected)**

1 **VERB** If something **reflects** an attitude or situation, it shows that the attitude or situation exists or it shows what it is like. ○ *The Los Angeles riots reflected the bitterness between the black and Korean communities in the city.* ○ *Concern at the economic situation was reflected in the government's budget.*

▶ **COLLOCATIONS:**
a **view/concern/change/decision** reflects *something*
reflect a **fact/value/belief/interest**
clearly reflect *something*

▶ **SYNONYM:** show

2 **VERB** When light, heat, or other rays **reflect** off a surface or when a surface **reflects** them, they are sent back from the surface and do not pass through it. ○ *The sun reflected off the snow-covered mountains.* ○ *The glass appears to reflect light naturally.*

▶ **COLLOCATIONS:**
reflect **off** *something*
reflect off a **surface/window**
reflect off **water**
reflect **light/sunlight/heat**
reflect an **image**

re|flec|tion /rɪflɛkʃ°n/ **(reflections)**

1 **NOUN** If you say that something is a **reflection of** a particular person's attitude or **of** a situation, you mean that it is caused by that attitude or situation and therefore reveals something about it. ○ [+ of] *Inhibition in adulthood seems to be very clearly a reflection of a person's experiences as a child.*

▶ **COLLOCATIONS:**
a reflection **of** *something*
a reflection of a **fact/attitude/trend**
a **direct/clear/obvious** reflection of *something*

▶ **SYNONYM:** indication

2 **NONCOUNT NOUN** **Reflection** is when light, heat, or other rays are sent back from a surface and do not pass through it. ○ [+ of] *the reflection of a beam of light off a mirror*

▶ **COLLOCATIONS:**
the reflection **of** *something*
the reflection of **light/sunlight/heat**

---

re|gard /rɪɡɑ́rd/ (regards, regarding, regarded)

1 **VERB** If you **regard** someone or something **as** being a particular thing or **as** having a particular quality, you believe that they are that thing or have that quality. ○ [+ as] *He was regarded as the most successful Chancellor of modern times.* ○ [+ as] *I regard creativity both as a gift and as a skill.*

▶ **COLLOCATIONS:**
regard *someone/something* **as** *something*
regard *someone* as a **contender/outsider**
regard *something* as a **classic**

2 **PHRASE** You can use **as regards** to indicate the subject that is being talked or written about. ○ *As regards the war, Haig believed in victory at any price.* ○ *A complete revolution of opinion has taken place as regards the formation of mountain chains.*

▶ **SYNONYMS:** concerning, regarding, relating to

3 **PHRASE** You can use **with regard to** or **in regard to** to indicate the subject that is being talked or written about. ○ *The department is reviewing its policy with regard to immunisation.* ○ *The prognosis is looking good, particularly in regard to her physical condition.*

▶ **SYNONYMS:** concerning, regarding

4 **PHRASE** You can use **in this regard** or **in that regard** to refer back to something that you have just said. ○ *In this regard nothing has changed.* ○ *I may have made a mistake in that regard.*

▶ **SYNONYMS:** on this/that point, in this/that respect

re|gard|ing /rɪɡɑ́rdɪŋ/

PREPOSITION You can use **regarding** to indicate the subject that is being talked or written about. ○ *He refused to divulge any information regarding the man's whereabouts.* ○ *There are conflicting reports regarding the number of terrorists involved.*

▶ **SYNONYM:** concerning

BUSINESS CORRESPONDENCE: *regarding* **and** *concerning*?

In business correspondence, the words **regarding** and **concerning** are often used to indicate the subject you are writing about.

○ *For questions regarding delivery times, please contact Customer Service.*
○ *This letter is in response to your inquiry concerning home insurance.*

The abbreviation **re:** is often used in notes, headings and informal
communications. ○ *Re: Meeting June 21*

---

re|gion /rˈiːdʒ³n/ (regions)

NOUN A **region** is a large area of land that is different from other areas of
land, for example because it is one of the different parts of a country with
its own customs and characteristics, or because it has a particular
geographical feature. ○ *Barcelona, capital of the autonomous region of
Catalonia* ○ *a remote mountain region*

▶ COLLOCATIONS:
  tour/visit/explore a region
  affect/destabilize/devastate/dominate a region
  divide/surround a region
  a **mountain/mountainous/industrial/mining** region
  a **barren/icy/remote/coastal** region
  a **disputed/autonomous/troubled** region
  a **border/frontier/desert/farming** region

▶ SYNONYMS: area, province, country

---

reg|is|ter /rˈɛdʒɪstər/ (registers, registering, registered)

1 VERB If you **register** to do something, you put your name on an official
list. ○ [+ to-inf] *Thousands lined up to register to vote.* ○ [+ for] *Many students
register for these courses to widen skills for use in their current job.* ○ *registered
voters*

▶ COLLOCATIONS:
  register **for/with** something
  register with a **dentist/authority/agency/embassy**
  register for a **service/election**
  a registered **voter/adviser/subscriber/nurse**
  officially register

▶ SYNONYMS: enroll, enlist, sign up

2 VERB If you **register** something, you have it recorded on an official list.
  ○ *In order to register a car in Japan, the owner must have somewhere to park it.*
  ○ *They registered his birth.* ○ *a registered charity*

r

▶ **COLLOCATIONS:**
a registered **trademark/logo/firearm/charity**
register a **birth/complaint**
officially registered

▶ **SYNONYMS:** license, record

3 VERB When something **registers on** a scale or measuring instrument, it shows on the scale or instrument. You can also say that something **registers** a certain amount or level **on** a scale or measuring instrument. ○ [+ on] *It will only register on sophisticated X-ray equipment.* ○ *The earthquake registered 5.3 points on the Richter scale.* ○ *The scales registered a gain of 1.3 pounds.*

▶ **COLLOCATIONS:**
register **on** *something*
register on a **radar/scale**
a **sensor** registers *something*
a **tremor/earthquake** registers *x*
register a **gain/increase/decline**
barely register

▶ **SYNONYM:** show

reg|is|tra|tion /rɛdʒɪstreɪʃən/

NONCOUNT NOUN The **registration** of something such as a person's name or the details of an event is the recording of it on an official list. ○ [+ of] *They have campaigned strongly for compulsory registration of dogs.* ○ *With the high voter registration, many will be voting for the first time.* ○ *fill in the registration forms*

▶ **COLLOCATIONS:**
the registration **of** *something*
the registration of **dogs/guns/firearms/interest**
voter/vehicle/car registration
initial/compulsory/online registration
a registration **form/requirement/number/process/fee**

▶ **SYNONYM:** licensing

regu|lar /rɛgyələr/

ADJECTIVE Regular events have equal amounts of time between them, so that they happen, for example, at the same time each day or each week. ○ *Get regular exercise.* ○ *We're going to be meeting there on a regular basis.* ○ *The cartridge must be replaced at regular intervals.*

▶ **COLLOCATIONS:**
regular **breathing/rhythm/exercise**
a regular **visitor/contributor/user/customer**
regular **intervals/updates**
regular **meetings/appointments/check-ups/visits**
a regular **occurrence/incident/feature/schedule**

▶ **PHRASE:** on a regular basis

▶ **SYNONYM:** frequent

regu|lar|ly /rɛgyələrli/

ADVERB ○ *Exercise regularly.* ○ *He also writes regularly for "International Management" magazine.*

▶ **COLLOCATIONS:**
happen/occur/meet/check/update/pause regularly
exercise/appear/visit regularly

▶ **SYNONYMS:** frequently, routinely

---

regu|late /rɛgyəleɪt/ (regulates, regulating, regulated)   `LEGAL`

VERB To **regulate** an activity or process means to control it, especially by means of rules. ○ *The powers of the European Commission to regulate competition are increasing.* ○ *regulating cholesterol levels*

▶ **COLLOCATIONS:**
regulate a **use/activity/industry**
a **law/state/government** regulates *something*

▶ **SYNONYMS:** control, manage

regu|la|tion /rɛgyəleɪʃən/ (regulations)

NONCOUNT NOUN ○ *AGT opposed the application and claimed immunity from federal regulation.*

▶ **COLLOCATIONS:**
federal/government/state/official regulation
financial regulation
strict/tighter regulation

▶ **SYNONYM:** control

regu|la|tory /rɛgyələtɔri/

ADJECTIVE ○ *the U.K.'s financial regulatory system* ○ *This new regulatory regime was designed to protect the public.*

r

▸ **COLLOCATIONS:**
a regulatory **system/regime/body/agency/authority**
a regulatory **requirement/framework**
regulatory **approval/reform**

---

re|hearse /rɪhɜrs/ **(rehearses, rehearsing, rehearsed)** `OFFICE`

VERB When people **rehearse** a performance, they practice it. ○ *The actors are rehearsing a play.*

▸ **COLLOCATIONS:**
rehearse a **play/scene/speech/dance**
a **dancer/actor/musician/band** rehearses

▸ **SYNONYM:** practice

---

re|inforce /riɪnfɔrs/ **(reinforces, reinforcing, reinforced)**

1 VERB If something **reinforces** a feeling, situation, or process, it makes it stronger or more intense. ○ *A stronger European Parliament would, they fear, only reinforce the power of the larger countries.* ○ *This sense of privilege tends to be reinforced by the outside world.*

▸ **COLLOCATIONS:**
reinforce a **perception/view/impression/belief**
mutually/powerfully/constantly/further reinforce *something*

▸ **SYNONYM:** strengthen

2 VERB If something **reinforces** an idea or point of view, it provides more evidence or support for it. ○ *The delegation hopes to reinforce the idea that human rights are not purely internal matters.*

▸ **COLLOCATIONS:**
reinforce a **notion/message/stereotype**
powerfully/further reinforce *something*

▸ **SYNONYM:** support

---

re|ject /rɪdʒɛkt/ **(rejects, rejecting, rejected)**

VERB If you **reject** something such as a proposal, a request, or an offer, you do not accept it or you do not agree to it. ○ *Seventeen publishers rejected the manuscript before Jenks saw its potential.* ○ *reject the possibility of failure*

▸ **COLLOCATIONS:**
voters/shareholders reject *something*
a **board/parliament/union/committee** rejects *something*
a **judge/jury/court** rejects *something*

reject a **proposal/idea/offer/suggestion/claim/call**
flatly/firmly/unanimously/angrily reject *something*
reject *something* **outright**

▶ **SYNONYMS:** deny, turn down, decline

re|jec|tion /rɪdʒɛkʃən/

NONCOUNT NOUN ○ [+ *of*] *The rejection of such initiatives indicates that voters*
are unconcerned about the environment. ○ *the chances of criticism and rejection*

▶ **COLLOCATIONS:**
the rejection **of** *something*
prevent/fear/avoid/face/risk rejection
overwhelming/repeated/initial rejection

▶ **PHRASE:** a letter of rejection

▶ **SYNONYM:** denial

---

re|late /rɪleɪt/ (relates, relating, related)

1 VERB If something **relates to** a particular subject, it concerns that
subject. ○ [+ *to*] *Other recommendations relate to the details of how such data*
is stored. ○ [+ *to*] *It does not matter whether the problem you have relates to*
food, drink, smoking, or just living.

▶ **COLLOCATIONS:**
relate **to** *something*
a **document/issue/matter** relates to *something*
a **rule/allegation/charge** relating to *something*
information relating to *something*

▶ **SYNONYMS:** concern, involve

2 VERB The way that two things **relate**, or the way that one thing **relates**
to another, is the kind of connection that exists between them. ○ *More*
studies will be required before we know what the functions of these genes are
and whether they relate to each other. ○ [+ *to*] *Cornell University offers a course*
that investigates how language relates to particular cultural codes.

▶ **COLLOCATION:** relate **to** *something*

▶ **SYNONYM:** connect

re|lat|ed /rɪleɪtɪd/

ADJECTIVE If two or more things are **related**, there is a connection
between them. ○ *The philosophical problems of chance and of free will are*
closely related. ○ *equipment and accessories for diving and related activities*

▶ **COLLOCATIONS:**
related **activities/information/matters/developments**
closely/directly/inversely related

▶ **SYNONYM:** connected

re|la|tion /rɪleɪʃən/ (relations)

1 NOUN Relations between people, groups, or countries are contacts
between them and the way in which they behave toward each other.
○ [+ with] Greece has established full diplomatic relations with Israel.
○ [+ between] Apparently relations between husband and wife had not
improved. ○ The company has a track record of good employee relations.

▶ **COLLOCATIONS:**
relations **with** someone
relations **between** people
relations **improve/deteriorate/worsen**
improve/establish/normalize/restore relations
diplomatic/public/industrial/international relations
race/gender/community relations
normal/friendly/poor/close relations

▶ **SYNONYMS:** contact, link

USAGE: *relations* or *relationship*?

You use **relationship** to talk about the family and personal
connections and friendships between individuals. ○ She had a close
relationship with her grandfather.

You can use **relations** or **relationship** to talk about connections
between groups of people and countries. You use **relations**
particularly to refer to the way that two groups or countries
communicate or deal with each other. ○ the delicate diplomatic relations
between the two countries

You use **relationship** more to talk about the connection between
two groups or countries that develops over time. ○ Companies feel call
centers can improve their relationship with customers.

---

2 NOUN If you talk about the **relation of** one thing **to** another, you are
talking about the ways in which they are connected. ○ [+ of] It is a
question of the relation of ethics to economics. ○ [+ between] a relation between
unemployment and drug-related offenses ○ [+ to] This theory bears no relation
to reality.

▶ **COLLOCATIONS:**
the relation **of** something **to** something
the relation **between** things

▶ **SYNONYMS:** concerning, regarding, with regard to, in respect of

3 PHRASE You can talk about something **in relation to** something else when you want to compare the size, condition, or position of the two things. ○ *The money he'd been ordered to pay was minimal in relation to his salary.* ○ *women's position in relation to men in the context of the family*

▶ **SYNONYM:** in comparison to

re|la|tion|ship /rɪleɪʃ°nʃɪp/ (relationships)

1 NOUN The **relationship** between two people or groups is the way in which they feel and behave toward each other. ○ *the friendly relationship between France and Britain* ○ *family relationships*

▶ **COLLOCATIONS:**
a relationship **between** people
personal relationships
a **professional/working/strong** relationship
a **good/healthy/close/intimate** relationship
a **romantic/loving/sexual** relationship
a **lesbian/homosexual/same-sex** relationship
a **meaningful/abusive/love-hate** relationship
a **stable/long-term/lasting/long-standing** relationship
develop/start/form/establish a relationship
build/maintain a relationship
strengthen/improve/sustain a relationship

▶ **SYNONYMS:** bond, partnership

2 NOUN The **relationship** between two things is the way in which they are connected. ○ [+ between] *There is a relationship between diet and cancer.* ○ [+ to] *an analysis of market mechanisms and their relationship to state capitalism and political freedom*

▶ **COLLOCATIONS:**
a relationship **between** things
a relationship **to** something
analyze/understand a relationship
a **close/strong/important/complex** relationship
a **cause-and-effect** relationship

▶ **SYNONYMS:** connection, association, link

r

rela|tive /rɛlətɪv/ (relatives)

1 NOUN Your **relatives** are the members of your family. ○ *We need to inform his relatives.* ○ *I was taken in by my mother's only relative.* ○ *a counseling service for relatives and friends as well as the drug abusers themselves*

▸ **COLLOCATIONS:**
a **close/near/distant/long-lost** relative
a **sick/elderly** relative
a **living/dead/surviving/blood** relative
grieving/bereaved relatives
visit/contact/trace relatives

▸ **PHRASE:** friends and relatives

▸ **SYNONYM:** relation

2 ADJECTIVE You use **relative** to say that something is true to a certain degree, especially when compared with other things of the same kind. ○ *The fighting resumed after a period of relative calm.* ○ *It is a cancer that can be cured with relative ease.*

3 ADJECTIVE You use **relative** when you are comparing the quality or size of two things. ○ *They chatted about the relative merits of London and Paris as places to live.* ○ *I reflected on the relative importance of education in 50 countries.*

▸ **COLLOCATIONS:**
relative **calm/obscurity/importance/safety**
relative **merits/advantages/strength**

▸ **SYNONYMS:** comparative, corresponding

4 PHRASE Relative to something means with reference to it or in comparison with it. ○ *House prices now look cheap relative to earnings.* ○ *The satellite remains in one spot relative to the earth's surface.*

▸ **SYNONYM:** in relation to

---

re|lease /rɪliːs/ (releases, releasing, released)

1 VERB If a person or animal **is released** from somewhere where they have been locked up or looked after, they are set free or allowed to go. ○ *[+ from] He was released from custody the next day.* ○ *[+ from] He is expected to be released from the hospital today.* ○ *He was released on bail.*

▸ **COLLOCATIONS:**
released **from** something
released from **prison/jail/custody**
a **prisoner/detainee/patient** is released
police/kidnappers release someone

▶ **PHRASE:** released someone on bail

▶ **SYNONYMS:** set free, free, liberate

- **Release** is also a noun. ○ [+ of] *He called for the immediate release of all political prisoners.* ○ [+ from] *Serious complications have delayed his release from the hospital.*

  ▶ **COLLOCATIONS:**
  release **from** *something*
  the release **of** *someone*
  release from **prison/jail/custody**
  the release of a **prisoner/hostage**
  immediate/imminent/early release
  call for/demand/secure *someone's* release

  ▶ **SYNONYMS:** liberation, discharge

2 VERB If someone in authority **releases** something such as a document or information, they make it available. ○ *They're not releasing any more details yet.* ○ *Figures released yesterday show retail sales were down in March.*

  ▶ **COLLOCATIONS:**
  release a **document/transcript**
  release **figures/details**
  officially release *something*

  ▶ **SYNONYMS:** issue, publish, announce

- **Release** is also a noun. ○ [+ of] *Action had been taken to speed up the release of checks.*

  ▶ **COLLOCATIONS:**
  the release **of** *something*
  the release of a **document/transcript**
  the **official** release of *something*
  a **press** release

  ▶ **SYNONYMS:** issue, publication, announcement

3 VERB If something **releases** gas, heat, or a substance, it causes it to leave its container or the substance that it was part of and enter the surrounding atmosphere or area. ○ *a weapon which releases toxic nerve gas* ○ *The contraction of muscles uses energy and releases heat.*

  ▶ **COLLOCATIONS:**
  release **chemicals/toxins/adrenaline/hormones**
  release *something* **accidentally/simultaneously**

  ▶ **SYNONYM:** discharge

- **Release** is also a noun. ○ [+ of] *Under the agreement, releases of cancer-causing chemicals will be cut by about 80 percent.*

▶ **COLLOCATIONS:**
the release **of** *something*
the release of **chemicals/toxins/adrenaline/hormones**
the **accidental/simultaneous** release of *something*

▶ **SYNONYM:** discharge

rel|evant /rɛləvᵊnt/

ADJECTIVE Something that is **relevant to** a situation or person is important or significant in that situation or to that person. ○ [+ *to*] *Is socialism still relevant to people's lives?* ○ *We have passed all relevant information on to the police.*

▶ **COLLOCATIONS:**
relevant **to** *someone/something*
directly/highly/especially relevant
relevant **information/experience**
a relevant **qualification/document/article**
the relevant **authorities**

▶ **SYNONYM:** pertinent

rel|evance /rɛləvᵊns/

NONCOUNT NOUN ○ [+ *to*] *Politicians' private lives have no relevance to their public roles.* ○ [+ *to*] *There are additional publications of special relevance to new graduates.*

▶ **COLLOCATIONS:**
relevance **to** *someone/something*
the relevance **of** *something*
question/determine the relevance of *something*
lack/have relevance
have **little** relevance
contemporary/social/practical relevance
particular/direct/immediate relevance

▶ **SYNONYM:** appropriateness

re|lieved /rɪlivd/

ADJECTIVE If you are **relieved**, you are feeling happy because something unpleasant has stopped or not happened. ○ [+ *that*] *Officials are relieved that the rise in prices has slowed.*

▶ **COLLOCATIONS:**
relieved **at** *something*

look/feel/seem relieved
greatly/extremely/much relieved

---

re|lin|quish /rɪlɪŋkwɪʃ/ **(relinquishes, relinquishing, relinquished)**

VERB If you **relinquish** something such as power or control, you give it up.
[FORMAL] ○ *He does not intend to relinquish power.*

▶ **COLLOCATIONS:** relinquish **control/power**

▶ **SYNONYMS:** give up, yield

---

re|lo|cate /rɪloʊkeɪt/ **(relocates, relocating, relocated)**   PERSONNEL

VERB If people or businesses **relocate** or if someone **relocates** them, they
move to a different place. ○ *If the company was to relocate, most employees
would move.* ○ *[+ to] The real estate investment trust relocated its principal
office to downtown Austin, Texas.*

▶ **COLLOCATIONS:**
relocate **to** *somewhere*
a **business/company/office/employee** relocates
relocate a **business/company/office/headquarters/employee**

▶ **SYNONYM:** move

re|lo|ca|tion /rɪloʊkeɪʃən/

NONCOUNT NOUN ○ *The company says the cost of relocation will be negligible.*

▶ **COLLOCATIONS:**
a **corporate** relocation
relocation **costs/expenses**
a relocation **package**
forced/proposed relocation

▶ **SYNONYM:** moving

---

re|luc|tant /rɪlʌktənt/

ADJECTIVE If you are **reluctant to** do something, you are unwilling to do it
and hesitate before doing it, or do it slowly and without enthusiasm.
○ *Mr. Spero was reluctant to ask for help.* ○ *The police are very reluctant to get
involved in this kind of thing.*

▶ **COLLOCATIONS:**
reluctant to **admit/discuss/accept** *something*
reluctant to **talk/invest/comment/act**

a reluctant **hero/ally/reader/witness**
initially/increasingly/understandably reluctant

▶ **SYNONYM:** unwilling

re|luc|tance /rɪlʌktəns/

NONCOUNT NOUN ○ *Ministers have shown extreme reluctance to explain their
position to the media.* ○ *Officials have indicated reluctance to quickly lift
the ban.*

▶ **COLLOCATIONS:**
show/express reluctance
overcome/indicate/explain *someone's* reluctance
growing/increasing reluctance
initial/apparent/marked/understandable reluctance

▶ **SYNONYM:** unwillingness

re|luc|tant|ly /rɪlʌktəntli/

ADVERB ○ *We have reluctantly agreed to let him go.* ○ *Rescuers reluctantly ended
their search Thursday morning.*

▶ **COLLOCATIONS:** reluctantly **agree/accept/decide/admit**

▶ **SYNONYMS:** unwillingly, grudgingly

---

rely /rɪlaɪ/ (relies, relying, relied)

VERB If you **rely on** someone or something, you need them and depend on
them in order to live or work properly. ○ [+ *on/upon*] *They relied heavily on
the advice of their professional advisers.* ○ [+ *on/upon*] *The Association relies
on member subscriptions for most of its income.*

▶ **COLLOCATIONS:**
rely **on/upon** *something/someone*
rely on *someone/something* **for** *something*
manufacturers/employers/farmers rely on *someone/something*
rely **heavily** on *someone/something* ·
rely on **support/technology/donations/volunteers**

▶ **SYNONYM:** depend

re|li|able /rɪlaɪəbəl/

ADJECTIVE Information that is **reliable** or that is from a **reliable** source is
very likely to be correct. ○ *There is no reliable information about civilian
casualties.* ○ *It's very difficult to give a reliable estimate.* ○ *We have reliable
sources.*

▶ **COLLOCATIONS:**
a reliable **statistic/prediction/indication/guide**
a reliable **source/informant/predictor/barometer**
reliable **intelligence/evidence/information**

▶ **SYNONYM:** trustworthy

re|li|abil|ity /rɪlaɪəbɪlɪti/

NONCOUNT NOUN ○ [+ *of*] *Both questioned the reliability of recent opinion polls.* ○ [+ *of*] *the reliability of her testimony* ○ [+ *of*] *Check the figures and set them beside other data to get some idea of their reliability.*

▶ **COLLOCATIONS:**
the reliability **of** *something*
the reliability of the **testimony/evidence/intelligence**
question/assure/assess/test the reliability of *something*
questionable/dubious/utter reliability

▶ **SYNONYM:** trustworthiness

---

re|main /rɪmeɪn/ (remains, remaining, remained)

VERB If someone or something **remains** in a particular state or condition, they stay in that state or condition and do not change. ○ *The three men remained silent.* ○ *The government remained in control.* ○ *He remained a formidable opponent.*

▶ **COLLOCATIONS:**
remain a **mystery/threat/secret/priority**
remain a **possibility/favorite**
remain **unchanged/silent/open/unclear**

▶ **SYNONYM:** continue

re|main|ing /rɪmeɪnɪŋ/

ADJECTIVE The **remaining** things or people are the things or people that are still there. ○ *The remaining shares were sold to outside investors.*

▶ **COLLOCATIONS:** remaining **shares/parts/ingredients**

▶ **SYNONYM:** leftover

---

re|mark|able /rɪmɑrkəbəl/

ADJECTIVE If something is **remarkable**, it is very unusual or surprising in a good way. ○ *They encouraged the growth of private businesses, with remarkable success.*

▶ **COLLOCATIONS:**
a remarkable **feat/achievement/result/story/career**
a remarkable **recovery/comeback/turnaround**
remarkable **success/ability**
quite/truly remarkable

▶ **SYNONYM:** extraordinary

---

rem|edy /rɛmədi/ (remedies)   [HEALTH & FITNESS]

1 **NOUN** A **remedy** is a successful way of dealing with a problem. ○ *The remedy lies in the hands of the government.* ○ [+ for] *a remedy for economic ills*

▶ **COLLOCATIONS:**
a remedy **for** something
propose/suggest/devise a remedy

▶ **SYNONYM:** solution

2 **NOUN** A **remedy** is something that is intended to cure you when you are ill or in pain. ○ [+ to-inf] *natural remedies to help overcome winter infections* ○ [+ for] *St John's wort is a popular herbal remedy for depression.*

▶ **COLLOCATIONS:**
a remedy **for** something
a remedy for **depression/disease/illness/pain**
a **herbal/homeopathic/natural** remedy
an **alternative/effective** remedy
a **cough/cold/indigestion** remedy

▶ **SYNONYMS:** cure, treatment

---

re|mind /rɪmaɪnd/ (reminds, reminding, reminded)

1 **VERB** If someone **reminds** you of something or **reminds** you **to** do something, they say something that makes you think about it or remember to do it. ○ [+ of] *She reminded Tim of the last time they met.* ○ [+ to -inf] *Can you remind me to call Jim?*

▶ **COLLOCATIONS:**
remind *someone* **of/about** something
constantly/gently remind

2 **VERB** If someone or something **reminds** you **of** another person or thing, they are similar to them and they make you think about them. ○ [+ of] *She reminds me of your sister.*

▶ **COLLOCATIONS:** **strongly/vividly** remind *someone*

re|mote /rɪmˈoʊt/ (remoter, remotest)

ADJECTIVE Remote areas are far away from cities and places where most people live, and are therefore difficult to get to. ○ *Landslides have cut off many villages in remote areas.* ○ *a remote farm in Vermont*

▶ **COLLOCATIONS:**
a remote **location/community/part**
a remote **area/region/place/corner**
a remote **island/mountain/village/town**

▶ **SYNONYMS:** isolated, inaccessible

re|mote|ly /rɪmˈoʊtli/

ADVERB You use **remotely** to emphasize the negative meaning of a sentence. ○ *He wasn't remotely interested in her.*

▶ **COLLOCATIONS:**
remotely **possible/likely/plausible**
remotely **interested**
remotely **funny/interesting**
remotely **similar/comparable**

---

re|move /rɪmˈuv/ (removes, removing, removed)

VERB If you **remove** something from a place, you take it away. [WRITTEN] ○ [+ from] *attempts to remove carbon dioxide from the atmosphere* ○ [+ from] *Three bullets were removed from his wounds.*

▶ **COLLOCATIONS:**
remove *something* **from** *somewhere*
surgically/forcibly/carefully/completely remove *something*
remove a **tumor/organ/layer/lump**
remove **tissue/skin/fat**
remove a **barrier/restriction/reference**

▶ **SYNONYMS:** take away, take out, extract

re|mov|al /rɪmˈuvˀl/

NONCOUNT NOUN ○ [+ of] *The removal of a small lump turned out to be major surgery.* ○ *The most common type of oxidation involves the removal of hydrogen atoms from a substance.*

▶ **COLLOCATIONS:**
removal **of** *something*
stain/garbage/hair removal

surgical/immediate/complete removal
a removal **cost/process**

▶ **PHRASE:** removal and replacement

▶ **SYNONYMS:** extraction, eradication

---

re|mu|nera|tion /rɪmyunəreɪʃən/ (remunerations)　`PERSONNEL`

NOUN **Remuneration** is the amount of money that a person is paid for the work that they do. [FORMAL ○ [+ of] *the continuing marked increases in the remuneration of the company's directors*

▶ **COLLOCATIONS:**
a remuneration **package/policy**
generous remuneration

▶ **SYNONYM:** payment

---

re|new /rɪnu/ (renews, renewing, renewed)

1 **VERB** If you **renew** an activity, you begin it again. ○ *He renewed his attack on government policy toward Europe.*

▶ **COLLOCATIONS:**
renew **hostilities**
renew an **attack/assault**

▶ **SYNONYM:** resume

2 **VERB** If you **renew** a relationship **with** someone, you start it again after you have not seen them or have not been friendly with them for some time. ○ *When the two men met again after the war they renewed their friendship.*

▶ **COLLOCATIONS:** renew a **friendship/acquaintance**

▶ **SYNONYM:** revive

re|new|able /rɪnuəbəl/

ADJECTIVE **Renewable** resources are natural ones such as wind, water, and sunlight that are always available. ○ *Wind turbines are devices which make use of renewable energy sources.* ○ *each winter's endlessly renewable supply of frozen water*

▶ **COLLOCATIONS:** a renewable **resource/fuel/source**

▶ **PHRASE:** a renewable energy source

re|new|al /rɪnuəl/ (renewals)

NOUN If there is a **renewal of** an activity or a situation, it starts again.
○ *They will discuss the possible renewal of diplomatic relations.*

▶ **COLLOCATION:** the renewal **of** *something*

---

re|nown /rɪnaʊn/

NONCOUNT NOUN A person **of renown** is well known, usually because they do or have done something good. ○ *a singer of renown* ○ *Despite his international renown, he was not qualified as an architect.*

▶ **COLLOCATIONS:**
international/worldwide/great renown
gain/achieve/win renown

▶ **SYNONYM:** fame

---

rent /rɛnt/   LOGISTICS & DISTRIBUTION

NONCOUNT NOUN Rent is the amount of money that you pay to use something that belongs to someone else. ○ *She worked hard to pay the rent on the apartment.*

▶ **COLLOCATIONS:**
pay/afford the rent
collect/raise the rent
charge/owe rent
affordable/low/high/fixed rent

▶ **PHRASE:** for rent

---

reorder /riɔrdər/ (reorders, reordering,   LOGISTICS & DISTRIBUTION
reordered)

VERB If you **reorder** goods, you order more of them from a supplier.
○ *Retailers can reduce their initial orders and reorder what they need.*

▶ **COLLOCATIONS:** reorder **goods/merchandise**

---

re|pair /rɪpɛər/ (repairs, repairing, repaired)

VERB If you **repair** something that is damaged, you fix it. ○ *Goldman has repaired the roof.*

▶ **COLLOCATIONS:**
repair a **roof/car/road/equipment**
repair **damage**
repair a **relationship/problem**

▶ **SYNONYM:** fix

re|pay /rɪpeɪ/ (repays, repaying, repaid)   `BANKING & FINANCE`

VERB If you **repay** a debt, you pay back the money that you borrowed.
○ *They may have difficulty repaying the mortgage interest.*

▶ **COLLOCATIONS:**
repay a **debt/loan/mortgage/money**
repay **interest/principal/capital**
repay a **creditor**
fully repay

re|pay|ment /rɪpeɪmənt/ (repayments)

NONCOUNT NOUN The **repayment of** money is the act or process of paying it back to the person you borrowed it from. ○ [+ *of*] *The bank will expect the repayment of the $114 million loan.* ○ *He took a loan with small, frequent repayments.*

▶ **COLLOCATIONS:**
repayment **of** $x
repayment of a **debt/loan/mortgage**
demand/make/seek repayment
monthly/early repayment
a repayment **schedule/term/period**

---

re|peat /rɪpit/ (repeats, repeating, repeated)

1 VERB If you **repeat** something, you say or write it again. ○ [+ *that*] *He repeated that he had been misquoted.* ○ *The man repeated his question impatiently.*

▶ **COLLOCATIONS:**
repeat a **word/phrase/warning/allegation/accusation**
repeat something **verbatim**

▶ **SYNONYMS:** reiterate, restate

2 VERB If you **repeat** an action, you do it again. ○ *The next day I repeated the procedure.* ○ *He said Japan would never repeat its mistakes.* ○ *Hold this position for 30 seconds, release, and repeat on the other side.*

▶ **COLLOCATIONS:**
repeat a **cycle/pattern**
repeat the **process/exercise/mistake/feat/success**
endlessly repeat

▶ **PHRASE:** history repeats itself

rep|eti|tion /rɛpɪtɪʃən/ (repetitions)

1 **NOUN** If there is a **repetition of** an event, it happens again. ○ [+ of] Today the city government has taken measures to prevent a repetition of last year's confrontation. ○ He wants to avoid repetition of the confusion that followed the discovery of the cystic fibrosis gene.

2 **NONCOUNT NOUN** **Repetition** means using the same words again. ○ He could also have cut out much of the repetition and thus saved many pages. ○ Unnecessary repetition weakens sentences.

▶ COLLOCATIONS:
repetition **of** something
avoid/prevent (a) repetition
endless/constant/sheer/relentless repetition
mere/frequent/unnecessary repetition

▶ SYNONYMS: duplication, reiteration, recurrence

---

re|place /rɪpleɪs/ (replaces, replacing, replaced)

VERB To **replace** a person or thing means to put another person or thing in their place. ○ [+ with] They were planning to pull down the building and replace it with shops and offices. ○ A cable replaces a traditional copper wire. ○ [+ as] A lawyer replaced Bob as chairman of the company.

▶ COLLOCATIONS:
replace someone **as** something
replace something/someone **with** something/someone
be replaced **by** something/someone
be replaced by a **newcomer**
replace a **battery/bulb/window/pipe/system**
replace **equipment**

▶ PHRASE: remove and replace

▶ SYNONYM: substitute

re|place|ment /rɪpleɪsmənt/

NONCOUNT NOUN ○ [+ of] the replacement of damaged or lost books

▶ COLLOCATIONS:
the replacement **of** something
require replacement
complete/partial replacement
hormone replacement
replacement **therapy/surgery/cost**

▶ SYNONYMS: substitution, exchange

r

re|port /rɪpɔ̱rt/ (reports, reporting, reported)

1 NOUN A **report** is an official document that a group of people issue after investigating a situation or event. ○ *After an inspection, the inspectors must publish a report.* ○ *[+ by] A report by the Association of University Teachers finds that only 22 percent of lecturers in our universities are women.*

▶ **COLLOCATIONS:**
a report **by** *someone*
a report **on** *something*
produce/present/publish/release a report
commission/compile/prepare a report
a report **suggests/concludes/recommends/says** *something*
a report **shows/reveals/finds/claims** *something*
a **recent/annual/special** report
a **preliminary/quarterly/internal** report
a **detailed/confidential/independent** report
a **background/intelligence/progress/research** report
a **police/financial** report

▶ **SYNONYMS:** analysis, account

2 VERB If you **report** something that has happened, you tell people about it. ○ *[+ that] Researchers reported that the incidence of the condition was rising significantly.* ○ *New cases are being reported more accurately.* ○ *[+ as] The foreign secretary is reported as saying that force will have to be used if diplomacy fails.*

▶ **COLLOCATIONS:**
report a **profit/loss**
a **newspaper/company/study/researcher/witness** reports

▶ **SYNONYMS:** relate, inform, communicate

re|port|ed|ly /rɪpɔ̱rtɪdli/

ADVERB If you say that something is **reportedly** true, you mean that someone has said that it is true, but you have no direct evidence of it. [FORMAL] ○ *More than two hundred people have reportedly been killed in the past week's fighting.* ○ *Now Moscow has reportedly agreed that the sale can go ahead.* ○ *General Breymann had been shot dead, reportedly by one of his own men.*

rep|re|sent /rɛprɪze̱nt/ (represents, representing, represented)

1 VERB If you say that something **represents** a change, achievement, or victory, you mean that it is a change, achievement, or victory. [FORMAL or WRITTEN] ○ *These developments represented a major change in the established order.*

▶ COLLOCATIONS: represent a **difference/increase/shift/step**

2 VERB If a sign or symbol **represents** something, it is accepted as meaning that thing. ○ *a black dot in the middle of the circle is supposed to represent the source of the radiation*

▶ SYNONYMS: symbolize, signify

3 VERB If someone such as a lawyer or a politician **represents** a person or group of people, they act on behalf of that person or group. ○ *the politicians we elect to represent us* ○ *The offer was accepted by the lawyers representing the victims.*

▶ COLLOCATIONS:
a **lawyer/attorney** represents *someone*
a **politician/councilor** represents *people*
a **group/body** represents *people*
a **union/association/organization** represents *people*

rep|re|sen|ta|tion /rɛprɪzɛnteɪʃən/

NONCOUNT NOUN ○ [+ *in*] *These people have no representation in Congress.*

▶ COLLOCATIONS:
political/democratic/congressional representation
legal representation
strong/effective/adequate representation
equal/unequal representation
direct/indirect/proportional representation

rep|re|senta|tive /rɛprɪzɛntətɪv/ (representatives)

1 NOUN A **representative** is a person who has been chosen to act or make decisions on behalf of another person or a group of people. ○ *trade union representatives* ○ *Employees from each department elect a representative.*

▶ COLLOCATIONS:
a representative **from** *somewhere*
elect/appoint/send/invite/meet a representative
a **registered/elected/sole/legal/authorized** representative
a **special/senior/official** representative
a **union/sales/industry** representative
a **community/state** representative

▶ SYNONYM: agent

r

2 **ADJECTIVE** Someone who is typical of the group to which they belong can be described as **representative**. ○ [+ *of*] *He was in no way representative of dog-trainers in general.* ○ *fairly representative groups of adults*

▶ **COLLOCATIONS:**
representative **of** *someone/something*
representative of a **population/community**
a representative **sample/selection/range**
broadly representative

▶ **SYNONYMS:** typical, characteristic

---

re|quest /rɪkwɛst/ (requests, requesting, requested) [COMMUNICATIONS]

1 **VERB** If you **request** something, you ask for it politely or formally.
[FORMAL] ○ *The governor had requested a police presence to ensure external security.* ○ [+ *that*] *The Prime Minister requested that a State of Emergency be declared.*

▶ **COLLOCATIONS:**
request **information/anonymity/permission**
a **letter/customer** requests *something*
formally/respectfully/specifically request *something*

▶ **SYNONYM:** ask for

USAGE: *request* or *require*?

These two words sound similar and are easily confused. If you **request** something, you ask for it politely. ○ *I called my supervisor to request permission to be late the next week.*

If you **require** something, you need it or it is necessary. ○ *Should you require any additional information, please call ...*

---

2 **NOUN** If you make a **request**, you politely or formally ask someone to do something. ○ [+ *for*] *France had agreed to his request for political asylum.* ○ *Vietnam made an official request that the meeting be postponed.* ○ *a request, not a demand*

▶ **COLLOCATIONS:**
a request **for** *something*
a request for **information/assistance/help**
receive/reject/refuse/deny/grant a request

▶ **SYNONYM:** appeal

re|quire /rɪkwaɪər/ (requires, requiring, required)

1 VERB If you **require** something or if something **is required**, you need it or it is necessary. [FORMAL] ○ *If you require further information, you should consult the registrar.* ○ [+ to-inf] *This isn't the kind of crisis that requires us to drop everything else.*

▶ **COLLOCATIONS:**
require **surgery/treatment/attention**
require **information/effort/investment**

▶ **SYNONYM:** need

2 VERB If a law or rule **requires** you **to** do something, you have to do it. [FORMAL] ○ [+ to-inf] *The rules also require employers to provide safety training.* ○ [+ that] *The law now requires that parents serve on the committees that plan and evaluate school programs.* ○ [+ of] *Then he'll know exactly what's required of him.*

▶ **COLLOCATIONS:**
require *something* **of** *someone*
the **law/rules/regulations** require *something*
require *someone* to **pay/provide/attend/report**

▶ **SYNONYMS:** order, demand, oblige, instruct

re|quire|ment /rɪkwaɪərmənt/ (requirements)

1 NOUN A **requirement** is a quality or qualification that you must have in order to be allowed to do something or to be suitable for something. ○ *Its products met all legal requirements.* ○ [+ for] *A bachelor's degree is the minimum requirement for entry-level teaching jobs.*

▶ **COLLOCATIONS:**
a requirement **for** *something*
a requirement for **membership/entry**
meet/satisfy/fulfill/impose/set a requirement
the **minimum** requirement
a **legal/statutory/essential** requirement
entry/visa/registration/safety requirements

▶ **SYNONYMS:** condition, qualification, stipulation, specification

2 NOUN Your **requirements** are the things that you need. [FORMAL] ○ *Variations of this program can be arranged to suit your requirements.* ○ [+ of] *a packaged food which provides 100 percent of your daily requirement of one vitamin*

▶ **COLLOCATIONS:**
requirement **of** *something*

daily/minimum/basic/essential requirements

▸ **SYNONYMS:** necessity, essential

---

re|sale /ˈriːseɪl/ LOGISTICS & DISTRIBUTION

NONCOUNT NOUN The **resale** price of something that you own is the amount of money that you would get if you sold it. ○ *a well-maintained used car with a good resale value*

▸ **COLLOCATIONS:**
the resale **of** something
resale **price/value**

---

re|sched|ule /ˌriːˈʃɛdʒuːl, -dʒuəl/ LOGISTICS & DISTRIBUTION
(reschedules, rescheduling, rescheduled)

1 VERB If someone **reschedules** an event, they change the time at which it is supposed to happen. ○ *Since I'll be away, I'd like to reschedule the meeting.*

▸ **COLLOCATIONS:** reschedule a **meeting/appointment/date/game**

2 VERB To **reschedule** a debt means to arrange for it to be paid back over a longer period of time. ○ *Companies have gone bust or had to reschedule their debts.*

▸ **COLLOCATIONS:** reschedule a **debt/loan/payment**

---

re|search /rɪˈsɜːrtʃ, ˈriːsɜːrtʃ/ **(researches, researching, researched)** R&D

1 NONCOUNT NOUN Research is work that involves studying something and trying to discover facts about it. ○ *65 percent of the 1987 budget went to nuclear weapons research and production.* ○ *money spent on cancer research* ○ *[+ into] a center which conducts animal research into brain diseases*

▸ **COLLOCATIONS:**
research **into/on** something
conduct/undertake/carry out research
fund/publish research
research **suggests/shows/reveals/indicates** something
market/cancer/animal research
scientific/biological/clinical/medical research
current/recent/experimental research
a research **facility/scientist/laboratory**
research **findings/results/methods**
a research **report/paper/project/fellow**

▸ **PHRASE:** research and development

▶ **SYNONYMS:** analysis, investigation

2 VERB If you **research** something, you try to discover facts about it.
  ○ *She spent two years in South Florida researching and filming her documentary.*
  ○ *So far we haven't been able to find anything, but we're still researching.*
  ○ *a meticulously researched study*

  ▶ **COLLOCATIONS: thoroughly/meticulously** research *something*

  ▶ **SYNONYMS:** investigate, examine, explore, study, analyze

re|search and de|vel|op|ment /rɪsɜrtʃ ən dɪvɛləpmənt/

NONCOUNT NOUN Research and development is work that applies
scientific research to the development of new products. ○ *The
organization is encouraging companies to group together to finance research
and development projects.*

  ▶ **COLLOCATIONS:**
    research and development **project/costs**
    finance/support research and development

---

re|serve /rɪzɜrv/ (reserves)

NOUN A **reserve** is a supply of something that is available for use when it is
needed. ○ *The Gulf has 65 percent of the world's oil reserves.* ○ *[+ of] Having a
reserve of 24 hours' worth of water is the standard across Canada.*

  ▶ **COLLOCATIONS:**
    a reserve **of** *something*
    reserves of **energy/oil/gas/strength/courage**
    maintain/establish/deplete/replenish reserves
    oil/gas/currency/gold reserves

  ▶ **SYNONYMS:** store, stock, supply

---

resi|dent /rɛzɪdənt/ (residents)

NOUN The **residents** of a house or area are the people who live there.
  ○ *The Archbishop called upon the government to build more low-cost homes for
  local residents.* ○ *More than 10 percent of Munich residents live below the
  poverty line.*

  ▶ **COLLOCATIONS:**
    residents **of/in** *somewhere*
    evacuate/warn/advise residents
    residents **say/fear/complain about/want/report** *something*
    former/local/permanent/nearby/elderly residents

  ▶ **SYNONYMS:** inhabitant, citizen

resi|dence /rɛzɪdəns/ (residences)

NOUN A **residence** is the place where someone lives. [FORMAL] ○ *the president's official residence*

▶ **COLLOCATIONS:**
a **primary/main/permanent/temporary** residence
a **private/royal/official** residence
the **mayor's/governor's** residence

▶ **SYNONYM:** home

resi|den|tial /rɛzɪdɛnʃl/

ADJECTIVE A **residential** area contains houses rather than offices or stores. ○ *a fashionable residential area of Maryland* ○ *a residential street lined with houses and parked cars*

▶ **COLLOCATIONS:** a residential **area/neighborhood/street**

---

re|sign /rɪzaɪn/ (resigns, resigning, resigned)   `PERSONNEL`

VERB If you **resign** from a job, you tell your employer that you are leaving it. ○ *He was forced to resign.*

▶ **COLLOCATIONS:**
resign **from** *something*
resign from a **job/position/post**

▶ **SYNONYM:** quit

res|ig|na|tion /rɛzɪgneɪʃən/ (resignations)

NOUN Your **resignation** is when you tell your employer that you are leaving your job. ○ *Barbara offered her resignation this morning.*

▶ **COLLOCATIONS:**
resignation **from** *something*
resignation from a **job/position/post**
sudden/forced/unexpected/immediate resignation
offer/tender/announce/hand in/submit *your* resignation

▶ **PHRASE:** a letter of resignation

---

re|sist|ance /rɪzɪstəns/

NONCOUNT NOUN Resistance to something such as a change or a new idea is a refusal to accept it. ○ *The U.S. wants big cuts in European agricultural export subsidies, but this is meeting resistance.* ○ *[+ to] stubborn resistance to social reform*

▶ COLLOCATIONS:
resistance **to** something
armed/stubborn/fierce/stiff resistance
meet/face/encounter/overcome resistance

▶ SYNONYM: opposition

---

re|source /rɪsɔːs/ (resources)　 LOGISTICS & DISTRIBUTION

1 **NOUN** The **resources** of an organization or person are the materials,
money, and other things that they have and can use in order to function
properly. ○ *Some families don't have the resources to feed themselves properly.*
○ *There's a great shortage of resource materials in many schools.*

▶ COLLOCATIONS:
allocate/devote/commit/lack/stretch/limit resources
human/financial/limited resources
resource **management**

▶ SYNONYM: supplies

2 **NOUN** A country's **resources** are the things that it has and can use to
increase its wealth, such as coal, oil, or land. ○ *resources like coal, tungsten,
oil, and copper* ○ *Today we are overpopulated, straining the earth's resources.*

▶ COLLOCATIONS:
natural/water/energy/mineral resources
the **world's/earth's** resources
a **country's/nation's** resources

▶ SYNONYMS: assets, materials

---

re|spect|ed /rɪspɛktɪd/

ADJECTIVE Someone or something that is **respected** is admired and
considered important by many people. ○ *He is highly respected for his
novels and plays.*

▶ COLLOCATIONS:
internationally/highly/widely respected
a respected **journalist/figure/businessman**

---

re|spon|sible /rɪspɒnsɪbᵊl/　 PERSONNEL

1 **ADJECTIVE** If someone or something is **responsible for** a particular event
or situation, they are the cause of it or they can be blamed for it. ○ [+ *for*]
He still felt responsible for her death. ○ *I want you to do everything you can to
find out who's responsible.*

▶ **COLLOCATIONS:**
responsible **for** *something*
be/feel responsible
hold *someone* responsible
the **person/individual/terrorist/gang/organization** responsible
criminally responsible

▶ **SYNONYMS:** to blame, guilty

2 **ADJECTIVE** If you are **responsible for** something, it is your job or duty to deal with it and make decisions relating to it. ○ [+ *for*] *the Secretary responsible for the environment* ○ *The man responsible for finding the volunteers is Dr. Charles Weber.*

▶ **COLLOCATIONS:**
responsible **for** *something*
the **people/organization/agency/department/body** responsible
financially responsible
partly/solely/ultimately/largely/primarily/chiefly responsible
personally/indirectly/directly responsible

▶ **SYNONYM:** accountable

re|spon|sibil|ity /rɪspɒnsɪbɪlɪti/ (responsibilities)

1 **NONCOUNT NOUN** If you have **responsibility** for something or someone, or if they are your **responsibility**, it is your job or duty to deal with them and to take decisions relating to them. ○ [+ *for*] *Each manager had responsibility for just under 600 properties.* ○ [+ *for*] *We need to take responsibility for looking after our own health.* ○ *"She's not your responsibility," he said gently.*

▶ **COLLOCATIONS:**
responsibility **for** *something*
have/assume/be given/shoulder/carry responsibility
delegate/assign responsibility
financial/personal/moral/legal responsibility
parental/social/personal/corporate responsibility

▶ **SYNONYMS:** duty, obligation

2 **NONCOUNT NOUN** If you accept **responsibility for** something that has happened, you agree that you were to blame for it or you caused it. ○ [+ *for*] *No one admitted responsibility for the attacks.* ○ [+ *for*] *Someone had to give orders and take responsibility for mistakes.*

▶ **COLLOCATIONS:**
responsibility **for** *something*
accept/claim/bear/share/take responsibility

deny/admit/acknowledge responsibility
diminished/collective/full/individual responsibility

▶ SYNONYMS: accountability, guilt, blame, fault, liability

3 **PLURAL NOUN** Your **responsibilities** are the duties that you have because of your job or position. ○ [+ *as*] *He handled his responsibilities as a counselor in an intelligent and caring fashion.* ○ *programs to help employees balance work and family responsibilities*

▶ COLLOCATIONS:
responsibilities **as** *something*
family/community/adult responsibilities
share responsibilities

▶ SYNONYMS: duties, obligations

---

res|tau|rant /rɛstərənt, -tərɑnt, -trɑnt/ **(restaurants)**

NOUN A **restaurant** is a place where you can buy and eat a meal.
○ *an Italian restaurant*

▶ COLLOCATIONS:
a **French/Italian/Chinese** restaurant
a **fancy/expensive/inexpensive/cheap/nice** restaurant
a **large/small/noisy/crowded** restaurant
a **local/family** restaurant

---

re|strain /rɪstreɪn/ **(restrains, restraining, restrained)**

1 **VERB** If you **restrain** someone, you stop them from doing what they intended or wanted to do, usually by using your physical strength. ○ *One onlooker had to be restrained by police.* ○ *One senator was physically restrained during an argument with a representative.* ○ *the bare minimum of force necessary to restrain the attackers*

▶ COLLOCATIONS: **forcibly/physically** restrain *someone*

2 **VERB** To **restrain** something that is growing or increasing means to prevent it from getting too large. ○ *The radical 500-day plan was very clear on how it intended to try to restrain inflation.* ○ *In the 1970s, the government tried to restrain corruption.* ○ *to restrain the growth in state spending*

▶ COLLOCATIONS: restrain **spending/growth/inflation/costs**

▶ SYNONYMS: limit, check

r

re|strict /rɪstrɪkt/ (restricts, restricting, restricted)

1 VERB If you **restrict** something, you put a limit on it in order to reduce it or prevent it becoming too great. ○ *There is talk of raising the admission requirements to restrict the number of students on campus.* ○ [+ to] *The French, I believe, restrict Japanese imports to a maximum of 3 percent of their market.*

2 VERB To **restrict** the movement or actions of someone or something means to prevent them from moving or acting freely. ○ *Villagers say the fence would restrict public access to the hills.* ○ *These dams restricted the flow of the river downstream.*

▶ **COLLOCATIONS:**
restrict something **to** something
restrict **access** to something
a **law/regulation** restricts something
restrict **imports/ freedom/movement/use**
severely restrict

▶ **SYNONYMS:** limit, restrain

re|stric|tion /rɪstrɪkʃ°n/ (restrictions)

NOUN ○ [+ on] *Some restriction on funding was necessary.* ○ [+ of] *the justification for this restriction of individual liberty* ○ [+ on] *the lifting of restrictions on political parties*

▶ **COLLOCATIONS:**
a restriction **of/on** something
restrictions on **imports/trade**
impose/place/lift a restriction
necessary/tight/severe/legal restrictions
travel/investment/ownership/speed restrictions

▶ **SYNONYMS:** limitation, control

re|sult /rɪzʌlt/ (results, resulting, resulted)

1 NOUN A **result** is something that happens or exists because of something else that has happened. ○ [+ of] *Compensation is available for people who have developed asthma as a direct result of their work.* ○ *Cancer is the end result of a long degenerative process.*

▶ **COLLOCATIONS:**
a result **of** something
a **direct** result
the **end** result

▶ **PHRASE:** as a result

▶ **SYNONYMS:** by-product, consequence

2 NOUN A **result** is the number that you get when you do a calculation. ○ *They found their computers producing different results from exactly the same calculation.*

▶ **SYNONYM:** answer

3 NOUN A **result** is the information that you get when you carry out an experiment or some research. ○ *There were some experimental errors on my part, invalidating the results.* ○ [+ of] *Here he published the results of his meticulous research.*

▶ **COLLOCATIONS:**
the results **of** something
the results of a **study/survey/experiment/inquiry**
get/achieve/produce/yield results
await/expect results
report/announce/release/publish results
disappointing/surprising results
consistent/impressive/positive results

▶ **SYNONYM:** findings

4 VERB If something **results in** a particular situation or event, it causes that situation or event to happen. ○ [+ in] *Fifty percent of road accidents result in head injuries.* ○ [+ in] *Continuous rain resulted in the land becoming submerged.*

▶ **COLLOCATIONS:**
result **in** something
result in **death/arrest**
result in a **loss/reduction/increase**

▶ **SYNONYMS:** cause, lead to

5 VERB If something **results from** a particular event or action, it is caused by that event or action. ○ [+ from] *Many hair problems result from what you eat.* ○ *Ignore the early warnings and illness could result.*

▶ **COLLOCATIONS:**
result **from** something
result from **use/exposure**
result from a **failure/lack**

▶ **SYNONYMS:** follow, develop, ensue

---

ré|su|mé /rɛzʊmeɪ/ **(résumés)** also **resume**   `PERSONNEL`

NOUN Your **résumé** is a short description of your education and the jobs you have had.

▶ **COLLOCATIONS:**
a **brief/lengthy/impressive** résumé
send/submit/write/do/post a résumé

▶ **SYNONYM:** curriculum vitae

---

re|tail /ˈriːteɪl/
MARKETING & SALES

NONCOUNT NOUN Retail is the activity of selling goods directly to the public, usually in small quantities. ○ *retail stores* ○ *Retail sales grew just 3.8 percent last year.* ○ *The companies had come to sell - retail, wholesale, or export.*

▶ **COLLOCATIONS:** retail **sales/prices/stores**

▶ **RELATED WORD:** wholesale

---

re|tain /rɪˈteɪn/ (retains, retaining, retained)
PERSONNEL

VERB To **retain** something means to continue to have that thing. [FORMAL] ○ *The interior of the shop still retains a nineteenth-century atmosphere.* ○ *Other countries retained their traditional and habitual ways of doing things.*

→ see note at **maintain**

▶ **COLLOCATIONS:** retain **control/power/rights/links/moisture/heat**

▶ **SYNONYMS:** keep, maintain, preserve

re|ten|tion /rɪˈtɛnʃən/

NONCOUNT NOUN [FORMAL] ○ [+ *of*] *They supported the retention of a strong central government.* ○ *A deficiency in magnesium increases lead absorption and retention.*

▶ **COLLOCATIONS:**
the retention **of** *something*
the retention of **organs/staff/power**
cause/ensure the retention of *something*
improve/increase/reduce the retention of *something*
fluid/water/data/customer retention

▶ **PHRASE:** recruitment and retention

---

re|tire /rɪˈtaɪər/ (retires, retiring, retired)
PERSONNEL

VERB When older people **retire**, they leave their job and usually stop working completely. ○ *At the age when most people retire, he is ready to face* *a new career.* ○ *Many said they plan to retire at 50.* ○ [+ *from*] *In 1974 he retired from the museum.*

▶ **COLLOCATIONS:**
retire **at** *an age*
retire **from/as** *something*
retire at the **age** of *x*
retire from **football/politics/teaching/the chairmanship**
retire as **chairman/president/manager/head**

▶ **SYNONYMS:** finish, leave, stop, quit

▶ **RELATED WORD:** resign

re|tired /rɪtaɪərd/

ADJECTIVE ○ *I am a retired teacher.*

▶ **COLLOCATIONS:**
a retired **teacher/police officer/firefighter**
a retired **couple**

re|tire|ment /rɪtaɪərmənt/

NONCOUNT NOUN ○ *the proportion of the population who are over retirement age* ○ *The prison warden is to take early retirement.*

▶ **COLLOCATIONS:**
near retirement
early/mandatory/impending/premature retirement
contemplate/approach/consider retirement
announce *someone's* retirement
retirement **age/savings/income/benefits**
a retirement **home/pension/fund**

▶ **RELATED WORD:** resignation

---

re|trench /rɪtrɛntʃ/ (retrenches, retrenching,   `BANKING & FINANCE`
retrenched)

VERB If a person or organization **retrenches**, they spend less money. [FORMAL] ○ *Shortly afterward, cuts in defense spending forced the aerospace industry to retrench.*

▶ **COLLOCATIONS:** a **company/business/organization** retrenches

---

re|trieve /rɪtriv/ (retrieves, retrieving, retrieved)

VERB To **retrieve** information from a computer or from your memory means to get it back. ○ *Computers can instantly retrieve millions of*

information bits. ○ *As the child gets older, so his or her strategies for storing and retrieving information improve.*

▶ **COLLOCATIONS:** retrieve **information/data**

▶ **PHRASE:** store and retrieve

re|triev|al /rɪtriːvᵊl/

NONCOUNT NOUN ○ *electronic storage and retrieval systems* ○ [+ *of*] *the study of the organization and retrieval of memories*

▶ **COLLOCATIONS:**
the retrieval **of** *something*
data/image/information retrieval

▶ **PHRASE:** storage and retrieval

retro|spect /rɛtrəspɛkt/

PHRASE When you consider something **in retrospect**, you think about it afterwards, and often have a different opinion about it from the one that you had at the time. ○ *In retrospect, I wish that I had thought about alternative courses of action.* ○ *In retrospect, it was a role he should have avoided, but fatigue and a lack of direction played their part in the choice.*

▶ **SYNONYM:** with hindsight

re|turn /rɪtɜːrn/ **(returns)**

NOUN The **return on** an investment is the profit that you get from it. ○ *Profits have picked up this year but the return on capital remains tiny.* ○ *Higher returns and higher risk usually go hand in hand.*

▶ **COLLOCATIONS:**
generate/expect/earn/achieve a return
diminish/maximize a return
a **high/average/annual/total** return

▶ **SYNONYM:** profit

re|unite /riːyuːnaɪt/ **(reunites, reuniting, reunited)**

VERB If people **are reunited**, they see each other again after a long time. ○ [+ *with*] *She was finally reunited with her family.*

▶ **COLLOCATION:** reunite *someone* **with** *someone*

▶ **SYNONYM:** rejoin

re|veal /rɪvil/ (reveals, revealing, revealed)

VERB To **reveal** something means to make people aware of it. ○ *She has refused to reveal the whereabouts of her daughter.* ○ [+ that] *A survey of the American diet has revealed that a growing number of people are overweight.* ○ [+ how] *No test will reveal how much of the drug was taken.*

▶ **COLLOCATIONS:**
reveal a **secret/identity/plan**
reveal **details/information**
a **report/study/investigation/examination** reveals *something*
publicly/sensationally/exclusively reveal *something*

▶ **SYNONYMS:** disclose, divulge, uncover

re|verse /rɪvɜrs/ (reverses, reversing, reversed)

1 VERB When someone or something **reverses** a decision, policy, or trend, they change it to the opposite decision, policy, or trend. ○ *They have made it clear they will not reverse the decision to increase prices.* ○ *The rise, the first in 10 months, reversed the downward trend in Belgium's jobless rate.*

▶ **COLLOCATIONS:**
reverse a **decision/policy/ruling**
a **court** reverses *something*
reverse a **situation/trend/decline**

▶ **SYNONYMS:** change, overrule, overturn

2 VERB If you **reverse** the order of a set of things, you arrange them in the opposite order, so that the first thing comes last. ○ *The normal word order is reversed in passive sentences.*

▶ **COLLOCATIONS:** reverse the **order/direction**

3 ADJECTIVE Reverse means opposite to what you expect or to what has just been described. ○ *The wrong attitude will have exactly the reverse effect.*

▶ **COLLOCATION:** the reverse **effect**

▶ **SYNONYM:** opposite

re|ver|sal /rɪvɜrsᵊl/ (reversals)

NOUN A **reversal of** a process, policy, or trend is a complete change in it. ○ [+ of] *The Financial Times says the move represents a complete reversal of previous U.S. policy.* ○ [+ of] *This marked a 7% increase on the previous year and the reversal of a steady five-year downward trend.*

▶ **COLLOCATIONS:**
a reversal **of** *something*

a reversal of a **policy/position/trend**
mark/represent/cause/experience/suffer a reversal
a reversal **occurs/comes**
a **dramatic/complete/sudden/sharp** reversal

---

re|vise /rɪvaɪz/ (revises, revising, revised)

VERB If you **revise** something, you alter it to make it better or more accurate. ○ *He soon came to revise his opinion of the profession.* ○ *The United Nations has been forced to revise its estimates of population growth upwards.* ○ *[+ for] the work of revising articles for publication* ○ *The staff should work together to revise the school curriculum.*

▶ COLLOCATIONS:
revise something **for** something
a revised **version/edition/estimate/figure/offer**
revise a **forecast/plan/rule/proposal**
a **government/official/analyst** revises something
revise something **upward/downward**

▶ SYNONYMS: change, alter, amend

re|vi|sion /rɪvɪʒ³n/ (revisions)

NOUN ○ *The phase of writing that is actually most important is revision.* ○ *[+ of] A major addition to the earlier revisions of the questionnaire is the job requirement exercise.*

▶ COLLOCATIONS:
a revision **of** something
revision of **history/policy/rules/laws**
need/require/undergo revision
propose/undertake/approve a revision
minor/substantial/extensive/radical revision

▶ SYNONYMS: editing, correction, alteration

---

re|voke /rɪvouk/ (revokes, revoking, revoked)   `LEGAL`

VERB When people in authority **revoke** something such as a license, a law, or an agreement, they cancel it. [FORMAL] ○ *The government revoked her husband's license to operate migrant-labor crews.*

▶ COLLOCATIONS: revoke someone's **citizenship/bail/parole**

re|volve /rɪvɒlv/ (revolves, revolving, revolved)

1 **VERB** If you say that one thing **revolves around** another thing, you mean that the second thing is the main feature or focus of the first thing.
○ [+ around] *Since childhood, her life has revolved around tennis.*

▶ **COLLOCATIONS:** someone's **life/marriage** revolves **around** something

2 **VERB** If a discussion or conversation **revolves around** a particular topic, it is mainly about that topic. ○ [+ around] *The debate revolves around specific accounting techniques.*

▶ **COLLOCATIONS:** a **case/discussion/debate** revolves **around** something

3 **VERB** If one object **revolves around** another object, the first object turns in a circle around the second object. ○ [+ around] *The satellite revolves around the earth once every hundred minutes.* ○ [+ around] *It is common knowledge that the Earth revolves around the Sun.*

▶ **COLLOCATIONS:** a **planet/satellite** revolves **around** something

4 **VERB** When something **revolves** or when you **revolve** it, it moves or turns in a circle around a central point or line. ○ *The wheel revolves very rapidly and makes a deafening noise when it is cutting.*

▶ **COLLOCATIONS:** a **wheel/door** revolves

▶ **SYNONYMS:** turn, spin

re|ward /rɪwɔrd/ (rewards)

NOUN A **reward** is something that you are given, for example because you have behaved well, worked hard, or provided a service to the community.
○ [+ for] *He was given the job as a reward for running a successful leadership bid.*

▶ **COLLOCATIONS:**
a reward **for** something
a reward for **good behavior/information**
a reward for **performance/achievement**
give/offer/get/receive/earn/deserve a reward
a **financial/just/fitting/tangible** reward
a **cash/material/million-dollar** reward
a reward **program/system**
reward **money**

▶ **PHRASES:**
as a reward
risk and reward

▶ **SYNONYMS:** bonus, prize

re|ward|ing /rɪwɔ́rdɪŋ/

ADJECTIVE Something that is **rewarding** gives you satisfaction. ○ *I have a job that is very rewarding.*

▶ **COLLOCATIONS:**
a rewarding **career/job/relationship/experience/life**
financially/personally/spiritually/emotionally rewarding

---

re|work /rɪwɜ́rk/ **(reworks, reworking, reworked)**

VERB If you **rework** an idea or a piece of writing, you make changes in order to improve it or bring it up to date. ○ *Keep reworking your résumé until you can't improve it anymore.*

▶ **COLLOCATIONS:**
rework a **story/idea/paragraph/résumé**
a reworked **version**

---

rig|or /rɪ́gər/

NONCOUNT NOUN If something is done with **rigor**, it is done in a strict, thorough way. ○ *The new current affairs series promises to address challenging issues with freshness and rigor.* ○ *They must believe you will pursue injustice with rigor and not be nudged off course.*

▶ **COLLOCATION:** *do something* **with** rigor

▶ **SYNONYMS:** strictness, thoroughness

rig|or|ous /rɪ́gərəs/

ADJECTIVE A test, system, or procedure that is **rigorous** is very thorough and strict. ○ *The selection process is based on rigorous tests of competence and experience.* ○ *a rigorous system of blood analysis* ○ *rigorous military training*

▶ **COLLOCATIONS:** rigorous **testing/scrutiny/analysis/examination**

▶ **SYNONYMS:** thorough, strict, tough

---

risk /rɪsk/ **(risks)**

1 NOUN If there is a **risk of** something unpleasant, there is a possibility that it will happen. ○ [+ *of*] *There is a small risk of brain damage from the procedure.* ○ [+ *that*] *In all the confusion, there's a serious risk that the main issues will be forgotten.* ○ *People do it because there is that element of danger and risk.*

2 **NOUN** If something that you do is a **risk**, it might have unpleasant or undesirable results. ○ *You're taking a big risk showing this to Kravis.* ○ *This was one risk that paid off.*

3 **NOUN** If you say that something or someone is a **risk**, you mean they are likely to cause harm. ○ *It's being overfat that constitutes a health risk.* ○ *The restaurant has been refurbished – it was found to be a fire risk.* ○ [+ *to*] *a risk to national security*

▶ COLLOCATIONS:
a risk **of** something
a risk **to** something/someone
a risk of **cancer/disease/injury**
a risk of **failure/attack**
a **serious/associated/high/low/great/potential** risk
pose/reduce/increase a risk
assess/involve/run/take a risk
a **health/fire/security** risk
risk **factor/assessment/management**

▶ SYNONYMS: gamble, danger, hazard

---

ri|val|ry /ˈraɪvəlri/ (rivalries)

NOUN **Rivalry** is competition or conflict between people, businesses, or organizations in the same area or for the same things. ○ [+ *between*] *the rivalry between the Inkatha and the ANC* ○ [+ *among*] *The rivalry among her peers was intense.* ○ *a city torn by deep ethnic rivalries*

▶ COLLOCATIONS:
rivalry **between/among** people
rivalry **exists/grows/begins/continues/develops**
intensify/fuel/spark/overcome rivalry
intense/fierce/bitter/ethnic rivalry
friendly/sporting/sibling/clan rivalry

▶ SYNONYMS: competition, competitiveness

---

ro|tate /rəʊˈteɪt/ (rotates, rotating, rotated)

VERB When something **rotates** or when you **rotate** it, it turns with a circular movement. ○ *The Earth rotates round the sun.* ○ *Take each foot in both your hands and rotate it to loosen and relax the ankle.*

▶ COLLOCATIONS:
the **Earth/sun** rotates

something rotates a **blade/cylinder/disc**
rotate **gently/constantly/rapidly/clockwise**

▶ **SYNONYMS:** revolve, turn, spin

ro|ta|tion /rəʊteɪʃ°n/ (rotations)

NOUN ○ [+ of] the daily rotation of the earth upon its axis ○ [+ of] the point of rotation of the lever arms

▶ **COLLOCATIONS:**
the rotation **of** something
a **daily/rapid/clockwise** rotation

▶ **SYNONYMS:** revolution, gyration, spinning

---

rou|tine /ruːtiːn/ (routines)

1 NOUN A **routine** is the usual series of things that you do at a particular time. ○ He followed the same routine he'd used on the previous Wednesday.

▶ **COLLOCATIONS:**
the **same** routine
someone's **regular/normal/usual/daily/morning** routine
a **different/boring/new** routine
a **fixed/set** routine
establish/follow/break/change/vary a routine
an **exercise** routine

▶ **SYNONYM:** regimen

2 ADJECTIVE You use **routine** to describe activities that are done as a normal part of a job or process. ○ The operator has to be able to carry out routine maintenance of the machine.

▶ **COLLOCATIONS:** routine **maintenance/repairs**

---

roy|al|ty /rɔɪəlti/ (royalties) `BANKING & FINANCE`

PLURAL NOUN Royalties are payments made to authors and musicians when their work is sold or performed. ○ [+ on] I lived on about £3,000 a year from the royalties on my book.

▶ **COLLOCATIONS:**
royalties **on** something
royalties on a **book/song**
a royalty **check/payment**
pay/earn/receive royalties
royalties **accrue**

Ss

sac|ri|fice /sǽkrɪfaɪs/ (sacrifices, sacrificing, sacrificed)

VERB If you **sacrifice** something that is valuable or important, you give it up, usually to obtain something else for yourself or for other people. ○ *She sacrificed family life to her career.* ○ *Kitty Aldridge has sacrificed all for her first film.*

  ▶ **COLLOCATIONS:** sacrifice *someone/something* **to/for** *someone/something*

  ▶ **SYNONYM:** give up

● **Sacrifice** is also a noun. ○ *She made many sacrifices to get Anita a good education.*

safe|ty /séɪfti/   `PERSONNEL`

NONCOUNT NOUN **Safety** is the state of not being in danger. ○ *We need to improve safety on our building sites.*

  ▶ **COLLOCATIONS:**
  the safety **of** *something/someone*
  protect/threaten/compromise the safety of *something/someone*
  improve/ensure/guarantee/enhance/increase safety
  relative/added/greater/extra safety
  public/personal/child safety
  road/food/air/water/fire safety

  ▶ **PHRASE:** health and safety

sala|ry /sǽləri/ (salaries)   `PERSONNEL`

NOUN A **salary** is the money that someone is paid each month by their employer, especially when they are in a profession such as teaching, law, or medicine. ○ *The lawyer was paid a huge salary.* ○ *The government has decided to increase salaries for all civil servants.* ○ [+ of] *IT directors can expect to earn average salaries of between $85,000 and $125,000.*

  ▶ **COLLOCATIONS:**
  a salary **of** *x*

a **monthly/annual/average/$x** salary
earn a salary
be **paid** a salary
a salary **increase**

▶ **SYNONYMS:** wage, earnings, income

---

sales fig|ures /seɪlz fɪgyərz/   MARKETING & SALES

PLURAL NOUN **Sales figures** are the numbers of a product or products that
have been sold and the money resulting from these sales. ○ *He pointed to
disappointing sales figures in Poland.*

▶ **COLLOCATIONS:**
   disappointing/dismal/strong/impressive sales figures
   projected/recent/monthly/weekly sales figures

---

sales|person /seɪlzpɜrsᵊn/ (salespeople or   MARKETING & SALES
salespersons)

NOUN A **salesperson** is a person whose job is to sell things. ○ *They will
usually send a salesperson out to measure your bathroom.*

▶ **COLLOCATIONS:**
   a **commissioned** salesperson
   a **good/experienced** salesperson

▶ **SYNONYMS:** salesman, saleswoman

---

sales tax /seɪlz tæks/ (sales taxes)   MARKETING & SALES

NOUN **Sales tax** is the percentage of money that you pay to the local or
state government when you buy things. ○ *The state's unpopular sales tax
on snacks has ended.*

▶ **COLLOCATIONS:**
   state/local sales tax
   charge/collect/owe/pay sales tax
   raise/lower the sales tax

---

sam|ple /sæmpᵊl/ (samples)   R&D

1 **NOUN** A **sample** of a substance is a small amount of it that is examined
and analyzed scientifically. ○ [+ *of*] *Samples of blood were taken for DNA
testing.* ○ *a robotic mission that would collect rock and soil samples for more
detailed analysis*

▶ **COLLOCATIONS:**
a sample **of** something
a sample of **blood/fluid/saliva**
a **urine/tissue/blood/soil** sample
take/collect/analyze/test a sample

▶ **SYNONYM:** specimen

2 NOUN A **sample** of people or things is a number of them chosen out of a larger group and then used in tests or used to provide information about the whole group. ○ [+ of] We based our analysis on a random sample of more than 200 males. ○ The sample size used in the study was too small.

▶ **COLLOCATIONS:**
a sample **of** people
a sample of **adults/voters**
a **random** sample
sample **size**

▶ **SYNONYM:** selection

---

sat|is|fy /sǽtɪsfaɪ/ (satisfies, satisfying, satisfied)

1 VERB To **satisfy** someone **that** something is true or has been done properly means to convince them by giving them more information or by showing them what has been done. ○ [+ that] He has to satisfy the environmental lobby that real progress will be made to cut emissions. ○ [+ that] The statisticians were satisfied that the sample and the evidence were sufficient.

▶ **SYNONYMS:** convince, persuade

2 VERB If you **satisfy** the requirements for something, you are good enough or have the right qualities to fulfill these requirements. ○ The procedures should satisfy certain basic requirements.

▶ **COLLOCATIONS:**
satisfy **requirements/objectives**
fully/reasonably/completely satisfy

▶ **SYNONYMS:** fulfill, meet

sat|is|fied /sǽtɪsfaɪd/

1 ADJECTIVE If you are **satisfied with** something, you are happy because you have gotten what you wanted or needed. ○ [+ with] We are not satisfied with these results. ○ asking for referrals from satisfied customers

2 ADJECTIVE If you are **satisfied that** something is true or has been done properly, you are convinced about this after checking it. ○ [+ that] People must be satisfied that the treatment is safe.

▶ **COLLOCATIONS:**
satisfied **with** *something*
reasonably/completely/very satisfied
a satisfied **customer/user**

▶ **SYNONYMS:** pleased, contented

sat|is|fac|tion /sætɪsfækʃən/

NONCOUNT NOUN If you feel **satisfaction**, you feel pleased to do or get something. ○ *It gives me a real sense of satisfaction when I close a deal.*

▶ **COLLOCATIONS:**
complete/great/deep/immense/tremendous satisfaction
personal/customer/employee/job satisfaction
feel/derive/find/get/express satisfaction
guarantee satisfaction

▶ **PHRASE:** a sense of satisfaction

▶ **SYNONYM:** contentment

sat|is|fac|tory /sætɪsfæktəri/

ADJECTIVE Something that is **satisfactory** is acceptable to you or fulfills a particular need or purpose. ○ *The concept of instinct is not a satisfactory explanation of human behavior.* ○ *It seemed a very satisfactory arrangement.*

▶ **COLLOCATIONS:**
a satisfactory **conclusion/answer/outcome/solution**
a satisfactory **explanation/condition**
mutually/wholly/entirely satisfactory

▶ **SYNONYMS:** acceptable, adequate

---

satu|rat|ed /sætʃəreɪtɪd/

ADJECTIVE **Saturated** fats are types of fat that are found in some foods, especially meat, eggs, and things such as butter and cheese. They are believed to cause heart disease and some other illnesses if eaten too often. ○ *foods rich in cholesterol and saturated fats*

▶ **COLLOCATIONS:** saturated **fats/compounds**

satu|ra|tion /sætʃəreɪʃən/

NONCOUNT NOUN **Saturation** is the process or state that occurs when a place or thing is filled completely with people or things, so that no more can be added. ○ [+ *of*] *Japanese car makers have been equally blind to the* *saturation of their markets at home and abroad.*

▸ COLLOCATIONS: **reach/approach** saturation

---

scarce /skɛərs/ (scarcer, scarcest)

ADJECTIVE If something is **scarce**, there is not enough of it. ○ *Food was scarce and expensive.* ○ *Jobs are becoming increasingly scarce.* ○ *the allocation of scarce resources*

▸ COLLOCATIONS:
   increasingly/relatively/extremely scarce
   scarce **resources/commodities/supplies**
   scarce **food/money/employment/jobs**

scarce|ly /skɛərsli/

1 ADVERB You use **scarcely** to emphasize that something is only just true or only just the case. ○ *He could scarcely breathe.* ○ *I scarcely knew him.*

▸ SYNONYM: barely

2 ADVERB You can use **scarcely** to say that something is not true or is not the case, in a humorous or critical way. ○ *It can scarcely be coincidence.*

▸ SYNONYM: hardly

---

scat|tered /skætərd/

ADJECTIVE **Scattered** things are spread over an area in an untidy or irregular way. ○ *He picked up the scattered toys.* ○ *[+ with] Every surface is scattered with photographs.*

▸ COLLOCATIONS:
   scattered **with** *something*
   scattered **throughout/among** *something*

---

sched|ule /skɛdʒul, -uəl/ (schedules)   PERSONNEL

NOUN A **schedule** is a plan that gives a list of events or tasks and the times at which each one should happen or be done. ○ *He has been forced to adjust his schedule.* ○ *We both have such hectic schedules.*

▸ COLLOCATIONS:
   a **busy/hectic/tight** schedule
   a **punishing/grueling/heavy** schedule
   adjust/rearrange/disrupt a schedule

▸ SYNONYM: timetable

scheme | 576

scheme /skim/ (schemes)

NOUN A **scheme** is a plan for achieving something, especially something
that will bring you some benefit. ○ *a quick money-making scheme*

▶ **COLLOCATIONS**: **devise/concoct/hatch** a scheme

▶ **SYNONYM**: plot

sci|en|tif|ic /saɪəntɪfɪk/ **Scientific** is used to describe things `R&D`
that relate to the study of nature and behavior of natural things. ○ *There
has been a certain amount of scientific research into meditation* ○ *the use of
animals in scientific experiments*

▶ **COLLOCATIONS:**
scientific **research/evidence/discovery/study**
the scientific **community**

scru|ti|nize /skrutᵊnaɪz/ (scrutinizes, scrutinizing, scrutinized)

VERB If you **scrutinize** something, you examine it very carefully, often to
find out some information from it or about it. [in BRIT, also use
scrutinise] ○ *The events that are scrutinized range from large data series on
insurance company accident claims to single cases.* ○ *Lloyds' results were
carefully scrutinised as a guide to what to expect from the other banks.*

▶ **COLLOCATIONS:**
closely/carefully/heavily scrutinize *something*
scrutinize **spending/legislation/expenditure**
scrutinize a **decision/application/bill/proposal**
a **committee/investigator/authority** scrutinizes *something*

▶ **SYNONYM**: examine

search en|gine /sɜrtʃ ɛndʒɪn/ (search engines) `COMMUNICATIONS`

NOUN A **search engine** is a computer program that you use to search for
information on the Internet. ○ *Search engines build their databases by
systematically following the links they find on web pages.*

▶ **COLLOCATIONS:**
an **Internet/Web** search engine
a **powerful/popular** search engine
use a search engine

sec|ond|ary /sɛkəndɛri/

ADJECTIVE If you describe something as **secondary**, you mean that it is less important than something else. ○ *The street erupted in a huge explosion, with secondary explosions in the adjoining buildings.* ○ *The actual damage to the brain cells is secondary to the damage caused to the blood supply.*

▶ **COLLOCATIONS:**
  a secondary **objective/market/explosion**
  seem/become secondary

▶ **PHRASE:** of secondary importance

▶ **RELATED WORD:** primary

se|cre|cy /sikrəsi/

NONCOUNT NOUN Secrecy is a situation in which you do not tell anyone about something. ○ *They met in complete secrecy.*

▶ **COLLOCATIONS:**
  in secrecy
  shrouded/cloaked in secrecy
  great/complete/absolute/total secrecy
  maintain/preserve secrecy

▶ **SYNONYM:** privacy

sec|tion /sɛkʃən/ (sections)

NOUN A **section** of something is one of the parts into which it is divided or from which it is formed. ○ [+ of] *He said it was wrong to single out any section of society for AIDS testing.* ○ *a large orchestra, with a vast percussion section* ○ *the Georgetown section of Washington, D.C.*

▶ **COLLOCATIONS:**
  a section **of** something
  a section of **society/the community/the population**
  a section of a **chapter**
  a **separate/entire/special** section
  the **relevant/preceding** section
  insert/amend a section
  a **percussion/brass/string** section

▶ **SYNONYM:** part

S

sec|tor /sɛktər/ **(sectors)**   `ORGANIZATION`

NOUN A particular **sector** of a country's economy is the part connected with that specified type of industry. ○ *the nation's manufacturing sector* ○ *the service sector of the Hong Kong economy*

▶ **COLLOCATIONS:**
a sector **of** *something*
a sector of **industry/the economy**
the **private/public/voluntary** sector
the **manufacturing/technology/service/banking/retail** sector

---

se|cure /sɪkyʊər/ **(secures, securing, secured)**

1 ADJECTIVE A **secure** place is tightly locked or well protected, so that people cannot enter it or leave it. ○ *We shall make sure our home is as secure as possible from now on.* ○ *The building has secure undercover parking for 27 vehicles.*

▶ **COLLOCATIONS:**
secure **parking/accommodation**
a secure **unit/place/area/location**
make *something* secure

▶ **PHRASE:** safe and secure

▶ **SYNONYMS:** safe, guarded, protected

2 VERB If you **secure** something that you want or need, you obtain it, often after a lot of effort. [FORMAL] ○ *Federal leaders continued their efforts to secure a ceasefire.* ○ *Graham's achievements helped secure him the job.*

▶ **COLLOCATIONS:**
secure a **victory/conviction/place/win/deal**
secure the **approval/support/backing** of *someone*
secure **funding/peace**

▶ **SYNONYM:** obtain

se|cu|rity /sɪkyʊərɪti/

NONCOUNT NOUN **Security** refers to all the measures that are taken to protect a place, or to ensure that only people with permission enter it or leave it. ○ *They are now under a great deal of pressure to tighten their airport security.* ○ *Strict security measures are in force in the capital.*

▶ **COLLOCATIONS:**
national/airport/border security
tight/lax security
tighten/improve/increase security

security **measures**
a security **adviser/official/guard**

USAGE: *safety* or *security*?

You usually use **safety** to talk about keeping individuals away from physical harm. ○ *regulations on health and safety at work* ○ *concerns for their personal safety*

You use **security** to talk more generally about protecting a place or a group of people. ○ *Airlines have substantially increased security in recent years.*

---

seg|ment /sɛgmənt/ (segments)

1 NOUN A **segment of** something is one part of it, considered separately from the rest. ○ [+ *of*] *the poorer segments of society* ○ [+ *of*] *the third segment of his journey*

▶ **COLLOCATIONS:**
a segment **of** *something*
a segment of **society**
a segment of the **population/public**

▶ **SYNONYMS:** section, part

2 NOUN A **segment** of a circle is one of the two parts into which it is divided when you draw a straight line through it. ○ *Divide the circle into segments like an orange.* ○ *The pie chart is divided into equal segments.*

▶ **COLLOCATIONS:**
a segment **of** *something*
a segment of a **circle/pie chart**

▶ **PHRASE:** divided into segments

3 NOUN A **segment** of a market is one part of it, considered separately from the rest. ○ [+ *of*] *Three-to-five day cruises are the fastest-growing segment of the market.* ○ *Women's tennis is the market leader in a growing market segment – women's sports.*

▶ **COLLOCATIONS:**
a segment **of** *something*
a segment of a **market/industry**
a **fast-growing/mid-sized/profitable** segment

▶ **SYNONYMS:** niche, sector

S

sel|dom /sɛldəm/

ADVERB If something **seldom** happens, it happens only occasionally.
○ *They seldom speak.* ○ *Hypertension can be controlled but seldom cured.*
○ *The fines were seldom sufficient to force any permanent change.*

▶ **SYNONYMS:** rarely, hardly ever, infrequently

se|lect /sɪlɛkt/ (selects, selecting, selected)

VERB If you **select** something, you choose it from a number of things of the same kind. ○ *Voters are selecting candidates for both U.S. Senate seats and for 52 congressional seats.* ○ *a randomly selected sample of school children*

▶ **COLLOCATIONS:**
select **for/from** *something*
select for **inclusion/testing/training**
select from a **list/shortlist/menu/range**
select a **candidate/delegate/winner/sample/option**
randomly/carefully/specially selected

▶ **SYNONYMS:** choose, pick out

se|lec|tion /sɪlɛkʃən/ (selections)

1 NONCOUNT NOUN Selection is the act of selecting one or more people or things from a group. ○ *Darwin's principles of natural selection* ○ *Dr. Sullivan's selection to head the Department of Health was greeted with satisfaction.*

▶ **COLLOCATIONS:**
the selection **of** *someone/something*
a selection **process/committee**

2 NOUN A **selection of** or **from** people or things is a set of them that have been selected from a larger group. ○ [+ *of*] *this selection of popular songs* ○ [+ *from*] *a handpicked selection from our top team*

▶ **COLLOCATIONS:** a **varied/eclectic** selection

3 NOUN The **selection of** goods in a store is the particular range of goods that it has available and from which you can choose what you want. ○ *It offers the widest selection of antiques of every description in a one day market.*

▶ **COLLOCATIONS:** a **wide/huge** selection

▶ **SYNONYM:** range

4 NOUN In computing, a **selection** is an area of the screen that you have highlighted, for example because you want to copy it to another file. ○ *On the TV, you'll see the selections change, left/right/up/down, in the direction you drag on the iPhone.*

se|lec|tive /sɪlɛktɪv/

1 **ADJECTIVE** A **selective** process applies only to a few things or people. ○ *selective admissions policies where students compete to enroll based on academic performance*

▶ **COLLOCATION:** **highly** selective

2 **ADJECTIVE** When someone is **selective**, they choose things carefully, for example, the things that they buy or do. ○ *Sales still happen, but buyers are more selective.*

▶ **COLLOCATION:** a selective **memory**

self-employed /sɛlfɪmplɔɪd/ `PERSONNEL`

ADJECTIVE If you are **self-employed**, you are working for yourself, rather than for a company. ○ *There are no paid holidays or sick leave if you are self-employed.* ○ *a self-employed builder*

▶ **COLLOCATIONS:** a self-employed **worker/tradesman/contractor**

semi|nar /sɛmɪnɑr/ (seminars) `PERSONNEL`

1 **NOUN** A **seminar** is a meeting where a group of people discuss a problem or topic. ○ *a series of half-day seminars to help businessmen get the best value from investing in information technology* ○ [+ on] *We conduct seminars on Immigration and Discrimination Law.*

2 **NOUN** A **seminar** is a class at a college or university in which the teacher and a small group of students discuss a topic. ○ *Students are asked to prepare material in advance of each weekly seminar.* ○ [+ on] *a seminar on a topic closely related to the course*

▶ **COLLOCATIONS:**
a seminar **on** *something*
attend/organize/conduct/hold a seminar
a seminar **room/topic/series/program**
a **weekly/two-hour/three-day** seminar

▶ **SYNONYMS:** meeting, tutorial, workshop

semi-skilled /sɛmɪskɪld, sɛmaɪ-/ also **semiskilled** `PERSONNEL`

ADJECTIVE A **semi-skilled** worker has some training and skills, but not enough to do specialized work. ○ *The region's advantage in semi-skilled and unskilled labor costs will continue for an indefinite period.*

▶ **COLLOCATIONS:** semi-skilled **workers/labor/jobs/work**

sen|ior /sínyər/

ADJECTIVE The **senior** people in an organization or profession have the highest and most important jobs. ○ *senior officials in the Israeli government* ○ *The budget was reviewed by senior management.* ○ *Television and radio needed many more women in senior jobs.*

▶ **COLLOCATIONS:**
  a senior **official/executive/manager**
  a senior **editor/analyst/politician**
  senior **management**
  a senior **job/position**

▶ **SYNONYMS:** chief, head

---

sepa|rate (separates, separating, separated)

The adjective is pronounced /sɛpərɪt/. The verb is pronounced /sɛpəreɪt/.

1 ADJECTIVE If one thing is **separate from** another, there is a barrier, space, or division between them, so that they are clearly two things. ○ *The financial review includes a separate section concerning exchange rates.* ○ *They are now making plans to form their own separate party.* ○ *[+ from] Business bank accounts were kept separate from personal ones.*

2 ADJECTIVE If you refer to **separate** things, you mean several different things, rather than just one thing. ○ *They repeated the experiment on three separate occasions, with the same results.* ○ *Men and women have separate exercise rooms.* ○ *The authorities say six civilians have been killed in two separate attacks.*

▶ **COLLOCATIONS:**
  separate **from** *something*
  separate from **the rest of** *something*
  a separate **section/unit**
  a separate **room/bedroom/toilet/entrance**
  a separate **incident/occasion/attack**
  entirely/completely/totally separate

▶ **SYNONYMS:** distinct, different, discrete

3 VERB If you **separate** people or things that are together, or if they **separate**, they move apart. ○ *Police moved in to separate the two groups.* ○ *[+ from] The front end of the car separated from the rest of the vehicle.* ○ *[+ from] a process in which small molecules are separated from larger ones*

4 VERB If you **separate** people or things that have been connected, or if
one **separates from** another, the connection between them is ended.
○ [+ *from*] *They want to separate teaching from research.* ○ *It's very possible that
we may see a movement to separate the two parts of the country.*

▶ **COLLOCATIONS:**
separate *something* **from** *something*
surgically/physically/forcibly/successfully separate

▶ **SYNONYMS:** disconnect, sever, split

sepa|rate|ly /sɛpərɪtli/

ADVERB If people or things are dealt with **separately** or do something
separately, they are dealt with or do something at different times or
places, rather than together. ○ *The software is sold separately.* ○ [+ *from*]
Acid fruits are best eaten separately from sweet fruits.

▶ **COLLOCATIONS:**
separately **from** *something*
sold/bought/purchased separately
calculated/analyzed separately

▶ **SYNONYM:** distinctly

---

se|quence /sikwəns/ **(sequences)**

1 NOUN A **sequence of** events or things is a number of events or things
that come one after another in a particular order. ○ [+ *of*] *the sequence of
events which led to the murder* ○ [+ *of*] *A flow chart displays the chronological
sequence of steps in a process.*

2 NOUN A particular **sequence** is a particular order in which things
happen or are arranged. ○ *the color sequence yellow, orange, purple, blue,
green and white* ○ *The chronological sequence gives the book an element of
structure.* ○ *a simple numerical sequence*

▶ **COLLOCATIONS:**
a sequence **of** *things*
a sequence of **events/letters/movements/steps**
a **chronological/logical/narrative/linear/numerical** sequence

▶ **SYNONYM:** series

se|quen|tial /sɪkwɛnʃᵊl/

ADJECTIVE Something that is **sequential** follows a fixed order. [FORMAL]
○ *the sequential story of the universe* ○ *In this way the children are introduced to
sequential learning.*

S

▶ **COLLOCATIONS:**
sequential **reasoning/logic**
a sequential **narrative**

▶ **SYNONYMS:** consecutive, in order

---

se|ries /sɪəriz/ (series)

NOUN A **series of** things or events is a number of them that come one after the other. ○ [+ of] *a series of meetings with students and political leaders* ○ [+ of] *a series of explosions*

▶ **COLLOCATIONS:**
a series **of** *things*
a series of **events/meetings/interviews**
a series of **attacks/bombings/explosions**

▶ **SYNONYMS:** succession, set, chain

---

se|ri|ous /sɪəriəs/

ADJECTIVE Serious problems or situations are very bad and cause people to be worried or afraid. ○ *Crime is an increasingly serious problem in Russian society.* ○ *Doctors said his condition was serious but stable.*

▶ **COLLOCATIONS:**
a serious **problem/difficulty/situation**
a serious **accident/injury/illness/condition**
a serious **crime/threat**
potentially/extremely/increasingly serious

se|ri|ous|ness /sɪəriəsnəs/

NONCOUNT NOUN ○ [+ of] *They don't realize the seriousness of the crisis.*

▶ **COLLOCATIONS:**
the seriousness **of** *something*
understand/realize/recognize the seriousness of *something*
the seriousness of the **situation/problem/offense/charge**

▶ **SYNONYM:** gravity

---

ser|vices /sɜrvɪsɪz/ `ORGANIZATION`

PLURAL NOUN Services are activities such as tourism, banking, and selling things that are part of a country's economy, but are not concerned with producing or manufacturing goods. ○ *Mining rose by 9.1%, manufacturing by 9.4% and services by 4.3%.*

▶ **COLLOCATIONS: public/financial/banking** services

▶ **PHRASE:** goods and services

---

set|tle /sɛtᵊl/ (settles, settling, settled)

1 VERB If people **settle** an argument or problem, or if something **settles** it, they solve it, for example, by making a decision about who is right or about what to do. ○ *They agreed to try to settle their dispute by negotiation.*

▶ **COLLOCATIONS:** settle a **dispute/score/argument/conflict**

▶ **SYNONYM:** resolve

2 VERB If people **settle** a legal dispute or if they **settle**, they agree to end the dispute without going to a court of law, for example, by paying some money or by apologizing. ○ *In an attempt to settle the case, Molken has agreed to pay restitution.* ○ *If she just offered to settle out of court, she was sure they could come to some sort of agreement.*

▶ **COLLOCATIONS:** settle a **lawsuit/case/suit**

▶ **PHRASE:** settle out of court

3 VERB If something **is settled**, it has all been decided and arranged. ○ *As far as we're concerned, the matter is settled.*

▶ **SYNONYM:** decide

4 VERB When people **settle** a place or in a place, or when a government **settles** them there, they start living there permanently. ○ *Refugees settling in a new country suffer from a number of problems.* ○ *He visited Paris and eventually settled there.*

▶ **COLLOCATION:** settle **in** *a place*

5 VERB When birds or insects **settle on** something, they land on it from above. ○ [+ on] *Moths flew in front of it, eventually settling on the rough painted metal.*

▶ **COLLOCATION:** settle **on** *something*

▶ **SYNONYMS:** land, light

set|tle|ment /sɛtᵊlmənt/ (settlements)

1 NOUN A **settlement** is an official agreement between two sides who were involved in a conflict or argument, often in a court of law in order to end a dispute by offering someone money. ○ *Our objective must be to secure a peace settlement.* ○ *She accepted an out-of-court settlement of $40,000.*

▶ **COLLOCATIONS:**
negotiate/propose/accept/secure a settlement
a **peaceful/amicable/permanent/informal** settlement

2 NOUN A **settlement** is a place where people have come to live and have built homes. ○ *The village is a settlement of just fifty houses.*

▶ **COLLOCATIONS:** a **nearby/isolated** settlement

▶ **SYNONYM:** community

---

sev|en|teen /sɛvᵊntin/

NUMBER Seventeen is the number 17. ○ *She will be seventeen next week.* ○ *a man the clinic had employed seventeen years ago.*

▶ **COLLOCATIONS:**
someone **is** seventeen
seventeen **dollars/euros**
seventeen **miles/kilometers**
seventeen **minutes/seconds**

▶ **PHRASE:** sixteen or seventeen

---

sev|en|ty /sɛvᵊnti/

NUMBER Seventy is the number 70. ○ *My cousin will be seventy in March.* ○ *a convoy of seventy ships leaving for England*

▶ **COLLOCATIONS:**
someone **is** seventy
seventy **dollars/euros**
seventy **miles/kilometers**
seventy **minutes/years**

▶ **PHRASE:** sixty or seventy

---

sev|er|ance pay /sɛvrəns peɪ, -ərəns/ `PERSONNEL`

NONCOUNT NOUN Severance pay is a sum of money that a company gives to its employees when it has to stop employing them. ○ *We were offered 13 weeks' severance pay.*

▶ **COLLOCATIONS:**
severance pay **of** $x
offer/collect/receive severance pay

---

sharp|en /ʃɑrpən/ (sharpens, sharpening, sharpened)

VERB If you **sharpen** something, you make its edge very thin or its end pointed. ○ *Mike had to sharpen the pencils every morning.*

▶ **COLLOCATIONS:** sharpen a **pencil/knife/blade/tool**

shift /ʃɪft/ (shifts, shifting, shifted)

1 **VERB** If you **shift** something or if it **shifts**, it moves slightly. ○ *He shifted from foot to foot.* ○ [V-ing] *Firefighters have been hampered by high temperatures and shifting winds.*

▸ **COLLOCATIONS:**
shift **uncomfortably/restlessly/uneasily**
shift *one's* **weight/position**

▸ **SYNONYM:** move

2 **VERB** If someone's opinion, a situation, or a policy **shifts** or **is shifted**, it changes slightly. ○ *Attitudes to mental illness have shifted in recent years.* ○ *The emphasis should be shifted more towards Parliament.*

▸ **COLLOCATIONS:** shift the **focus/emphasis/balance**

▸ **SYNONYMS:** alter, change, adjust

● **Shift** is also a noun. ○ [+ in] *a shift in government policy* ○ *The migration towards technology as a service is a cultural shift.*

▸ **COLLOCATIONS:**
a shift **in** *something*
a shift in **focus/emphasis/power/priorities/attitudes**
a **sudden/major/cultural** shift

▸ **SYNONYM:** change

ship|ment /ʃɪpmənt/ (shipments) `LOGISTICS & DISTRIBUTION`

NOUN A **shipment** is an amount of a particular kind of cargo that is sent to another country on a ship, train, airplane, or other vehicle. ○ *Food shipments to the port could begin in a matter of weeks.*

▸ **COLLOCATIONS:**
a shipment **of** *something*
a shipment of **petroleum/grain**
authorize/ban a shipment
seize/unload a shipment

▸ **SYNONYMS:** consignment, delivery

short|age /ʃɔrtɪdʒ/ (shortages) `LOGISTICS & DISTRIBUTION`

NOUN If there is a **shortage of** something, there is not enough of it. ○ [+ of] *A shortage of funds is preventing the U.N. from monitoring relief.* ○ *Vietnam is suffering from a food shortage.*

▶ **COLLOCATIONS:**
a shortage **of** *something*
a shortage of **labor/housing/food/teachers/doctors**
a **food/labor/skills/housing/fuel** shortage
a **chronic/severe/acute/dire** shortage
ease/alleviate/address/face/experience a shortage

▶ **SYNONYM:** lack

short-handed /ʃɔːrthændɪd/ also **shorthanded** `PERSONNEL`

ADJECTIVE If a company or an organization is **short-handed**, it does not have enough people to work on a particular job or for a particular purpose. ○ *We're actually a bit short-handed at the moment.*

▶ **COLLOCATIONS:** a **company/organization/team** is short-handed

▶ **SYNONYMS:** short-staffed, understaffed

short|list /ʃɔːrtlɪst/ (shortlists, shortlisting, shortlisted) `PERSONNEL`
also **short list**

1 NOUN A **shortlist** is a list of a few suitable applicants for a job from which the successful person will be chosen. ○ *If you've been asked for an interview you are probably on a shortlist of no more than six.*

▶ **COLLOCATIONS:**
a shortlist **of** *x people*
a shortlist of **candidates**
make/draw up/compile/announce a shortlist
the **final** shortlist

▶ **RELATED WORD:** long list

2 VERB If someone or something **is shortlisted for** a job, they are put on a shortlist. ○ [+ *for*] *He was shortlisted for the job.*

▶ **COLLOCATIONS:**
be shortlisted **for** *something*
be shortlisted for a **job/post/position**

short-term /ʃɔːrttɜːrm/

ADJECTIVE **Short-term** is used to describe things that will last for a short period of time. ○ *The company has 90 staff, almost all on short-term contracts.*

▶ **COLLOCATIONS:**
a short-term **contract/deal/investment/loan**
short-term **debt/interest rates**

short-term **gains/profits/losses**
a short-term **strategy/fix/solution/effect**
short-term **employment**

▶ **RELATED WORD:** long-term

---

shrink /ʃrɪŋk/ (shrinks, shrinking, shrank, shrunk)

VERB If something **shrinks** or something else **shrinks** it, it becomes
smaller. ○ *The vast forests of West Africa have shrunk.* ○ *Hungary may have to
lower its hopes of shrinking its state sector.*

▶ **COLLOCATIONS:**
a **workforce/economy/deficit** shrinks
drastically/dramatically/steadily shrink

▶ **SYNONYM:** decrease

---

shut|down /ʃʌtdaʊn/ (shutdowns)   LOGISTICS & DISTRIBUTION

NOUN A **shutdown** is the closing of a factory, store, or other business.
○ *The shutdown is the latest in a series of painful budget measures.*

▶ **COLLOCATIONS:**
the shutdown **of** *something*
the shutdown of a **factory**
a **government/factory/plant** shutdown
a **temporary/total/emergency** shutdown
force/order/cause a shutdown

---

side-effect /saɪdɪfɛkt/ (side-effects) also side   HEALTH & FITNESS
effect

NOUN The **side-effects** of a drug are the effects, usually bad ones, that
the drug has on you in addition to its function of curing illness or pain.
○ *The treatment has a whole host of extremely unpleasant side-effects including
weight gain, acne, skin rashes and headaches.* ○ *Most patients suffer no
side-effects.*

▶ **COLLOCATIONS:**
experience/suffer/have side-effects
serious/adverse/unpleasant/possible side-effects
side-effects **include** *something*

▶ **SYNONYM:** reaction

side|ways /saɪdweɪz/

ADVERB **Sideways** means from or toward the side of something or someone. ○ *Piercey glanced sideways at her.* ○ *The ladder blew sideways.*

▶ **COLLOCATIONS:** **move/look a little** sideways

● **Sideways** is also an adjective. ○ *Alfred shot him a sideways glance.*

▶ **COLLOCATIONS:** a sideways **glance/look/movement/move**

▶ **SYNONYM:** lateral

sight|see|ing /saɪtsiːɪŋ/ `TRAVEL`

NONCOUNT NOUN **Sightseeing** is visiting places that tourists usually go to. ○ *We had a day's sightseeing in Venice.*

▶ **COLLOCATIONS:**
go/do sightseeing
a sightseeing **trip/excursion**
a **day's** sightseeing

▶ **PHRASE:** a week of sightseeing

sig|nal /sɪgnəl/ **(signals)**

NOUN A **signal** is a series of radio waves, light waves, or changes in electrical current which may carry information. ○ *high-frequency radio signals* ○ *a means of transmitting television signals using microwave frequencies*

▶ **COLLOCATIONS:**
send/transmit/emit/broadcast a signal
receive/detect/decode a signal
a **clear/strong/digital/analog/radio/satellite** signal
signal **processing**

sig|na|ture /sɪgnətʃər, -tʃʊər/ **(signatures)** `COMMUNICATIONS`

NOUN Your **signature** is your name, written by you. ○ *I put my signature at the bottom of the page.*

▶ **COLLOCATIONS:**
witness/forge/verify a signature
write/affix/add *someone's* signature
collect/gather/get signatures
a **legible/illegible/valid** signature
a **digital/electronic** signature

sig|ni|fy /sɪgnɪfaɪ/ (signifies, signifying, signified)

VERB If an event, a sign, or a symbol **signifies** something, it is a sign of that thing or represents that thing. ○ *The contrasting approaches to Europe signified a sharp difference between the major parties.* ○ [+ that] *The symbol displayed outside a restaurant signifies there's excellent cuisine inside.*

▶ **COLLOCATIONS:**
signify a **shift** in *something*
signify the **beginning/end** of *something*

▶ **SYNONYM:** indicate

sig|nifi|cance /sɪgnɪfɪkəns/

NONCOUNT NOUN The **significance** of something is the importance that it has, usually because it will have an effect on a situation or shows something about a situation. ○ [+ of] *Ideas about the social significance of religion have changed over time.* ○ *The difference did not achieve statistical significance.*

▶ **COLLOCATIONS:**
the significance **of** *something*
the significance of a **discovery/event/occasion/finding**
cultural/historical/political/religious significance
great/special/symbolic/statistical significance
attach significance to *something*
downplay/understand/appreciate the significance of *something*
assume/acquire significance

▶ **SYNONYM:** importance

sig|nifi|cant /sɪgnɪfɪkənt/

1 ADJECTIVE A **significant** amount or effect is large enough to be important or affect a situation to a noticeable degree. ○ *A small but significant number of 11-year-olds are illiterate.* ○ *foods that offer a significant amount of protein* ○ *The study is too small to show whether this trend is statistically significant.*

→ see note at **dramatic**

2 ADJECTIVE A **significant** fact, event, or thing is one that is important or shows something. ○ *Time would appear to be the significant factor in this whole drama.* ○ *a very significant piece of legislation*

▶ **COLLOCATIONS:**
a significant **amount/proportion/difference/improvement**
a significant **change/increase/effect/factor**
a significant **number** of *people/things*

seem/prove/become significant
statistically significant

▶ **SYNONYMS:** important, large

---

simi|lar /sɪmɪlər/

ADJECTIVE If one thing is **similar to** another, or if two things are **similar**, they have features that are the same. ○ [+ to] *The accident was similar to one that happened in 1973.* ○ *a group of similar pictures*

▶ **COLLOCATIONS:**
  similar **to/in** *something*
  similar in **size/style**
  a similar **situation/incident/amount**
  similar **circumstances**
  strikingly/remarkably similar

▶ **SYNONYM:** alike

simi|lar|ity /sɪmɪlærɪti/ (similarities)

NOUN ○ [+ in] *There was a very basic similarity in our philosophy.* ○ *The film bears some similarities to Spielberg's "A.I."* ○ [+ between] *The similarities between Mars and Earth were enough to keep alive hopes of some form of Martian life.*

▶ **COLLOCATIONS:**
  similarity **to/in** *something*
  similarities **between** *things*
  bear a similarity to *something*
  share similarities
  a **striking/remarkable/uncanny/superficial** similarity

---

sim|pli|fy /sɪmplɪfaɪ/ (simplifies, simplifying, simplified)

VERB If you **simplify** something, you make it easier to understand or you remove the things which make it complex. ○ *a plan to simplify the complex social security system* ○ *technology for simplifying trade procedures* ○ *a simplified version of the formula*

▶ **COLLOCATIONS:**
  simplify a **procedure/process/diagram/task**
  a simplified **version**
  greatly/radically/vastly simplified

simu|late /sɪmyəleɪt/ (simulates, simulating, simulated)

VERB If you **simulate** a set of conditions, you create them artificially, for example in order to conduct an experiment. ○ *The scientist developed one model to simulate a full year of the globe's climate.* ○ *Cars are tested to see how much damage they suffer in simulated crashes.*

▶ **COLLOCATIONS:** simulate **conditions/altitude/gravity**

▶ **SYNONYMS:** replicate, reproduce, model

simu|la|tion /sɪmyəleɪʃᵊn/ (simulations)

NOUN ○ [+ of] *Training includes realistic simulation of casualty procedures.* ○ [+ of] *a simulation of the greenhouse effect*

▶ **COLLOCATIONS:**
simulation **of** something
computer simulation
a simulation **model/tool**

sim|ul|ta|neous /saɪməlteɪniəs/

ADJECTIVE Things that are **simultaneous** happen or exist at the same time. ○ *the simultaneous release of the book and the album* ○ *The theater will provide simultaneous translation in both English and Chinese.*

▶ **COLLOCATIONS:** simultaneous **translation/attacks/actions**

▶ **SYNONYM:** concurrent

sin|gu|lar /sɪŋgyələr/

1 ADJECTIVE The **singular** form of a word is the form that is used when referring to one person or thing. ○ *the fifteen case endings of the singular form of the Finnish noun*

▶ **COLLOCATIONS:** a singular **noun/verb/pronoun**

2 NOUN The **singular** of a noun is the form of it that is used to refer to one person or thing. ○ *The inhabitants of the Arctic are known as the Inuit. The singular is Inuk.*

s

situ|at|ed /sɪtʃueɪtɪd/

ADJECTIVE If something is **situated** in a particular place or position, it is in that place or position. ○ [+ in] *His hotel is situated in one of the loveliest places on the Loire.*

▶ **COLLOCATIONS:** situated **in the middle of/on the edge of** *something*

▶ **SYNONYM:** located

situa|tion /sɪtʃueɪʃ°n/ (situations)

NOUN You use **situation** to refer generally to what is happening in a particular place at a particular time, or to refer to what is happening to you. ○ *Army officers said the situation was under control.* ○ *The local authority faced a difficult financial situation.* ○ *If you want to improve your situation, you must adopt a positive mental attitude.*

▶ **COLLOCATIONS:**
the **current/present** situation
a **financial/economic/political** situation
a **dangerous/difficult/tense** situation
describe/discuss a situation
handle/improve/understand a situation
a situation **improves/changes/deteriorates**

▶ **SYNONYM:** circumstances

---

six|teen /sɪkstin/

NUMBER Sixteen is the number 16. ○ *She will be sixteen this Wednesday.*
○ *Sixteen people were injured.*

▶ **COLLOCATIONS:**
someone **is** sixteen
sixteen **dollars/cents**
sixteen **miles/kilometers**
sixteen **months/weeks**

▶ **PHRASE:** fifteen or sixteen

---

six|ty /sɪksti/

NUMBER Sixty is the number 60. ○ *She will be sixty next birthday.* ○ *Over sixty cars were set alight.*

▶ **COLLOCATIONS:**
someone **is** sixty
sixty **dimes/quarters**
sixty **miles/kilometers**
sixty **minutes/years**

▶ **PHRASE:** fifty or sixty

skill /skɪl/ (skills)

PERSONNEL

NOUN A **skill** is a type of work or activity that requires special training and knowledge. ○ *an opportunity to learn new computer skills* ○ *Trainees will be taught basic practical skills.*

▶ COLLOCATIONS:
learn/acquire/develop/teach a skill
a **basic/essential/technical/practical/transferable** skill
communication/interpersonal/literacy/numeracy skills
a skills **shortage/gap**
skills **development/training**

▶ SYNONYMS: ability, technique

skill|ful /skɪlfəl/

ADJECTIVE If you are **skillful**, you are able to do something very well. ○ *We need skillful, hands-on managers.*

▶ COLLOCATIONS:
skillful **at** *something*
a skillful **manager/artist/player**

▶ SYNONYM: expert

slow|down /sloʊdaʊn/ (slowdowns)

BANKING & FINANCE

NOUN A **slowdown** is a reduction in speed or activity. ○ [+ *in*] *a slowdown in economic growth*

▶ COLLOCATIONS:
a slowdown **in** *something*
a **industry/economic/market/housing/business** slowdown
a **sharp/marked/global** slowdown

so|ci|ety /səsaɪɪti/ (societies)

1 NONCOUNT NOUN Society is people in general, thought of as a large organized group. ○ *This reflects attitudes and values prevailing in society.* ○ *He maintains Islam must adapt to modern society.*

2 NOUN A **society** is the people who live in a country or region, their organizations, and their way of life. ○ *Debate is fundamental to a democratic society.* ○ *those responsible for destroying our African heritage and the fabric of our society* ○ *the complexities of South African society*

▶ COLLOCATIONS:
modern/contemporary society

a **democratic/capitalist/industrial** society
Western/American society

▸ **SYNONYM:** community

---

soft|ware /sɔ̲ftwɛər/   `OFFICE`

NONCOUNT NOUN Computer programs are referred to as **software**. ○ *the people who write the software for big computer projects* ○ *the latest software development technologies*

▸ **COLLOCATIONS:**
install/use/download software
design/develop software
computer/antivirus software
software **development**
a software **developer/company**

▸ **RELATED WORD:** hardware

---

so|lar /so̲ʊlər/

1 ADJECTIVE Solar is used to describe things relating to the sun. ○ *a total solar eclipse* ○ *Snow and ice reflect 80% to 90% of solar radiation back into space.*

▸ **COLLOCATIONS:**
a solar **eclipse/storm**
solar **radiation**

▸ **PHRASE:** the solar system

2 ADJECTIVE Solar power is obtained from the sun's light and heat.
○ *a government effort to promote solar power* ○ *A solar water heater reduces electricity consumption.*

▸ **COLLOCATIONS:**
solar **power/energy**
a solar **panel/cell/heater**

---

sole /so̲ʊl/

1 ADJECTIVE The **sole** thing or person of a particular type is the only one of that type. ○ *Their sole aim is to destabilize the Indian government.* ○ *It's the sole survivor of an ancient family of plants.*

▸ **COLLOCATIONS:**
the sole **purpose/aim/responsibility**
a sole **survivor**

▸ **SYNONYM:** only

2 ADJECTIVE If you have **sole** charge or ownership of something, you are the only person in charge of it or who owns it. ○ *Many women are left as the sole providers in families after their husband has died.* ○ *Chief Hart had sole control over that fund.*

▶ COLLOCATIONS:
sole **possession/responsibility/custody**
a sole **proprietor/representative/breadwinner**

sole|ly /soʊlli/

ADVERB If something involves **solely** one thing, it involves only this thing and no others. ○ *Too often we make decisions based solely upon what we see in the magazines.* ○ *This program is a production of NPR, which is solely responsible for its content.*

▶ COLLOCATIONS:
rely/concentrate/focus solely on *something*
based solely on *something*
solely **responsible**

▶ SYNONYM: only

solve /sɒlv/ (solves, solving, solved)

VERB If you **solve** a problem or a question, you find a solution or an answer to it. ○ *Their domestic reforms did nothing to solve the problem of unemployment.* ○ *We may now be able to get a much better idea of the true age of the universe, and solve one of the deepest questions of our origins.*

▶ COLLOCATIONS:
solve a **problem/conflict/crisis**
solve a **puzzle/riddle/equation**
attempt/try to solve *something*

▶ SYNONYM: work out

so|lu|tion /səluʃ°n/ (solutions)

NOUN A **solution to** a problem or difficult situation is a way of dealing with it so that the difficulty is removed. ○ *Although he has sought to find a peaceful solution, he is facing pressure to use greater military force.* ○ *[+ to] the ability to sort out simple, effective solutions to practical problems* ○ *The real solution lay in providing affordable accommodations.*

▶ COLLOCATIONS:
a solution **to** a problem
a **peaceful/diplomatic/political** solution
a **simple/ideal/temporary** solution

the **best** solution
find/offer/provide a solution
the solution **lies in** *something*

▶ SYNONYM: answer

---

source /sɔrs/ (sources)

1 NOUN The **source of** something is the person, place, or thing that you get it from. ○ *Renewable sources of energy must be used where practical.* ○ *Tourism, which is a major source of income for the city, may be seriously affected.*

▶ COLLOCATIONS:
a source **of** *something*
a source of **information/inspiration**
a source of **income/revenue/funding**
a **heat/food/energy** source
a **renewable/alternative/major/main** source

2 NOUN A **source** is a person or book that provides information for a news story or for a piece of research. ○ *Military sources say the boat was heading south at high speed.* ○ *Carson (1970) made extensive use of secondary data sources.*

▶ COLLOCATIONS:
a source **of** *something*
a **primary/secondary** source
police/intelligence sources
a **reliable/senior/unnamed/unidentified** source
identify/locate/quote/cite a source
sources **say/confirm/tell** *things*

3 NOUN The **source of** a difficulty is its cause. ○ [+ *of*] *Reactions to ointments are a common source of skin problems.*

▶ COLLOCATIONS:
a source **of** *something*
the source of a **problem**

▶ SYNONYMS: root, cause, origin

---

spa|cious /speɪʃəs/

ADJECTIVE A **spacious** room or other place is large in size or area, so that you can move around freely in it. ○ *The house has a spacious kitchen and dining area.*

▶ COLLOCATIONS: a spacious **bedroom/apartment/kitchen/interior**

▶ SYNONYM: roomy

---

span /spæn/ (spans)

1 NOUN A **span** is the period of time between two dates or events during which something exists, functions, or happens. ○ [+ of] *The batteries had a life span of six hours.* ○ [+ between] *Gradually the time span between sessions will increase.*

▶ COLLOCATIONS:
a span **of** *something*
the span **between** *things*
a **life/time** span
a **short/four-year/five-minute** span

2 NOUN Your concentration **span** or your attention **span** is the length of time you are able to concentrate on something or be interested in it. ○ *His ability to absorb information was astonishing, but his concentration span was short.* ○ *Young children have a limited attention span and can't concentrate on one activity for very long.*

▶ COLLOCATIONS: a **concentration/attention** span

---

spe|cial /spɛʃ^əl/

ADJECTIVE If someone or something is **special**, they are better or more important than normal people or things. ○ *My special guest will be Zac Efron.*

▶ COLLOCATIONS:
a special **friend/guest/relationship**
a special **event/meeting/occasion/day**
a special **place/quality**
a special **price/offer/deal**
special **attention/care/concern/treatment**

spe|cial|ize /spɛʃəlaɪz/ (specializes, specializing, specialized)

VERB If you **specialize in** something, you spend most of your time studying it or doing it. [in BRIT, also use **specialise**] ○ [+ in] *They work for banks or law firms that specialize in business.*

▶ COLLOCATIONS:
specialize **in** *something*
specialize in **business**

a **company/lawyer/doctor/writer** specializes

highly specialized

spe|cial|ty /ˈspɛʃəlti/ (specialties)

NOUN Someone's **specialty** is something that they do particularly well, or a subject that they know a lot about. [in BRIT, use **speciality**]
○ *His specialty is international law.*

▶ **COLLOCATION:** a **medical** specialty

▶ **SYNONYM:** forte

---

spe|cif|ic /spɪsɪfɪk/

ADJECTIVE You use **specific** to refer to a particular fixed area, problem, or subject. ○ *Massage may help to increase blood flow to specific areas of the body.* ○ *There are several specific problems to be dealt with.* ○ *the specific needs of the individual*

▶ **COLLOCATIONS:**
a specific **area/location/target/group**
a specific **problem/need/issue/question/purpose**

▶ **SYNONYM:** particular

spe|cifi|cal|ly /spɪsɪfɪkli/

ADVERB ○ *the first nursing home designed specifically for people with AIDS* ○ *brain cells, or more specifically, neurons*

▶ **COLLOCATIONS:**
specifically **designed/targeted/aimed**
specifically **state/mention/exclude**

▶ **SYNONYM:** particularly

speci|fy /spɛsɪfaɪ/ (specifies, specifying, specified)

1 VERB If you **specify** something, you give information about what is required or should happen in a certain situation. ○ *They specified a spacious entrance hall.* ○ [+ what] *He has not specified what action he would like them to take.*

2 VERB If you **specify** what should happen or be done, you explain it in an exact and detailed way. ○ *Each recipe specifies the size of egg to be used.* ○ [+ that] *One rule specifies that student drivers must be supervised by adults.* ○ *Patients eat together at a specified time.*

▶ **COLLOCATIONS:**
specify a **date/size/time/period**
exactly/explicitly specify *something*

spec|tacu|lar /spɛktækyələr/

ADJECTIVE Something that is **spectacular** is very big and dramatic.
○ *We had spectacular views of Sugar Loaf Mountain.*

▶ **COLLOCATIONS:**
a spectacular **view/scenery/sunset**
a spectacular **performance/show**
a spectacular **success/failure/result/recovery**
truly/quite spectacular

▶ **SYNONYM:** striking

spec|ta|tor /spɛkteɪtər/ (spectators)

NOUN A **spectator** is someone who watches something, especially a sports event. ○ *Thirty thousand spectators watched the final game.*

▶ **COLLOCATIONS:**
spectators **applaud/cheer**
attract/astonish/thrill spectators

▶ **SYNONYMS:** onlooker, supporter

spec|trum /spɛktrəm/ (spectra or spectrums)

1 **NOUN** The **spectrum** is the range of different colors that is produced when light passes through a glass prism or through a drop of water. A rainbow shows the colors in the spectrum. ○ *lights known as ultraviolet because on the color spectrum they lie above violet* ○ *Yellow is the most luminous of the color spectrum.*

▶ **PHRASE:** the color spectrum

2 **NOUN** A **spectrum** is a range of a particular type of thing. ○ *She'd seen his moods range across the emotional spectrum.* ○ *Politicians across the political spectrum have denounced the act.* ○ *[+ of] The term "special needs" covers a wide spectrum of problems.*

▶ **COLLOCATIONS:**
a spectrum **of** something
a **broad/wide/entire** spectrum
the **political/emotional** spectrum

▶ **SYNONYM:** range

3 **NOUN** A **spectrum** is a range of light waves or radio waves within particular frequencies. ○ *Vast amounts of energy, from X-rays right through the spectrum down to radio waves, are escaping into space.* ○ *The individual*

colors within the light spectrum are believed to have an effect on health. ○ *the ultraviolet spectra of hot stars*

▶ COLLOCATIONS: the **light/ultraviolet/radio** spectrum

---

specu|late /spɛ́kyəleɪt/ (speculates, speculating, speculated)

VERB If you **speculate** about something, you make guesses about its nature or identity, or about what might happen. ○ [+ *about*] *Critics of the project speculate about how many hospitals could be built instead.* ○ [+ *that*] *The doctors speculate that he died of a cerebral haemorrhage caused by a blow on the head.*

▶ COLLOCATIONS:
speculate **about** something
analysts/observers/researchers/experts speculate

specu|la|tion /spɛ́kyəleɪʃən/ (speculations)

NOUN ○ [+ *over*] *The President has gone out of his way to dismiss speculation over the future of the economy minister.* ○ [+ *about*] *I had published my speculations about the future of the universe in the Review of Modern Physics.*

▶ COLLOCATIONS:
speculation **about/over** something
fuel/prompt/spark/dismiss speculation
intense/widespread/pure speculation
media/press speculation
speculation **mounts/continues/grows**

specu|la|tive /spɛ́kyəleɪtɪv, -lətɪv/

ADJECTIVE Speculative investment involves buying goods or shares in the hope of being able to sell them again at a higher price and make a profit. ○ *Thousands of retirees were persuaded to mortgage their homes to invest in speculative bonds.*

▶ COLLOCATIONS:
speculative **investments/funds/bonds/stocks**
a speculative **boom/bubble**
speculative **buying/trading**

---

sphere /sfɪ́ər/ (spheres)

1 NOUN A **sphere** is an object that is completely round in shape like a ball. ○ *the volume of a hollow sphere*

▶ **COLLOCATIONS:** a **celestial/heavenly/microscopic/crystal** sphere

▶ **SYNONYM:** globe

2 NOUN A **sphere of** activity or interest is a particular area of activity or interest. ○ [+ *of*] *the sphere of international politics* ○ [+ *of*] *nurses, working in all spheres of the health service*

▶ **COLLOCATIONS:**
a sphere **of** *something*
a sphere of **activity/influence/life**

▶ **SYNONYM:** field

---

spokes|person /spoʊkspɜrsᵊn/ (spokespersons or   `JOBS`
spokespeople)

NOUN A **spokesperson** is a person who speaks as the representative of a group or organization. ○ *A spokesperson for Amnesty, Norma Johnston, describes some cases.* ○ *A company spokesperson confirmed the dismissal.*

▶ **COLLOCATIONS:**
a spokesperson **for** *something*
a spokesperson for a **department/company/agency/group**
a **police/official/military/departmental** spokesperson
a spokesperson **says/confirms/denies** *things*

▶ **SYNONYMS:** speaker, representative

USAGE: Gender neutral language

In modern usage, especially in formal contexts, it is considered better to use words for jobs and roles that do not specify whether it is a man or a woman. This shows that the person's gender is less important than their profession or position. For example **spokesperson** is preferred to **spokesman** or **spokeswoman**. Other gender neutral words include:

Salesperson instead of **salesman/saleswoman**

Chairperson or **chair** instead of **chairman/chairwoman**

Police officer instead of **policeman/policewoman**

---

spon|sor /spɒnsər/ (sponsors, sponsoring,   `MARKETING & SALES`
sponsored)

VERB If an organization or a person **sponsors** an event, they pay for it. ○ *A local bank is sponsoring the race.*

▶ COLLOCATIONS:
sponsor a **race/event/contest/conference/program**
a **company/government/bank/group** sponsors *something*

▶ SYNONYM: back

● **Sponsor** is also a noun. ○ [+ *of*] *Our company is proud to be the sponsor of this event.*

▶ COLLOCATIONS:
a sponsor **of/for** *something*
a sponsor of a **race/event/contest**
a **main/major/official/corporate** sponsor
become/find/get/attract/seek a sponsor

▶ SYNONYM: backer

---

spon|ta|neous /spɒnteɪniəs/

1 ADJECTIVE **Spontaneous** acts are not planned or arranged, but are done because someone suddenly wants to do them. ○ *Diana's house was crowded with happy people whose spontaneous outbursts of song were accompanied by lively music.*

▶ COLLOCATIONS:
spontaneous **applause**
a spontaneous **outburst/gesture**

2 ADJECTIVE A **spontaneous** event happens because of processes within something rather than being caused by things outside it. ○ *I had another spontaneous miscarriage at around the 16th to 18th week.*

▶ COLLOCATIONS:
spontaneous **combustion**
a spontaneous **miscarriage/abortion**

spon|ta|neous|ly /spɒnteɪniəsli/

ADVERB ○ *People spontaneously stood up and cheered.*

▶ COLLOCATIONS: **laugh/act** spontaneously

---

spo|rad|ic /spəræðɪk/

ADJECTIVE **Sporadic** occurrences of something happen at irregular intervals. ○ *a year of sporadic fighting in the north of the country*

▶ COLLOCATIONS: sporadic **violence/fighting/gunfire/clashes**

▶ SYNONYM: intermittent

spread /sprɛd/ (spreads, spreading, spread) `OFFICE`

1 **VERB** If something **spreads** or **is spread** by people, it gradually reaches or affects a larger and larger area or more and more people. ○ *The industrial revolution which started a couple of hundred years ago in Europe is now spreading across the world.* ○ *the sense of fear spreading in residential neighborhoods* ○ *He was fed-up with the lies being spread about him.*

● **Spread** is also a noncount noun. ○ *The greatest hope for reform is the gradual spread of information.* ○ *Thanks to the spread of modern technology, trained workers are now more vital than ever.*

2 **VERB** If something such as a liquid, gas, or smoke **spreads** or **is spread**, it moves outwards in all directions so that it covers a larger area. ○ *Fire spread rapidly after a chemical truck exploded.* ○ *A dark red stain was spreading across his shirt.* ○ *In Northern California, a wildfire has spread a haze of smoke over 200 miles.*

● **Spread** is also a noncount noun. ○ *The situation was complicated by the spread of a serious forest fire.*

▶ **COLLOCATIONS:**
the spread **of** something
the spread of **disease**
spread **gossip/lies/the word**
spread a **virus/disease/infection**
a **rumor/virus/disease** spreads
word spreads that…
prevent/stop/halt the spread of *something*
wide/rapid/global spread
spread **evenly/thinly**

▶ **SYNONYM:** circulate

spread|sheet /sprɛdʃit/ (spreadsheets)

NOUN A **spreadsheet** is a computer program that arranges numbers and information in rows and can be used for calculating and planning.

▶ **COLLOCATIONS:**
an **accounting** spreadsheet
use/create a spreadsheet
a spreadsheet **program/application**

sta|ble /steɪbəl/ (stabler, stablest)

ADJECTIVE If something is **stable**, it is not likely to change or come to an end suddenly. ○ *The price of oil should remain stable for the rest of the year.* ○ *a stable marriage*

▶ **COLLOCATIONS:**
a stable **environment/condition/relationship/marriage**
financially/politically/relatively/fairly stable
remain/become stable

▶ **SYNONYM:** steady

sta|bil|ity /stəbɪlɪti/

NONCOUNT NOUN ○ *It was a time of political stability and progress.* ○ *UN peacekeepers were dispatched to ensure stability in the border region.*

▶ **COLLOCATIONS:**
stability **of/in** *something*
the stability of a **region/area/country**
restore/maintain/ensure/threaten stability
long-term/relative/regional stability
political/social/economic/financial stability

▶ **PHRASE:** peace and stability

sta|bi|lize /steɪbɪlaɪz/ (stabilizes, stabilizing, stabilized)

VERB If something **stabilizes**, or **is stabilized**, it becomes stable. [in BRIT, also use **stabilise**] ○ *Although her illness is serious, her condition is beginning to stabilize.* ○ *Officials hope the move will stabilize exchange rates.*

▶ **COLLOCATIONS:**
stabilize a **country/situation**
a **condition/market/economy** stabilizes

▶ **SYNONYM:** steady

---

stack /stæk/ (stacks)

NOUN A **stack of** things is a pile of them. ○ [+ of] *There were stacks of books on the bedside table and floor.*

▶ **COLLOCATIONS:**
a stack **of** *something*
a stack of **tires/crates/pancakes**
neat stacks

> **EXTEND YOUR VOCABULARY**
>
> A **stack** of things is usually tidy, and often consists of flat objects placed directly on top of each other. ○ *a neat stack of boxes*
>
> A **heap** of things is usually untidy, and often has the shape of a hill or mound. ○ *Now, the building is a heap of rubble.*
>
> A **pile** can be tidy or untidy ○ *a pile of untouched paperwork*

stand-alone /stændəloʊn/ `ORGANIZATION`

ADJECTIVE A **stand-alone** business or organization is independent and does not receive financial support from another organization. ○ *They plan to relaunch it as a stand-alone company.*

▶ **COLLOCATIONS:** a stand-alone **company/organization/store**

stand|ard /stændərd/ (standards)

1 NOUN A **standard** is a level of quality or achievement, especially a level that is thought to be acceptable. ○ [+ *of*] *improvements in the general standard of living* ○ *There will be new national standards for hospital cleanliness.*

2 NOUN A **standard** is something that you use in order to judge the quality of something else. ○ *systems that were by later standards absurdly primitive*

▶ **COLLOCATIONS:**
  a standard **of** *something*
  a standard of **excellence/living/conduct/behavior**
  set/raise/maintain/meet a standard
  industry/safety/living standards
  a **high/minimum/strict/national/professional** standard
  the standard **required**

▶ **SYNONYMS:** guideline, level

3 ADJECTIVE You use **standard** to describe things which are usual and normal. ○ *It was standard practice for untrained clerks to advise in serious cases such as murder.* ○ *the standard format for a scientific paper*

▶ **COLLOCATIONS:**
  a standard **model/feature/format/rate/size**
  standard **equipment/practice/procedure**

▶ **PHRASE:** standard English

▶ **SYNONYMS:** normal, regular, usual

stand|ard|ize /stændərdaɪz/ (standardizes, standardizing, standardized)

VERB To **standardize** things means to change them so that they all have the same features. [in BRIT, also use **standardise**] ○ *There is a drive both to standardize components and to reduce the number of models.*

▶ **COLLOCATIONS:**
  standardize **parts/components**
  a standardized **test/procedure**

▶ **SYNONYM:** regularize

S

stand|ardi|za|tion /stændərdɪzeɪʃən/

NONCOUNT NOUN ○ [+ of] the standardization of working hours

▸ **COLLOCATION:** standardization **of** something

stand|ard of liv|ing /stændərd əv lɪvɪŋ/ (standards of living)

NOUN Your **standard of living** is your quality of life and the amount of money that you have. ○ We're all trying to improve our standard of living.

▸ **COLLOCATIONS:**
a **high/low** standard of living
improve/raise/lower someone's standard of living

---

start-up /stɑrtʌp/ (start-ups)　　R&D

1 **ADJECTIVE** A **start-up** company is a small business that has recently been started by someone. ○ Thousands of start-up firms have entered the computer market.

▸ **COLLOCATIONS:** a start-up **company/business**

2 **NOUN** A **start-up** is a small business that has recently been started by someone. ○ For now the only bright spots in the labor market are small businesses and high-tech start-ups.

▸ **COLLOCATIONS:**
a **business/Internet/high-tech** start-up
a **successful/small** start-up
launch/finance/fund a start-up

---

state|ment /steɪtmənt/ (statements)　　COMMUNICATIONS

NOUN A **statement** is something that you say or write which gives information in a formal or definite way. ○ "Things are moving ahead." — I found that statement vague and unclear. ○ The 350-page report was based on statements from witnesses to the events.

▸ **COLLOCATIONS:**
make/issue/release a statement
a **brief/formal/written/official/public** statement

---

sta|tion|ary /steɪʃənɛri/

ADJECTIVE Something that is **stationary** is not moving. ○ I had run my bike into a stationary car because I wasn't looking where I was going

▸ **SYNONYMS:** motionless, still

sta|tis|tics /stətɪstɪks/

1 **PLURAL NOUN** **Statistics** are facts which are obtained from analyzing information expressed in numbers, for example information about the number of times that something happens. ○ *Official statistics show real wages declining by 24%.* ○ *There are no reliable statistics for the number of deaths in the battle.*

▶ **COLLOCATIONS:**
official/economic/national statistics
statistics **show/indicate/reveal/suggest** *things*
compile/collect/release/publish statistics

▶ **SYNONYMS:** figures, numbers

2 **NONCOUNT NOUN** **Statistics** is a branch of mathematics concerned with the study of information that is expressed in numbers. ○ *a professor of Mathematical Statistics*

sta|tis|ti|cal /stətɪstɪkəl/

ADJECTIVE ○ *The report contains a great deal of statistical information.* ○ *Other controls accounting for measurement noise confirmed the statistical significance of the relationship.*

▶ **COLLOCATIONS:**
statistical **analysis/data/evidence/figures/information**
statistical **significance/probability/correlation**
a statistical **method/technique**

▶ **SYNONYM:** numerical

steady /stɛdi/ (steadier, steadiest)

ADJECTIVE A **steady** situation continues or develops gradually without any interruptions and is not likely to change quickly. ○ *Despite the steady progress of building work, the campaign against it is still going strong.* ○ *The improvement in standards has been steady and persistent.* ○ *a steady stream of traffic*

▶ **COLLOCATIONS:**
steady **progress/decline/improvement/growth**
a steady **supply/stream/trickle/rise/increase**

▶ **SYNONYMS:** regular, even

steadi|ly

ADVERB ○ *Overseas student numbers in Britain have been rising steadily for a decade.* ○ *The company has steadily been losing market share to Boeing and Airbus.*

▶ **COLLOCATIONS:**
climb/rise/grow/increase/improve steadily
decrease/decline/fall/breathe/rain steadily

▶ **SYNONYM:** evenly

---

steep /stiːp/ (steeper, steepest)

1 ADJECTIVE A **steep** slope rises at a very sharp angle and is difficult to go up. ○ *San Francisco is built on 40 hills and some are very steep.* ○ *a narrow, steep-sided valley*

2 ADJECTIVE A **steep** increase or decrease in something is a very big increase or decrease. ○ *Consumers are rebelling at steep price increases.* ○ *Many smaller emerging Asian economies are suffering their steepest economic declines for half a century.*

→ see note at **dramatic**

▶ **COLLOCATIONS:**
a steep **hill/slope/descent/gradient**
a steep **rise/increase/fall/decline/curve**

▶ **SYNONYMS:** sharp, sheer

---

stimu|late /stɪmyəleɪt/ (stimulates, stimulating, stimulated)

1 VERB To **stimulate** something means to encourage it to begin or develop further. ○ *America's priority is rightly to stimulate its economy.* ○ *The Russian health service has stimulated public interest in home cures.*

▶ **COLLOCATIONS:**
stimulate the **economy**
stimulate **growth/demand/production**

▶ **SYNONYM:** encourage

2 VERB If something **stimulates** a part of a person's body, it causes it to move or start working. ○ *Exercise stimulates the digestive and excretory systems.* ○ [+ to-inf] *The body is stimulated to build up resistance.*

▶ **COLLOCATIONS:**
stimulate **circulation/nerves/glands**
stimulate the **appetite**

stimu|la|tion /stɪmyəleɪʃən/

NONCOUNT NOUN ○ *an economy in need of stimulation* ○ *physical stimulation* ○ [+ of] *the chemical stimulation of drugs*

▶ **COLLOCATIONS:**
stimulation **of** *something*
provide/need/require stimulation
physical/sexual/nerve/brain stimulation

stimu|lus /stɪmyələs/ (stimuli)

NOUN A **stimulus** is something that encourages activity in people or things. ○ *Interest rates could fall soon and be a stimulus to the U.S. economy.* ○ *It is through our nervous system that we adapt ourselves to our environment and to all external stimuli.*

▶ **COLLOCATIONS:**
a **conditioned/sensory/external/short-term** stimulus
a **fiscal/monetary/economic** stimulus
a stimulus **package/plan**

---

stipu|late /stɪpyleɪt/ (stipulates, stipulating, stipulated)

VERB If you **stipulate** a condition or **stipulate that** something must be done, you say clearly that it must be done. ○ [+ *that*] *She could have stipulated that she would pay when she received the computer.*

▶ **SYNONYM:** specify

stipu|la|tion /stɪpyəleɪʃ°n/ (stipulations)

NOUN ○ *Clifford's only stipulation is that his clients obey his advice.*

▶ **SYNONYM:** condition

---

stock /stɒk/ (stocks)　　**BANKING & FINANCE**

1 NOUN Stocks are shares in the ownership of a company, or investments on which a fixed amount of interest will be paid. ○ *the buying and selling of stocks and shares*

▶ **COLLOCATIONS:**
buy/sell/trade/own stock
a stock **falls/rises/closes**

▶ **PHRASES:**
stocks and shares
the stock market

2 NONCOUNT NOUN A company's **stock** is the amount of money which the company has through selling shares. ○ *At its peak, shareholders held stock valued at $180 billion.*

3 **NOUN** If you have a **stock of** things, you have a supply of them stored in a place ready to be used. ○ *I keep a stock of CDs describing various relaxation techniques.*

▶ **COLLOCATIONS:**
a stock **of** *something*
a stock of **grain/weapons**

▶ **SYNONYMS:** supply, hoard

stock ex|change /stɒk ɪkstʃeɪndʒ/ (stock exchanges)

1 **NOUN** A **stock exchange** is a place or organization where people buy and sell stocks. ○ *In late trading on London's stock exchange, the shares were quoted at 833 pence.*

▶ **COLLOCATIONS:**
the **New York/London** stock exchange
domestic/international stock exchanges

2 **NOUN** The **stock exchange** is the prices or trading activity of a stock exchange. ○ *The stock exchange fell heavily today.*

▶ **COLLOCATIONS:**
the stock exchange **rises/rallies/recovers**
the stock exchange **falls/crashes/plunges**

stock mar|ket /stɒk mɑrkɪt/ (stock markets)

NOUN The **stock market** is the activity of buying stock, or the place where this is done. ○ *The company's shares promptly fell on the stock market.* ○ *This is a practical guide to investing in the stock market.*

▶ **COLLOCATIONS:**
on/in the stock market
the stock market **rises/rallies/goes up**
the stock market **falls/drops/crashes/plunges**
the stock market **opens/closes**
play the stock market
a stock market **bubble/boom/crash**

stop|page /stɒpɪdʒ/ (stoppages)   `PERSONNEL`

NOUN A **stoppage** is an occasion when people stop working because of a disagreement with their employers. ○ *Mineworkers in the Ukraine have voted for a one-day stoppage next month.*

▶ **COLLOCATIONS:**
  a **work/labor** stoppage
  a **one-day** stoppage
  call/end/threaten a stoppage

---

straight|forward /streɪtfɔrwərd/

ADJECTIVE If you describe something as **straightforward**, you approve of
  it because it is easy to do or understand. ○ *Cost accounting is a relatively*
  straightforward process. ○ *The question seemed straightforward enough.*
  ○ *simple straightforward language*

▶ **COLLOCATIONS:**
  fairly/relatively/pretty straightforward
  a straightforward **narrative/task/explanation/answer**

▶ **SYNONYMS:** uncomplicated, clear

---

strat|egy /strætədʒi/ (strategies)   `R&D`

NOUN A **strategy** is a general plan or set of plans intended to achieve
  something, especially over a long period. ○ *Next week, health officials*
  gather in Amsterdam to agree on a strategy for controlling malaria.
  ○ *a customer-led marketing strategy*

▶ **COLLOCATIONS:**
  a strategy **for** *something*
  devise/adopt/pursue/implement/develop a strategy
  a **long-term/overall/national** strategy
  a **marketing/pricing/investment/growth/economic** strategy

▶ **SYNONYMS:** policy, plan

stra|tegic /strətidʒɪk/   **s**

ADJECTIVE **Strategic** means relating to the most important, general
  aspects of something such as a military operation or political policy,
  especially when these are decided in advance. ○ *the new strategic thinking*
  which NATO leaders produced at the recent London summit ○ *The island is of*
  strategic importance to France.

▶ **COLLOCATIONS:**
  strategic **planning/thinking/marketing/importance**
  a strategic **plan/point/position/site**

▶ **SYNONYMS:** important, critical, key

stra|tegi|cal|ly /strətiʤɪkəli/

ADVERB ○ *strategically important roads, bridges, and buildings*

▶ **COLLOCATIONS:**
strategically **important**
strategically **located/placed**

---

strength /strɛŋkθ, strɛŋθ/

1 **NONCOUNT NOUN** The **strength** of an object or material is its ability to be treated roughly, or to carry heavy weights, without being damaged or destroyed. ○ [+ *of*] *He checked the strength of the cables.* ○ *the properties of a material, such as strength or electrical conductivity*

▶ **COLLOCATION:** the strength **of** *something*

2 **NONCOUNT NOUN** Your **strength** is the physical energy that you have, which gives you the ability to perform various actions. ○ [+ *of*] *She has always been encouraged to swim to build up the strength of her muscles.*

3 **NONCOUNT NOUN** The **strength** of a person, organization, or country is the power or influence that they have. ○ *America values its economic leadership, and the political and military strength that goes with it.* ○ *The Alliance in its first show of strength drew a hundred thousand-strong crowd to a rally.* ○ *They have their own independence movement which is gathering strength.*

▶ **COLLOCATIONS:**
a **show of** strength
military/economic/political strength
gather/gain strength

▶ **SYNONYM:** power

4 **NONCOUNT NOUN** If you refer to the **strength of** a feeling, opinion, or belief, you are talking about how deeply it is felt or believed by people, or how much they are influenced by it. ○ [+ *of*] *He was surprised at the strength of his own feeling.* ○ [+ *of*] *What makes a mayor successful in Los Angeles is the strength of his public support.*

▶ **COLLOCATION:** the strength **of** *something*

▶ **SYNONYMS:** intensity, depth

strength|en /strɛŋθəʳn/ (strengthens, strengthening, strengthened)

VERB To **strengthen** something means to make it stronger. If something **strengthens**, it becomes stronger. ○ *The dollar strengthened against most other currencies.* ○ *Community leaders want to strengthen controls at external frontiers.* ○ *Yoga can be used to strengthen the immune system.*

▶ COLLOCATIONS:
strengthen **ties/unity/cooperation/democracy/resolve**
strengthen a **relationship/bond/argument**
strengthen the **economy**
strengthen **muscles/bones**
the **economy/dollar/pound/yen** strengthens
greatly/immeasurably/further strengthen

▶ SYNONYMS: reinforce, enhance, fortify

---

stress /strɛs/ (stresses, stressing, stressed)   [HEALTH & FITNESS]

1 **VERB** If you **stress** a point in a discussion, you put extra emphasis on it because you think it is important. ○ [+ that] *The spokesman stressed that the measures did not amount to an overall ban.* ○ *They also stress the need for improved employment opportunities, better transport and health care.*

▶ COLLOCATIONS:
stress the **importance/significance/urgency** of something
stress the **need** for something
repeatedly stress

▶ SYNONYM: emphasize

● **Stress** is also a noun. ○ [+ on] *Japanese car makers are laying even more stress on European sales.*

▶ COLLOCATIONS:
a stress **on** something
lay/place stress on something

▶ SYNONYM: emphasis

2 **NONCOUNT NOUN** If you feel under **stress**, you feel worried and tense because of difficulties in your life. ○ *Individuals develop colds, backache, or eczema when they are under stress.* ○ *a wide range of stress-related problems* ○ *Relaxation exercises can relieve stress.*

▶ COLLOCATIONS:
under stress
cope with/deal with/handle stress
cause/experience/relieve/reduce stress
emotional/mental/psychological/work-related stress
chronic/severe/extreme stress
stress **related**

▶ PHRASES:
stress and anxiety
post-traumatic stress disorder

▶ SYNONYMS: anxiety, worry, strain

3 **NOUN** **Stresses** are strong physical pressures applied to an object.
○ *Earthquakes happen when stresses in rock are suddenly released as the rocks fracture.*

stress|ful /strɛsfəl/

ADJECTIVE If a situation or experience is **stressful**, it makes you feel worried. ○ *I have one of the most stressful jobs there is.*

▶ **COLLOCATIONS:**
a stressful **experience/situation/event/job/life**
a stressful **time/period/week/day**
extremely/highly stressful

▶ **PHRASE:** difficult and stressful

---

stretch /strɛtʃ/ (stretches, stretching, stretched)

1 **VERB** Something that **stretches** over an area or distance covers or exists in the whole of that area or distance. ○ [+ *for*] *The procession stretched for several miles.*

▶ **SYNONYM:** extend

2 **VERB** If something **stretches from** one time **to** another, it begins at the first time and ends at the second, which is longer than expected.
○ [+ *from N to N*] *a working day that stretches from seven in the morning to eight at night*

▶ **SYNONYM:** continue

3 **VERB** If a group of things **stretch from** one type of thing **to** another, the group includes a wide range of things. ○ [+ *from N to N*] *a trading empire, with interests that stretched from chemicals to sugar*

▶ **SYNONYM:** range

---

strict /strɪkt/ (stricter, strictest)

ADJECTIVE A **strict** rule or order is very clear and precise or severe and must always be obeyed completely. ○ *The officials had issued strict instructions that we were not to get out of the Jeep.* ○ *French privacy laws are very strict.* ○ *All your replies will be treated in the strictest confidence.*

▶ **COLLOCATIONS:**
a strict **rule/instruction/law/guideline/regulation/limit**
a strict diet
strict **adherence** to *something*

▶ **PHRASE:** in strict confidence

▶ **SYNONYMS:** austere, severe

strict|ly /strɪktli/

ADVERB ○ *The number of new members each year is strictly monitored.* ○ *The government is strictly controlling credit expansion.*

▶ **COLLOCATIONS:**
strictly **control/limit/regulate/enforce**
strictly **adhere to** *something*
strictly **forbidden/prohibited**

---

struc|ture /strʌktʃər/ (structures, structuring, structured)   `ORGANIZATION`

1 NONCOUNT NOUN The **structure of** something is the way in which it is made, built, or organized. ○ [+ *of*] *The typical family structure of Freud's patients involved two parents and two children.* ○ [+ *of*] *The chemical structure of this particular molecule is very unusual.*

▶ **COLLOCATIONS:**
the structure **of** *something*
the structure of a **molecule/protein/atom**
organizational/hierarchical structure
social/management structure
the structure of **society**

▶ **SYNONYMS:** organization, arrangement

2 VERB If you **structure** something, you arrange it in a careful, organized pattern or system. ○ *By structuring the course this way, we're forced to produce something the companies think is valuable.*

▶ **COLLOCATIONS:**
structure a **narrative/essay**
structure a **course/examination/curriculum**
society is structured
tightly/rigidly/loosely/hierarchically structured

▶ **SYNONYM:** organize

---

strug|gle /strʌgəl/ (struggles, struggling, struggled)

1 VERB If you **struggle to** do something, you try hard to do it, even though other people or things may be making it difficult for you to succeed. ○ *They had to struggle against all kinds of adversity.* ○ [+ *to*-inf] *Those who have lost their jobs struggle to pay their supermarket bills.*

▶ **COLLOCATIONS:**
struggle **against** *something*
struggle to **cope/survive/recover**

struggle to **overcome/maintain/keep/find** *something*

▶ **PHRASE:** struggle against the odds

▶ **SYNONYMS:** battle, fight

2 NOUN A **struggle** is a long and difficult attempt to achieve something such as freedom or political rights. ○ [+ *for*] *India's struggle for independence* ○ *IT directors now face an uphill struggle to win back respect from their business peers.*

▶ **COLLOCATIONS:**
a struggle **for/against** *something*
a struggle **with** *someone/something*
a struggle for **survival/independence/freedom/democracy**
a struggle against **terrorism/apartheid**
a struggle with **cancer/illness/addiction**
a **constant/ongoing/uphill/bitter/long** struggle
a **power/class/freedom/political** struggle

▶ **SYNONYM:** battle

---

sub|con|tract /sʌbkəntrækt/ **(subcontracts,** **ORGANIZATION**
subcontracting, subcontracted)

VERB If one company **subcontracts** part of its work **to** another company, it pays the other company to do part of the work that it has been employed to do. ○ *The company is subcontracting production of most of the parts.*

▶ **COLLOCATIONS:**
subcontract *something* **to** *someone*
subcontract **work/production**
a **company** subcontracts

sub|con|trac|tor /sʌbkɑntræktər/ **(subcontractors)** also
sub-contractor

NOUN A **subcontractor** is a person or company that has a contract to do part of a job that another company is responsible for. ○ *The company was considered as a possible subcontractor to build the airplane.*

▶ **COLLOCATIONS:**
a **building/construction** subcontractor
hire/fire/use a subcontractor

sub|mit /səbˈmɪt/ (submits, submitting, submitted) `COMMUNICATIONS`

VERB If you **submit** a proposal, report, or request **to** someone, you formally send it to them so that they can consider it or decide about it. ○ [+ to] *They submitted their reports to the Chancellor yesterday.* ○ *Head teachers yesterday submitted a claim for a 9 percent pay rise.*

▶ **COLLOCATIONS:**
submit *something* **to** *someone*
submit a **proposal/bid/request/application/claim**
submit a **report/document/sample**
submit *one's* **resignation**

▶ **SYNONYMS:** present, hand in

sub|scribe /səbˈskraɪb/ (subscribes, subscribing, subscribed)

VERB If you **subscribe to** an opinion or belief, you are one of a number of people who have this opinion or belief. ○ [+ to] *I've personally never subscribed to the view that either sex is superior to the other.*

▶ **COLLOCATIONS:**
subscribe **to** *something*
subscribe to a **view/belief/theory/opinion**

sub|se|quent /ˈsʌbsɪkwənt/

ADJECTIVE You use **subsequent** to describe something that happened or existed after the time or event that has just been referred to. [FORMAL] ○ *the increase of population in subsequent years* ○ *Those concerns were overshadowed by subsequent events.*

▶ **COLLOCATIONS:**
a subsequent **year/event/period/generation**
a subsequent **investigation/inquiry/purchase**

▶ **SYNONYMS:** following, next

sub|se|quent|ly

ADVERB ○ *She subsequently became the Faculty's President.* ○ *Kermes were then believed to be berries, but were subsequently discovered to be scale insects.*

▶ **COLLOCATIONS:** subsequently **discover/withdraw/arrest/release**

▶ **SYNONYM:** later

S

sub|sidi|ary /səbsɪdiɛri/ (subsidiaries) `ORGANIZATION`

1 **NOUN** A **subsidiary** or a **subsidiary** company is a company that is part of a larger and more important company. ○ [+ *of*] *British Asia Airways, a subsidiary of British Airways* ○ *It's one of ten companies that are subsidiaries of Cossack Holdings.*

▶ **COLLOCATIONS:**
a subsidiary **of** *something*
a subsidiary of a **company/conglomerate/bank**
a subsidiary **company/corporation/bank**
a **fully-owned/majority-owned** subsidiary

2 **ADJECTIVE** If something is **subsidiary**, it is less important than something else with which it is connected. ○ *The marketing department has increasingly played a subsidiary role to the sales department.* ○ *This character may be pushed into a subsidiary position or even abandoned altogether.*

▶ **COLLOCATIONS:** a subsidiary **role/position**

▶ **SYNONYM:** secondary

sub|si|dy /sʌbsɪdi/ (subsidies) `BANKING & FINANCE`

NOUN A **subsidy** is money that is paid by a government or other authority in order to help an industry or business, or to pay for a public service. ○ *European farmers are planning a massive demonstration against farm subsidy cuts.* ○ *They've also slashed state subsidies to utilities and transportation.*

▶ **COLLOCATIONS:**
a **farm/agricultural/export** subsidy
a **state/public/government/federal** subsidy
provide/receive/cut/reduce/eliminate a subsidy
subsidy **cuts**

▶ **SYNONYMS:** grant, aid

sub|si|dize /sʌbsɪdaɪz/ (subsidizes, subsidizing, subsidized)

VERB If a government or other authority **subsidizes** something, they pay part of the cost of it. [in BRIT, also use **subsidise**] ○ *Around the world, governments have subsidized the housing of middle- and upper-income groups.* ○ *pensions that are subsidized by the government*

▶ **COLLOCATIONS:**
the **government** subsidizes *something*
heavily/unfairly subsidized

▶ **SYNONYM:** support

sub|stance /sˈʌbstəns/ (substances)

NOUN A **substance** is a solid, powder, liquid, or gas with particular properties. ○ *There's absolutely no regulation of cigarettes to make sure that they don't include poisonous substances.* ○ *The substance that's causing the problem comes from the barley.*

▶ **COLLOCATIONS:**
a **toxic/hazardous/poisonous** substance
a **banned/illegal** substance
a **chemical/powdery/waxy/oily** substance

▶ **PHRASE:** substance abuse

sub|stan|tial /səbstænʃᵊl/

ADJECTIVE **Substantial** means large in amount or degree. [FORMAL] ○ *A substantial number of products will have to change their labels.* ○ *a very substantial improvement*

▶ **COLLOCATIONS:**
a substantial **number/amount/sum/portion/proportion**
a substantial **increase/improvement/gain**
substantial **damage**

▶ **SYNONYMS:** significant, considerable

---

sub|sti|tute /sˈʌbstɪtut/ (substitutes, substituting, substituted)

1 VERB If you **substitute** one thing **for** another, or if one thing **substitutes for** another, it takes the place or performs the function of the other thing. ○ [+ for] *They were substituting violence for dialogue.* ○ *He substituted different isotopes into the model and charted the changes.*

▶ **COLLOCATION:** substitute *something* **for** *something*

▶ **SYNONYMS:** change, replace

2 NOUN A **substitute** is something that you have or use instead of something else. ○ [+ for] *the increased use of nuclear energy as a substitute for fossil fuels* ○ *tests on humans to find a blood substitute made from animal blood*

▶ **COLLOCATIONS:**
a substitute **for** *something*
use/find/become a substitute
a **blood/sugar/milk** substitute
a **poor/suitable/adequate** substitute

▶ **SYNONYMS:** replacement, equivalent

S

sub|sti|tu|tion /sʌbstɪtuːʃⁿn/ (substitutions)

NOUN ○ [+ of] *safety concerns over the substitution of ingredients* ○ *the nature and pace of technology substitution*

▶ **COLLOCATIONS:**
the substitution **of** *something*
crop/import/technology substitution
make a substitution

---

sub|tract /səbtrækt/ (subtracts, subtracting, subtracted)

VERB If you **subtract** one number **from** another, you do a calculation in which you take it away from the other number. For example, if you subtract 3 from 5, you get 2. ○ [+ from] *Mandy subtracted the date of birth from the date of death.* ○ *We have subtracted $25 per adult to arrive at a basic room rate.*

▶ **COLLOCATIONS:**
subtract *something* **from** *something*
subtract a **number/value/cost**

▶ **SYNONYM:** take away

sub|trac|tion /səbtrækʃⁿn/ (subtractions)

NOUN ○ *She's ready to learn simple addition and subtraction.* ○ *I looked at what he'd given me and did a quick subtraction.*

▶ **COLLOCATION: do** a subtraction

▶ **PHRASE:** addition and subtraction

---

suc|ceed /səksiːd/ (succeeds, succeeding, succeeded)

1 VERB If you **succeed**, or if you **succeed in** doing something, you achieve the result that you wanted. ○ [+ in] *We have already succeeded in working out ground rules with the Department of Defense.* ○ [+ in] *Some people will succeed in their efforts to stop smoking.* ○ *the skills and qualities needed to succeed in small- and medium-sized businesses*

2 VERB If something **succeeds**, it works in a satisfactory way or has the result that is intended. ○ *If marriage is to succeed in the 1990s, then people have to recognize the new pressures it is facing.* ○ *a move which would make any future talks even more unlikely to succeed*

▶ **COLLOCATIONS:**
succeed **in/as** *something*
a **bid/negotiation/experiment** succeeds

succeed **admirably/brilliantly/academically**
finally/eventually succeed

▶ **SYNONYMS:** accomplish, manage

suc|cess /səksɛs/

NONCOUNT NOUN Success is the achievement of something that you have
been trying to do. ○ [+ of] *the success of European business in building a
stronger partnership between management and workers* ○ *Nearly all of the
young people interviewed believed that work was the key to success.*

▶ **COLLOCATIONS:**
the success **of** something
success **as** something
enjoy/achieve/taste success
success **depends on/lies in** something
huge/great success
the success **rate**

▶ **PHRASES:**
the key to success
success or failure

suc|cess|ful /səksɛsfəl/

ADJECTIVE Someone or something that is **successful** achieves a desired
result or performs in a satisfactory way. ○ *I am looking forward to a long and
successful partnership with him.* ○ [+ in] *Women do not necessarily have to
imitate men to be successful in business.* ○ *She is a successful lawyer.*

▶ **COLLOCATIONS:**
be successful **in/as** something
hugely/highly/enormously successful
commercially/financially successful
a successful **career/launch/campaign**
a successful **outcome/conclusion**
a successful **businessman/businesswoman/applicant**
prove/become successful

suc|cess|ful|ly /səksɛsfəli/

ADVERB ○ *All three laser systems have been successfully tested on the eyes of blind
patients.*

▶ **COLLOCATIONS:**
successfully **complete/defend/challenge/negotiate/launch**
compete/work/operate/treat/use successfully

suc|ces|sive /səksɛsɪv/

ADJECTIVE **Successive** means happening or existing one after another without a break. ○ *Jackson was the winner for a second successive year.* ○ *Britain was suffering from the failure of successive governments to coordinate a national transportation policy.*

▶ COLLOCATIONS:
the **second/third/fourth** successive *something*
successive **governments/defeats/wins/generations**

suc|cinct /səksɪŋkt/

ADJECTIVE Something that is **succinct** expresses facts or ideas clearly and in few words. ○ *The book gives an admirably succinct account of the technology and its history.* ○ *If you have something to say make sure that it is accurate, succinct, and to the point.*

▶ COLLOCATIONS:
a succinct **summary/description/statement**
a succinct **account/verdict**

sud|den /sʌdᵊn/

ADJECTIVE **Sudden** means happening quickly and unexpectedly. ○ *There has been a sudden increase in costs.*

▶ COLLOCATIONS:
a sudden **drop/rise/decrease/increase/loss/change/shift**
a sudden **noise/rush/movement**
a sudden **decision/departure/appearance/attack**
a sudden **interest/urge**
a sudden **death**

▶ SYNONYM: abrupt

sud|den|ly /sʌdənli/

ADVERB ○ *Her expression suddenly changed.*

▶ COLLOCATIONS:
suddenly **change/find/feel/realize/appear/decide**
die suddenly
stop/start/happen suddenly

▶ SYNONYM: abruptly

suf|fi|cient /səfɪʃᵊnt/

ADJECTIVE If something is **sufficient for** a particular purpose, there is enough of it for the purpose. ○ [+ to-inf] *One meter of fabric is sufficient to cover the exterior of an 18-inch-diameter hatbox.* ○ *There was not sufficient evidence to secure a conviction.*

▶ **COLLOCATIONS:**
sufficient **for** *something*
sufficient to **cover/justify/warrant** *something*
sufficient **evidence/resources/funding**
a sufficient **quantity/number/reason**

▶ **SYNONYM:** enough

sug|ges|tion /səgdʒɛstʃᵊn/ (suggestions)　　COMMUNICATIONS

NOUN If you make a **suggestion**, you put forward an idea or plan for someone to think about. ○ *The dietitian was helpful, making suggestions as to how I could improve my diet.* ○ [+ of] *Perhaps he'd followed her suggestion of a stroll to the river.*

▶ **COLLOCATIONS:**
a suggestion **of/for** *something*
suggestions for **improvement**
make/have/offer/put forward a suggestion
dismiss/reject/welcome a suggestion
a **constructive/practical** suggestion

▶ **SYNONYMS:** proposal, recommendation, idea, plan

suit|able /suːtəbᵊl/

ADJECTIVE Someone or something that is **suitable for** a particular purpose or occasion is right or acceptable for it. ○ [+ for] *Employers usually decide within five minutes whether someone is suitable for the job.* ○ *The authority must make suitable accommodation available to the family.*

▶ **COLLOCATIONS:**
suitable **for** *something*
eminently/perfectly/particularly suitable
a suitable **candidate/applicant**
a suitable **location/venue/site**
a suitable **alternative/substitute**

▶ **SYNONYMS:** appropriate, right

sum|mary /sʌ́məri/ (summaries)   `COMMUNICATIONS`

NOUN A **summary of** something is a short account of it, which gives the main points but not the details. ○ [+ of] *What follows is a brief summary of the process.* ○ *In summary, it is my opinion that this complete treatment process was very successful.*

▸ **COLLOCATIONS:**
   a summary **of** something
   a **brief/written/executive** summary

▸ **PHRASE:** in summary

▸ **SYNONYMS:** résumé, abstract, précis

sum|ma|rize /sʌ́məraɪz/ (summarizes, summarizing, summarized)

VERB If you **summarize** something, you give a summary of it. [in BRIT, also use **summarise**] ○ *Table 3.1 summarizes the information given above.* ○ *Basically, the article can be summarized in three sentences.*

▸ **COLLOCATIONS:**
   summarize **information/findings/data/results**
   summarize a **discussion/argument**
   succinctly/briefly summarize

▸ **SYNONYMS:** sum up, outline

su|perb /supɜ́rb/

ADJECTIVE If something is **superb**, it is extremely good. ○ *There is a superb golf course 6 miles away.*

▸ **COLLOCATIONS:**
   a superb **performance/job/effort/view**
   superb **quality/value**

▸ **SYNONYM:** excellent

super|in|ten|dent /supərɪntɛ́ndənt, suprɪn-/   `JOBS`
(superintendents)

NOUN A **superintendent** is a person whose job is to take care of a large building such as an apartment building. ○ *a shortage of candidates willing to take on the responsibilities of school superintendents*

▸ **COLLOCATIONS:** a **building/school** superintendent

su|peri|or /supɪəriər/ (superiors) `JOBS`

1 ADJECTIVE If you describe something as **superior**, or that one thing or person is **superior to** another, you mean that it is good and better than other things of the same kind. ○ *A few years ago it was virtually impossible to find superior quality coffee in local shops.* ○ [+ to] *We have a relationship infinitely superior to those of many of our friends.*

▶ **COLLOCATIONS: far/vastly** superior

2 ADJECTIVE A **superior** person or thing is more important than another person or thing in the same organization or system. ○ *negotiations between the mutineers and their superior officers*

su|peri|or|ity /supɪəriɔriti/

NONCOUNT NOUN The **superiority** of something refers to its advantage or importance over other things of the same kind. ○ *The technical superiority of laser discs over tape is well established.* ○ *a false sense of his superiority over mere journalists*

super|vise /supərvaɪz/ (supervises, supervising, supervised) `PERSONNEL`

1 VERB If you **supervise** an activity or a person, you make sure that the activity is done correctly or that the person is doing a task or behaving correctly. ○ *College professors have refused to supervise students' examinations.* ○ *He supervised and trained more than 400 volunteers.*

2 VERB If you **supervise** a place where work is done, you ensure that the work there is done properly. ○ *He makes the wines and supervises the vineyards.*

▶ **COLLOCATIONS:**
supervise the **installation/construction/preparation** of *something*
supervise a **transition/operation**
supervise **properly/adequately**
be supervised by a **teacher/manager/coach/adult**

▶ **SYNONYMS:** oversee, direct

super|vi|sion /supərvɪʒ⁰n/

NONCOUNT NOUN ○ *A toddler requires close supervision and firm control at all times.* ○ [+ of] *The plan calls for a cease-fire and U.N. supervision of the country.* ○ *First-time license holders have to work under supervision.*

▶ **COLLOCATIONS:**
the supervision **of** *something*
be **under** supervision

parental/medical/adult supervision
close/strict/constant/proper supervision
exercise/provide/receive/need supervision

▶ **SYNONYMS:** control, management

super|vi|sor /ˈsuːpərvaɪzər/ (supervisors)

NOUN A **supervisor** is a person who supervises activities or people, especially workers or students. ○ *a full-time job as a supervisor in a factory* ○ *Each student has a supervisor to advise on the writing of the dissertation.*

sup|plement /ˈsʌplɪmənt/ (supplements, supplementing, supplemented)

VERB If you **supplement** something, you add something to it in order to improve it. ○ *people doing extra jobs outside their regular jobs to supplement their incomes* ○ [+ with] *I suggest supplementing your diet with vitamins E and A.*

▶ **COLLOCATIONS:**
supplement *something* **with** *something*
supplement a **diet/income**

▶ **SYNONYMS:** augment, enhance, enrich

● **Supplement** is also a noun. ○ [+ to] *Business sponsorship must be a supplement to, not a substitute for, public funding.*

▶ **COLLOCATION:** a supplement **to** *something*

▶ **SYNONYM:** addition

sup|plemen|ta|ry /ˌsʌplɪˈmɛntəri, -tri/

ADJECTIVE Supplementary things are added to something in order to improve it. ○ *the question of whether or not we need to take supplementary vitamins* ○ *Provide them with additional background or with supplementary information.*

▶ **COLLOCATIONS:**
supplementary **food/vitamins/oxygen/information**
a supplementary **question/fee/grant/budget**

▶ **SYNONYMS:** extra, additional

sup|ply /səˈplaɪ/ (supplies, supplying, supplied) `LOGISTICS & DISTRIBUTION`

1 VERB If you **supply** someone with something that they want or need, you give them a quantity of it. ○ *an agreement not to produce or supply* *chemical weapons* ○ [+ *with*] *a pipeline which will supply the major Greek cities with Russian natural gas* ○ [+ *to*] *the blood vessels supplying oxygen to the brain*

▶ **COLLOCATIONS:**
supply *someone/something* **with** *something*
supply *something* **to** *something/someone*
a **company/firm/institution** supplies *things*
supply **food/arms/oxygen/electricity/equipment/data**
supply a **product**

2 **NOUN** A **supply of** something is an amount of it that someone has or that is available for them to use. ○ [+ *of*] *The brain requires a constant supply of oxygen.* ○ *Most urban water supplies in the United States now contain fluoride in varying amounts.*

▶ **COLLOCATIONS:**
a supply **of** *something*
a supply of **oxygen/electricity/fuel**
a **plentiful/abundant/adequate/limited** supply
water/gas/electricity/oxygen/medical supplies

3 **NONCOUNT NOUN** **Supply** is the quantity of goods and services that can be made available for people to buy. ○ *Prices change according to supply and demand.*

▶ **PHRASE:** supply and demand

---

sup|port /səpɔ̲rt/ (supports, supporting, supported)

1 **VERB** If you **support** someone or their ideas or aims, you agree with them, and perhaps help them because you want them to succeed. ○ *The vice president insisted that he supported the hard-working people of New York.* ○ *The National Union of Mineworkers pressed the party to support a total ban on imported coal.*

▶ **COLLOCATIONS:**
support a **proposal/effort/idea/war/ban**
support **legislation**
strongly/actively/fully/wholeheartedly support

▶ **SYNONYMS:** back, endorse

• **Support** is also a noncount noun. ○ *The prime minister gave his full support to the government's reforms.* ○ *They are prepared to resort to violence in support of their beliefs.*

▶ **COLLOCATIONS:**
support **for** *something*

S

give/offer support
full/strong/public support

▶ **PHRASE:** in support of

▶ **SYNONYMS:** backing, endorsement

2 NONCOUNT NOUN Financial **support** is money provided to enable an organization to continue. This money is usually provided by the government. ○ *the government's proposal to cut agricultural support by only about 15%*

▶ **COLLOCATIONS:**
support **for** *something/someone*
financial/material support
provide/withdraw support

▶ **SYNONYM:** funding

3 VERB If you **support** someone, you provide them with money or the things that they need. ○ *I have children to support, money to be earned, and a home to be maintained.* ○ *She sold everything she'd ever bought in order to support herself through art school.*

▶ **COLLOCATIONS:** support **children/a family**

▶ **SYNONYMS:** finance, fund

4 VERB If a fact **supports** a statement or a theory, it helps to show that it is true or correct. ○ *The Freudian theory about daughters falling in love with their father has little evidence to support it.* ○ *This observation is supported by the archaeological evidence.*

→ see note at **confirm**

▶ **COLLOCATIONS:**
support a **view/notion/idea/theory**
evidence/data/findings support *something*

▶ **SYNONYMS:** substantiate, back up

• **Support** is also a noncount noun. ○ *[+ for] History offers some support for this view.* ○ *The study did not lend support to the hypothesis.*

▶ **COLLOCATIONS:**
support **for** *something*
offer/lend support

▶ **SYNONYM:** evidence

sup|posed

Pronounce /səpoʊzd/ or /səpoʊst/ for meanings **1** and **2**, and /səpoʊzd/ for meanings **3** and **4**.

1 If you **are supposed to** do or have something, you should do or have it. ○ [+ *to*] *We are supposed to have an hour for lunch.*

2 If something **is supposed to** happen, it is planned or expected. ○ [+ *to*] *Mr. Stewart is supposed to authorize the bank's electronic payments.*

3 If something **is supposed to** be true, many people say it is true. ○ [+ *to*] *"Avatar" is supposed to be a really great movie.*

4 **ADJECTIVE** You can use **supposed** to suggest that something may not be what people say it is. ○ *the supposed cause of the accident*

▶ **COLLOCATIONS:**
the supposed **cause/motive/reason**
a supposed **cure/solution**
a supposed **friend/ally/rival/expert**

sup|pos|ed|ly /səpoʊzɪdli/

ADVERB ○ *It was supposedly his own work.*

▶ **COLLOCATIONS:**
supposedly **independent/true/safe/secure**
supposedly **represent** *something*

sur|charge /sɜrtʃɑrdʒ/ (surcharges) · BANKING & FINANCE

NOUN A **surcharge** is an extra payment of money in addition to the usual payment for something. ○ [+ *on*] *The government introduced a 15% surcharge on imports.*

▶ **COLLOCATIONS:**
a surcharge **on** *something*
introduce/impose/add/levy a surcharge
a *x* **percent** surcharge
a **monthly/additional/small/temporary** surcharge
a **tax/fuel/ticket** surcharge
pay a surcharge

sur|face /sɜrfɪs/ (surfaces)

NOUN The **surface** of something is the flat top part of it or the outside of it. ○ *Ozone forms a protective layer between 12 and 30 miles above the Earth's* *surface.* ○ *tiny little waves on the surface of the water* ○ *Its total surface area was seven thousand square feet.*

▶ COLLOCATIONS:
the surface **of** *something*
on the surface
the **earth's/moon's** surface
a **smooth/slippery/flat** surface
a surface **area/temperature/layer**

---

sur|plus /sɜ́ːrplʌs, -pləs/ **(surpluses)**　　[LOGISTICS & DISTRIBUTION]

NOUN A **surplus** is more than you need of something. ○ [+ *of*] *There was a surplus of food.*

▶ COLLOCATIONS:
a surplus **of** *something*
a surplus of **food/workers**
a **budget/trade/account/cash** surplus
run/project/produce/expect/generate a surplus

▶ SYNONYM: excess

---

sur|prise /sərpráɪz/ **(surprises)**

NOUN A **surprise** is an unexpected event or fact. ○ [+ *for*] *I have a surprise for you: We are moving to Switzerland!*

▶ COLLOCATIONS:
a surprise **for** *someone*
a **big/nice/pleasant/unexpected/nasty** surprise
spring/have/get a surprise

● **Surprise** is also an adjective. ○ *a surprise visit*

▶ COLLOCATIONS:
a surprise **visit/announcement/attack/move/appearance**
a surprise **party**

sur|pris|ing /sərpráɪzɪŋ/

ADJECTIVE ○ *The focus on health-care benefits isn't surprising.*

▶ COLLOCATIONS:
a surprising **result/fact**
very/somewhat surprising

sur|round|ings /səraʊndɪŋz/

PLURAL NOUN When you are describing the place where you are at the moment, or the place where you live, you can refer to it as your **surroundings**. ○ *The child's need to interact with immediate surroundings is critical to language development.* ○ *Schumacher adapted effortlessly to his new surroundings.*

▶ **COLLOCATIONS:** **natural/beautiful/familiar** surroundings

▶ **SYNONYMS:** environment, location, setting

sur|tax /sɜrtæks/ BANKING & FINANCE

NONCOUNT NOUN **Surtax** is an additional tax on incomes higher than the level at which ordinary tax is paid. ○ *[+ for] a 10% surtax for Americans earning more than $250,000 a year*

sus|pend /səspɛnd/ (suspends, suspending, suspended)

1 VERB If you **suspend** something, you delay it or stop it from happening for a while or until a decision is made about it. ○ *The union suspended strike action this week.* ○ *[+ until] A U.N. official said aid programs will be suspended until there's adequate protection for relief convoys.*

▶ **COLLOCATIONS:**
suspend *something* **until** *a time*
immediately/temporarily/indefinitely suspend *something*
suspend **aid/trading/operations**
suspend a **flight/shipment/sentence**

▶ **PHRASE:** suspend disbelief

▶ **SYNONYM:** delay

2 VERB If something **is suspended** from a high place, it is hanging from that place. ○ *a mobile of birds or nursery rhyme characters which could be suspended over the cot* ○ *chandeliers suspended on heavy chains from the ceiling*

▶ **COLLOCATIONS:**
suspended **from/by/over/above** *something*
suspended from a **ceiling/rafter/hook**
suspended by **wire/rope**
suspended above the **floor/ground**

▶ **SYNONYM:** hang

sus|tain /səsteɪn/ **(sustains, sustaining, sustained)** `R&D`

VERB If you **sustain** something, you continue it or maintain it for a period
of time. ○ *Euphoria cannot be sustained indefinitely.* ○ *a period of sustained
economic growth throughout 1995*

→ see note at **maintain**

▶ **COLLOCATIONS:**
sustained **growth**
a sustained **attack**
indefinitely/artificially sustained

▶ **SYNONYMS:** maintain, continue

sus|tain|able /səsteɪnəbəl/

1 ADJECTIVE You use **sustainable** to describe the use of natural resources
when this use is kept at a steady level that is not likely to damage the
environment. ○ *the management, conservation and sustainable
development of forests* ○ *Try to buy wood that you know has come from a
sustainable source.*

▶ **COLLOCATIONS:**
sustainable **agriculture/fishery/forestry**
a sustainable **forest/future/source**
ecologically/environmentally sustainable

▶ **SYNONYMS:** environmentally friendly, ecological

2 ADJECTIVE A **sustainable** plan, method, or system is designed to
continue at the same rate or level of activity without any problems.
○ *the creation of an efficient and sustainable transportation system*
○ *a sustainable recovery in consumer spending*

▶ **COLLOCATIONS:**
sustainable **recovery/growth/development**
a sustainable **policy**

sus|tain|abil|ity /səsteɪnəbɪlɪti/

NONCOUNT NOUN ○ *the growing concern about environmental sustainability*
○ *[+ of] doubts about the sustainability of the current economic expansion*

▶ **COLLOCATIONS:**
the sustainability **of** something
ecological/environmental/long-term sustainability

sym|bol /sɪmbᵊl/ (symbols)

1 NOUN Something that is a **symbol of** a society or an aspect of life seems to represent it because it is very typical of it. ○ *To them, the monarchy is the special symbol of nationhood.*

2 NOUN A **symbol of** something such as an idea is a shape or design that is used to represent it. ○ *Later in this same passage Yeats resumes his argument for the Rose as an Irish symbol.*

3 NOUN A **symbol for** an item in a calculation or scientific formula is a number, letter, or shape that represents that item. ○ *mathematical symbols and operations*

▶ **COLLOCATIONS:**
a symbol **of/for** *something*
a symbol of **strength/resistance/hope/unity/freedom**
a **potent/powerful/visible/religious/status/sex** symbol
a symbol **denotes/indicates** *something*

▶ **SYNONYMS:** sign, representation

sym|bol|ic /sɪmbɒlɪk/

1 ADJECTIVE If you describe an event, action, or procedure as **symbolic**, you mean that it represents an important change, although it has little practical effect. ○ *A lot of Latin-American officials are stressing the symbolic importance of the trip.*

▶ **COLLOCATIONS:**
a symbolic **gesture/act**
highly/largely/purely symbolic

2 ADJECTIVE Something that is **symbolic of** a person or thing is regarded or used as a symbol of them. ○ [+ *of*] *Yellow clothes are worn as symbolic of spring.*

▶ **COLLOCATIONS:** symbolic **significance/importance/value**

▶ **SYNONYMS:** representative, iconic, metaphorical

3 ADJECTIVE **Symbolic** is used to describe things involving or relating to symbols. ○ *symbolic representations of landscape*

sym|bol|ize /sɪmbəlaɪz/ (symbolizes, symbolizing, symbolized)

VERB If one thing **symbolizes** another, it is used or regarded as a symbol of it. [in BRIT, also use **symbolise**] ○ *The fall of the Berlin Wall symbolised the end of the Cold War between East and West.*

▶ **COLLOCATIONS:** symbolize **unity/oppression/hope**

▶ **SYNONYMS:** represent, signify

sys|tem /sɪstəm/ (systems)

1 **NOUN** A **system** is a way of working, organizing, or doing something that follows a fixed plan or set of rules. You can use **system** to refer to an organization or institution that is organized in this way. ○ *a flexible and relatively efficient filing system* ○ [+ of] *a multiparty system of government*

▶ **COLLOCATIONS:**
a system **of** something
a system of **government/education**
a **health/education/management/justice/banking** system
a **filing/storage** system
design/develop/implement/use a system
a system **works/operates/fails**

▶ **SYNONYMS:** arrangement, organization

2 **NOUN** A **system** is a set of devices powered by electricity, for example a computer or an alarm. ○ *Viruses tend to be good at surviving when a computer system crashes.*

▶ **COLLOCATIONS:**
install a system
a **computer/alarm/electronic** system

▶ **SYNONYMS:** representative, iconic, metaphorical

sys|tem|at|ic /sɪstəmætɪk/

ADJECTIVE Something that is done in a **systematic** way is done according to a fixed plan, in a thorough and efficient way. ○ *A systematic review was carried out.* ○ *They had not found any evidence of a systematic attempt to rig the ballot.*

▶ **COLLOCATIONS:** a systematic **way/attempt/approach/review**

▶ **SYNONYMS:** orderly, methodical

S

Tt

---

take|over /teɪkoʊvər/ **(takeovers)** ORGANIZATION

NOUN A **takeover** is the act of gaining control of a company by buying more of its shares than anyone else. ○ [+ of] *the government's takeover of the Bank of New England Corporation* ○ *a hostile takeover bid for NCR, America's fifth-biggest computer-maker*

▶ **COLLOCATIONS:**
a takeover **of** *something*
propose/complete/finance a takeover
a **$**x takeover
a **corporate/hostile/friendly** takeover
a takeover **bid/offer**

▶ **SYNONYM:** buyout

▶ **RELATED WORD:** merger

---

tal|ent /tælənt/ PERSONNEL

NONCOUNT NOUN **Talent** is your natural ability to do something well. ○ *He's got lots of talent.*

▶ **COLLOCATIONS:**
nurture/possess/have/develop talent
homegrown/musical/creative/young/fresh/raw talent
a talent **scout/show/agency/search**

▶ **SYNONYM:** ability

tal|ent|ed /tæləntɪd/

ADJECTIVE If someone is **talented**, they have a natural ability to do something well. ○ *Mr. Diefenbach is a talented executive.*

▶ **COLLOCATIONS:** a talented **player/artist/musician/individual**

▶ **PHRASE:** young and talented

▶ **SYNONYM:** expert

tan|gible /tændʒɪbəl/

ADJECTIVE If something is **tangible**, it is clear enough or definite enough to be easily seen, felt, or noticed. ○ *There should be some tangible evidence that the economy is starting to recover.*

▶ COLLOCATIONS:
a tangible **benefit/asset**
tangible **proof/evidence**

▶ SYNONYMS: palpable, real

---

tar|get /tɑrgɪt/ (targets, targeting or targetting, targeted or targetted)   `MARKETING & SALES`

1 **NOUN** A **target** is a result that you are trying to achieve. ○ *The budgets should be based on company objectives, and set realistic targets.* ○ *an exports target of $5 billion a year*

▶ COLLOCATIONS:
a target **of** x
set/achieve/meet/reach/miss/exceed a target
a **realistic/tough/ambitious** target
a **government** target
a **performance/growth/sales/profit/financial** target
a target **rate/weight/time**

▶ SYNONYMS: objective, goal

2 **VERB** To **target** a particular person or thing means to decide to attack or criticize them. ○ *He targets the economy as the root cause of the deteriorating law and order situation.* ○ *Supermarkets have attached security tags to small, valuable items targeted by thieves.*

▶ COLLOCATIONS:
targeted **by** someone
targeted by **vandals/thieves/fraudsters/terrorists**
target **foreigners/militants/drinkers**
specifically/aggressively/unfairly target

▶ SYNONYMS: attack, blame, criticize

● **Target** is also a noun. ○ [+ *of*] *In the past they have been the target of racist abuse.* ○ [+ *for*] *The professor has been a frequent target for animal rights extremists.*

▶ COLLOCATIONS:
the target **of** something
a target **for** someone
a **soft/easy/legitimate/potential/possible** target
the **main/prime** target

a target of **attack/criticism/abuse/violence**

3 **VERB** If you **target** a particular group of people, you try to appeal to those people or affect them. ○ *The campaign will target American insurance companies.* ○ *The company has targeted adults as its primary customers.*

▶ **COLLOCATIONS:**
targeted **at** *someone*
targeted at **consumers/voters/investors/teenagers**
primarily/mainly/actively target *someone*

▶ **SYNONYMS:** aim at, focus on

● **Target** is also a noun. ○ *a prime target group for marketing strategies*

▶ **COLLOCATIONS:**
a target **for** *someone/something*
a **main/prime** target
a target **group/market/audience**

tar|get mar|ket /tɑrgɪt mɑrkɪt/ (target markets)

NOUN A **target market** is a market in which a company is trying to sell its products or services. ○ *We decided that we needed to change our target market from the over-45's to the 35-45's.*

---

tar|iff /tærɪf/ (tariffs)   `BANKING & FINANCE`

NOUN A **tariff** is a tax that a government collects on goods coming into a country. ○ [+ on] *America wants to eliminate tariffs on items such as electronics.* ○ *a rise in import tariffs*

▶ **COLLOCATIONS:**
a tariff **on** *something*
a tariff on **imports/goods/products**
a **trade/import/lumber/steel** tariff
a **punitive/protective** tariff
impose/levy/reduce/raise a tariff
tariff **reduction/cuts**

▶ **SYNONYMS:** tax, duty

---

task /tæsk/ (tasks)

NOUN A **task** is an activity or piece of work that you have to do, usually as part of a larger project. ○ [+ of] *the massive task of reconstruction after the war* ○ *She used the day to catch up with administrative tasks.*

▶ **COLLOCATIONS:**
the task **of** *something*

the task of **management/leadership/reconstruction**
face/undertake/accomplish/perform a task
assign/give *someone* a task
a **daunting/difficult/unenviable/thankless/easy** task
a **household/administrative/computing** task
the task **ahead**

▶ **SYNONYMS:** chore, job, assignment, duty, responsibility

taxa|tion /tækseɪʃᵊn/ BANKING & FINANCE

NONCOUNT NOUN Taxation is the system by which a government takes money from people and spends it on things such as education, health, and defense. ○ [+ on] *a proposal to increase taxation on fuel*

▶ **COLLOCATIONS:**
taxation **of/on** *something*
taxation of/on **income/dividends**
increase/raise/introduce taxation
reduce/avoid taxation
a taxation **system/policy**
income/interest/business/personal taxation
general/indirect/double taxation

tax|able /tæksəbᵊl/

ADJECTIVE Taxable income is income on which you have to pay taxation.
○ *It is worth consulting the guide to see whether your income is taxable.*

▶ **COLLOCATIONS:** taxable **income/benefits**

team|work /tiːmwɜrk/ PERSONNEL

NONCOUNT NOUN Teamwork is the ability of a group of people to work well together. ○ *She knows the importance of teamwork.*

▶ **COLLOCATIONS: require/promote/foster/involve** teamwork

▶ **PHRASE:** leadership and teamwork

▶ **SYNONYM:** cooperation

tech|ni|cal /tɛknɪkᵊl/ JOBS

1 ADJECTIVE Technical means involving the sorts of machines, processes, and materials that are used in industry, transportation, and communications. ○ *In order to reach this limit a number of technical problems will have to be solved.* ○ *jobs that require technical knowledge*

▶ COLLOCATIONS:
technical **assistance/knowledge/expertise**
a technical **problem/glitch/fault**
highly technical

▶ SYNONYMS: high-tech, technological, mechanical

2 ADJECTIVE **Technical** language involves using special words to describe the details of a specialized activity. ○ *The technical term for sunburn is erythema.* ○ *He's just written a book: large format, nicely illustrated, and not too technical.*

▶ COLLOCATIONS:
a technical **term/word**
technical **jargon**

tech|ni|cian /tɛknɪʃən/ (technicians)

NOUN A **technician** is someone whose job involves working with special equipment or machines. ○ *He works as a laboratory technician.*

▶ COLLOCATIONS: a **medical/dental/lab/computer** technician

tech|nique /tɛkniːk/ (techniques)   `R&D`

NOUN A **technique** is a particular method of doing an activity, usually a method that involves practical skills. ○ *tests performed using a new technique* ○ *developments in the surgical techniques employed*

▶ COLLOCATIONS:
a technique **of** something
a technique of **analysis/management/production**
a **sophisticated/modern/innovative/traditional** technique
a **surgical/mathematical/investigative** technique
a **breathing/relaxation/survival** technique
develop/perfect/master/learn a technique
employ/use/apply a technique

▶ SYNONYMS: method, style, system, way

USAGE: *technique, technology,* or *technical*?

A **technique** is a practical way of doing something. **Technique** is a countable noun. ○ *a common Internet marketing technique*

Technology refers to systems, devices, and methods that make use of scientific knowledge. You can use **technology** as a noncount noun to talk about the uses of science generally. ○ *Thanks to modern technology, many people are able to work from home.*

t

You can also use **technology** as a countable noun to talk about particular systems and devices. ○ *the development of new technologies to produce cleaner energy*

Technological is an adjective to describe things that involve the use of new scientific ideas. ○ *the latest technological advances*

You can also use the adjective **technical** to describe things that more generally involve machines or specialist knowledge. ○ *The flight was delayed by a technical fault.*

---

tech|nol|ogy /tɛknɒlədʒi/ (technologies) `R&D`

NOUN Technology refers to methods, systems, and devices that are the result of scientific knowledge being used for practical purposes.
○ *Technology is changing fast.* ○ *They should be allowed to wait for cheaper technologies to be developed.* ○ *nuclear weapons technology*

→ see note at **technique**

▶ **COLLOCATIONS:**
   develop/use/embrace technology
   advanced/modern/new technology
   the **latest** technology
   digital/wireless/mobile/nuclear technology
   information/computer technology
   technology **advances/changes/improves**
   technology **enables/allows** *something*
   the technology **sector**

▶ **PHRASE:** science and technology

▶ **SYNONYMS:** electronics, mechanization

---

tele|con|fer|ence /tɛlɪkɒnfərəns, -frəns/ `COMMUNICATIONS`
(teleconferences)

NOUN A **teleconference** is a meeting involving people in different places who use telephones or video links to communicate with each other.
○ *Managers at their factory hold a two-hour teleconference with head office every day.*

▶ **COLLOCATIONS: hold/handle/conduct** a teleconference

tele|gram /ˈtɛlɪɡræm/ (telegrams) `COMMUNICATIONS`

NOUN A **telegram** is a message that is sent by telegraph and then printed and delivered to someone's home or office. ○ *The president received a briefing by telegram.*

▶ **COLLOCATIONS: send/receive/read** a telegram

tele|mar|ket|ing /ˈtɛlɪmɑrkɪtɪŋ/ `MARKETING & SALES`

NONCOUNT NOUN Telemarketing is a method of selling in which someone telephones people to try to persuade them to buy products or services. ○ *As postal rates go up, many businesses have been turning to telemarketing as a way of contacting new customers.*

tem|po|rary /ˈtɛmpəreri/ `PERSONNEL`

ADJECTIVE Something that is **temporary** lasts for only a limited time. ○ *His job here is only temporary.* ○ *a temporary loss of memory*

▶ **COLLOCATIONS:**
temporary **accommodations/shelter**
a temporary **injunction/ban**
a temporary **measure/reprieve/setback**
a temporary **visa/permit**

▶ **PHRASE:** on a temporary basis

▶ **SYNONYM:** short-term

tem|po|rari|ly /ˌtɛmpəˈrɛrɪli/

ADVERB ○ *The peace agreement has at least temporarily halted the civil war.* ○ *Checkpoints between the two zones were temporarily closed.*

▶ **COLLOCATIONS:**
temporarily **suspended/halted/closed/blocked/shut/unavailable**
temporarily **insane/homeless/unemployed/blind**

temp|ta|tion /tɛmpˈteɪʃən/

NONCOUNT NOUN Temptation is the feeling that you want to do something or to have something, when you know you should not. ○ *Try to resist the temptation to eat snacks.*

▶ **COLLOCATIONS:**
resist/avoid/overcome temptation
great/irresistible temptation

▶ **SYNONYM:** seduction

ten|den|cy /tɛndənsi/ (tendencies)

NOUN A **tendency** is a worrying or unpleasant habit or action that keeps occurring. ○ [+ toward] *the government's tendency toward secrecy in recent years*

▶ **COLLOCATIONS:**
a tendency **toward** something
exhibit/display/curb/increase a tendency

▶ **SYNONYMS:** trend, habit, disposition

ten|sion /tɛnʃən/

1 NONCOUNT NOUN Tension is the feeling that is produced in a situation when people are anxious and do not trust each other, and when there is a possibility of sudden violence or conflict. ○ [+ between] *The tension between the two countries is likely to remain.* ○ *years of political tension and conflict*

▶ **COLLOCATIONS:**
tension **between** things
create/cause/increase/raise/heighten tension
ease/reduce/defuse tension
racial/political/religious/ethnic/social tension
growing/rising/increasing/escalating/mounting tension

▶ **PHRASE:** tension is high

▶ **SYNONYM:** anxiety

2 NONCOUNT NOUN The **tension** in something such as a rope or wire is the extent to which it is stretched tight. ○ *The reassuring tension of the rope moved with him, neither too tight nor too loose.* ○ *the tension created when tightening the wire*

▶ **SYNONYM:** tightness

ten|ta|tive /tɛntətɪv/

ADJECTIVE Tentative agreements, plans, or arrangements are not definite or certain, but have been made as a first step. ○ *Political leaders have reached a tentative agreement to hold a preparatory conference next month.* ○ *Such theories are still very tentative.* ○ *The study was adequate to permit at least tentative conclusions.*

→ see note at **inconclusive**

▶ **COLLOCATIONS:**
a tentative **step/agreement/settlement/deal**
a tentative **conclusion/thesis/theory**

▶ **SYNONYMS:** provisional, conditional, indefinite

ter|ri|tory /tɛrətɔri/

1 NONCOUNT NOUN Territory is land that is controlled by a particular country or ruler. ○ *The government denies that any of its territory is under rebel control.* ○ *India and Pakistan have fought wars over the disputed territory of Kashmir.* ○ *Russian territory*

▶ **COLLOCATIONS:**
enter/seize/conquer/occupy/control territory
occupied/disputed/neutral territory

▶ **SYNONYM:** land

2 NONCOUNT NOUN An animal's **territory** is an area that it regards as its own and that it defends when other animals try to enter it. ○ *The territory of a cat only remains fixed for as long as the cat dominates the area.*

text mes|sage /tɛkst mɛsɪdʒ/ (text messages) COMMUNICATIONS

NOUN A **text message** is a message that you write and send using a cellphone. ○ *one person might think it's harmless to look at another person's text messages or emails, while others would be appalled.*

▶ **COLLOCATIONS:** **send/receive** a text message

thir|teen /θɜrtin/

NUMBER Thirteen is the number 13. ○ *My nephew is thirteen.*

▶ **COLLOCATIONS:**
someone **is** thirteen
thirteen **dollars/euros**
thirteen **miles/kilometers**
thirteen **minutes/seconds**

▶ **PHRASE:** thirteen or fourteen

thir|ty /θɜrti/

NUMBER Thirty is the number 30. ○ *There are thirty days in November*

▶ **COLLOCATIONS:**
someone **is** seventy

t

thirty **dollars/euros**
thirty **miles/kilometers**
thirty **minutes/years**

▶ **PHRASE:** twenty or thirty

---

thor|ough /θ<u>ɜ</u>roʊ/

ADJECTIVE A **thorough** action or activity is one that is done very carefully and in a detailed way so that nothing is forgotten. ○ *We are making a thorough investigation.* ○ *This very thorough survey goes back to 1784.* ○ *How thorough is the assessment?*

▶ **COLLOCATIONS:**
a thorough **investigation/review/examination/search/analysis**
a thorough **job**
thorough **understanding/knowledge**
painstakingly/exceedingly thorough

▶ **SYNONYMS:** careful, detailed, exhaustive

---

through|out /θru<u>aʊ</u>t/

PREPOSITION If something is **throughout** somewhere, it is in all parts of that place. ○ *Such a failure creates problems throughout the financial system.*

▶ **SYNONYMS:** right through, from beginning to end

---

tight|en /t<u>aɪ</u>tᵊn/ (tightens, tightening, tightened)

VERB If you **tighten** something, you make it tighter. ○ *She tightened the belt on her robe.*

▶ **COLLOCATIONS:**
tighten a **screw/throat/noose/grip**
tighten **restrictions/security/regulations**

▶ **SYNONYMS:** close, fasten

---

time zone /t<u>aɪ</u>m z<u>oʊ</u>n/ (time zones) TRAVEL

NOUN A **time zone** is one of the areas that the world is divided into for measuring time. ○ *Their wives are thousands of miles away in a different time zone.*

▶ **COLLOCATIONS:**
a **different/new** time zone
cross a time zone

ti|tle /taɪtᵊl/ **(titles)**

NOUN The **title** of a book, play, film, or piece of music is its name. ○ *Patience and Sarah was first published in 1969 under the title A Place for Us.*

▶ **COLLOCATIONS:**
the title **of** something
the title of a **book/novel/article/essay**

top man|age|ment /tɒp mænɪdʒmənt/ or **senior**   JOBS
management

NONCOUNT NOUN The **top management** of an organization or business is its most senior staff. ○ *He insists top management didn't exert any pressure on its researchers to cheat.*

▶ **SYNONYM:** administration

tra|di|tion /trədɪʃᵊn/ **(traditions)**

NOUN A **tradition** is a custom or belief that has existed for a long time. ○ [+ *of*] *the rich traditions of Afro-Cuban music, and dance* ○ [+ *of*] *Mary has carried on the family tradition of giving away plants.* ○ *The story of King Arthur became part of oral tradition.*

▶ **COLLOCATIONS:**
a tradition **of** something
a tradition of **tolerance/storytelling/poetry/worship**
uphold/maintain/preserve/continue a tradition
keep a tradition **alive**
a **long/proud/ancient/oral** tradition
a **family/folk/religious/Christian** tradition
tradition **dictates** something

▶ **SYNONYMS:** custom, heritage, culture, practice, ritual

trans|form /trænsfɔrm/ **(transforms, transforming, transformed)**

1 VERB To **transform** something **into** something else means to change or convert it into that thing. ○ [+ *into*] *Your metabolic rate is the speed at which your body transforms food into energy.* ○ [+ *from/into*] *Delegates also discussed transforming them from a guerrilla force into a regular army.*

2 VERB To **transform** something or someone means to change them completely and suddenly so that they are much better or more attractive. ○ *The spread of the Internet and mobile technology have* *transformed society.* ○ [+ into] *Yeltsin was committed to completely transforming Russia into a market economy.*

▶ **COLLOCATIONS:**
transform *something* **from/into** *something*
completely/magically/dramatically transform
transform **society**
transform a **country/business/area**
transform the **economy/landscape/country/world**

▶ **SYNONYMS:** change, convert

trans|for|ma|tion /trænsfəmeɪʃ°n/ (transformations)

NOUN ○ *one of the most astonishing economic transformations seen since the second world war* ○ *After 1959, the Spanish economy underwent a profound transformation.*

▶ **COLLOCATIONS:**
the transformation **of** *something*
undergo/see/make a transformation
a transformation **occurs/takes place**
a **radical/dramatic/profound/complete** transformation
a **social/economic/personal/political/cultural** transformation

▶ **SYNONYM:** change

---

trans|late /trænzleɪt/ (translates, translating, translated) `COMMUNICATIONS`

VERB If something that someone has said or written **is translated from** one language **into** another, it is said or written again in the second language. ○ [+ into/from] *Only a small number of Kadare's books have been translated into English.* ○ [+ into/from] *Martin Luther translated the Bible into German.* ○ [+ as] *The Celtic word "geis" is usually translated as "taboo".*

▶ **COLLOCATIONS:**
translate *something* **from/into** a language
translate *something* **as** *something*
translate a **word/text/poem/passage**
translate **loosely/roughly/literally**

▶ **SYNONYMS:** interpret, gloss, render

trans|la|tion /trænzleɪʃ°n/ (translations)

NOUN ○ *The papers have been sent to Saudi Arabia for translation.* ○ [+ of] *MacNiece's excellent English translation of "Faust"* ○ *I've only read Solzhenitsyn in translation.*

▶ **COLLOCATIONS:**
a translation **of** something
a translation of a **poem/novel/article/word/phrase**
a **literal/faithful/accurate/rough** translation
a **French/English/Russian** translation

▶ **PHRASE:** lose something/be lost in (the) translation

---

trans|mit /trænzmɪt/ (transmits, transmitting, transmitted)

VERB If one person or animal **transmits** a disease to another, they have the disease and cause the other person or animal to have it. [FORMAL] ○ [+ to] *mosquitoes that transmit disease to humans* ○ [+ through] *There was no danger of transmitting the infection through operations.* ○ *the spread of sexually transmitted diseases*

▶ **COLLOCATIONS:**
transmit something **to** someone/something
transmitted **by/through** something
transmitted by **mosquitoes/contact/transfusion**
transmit a **disease/infection/virus**
sexually/orally/genetically transmitted

▶ **SYNONYMS:** pass, spread

---

trans|par|en|cy /trænspɛərənsi, -pær-/

1 **NONCOUNT NOUN Transparency** is the quality that an object or substance has when you can see through it. ○ [+ of] *Cataracts is a condition that affects the transparency of the lenses.*

▶ **COLLOCATION:** the transparency **of** something

2 **NONCOUNT NOUN** The **transparency** of a process, situation, or statement is its quality of being easily understood or recognized, for example because there are no secrets connected with it, or because it is expressed in a clear way. ○ [+ in] *openness and transparency in the Government's economic decision-making*

▶ **COLLOCATIONS:**
transparency **in** something
increase/improve/ensure transparency
greater/full transparency

▶ **PHRASES:**
transparency and accountability
openness and transparency

▶ **SYNONYM:** clarity

trans|port /trænspɔrt/ (transports, transporting, transported)

LOGISTICS & DISTRIBUTION

VERB To **transport** people or goods somewhere is to take them from one place to another in a vehicle. ○ *There's no gas, so it's very difficult to transport goods.* ○ *They use tankers to transport the oil to Los Angeles.*

▸ **COLLOCATIONS:**
transport *something* **by** *something*
transport *something* by **airplane/helicopter/rail**
transport **freight/cargo/goods**
ferries/ships/trucks transport *things*

▸ **SYNONYMS:** move, ship

trans|por|ta|tion /trænspərteɪʃⁿn/

NONCOUNT NOUN **Transportation** is the moving of people or goods from one place to another, for example using buses or trains. [in BRIT, use **transport**] ○ *The extra money could be spent on improving public transportation.* ○ *An efficient transportation system is critical to the long-term future of the city.* ○ *Local production virtually eliminates transportation costs.*

▸ **COLLOCATIONS:**
public/rail/air/road/passenger transportation
improve/provide/use transportation
a transportation **system/link/infrastructure**

▸ **SYNONYM:** carriage

---

trav|el /trævⁿl/ (travels, traveling, traveled) [in BRIT, use travelling, travelled]

TRAVEL

VERB If you **travel**, you go on a trip. ○ *I've been traveling all day.*

▸ **COLLOCATIONS:**
non-essential/unlimited/overseas/foreign/first-class travel
air/business/space/train travel

trav|el|er's check /trævⁿlərz tʃɛk/ (traveler's checks)

NOUN A **traveler's check** is a check that is sold to people traveling abroad and can be exchanged for cash. [in BRIT, use **traveller's cheque**] ○ *He paid me in traveler's checks, and I gave $2,000 to Ivan.*

▸ **COLLOCATIONS:** **get/cash/have** a traveler's check

t

treat|ment /trịtmənt/ (treatments) `HEALTH & FITNESS`

1 **NOUN** **Treatment** is medical attention given to a sick or injured person or animal. ○ *Many patients are not getting the medical treatment they need.* ○ [+ *of*] *a veterinary surgeon who specializes in the treatment of cage birds* ○ [+ *for*] *an effective treatment for eczema*

▶ **COLLOCATIONS:**
treatment **for** *something*
the treatment **of** *something*
treatment for **addiction/cancer/depression**
the treatment of a **disease/disorder**
medical/dental/fertility/hospital treatment
an **effective** treatment
successful/unsuccessful treatment
AIDS/cancer treatment
give/get/undergo/receive/prescribe treatment

▶ **SYNONYMS:** cure, medicine, therapy

2 **NONCOUNT NOUN** Your **treatment** of someone is the way you behave towards them or deal with them. ○ *We don't want any special treatment.* ○ [+ *of*] *the government's responsibility for the humane treatment of prisoners*

▶ **COLLOCATIONS:**
the treatment **of** *someone*
the treatment of **prisoners/offenders/asylum seekers**
special/preferential/equal/fair/unfair treatment
harsh/humane treatment

▶ **SYNONYM:** behavior

trea|ty /trịti/ (treaties) `LEGAL`

NOUN A **treaty** is a written agreement between countries in which they agree to do a particular thing or to help each other. ○ [+ *of*] *the Treaty of Rome, which established the European Community* ○ [+ *on*] *negotiations over a 1992 treaty on global warming* ○ *A peace treaty was signed between France and Russia.*

▶ **COLLOCATIONS:**
the treaty **of** *something*
a treaty **on** *something*
a **peace/arms/nuclear/climate** treaty
a **draft/formal/global** treaty
negotiate/sign/ratify/approve a treaty
violate/reject a treaty

▶ **SYNONYMS:** pact, agreement

tre|men|dous /trɪmɛndəs/

ADJECTIVE If something is **tremendous**, it is very large in amount or level.
○ *There is tremendous pressure to keep down commercial rates.*

▶ **COLLOCATIONS:** a tremendous **amount/opportunity/success**

▶ **SYNONYM:** huge

trend /trɛnd/ (trends)

NOUN A **trend** is a change or development towards something new or different. ○ *This is a growing trend.* ○ *[+ toward] There has been a trend toward part-time employment.* ○ *the downward trend in gasoline prices*

▶ **COLLOCATIONS:**
a trend **toward** *something*
buck/defy/reverse/reflect/continue a trend
a **growing/emerging/new/recent** trend
the **latest/current** trend
a **general/underlying/overall/global/international** trend
a **social/economic/cultural** trend
a **downward/upward/disturbing/worrying** trend

▶ **SYNONYMS:** tendency, movement

tri|ple /trɪpᵊl/ (triples, tripling, tripled)

1 ADJECTIVE Something that is **triple** consists of three things or parts.
○ *The property includes a triple garage.*

▶ **SYNONYM:** triplicate

2 VERB Something that **triples** becomes three times as large. ○ *My salary tripled.*

trouble|shoot|ing /trʌbᵊlʃutɪŋ/ [R&D]

NONCOUNT NOUN **Troubleshooting** is the activity or process of solving major problems or difficulties that occur in a company or government.
○ *The purpose of remotely accessing a PC isn't just file retrieval or troubleshooting.*

turn|around /tɜrnəraʊnd/ (turnarounds) [BANKING & FINANCE]

NOUN A **turnaround** is a sudden improvement, especially in the success of a business or a country's economy. ○ *The company has been enjoying a turnaround in recent months.*

► **COLLOCATIONS:**
  engineer/achieve/mark/represent a turnaround
  a **remarkable/dramatic/quick** turnaround

---

turn|over /ˈtɜrnoʊvər/ **(turnovers)**   `BANKING & FINANCE`

NOUN The **turnover** of a company is the value of the goods or services sold during a particular period of time. ○ [+ of] *The company had a turnover of $3.8 million.* ○ *Group turnover rose by 13 percent to $1 million.*

► **COLLOCATIONS:**
  a turnover **of** $x
  total/annual/average turnover
  turnover **rises/grows/falls**

► **SYNONYM:** revenue

---

twen|ty /ˈtwɛnti/

NUMBER **Twenty** is the number 20. ○ *She has written twenty novels.* ○ *a young man of about twenty*

► **COLLOCATIONS:**
  someone **is** twenty
  twenty **dollars/euros**
  twenty **miles/kilometers**
  twenty **minutes/years**

---

typi|cal /ˈtɪpɪkəl/

ADJECTIVE If someone or something is **typical**, it has the normal and expected characteristics of someone or something. ○ *These products followed a typical sales pattern.*

► **COLLOCATIONS:** a typical **story/attitude/pattern/example/style**

► **SYNONYMS:** usual, conventional

t

Uu

ul|ti|mate /ˈʌltɪmɪt/

1 **ADJECTIVE** You use **ultimate** to describe the final result or aim of a long series of events. ○ *He said it is still not possible to predict the ultimate outcome.* ○ *The ultimate aim is to expand the network further.*

▶ **COLLOCATIONS:**
the ultimate **aim/goal/objective**
the ultimate **fate/outcome/result/destination**

▶ **SYNONYMS:** eventual, final

2 **ADJECTIVE** You use **ultimate** to describe the most important or powerful thing of a particular kind. ○ *the ultimate power of the central government* ○ *Of course, the ultimate authority remained the presidency.*

▶ **COLLOCATIONS:**
the ultimate **control/power/authority**
the ultimate **challenge/responsibility**

▶ **SYNONYMS:** most important, highest

ul|ti|mate|ly /ˈʌltɪmɪtli/

1 **ADVERB** **Ultimately** means finally, after a long and often complicated series of events. ○ *Whatever the scientists ultimately conclude, all of their data will immediately be disputed.* ○ *It was a tough but ultimately worthwhile struggle.*

▶ **COLLOCATIONS:** ultimately **decide/conclude/succeed**

▶ **SYNONYMS:** eventually, in the end

2 **ADVERB** You use **ultimately** to indicate that what you are saying is the most important point in a discussion. ○ *Ultimately, Bismarck's revisionism scarcely affected or damaged British interests at all.*

un|ac|cep|table /ˌʌnəkˈsɛptəbᵊl/

ADJECTIVE Something that is **unacceptable** is too bad or wrong to be allowed. ○ *He took an unacceptable risk by investing so heavily in industry.*

▶ **COLLOCATIONS:**
unacceptable **behavior/conduct**
an unacceptable **situation/proposal/risk**
totally/completely/simply/socially unacceptable

▶ **SYNONYMS:** unsatisfactory, inappropriate

---

under|es|ti|mate /ˌʌndərɛstɪmeɪt/ (underestimates, underestimating, underestimated)

VERB If you **underestimate** something, you do not realize how large or great it is or will be. ○ *Marx clearly underestimated the importance of population growth.* ○ [+ how] *The most common mistake students make in library research is underestimating how long it will take to find the sources they need.*

▶ **COLLOCATIONS:**
underestimate the **seriousness/importance** of *something*
underestimate the **extent/complexity** of *something*
grossly/vastly/seriously underestimate

▶ **SYNONYM:** undervalue

---

under|go /ˌʌndərɡoʊ/ (undergoes, undergoing, underwent, undergone)

VERB If a person or thing **undergoes** something necessary or unpleasant, it happens to them. ○ *New recruits have been undergoing training in recent weeks.* ○ *When cement powder is mixed with water it undergoes a chemical change and sets hard.*

▶ **COLLOCATIONS:**
undergo an **operation**
undergo **surgery/treatment/therapy/training**
undergo **refurbishment/restoration/repairs**
undergo a **change/transformation/facelift/reaction**
undergo a **review/assessment/evaluation/test/check**

---

under|ly|ing /ˌʌndərlaɪɪŋ/

ADJECTIVE The **underlying** features of an object, event, or situation are not obvious, and it may be difficult to discover or reveal them. ○ *To stop a problem you have to understand its underlying causes.* ○ *I think that the underlying problem is education, unemployment and bad housing.*

▶ **COLLOCATIONS:**
an underlying **cause/reason/problem/issue**

an underlying **principle/assumption/theme/philosophy**
an underlying **trend**

▸ SYNONYMS: basic, fundamental

---

un|em|ployed /ˌʌnɪmˈplɔɪd/ 　　　　　　　PERSONNEL

ADJECTIVE Someone who is **unemployed** does not have a job. ○ *Millions of
people are unemployed.* ○ *This workshop helps young unemployed people in the
city.* ○ [+ for] *Have you been unemployed for over six months?*

▸ COLLOCATIONS:
unemployed **for** *a time*
become/remain unemployed
unemployed **workforce/population/workers/youth**
currently/newly/temporarily unemployed

▸ SYNONYM: out of work

un|em|ploy|ment /ˌʌnɪmˈplɔɪmənt/

NONCOUNT NOUN **Unemployment** is the fact that people who want jobs
cannot get them. ○ *an area that had the highest unemployment rate in
Western Europe* ○ *Unemployment is damaging both to individuals and to
communities.*

▸ COLLOCATIONS:
a **rise/fall** in unemployment
reduce/increase/tackle unemployment
high/low/mass/long-term/widespread unemployment
youth unemployment
unemployment **benefits/figures/levels**
the unemployment **rate**

---

uni|ver|sal /ˌyuːnɪˈvɜrsəl/

1 ADJECTIVE Something that is **universal** relates to everyone in the world
or everyone in a particular group or society. ○ *The insurance industry has
produced its own proposals for universal health care.* ○ *The desire to look
attractive is universal.*

▸ COLLOCATIONS:
universal **childcare/health care/suffrage/literacy**
a universal **language/truth**
universal **appeal**

2 ADJECTIVE Something that is **universal** affects or relates to every part of
the world or the universe. ○ *universal diseases* ○ *the law of universal gravitation*

▶ **SYNONYM:** worldwide

---

un|known /ʌnnoʊn/

ADJECTIVE If something is **unknown**, it is not known. ○ *The cost of their product is unknown.*

▶ **COLLOCATIONS:**
an unknown **quantity/number/origin**
previously/hitherto/virtually/relatively/still unknown

▶ **PHRASE:** for reasons unknown

▶ **SYNONYM:** unidentified

---

un|like|ly /ʌnlaɪkli/ (unlikelier, unlikeliest)

ADJECTIVE If you say that something is **unlikely** to happen or **unlikely** to be true, you believe that it will not happen or that it is not true, although you are not completely sure. ○ *A military coup seems unlikely.* ○ [+ to-inf] *As with many technological revolutions, you are unlikely to be aware of it.* ○ [+ that] *It's now unlikely that future parliaments will bring back the death penalty.*

▶ **COLLOCATIONS:**
seem/look unlikely
highly/most/increasingly/very unlikely
an unlikely **event/breakthrough/move/combination**
an unlikely **scenario/setting/source**

---

un|nec|es|sary /ʌnnɛsəsɛri/

ADJECTIVE If you describe something as **unnecessary**, you mean that it is not needed or does not have to be done, and is undesirable. ○ [+ to-inf] *She explained that it is quite unnecessary to hurt a patient.* ○ *The slaughter of whales is unnecessary.* ○ *Don't take any unnecessary risks.*

→ see note at **unlikely**

▶ **COLLOCATIONS:**
unnecessary **suffering/risk/expense**
unnecessary **legislation/regulation/treatment**
totally/completely/quite unnecessary

▶ **SYNONYM:** needless

u

un|pre|dict|able /ˌʌnprɪdɪ́ktəbᵊl/

ADJECTIVE If you describe someone or something as **unpredictable**, you mean that you cannot tell what they are going to do or how they are going to behave. ○ *In macular surgery, outcomes are unpredictable.* ○ *Adding more elements into the equation might have unpredictable consequences.* ○ *an unpredictable work environment*

▸ **COLLOCATIONS:**
a **result/outcome/situation** is unpredictable
unpredictable **behavior/weather/consequences**

▸ **SYNONYM:** changeable

un|usual /ʌnyúːʒuəl/

ADJECTIVE If something is **unusual**, it does not happen or exist very often. ○ *Waiting lists of a month aren't unusual for popular models.*

▸ **COLLOCATIONS:**
nothing/anything/something unusual
highly/somewhat/extremely unusual
an unusual **step/move/punishment**

▸ **SYNONYM:** rare

un|usu|al|ly /ʌnyúːʒuəli/

ADVERB ○ *The industry benefited from unusually strong demand in the second quarter.*

▸ **COLLOCATIONS:** unusually **quiet/warm/high/large/strong/heavy**

▸ **SYNONYM:** exceptionally

up|date /ʌpdéɪt, ʌ́pdeɪt/ (updates, updating, updated)

VERB If you **update** something, you make it more modern, usually by adding new parts to it or giving new information. ○ *He was back in the office, updating the work schedule on the computer.* ○ *The guide was updated last year.* ○ *an updated edition of the book*

▸ **COLLOCATIONS:**
an updated **version/edition/database/list/forecast**
updated **information/software/guidelines**
regularly/constantly/automatically updated

▸ **PHRASE:** revised and updated

▸ **SYNONYM:** modernize

up|grade /ˈʌpgreɪd, -ˈgreɪd/ (upgrades, upgrading, upgraded)

VERB If you **upgrade** something, you improve it or replace it with a better one. ○ *The road into town is being upgraded.* ○ *I recently upgraded my computer.*

▸ **COLLOCATIONS:** upgrade a **facility/version/network**

▸ **SYNONYM:** improve

up|turn /ˈʌptɜrn/ (upturns)   BANKING & FINANCE

NOUN An **upturn** is an improvement in the economy or in a business.
○ *They do not expect an upturn in the economy until the end of the year.*

▸ **COLLOCATIONS:**
an upturn **in** *something*
an upturn in **business/sales/demand**
an **economic** upturn
a **sharp/sustained/strong/slight** upturn

▸ **SYNONYM:** rise

uti|lize /ˈyutɪlaɪz/ (utilizes, utilizing, utilized)

VERB If you **utilize** something, you use it. [FORMAL] [in BRIT, also use **utilise**] ○ *Sound engineers utilize a range of techniques to enhance the quality of the recordings.* ○ *Minerals can be absorbed and utilized by the body in a variety of different forms.*

▸ **COLLOCATIONS:**
utilize a **strategy/method/approach/service/resource**
utilize **technology/energy/power**
fully/effectively utilize *something*

▸ **SYNONYMS:** use, employ

u

Vv

va|cant /ˈveɪkənt/

ADJECTIVE If something is **vacant**, it is not being used by anyone. ○ *Halfway down the bus was a vacant seat.*

▶ **COLLOCATIONS:**
a vacant **position/seat/job/lot/building**
vacant **land**
mostly/largely/currently vacant

▶ **SYNONYM:** empty

va|can|cy /ˈveɪkənsi/ (vacancies)

1 NOUN A **vacancy** is a room in a hotel that is available. ○ *The hotel still has a few vacancies.*

2 NOUN A **vacancy** is a job that has not been filled. ○ *We have a vacancy for an assistant.*

▶ **COLLOCATIONS:**
fill/leave/have/create a vacancy
a vacancy **arises/occurs/exists/remains**

▶ **SYNONYM:** opening

va|ca|tion /veɪˈkeɪʃən/ (vacations)

NOUN A **vacation** is a period of time when you relax and enjoy yourself away from home. ○ *They planned a vacation in Europe.*

▶ **COLLOCATIONS:**
take/plan/spend/need a vacation
a **summer/winter/family** vacation
a vacation **spot/package/home**

▶ **SYNONYM:** break

value /ˈvælyu/ (values, valuing, valued) BANKING & FINANCE

1 NONCOUNT NOUN The **value** of something is how much money it is worth. ○ [+ of] *The value of his investment has risen by more than $50,000.* ○ *The country's currency went down in value by 3.5 percent.* ○ *It might contain something of value.*

▶ **COLLOCATIONS:**
the value **of** something
change **in** value
something **of** value
the **actual/present/current** value of *something*
of **equal/great/no** value
go up/increase/go down in value

▶ **PHRASE:** be of value

▶ **SYNONYMS:** cost, price, worth

2 NONCOUNT NOUN The **value** of something such as a quality, attitude, or method is its importance or usefulness. If you place a particular **value** on something, that is the importance or usefulness you think it has. ○ *Further studies will be needed to see if these therapies have any value.* ○ *Current sales figures tell us something of value about what is really going on.*

▶ **COLLOCATIONS:**
place/put a value on *something*
artistic/actual/real/true/great value
a value **judgment**

▶ **PHRASE:** of (no) value

▶ **SYNONYM:** worth

3 VERB If you **value** something or someone, you think that they are important and you appreciate them. ○ *a culture in the workplace which values learning and development* ○ *Authority is rooted in a patriarchal system; males are highly valued.*

▶ **COLLOCATIONS:**
value a **contribution/input/opinion**
value **freedom/diversity/friendship/support/life**
value a **skill/opportunity/experience**
value *something/someone* **greatly/highly**

▶ **SYNONYMS:** admire, approve of

4 PLURAL NOUN The **values** of a person or group are the moral principles and beliefs that they think are important. ○ *The countries of South Asia also share many common values.* ○ *The Health Secretary called for a return to traditional family values.*

▶ **COLLOCATIONS:**
share/reflect values
modern/traditional/moral/cultural/social/family values

▶ **SYNONYMS:** beliefs, morals

5 NOUN A **value** is a particular number or amount. ○ *Normal values lie between 1.0 and 3.0 mg per 100 ml blood serum.* ○ *These calculations were based on average values for velocity and acceleration.*

▶ **SYNONYMS:** number, amount, figure

valu|able /vǽlyuəbᵊl/

ADJECTIVE If you describe something or someone as **valuable**, you mean that they are very useful and helpful. ○ *Many of our teachers also have valuable academic links with Heidelberg University.* ○ *The experience was very valuable.*

▶ **COLLOCATIONS:**
extremely/less/very valuable
prove/become valuable
a valuable **asset/lesson/resource/experience**
a valuable **contribution/item**
valuable **property/information/advice**

▶ **SYNONYMS:** useful, helpful

---

vary /vɛ́əri/ (varies, varying, varied)

1 VERB If things **vary**, they are different from each other in size, amount, or degree. ○ *Assessment practices vary in different schools or colleges.* ○ [+ from] *The text varies from the earlier versions.* ○ [V-ing] *Different writers will prepare to varying degrees.*

2 VERB If something **varies** or if you **vary** it, it becomes different or changed. ○ *The cost of the alcohol tax varies according to the amount of wine in the bottle.* ○ *Company officials should make sure that security routines are varied.*

→ see note at **fluctuate**

▶ **COLLOCATIONS:**
vary **from** *something*
vary from *something* **to** *something*
vary from **region to region/person to person**
vary **considerably/enormously/greatly/widely**
opinions/prices/estimates/practices vary
varying **degrees/sizes/lengths/amounts**

▶ **SYNONYMS:** differ, change

vari|able /vɛəriəbəl/ (variables)

NOUN A **variable** is a factor that can change in quality, quantity, or size, that you have to take into account in a situation. ○ *Decisions could be made on the basis of price, delivery dates, after-sales service or any other variable.* ○ *Other variables in making forecasts for the industry include the weather and the general economic climate.*

▶ **COLLOCATIONS:**
a **dependent/independent** variable
demographic/socioeconomic/extraneous variables
manipulate/measure/identify/examine variables
variables **determine/influence/cause** *something*

▶ **SYNONYM:** factor

vari|ation /vɛərieɪʃən/ (variations)

NOUN A **variation** is a change or slight difference in a level, amount, or quantity. ○ [+ *in*] *The survey found a wide variation in the prices charged for canteen food.* ○ *The employment rate shows significant regional variations.*

▶ **COLLOCATIONS:**
variation **in** *something*
seasonal/genetic/regional variation
wide/considerable/slight variation
show variation

▶ **SYNONYMS:** difference, diversity

var|ied /vɛərid/

ADJECTIVE Something that is **varied** consists of things of different types, sizes, or qualities. ○ *It is essential that your diet is varied and balanced.* ○ *Before his election to the presidency, Mitterrand had enjoyed a long and varied career.*

▶ **COLLOCATIONS:**
extremely/richly varied
a varied **menu/diet/career**
a varied **landscape/coastline**

▶ **SYNONYM:** diverse

vari|ous /vɛəriəs/

ADJECTIVE If you say that there are **various** things, you mean there are several different things of the type mentioned. ○ *He found various species of animals and plants, each slightly different.* ○ *The school has received various grants from the education department.*

V

▶ **COLLOCATIONS:**
various **artists/groups/locations**
various **types/forms/kinds/parts/species**
various **elements/components/categories**

▶ **SYNONYM:** different

---

vast /væst/ **(vaster, vastest)**

ADJECTIVE Something that is **vast** is extremely large. ○ *Afrikaner farmers who own vast stretches of land*

▶ **COLLOCATIONS:**
vast **amounts/quantities/knowledge**
a vast **distance/expanse/majority**
a vast **number of** *something*

▶ **SYNONYMS:** broad, endless, huge, massive

---

ve|hi|cle /viːɪkᵊl/ **(vehicles)**

NOUN A **vehicle** is a machine such as a car, bus, or truck that has an engine and is used to carry people from place to place. ○ *The vehicle would not be able to make the journey on one tank of fuel.* ○ *a vehicle that was somewhere between a tractor and a truck*

▶ **COLLOCATIONS:**
a **military/armored/commercial** vehicle
a **motor/utility/sport/emergency** vehicle
a **stolen** vehicle

---

ven|ture /vɛntʃər/ **(ventures)**   **BANKING & FINANCE**

NOUN A **venture** is a business activity that may or may not be successful. ○ *He gambled his family business on a new venture.*

▶ **COLLOCATIONS:**
form/launch/announce a venture
a **commercial/new/joint/late/successful** venture
a **business/Internet** venture

▶ **SYNONYM:** project

ven|ture capi|tal /vɛntʃər kæpɪtᵊl/

NONCOUNT NOUN **Venture capital** is money that is invested in projects that have a high risk of failure, but that will bring large profits if they are successful. ○ *Successful venture capital investment is a lot harder than it sometimes looks.*

▶ COLLOCATIONS:
raise/provide venture capital
a venture capital **firm/community/fund/investment**

---

venue /vɛnyu/ (venues) `OFFICE`

NOUN A **venue** is the place where an event or activity will happen.
○ *Fenway Park will be used as a venue for the rock concert.*

▶ COLLOCATIONS:
choose/switch/visit a venue
a **popular/alternative/live/perfect** venue
a **concert/entertainment/music** venue

---

ver|sa|tile /vɜrsətᵊl/

ADJECTIVE A tool, machine, or material that is **versatile** can be used for many different purposes. ○ *Never before has computing been so versatile.* ○ *The most versatile domesticated plant is the coconut palm.*

▶ SYNONYMS: adaptable, flexible

ver|sa|til|ity /vɜrsətɪlɪti/

NONCOUNT NOUN ○ [+ *of*] *the versatility of the software*

▶ COLLOCATIONS:
the versatility **of** *something*
offer/provide versatility
great versatility

▶ SYNONYMS: adaptability, flexibility

---

vi|able /vaɪəbᵊl/

ADJECTIVE Something that is **viable** is capable of doing what it is intended to do. ○ *Cash alone will not make Eastern Europe's banks viable.* ○ *commercially viable products* ○ *the argument that plastic is a viable alternative to traditional building materials*

▶ COLLOCATIONS:
commercially/economically/financially viable
a viable **alternative/option/solution/proposition**
make *something* viable

▶ SYNONYMS: feasible, possible, reasonable

vi|abil|ity /vaɪəbɪlɪti/

NONCOUNT NOUN ○ [+ of] the shaky financial viability of the nuclear industry ○ The philosophy behind the development managers is to ensure long-term viability, profitability, and sustainability.

▶ **COLLOCATIONS:**
the viability **of** something
the viability of a **project/strategy/industry**
financial/commercial/economic/long-term viability
assess/ensure/threaten the viability of something

▶ **SYNONYM:** feasibility

vi|brant /vaɪbrənt/

ADJECTIVE Someone or something that is **vibrant** is full of life, energy, and enthusiasm. ○ Tom felt himself being drawn toward her vibrant personality. ○ Her voice was vibrant and color lighted her cheeks.

▶ **COLLOCATIONS:** a vibrant **scene/culture/color/atmosphere**

▶ **SYNONYM:** lively

vi|bran|cy /vaɪbrənsi/

NONCOUNT NOUN ○ She was a woman with extraordinary vibrancy and extraordinary knowledge.

▶ **COLLOCATIONS:** **bring/add** vibrancy

▶ **SYNONYM:** vitality

video con|fer|enc|ing /vɪdioʊ kɒnfrənsɪŋ/ `COMMUNICATIONS`
also **video-conferencing** or **videoconferencing**

NONCOUNT NOUN **Video conferencing** is a system that allows people in different places to have a meeting by seeing and hearing each other on a screen. ○ We also hope to use video conferencing to train and supervise staff.

▶ **COLLOCATIONS:** **set up/use/allow/add** video conferencing

vig|or|ous /vɪgərəs/

1 ADJECTIVE **Vigorous** physical activities involve using a lot of energy, usually to do short and repeated actions. ○ Very vigorous exercise can increase the risk of heart attacks.

▶ **COLLOCATIONS:**
vigorous **exercise**

a vigorous **workout**

▶ **SYNONYM:** energetic

2 ADJECTIVE A **vigorous** person does things with great energy and enthusiasm. A **vigorous** campaign or activity is done with great energy and enthusiasm. ○ *Theodore Roosevelt was a strong and vigorous politician.*

▶ **COLLOCATIONS:**
a vigorous **campaigner/supporter**
a vigorous **debate/defense**

▶ **SYNONYM:** forceful

---

vio|late /vaɪəleɪt/ (violates, violating, violated)

VERB If someone **violates** an agreement, law, or promise, they break it. [FORMAL] ○ *They went to prison because they violated the law.* ○ *They violated the ceasefire agreement.*

▶ **COLLOCATIONS:**
violate the **law/constitution**
violate a **rule/principle/agreement**
violate **probation/copyright**

▶ **SYNONYMS:** breach, break, disobey

vio|la|tion /vaɪəleɪʃən/ (violations)

NOUN ○ [+ *of*] *This could constitute a violation of international law.* ○ [+ *of*] *He was in violation of his contract.* ○ *allegations of human rights violations*

▶ **COLLOCATIONS:**
a violation **of** *something*
a violation of the **law**
a violation of a **rule/agreement/contract**
a **human rights/copyright/parole** violation
a **gross/alleged/flagrant** violation
constitute a violation
commit/report a violation

▶ **PHRASE:** in violation of *something*

---

vir|tual /vɜrtʃuəl/

1 ADJECTIVE You can use **virtual** to indicate that something is so nearly true that for most purposes it can be regarded as true. ○ *the virtual disappearance of marriage as an institution among poor black people* ○ *conditions of virtual slavery*

▶ **COLLOCATIONS:**
a virtual **certainty/impossibility**
a virtual **prisoner/standstill/monopoly**
the virtual **disappearance/elimination** of *something*

▶ **SYNONYM:** near

2 **ADJECTIVE** **Virtual** objects and activities are generated by a computer to simulate real objects and activities. ○ *software that generates virtual environments of war zones* ○ *a virtual shopping center*

▶ **COLLOCATIONS:**
virtual **reality**
a virtual **environment/world/community/tour/network**

▶ **SYNONYMS:** computerized, online

---

vis|ible /vɪzɪbəl/

1 **ADJECTIVE** If something is **visible**, it can be seen. ○ *The warning lights were clearly visible.* ○ [+ to] *They found a bacterium visible to the human eye.*

2 **ADJECTIVE** You use **visible** to describe something or someone that people notice or recognize. ○ *The most visible sign of the intensity of the crisis is unemployment.* ○ *The cabinet is a highly visible symbol of the executive branch of the United States government.*

▶ **COLLOCATIONS:**
visible **to/from** *something*
barely/plainly/clearly/highly/very visible
less/more/still visible
a visible **sign/symbol/reminder/presence/manifestation**
make *something* visible

▶ **SYNONYMS:** clear, evident, noticeable

▶ **RELATED WORDS:** audible, tangible

vis|ibil|ity /vɪzɪbɪlɪti/

NONCOUNT NOUN **Visibility** means how far or how clearly you can see. ○ *Visibility was poor.*

▶ **COLLOCATIONS:**
reduce/increase/improve visibility
poor/good/high/low visibility

visi|tor /vɪzɪtər/ (visitors)   `PERSONNEL`

NOUN A **visitor** is someone who is visiting a person or place. ○ *We had some visitors from Milwaukee.*

▶ **COLLOCATIONS:**
invite/entertain/welcome/greet a visitor
a visitor **arrives/attends/stays** *somewhere*
a **special/uninvited/regular** visitor

▶ **SYNONYM:** guest

vi|tal /vaɪtᵊl/

ADJECTIVE If you say that something is **vital**, you mean that it is necessary or very important. ○ [+ *to*] *The port is vital to supply relief to millions of drought victims.* ○ *It is vital that records are kept.*

▶ **COLLOCATIONS:**
vital **to/for** *something*
vital **information**
a vital **role/service/contribution**
a vital **part/component/element/ingredient/link/organ**
strategically/politically/economically/absolutely vital

▶ **PHRASE:** of vital importance

▶ **SYNONYMS:** crucial, essential

viv|id /vɪvɪd/

ADJECTIVE If you describe memories and descriptions as **vivid**, you mean that they are very clear and detailed. ○ *The play is a vivid portrait of black America in 1969.* ○ *The poems are full of vivid imagery.*

▶ **COLLOCATIONS:**
a vivid **description/portrait/portrayal**
vivid **imagery**
a vivid **memory/recollection/dream**

▶ **SYNONYMS:** clear, intense

V

vol|un|tary /vɒləntɛri/   `PERSONNEL`

1 ADJECTIVE Voluntary actions or activities are done because someone chooses to do them and not because they have been forced to do them. ○ *The program, due to begin next month, will be voluntary.*

▶ **COLLOCATIONS:**
voluntary **redundancy/retirement/euthanasia**
a voluntary **contribution/action/program/test/course**

▶ **SYNONYM:** optional

2 ADJECTIVE Voluntary work is done by people who are not paid for it, but who do it because they want to do it. ○ *charities and voluntary organizations* ○ *He'd been working at the local hostel for the homeless on a voluntary basis.*

▶ **COLLOCATIONS:**
a voluntary **organization/group**
voluntary **work**
the voluntary **sector**

▶ **PHRASE:** on a voluntary basis

▶ **SYNONYM:** charitable

---

vul|ner|able /vʌlnərəbəl/

1 ADJECTIVE Someone who is **vulnerable** is weak and without protection, with the result that they are easily hurt physically or emotionally. ○ *Old people are particularly vulnerable members of our society.*

2 ADJECTIVE If someone or something is **vulnerable to** something, they have some weakness or disadvantage which makes them more likely to be harmed or affected by that thing. ○ *[+ to] People with high blood pressure are especially vulnerable to diabetes.*

▶ **COLLOCATIONS:**
vulnerable **to** *something*
vulnerable to **attack/damage/fire**
vulnerable **children/women/people**
a vulnerable **position**
especially/highly/increasingly vulnerable
become/remain vulnerable

▶ **SYNONYMS:** weak, prone, susceptible, exposed

v

Ww

---

wage /weɪdʒ/ **(wages)**　　

NOUN Someone's **wages** are the amount of money that is regularly paid to them for the work that they do. ○ *His wages have gone up.* ○ *This may end efforts to set a minimum wage well above the poverty line.*

▶ **COLLOCATIONS:**
  earn/pay/raise/increase/cut wages
  a wage **increase/cut**
  a **low/high/basic/minimum** wage
  a wage **demand/earner**

▶ **SYNONYMS:** salary, pay, earnings, income

Wall Street /wɔl striːt/　　

NOUN **Wall Street** is a street in New York where the Stock Exchange and important banks are. **Wall Street** is often used to refer to the financial business carried out there and to the people who work there. ○ *On Wall Street, stocks closed at their second highest level today.* ○ *Wall Street seems to be ignoring the fact that consumers are spending less.*

▶ **COLLOCATIONS:** a Wall Street **broker/trader/banker/lawyer/firm**

▶ **PHRASES:**
  on Wall Street
  the Wall Street crash

---

ware|house /wɛərhaʊs/ **(warehouses)**　　

NOUN A **warehouse** is a large building where goods are stored before they are sold. ○ *A big warehouse will deliver groceries to households throughout London.*

▶ **COLLOCATIONS:**
  a **bonded/wholesale** warehouse
  a **furniture/tobacco/chemical** warehouse

build/convert/abandon a warehouse
a warehouse **building/complex/facility**

---

war|ran|ty /wɔrənti/ (warranties)　　LOGISTICS & DISTRIBUTION

NOUN A **warranty** is a promise by a company that if you find a fault in
something they have sold you, they will repair it or replace it. ○ *The TV
comes with a twelve-month warranty.* ○ *The equipment is still under warranty.*

▶ **COLLOCATIONS:**
a warranty **expires/runs out**
a warranty **covers** *something*
offer/extend/provide a warranty
a **lifetime** warranty
a **basic/extended/limited** warranty

▶ **PHRASES:**
under warranty
breach of warranty

---

wealthy /wɛlθi/ (wealthier, wealthiest)

ADJECTIVE Someone who is **wealthy** has a large amount of money,
property, or valuable possessions. ○ *a wealthy international businessman*

▶ **COLLOCATIONS:**
fabulously/extremely/very/relatively wealthy
a wealthy **businessman/individual/nation/family**
a wealthy **landowner/donor/client**

▶ **SYNONYMS:** affluent, well-off, rich

---

weath|er /wɛðər/

NONCOUNT NOUN The **weather** is the temperature and conditions
outside, for example if it is raining, hot, or windy. ○ *I like cold weather.*

▶ **COLLOCATIONS:**
cold/warm/mild/beautiful/perfect/terrible/freezing weather
the weather **improves/clears up**
a weather **forecast/report/forecaster**
predict/forecast the weather

▶ **PHRASES:**
How is the weather?
What's the weather?

w

web|site /wɛbsaɪt/ (websites) also **web site** `COMMUNICATIONS`

NOUN A **website** is a set of information about a particular subject that is available on the Internet. ○ *Every time you visit a website, you leave a record showing you were there.*

▶ **COLLOCATIONS:**
launch/create/build/design/run a website
visit/access a website
an **official/personal** website
a **news/travel/financial/government** website

weigh /weɪ/ (weighs, weighing, weighed)

1 VERB If someone or something **weighs** a particular amount, this amount is how heavy they are. ○ *It weighs nearly 27 kilos (about 65 pounds).* ○ *This little ball of gold weighs a quarter of an ounce.*

▶ **COLLOCATIONS:**
weigh **exactly/roughly** *an amount*
weigh **less than/more than** *an amount*
weigh *x* **pounds/ounces/kilos/tons**

2 VERB If you **weigh** something or someone, you measure how heavy they are. ○ *The scales can be used to weigh other items such as packages.* ○ *Each sample was accurately weighed.*

▶ **COLLOCATIONS:** weigh *something* **carefully/accurately**

▶ **SYNONYM:** measure

weight /weɪt/ (weights)

NOUN The **weight** of a person or thing is how heavy they are, measured in units such as ounces, pounds, or tons. ○ *What is your height and weight?* ○ *This reduced the weight of the load.* ○ *[+ of] Turkeys can reach enormous weights of up to 50 pounds.*

▶ **COLLOCATIONS:**
a weight **of** *an amount*
lose/gain/put on weight
weight **gain/loss**
body weight
excess/ideal/healthy/normal weight

▶ **PHRASE:** height and weight

W

well-known /wɛlnoʊn/

ADJECTIVE A **well-known** person or thing is famous or familiar. ○ *She was a very well-known author.*

▸ **COLLOCATIONS:** a well-known **author/celebrity/actor**

wheth|er /wɛðər/

CONJUNCTION You use **whether** when you are talking about a choice between two or more things. ○ *I have to decide whether or not to take the job.*

▸ **COLLOCATIONS:**
decide/see whether
whether *to do something*

▸ **PHRASE:** whether or not

whole|sale /hoʊlseɪl/　　　LOGISTICS & DISTRIBUTION

NONCOUNT NOUN Wholesale is the activity of buying and selling goods in large quantities and therefore at cheaper prices, usually to stores who then sell them to the public. ○ *Warehouse clubs allow members to buy goods at wholesale prices.*

▸ **COLLOCATIONS:**
a wholesale **price/merchant/dealer/business**
a wholesale **distributor/customer**
the wholesale **market**

● **Wholesale** is also an adverb. ○ *The fabrics are sold wholesale to retailers, fashion houses, and other manufacturers.*

▸ **COLLOCATIONS:** **sell/buy** wholesale

▸ **RELATED WORD:** retail

wind|fall /wɪndfɔl/ **(windfalls)**　　　BANKING & FINANCE

NOUN A **windfall** is a sum of money that you receive unexpectedly. ○ *the man who received a $250,000 windfall after a banking error*

▸ **COLLOCATIONS:**
get/receive a windfall
an **unexpected** windfall

w

wire|less /ˈwaɪərlɪs/ `COMMUNICATIONS`

ADJECTIVE Wireless technology uses radio waves rather than electricity and therefore does not require any wires. ○ *the fast-growing wireless communication market* ○ *transmitting data across a wireless network* ○ *The company is going wireless.*

▶ **COLLOCATIONS:**
  a wireless **phone/telephone/device**
  a wireless **frequency/signal/zone**
  a wireless **network/connection/infrastructure**
  wireless **applications/equipment**
  wireless **communications/systems/technology**
  go wireless

with|draw /wɪðˈdrɔː, wɪθ-/ (withdraws, `BANKING & FINANCE`
withdrawing, withdrew, withdrawn)

1 VERB If you **withdraw** something, you remove it or take it away.
[FORMAL] ○ *The university rarely withdraws offers of admission.* ○ *government plans to withdraw financial support*

2 VERB If you **withdraw from** an activity or organization, you stop taking part in it. ○ [+ *from*] *The African National Congress threatened to withdraw from the talks.* ○ [+ *from*] *The team has withdrawn from the tournament due to high cost of travel.*

▶ **COLLOCATIONS:**
  withdraw *something* **from** *something*
  withdraw from a **treaty/tournament/race**
  withdraw from **participation/talks**
  withdraw **support/funding**
  withdraw a **request/offer**
  hastily/gradually/temporarily withdraw

▶ **SYNONYM:** remove

with|draw|al /wɪðˈdrɔːəl, wɪθ-/ (withdrawals)

1 NOUN The **withdrawal of** something is the act or process of removing it, or ending it. [FORMAL] ○ [+ *of*] *If you experience any unusual symptoms after withdrawal of the treatment then contact your doctor.*

2 NONCOUNT NOUN Someone's **withdrawal from** an activity or an organization is their decision to stop taking part in it. ○ *his withdrawal from government in 1946*

W

► COLLOCATIONS:
withdrawal **of/from** *something*
withdrawal of **support**

► SYNONYM: removal

---

work|place /wɜrkpleɪs/ (workplaces) `OFFICE`
also **work place**

NOUN Your **workplace** is the place where you work. ○ *the difficulties facing women in the workplace* ○ *Workplace cafeterias are offering healthier foods than ever before.*

► COLLOCATIONS:
in the workplace
workplace **safety/agreements**
a workplace **cafeteria**
a **modern/family-friendly/safe** workplace

---

work|shop /wɜrkʃɒp/ (workshops) `PERSONNEL`

NOUN A **workshop** is a period of discussion or practical work on a particular subject in which a group of people share their knowledge or experience.
○ [+ *for*] *Trumpeter Marcus Belgrave ran a jazz workshop for young artists.*
○ *a one-day performance evaluation workshop* ○ [+ *on*] *Students attend a variety of workshops on topics ranging from public speaking to managing stress.*

► COLLOCATIONS:
a workshop **for** *people*
a workshop **on** *something*
a workshop for **beginners/adults/children/teachers**
a workshop on a **topic/subject**
hold/run/conduct/attend a workshop
a **one-day/two-day/intensive** workshop
a **practical/hands-on/interactive** workshop

► SYNONYMS: seminar, master class, tutorial

World Wide Web /wɜrld waɪd wɛb/ `COMMUNICATIONS`

NOUN The **World Wide Web** is a computer system that allows you to see information from all over the world on your computer. ○ *the rapid growth in the use of the World Wide Web* ○ *Buyers spotted her ads on the World Wide Web.*

► COLLOCATIONS: **surf/browse/access** the World Wide Web

► RELATED WORD: Internet

worth|while /wɜrθwaɪl/

ADJECTIVE If something is **worthwhile**, it is enjoyable or useful, and worth the time, money, or effort that is spent on it. ○ *The President's trip to Washington this week seems to have been worthwhile.* ○ *an interesting and worthwhile project* ○ [+ to-inf] *It might be worthwhile to consider an insurance policy.*

▶ **COLLOCATIONS:**
the **sacrifice/effort/exercise/work** is worthwhile
a worthwhile **endeavor/cause/project/initiative/exercise**
a worthwhile **investment/contribution/addition/improvement**
financially worthwhile

▶ **SYNONYMS:** useful, helpful, valuable

W

Word lists

Organizations

company (noun)
conglomerate (noun)
corporate (adj)
corporation (noun)
enterprise (noun)
establish (verb)
  establishment (noun)
firm (noun)
institute (noun)
  institution (noun)
organize (verb)
  organized (adj)
  organization (noncount, noun)

Sectors

agricultural (adj)
commerce (noncount)
  commercial (adj)
factory (noun)
industry (noncount, noun)
  industrial (adj)
manufacture (verb)
  manufacturer (noun)
  manufacturing (noncount)
private sector (noun)
privatize (verb)
sector (noun)
services (plural)

Structure

committee (noun)
founder (noun)
franchise (noun, verb)
joint venture (noun)
merge (verb)
  merger (noun)
multinational (adj, noun)
network (noun)
owner (noun)
  ownership (noncount)
parent company (noun)
partner (noun)
  partnership (noun)
private company (noun)
stand-alone (adj)
structure (noncount, verb)
subcontract (verb)
  subcontractor (noun)
subsidiary (adj, noun)
takeover (noun)

Import-export

bill of lading (noun)
customs (noun)
export (noun, verb)
import (noncount, noun, verb)
shipment (noun)

Orders & distribution

deliver (verb)
  delivery (noun)
distribute (verb)
  distribution (noncount, noun)
overdue (adj)
reorder (verb)
resale (noncount)
reschedule (verb)
transport (verb)
  transportation (noncount)
warehouse (noun)
wholesale (adv, noncount)
warranty (noun)

Structure

agent (noun)
infrastructure (noun)
in-house (adj, adv)

merchant (noun)
middleman (noun)
operate (verb)
  operational (adj)
  operating budget (noun)
outlet (noun)
outsource (verb)
overhead (noncount)
rent (noncount)

Supply

glut (noun)
inventory (noun)
overcapacity (noncount)
quota (noun)
raw materials (plural)
resource (noun)
shortage (noun)
shutdown (noun)
supply (noncount, noun, verb)
surplus (noun)

Finance

asset (noun, plural)

bankrupt (adj)
  bankruptcy (noncount)

billable (adj)

borrow (verb)
  borrower (noun)

buyout (noun)

capital (noncount, noun)
  capitalize (verb)

commission (noncount, noun, verb)

cost-effective (adj)

counteroffer (noun)

debt (noncount, noun)

deduct (verb)

depreciate (verb)
  depreciation (noun)

donate (verb)
  donation (noun)

down payment (noun)

figure (noun)

finance (noncount)
  financial (adj)

foreclosure (noun)

fortune (noun)

fund (plural, verb)

installment (noun)

leverage (noncount)

liability (noncount)

line of credit (noun)

liquidate (verb)
  liquidation (noun)

lose (verb)
  loss (noun)

lucrative (adj)

lump sum (noun)

mortgage (noun)
  mortgage rate (noun)

payable (adj)

payment (noncount, noun)

proceeds (plural)

receive (verb)
  receipt (noun)

refinancing (noncount)

repay (verb)
  repayment (noncount)

retrench (verb)

royalty (plural)

subsidy (noun)
  subsidize (verb)

surcharge (noun)

value (noncount, noun, plural, verb)
  valuable (adj)

windfall (noun)

Accounting

account (noun)
  accounting (noncount)

balance (noun, verb)
  balanced (adj)
  balance sheet (noun)

bookkeeping (noncount)
  bookkeeper (noun)

breakeven point (noun)

budget (noun, verb)

cash flow (noncount)

comptroller (noun)

deficit (noun)

expenditure (noncount)

expense (noncount, plural)
  expensive (adj)
  expense account (noun)

profit (noun, verb)
profitable (adj)
quarter (noun)
quarterly (adj)
turnover (noun)

Banking

bank account (noun)
blank check (noun)
charge (noun, verb)
charge card (noun)
checking account (noun)
collateral (noncount)
credit (noncount)
credit card (noun)
debit (verb)
debit card (noun)
deposit (noun, verb)
interest (noncount, noun, verb)
interest rate (noun)
letter of credit (noun)
overdraft (noun)
prime (adj)
prime rate (noun)
withdraw (verb)
withdrawal (noncount, noun)

Currency

currency (noun)
dollar (noun)
euro (noun)
exchange (verb)
exchange rate (noun)
foreign (adj)
foreign exchange (noncount, plural)

monetary (adj)

Economics

boom (noun, verb)
bubble (noun)
depressed (adj)
downturn (noun)
economy (noun)
economical (adj)
economically (adv)
fiscal (adj)
GDP (noun)
GNP (noun)
inflation (noncount)
law of supply and demand
(noncount)
meltdown (noncount)
per capita (adj)
recession (noun)
slowdown (noun)
turnaround (noun)
upturn (noun)

Insurance

insurance (noncount)
policy (noun)
policyholder (noun)
premium (noun)

Investment

bear market (noun)
bondholder (noun)
bricks and mortar (noncount)

bull market (noun)
buyer's market (noun)
closing price (noun)
commodity (noun)
dividend (noun)
Dow Jones average (noun)
invest (verb)
   investment (noncount, noun)
   investor (noun)
Nikkei Stock Average (noncount)
stock (noncount, noun)
   stock exchange (noun)
   stock market (noun)
venture (noun)
   venture capital (noncount)
Wall Street (noun)

Taxes

deductible (adj, noun)
duty (noun)
rebate (noun)
surtax (noncount)
tariff (noun)
taxation (noncount)
   taxable (adj)

General

compensate (verb)
  compensation (noncount)
comply (verb)
copyright (noun)
deregulate (verb)
  deregulation (noncount)
enforce (verb)
  enforcement (noncount)
illegal (adj)
lawyer (noun)
legal (adj)
  legalize (verb)
legitimate (adj)
offense (noun)
  offend (verb)
penalty (noun)
regulate (verb)
  regulation (noncount)
  regulatory (adj)
revoke (verb)
treaty (noun)

Marketing

advertise (verb)
  advertisement (noun)
  advertising agency (noun)
brand (noun)
  brand loyalty (noncount)
  brand name (noun)
  brand-new (adj)
  brand recognition (noncount)
brochure (noun)
campaign (noun, verb)
catalog (verb)
endorse (verb)
  endorsement (noun)
exhibit (verb)
  exhibition (noun)
image (noun)
launch (noun, verb)
logo (noun)
publicity (noncount)
sponsor (noun, verb)
telemarketing (noncount)

Markets

captive market (noun)
client (noun)
consumer behavior (noncount)
consumerism (noncount)
customer (noun)
  customer service (noncount)
demand (noncount)
demographic (adj, noun, plural)
domestic (adj)
  domestic market (noun)

emerge (verb)
  emerging market (noun)
global (adj)
  global market (noun)
market (noun, verb)
  marketable (adj)
  marketplace (noun)
  market research (noncount)
  market sector (noun)
  market value (noun)
monopolize (verb)
niche market (noun)
target (noun, verb)
  target market (noun)

Prices

affordable (adj)
bargain (noun)
discount (verb)
list price (noun)
markdown (noun)
overcharge (verb)

Sales

bar code (noun)
best-seller (noun)
  best-selling (adj)
mail order (noncount)
merchandise (noncount)
money-maker (noun)
nonrefundable (adj)
online (adj)
  online shopping (noncount)
package (noun, verb)

product (noun)
purchase (noun, verb)
retail (noncount)
sales figures (plural)
sales tax (noun)
salesperson (noun)

Business planning

benchmark (noun)
business cycle (noun)
business model (noun)
business objective (noun)
business plan (noun)
competition (noncount)
  competitor (noun)
diversify (verb)
  diversification (noun)
dominate (verb)
  dominant (adj)
expand (verb)
  expansion (noncount)
forecast (noun, verb)
implement (verb)
  implementation (noncount)
improve (verb)
  improvement (noun)
model (noun, verb)
outlook (noun)
project (noun, verb)
  projection (noun)
strategy (noun)
  strategic (adj)
  strategically (adv)
sustain (verb)
  sustainable (adj)
  sustainability (noncount)
troubleshooting (noncount)

Innovation

devise (verb)
innovation (noncount, noun)
  innovative (adj)
modern (adj)
  modernize (verb)

obsolete (adj)
origin (noun)
  original (adj)
  originally (adv)
  originate (verb)
start-up (adj, noun)

Research

advance (noun, verb)
  advanced (adj)
breakthrough (noun)
develop (verb)
  developed (adj)
  developing (adj)
  development (noun)
  developmental (adj)
device (noun)
discovery (noun)
formula (noun)
  formulate (verb)
gadget (noun)
high-tech (adj)
hybrid (noun)
instrument (noun)
invent (verb)
  invention (noun)
laboratory (noun)
leading edge (noun)
patent (noun, verb)
research (noncount, verb)
  research and development (noncount)
sample (noun)
scientific
spectrum (noun)
technique (noun)
technology (noun)

Management

board of directors (noun)
CEO (noun)
CFO (noun)
chairperson (noun)
chief executive officer (noun)
chief financial officer (noun)
director (noun)
executive (noun)
manage (verb)
   managing (adj)
   management (noncount, noun)
   manager (noun)
   managerial (adj)
senior (adj)
superior (adj)
   superiority (noncount)
top management (noncount)

Professions

architect (noun)
diplomat (noun)
electrician (noun)
engineer (noun)
professional (adj)

Roles

administrative (adj)
   administrative assistant (noun)
coach (verb)
consult (verb)
   consultant (noun)
   consultation (noun)
entrepreneur (noun)
   entrepreneurial (adj)
expert (noun)
   expertise (noncount)
instructor (noun)
manual (adj)
messenger (noun)
receptionist (noun)
spokesperson (noun)
superintendent (noun)
technical (adj)
   technician (noun)

People

colleague (noun)
co-worker (noun)
delegate (noun, verb)
  delegation (noncount)
predecessor (noun)
supervise (verb)
  supervision (noncount)
  supervisor (noun)
visitor (noun)

Recruitment

apply (verb)
  applicant (noun)
  application (noun)
  application form (noun)
candidate (noun)
entry-level (adj)
interview (noun, verb)
job description (noun)
portfolio (noun)
position (noun)
recruit (verb)
  recruitment (noncount)
résumé (noun)
retain (verb)
  retention (noncount)
shortlist (noun, verb)
vacant (adj)
  vacancy (noun)

Skills

competence (noncount)
  competent (adj)

experience (noncount, noun, verb)
  experienced (adj)
leadership (noun)
overqualified (adj)
qualify (verb)
  qualification (noun)
semi-skilled (adj)
skill (noun)
  skillful (adj)
talent (noncount)
  talented (adj)
teamwork (noncount)

Training

apprenticeship (noun)
in-service (adj)
intern (noun, verb)
  internship (noun)
on-the-job training (noncount)
seminar (noun)
workshop (noun)

Career development

career (noun)
downgrade (verb)
occupation (noun)
  occupational (adj)
promote (verb)
  promotion (noncount)
responsible (adj)
  responsibility (noncount, plural)

Remuneration

basic wage (noun)
living wage (noun)
minimum (adj, noun)
  minimum wage (noun)
paycheck (noun)
payday (noun)
payroll (noun)
remuneration (noun)
salary (noun)
wage (noun)

HR

best practice (noncount, plural)
confidential (adj)
  confidentiality (noncount)
department (noun)
  departmental (adj)
human resources (noncount)
official (adj, noun)
relocate (verb)
  relocation (noncount)
safety (noncount)
schedule (noun)
stoppage (noun)

Staffing

employ (verb)
  employee (noun)
  employment (noncount)
labor (noncount)
  labor force (noun)
  labor-intensive (adj)
manpower (noncount)

overstaffed (adj)
personnel (plural)
self-employed (adj)
short-handed (adj)
unemployed (adj)
  unemployment (noncount)

Terms & conditions

absent (adj)
  absence (noun)
benefit (noun, verb)
  benefits package (noun)
contract (noun, verb)
dress code (noun)
leave of absence (noun)
moonlight (verb)
  moonlighting (noncount)
nine-to-five job (noun)
overtime (adv)
part-time (adj, adv)
permanent (adj)
temporary (adj)
  temporarily (adv)
vacation (noun)
voluntary (adj)

Leaving

dismiss (verb)
  dismissal (noncount)
downsize (verb)
  downsizing (noncount)
layoff (noun)
pension (noun)
  pension plan (noun)
pink slip (noun)

quit (verb)
resign (verb)
    resignation (noun)
retire (verb)
    retired (adj)
    retirement (noncount)
severance pay (noncount)

Building

access (noncount, verb)
  accessible (adj)
boardroom (noun)
cafeteria (noun)
elevator (noun)
entrance (noun)
escalator (noun)
facility (noun)
lobby (noun)
office (noun)
parking lot (noun)
workplace (noun)

Office supplies

briefcase (noun)
bulletin board (noun)
calculator (noun)
calendar (noun)
diary (noun)
drawer (noun)
envelope (noun)
equipment (noncount)
machinery (noncount)

IT

CD-ROM (noun)
compact disc (noun)
computer (noun)
disk (noun)
  disk drive (noun)
document (noun, verb)
download (noun, verb)
DVD (noun)
file (noun)
flash drive (noun)
floppy disk (noun)
hard drive (noun)
memory (noun)
  memory stick (noun)
personal computer (noun)
printer (noun)
software (noncount)
spreadsheet (noun)

Meetings & conferences

arrangement (noun)
assembly (noncount, noun)
attendance (noncount, noun)
auditorium (noun)
conference (noun)
meeting (noun)
microphone (noun)
participate (verb)
  participation (noncount)
  participant (noun)
platform (noun)
present (adj, noun, verb)
  presentation (noun)
rehearse (verb)
venue (noun)

Tasks

bureaucracy (noncount)
  bureaucratic (adj)
deadline (noun)
paperwork (noncount)
photocopy (noun, verb)

General

advice (noncount)
translate (verb)
  translation (noncount)

Correspondence

abbreviate (verb)
  abbreviation (noun)
apologize (verb)
attach (verb)
  attachment (noun)
clarify (verb)
complaint (noun)
confirm (verb)
  confirmation (noncount)
congratulate (verb)
  congratulations
contact (noncount, verb)
cover letter (noun)
cut and paste (verb)
dictate (verb)
draft (noun)
inform (verb)
inquire (verb)
  inquiry (noun)
paragraph (noun)
request (noun, verb)
signature (noun)
submit (verb)

Discussion

accent (noun)
comment (noun, verb)
debate (noun, verb)

discuss (verb)
  discussion (noun)
explain (verb)
  explanation (noun)
express (verb)
suggestion (noun)

Information

access (noncount, verb)
  accessible (adj)
according to
bar graph (noun)
data (noncount)
diagram (noun)
graphics (plural)
information (noncount)
  informative (adj)

Means of communication

announcement (noun)
blog (noun)
cellphone (noun)
communicate (verb)
  communication (noncount, plural)
conference call (noun)
disconnect (verb)
email (noncount, noun, verb)
fax (noun)
feedback (noncount)
forward (verb)
handshake (noun)
instant messaging (noncount)
Internet (noun)

junk mail (noncount)
media (noun)
medium (noun)
memo (noun)
message (noun)
multimedia (adj, noncount)
newsletter (noun)
newspaper (noun)
pamphlet (noun)
phone call (noun)
publication (noncount, noun)
publish (verb)
   publisher (noun)
search engine (noun)
statement (noun)
summary (noun)
   summarize (verb)
teleconference (noun)
telegram (noun)
text message (noun)
video conferencing (noncount)
website (noun)
wireless (adj)
World Wide Web (noun)

General

accommodate (verb)
accommodations (plural)
car pool (noun, verb)
commute (verb)
commuter (noun)
driver's license (noun)
hotel (noun)
sightseeing (noncount)
time zone (noun)
travel (verb)
traveler's check (noun)

Foreign travel

abroad (adv)
airport (noun)
baggage (noncount)
departure (noun)
jet lag (noncount)
lounge (noun)
luggage (noncount)
overseas (adj)
passport (noun)

General

casualty (noun)

diagnose (verb)
  diagnosis (noun)

diet (noun)

health care (noncount)

injury (noun)

patient (noun)

prescription (noun)

recover (verb)
  recovery (noun)

remedy (noun)

side-effect (noun)

stress (noncount, noun, verb)
  stressful (adj)

treatment (noncount, noun)

Actions

accompany (verb)
acquire (verb)
   acquisition (noncount, noun)
analyze (verb)
   analysis (noun)
assist (verb)
   assistance (noncount)
authorize (verb)
behave (verb)
   behavior (noncount)
capture (noncount, verb)
certify (verb)
   certificate (noun)
combine (verb)
   combination (noun)
commit (verb)
   commitment (noun)
conceal (verb)
conduct (verb)
conserve (verb)
contribute (verb)
   contribution (noun)
control (noncount, verb)
deal (noun)
   dealings (plural)
deceive (verb)
   deception (noncount)
defend (verb)
   defense (noun)
demonstrate (verb)
   demonstration (noun)
deprive (verb)
   deprivation (noun)
detect (verb)
   detection (noncount)

discard (verb)
discharge (noun, verb)
disrupt (verb)
   disruption (noun)
disturb (verb)
   disturbance (noncount)
divide (verb)
dodge (verb)
enclose (verb)
engage (verb)
enroll (verb)
errand (noun)
execute (verb)
   execution (noncount)
exercise (noun)
gather (verb)
generate (verb)
imitate (verb)
   imitation (noun)
impose (verb)
   imposition (noncount)
input (noun, verb)
insert (verb)
inspect (verb)
   inspection (noun)
interact (verb)
   interactive (adj)
interfere (verb)
   interference (noncount)
investigate (verb)
isolate (verb)
   isolation (noncount)
mass-produce (verb)
   mass-produced (adj)
   mass production (noncount)
method (noun)
monitor (noun, verb)

note (noun, verb)
  notable (adj)
notice (verb)
  noticeable (adj)
observe (verb)
  observation (noncount)
obtain (verb)
occupy (verb)
  occupied (adj)
  occupancy (noncount)
  occupant (noun)
omit (verb)
optimize (verb)
overcome (verb)
overlook (verb)
participate (verb)
  participation (noncount)
  participant (noun)
perform (verb)
  performance (noun)
practice (noun, verb)
prepared (adj)
  preparation (noncount, plural)
preserve (verb)
procedure (noun)
  procedural (adj)
provide (verb)
  provided (conj)
pursue (verb)
  pursuit (noncount)
recognize (verb)
  recognition (noncount)
recycle (verb)
register (verb)
  registration (noncount)
reject (verb)
  rejection (noncount)

release (noun, verb)
relinquish (verb)
rely (verb)
  reliable (adj)
  reliability (noncount)
remove (verb)
  removal (noncount)
renew (verb)
  renewable (adj)
  renewal (noun)
repeat (verb)
  repetition (noncount, noun)
replace (verb)
  replacement (noncount)
retrieve (verb)
  retrieval (noncount)
return (noun)
reunite (verb)
reveal (verb)
reverse (adj, verb)
  reversal (noun)
revise (verb)
  revision (noun)
rework (verb)
sacrifice (noun, verb)
scrutinize (verb)
sharpen (verb)
simplify (verb)
simulate (verb)
  simulation (noun)
subscribe (verb)
substitute (noun, verb)
  substitution (noun)
task (noun)
tighten (verb)
utilize (verb)

States & processes

deserve (verb)
display (noun, verb)
effect (noun)
encounter (verb)
fare (verb)
indicate (verb)
loom (verb)
outweigh (verb)
reflect (verb)
    reflection (noncount, noun)
represent (verb)
    representation (noncount)
    representative (adj, noun)
revolve (verb)

absorb (verb)
condense (verb)
drain (verb)
exposure (noncount)
fade (verb)
    faded (adj)
function (noun, verb)
    functional (adj)
integrate (verb)
    integration (noncount)
occur (verb)
    occurrence (noun)
penetrate (verb)
    penetration (noncount)
process (noun)
reinforce (verb)
saturated (adj)
    saturation (noncount)
stretch (verb)

transmit (verb)
undergo (verb)

background (noun)
circumstance (noun, plural)
    circumstantial (adj)
condition (noun, plural)
default (adj, noncount)
empty (adj)
incident (noun)
instance (noun)
present (adj, noun, verb)
    presence (noncount)
privacy (noncount)

maintain (verb)
    maintenance (noncount)
prevail (verb)
    prevalent (adj)
    prevalence (noncount)
recur (verb)
remain (verb)
    remaining (adj)

belong (verb)
inherit (verb)
possess (verb)
    possession (noncount, noun)

Change

adapt (verb)
    adaptability (noncount)
    adaptation (noncount)
adjust (verb)
    adjustment (noun)

adopt (verb)
  adoption (noncount)
alter (verb)
  alteration (noun)
convert (verb)
customize (verb)
fluctuate (verb)
  fluctuation (noun)
innovation (noncount, noun)
  innovative (adj)
manipulate (verb)
modern (adj)
  modernize (verb)
modify (verb)
  modification (noun)
shift (noun, verb)
transform (verb)
  transformation (noun)
trend (noun)
update (verb)
upgrade (verb)

extend (verb)
  extension (noncount)
  extensive (adj)
  extent (noun)
heighten (verb)
increase (noun, verb)
  increasingly (adv)
magnify (verb)
  magnification (noncount, noun)
raise (verb)
stimulate (verb)
  stimulation (noncount)
  stimulus (noun)
strength (noncount)
  strengthen (verb)
stretch (verb)
supplement (noun, verb)
  supplementary (adj)
upturn (noun)

Increasing

accelerate (verb)
accumulate (verb)
  accumulation (noun)
augment (verb)
  augmentation (noncount)
boom (noun, verb)
broaden (verb)
deepen (verb)
enlarge (verb)
exaggerate (verb)
  exaggeration (noun)
expand (verb)
  expansion (noncount)

Decreasing

decline (noun, verb)
decrease (noun, verb)
deduct (verb)
deplete (verb)
depreciate (verb)
  depreciation (noun)
deteriorate (verb)
  deterioration (noncount)
diminish (verb)
downsize (verb)
  downsizing (noncount)
downturn (noun)
lose (verb)
  loss (noun)
minimize (verb)

plummet (verb)
reduce (verb)
  reduction (noun)
shrink (verb)
slowdown (noun)
subtract (verb)
  subtraction (noun)

Stopping

abandon (verb)
cancel (verb)
  cancellation (noun)
cease (verb)
dispose (verb)
  disposable (adj)
  disposal (noncount)
eliminate (verb)
  elimination (noncount)
quit (verb)
suspend (verb)

impede (verb)
  impediment (noun)
obstruct (verb)
prevent (verb)
  prevention (noncount)
prohibit (verb)
restrain (verb)
restrict (verb)
  restriction (noun)

Mental processes

appreciate (verb)
  appreciation (noun)

assess (verb)
  assessment (noun)
assume (verb)
  assumption (noun)
awareness (noncount)
believe (verb)
comprehend (verb)
conceive (verb)
contemplate (verb)
  contemplation (noncount)
dedicate (verb)
  dedication (noun)
deduce (verb)
determine (verb)
  determination (noncount)
  determined (adj)
disregard (noncount, verb)
distinguish (verb)
distract (verb)
  distraction (noun)
evaluate (verb)
  evaluation (noun)
expect (verb)
  expectations (plural)
guarantee (noun, verb)
identify (verb)
  identification (noncount)
imagine (verb)
  imagination (noun)
intend (verb)
  intent (adj, noun)
  intentional (adj)
perceive (verb)
  perception (noun)
ponder (verb)
presume (verb)
  presumably (adv)

realize (verb)
re-evaluate (verb)
regard (verb)

Ideas & opinions

basis (noun)
concept (noun)
phenomenon (noun)
principle (noun)
underlying (adj)

approach (noun, verb)
bias (noun, verb)
  biased (adj)
conservative (adj)
impartial (adj)
  impartiality (noncount)
mainstream (noun)
opinion (noun)
perspective (noun)
radical (adj)
  radically (adv)
resistance (noncount)

Feelings & reactions

ambivalent (adj)
  ambivalence (noncount)
caution (noncount)
  cautious (adj)
cope (verb)
react (verb)
  reaction (noun)
surprise (adj, noun)
  surprising (adj)
temptation (noncount)

amazement (noncount)
attraction (noncount, noun)
delighted (adj)
devoted (adj)
enthusiasm (noncount)
positive (adj)
  positively (adv)
relieved (adj)
remarkable (adj)
satisfy (verb)
  satisfied (adj)
  satisfaction (noncount)
  satisfactory (adj)

anxious (adj)
confuse (verb)
  confused (adj)
  confusing (adj)
  confusion (noncount)
desperate (adj)
  desperately (adv)
disappoint (verb)
  disappointment (noncount)
impatient (adj)
  impatience (noncount)
negative (adj)
  negatively (adv)
offense (noun)
  offensive (adj, noun)
  offend (verb)
reluctant (adj)
  reluctance (noncount)
  reluctantly (adv)
tension (noncount)
unacceptable (adj)

Choices & decisions

assign (verb)
decide (verb)
  decision (noun)
  decision-making (noncount)
dilemma (noun)
elect (verb)
  election (noun)
nominate (verb)
  nomination (noun)
opt (verb)
option (noun)
  optional (adj)
prefer (verb)
  preferable (adj)
  preference (noun)
select (verb)
  selection (noncount, noun)
  selective (adj)

Speech & writing

assure (verb)
claim (noun, verb)
compliment (noun, verb)
contend (verb)
convey (verb)
convince (verb)
declare (verb)
define (verb)
definition (noun)
describe (verb)
  description (noun)
discourage (verb)
emphasis (noun)
  emphasize (verb)

encourage (verb)
  encouragement (noncount)
  encouraging (adj)
exaggerate (verb)
  exaggeration (noun)
highlight (verb)
illustrate (verb)
  illustration (noun)
imply (verb)
interruption (noncount)
introduction (noun)
  introductory (adj)
mention (verb)
misunderstand (verb)
negotiate (verb)
  negotiable (adj)
  negotiation (noun)
outline (noun)
persuade (verb)
promise (noun, verb)
propose (verb)
  proposal (noun)
  proposition (noun)
reassure (verb)
  reassurance (noncount)
recommend (verb)
  recommendation (noun)
refer (verb)
  reference (noun)
remind (verb)
stipulate (verb)
  stipulation (noun)
succinct (adj)
symbolic (adj)
  symbolize (verb)

fluent (adj)

interpret (verb)
  interpretation (noun)

present (adj, noun, verb)
  presentation (noun)

directory (noun)

e.g. (adv)

edition (noun)

index (noun)

label (noun, verb)

magazine (noun)

margin (noun)

passage (noun)

petition (noun, verb)

quote (noun, verb)

record (noun, verb)

report (noun, verb)
  reportedly (adv)

symbol (noun)

title (noun)

Agreement

accept (verb)
  acceptable (adj)
  acceptance (noncount, noun)

agreement (noncount)

compromise (noun, verb)

concede (verb)

concession (noun)

consensus (noun)

consent (noncount, verb)

cooperate (verb)
  cooperation (noncount)

coordinate (verb)
  coordination (noncount)

mutual (adj)

settle (verb)
  settlement (noun)

support (noncount, verb)

Disagreement

argument (noun)

clash (noun, verb)

conflict (noncount, noun, verb)

confront (verb)

contradict (verb)
  contradiction (noun)
  contradictory (adj)

contrary (adj)

critical (adj)

criticize (verb)
  criticism (noncount, noun)

deny (verb)

disagree (verb)
  disagreement (noncount, noun)

disapprove (verb)
  disapproval (noncount)

dispute (noun, verb)

object (noun, verb)
  objection (noun)

offense (noun)
  offensive (adj, noun)
  offend (verb)

oppose (verb)
  opposed (adj)
  opposing (adj)
  opposition (noncount)

resistance (noncount)

rivalry (noun)

Achievement

accomplish (verb)
accomplishment (noun)
achievement (noun)
championship (noun)
goal (noun)
incentive (noun)
inspiration (noncount)
motivate (verb)
motivated (adj)
motivation (noncount)
object (noun, verb)
objective (adj, noun)
opportunity (noun)
progress (noncount, verb)
reach (verb)
succeed (verb)
success (noncount)
successful (adj)
successfully (adv)

People

acquaintance (noun)
anonymous (adj)
celebrity (noun)
citizen (noun)
contingent (noun)
dignitary (noun)
finalist (noun)
individual (adj, noun)
inhabitant (noun)
member (noun)
membership (noncount)
native (adj)
novice (noun)

occupant (noun)
participant (noun)
pedestrian (adj)
population (noun)
resident (noun)
residence (noun)
residential (adj)
rivalry (noun)
society (noncount, noun)
spectator (noun)

Recreation

beverage (noun)
celebration (noun)
ceremony (noun)
lottery (noun)
makeup (noncount)
recreation (noncount)
restaurant (noun)

Education

academic (adj)
classroom (noun)
college (noun)
degree (noun)
dictionary (noun)
diploma (noun)
examine (verb)
examination (noun)
exam (noun)
grade (noun, verb)
seminar (noun)

Politics & issues

bureaucracy (noncount)
  bureaucratic (adj)
Cabinet (noun)
campaign (noun, verb)
elect (verb)
  election (noun)
embassy (noun)
endorse (verb)
  endorsement (noun)
government (noun)
nominate (verb)
  nomination (noun)
official (adj, noun)
party (noun)
represent (verb)
  representation (noncount)
  representative (adj, noun)

agenda (noun)
inflation (noncount)
policy (noun)
recession (noun)

conservative (adj)
controversy (noun)
  controversial (adj)
dilemma (noun)
mainstream (noun)
radical (adj)
  radically (adv)

Rules & regulations

allow (verb)
  allowable (adj)
  allowance (noun)

approve (verb)
  approval (noncount)
code (noun)
compel (verb)
comply (verb)
compulsory (adj)
condition (noun, plural)
deregulate (verb)
  deregulation (noncount)
disqualify (verb)
eligible (adj)
  eligibility (noncount)
enforce (verb)
  enforcement (noncount)
exclude (verb)
  excluding (prep)
  exclusion (noun)
  exclusive (adj)
license (noun)
obligation (noun)
oblige (verb)
  obligatory (adj)
permit (noun, verb)
  permission (noncount)
regulate (verb)
  regulation (noncount)
  regulatory (adj)
require (verb)
  requirement (noun)
standard (adj, noun)
  standardize (verb)
  standardization (noncount)
  standard of living (noun)
strict (adj)
  strictly (adv)

Problems & solutions

burden (noun)
challenge (noun, verb)
deficiency (noun)
defective (adj)
disaster (noun)
  disastrous (adj)
fail (verb)
  failure (noun)
mistake (noun, verb)
  mistaken (adj)
problem (noun)
struggle (noun, verb)

correction (noun)
recover (verb)
  recovery (noun)
remedy (noun)
repair (verb)
solve (verb)
  solution (noun)
troubleshooting (noncount)

Damage

accidental (adj)
breakdown (noun)
collide (verb)
  collision (noun)
crash (noun, verb)
damage (noncount, verb)
  damaging (adj)
defective (adj)
deficiency (noun)
demolish (verb)
  demolition (noun)

dent (verb)
destroy (verb)
  destruction (noncount)
deteriorate (verb)
  deterioration (noncount)
injury (noun)
jeopardy
  jeopardize (verb)
neglect (verb)
violate (verb)
  violation (noun)

Equipment

appliance (noun)
breakdown (noun)
device (noun)
digital (adj)
disconnect (verb)
electricity (noncount)
  electrical (adj)
equipment (noncount)
gadget (noun)
high-tech (adj)
instrument (noun)
machinery (noncount)
magnetic (adj)
magnify (verb)
  magnification (noncount, noun)
mechanism (noun)
  mechanical (adj)
nuclear (adj)
output (noncount)
photograph (noun, verb)
signal (noun)
technology (noun)

Natural world

climate (noun)
coastal (adj)
continent (noun)
   continental (adj)
desert (noun)
diamond (noun)
ecology (noncount)
environment (noun)
   environmental (adj)
host (noun)
nature (noncount, noun)
   natural (adj)
ocean (noun)
pollution (noncount)
solar (adj)
weather (noncount)

Objects

container (noun)
material (adj, noun, plural)
object (noun, verb)
property (noncount, noun)
real estate (noncount)
stack (noun)
substance (noun)
surface (noun)
vehicle (noun)

Position

adjacent (adj)
beneath (prep)
boundary (noun)

brink (noun)
elsewhere (adv)
external (adj)
indoors (adv)
internal (adj)
parallel (adj)
proximity (noncount)
scattered (adj)
situated (adj)
   situation (noun)
steep (adj)

Appearance

appearance (noun)
black and white (adj)
decorate (verb)
   decoration (noncount)
   decorative (adj)
delicate (adj)
distinctive (adj)
image (noun)
pattern (noun)
sphere (noun)

Location

abroad (adv)
district (noun)
foreign (adj)
international (adj)
local (adj)
locate (verb)
   located (adj)
   location (noun)
long-distance (adj)

metropolitan (adj)
municipal (adj)
national (adj)
  nationality (noun)
nationwide (adj)
overseas (adj)
region (noun)
remote (adj)
  remotely (adv)
surroundings (plural)
territory (noncount)
throughout (adv, prep)

column (noun)
component (noun)
detail (noun, plural)
element (noun)
example (noun)
feature (noun)
gap (noun)
installment (noun)
phase (noun)
portion (noun)
section (noun)
segment (noun)

Structure

compose (verb)
  composition (noncount)
miscellaneous (adj)
order (noun, verb)
separate (adj, verb)
  separately (adv)
source (noun)

collection (noncount, noun)
form (noun, verb)
format (noun)
framework (noun)
program (noun, verb)
scheme (noun)
series (noun)
system (noun)
  systematic (adj)

category (noun)
  categorize (verb)
classify (verb)
  classification (noncount)

Movement

circulate (verb)
  circulation (noncount)
distribute (verb)
  distribution (noncount, noun)
propel (verb)
rotate (verb)
  rotation (noun)
spread (verb)
transport (verb)
  transportation (noncount)
travel (verb)
clockwise (adv)
mobile (adj)
motion (noncount)
movement (noun)
sideways (adj, adv)
stationary (adj)

Measurements

centimeter (noun)
degree (noun)
dense (adj)
  density (noun)
depth (noun)
diameter (noun)
dimension (noun)
distance (noun)
length (noun)
  lengthy (adj)
magnitude (noncount)
measure (plural, verb)
  measurement (noun)
strength (noncount)
  strengthen (verb)
weigh (verb)
  weight (noun)

Numbers

calculate (verb)
  calculation (noun)
  calculator (noun)
digit (noun)
figure (noun)
minus (adj, Conj)
statistics (noncount, plural)
  statistical (adj)
value (noncount, noun, plural, verb)
eighteen (num)
eighty (num)
fifteen (num)
fifty (num)
forty (num)
fourteen (num)

nineteen (num)
ninety (num)
seventeen (num)
seventy (num)
sixteen (num)
sixty (num)
thirteen (num)
thirty (num)
twenty (num)
  twentieth (adj, adv)

Size & amount

approximate (adj, verb)
  approximately (adv)
capacity (noncount, noun)
equal (adj, verb)
precise (adj)
  precisely (adv)
underestimate (verb)

dozen (quant)
multiple (adj)
  multiply (verb)
percent (noun)
  percentage (noun)
proportion (noun)
range (noun, verb)
ratio (noun)
triple (adj, verb)

ample (adj)
bulk (quant)
concentration (noncount, noun)
considerable (adj)
  considerably (adv)
extreme (adj)
  extremely (adv)

inordinate (adj)
maximum (adj, noun)
  maximize (verb)
numerous (adj)
substantial (adj)

exceed (verb)
  excess (noun)
extra (adj)
additional (adj)
reserve (noun)

average (adj, noun)
sufficient (adj)

barely (adv)
deficiency (noun)
insignificant (adj)
insufficient (adj)
lack (noncount, verb)
minimal (adj)
negligible (adj)
nominal (adj)
singular (adj, noun)
sole (adj)
  solely (adv)

compact (adj)
miniature (adj)
minute (adj)
vast (adj)

Degree

absolutely (adv)
appreciable (adj)

definite (adj)
  definitely (adv)
dramatic (adj)
  dramatically (adv)
drastic (adj)
entirely (adv)
extensive (adj)
  extent (noun)
indeed (adv)
intense (adj)
largely (adv)
really (adv)

basically (adv)
comparative (adj)
  comparatively (adv)
limit (noun, verb)
  limited (adj)
moderate (adj)
  moderately (adv)
partial (adj)
  partially (adv)
rather (conj)
tentative (adj)
virtual (adj)

generally (adv)
  generalize (verb)
  generalization (noun)
overall (adj)
particular (adj)
  particularly (adv)
specific (adj)
  specifically (adv)
  specify (verb)
universal (adj)

Importance

crucial (adj)
essential (adj)
fundamental (adj)
important (adj)
  importance (noncount)
major (adj)
  majority (noun)
necessary (adj)
  necessarily (adv)
  necessity (noun)
primary (adj)
  primarily (adv)
principal (adj)
priority (noun)
  prioritize (verb)
prominent (adj)
relevant (adj)
  relevance (noncount)
serious (adj)
  seriousness (noncount)

significance (noncount)
  significant (adj)

special (adj)
  specialize (verb)
  specialty (noun)
vital (adj)

minor (adj)
  minority (noun)
secondary (adj)
unnecessary (adj)

Linking words

besides (prep)
except (prep)
  exception (noun)
  exceptional (adj)
however (adv)
moreover (adv)
nevertheless (adv)
nonetheless (adv)
otherwise (adv)
whether (conj)

Links & connections

affect (verb)
concern (verb)
  concerned (adj)
  concerning (prep)
connect (verb)
  connection (noun)
consequence (noun)
  consequently (adv)
corresponding (adj)
effect (noun)
impact (noun, verb)
influence (noun, verb)
  influential (adj)
involve (verb)
joint (adj)
link (noun, verb)
logic (noncount)
reason (noncount, noun)
  reasoning (noncount)
regarding (prep)
relate (verb)
  related (adj)

relation *(noun)*
relationship *(noun)*
relative *(adj, noun)*
result (noun, verb)

Similar & different

compare (verb)
  comparison (noun)
neither (adj)

contrast (noun, verb)
deviate (verb)
dichotomy (noun)
differ (verb)
  difference (noun)
  different (adj)
  differentiate (verb)
disparity (noun)
distinct (adj)
  distinction (noun)
  distinctive (adj)
vary (verb)
  variable (noun)
  variation (noun)
  varied (adj)
  various (adj)

comparable (adj)
complement (verb)
likewise (adv)
similar (adj)
  similarity (noun)

Probability & certainty

actually (adv)
apparent (adj)
  apparently (adv)
arbitrary (adj)
conclusive (adj)
likelihood (noncount)
luckily (adv)
perhaps (adv)
possible (adj)
  possibility (noun)
  possibly (adv)
potential (noncount)
  potentially (adv)
probable (adj)
  probability (noun)
random (adj)
risk (noun)
supposed (adj)
  supposedly (adv)
tendency (noun)
unlikely (adj)
unpredictable (adj)

Predictions

anticipate (verb)
forecast (noun, verb)
outcome (noun)
outlook (noun)
predict (verb)
  predictable (adj)
  prediction (noun)
project (noun, verb)
  projection (noun)

GENERAL

prospect (noun)
prospective (adj)
short-term *(adj)*
speculate (verb)
speculation (noun)
speculative (adj)

Time

beforehand (adv)
former (adj, pron)
formerly (adv)
old-fashioned (adj)
precede (verb)
precedent (noun)
previous (adj)
previously (adv)
recent (adj)
retrospect
tradition (noun)

current (adj, noun)
lately (adv)
nowadays (adv)
ongoing (adj)
present (adj, noun, verb)

due
pending (adj)
postpone (verb)
postponement (noun)
short-term (adj)
subsequent (adj)
subsequently (adv)

annual (adj)
frequently (adv)

intermittent (adj)
interval (noun)
monthly (adj)
often (adv)
regular (adj)
regularly (adv)
seldom (adv)
sporadic (adj)

daytime (noun)
decade (noun)
delay (noun, verb)
duration (noncount)
interim (adj)
lifetime (noun)
meantime
meanwhile (adv)
moment (noun)
occasion (noun)
occasional (adj)
occasionally (adv)
o'clock (adv)
permanent (adj)
span (noun)
temporary (adj)

chronological (adj)
coincide (verb)
coincidence (noun)
consecutive (adj)
finally (adv)
following (adj, prep, pron)
initial (adj)
initially (adv)
intermediate (adj)
latter (adj, pron)
preliminary (adj)

routine (adj, noun)

sequence (noun)
  sequential (adj)

simultaneous (adj)

successive (adj)

ultimate (adj)
  ultimately (adv)

abrupt (adj)
  abruptly (adv)

eventually (adv)

gradual (adj)
  gradually (adv)

immediately (adv)

pace (noun)

prompt (verb)
  promptly (adv)

quick (adj)
  quickly (adv)

rapid (adj)
  rapidly (adv)

rate (noun)

spontaneous (adj)
  spontaneously (adv)

sudden (adj)
  suddenly (adv)

Qualities & characteristics

characteristic (adj, noun)

concrete (adj)

dependent (adj)
  dependence (noncount)

direct (adj)

distinctive (adj)

evident (adj)

extravagant (adj)

feasible (adj)
  feasibility (noncount)

flexible (adj)
  flexibility (noncount)

formal (adj)

inconclusive (adj)

independent (adj)

indirect (adj)

informal (adj)

instinct (noun)

interchangeable (adj)

obvious (adj)
  obviously (adv)

persistent (adj)

rational (adj)

reality (noncount)
  realistic (adj)

rigor (noncount)
  rigorous (adj)

secrecy (noncount)

secure (adj, verb)
  security (noncount)

stable (adj)
  stability (noncount)
  stabilize (verb)

steady (adj)
  steadily (adv)

tangible (adj)

vigorous (adj)

vivid (adj)

available (adj)

conventional (adj)

daring (adj)

norm (noun)
  normally (adv)

ordinary (adj)
orthodox (adj)
rare (adj)
scarce (adj)
  scarcely (adv)
typical (adj)
unusual (adj)
  unusually (adv)

complex (adj)
complicated (adj)
comprehensive (adj)
elaborate (adj, verb)
intricate (adj)
straightforward (adj)
thorough (adj)

affluent (adj, plural)
creative (adj)
intelligent (adj)
prosperous (adj)
wealthy (adj)
well-known (adj)

artificial (adj)
crowded (adj)
loose (adj)
  loosely (adv)
mobile (adj)
physical (adj)
spacious (adj)
transparency (noncount)
visible (adj)
  visibility (noncount)

familiar (adj)
famous (adj)

popular (adj)
renown (noncount)
unknown (adj)

inferior (adj)
mediocre (adj)
neutral (adj)
okay (adj, adv)
quality (noncount, noun)
satisfactory (adj)

able (phrase)
  ability (noun)
beginner (noun)
caliber (noncount)
capable (adj)
  capability (noun)
concentration (noncount, noun)

Negative qualities

aggressive (adj)
ambiguous (adj)
ambivalent (adj)
  ambivalence (noncount)
chaos (noncount)
  chaotic (adj)
chronic (adj)
dangerous (adj)
deceptive (adj)
difficult (adj)
disadvantage (noun)
hazardous (adj)
impossible (adj)
impractical (adj)
inaccessible (adj)

inaccurate (adj)
  inaccuracy (noun)
inactive (adj)
inadequate (adj)
incapable (adj)
inconvenient (adj)
invalid (adj)
negative (adj)
  negatively (adv)
unacceptable (adj)
vulnerable (adj)

Positive qualities

accurate (adj)
  accuracy (noncount)
  accurately (adv)
adequate (adj)
  adequately (adv)
advantage (noncount, noun)
  advantageous (adj)
appealing (adj)
appropriate (adj)
  appropriately (adv)
authentic (adj)
brilliant (adj)
candid (adj)
coherent (adj)
  coherence (noncount)
comfortable (adj)
compatible (adj)
concise (adj)
considerate (adj)
  consideration (noncount)
consistent (adj)
  consistently (adv)
convenient (adj)

credible (adj)
decent (adj)
desirable (adj)
diligent (adj)
effective (adj)
efficient (adj)
  efficiently (adv)
enthusiasm (noncount)
extraordinary (adj)
favorable (adj)
first-class (adj, adv)
genuine (adj)
impartial (adj)
  impartiality (noncount)
indispensable (adj)
outstanding (adj)
perfect (adj)
positive (adj)
  positively (adv)
practical (adj)
  practically (adv)
precious (adj)
respected (adj)
reward (noun)
  rewarding (adj)
spectacular (adj)
suitable (adj)
superb (adj)
tremendous (adj)
versatile (adj)
  versatility (noncount)
viable (adj)
  viability (noncount)
vibrant (adj)
  vibrancy (noncount)
worthwhile (adj)

Key to grammatical labels in word lists

adj	adjective
adv	adverb
conj	conjunction
noncount	noncount noun
noun	noun
num	number
phrase	phrase
plural	plural noun
prep	preposition
pron	pronoun
quant	quantifier
verb	verb